with every good wish

John Morris

One Equall Light

And into that gate they shall enter, and in that house they shall dwell, where there shall be no Cloud nor Sun, no darknesse nor dazling, but *one equall light*, no noyse nor silence, but one equall musick, no fears nor hopes, but one equall possession, no foes nor friends, but one equall communion and Identity, no ends nor beginnings, but one equall eternity.

A Sermon Preached at White-hall February 29th 1628.

One Equall Light

*An anthology of the writings of
John Donne*

*Compiled and edited
and with introductory essays by*
John Moses
Dean of St Paul's

Foreword by
Rowan Williams
Archbishop of Canterbury

WILLIAM B. EERDMANS PUBLISHING COMPANY
GRAND RAPIDS, MICHIGAN / CAMBRIDGE, U.K.

Originally published 2003 in the United Kingdom by
the Canterbury Press Norwich
(a publishing imprint of Hymns Ancient & Modern Limited,
a registered charity)
St Mary's Works, St Mary's Plain,
Norwich, Norfolk, NR3 3BH
www.scm-canterburypress.co.uk

This edition published 2004 in the United States of America by
Wm. B. Eerdmans Publishing Company
255 Jefferson Ave. S.E., Grand Rapids, Michigan 49503 /
P.O. Box 163 Cambridge CB3 9PU U.K.
www.eerdmans.com

08 07 06 05 04   5 4 3 2 1

ISBN 0-8028-2772-1

Manufactured in the UK

CONTENTS

Contents

Contents

Contents

FOR SUSAN

Were her first yeares the *Golden Age*; that's true,
But now shee's *gold* oft tried, and ever new.

Elegie IX. The Autumnall.

ACKNOWLEDGEMENTS

I am glad to acknowledge at the outset my indebtedness to the Archbishop of Canterbury for the *Foreword* that he has so generously provided.

I am grateful to the Worshipful Company of Weavers in the City of London for the invitation to give the Limborough Lecture in 2002 which appears in this *Anthology* as the first part of the *Introduction to John Donne*.

I am glad to acknowledge the permission that has been granted to quote directly from several published works. Every attempt has been made to secure permission to use copyright material, and all such material is acknowledged in the *Notes* at the end of the book.

But my chief word of gratitude and appreciation must be to Mrs Anita Butt, who has recently retired as my private secretary after fourteen years, and for whom the preparation of the manuscript has been – most certainly for me – the last labour of greatly valued work.

FOREWORD

THE ARCHBISHOP OF CANTERBURY

'The English Church had gain'd a second St Austin', says Izaak
Walton about John Donne's ordination; and generations since have
not disputed this. Walton seems to have been thinking about the com-
parable reputations of both men before conversion, but there is far
more to it than that. Both men have the capacity to deposit a phrase in
the mind that will echo for years. Both, in the simple balance of an
antithesis or a trick of assonance can make you feel that something
about the Christian faith has been said once and for all, that no explanation will ever tell you as much as these few words.

They are not ashamed to aim for the most volatile emotional
regions, and to put a deeply erotic imagination to work for Christ. Yet
no one would call either of them indulgent, sentimental or titillating;
they can shock, but they do not exploit. Both are eloquently aware
both of their own skill and of their own fallibility. They know how
wonderfully, fantastically persuasive they can be and they know the
seductions of that persuasiveness and struggle not to disappear behind
their own hypnotic voice. That we still read them and are disturbed
by them testifies to the fact that they are more than just virtuosos of
rhetoric. We ask continually about the human experience behind these
words; we know they are not cheaply said.

Donne's contribution to the language is unusual; not many have left
a legacy that is equally significant in prose and poetry, in secular and
in religious writing. But those who most want to celebrate Donne do
so not because of this, but because of what the language allows to
'show through'. Odd as it sounds, the more highly worked Donne's
language becomes, the more you start wondering seriously what kind
of reality it is that can prompt and sustain quite such extraordinary
musical and conceptual patternings without absurdity. The answer is
– of course – that Donne believed what all Christians then believed:

that we were created by love, that we ruined ourselves by choice, that we are restored by sacrifice, that the human destiny is to share in the life of the Trinity in bliss. If modern Christians often believe less, or less fervently, they may be forced by Donne to ask how the very rhythms of their speech are weakened and shrunk by the change.

He is not an apologist, then; but by showing how a mercurial personality and a wildly extravagant and often dark imagination can be made the vehicles for Christian orthodoxy, he puts a serious challenge to all his readers. To paraphrase what was said about a great but flawed nineteenth-century Christian, the surprise is not that a saint should have the temperament of a Donne, but that someone with the temperament of a Donne should be able to receive at least some of the graces of holiness. When we have read Donne, we may have a healthier respect for the tradition of doctrine and prayer in which he made his home.

That tradition was, ultimately and not without struggle, the Church of England. From our perspective, fairly familiar with modern Anglicanism, it is not always easy to recognize the Anglican atmosphere of the early seventeenth century. This is not simply a gentle, learned and tolerant piety, but an intellectually complex, thoroughly demanding world of thought. Donne's contribution to the definition of Anglicanism is not in terms of an ethos of cultivated inclusiveness, and it is a pity that the great age of Anglican preaching and poetry has acquired that sort of reputation. It is more in terms of a balance between passion and irony that has very deep roots in Augustine and which in Donne's time had been given added energy both by Calvin and by some of his Catholic critics. It is emphatically there just under the less craggy surface of those apparently 'softer' spirits, Hooker and Herbert. It is the voice we can hear in Eliot nearer our own day, Eliot for whom Donne was so transforming a discovery.

He was prolific, and inevitably uneven, and we need guides to help us around the territory. Dr John Moses here offers a superb selection, introduced and expounded with authority. I hope that this volume will be an orientation not only to Donne but to all of that robust and exhilarating world of mind and spirit to which he belonged – a world whose resourcefulness can and must still be quarried if we are to present faith as a real kindling of language and so of life.

Rowan Cantuar:

PREFACE

The starting point for this Anthology has been John Donne's continuing fascination for large numbers of people. His poetry is well known; but his sermons are largely unknown, although they are judged to be masterpieces of the preaching of the English Church. What has therefore been attempted is a comprehensive overview which, drawing in large measure upon his sermons, provides the general reader with an introduction to his thought.

It was Donne's conviction as a preacher that 'our mortality and our immortality . . . are the two reall Texts and Subjects of all our Sermons'.[1] It is this word which provides whatever justification might be needed for an Anthology which is compiled around the central themes of *Humanity* and *Divinity*. The former encompasses those things that relate to our human nature; the latter pertains to those things that relate to our eternal destiny. It is a distinction that Donne would have understood, but it is not one that he would have pressed too far. No one knew more clearly than John Donne the extent to which the secular and the sacred penetrate and inform each other.

'One equall light' stands in Donne's preaching alongside one equal music, one equal possession, one equal communion and one equal eternity. They are the phrases by which he speaks of the life of heaven; and they stand in sharp contrast to the contradictions of our experience: darkness and dazzling, noise and silence, fears and hopes, foes and friends, endings and beginnings.[2] All these things are brought into the light – in poetry and in sermons – by Donne's creative, restless imagination. He speaks of the human predicament, of the vanities of the world, of the desires of the flesh, of the delights of friendship, of the mysteries of faith, of the gospel of grace, of the fact and fear of death, of the hope of immortality.

The Anthology is preceded by Introductory Essays which tell something of the story of the man and his meaning for us today; of the distinctive characteristics of his writings as a poet, a propagandist and a preacher; and of his final years as Dean of St Paul's. It is the Anthology, however, which enables Donne to speak for himself. The shape of the Anthology has been determined by Donne's writings, and the thematic approach which has been adopted should give direction and focus to those who are reading Donne at any depth for the first time.

There are nearly one thousand quotations in this Anthology – of which eight hundred are taken from his sermons – and they provide ample illustration of Donne's observance of life, his wit, his awareness of God, his affirmations of faith, the wealth of imagery he employed, his tricks of style and his rhetoric. It is, however, the mind of the man which is our primary concern. He was not an original thinker; he was not a systematic theologian; but the quotations provide some insight into the thoughts, feelings, passions, insecurities, aspirations and convictions of the man. If it is true that Donne had things to say about humanity and divinity, it is no less the case that he had much to say about himself. The light of his mind, of his pen, of his tongue is constantly turned inwards. He is the inescapable presence – magical, mercurial, melancholic – whose fascination consists in part in the extent to which he intrudes, showing us something of himself, becoming known and yet remaining unknown.

In the selection of quotations from Donne's writings, regard has been paid to content and style, to gospel and poetry; but there are nonetheless important caveats that must be made. A selection which is arranged thematically can easily give the impression that the poetry, the prose works and the sermons possess a greater degree of coherent, integrated thought than is actually the case. Donne's writings – like the man himself – do not always fit tidily into clearly defined compartments; and the arrangement is therefore not so systematic that one quotation inevitably leads into the next. It is, rather, a grouping of quotations around a common theme.

Some quotations are very short – a line or two – but such a selection can be justified, in spite of the acknowledged risk of taking the words out of their context, if what is then presented encapsulates succinctly the argument, the subject, the mood, the theme of a longer passage. Any compiler of Donne's writings will guard against 'the lure of the glittering fragments at the expense of the whole';[3] but poetic quality has not been the sole concern. It is important not to wrench a passage from its context; but it can also be important to set a passage free – and especially when the context consists of long and indigestible sentences, classical allusions, and extensive quotations from the Fathers and the Schoolmen – so that it might speak with simplicity and directness.

There is inevitably a good deal of interpretation where the meaning of some of Donne's writings is concerned. An Anthology presents a broad cross-section, and it allows the reader to take what is presented at face value, or to look beneath the surface, or to be prompted to find the commentaries of scholars. The quotations are of varying quality. Some will give pause for thought as Donne's melancholy turn of mind dominates what he has to say. Some will delight by their exuberance, their vitality, their love of love and of life. Some will give good reason to reflect in silence and in prayer.

Donne comes down to us from a golden age of letters; but the thought-forms, the vocabulary, the sentence construction and the imagery are not those with which we are familiar today. It is even more true that those who turn to his sermons will not necessarily find it easy to engage with a preacher who speaks unambiguously of sin, of death, and of judgement. But Donne's words still have the power to raise our sights, to penetrate our defences, and to put us in touch with the fundamentals of faith.

Scripture, tradition and reason: these provide the parameters within which Donne stands in his preaching. It is not the least of his merits that he challenges his readers today to reflect upon the contemporary culture in which our lives are lived. It is therefore hoped that the Anthology will serve as a basis for personal reflection and meditation – perhaps during the season of Lent, or in a time of retreat, or in those private moments when we are convicted by God, by sin, by grace. It is especially the case that Donne's words concerning the office of a priest and of a preacher provide ample scope for critical self-examination. *One Equall Light*, an Anthology of the writings of John Donne, brings us to that deep well of biblical theology and Christian piety from which he drew so freely as he expounded the gospel of grace.

John Moses
London 2003

AN INTRODUCTORY NOTE

Quotations from Donne's *Poems* are taken from *John Donne: Complete English Poems*, edited by C.A. Patrides, Everyman's Library, 1991.

Quotations from Donne's *Sermons* are taken from *The Sermons of John Donne*, edited by Evelyn M. Simpson & George R. Potter, 10 volumes, University of California Press, 1953–62.

Donne's sentence construction and spelling have been retained together with his use of capital letters, italics, and punctuation.

Brief explanatory words have been provided as footnotes to the text by courtesy of Everyman's Library where these are judged to be helpful.

It might be helpful, however, to note that there has been no amendment of Donne's use of 'then', although the reader might be glad to know at the outset that the word would very frequently (but not invariably) be rendered as 'than' in our speaking and writing today.

AN INTRODUCTION TO
JOHN DONNE

THE MAN AND HIS
MEANING

Reputations are elusive, unpredictable. They rise and fall and rise again. Few English writers have been victims of greater fluctuations in fashion, in critical thought, in popular esteem than John Donne – poet, preacher and sometime Dean of St Paul's. One introduction to his poetry suggests that 'Donne was much praised in his life time, under-praised thereafter, and over-praised (in the twentieth century)'.[1]

Certainly there have been from the beginning seriously conflicting judgements concerning the quality and the enduring value of Donne's writings. For Ben Jonson, Donne was 'the first poet in the World in some things'.[2] For Alexander Pope, it would have been necessary 'to translate (Donne) into "correct" verse if a more polished age was to give him a hearing'.[3] For Samuel Taylor Coleridge, Donne's poetry possessed 'Wonder-exciting vigour, intenseness and peculiarity of thought'.[4] For T.S. Eliot, 'Donne's poetry is the concern of the present and of the recent past rather than of the future!'[5]

Donne was a restless, passionate, worldly, self-seeking man. The apparent contradictions of his life are to be found in his writings. It is scarcely surprising that there has rarely been a consensus of opinion. Popular knowledge of Donne today is confined to his poetry. His letters and his prose works and his sermons are largely unknown; but Donne would be judged by many to be not merely one of the major English poets, but also one of the great preachers of the English Church.

The last two or three generations have seen a vast upsurge of inter-est – and not least of all in North America – in Donne's writings. Indeed, visitors from the United States who come to St Paul's Cathedral will often ask as one of their first questions if they might see Donne's effigy. What, therefore, is the basis of this man's continuing fascination to so many people? What is his meaning today? These are questions that can only be considered in the context of his life and work.

John Donne was born in 1572 in Bread Street in the City of London, within sight and sound of Old St Paul's. His father, who died when Donne was scarcely four years old, was a prosperous merchant, a senior member of the Worshipful Company of Ironmongers. It seems probable that Donne was educated at home by private tutors before he matriculated at Oxford in 1584. He may well have spent some time on the continent – perhaps in Italy and Spain – in the late 1580s and the early 1590s, either as a traveller or possibly as a gentleman volunteer in military service.

By 1591, Donne had returned to London and, having completed a year's preliminary study at Thadies Inn, was admitted to Lincoln's Inn in May 1592. In later life Donne criticized himself for neglecting his study of the law, but he continued to read widely and to achieve something of a reputation even as a young man for the quality of his mind and for his wide-ranging studies. He was clearly a man of wit and great personal charm and, although he was never called to the bar, the friendships that he made during these early years remained throughout much of his life.

The legacy Donne had received from his father maintained him financially during these years, but the legacy he had received from his mother was no less important. Donne had been born – at least on his mother's side – into a devout and prominent Roman Catholic family, for whom imprisonment, exile and execution were all part of the family tradition. Theological enquiry was an important ingredient in the mix for Donne throughout the whole of his life, and not least of all at this time as he wrestled with the conflicting pressures of family loyalties and of an unavoidably heavy-handed religious settlement in England.

Study and theological enquiry did not constitute the whole of his life. In common with young men of his age at any time in history, he used these early years to push out the boundaries, to enjoy life. He appears to have presented himself at Court from time to time; and he was described at a later date as having been at this time 'a great visiter of Ladies, a great frequenter of Playes, a great writer of conceited Verses'.[6]

Many would sustain the charge of 'conceited Verses'. Arrogance, self-centredness, scepticism, irreverence: all these words have been used in one form or another by scholars who have attempted to understand this gifted, restless man. It was, of course, a golden age. These were the years of Spenser, of Marlowe, of Shakespeare, of Ben Jonson; and Donne must properly be seen as part of that renaissance of letters in the written and the spoken word. Time and again he displays an exquisite turn of phrase, an eloquence, an earthiness, an intensity of feeling, a positive rejoicing in the delights of love. There may be dross, but there is also gold.

One of the problems in attempting a life of Donne is that there is no certainty concerning the dates when many of his poems were written. Donne never sought the printing and circulation of his poetry. It is very probable that many of his poems have been lost or destroyed. It may be that Donne saw them in later life as nothing more than the playful musings of his younger years. Ben Jonson believed that Donne had written 'all his best Pieces' before he was twenty-five;[7] and it is, of course, from these early years that so much of his love poetry can be traced. Donne had a great agility with words, and the sensuality – indeed, the blatantly erotic sexuality – of some of his poetry is one of its abiding hallmarks. He could be playful. He could be tender. He could be erotic. He could be promiscuous. He could be cynical. He could be brutal. It is, some would suggest, precisely here – in 'the expression of free thoughts and uncensored moods' – that we find 'the glory of his greatest poetry'.[8]

Important questions remain. Was Donne as a young man as promiscuous as some of his poems suggest? Or were they the products of a fevered imagination? Or did he make a little go a long way? Was he writing to tease, to shock, to amuse, to impress? Were so many of his poems – as Donne himself wrote of an early prose work – 'but swaggerers . . . made . . . rather to deceive time than her daughter truth'?[9] The years that followed immediately upon Donne's studies at Lincoln's Inn were dominated by two activities. There was in the first place his foreign adventures in 1596 and 1597 when he volunteered for military service in the expeditions to Cadiz and the Azores. Donne was one of the large number of young men in fashionable London circles who came forward to take part in these episodes in the long drawn out struggle between England and Spain. There was secondly – and perhaps as a direct consequence of these expeditions – the appointment that might well have proved to be for Donne the first and all-important rung on the ladder of preferment in the service of the Crown and of the state.

One of Donne's companions on the expedition to the Azores – a fellow student from Lincoln's Inn days – was the elder son of Sir Thomas Egerton, Lord Keeper of the Great Seal, Master of the Roll and a Privy Counsellor. Egerton's duties brought him into close contact with the Court, with the Privy Council, with Parliament and with the law. Donne was employed on his return to England as one of Egerton's secretaries. His legal training would have assisted him as he went about the routine duties of a public servant in the household of one of the Crown's most senior law officers. Egerton and Donne appear to have had a good regard for each other; and the appointment was one that could not fail to broaden Donne's horizons. It introduced him to men of influence, and prepared him for greater responsibilities over the years ahead. It was on the strength of the Egerton family interest that Donne was returned to Parliament as the Member for Brackley, in Northamptonshire, in 1601.

Whatever hopes Donne might have entertained for a career in the public service were destroyed at a stroke in the weeks just before Christmas 1601 when he married in a secret ceremony Ann, the daughter of Sir George More, and the niece of his employer, Sir Thomas Egerton. Donne had first met Ann when she stayed in London with Lady Egerton, following upon the death of her mother. She could only have been a girl of fifteen at the time. She had returned to the family home after the death of Lady Egerton in January 1600 and did not return to London again for another twenty months. It is tempting to ask if Donne used his poetry – perhaps through smuggled letters – to court Ann and stay in touch. Indeed, some have suggested that a number of Donne's love poems were addressed to Ann before and after their marriage. What is certain is that they married within weeks of Ann's return to London in October 1601, and the little evidence that has survived suggests that they were deeply in love with each other and remained so throughout their marriage.

The marriage violated every convention and the offence could only have been compounded by Donne's decision to wait for several weeks before he wrote to inform Ann's father that 'yt is irremediably done'.[10] The response was uncompromising. Sir George More refused to make any financial settlement and demanded that the marriage should be annulled. Donne, together with the officiating minister and the witnesses, was arrested and imprisoned for a week or so. Sir Thomas Egerton dismissed Donne from his service.

One tradition suggests that a subsequent letter to Ann's father concluded with the names, 'John Donne . . . Ann Donne . . . Un-done'.[11] The story is almost certainly apocryphal, but the word 'Un-done' captures precisely the situation in which Donne and his wife now found themselves. It is true that the validity of the marriage was upheld, and that after the passing of some years some modest financial support was provided for Ann and her children; but Donne had condemned himself and his wife to long years of poverty. Donne's legacy was nearly exhausted; he was almost certainly in debt; and he would no longer be considered seriously for the employment that he sought.

The explanation of the marriage can only be Donne's certain knowledge that the proposed union would have been refused by Ann's father. But what is the truth of the matter? Was Donne simply reckless in his love for Ann More? Or was the marriage a calculated move – a gambler's throw of the dice – in the vain hope that he might thereby secure wealth and place and position in society? Was he a victim of his overweening self-confidence?

What can be said is that the marriage, which proved to be the sheet-anchor of Donne's life, asks all students to acknowledge some of the contradictions that are posed by this extraordinary man. He was ambitious for worldly success, but he threw everything away for love. The evidence of some of his early poems suggests at the very least a degree of promiscuity and some cynicism concerning the institution of marriage; but his enduring love for Ann – and his fidelity in marriage – have never been called in question.

The long wilderness years now stretched ahead. Accommodation was provided for Donne and his young wife and their rapidly growing family at Pyrford in Surrey. Donne no doubt assisted with the management of the estate, but study – long hours of comprehensive, rigorous, meticulous study – was the major preoccupation to which he repeatedly returned with great self-discipline. Friends came to visit and Donne was an active correspondent, but he and Ann were dependent on the hospitality and generosity of others and there was no sense of focus or direction.

It was a friend who encouraged Donne to come to London in 1603 at the beginning of a new reign and to seek his fortune at Court. Donne had found his exile from London unbearable, and he renewed his efforts to secure employment. He was constantly seeking new openings and new patrons. Employment, income, status, influence – these were his requirements. There were increasingly large numbers of men and women to whom Donne could turn, but none proved able or willing to provide the appointments he sought. Journeys abroad in 1605–6 and 1611–12 involved long periods of separation from Ann and the children, but they provided some outlet, serving as travelling companion, as secretary, as translator to wealthy patrons.

Donne acquired a small house at Mitcham towards the end of 1606, together with a small apartment in London. Poverty was obviously a relative term, but it was nonetheless oppressive for Donne and for his wife and family. He spent a great deal of time in London, following the Court, cultivating new patrons, living by his wits, enjoying the camaraderie of the *Mitre* and the *Mermaid*, spending long hours in studying canon and civil law, exploring questions relating to divinity and the religious settlement, submitting theological pamphlets to the King and flattering poems to ladies of wealth. It is from these years that we date some of his finest poetry and most of his prose writing,[12] including many of his letters; but Donne nonetheless came close to despair. There were periods of ill health throughout his life, and the later years of the first decade of the seventeenth century saw Donne brought down by a deep melancholy, even perhaps by thoughts of suicide. He expressed very succinctly the burden of his complaint: 'I would feign do something; but that I cannot tell what, is no wonder. For to chuse is to do: but to be no part of any body, is to be nothing'.[13]

Ordination was suggested to Donne at this period of his life, and Donne certainly took his theological studies very seriously; but his heart was still in the service of the Crown and he sought instead appointments which depended on the King's favour – in the Queen's household, in the English Civil Service for Ireland, as Secretary to the Virginia Company, as English Ambassador to Venice. Donne could observe with some truth that 'no one attends Court fortunes with more impatience than I do';[14] but every door was closed, and the perennial struggle to make ends meet – let alone to be someone, to do something – continued unabated.

The backcloth to these years may well have been unemployment and penury, but personal qualities of a high order are displayed in the self-imposed discipline of study and writing. It is from these years that we can trace the majority of the *Divine Poems* and four major prose works. There is a new seriousness in much of his writing, and he demonstrates an extraordinarily wide range of knowledge that goes far beyond any formal training he had previously received, drawing upon the literature and the philosophy of the biblical and the classical, the ancient and the medieval, worlds.

Donne was well able to write to order and for payment, and his most ambitious and controversial poems – *The Anniversaries* and *A Funerall Elegie* – written to commemorate the daughter of Sir Robert Drury who died in 1610 at the age of fourteen, must be considered in that light; but *The First Anniversarie* is important also in the sense that it takes as its starting point 'the frailty and the decay of his whole World'. Donne has been valued for his celebration of love, but it ought not to be forgotten that he is also 'the foremost English poet – as well as the greatest prose writer – of death'.[15] It is, of course, the human condition to which Donne continually returns in his writing. His delight in the pleasures of the flesh must be set alongside everything he has to say about the fragility of our human nature, our mortality, the fact and fear of death, and the hope of heaven. Certainly it is in the *Divine Poems*, and especially the *Holy Sonnets*, that all these things are brought together as his poetry finds its highest expression.

By contrast with his poems, the prose works that belong to this period are intended to instruct or persuade, and perhaps even to enable Donne to think through matters of concern. The despair of these years is to be found in his treatise on suicide;[16] but it is the religious controversies of the age that increasingly dominate his studies. His work has been described by one scholar as a contribution to the 'Anglican propaganda machine'.[17] No one would deny that *Pseudo-Martyr* and *Ignatius His Conclave* were anything more than works of religious propaganda, and Donne was certainly concerned to commend himself to the Protestant King James; but let it also be recognized that his wide-ranging studies, his legal training, and his capacity to master an argument and express himself cogently made him a natural protagonist. But thinking through the issues for himself also mattered, and his *Essayes in Divinitie*, written a year or so before he took holy orders although not actually published until twenty years after his death, represents his attempt to think through his theology and demonstrates an intimate working knowledge of the Bible, the commentaries, the writings of the Fathers and the theologians of the medieval world.

Disappointment, frustration, despair and poverty formed the background to the decision that was taken in the closing weeks of 1614 to take holy orders. Even while he had been seeking an appointment – any appointment – at Court in the early months of 1613, Donne had written to his chosen patron that he had 'resolved to make my Profession Divinitie'.[18] But it was only when he was fully persuaded of the futility of seeking any secular appointment that Donne was prepared to take seriously the advice of the King to take orders, and even then he was anxious to secure in the first instance whatever assurance the King might give concerning the possibility of preferment.

It is, then, scarcely surprising that the charge of hypocrisy has been brought against Donne by some scholars both in respect of his abandonment of his Roman Catholic heritage and of his priestly vocation and preaching ministry in the Church of England.[19] It is never easy to know the truth about another person's spiritual journey. Donne undoubtedly moved towards the Church of England at a relatively early stage in his life, but he never denied the legacy of persecution to which members of his family had been subjected. Nor did he ever distance himself in private devotion or public preaching from the riches of the Catholic tradition of spirituality. He certainly commenced his theological studies in the early 1590s, and it may well have been that in troubled times the peace of the realm and the sovereignty of nation states had more to do with his movement towards the Church of England than any doctrinal differences. One other thing should be said: whatever the reasons for his abandonment of his family's Roman Catholic tradition of faith, Donne nevertheless retained 'an unquestioning acceptance of the claim of religion'.[20]

The Latin epitaph, which Donne himself composed and which is to be found today above his effigy in the south quire aisle of St Paul's Cathedral, records that he 'entered Holy Orders under the influence and pressure of the Holy Spirit and by the advice and exhortation of King James'.[21] It is a statement that acknowledges the influences – spiritual and secular – that were brought into play. Donne had long since been aware of a 'melancholy in the soule' and of a 'distrust of (God's) salvation';[22] but his *Essayes in Divinitie* hint at something more: 'Thou hast set up many candlesticks, and kindled many lamps in mee; but I have either blown them out, or carried them to guide me in by and forbidden ways. Thou hast given me a desire of knowledg, and some meanes to it, and some possession of it; and I have arm'd myself with thy weapons against thee. Yet, O God, have mercy upon me.'[23]

Donne is not the first person about whom questions might properly be asked when the issue of motivation is raised for discussion. St Paul, writing to the Church at Corinth in order to commend his apostleship, reminded his readers that 'we have this treasure (that is, the Gospel) in earthen vessels, to show that the transcendent power belongs to God and not to us'.[24] It may well be that what Donne represents is not merely the earthen-ness of the vessel, but also the experience of the man who has nowhere else to turn for the things that he wants, and who then – and only then – can find his true self.

Donne was ordained deacon and priest by the Lord Bishop of London in St Paul's Cathedral – the great medieval cathedral that is known as Old St Paul's – on 23 January 1615. He was appointed almost immediately as a Chaplain in Ordinary to the King; and the University of Cambridge, acting – albeit with some reluctance – in response to a royal mandate, conferred on Donne the degree of Doctor of Divinity. Donne was appointed Reader in Divinity at Lincoln's Inn in October 1616 and the Chapel provided the primary arena for his preaching ministry during these early years. In common with the custom of the age, Donne was appointed at various times to benefices in Huntingdonshire, Kent and Bedfordshire, on the clear understanding that residence would not be required and that pastoral duties would be performed by stipendiary curates. At a later date – and during his time at St Paul's – Donne was appointed to the vicarage of St Dunstan in the West, although here he appears to have been assiduous in his preaching and his pastoral work.

Something of the regard in which he was held can be inferred from the one foreign expedition in which he was involved during these years. It may well be that Donne – with the full knowledge of the king – had been engaged in correspondence with agents in Europe ever since his ordination. A revolt by Protestant subjects in Bohemia in 1618 raised large questions concerning the peace of Europe, the religious settlement in the German states, and the role of England in all these matters. Lord Doncaster was sent by the King as his ambassador to the German princes and Donne went as Doncaster's chaplain, although he would have used the opportunity to establish relations with some of the Protestant divines on the Continent.

These early years in orders were overshadowed for Donne by the death of his wife in August 1617. Ann died in the thirty-third year of her life a week after giving birth to a stillborn child. There were twelve known pregnancies during the sixteen years of their marriage: two children had been stillborn, three had died in infancy. Ann's lot had been that of many women down the centuries, but what cannot be evaluated is her influence upon her husband. Donne had written to her brother, Sir Robert More, three years before her death that 'we had not one another at so cheap a rate as that we should ever be weary of one another'.[25] The marriage appears to have been a love match from beginning to end in spite of the years of poverty, separation, disappointment and illness. It is tempting to speculate and to ask if Ann's influence had been a key factor in Donne's greater self-awareness, maturity, even vocation. Certainly there is some consensus among scholars that her death served to deepen Donne's awareness of God, his own sense of the rightness of his vocation, and the intensity of his religious feeling.[26]

None of these things was to inhibit Donne, however, in his search for preferment. He was already seen as a man who might well be appointed to a deanery when an appropriate vacancy occurred, and it is clear that he worked hard to ensure that his name was considered seriously for St Paul's. He wrote to the Duke of Buckingham, the King's favourite, in August 1621, expressing his hope that there might be 'a hole for so poore a worme as I ame to have crept in at'.[27]

Donne was installed as Dean of St Paul's in November 1621. He had achieved in less than seven years in orders all that he had sought throughout his adult life – secure employment, a comfortable income, a position of status and influence. The last nine years of his life were devoted in large measure to St Paul's. He was not a reforming dean. He made no attempt to change existing practices. The requirements of the fabric – and the concomitant problem of fund raising – were largely ignored. The nave of the cathedral continued to be a place of public assembly, largely unrestricted movement and commerce of many kinds. Donne presided over the affairs of the cathedral with integrity and competence. He took his place in the wider world – maintaining a large household, providing hospitality, sitting in the Court of Delegates and the Court of High Commission, serving as a governor of Charterhouse and as Prolocutor of the Convocation of Canterbury. Donne retained his links with the Court as a Chaplain to the King, and ensured that he visited his country parishes during the summer months.

Study remained his primary discipline and all his creative energy now went into his preaching. His name has come down as one of the great preachers of the English Church, and his sermons – one hundred and sixty of which have survived – are seen as 'one of the great glories of English literature'.[28] It is one of the curiosities of Donne's life that he was at great pains to preserve his sermons but took little account of his poetry. Donne himself distinguished between *Jack Donne* and *Doctor Donne*, between his earlier and his later years.[29] He referred to poetry as 'the Mistresse of my youth' and to divinity as 'the wife of my age'.[30] It seems as though there was some conscious disowning of himself – or at least of his past – as though his earlier writings, and especially his love poems, were somehow incompatible with what he had become and what he now felt he had to say.

Donne was absolutely clear about the authority of Scripture, the authority of the Church, and the authority of the preacher. The preparation and the delivery of his sermons constituted the most important part of his public ministry, and he preached regularly at St Paul's, at St Dunstan's, and before the Court. Donne preached, of course, in an age when a sermon was 'a full hour's closely reasoned discourse',[31] and he would have spoken without notes or with only the bare bones of his sermon in front of him. He prepared his sermons with meticulous care: choosing his text, consulting the commentaries, drawing upon the writings of the Fathers and the great expositors of Scripture, preparing his notes, and committing the sermon to memory.

Students of English literature will turn to Donne's sermons today and will recognize the intricacies of their structure, the dignity of the language, the wide-ranging employment of images. Students of preaching will acknowledge that the sermons are both expository and evangelistic: they are concerned to break open the word of Scripture and then to confront the hearer with the challenge of the gospel message. This is not to say that Donne's sermons are easy to read. They come down to us from another age: the sentence construction, the biblical and classical allusions, the Latin quotations, the wordiness, the denseness are all formidable impediments; and yet for those who persevere there are nuggets of pure gold. Donne's canvas is broad – God's purposes in creation, the reality of sin, the whole drama of redemption, the inescapable fact of death, the hope of heaven.

It is, however, the simplicity of phrase and the commonplace illustrations that are so telling. On the centrality of the cross he wrote: 'if I could dye a thousand times for Christ this were nothing if Christ had not died for me'.[32] On the vision of God: 'I shall not live til I see God, and when I have seen him I shall never die'.[33] On the love of God: 'whom God loves, hee loves to the end: and not onely to their own end, to their death, but to his end, and his end is, that he might love them still'.[34] Then, taking his illustrations from many spheres of life, he expands upon the flowering of the human soul in the life to come: 'there she reads without spelling, and knowes without thinking, and concludes without arguing; she is at the end of her race, without running; In her triumph without fighting; In her haven without sayling: A free-man without any prentiship; at full yeares, without any wardship; and a Doctor without any proceeding. She knows truly, and easily, and immediately, and entirely, and everlastingly; Nothing left out at first, nothing worne out at last, that conduces to her happiness.'[35]

Ill health had dogged Donne throughout his adult life, and his later years were overshadowed by the death of family and friends. He confided in a friend towards the end that, 'I have never had good temper, nor good pulse, nor good appetite, nor good sleep'.[36] He fell ill with fever in August 1630, and the rumour that he had died was greeted by Donne with characteristic wit: 'A man would almost be content to dye . . . to hear of so much sorrow, and so much good testimony from good men as I . . . did upon the report of my death'.[37] Donne returned to London to preach before the Court on the first Friday in Lent, 25 February 1631. His friends pleaded with him to withdraw from this commitment, but he persevered and his sermon – published as *Death's Duell* – was commented upon by observers as 'Dr Donne (preaching) his own Funeral Sermon'.[38] 'God doth not say', said Donne, 'Live well and thou shalt dye well, that is, an easie, a quiet death; But live well here, and thou shalt live well for ever'.[39]

Donne was exhausted and returned to his deanery and continued to deal with cathedral business for another month. It was during this time that the most bizarre of all incidents occurred when Donne made preparation for his effigy. Fires were lit in the study, his clothes were removed, and he wrapped himself in a burial shroud with only his emaciated face to be seen. A sketch was made and was subsequently used by the sculptor Nicholas Stone to create the effigy in which the shrouded figure is to be seen 'rising from the funeral urn . . . (with the suggestion) . . . that he is still rising and has not yet drawn himself erect'.[40] Donne left his study for the last time, and remained thereafter in his bedroom, conscious of growing weakness, and saying farewell to friends and colleagues who took their last leave of him. Izaak Walton, his friend and disciple and first biographer, records as his final words, 'I were miserable if I might not dye'; and then, 'Thy Kingdom come. Thy will be done'.[41]

Donne comes down to us with all his ambiguities and contradictions. He was an ambitious, self-serving, passionate, searching man; but he was able to write exquisite poetry and having taken Orders – admittedly as a last resort – he bequeathed to subsequent generations sermons of incomparable learning, depth and beauty. But the questions remain: What is the basis of his continuing fascination? What is his meaning today?

Something of the meaning must be found in the quality of his writing, and especially his poetry. It is not merely that he is one of the great exponents of sexual desire and erotic love. It is something to do with the exuberance, the wit, the irreverence. There is an overwhelming, unequivocal affirmation of the centrality of love. He knows the raw material of our humanity: its thoughts, its emotions, its lusts, its fragility, its torments, its aspirations. He allows us to see his inmost thoughts and feelings, and he holds up a mirror so that we might see our own. But his poetry, and especially his love poetry, points to something more. Rupert Brooke saw Donne as 'the one great lover-poet who was not afraid to acknowledge that he was composed of body, soul and mind, and one who faithfully recorded all the pitched battles, alarms, treaties, sieges and fanfares of that extraordinary triangular warfare'.[42] He understood the appetites, the desires, of the flesh, and yet he was able to affirm the integrity and the value of the world and to point beyond it.

Donne has the great merit that he does not conform to stereotypes of clerical figures, of Anglican divines. It could be argued that he brought to ordination and retained throughout his preaching ministry the mind and temper of a layman – informed, disciplined, worldly-wise, sensitive to political nuances, alert to the need for compromise, and yet able to preach the gospel. Certainly the paradoxes, the contradictions, remain. They are merely set now within the frame of priestly vocation, of public ministry.

There had been an element of compulsion in Donne's search for God, but his experience of God appears to have been tentative and hesitant, at least until the time of his ordination which was followed so closely by the death of his wife. It is as though he could not get God out of his system, and yet he could not quite bring everything together in the life of faith. It is nonetheless a sobering thought that if Donne had secured the appointments he had sought prior to ordination his sermons would never have been written; but the sermons that have survived – over and above their literary merit – are good instances of mature faith and experience. It is the depths that must have been there all along – waiting to be opened up, waiting to be explored, waiting to yield a rich harvest – that are so intriguing.

It is, however, the ambiguities of his life which continue to fascinate. He represents a type of Christian discipleship in which the flesh and the spirit, the secular and the sacred, the human and the divine, are locked into each other and are required to live in a continuing tension. There is a worldliness about Donne – *Jack Donne* and *Doctor Donne* – which is not always attractive, but the contradictions that he embodies are ones that can be easily recognized, and in an extraordinary way they make him more compelling as a man. Is it, perhaps, that we can see in him something of our foibles, our compromises, our struggles with the idea – and the ideal – of the Holy?

But Donne should be allowed to speak the last word. He understood the changing moods and rhythms of life, but he was able to point beyond all contrasts and contradictions to that final destiny 'where there shall be no Cloud nor Sun, no darknesse nor dazling, but one equall light, no noyse nor silence, but one equall musick, no fears nor hopes, but one equall possession, no foes nor friends but one equall communion and Identity, no ends nor beginnings, but one equall eternity.'[43]

POET, PROPAGANDIST, PREACHER

Every age is a time of transition, and the English writers of the late Elizabethan and Jacobean periods were mindful of moving in new directions. They had been nurtured in the traditions of the ancient and the medieval worlds, and their minds and their literary aspirations had initially been shaped by the natural sciences and philosophical speculations, the myths and legends, of earlier ages; but they were required to come to terms with new knowledge and to speak of their experience of life in new ways.

It was an age of extraordinary richness and versatility in English letters: Spenser, Sydney, Ralegh, Bacon, Marlowe, Shakespeare, Donne, Jonson. It is certainly the case that Donne declined to acknowledge in later life the poetry of his younger years, but he stands nonetheless as a distinguished representative of a generation of writers who embodied an English renaissance and who pointed forward into a new world.

Jonson and Marlowe are the two contemporaries with whom Donne is most closely identified, although in later years a younger generation of writers, and especially Herbert, looked towards him as their inspiration. But the influences – philosophical and literary – that informed Donne's mind included the Greek authors whom he had read in Latin translation – Plato, Aristotle, Plotinus, Plutarch; the Latin authors – Virgil, Horace, Juvenal, Martial and Seneca; French, Spanish and Italian writers – including especially Rabelais, Montaigne and Dante; together with the biblical, doctrinal and devotional writings of the Fathers, the Schoolmen and the controversialists – Roman Catholic and Protestant – of his own age.

Donne ranged widely in his reading, and his keen and acquisitive mind was alert to the changes that were taking place in the world-view that the more informed were bringing to their experience of life. The work of Copernicus and Galileo, the discoveries of the great sea-explorers, the place of reason in the search for knowledge, the emergence of the empirical sciences and the discerning of new insights in the field of medicine, the ordering of affairs in the nation state: all these find some acknowledgement in Donne's writings, and not least of all in his poetry.

This time of transition between the medieval and the modern worlds brought with it a new self-consciousness, a greater awareness of the range of human knowledge and experience, and – in the writings of the Metaphysical Poets – a sceptical, satirical turn of mind and phrase. One scholar who has claimed Donne as a renaissance man has done so on the grounds that he understood the importance of 'the freedom of the mind to seek in fact and experience the ultimate basis for the truth about the nature of things'.[1]

Donne is perhaps the foremost representative of a group of poets in the early years of the seventeenth century whose work has been loosely connected by their designation as the Metaphysical Poets. The term is misleading because none of the writers in question – Donne, Herbert, Crashaw, Vaughan, Marvell, Traherne – has any serious interest in metaphysics; but they were men of learning, eager to explore the whole range of human experience, ebullient in style, extravagant in their use of imagery, and well able to make unexpected connections.

Donne had the eye of the true artist. He would take whatever he wanted from any area of life and use it to illustrate his chosen subject. There is evidence of immaturity, of mere cleverness, of truculence, of cynicism; but Donne wrote as one who was completely involved. He was not merely observing or exploring. He was sharing in his subject; he was a living part of it. The repeated use of nautical and seafaring metaphors conveys the impression that Donne was consciously embarking – certainly in his early years as a poet – upon his own journey of discovery. Dame Helen Gardner suggests that, 'We seem to be overhearing something not meant for us to hear, something private, neither addressed to us, nor dressed up for our approval, or pleasure, or edification'.[2]

Mankind – to use Donne's word – was his chosen area for exploration. He would take his illustrations – analogy, metaphor, simile – from every part of life, but he was not an exponent of the beauty of nature or of idealized, romanticized love. Nor did he attempt to re-cast old myths in new forms. Perhaps his feet were set too firmly on the soil of London. But his primary concerns – the human condition, the way of the world, the love of men and women, our mortality – were illuminated by contrasting moods and styles. Donne could be logical and passionate, tortuous and incisive, analytical and emotional, detached and deeply involved.

But wherein lies the fascination of Donne's poetry? There is no scholarly consensus regarding the dating of much of his work, and individual poems cannot necessarily be ascribed to those periods of his life which are dominated by carefree living, by changing moods, by the fluctuations of fortune, by a growing religious awareness. It is probable that most of the *Satyres*, the *Elegies* and many of the *Songs and Sonnets* belong to the period before his marriage to Ann More in 1601; that the remainder of the *Elegies* and *Songs and Sonnets*, many of the verse letters and *Divine Poëms*, together with *The Anniversaries*, belong to the middle years between his marriage and his ordination in 1615; and that the rest of the *Divine Poëms* belong to the later years of his life.

There are certainly distinct periods in Donne's life, but his poetry cuts across so many of the predictable divides – a simple chronology, a bitter-sweet experience of life, the secular and the sacred. The poetic genius appears to reside in a combination of skills and characteristics, of themes and thoughts and feelings, of insecurities.

There are in the first place distinctive characteristics of pace, of temper, of style.

There is the use of one-syllable words in quick succession:

> View your fat Beasts, stretch'd Barnes, and labour'd fields,
>   Eate, play, ryde, take all joyes which all day yields.[3]

There is alliteration:

> A bracelet of bright haire about the bone.[4]

There is the rapid sequence of words:

> Love, let my body raigne[a] and let
> Me travel, sojourne, snatch, plot, have, forget.[5]

a. raigne (range)

[19]

There is the rapid sequence of questions:

> 'Tis true, 'tis day, what though it be?
> O wilt thou therefore rise from me?
> Why should we rise, because 'tis light?
> Did we lie downe, because t'was night?[6]

There is the speed with which a scene is captured and conveyed:

> But by his losse grow all our *orders* lesse;
> The name of *Father*, *Master*, *Friend*, the name
> Of *Subject* and of *Prince*, in one are lame;
> Faire mirth is dampt, and conversation black,
> The *household* widdow'd, and the *garter* slack;
> The *Chappell* wants an eare, *Councell* a tongue.[7]

There is the repeated refrain:

> Shee, shee is dead; shee's dead: when thou knowst this,
> Thou knowst how . . .[8]

There is directness of speech:

> For Godsake hold your tongue, and let me love.[9]

There is succinct characterization:

> Doe-bak'd men.
> Cloystrall Men.
> Spirituall Cholerique Critiqs.[10]

There are the changes of mood, of tone:

> He is starke mad, who ever sayes,
>   That he hath been in love an houre,
> Yet not that love so soone decayes,
>   But that it can tenne in lesse space devour;
> Who will believe mee, if I sweare
> That I have had the plague a yeare?
>   Who would not laugh at mee, if I should say,
>   I saw a flaske of *powder* burne a day?[11]

There are the contrasts that are drawn:

> Bee thine owne Palace, or the world's thy gaole.
> And in the worlds sea do not like corke sleepe.
> Upon the waters face; nor in the deepe
> Sinke like a lead without a line: but as
> Fishes glide, leaving no print where they passe,
> Nor making sound; so, closely thy course goe.[12]

There is no suggestion that all these characteristics repeat themselves in poem after poem; rather, it is that – taken cumulatively – they set the scene, they force the pace, they beguile – indeed, they besiege – the reader, by the fluidity, the energy of the language, and by their capacity to attract, to compel, to move on.

There is, secondly, the vast range of imagery upon which Donne drew in his poetry and, indeed, in his prose writings.

There are inevitably the biblical and theological images which provided the framework for so much of his thinking:

> Else, man not onely is the heard of swine,
>   But he's those devils too, which did incline
> Them to a headlong rage, and made them worse:
>   For man can adde weight to heavens heaviest curse:
> As Soules (they say) by our first touch, take in
>   The poysonous tincture of Originall sine,
> So, to the punishments which God doth fling,
>   Our apprehension contributes the sting.[13]

> Wee are but farmers of our selves, yet may,
> If we can stocke our selves and thrive uplay
> Much, much deare treasure for the great rent day.[14]

There are the geographical and nautical images which appear frequently. Two instances – one relating to his experience of life, and the other relating to a man's exploration of his lover's body – must suffice:

> Life is a voyage, and in our lifes wayes
> Countries, Courts, Towns are rockes or Remoraes;[a]
> They break or stop all ships, yet our state's such,
> That though then[b] pitch they staine worse, wee must touch.[15]

a. Remoraes (a sucking-fish)   b. then (than)

> The Nose (like to the first Meridian) runs
> Not 'twixt an East and West but 'twixt two suns;
> It leaves a Cheek, a rosie Hemisphere
> On either side, and then directs us where
> Upon the islands fortunate we fall,
> Not faynte *Canaries*, but *Ambrosiall*,
> Her swelling lips; To which when wee are come,
> We anchor there, and think our selves at home.[16]

Military images are also brought into service in exploring the delights of sexual desire:

> Here let mee warr; in these armes lett mee lye;
> Here let mee parlee, batter, bleede, and dye.
> Thy armes imprison mee, and myne armes thee,
> Thy hart thy ransome is: take myne for mee.[17]

There is poetry – a great deal of poetry – in Donne's prose writings, and his *Devotions upon Emergent Occasions* draws directly upon the natural world to explore the torments of sickness.

> Is this the honour which Man hath by being a *little world*, that he hath these *earthquakes* in him selfe, sodaine shakings; these *lightnings*, sodaine flashes; these *thunders*, sodaine noises; these *Eclypses*, sodaine offuscations, and darknings of his senses; these *Blazing stars,* sodaine fiery exhalations; these *Rivers of blood*, sodaine red waters?[18]

The human scene – as Donne captures it in his accounts of cities, of the courts of princes, and of the country – draws swiftly upon a variety of images: sepulchres, theatres, deserts.

> Cities are Sepulchers; they who dwell there
> Are carcases, as if no such there were.
> And Courts are Theaters, where some men play
> Princes, some slaves, all to one end, and of one clay.
> The country is a desert, where no good,
> Gain'd as habits, not borne is understood.[19]

The bleakness of life – the special bleakness of London at the time of the plague – is conveyed in these lines:

Thinke in how poore a prison thou didst lie
After, enabled but to sucke and crie.
Thinke, when t'was growne to most, T'was a poore Inne,
A Province pack'd up in two yards of skinne.[20]

As lancke and thin is every street and way
As a woman deliver'd yesterday.[21]

This handful of illustrations can scarcely do justice to the richness of Donne's imagery. He stamped his creativity, his individuality, upon his treatment of the human scene. The subject matter – or at least his interpretation – might be cheerless at times, and he could certainly be predictable in his writing; but the overall impression is of a mind that is ingenious, resourceful, provocative, straining and refreshing.

There is, thirdly, the dominance of certain themes – love and death – for which Donne is renowned. It is here that he gives full rein to his imagination and betrays so much of himself.

Donne explores the changing moods of human sexuality, of the love of men and women. He writes of desire, of ecstasy, of anxiety, of desolation. He provides an affirmation of the primacy of love.

When thou and I first one another saw:
All other things, to their destruction draw,
   Only our love hath no decay;
This, no to morrow hath, nor yesterday,
Running it never runs from us away,
But truly keepes his first, last, everlasting day.[22]

Donne writes with great simplicity, playfully and joyfully, of the delights of love.

I wonder by my troth, what thou, and I
Did till we lov'd? were we not wean'd til then?
But suck'd on countrey pleasures, childishly?
Or snorted we in the seaven sleepers den?
T'was so; But this all pleasures fancies bee
If ever any beauty I did see,
Which I desir'd, and got, twas but a dreame of thee.[23]

[23]

He is able to be sensual, flagrantly erotic.

> Licence my roaving hands, and let them go,
> Before, behind, between, above, below.[24]

But he is also well able to be promiscuous, cynical and brutal.

> Women are made for men, not him, nor mee.
> Foxes and goats; all beasts change when they please,
> Shall women, more hot, wiley, wild then[a] these,
> Be bound to one man, and did Nature then
> Idly make them apter to'endure then men?[25]

> Hope not for minde in women; at their best,
> Sweetnesse, and wit they'are, but, *Mummy*,[b] possest.[26]

> And at the Bridegroomes wish'd approach doth lye,
> Like an appointed Lambe when tenderly,
>   The priest comes on his knees t'embowell her.[27]

It is here that we see something of Donne's inability to enter into the mind and the feelings of a woman, and of his cynicism regarding the intimacies of sexuality and, indeed, of the institution of marriage. And yet he is capable also of speaking with great insight of the maturity in love to which men and women are able to aspire.

> No *Spring*, nor *Summer* Beauty hath such grace,
>   As I have seen in one *Autumnall* face.

> Were her first yeares the *Golden Age*; That's true,
> But now shee's *gold* oft tried and ever new.[28]

Love, the love of men and women, is an overwhelming preoccupation – intrusive, pervasive – and Donne pays tribute, homage.

> Love all alike, no season knowes nor clyme,
> No houres, dayes, months, which are the rags of time.[29]

But death takes its place alongside love as a subject of no less fascination for Donne. It was for him an obsession – 'undeviating, constant,

a. then (than)
b. Mummy (body without mind)

permanent, fixed'.[30] His awareness of our mortality stands – or appears to stand – in sharp contrast to the devil-may-care attitude of so many of his love poems; but it can only have its sombre, melancholy roots at some deep level within his psyche. His *Devotions upon Emergent Occasions* was written at a time of great sickness, but his overview of the human scene – 'the Earth . . . Cities . . . Men' – is that they have their 'common center . . . (in) . . . decay, ruine'.[31]

Death is 'strong and long-liv'd'.[32] The whole creation is subject to its sovereign power.

> Th'earths face is but thy Table; there are set
> Plants, cattell, men, dishes for Death to eate.[33]

Death encompasses our lives. Everything partakes of its destruction.

> Our births and lives, vices, and vertues, bee
> Wastefull consumptions, and degrees of thee.[34]

The philosophical mind-set within which all Donne's writings, including his poetry, must be set, is that provided by Christian faith and Christian hope. He does not hesitate to draw upon these resources to challenge death's supremacy.

> One short sleepe past, wee wake eternally,
> And death shall be no more, death thou shalt die.[35]

But nonetheless the fascination remains. Death and the fear of death – even when set within the context of Christian hope – bring an urgency, an intensity, into a good deal of Donne's poetry. Death is ever-present. It is climactic.

The continuing fascination of Donne's poetry lies in certain clearly established features: the distinctive characteristics of pace, of mood, of temper, of style; the vast range of imagery; the dominance of certain themes – love and death. It is in these ways that Donne clamours to secure our attention; displaying an imagination that is ingenious, provocative and resourceful; and sharing something of his own humanity – arrogant, restless, irreverent, cynical, intense, insecure. It is as though we are being admitted as spectators to a man's love affair with language, with all that impinges upon his consciousness, with love, with death, with God – and with himself.

[25]

J.E.V. Crofts writes of 'a man . . . unable to escape from his own drama'. He makes connections between Donne's treatment of love in his poetry and his treatment of death in his sermons. In the former, we find Donne writing 'not of love, but of himself loving'; and in the latter, it is not death that inspires his eloquence 'so much as the image of himself dying'. Crofts suggests that we have here something of the truth concerning 'the powerful fascination which (Donne's) writings exert . . . Every word is resonant with his voice; every line seems to bear the stamp of his peculiar personality'.[36]

A hymne to the Saints and to Marquesse Hamylton was written by Donne at the request of Sir Robert Carr in 1625. In a dedicatory letter to his friend and former patron, Donne belittles the poetry of his earlier years: 'you know my uttermost when it was best, and even then I did best when I had least truth for my subjects'. It is an intriguing statement. It might represent nothing more than Donne disowning – and not for the first time – the poetry of his youth; but it might also mean that for Donne – at least in the perspective of his later years – the poetry was little more than the work of his imagination, that the man who appears to give so much of himself is also mindful of how much he has held back.

Donne's complex mind and personality – tortured, energetic, intense, creative – do not easily lend themselves to any one interpretation. The ambiguities are too many. It is one of the paradoxes concerning Donne that although he is the first major English poet of whose life we know a great deal, yet it can also be maintained that 'no one in the history of English literature . . . is so difficult to realise, so impossible to measure'.[37]

There can be no evaluation of Donne's work as a propagandist without some acknowledgement of the prior question concerning his religious allegiance. Donne had been born into a Roman Catholic family which had suffered on his mother's side a history of imprisonment, exile and execution. Donne prefaced his book *Pseudo-Martyr* with an acknowledgement that he 'derived from such a stocke and race, as, I beleeve, no family (which is not of far longer extent and greater branches) hath endured and suffered more in their persons and fortunes, for obeying the Teachers of Romane Doctrine, then it hath done'.[38]

Donne's failure to proceed to his first degree at Oxford in the late

1580s was undoubtedly due to his inability as a Roman Catholic to subscribe to the Thirty-Nine Articles and to take the Oath of Supremacy. John Sparrow's study of Donne's religious development leads him to suggest that 'Donne was never, except nominally, a Roman Catholic'.[39] It is not easy to take this judgement at face value in the light of his family's story; but it is probable that the early 1590s was a time of eager theological enquiry on Donne's part. Izaak Walton writes of his beginning 'seriously to survey and consider the body of divinity, as it was then controverted betwixt the *Reformed* and the *Roman church*'.[40]

Donne was at pains in later years to insist that he 'used no inordinate hast nor precipitation in binding my conscience to any locall Religion'.[41] He was mindful of the fact that he 'had a longer work to doe than many other men; for I was first to blot out certaine impressions of the Roman religion, and to wrastle both against the examples and against the reasons, by which some hold was taken'.[42] Many scholars have drawn attention to *Satyre III*, and it may be that what is depicted there is Donne's pursuit of an understanding of the truth on which he might take his stand.

> . . . on a huge hill,
> Cragg'd, and steep, Truth stands, and hee that will
> Reach her, about must, and about must goe;
> And what the hills suddenes resists, winne so;
> Yet strive so, that before age death's twilight,
> Thy soule rest, for none can worke in that night.[43]

It is impossible to know if Donne was influenced in this journey by developments in his family's fortunes at this stage. It may be that the death of his younger brother Henry in 1593, while suffering imprisonment for his part in harbouring in his room a Roman Catholic priest, together with the decision of his mother and stepfather to go into exile in 1595, were final indications that if he sought advancement in the world then he must renounce his Roman Catholic faith. There is no evidence of any dramatic moment of conversion;[44] but there would almost certainly have been elements of self-preservation and self-seeking in his decision to forsake the Roman Catholic Church.

What can only be sustained with far greater difficulty is John Carey's interpretation of Donne's psychology and writings and ordained ministry on the basis of his 'apostacy'.[45] It is not self-evident that 'the first thing' – that is, *the most important thing* – 'to remember about Donne is that he was born a Catholic; (and) the second, that he betrayed his faith'.[46] There is good reason to speak of Donne's 'intractable egotism and of his determination to succeed'.[47] The evidence is abundant. It is certainly legitimate to write of Donne's becoming 'a part of the Anglican propaganda machine'.[48] There is justice in that charge. But the evidence of Donne's later life and of his preaching does not support without a good deal of qualification Carey's portrayal of 'Donne's need for a God who would make him suffer';[49] or of a man whose 'Christianity is dark and tormented';[50] or of Donne's finding 'in God and in his own position as God's spokesman, a final and fully adequate expression of his power lust';[51] or of Donne's having 'in his preaching something far more corrosive than satire with which to attack mankind, namely Christianity'.[52] It is scarcely surprising that David Edwards in his recent study of John Donne has levelled the charge of 'unfairness'.[53] There are depths in Donne's psyche which are not easily fathomed. There is – among many other things – a sombre, melancholy quality about the man. But it is difficult to justify on the basis of one hypothesis – and one which begs too many questions to be accepted uncritically – such a comprehensive interpretation of any man: his life, his writing, his preaching, his motivation.

The limited evidence provided by Donne's writings suggests that any change of allegiance was gradual.[54] Reference has already been made to *Satyre III*, and Helen Gardner's identification of the authority of conscience[55] – 'Keepe the truth which thou hast found'[56] – finds some resonance in Donne's letter to Sir Robert Ker towards the end of his life: 'My tenets are always for the Religion I was born in, and the peace of the State, and the rectifying of the conscience'.[57] Donne remained throughout his life 'a Catholic in the broadest sense of that word'.[58] His reading, his devotional life, his preaching provide ample proof of his continuing indebtedness to the Fathers and to the medieval Schoolmen. It remains the case, however, that other considerations – political and theological – weighed heavily in the balance and influenced his movement towards the Church of England.

The reformation divide dominated the politics of Western Europe and a continuing casualty was 'the peace of the State'. Conformity was required on both sides as a condition of unity. Neither Catholic nor Protestant princes had any monopoly of barbarity. Men and women were required to choose. The political element at the heart of the

English Reformation was an endorsement of the authority of the nation state – 'this realm of England is an Empire';[59] and the sovereign – the godly prince – was the symbol of the nation's unity and the final arbiter in all matters temporal and spiritual. The imperial pretensions of the papacy were rejected, and the heavy-handed response of the Roman see before and after the Council of Trent stiffened the resolve of those who were determined to secure peace and public order.

But the Reformation was also concerned with the purifying of religion. It was Queen Elizabeth I's proud boast to Parliament in 1598 that 'the estate and government of this Church of England as it now standeth in this reformation . . . both in form and doctrine . . . is agreeable with scriptures, with the most ancient general councils, with the practice of the primitive church, and with the judgement of all the old learned fathers'.[60] It was certainly Donne's complaint against the Roman Catholic Church that 'the Additional things exceed the Fundamentall; the Occasionall, the Originall; the Collaterall, the Direct; and the Traditions of men, the Commandments of God'.[61] It was an important emphasis in his work as a propagandist – both in the early 1600s and in his later preaching ministry – that 'our Church in the Reformation, proposed not that for her end, how shee might goe from Rome, but how she might come to the Truth'.[62]

One hundred and fifty years were to pass from the time of the Henrician Reformation in the 1530s to the Glorious Revolution of 1688. The English settlement remained precarious throughout the whole of that period, and the threat to its survival came as much from the Puritans as from the Roman Catholics. Donne identified himself entirely with the mainstream tradition of the English Church in emphasizing the *via media*. The path between the excesses of Rome and the abstinences of Geneva was one that Donne was well qualified to pursue. 'We need not clime up seven hills, nor wash our selves seven times in a Lake'.[63] Quite apart from doctrinal and political considerations – and in Donne's case no doubt some awareness of personal advantage – there was a feeling for the *via media* which expressed itself in the continuing dialogue between Scripture, tradition *and* reason; in the appeal to the authority of the early fathers *and* in an openness to new learning; in a commitment to the historic continuity of the catholic Church *and* in the freedom of the national churches. This is the background to Donne's encouragement to his hearers to 'trouble not thy selfe to know the formes and fashions of forraine particular Churches; neither of a Church in the lake, nor a Church upon seven hills; but since God hath planted thee in a Church, where all things necessary for salvation are administred to thee, and where no erronious doctrine . . . is affirmed and held, that is the Hill and that is the Catholique Church.'[64]

It appears from Izaak Walton that Donne's theological studies in the early 1590s had included the works of Cardinal Bellarmine,[65] and that these had been the subject of discussion in due course with Anthony Rudd, the Dean of Gloucester, to whom Donne might well have been referred for the purposes of critical oversight.[66] The following years were no doubt dominated for Donne by the expeditions to Cadiz and the Azores, by his employment in the household of Sir Thomas Egerton, and by his marriage to Ann More; but the long years of unemployment and poverty gave Donne some opportunity to make good use of his theological reading, his legal training and his aptitude for controversy. No self-appointed propagandist could have chosen with greater care a time in which his skills were to be more in demand.

A succession of smaller incidents in the early 1600s, culminating in the Gunpowder Plot of November 1605, brought the allegiance of Roman Catholic recusants into the forefront of public concern. Controversy centred around the re-imposition of the Oath of Allegiance, which in turn served to highlight differences of opinion within the Catholic community. Some Roman Catholic families would have been willing to make the necessary concessions, but resistance was strengthened by the obduracy of the Roman see, and King James the First was determined to bring out into the open 'the difference between the civilly-obedient Papists, and the perverse disciples of the Powder-Treason'.[67]

It was these controversies – the Gunpowder Plot, the imposition of new penalties and the publication of partisan tracts on both sides – which drew Donne into his work as a propagandist. Izaak Walton suggests that Donne now began to devote some considerable time to 'a constant study of some points of controversy betwixt the *English* and *Roman Church* and especially those of *Supremacy* and *Allegiance*'.[68] The two principal protagonists were Cardinal Bellarmine and Bishop Lancelot Andrewes, and they were joined at an early stage by Thomas Morton, who was appointed to the deanery of Gloucester in the summer of 1607. There is some difference of scholarly opinion concerning the degree to which Donne assisted Morton in the preparation of his writings,[69] but it is possible that Donne provided important background information concerning the various authorities quoted in the texts.[70]

It was the publication of *Pseudo-Martyr* in 1610 that established Donne as 'a serious controversialist'.[71] Izaak Walton suggests that it was written at the request of King James.[72] Certainly the book was dedicated to the King and served to enhance Donne's reputation and to point him – in the eyes of the King – towards ordination and preferment in the church. It was the first of Donne's prose works to be published, and it brought him into the forefront of the public debate.

Pseudo-Martyr does not attempt to offer a wide-ranging defence of the Church of England. Donne confined himself in large measure to questions relating to the royal supremacy, the Oath of Allegiance and the duty of subjects. Donne is persuaded that Roman Catholics should take the Oath of Allegiance, that any sufferings endured for failing to do so are self-inflicted, and that those who do suffer are therefore pseudo-martyrs and have no claim to the true dignity of martyrdom which belongs to those who have died for their faith.

Donne wrote with 'a studied moderation'.[73] He was concerned along the way to challenge the Pope's claim to temporal jurisdiction and the policy of uncompromising and subversive opposition to kings and nation states who had embraced the reformed religion. 'To offer our liues for defence of the catholique faith, hath euer beene a religious custome; but to call euery pretence of the Pope, Catholique faith, and to bleede to death for it, is a sicknesse and a medicine, which the Primitiue Church neuer understood'.[74]

There is also to be found in *Pseudo-Martyr* a clear statement of the position to which Donne had moved and which placed him within the mainstream of reformed thinking concerning the English religious settlement. Donne insists that his overriding purpose is 'the Vnity and peace' of the Church.[75] He argues that 'as when the roofe of the Temple rent assunder, not long after followed the ruine of the foundation it selfe: so if these two principal beames and toppe-rafters, *the Prince* and *the Priest*, rent assunder, the whole frame and Foundation of Christian Religion will be shaked'.[76] There is more than a hint here of Richard Hooker's *Res Publica Christiana*. Church and commonwealth are one, and they find their focus and their unity in the person of the king. Thus it is that Donne can go on to argue that 'if we distinguish not between Articles of faith and jurisdiction, but account all those super-edifications and furnitures, and ornaments which God hath afforded to His Church, for exteriour gouernment, to be equally the Foundation it selfe, there can bee no Church'.[77] Donne was to make it abundantly plain in the course of his subsequent ministry that the foundation is the authority of Christ in Scripture in his Church. What Donne resists are the totalitarian claims of the Roman imperium.

Pseudo-Martyr was followed in 1611 by the publication of *Ignatius His Conclave*. This book, which was published anonymously, was written by Donne in Latin, and then in English, and finally appeared in no less than three Latin and four English editions. It is a mischievous and scurrilous satire, which does not pretend to be anything more than an attack on the Jesuits. Its popularity at the time says something about the climate of opinion in which it appeared, but it has long since ceased to have any relevance except as an instance of Donne's tongue-in-the-cheek imagination and of the dubious gifts as a polemicist which he undoubtedly possessed.

Ignatius His Conclave takes the form of a dream in which Donne portrays the scene in hell as various candidates – including Copernicus, Paracelsus, Machiavelli and Columbus – come for admission. Their claims are resisted in every case by Ignatius Loyola who, seated near the Devil's chair, is determined to reserve all places in hell for members of the Society of Jesus. The Devil's patience is finally exhausted, and he suggests that the only way forward will be for Ignatius and all Jesuits to withdraw to the moon and establish a new empire there. The dream ends with a riot in hell as Ignatius Loyola attempts to dispossess Pope Boniface of his seat and place.

Few publications provide so eloquent a commentary upon the context in which Donne pursued his career as a propagandist. Those who appear for admission to hell are obviously representatives in many cases of new developments in astronomy, in philosophy, in political theory, in our knowledge of the world. But the primary objective of attack in *Ignatius His Conclave* is not the innate conservatism of the papacy and its resistance to all thought which it could not control; it is far more specifically the Jesuits, who were associated – certainly in England and France – with the policy of violence against kings who embraced the reformed religion and renounced the temporal jurisdiction of the papacy. There had been some alarm in England at the assassination of King Henri IV of France in 1610, and Donne, who was sceptical of the value of monasticism throughout his life, chose his target well, and may well have had the additional satisfaction of bringing the arch-rival protagonist, the Jesuit Cardinal Bellarmine, within his sights.

Donne would certainly have hoped that his public espousal of the king's concerns would lead to royal favour and to employment; but Izaak Walton, whose imaginative reconstructions of significant conversations at different times in Donne's life cannot be accepted uncritically, relates the king's judgement: 'I know Mr Donne is a learned man, has the abilities of a learned divine, and will prove a powerful preacher; and my desire is to prefer him that way, and in that way I would deny you nothing for him'. [78] It can only be inferred that King James had found in Donne someone who could be trusted to defend the ecclesiastical settlement and the royal prerogative.

The royal prerogative – the royal supremacy – was an important ingredient in Donne's thinking. Donne's position in due course as a Chaplain in Ordinary to the King required him to preach at court in the course of every year, over and above the public sermons that he gave in the presence of the King and of lords spiritual and temporal throughout his ministry at Paul's Cross. Donne always held back from any criticism of the King in the pulpit. He was adamant that kings are 'Lieutenants and Images of God'[79] and that judgement therefore belongs to God alone. Donne did not always enjoy easy relations with the Puritans, and his public intervention in defence of the King's newly published *Instructions to Preachers* in September 1622 could not have helped; but Donne took advantage of the opportunity to speak of the relationship between church and state, to justify the *Instructions* and the restrictions they attempted to impose upon Puritan preachers, and to win the King's approval for a sermon which was 'a piece of such perfection as could admit neither addition nor diminution'.[80]

Donne's intervention on this issue was occasioned by the King's request, but he would have entered the fray with some appetite and conviction. It was unquestionably the Separatists, the Independents, the Puritans, whom he had in mind when he urged that, 'Except there be errour in *fundamentall* points, such as make this Church no Church, let no man depart from that Church, and that religion, in which he delivered himself to the service of God at first'.[81]

Donne steers a middle course between the traditions of Rome and Geneva.

... the Church of God, is not so *beyond sea*, as that we must needs seek it *there* either in a *painted Church*, on one side, or in a *naked Church*, on another; a Church in a *dropsie*, overflowne with *Ceremonies*, or a Church in a *Consumption*, for want of such Ceremonies, as the primitive Church found usefull, and beneficiall, for the advancing of the glory of God, and the devotion, of the Congregation.[82]

Donne was unashamedly partisan in his defence of the English religious settlement.

And nearer to (God), and to the institution of his Christ, can no Church, no not of the Reformation, be said to have come closer than ours.[83]

Donne was stridently dismissive of the universal and exclusive claims of the Church of Rome.

... the uncharitableness of the *Church* of *Rome* toward us all, is not a *Torrent*, nor is it a Sea, but a generall *flood*, an universall *deluge*, that swallowes all the world ... and will not allowe a possibilitie of Salvation to the whole *Arke*, the whole Christian Church, but to one *Cabin* in that *Arke*, the *Church of Rome*; and then denie us this Salvation, not for any *Positive* Errour, that they ever charged us to affirme; not because wee affirme any thing, that they denie, but because wee denie somethings, which they in their afternoone are come to affirme.[84]

But his most vehement and abrasive expressions of disgust are reserved for the papacy itself.

There is a man, the man of sin at Rome, that pretends to be Christ, to all uses. And I would be content with that, and stop there, and not be a Hyper-Christus, Above Christ, more then Christ. I would he would not more trouble the peace of Christendome, no more occasion the assassination of Christian Princes, no more binde the Christian liberty, in forbidding meats, and marriage, no more slacken and dissolve Christian bands, by Dispensations and Indulgences, then Christ did, but if he will needs be more, if he will needs have an addition to the name of Christ, let him take heed of that addition, which some are apt enough to give him, however he deserve it, that he is Antichrist'.[85]

The times in which Donne lived demanded uncompromising statements of conviction. The divide in western Christendom was too recent, too fundamental, too raw, to encourage the courtesies of a later age. Donne took his place alongside a fair number of contemporaries on both sides of the divide who used their intellectual, literary and oratorical skills as unashamed apologists of the cause they espoused. But there is a hint – and a good deal more than a hint – of a broader vision. Dominic Baker-Smith finds that, 'Behind the mineral brilliance and irony there lies Donne's image of the true church, an image that holds in delicate relation the values of personal judgement and Catholic tradition'.[86] When it comes to personal piety, Donne is not afraid to be both Papist (in fasting and prayer and mortification of the flesh) and Puritan (in his detestation of blasphemy and of profaning the Sabbath).[87] And beyond these disciplines, there lies an inclusive vision that transcends all controversy and division.

> For all this separation, Christ Jesus is amongst us all, and in his time, will breake downe the wall too, these differences amongst Christians, and make us all glad of that name, the name of Christians, without affecting ourselves, or inflicting upon others, other names of envy, and subdivision.[88]

Nonetheless, Donne's work as a propagandist must stand alongside his poetry and his preaching as one aspect of a mind and a spirit that were lively, provocative, searching.

John Donne is renowned for his poetry, but he deserves to be no less well known for his sermons. His prose writings are of little more than historical interest, but his sermons have been described as 'the most significant prose ever uttered from an English pulpit, if not the most magnificent prose ever spoken in our tongue'.[89] Donne was – at least after the death of Lancelot Andrewes in 1626 – the most famous preacher of his day, and his sermons have come down as 'one of the earliest and best expositions of the divinity of (the) English Church'.[90]

The publication of some of Donne's poetry in 1633 was accompanied by a number of tributes – *Elegies Upon the Author* – contributed by friends. One of these – Mr R.B. (probably Mr Richard Busby, subsequently headmaster of Westminster School) – gives this impression of Donne the preacher.

> Mee thinkes I see him in the pulpit standing,
> Not eares, or eyes, but all mens hearts commanding,
> Where wee that heard him, to our selves did faine
> Golden Chrysostome was alive again;
> And never were we weari'd, till we saw
> His houre (and but an houre) to end did drawe.[91]

The virtues of Donne's sermons may not be immediately apparent. Henry Hart Milman, one of Donne's mid-nineteenth-century successors as Dean of St Paul's, wrote, 'It is difficult for a Dean of our rapid and restless days to imagine . . . a vast congregation in the Cathedral or at Paul's Cross, listening not only with patience but even with absorbed interest, with unflagging attention, even with delight and rapture, to these interminable disquisitions, to us teeming with laboured obscurity, false and misplaced wit, fatiguing antitheses. However set off, as by all accounts they were, by a most graceful and impressive delivery, it is astonishing to us that he should hold a London congregation enthralled, unwearied, unsatiated. Yet there can be no doubt that this was the case.'[92]

Donne brought to his work as a preacher his skill as a poet. He never lost his feel for words. It was in his sermons that his genius as a poet, as a word-artist, came to full maturity and expression. But their literary craftsmanship, their richness of language, their unrivalled use of metaphor, their pace and tone, their rhetoric, their eloquence do not obscure or compromise the preacher's portrayal of the human predicament, of the vanities of life, of the deceits of sin, of the gospel of grace and redemption. Their length, their denseness, their scriptural and classical allusions, their frequent quotations, their tricks of style do not conceal the direct appeal of the preacher to mind and heart and conscience.

The sermon was for Donne an exposition of Scripture *and* an evangelical call to penitence and holiness of life. Izaak Walton describes Donne as 'a preacher in earnest . . . always preaching to himself . . . (and) carrying some to heaven in holy raptures, and enticing others by a sacred art and courtship to amend their lives'.[93] Donne did not hesitate to reprove the man who 'heares but the Logique, or the Retorique, or the Ethique, or the poetry of the sermon', but fails to hear 'the Sermon of the Sermon'.[94] Donne's surviving sermons constitute a unique archive, both for any understanding of the man and for any appreciation of the preaching of the English Church in the early seventeenth century. Izaac Walton's statement that Donne preached 'once a week if not oftner'[95] may not be accurate, but there is no doubt that Donne preached with far greater frequency than many of his predecessors and successors in the deanery of St Paul's. Preaching was the first priority, the distinctive hallmark, of his public ministry; and he was determined to ensure that his sermons – or at least some of his sermons – would survive.

A sermon would customarily last for an hour and would be delivered by the preacher with reference only to notes. One hundred and forty five of Donne's sermons appeared in print in three folio volumes within thirty years of his death, and the complete edition of the one hundred and sixty extant sermons prepared by George Potter and Evelyn Simpson for publication by the University of California Press between 1953 and 1962 remains the definitive edition of Donne's preaching. The sermons that have survived are not word for word the sermons that Donne preached. Some would have taken two or three hours to deliver in the form in which they now stand. Donne prepared many of his sermons for printing, writing them out in full, correcting and enlarging upon any notes he had used in the pulpit.

Ordination had given Donne 'a new calling, new thoughts, and a new employment for his wit and eloquence'.[96] It was his boast that London had 'the ablest preaching Clergy of any City in Christendom';[97] and the sermon – the hour-long discourse: scholarly, meticulously prepared, with ample scope for literary and oratorical skills, and delivered with passion – might have been devised for Donne and the deployment of his talents. One contemporary wrote of the 'wealth of his unequalled wit, and yet more incomparable eloquence in the pulpit'.[98]

Donne brought to his public ministry a high sense of the dignity and the authority of the office of a preacher. He condemned the laziness and the ignorance and the vainglory of the preacher who made 'a pye of Plums without meat' or 'an Oration of Flowres and Figures, and Phrases without strength'.[99] Whatever the dynamics of his own personality, whatever the gifts he brought to ordination, whatever the apparent ease with which in due course he commanded the attention of his congregations, Donne was clear that 'a preachers end is not a gathering of fame to himselfe, but a gathering of soules to God'.[100]

Donne lived in an age of transition, but he was steeped in the scholarship and the traditions of the ancient and medieval worlds. His wide reading over the years had given him a detailed knowledge of the early Fathers, the medieval Schoolmen, and the theologians and controversialists – Roman Catholic and Protestant – of recent generations. There are repeated references in his sermons to Augustine, Ambrose, Tertullian, Bonaventure, Luther and Calvin; and Donne stands alongside the notable preachers and writers of his age – Richard Hooker, Lancelot Andrewes, William Laud, Jeremy Taylor – in his appeal to the Fathers and the Schoolmen.

Donne brought to his preaching his remarkable gift for words, but the ordering of his sermons reflects the traditions of an earlier age: a detailed examination of the text, an allegorical method of interpretation, the appeal to authority, the use of reason. But Donne breathes new life into the ordered method of exposition with an imagination and an intensity that are unparalleled: the fluidity of his language, the imagery, the parallelism, the repeated use of words and themes, the moral fervour.

Donne was not a systematic theologian. Nor was he an original or a speculative thinker. He remained firmly within the mainstream tradition of a reformed Catholicism. His originality lay in the images he employed to press home the appeal to conscience. He was essentially a moralist. 'Morall Divinity becomes all', he wrote, 'but Naturall Divinity and Metaphysical Divinity, almost all may spare.'[101] The moral intensity which can be found in his religious poetry becomes moral fervour in his preaching. 'His sermons are the work of an orator and a poet, whose strength lay in the reality of his own personal religious experience and in the power of imagination.'[102]

The methodical and well-ordered approach that was adopted by Donne in the presentation of his sermons can be well illustrated by reference to an early sermon preached at Lincoln's Inn in the spring or summer of 1618 on Psalm 38, verse 3. Donne introduces his text and then continues:

Which words we shall first consider . . . as they are historically, and literally to be understood of *David*; And secondly, in their *retrospect*, as they look back upon the first *Adam*, and so concern

Mankind collectively, and so *You*, and *I*, and all have our portion in these calamities; And thirdly, we shall consider them in their *prospect*, in their future relation to the *second Adam*, in *Christ Jesus*, in whom also all mankinde was collected.[103]

Thus the psalm from which his text is taken becomes for Donne 'a *historicall*, and *personall* Psalm, determin'd in *David* . . . a *Catholique* and *universall* Psalm, extended to the whole condition of *man* . . . a *Propheticall*, and *Evangelicall* Psalm, directed upon Christ'.[104]

There is nothing here, however, to indicate either the literary devices or the rhetoric and the passion by which Donne would capture the minds and hearts of his congregations. There is a far larger vocabulary in his sermons than in his poetry. There is the use of alliteration, of parallel structures, of antithesis. There is the repetition of key words from clause to clause, from sentence to sentence, enabling them to 'take fire from each other'.[105] There is metaphor and paradox and epigram. There is hyperbole. There is movement, rhythm, music. And there is passion. 'Ideas, theories, doctrines, quotations, allusions, imagery, are all devoted to this end, they are inherent, all caught up in the intensity of the emotion. The repetition and the alliteration, the internal resonances and rhythms, all drive inwards to its core.'[106]

It is in the generous use of imagery that Donne displays his genius as a poet in the pulpit. He takes his illustrations from everyday life, drawing his hearers into situations that they can well imagine, and enabling them to see the hidden purposes of God. The royal court, the university, the court of law, the theatre and the market place; the sea, the maps of the world, fishing and the seashore; the world of nature, the seasons, thunder and lightning, agriculture, the tree and its blossom; all these – and so many other – images are brought into play. The call to discipleship is illustrated by reference to recruitment for military service; private prayer by reference to the striking of a clock; public prayer by reference to the coinage of the realm; suffering for Christ by reference to the fires of Smithfield and the Courts of Justice; and the life of heaven by reference to spelling, knowledge, athletics, fighting, sailing, apprenticeship, wardship.

Donne's dramatic talents, combined with a melancholy turn of mind, an intensely personal approach, and great intellectual vitality, stamp his personality upon his sermons. He can argue, he can plead, he can challenge, he can confront. He can be laboured, artful, colloquial, incisive, direct. He can speak with complexity, subtlety, simplicity. There is a rigour, an austerity, about his preaching. He is uncompromising in his denunciation of sin, of complacency, of collusion. He knows the human condition and he penetrates its defences. And yet there is hope: the confidence of faith, the conviction of grace, the invitation to glory.

Donne's public ministry – and especially his preaching – must be set against the backcloth of a reformation settlement which was under attack from Papists and Puritans. The English Reformation had been concerned to establish within a reformed church polity the primary authority of the Scriptures, of the gospel sacraments, of the threefold orders of ministry, of the historic creeds, of the early ecumenical councils. It had been Richard Hooker's great achievement in his work *Of the Laws of Ecclesiastical Polity* to bring all these things within a wide-ranging theological and philosophical system, maintaining the essential continuities with the early and the medieval church, and holding fast to the theory and practice of a Christian commonwealth in which church and state are one.

It was exactly here that Donne took his stand, treading carefully the middle way between Rome and Geneva. He was true to the Scriptures. He was true to the traditions of the early church. He understood the dialogue of faith and reason. He preached with passion the touchstone doctrines of the incarnation and the atonement. There was – perhaps inevitably at this stage in the story of the English Church – something more than a dash of Calvinism in his teaching: election to salvation, the universal corruption of sin, the death of the cross as a substitutionary sacrifice, the corruptions of the Roman Church and the tentative but tell-tale designation of the Bishop of Rome as the Antichrist.

Donne was open to criticism from both sides, and not least of all from the Puritans for whom the complexity of his sermons, the subtlety of his arguments and the elegance of his language earned him the reputation of being 'a bad edifier'.[107] It may be as Evelyn Simpson suggests that, 'His theology was too medieval in some respects and too modern in others'.[108] There was undoubtedly a broader vision which enabled Donne to feel after something more inclusive than the rigid definitions of Catholic and Protestant orthodoxy; but what is established beyond all doubt is his full acceptance of the fundamental Christian doctrines and of the teaching and formularies of the English Church.

None of the literary and oratorical characteristics displayed in Donne's sermons – his method of proceeding with the exposition of a text, his literary skills, his craftsmanship, his pace, his rhetoric – obscured his proclamation of the gospel. What is conveyed in the sermons, in spite of their complexity and their ingenuity, is the whole drama of redemption. Faith and reason in the discernment of God, the life of the Holy Trinity, election and creation, the fall, the human predicament, the work of Christ, the church, the life of discipleship, the last things: all these are explored – or at the very least touched upon – as Donne's preaching ministry unfolds at Lincoln's Inn, at Paul's Cross, before the Court, at St Paul's Cathedral, at St Dunstan's in the West.

Donne's approach to Scripture was uncritical, unquestioning. It was in all its parts the revealed and transmitted word of God.

> . . . the *Christian doctrine necessary* for salvation was delivered at once, that is intirely in one spheare, in the body of the Scriptures.[109]

But the Scriptures cannot be detached from the life of the church and from the preaching of the word.

> The Scriptures are Gods Voyce; The Church is his Eccho; a redoubling, a repeating of some particular syllables, and accents of the same voice.[110]

> There is no salvation but by faith, nor faith but by hearing, nor hearing but by preaching.[111]

What is conveyed in the Scriptures is the biblical understanding of our humanity: elected to grace and glory; created in the image of God; fallen and enslaved by sin; redeemed by the birth, passion, death and resurrection of Jesus Christ.

> God hath elected certaine men, whom he intends to create, that he may elect them; that is, that he may declare his Election upon them. God had thee, before he made thee; he loved thee first, and then created thee, that thou loving him, he might continue his love to thee.[112]

> This then is the miserable state of the world, It might know, and does not, that it is wholly under an inundation, a deluge of sin.[113]

[41]

. . . before our bones were hardned, the canker and rust of *Adams* sin was in our bones . . . before we were a minute old, we have a sin in us that is six thousand years old.[114]

You see what you had, and how you lost it. If it might not bee recovered, God would not call you to it.[115]

The whole life of Christ was a continuall Passion . . . His birth and death were but one continuall act, and His Christmas-day and His Good Friday are but the evening and morning of one and the same day.[116]

. . . all sins, of all ages, all sexes, all places, al times, all callings, sins heavy in their substance, sins aggravated by their circumstances, all kinds of sins, and all particular sins of every kind, were upon him, upon Christ Jesus.[117]

. . . when I believe God in Christ, dead, and risen againe according to the Scriptures, I have nothing else to beleeve.[118]

Donne brought to his preaching his knowledge of the world and of his own frailty. He recalled only too easily the long years of self-seeking, of emptiness. He spoke therefore with understanding as he portrayed the human predicament and called his hearers to repentance.

All the foure changes of our life, Infancy, Youth, Middle-Age, and Old, have been spent and worne out in a continuall, and uninterrupted course of sin.[119]

Before Ambition, or Covetousnesse, or Licentiousnesse, is awake in us, Pride is working.[120]

We sin constantly, and we sin continually, and we sin confidently; and we finde so much pleasure and profit in sin, as that we have made a league, and sworn a friendship with sin; and we keep that perverse, and irreligious promise over-religiously; and the sins of our youth flow into other sins, when age disables us for them.[121]

There are complexions that cannot blush; there growes a blacknesse, a sootinesse, upon the soule, by customs in sin, which overcomes all blasting, all tendernesse.[122]

There is an urgency both about the preaching of the call to discipleship and the life of Christian obedience.

God . . . desires to have his kingdome well peopled; he would have *many*, he would have *all*, he would have *every one* of them have all.[123]

Our *criticall* day is *not* the *very day* of our *death*: but the whole course of our life. I thank him that *prayes* for me when my bell tolles, but I thank him more that *Catechises* mee, or *preaches* to mee, or *instructs* mee how to live.[124]

If I would not serve God, except I might be saved for serving him, I shall not be saved though I serve him; My first end in serving God, must not be my self, but he and his glory.[125]

There is in Donne's sermons an obsession with death and with the experience of dying. There is something morbid, even at times grotesque, by the standards of a later age; but Donne is in no doubt about the Christian hope and the true meaning of the torments of damnation.

My hope *before* death is, that this life is the *way*; my hope *at* death is, that my death shall be a *doore* into a better state.[126]

. . . but when we shall have given to those words, by which hell is expressed in the Scriptures, the heaviest significations, that either the nature of those words can admit, or as they are types and representations of hell, as *fire*, and *brimstone*, and *weeping*, and *gnashing*, and *darkness*, and *the worme* . . . when all is done, the hell of hels, the torment of torments is the everlasting absence of God, and the everlasting impossibility of returning to his presence.[127]

There is a sombre, melancholy feel to much of Donne's preaching, but it is shot through – surprisingly so at times – with affirmations of the joy of discipleship.

Religion is no sullen thing, it is not a melancholy, there is not so sociable a thing as the love of Christ Jesus.[128]

Beloved, good diet makes the best Complexion, and a good conscience is a continuall feast; A cheerful heart makes the best blood and peace with God is the true cheerfulnesse of heart.[129]

There are many . . . outward badges and marks, by which others may judge, and pronounce mee to be a true Christian; But the inward badge and marke, by which I know this in my self, is joy.[130]

But the joys of discipleship are merely an anticipation of the life of the world to come. Beyond all faith and hope there is the love in which the redeemed are united through Christ in God for all eternity.

In heaven, where we shall *know God*, there may be no use of *faith*; in heaven, where we shall *see God*, there may be no use of *hope*; but in heaven, where *God* the Father, and the *Son*, love one another in the Holy Ghost, the bond of charity shall everlastingly unite us together.[131]

The glory of Gods Saints in Heaven, is not so much to have a Crown, as to lay down that Crown at the Feet of the Lamb.[132]

The discipline that lay behind the long years of study can be seen in Donne's methodical approach to his sermons and in the sheer quantity of quotations that dominate the texts. The genius that has been apparent in the poetry of his earlier years is displayed in the literary and oratorical tricks of style, the extraordinarily wide range of imagery, and the rhetoric of the sermons. It is also possible to see something of the restless, striving – even tortured – man, who keeps faith with his priestly task, but who continues to show something of the wounds of his own passion.

Izaak Walton, who loses no opportunity to enlarge the reputation of his friend and pastor, speaks of Donne's movement towards ordination in extravagant terms. 'Now the *English church* had gained a second St. *Austin*; for I think none was so like him before his conversion; none so like St. *Ambrose* after it: and, if his youth had the infirmities of the one, his age had the excellencies of the other; the learning and holiness of both.'[133] But Walton's eulogy begs too many questions. Was the transition to holiness as thorough as Walton suggests? Was there no looking back at what might have been, or – more probably – no looking forward to what might still be? It is Donne's experience of life that makes his call to penitence so compelling. Is he not speaking out of his experience – his continuing experience – when he reminds his congregation that, 'Our life is a warfare, our whole life; it is not onely with lusts in our youth, and ambitions in our middle yeares, and indevotions in our age, but with agonies in our body and tentations in our spirit upon our death-bed, that we are to fight.'[134]

It is no disparagement of Donne's integrity to say that he becomes more and not less impressive because he had known the appetites of the flesh, the ambitions of the world, the weariness of life. It may well be that Donne, caught in the crossfire of flesh and spirit, had something approaching a love-hate relationship with life, with the world; but there are important consequences for his preaching. First, the delight in physical love, in sexual love, which was so explicit in some of his early poems, is now transmuted so that what is presented is God's love for man and man's love for God. But it is still love in its various manifestations that is at the heart of so much that he has to say. Secondly, the vast range of imagery upon which Donne draws suggests that for him all life is one. The world in its entirety is the arena of God's activity. Latter-day distinctions between the sacred and the secular are meaningless. God's purposes and grace and judgement can be discerned in all the circumstances of life.

Donne reveals himself to a remarkable degree, and 'the personality that emerges . . . is itself fluid and restless – always changing, expanding, struggling, developing – exploring new channels, sometimes tortuous, always original, into which to pour its restless energy'.[135] It is no small part of his originality that he transcends traditional categories – of theology, of ecclesiastical tradition – feeling after a broader and far more inclusive vision.

Scripture has for Donne a primary authority, but he recognizes that it admits 'diverse interpretations',[136] that the 'figurative sense' will often be 'the literall sense',[137] and that there is a 'Law of Liberty' which requires us 'charitably to lead others to their liberty if they differ from us, and not differ from Fundamentall Truths'.[138] Something of this broader vision is to be found also in his approach to the doctrine of Election.

> When God gives me accesse into his *Library*, leave to consider his proceedings with men, I find the first book of Gods making to be the *Book of Life*. The Book where all their names are written that are elect to Glory. But I find no such Book of Death.[139]

It may be Donne's experience of grace which determines his approach, but the question is confidently asked that if the whole of our humanity is in Christ, then 'can any man be excluded from a possibility of mercy?'[140]

The austerity that marks so much of Donne's preaching is absent when he comes from time to time to consider the ways in which God accomplishes the salvation of mankind.

> . . . though . . . there are an infinite number of *Stars* more than we can distinguish, and so, by Gods grace, there may be an infinite number of soules saved, more then those whose salvation, we discerne the *ways* and the meanes.[141]

> Let us embrace the way which God hath given us, which is the knowledge of his Sonne, Christ Jesus: what other way God may take with others . . . let us not inquire too curiously, determine too peremptorily, pronounce too uncharitably: God be blessed, for his declaring his good-will towards *us*, and *his will be done* his way upon others.[142]

It is the same spirit of generosity which informs Donne's appeal to Christian people to live in charity with one another.

> Go thou to heaven, in an humble thankfulnesse to God, and holy cheerfulnesse in that way that God hath manifested to thee; and do not pronounce too bitterly, too desperately, that every man is in an errour, that thinkes not just as thou thinkest, or in no way that is not in thy way.[143]

The law of liberty, the law of love, are both contained for Donne within an awareness of the universality of grace. 'Christ is come to call sinners, onely sinners, all sinners.'[144] Few preachers could have spoken these words with greater insight or greater feeling. The sermons constitute a remarkable testimony to the power of the wounded healer. There is nothing forced, nothing self-indulgent about Donne's abiding sense of unworthiness.

> I doubt not of mine own salvation; and in whom can I have so much occasion of doubt, as in my self? When I come to heaven, shall I be able to say to any there, Lord! how got you hither? Was any less likely to come thither then I?[145]

DEANE OF PAULES

John Donne was appointed to the deanery of St Paul's by King James I in the autumn of 1621. Izaak Walton gives an account, which may well be apocryphal, of how the King instructed Donne to attend him at dinner, and of how 'when his majesty was sat downe, before he had eaten any meat, he said . . . Dr. Donne, I have invited you to dinner; and, though you sit not down with me, yet I will carve you of a dish that I know you love well; for, knowing you love London, I do therefore make you Dean of Paul's; and when I have dined, then do you take your beloved dish home to your study, say grace there to your self, and much good may it do you.'[1]

Ordination had not assuaged Donne's ambition. He had been encouraged to believe that the King would advance him, but he left nothing to chance and worked hard to secure the influence of those who might assist. His name had been mentioned casually in connection with the deaneries of Salisbury and Gloucester in the summer of 1621, but in the event there was no vacancy in either place. He had pressed his name upon the Duke of Buckingham, the current favourite at Court, as one condemned to 'ly in a corner, as a clodd of clay, attending what kinde of vessell yt shall please you to make of'.[2] It may well be that Donne owed his appointment, which was made possible by the preferment of his predecessor, Dr Valentine Carey, to the see of Exeter, not merely to Buckingham but also to Dr John Williams who, retaining the deanery of Westminster, had also been recently appointed as Bishop of Lincoln and Lord Keeper of the Great Seal.

Donne's election, institution and installation took place on 22 November, and he took possession in due course of the deanery, 'a building of great extent . . . a desirable residence . . . a faire old mansion',[3] which stood on the south side of the cathedral. One of Donne's first tasks, undertaken no doubt at his own expense, was the repair and enrichment of the chapel annexed to the deanery.[4] Donne had previously encouraged the benchers of Lincoln's Inn during his years as Reader in Divinity to proceed with their plans for the rebuilding of their chapel; but these two activities with which Donne was closely associated – the building of the chapel of Lincoln's Inn and the refurbishment of the chapel annexed to the deanery – did not indicate any enthusiasm on his part for the long-neglected task of repairing the fabric of the cathedral.

The cathedral had been in serious need of extensive repair and restoration since 1561 when the spire of Old St Paul's was struck by lightning and completely destroyed, together with the roofs of the nave and the north and south aisles. Unavoidable repairs were carried out and new roofs were completed by 1566, but neglect and apathy then took over. Drawings and estimates for new repairs – to the nave, the aisles, the transepts, and the chapter house, together with the rebuilding of the spire – were provided in 1582 and again in 1608, but no work was set in hand. The cathedral is described as being 'almost ruinous',[5] and a Commission was appointed by King James in 1620 'to enquire into the decay of the Cathedral'.[6] There was no question of the financial burden falling solely upon the Dean and Chapter. A second Commission appointed in 1620 authorized the appointment of 'surveyors and other officers' and prepared the way for a nationwide appeal.[7] The Bishop of London provided monies for the purchase of stone, but again there appears to have been no resolve to pursue the work. Portland stone, which had been intended for some of the repairs, was 'borrowed by the Duke of Buckingham for his water-gate at York House'.[8] It is impossible to avoid asking if the stone was borrowed with a view to its being restored, or if Buckingham was extracting his price for any service he had rendered in securing the deanery for Donne a few years before.[9]

Judgements concerning what happened at the cathedral during Donne's tenure of office can often be based only upon reports which either precede or immediately follow his years as Dean. Certainly there is no evidence to suggest that Donne and his residentiary canons gave the repair of the building any priority, but the appointment of William Laud to the see of London in 1628 brought a new determination to bear. Within days of Donne's death in March 1631, the necessary steps were taken to ensure that funding was secured and administered on behalf of the Chapter, and Laud commended the proposals to the Privy Council on the grounds that it was the King's intention 'to have the Cathedral Church of St Paul, in London, repaired and beautified, being one of the goodliest and most ancient fabricks in Europe; but now a disgrace to o^r. country, and the citte, and a common imputacon and scandall laid upon o^r. Religion . . . it being growen into extreme decay, and like shortly to fall, if it be not prevented'.[10] Much was achieved in the following decade under the direction of Inigo Jones as Surveyor to the Fabric, but from the early 1640s everything was overtaken by the traumas of civil war and of the Commonwealth, and within a generation the cathedral, together with so much of the City of London, was destroyed in the Great Fire.

Any scandal pertaining to the decay of the fabric of the cathedral was more than compounded by a long history of desecration. *The Burnynge of Paules Church*, which had been published soon after the cathedral had been struck by lightning in 1561, spoke at that time of 'the South Alley for Usurye and Poperye, the North for Simony, and the Horse Faire in the middest for all kind of bargains, meetings, brawlings, murthers, conspiracies, and the Font for the ordinarie paymentes of money'.[11] The situation had scarcely improved by the time of Bishop Bancroft's visitation in 1598, when the response of the Dean and Chapter and of other officers of the cathedral to the Articles of Enquiry depicted a scene of 'greate disorder in the Churche, that Porters, Butchers, Waterberers, and who not? be suffred . . . to carrye and recarrye whatsoever, no man w^{t}hstandinge them or gaynsayenge them . . . and boyes . . . pissinge upon stones in the Churche by St Faithes doore to slide vpon as vpon ysse'.[12] It is evident that areas in the cathedral were 'hyred out for warehouses', and the nave and transepts – over and above their use as thoroughfares for tradesmen – had become 'a daily receptable for Roges and beggers howsoeur diseased'.[13] It was a frequent complaint that the noise in the main body of the cathedral disturbed the daily services in the quire.

By the time of Archbishop Laud's metropolitical visitation in 1636 there had been significant improvements. It was conceded that 'the church and churchyarde hath beene long before our times . . . a throughfayre, and is so still, much against our will', but it is also maintained that the 'officers of the church' have ensured that 'the passage through the church' – presumably from the south to the north transepts – is no longer used for 'portage'.[14] A commission, which had been appointed shortly after Donne's death to inquire into the profanation of the cathedral, placed the responsibility for any disrespect

[49]

and disorder entirely upon the Dean and Chapter, but the limited evidence suggests that Donne and his colleagues had attempted to contain the nuisance and taken some steps towards reforming the abuses.

It had also been a concern over many years that the behaviour of members of the musical foundation – the minor canons, the vicars choral and the choristers – had left much to be desired. Here again the replies to the visitations of Bishop Bancroft in 1598 and of Archbishop Laud in 1636 are telling. The earlier response tells of 'some of yᵉ Petticannons and Vicars . . . comming tardy, or beinge absent, or goinge oute (before the end of the service)',[15] and of the choristers 'talkinge and playinge, or els . . . ronning abowte the quiere to gentlemen and other poore men, for spurre money,[16] not lightlie leavinge them tell thaye have monye, or dryve them owt of the quier'.[17] But by 1636, the only complaint concerning the minor canons and the vicars choral is that some of them are absent far too frequently 'vnder pʳtence of their attendance at the King's Chappell', whereas the choristers are judged to be 'well ordered'.[18] It has to be inferred that the chapter under Donne's leadership played some part in the improvements that had taken place over a period of nearly forty years.

The reply of the Dean and Chapter to Laud's Articles of Enquiry in 1636 suggests that the Cathedral Foundation consisted of the dean; thirty prebendaries, of whom four were residentiary canons, although they did not themselves necessarily hold the ancient offices of precentor, treasurer and chancellor; five archdeacons; twelve minor canons; six vicars choral; an epistoler; an almoner; ten choristers; a sacrist; four virgers; and two bell ringers. There may well have been small variations from time to time, but this would have been for all practical purposes the Foundation over which Donne presided. The full Chapter of the cathedral would normally meet on St Barnabas Day, but the routine administration of the cathedral was entrusted to the Dean and the four residentiaries. Donne appears to have enjoyed good relations with his colleagues – Thomas Mountford, Thomas Whyte (who was succeeded on his death in 1623 by Thomas Winniff), Henry King and John King. They held numerous other offices in the church, and although no houses were provided for them by Chapter they appear (with the exception of John King who was rarely seen in London) to have despatched cathedral business – the management of chapter estates, the leasing of chapter properties, the collection of rents, the receiving of the accounts of their bailiffs, and the exercise of patronage – with due diligence.

From the time of the Reformation until the early years of the nineteenth century – with the exception of the Commonwealth period – the musical foundation normally consisted of twelve minor canons, six vicars choral, two additional officers who held the titles of epistoler and almoner, and ten choristers. The minor canons and the vicars choral were supported both by estate income and by stipends paid by the Dean and Chapter. The first minor canon, who was often known as the Sub Dean, had overall responsibility for the choir. The second and third minor canons, who held the titles of Senior and Junior Cardinal, were responsible for attendance, for discipline, and for ensuring that the choristers learned their catechism. The almoner was responsible for the education and welfare of the choristers, who lodged in the almonry house on the south side of the churchyard. When the choristers had secured the necessary degree of musical competence, they would go for their more formal education to Paules Schole for two hours in the morning and one hour in the afternoon in summer, and for one hour in the morning and one hour in the afternoon in winter. By Donne's time, the choristers had almost ceased to perform as child actors – the Children of Paules – although their predecessors in the early years of Elizabeth's reign and in the early years of the seventeenth century had been greatly regarded.

Donne – in common with all senior churchmen – did not confine his preferments or his activities to St Paul's. He had resigned the benefice of Keyston in Huntingdonshire shortly before his installation as Dean, but he continued to hold his appointment as a Chaplain in Ordinary to the King and he retained the benefice of Sevenoaks in Kent, and was preferred to the benefice of Blunham in Bedfordshire by the Earl of Kent in 1622. His predecessor as Dean had also held the Prebend of Chiswick and this passed to Donne in due course. The pastoral care of his country parishes was entrusted to curates, although Donne appears to have been conscientious in visiting the parishes for short periods in the summer and in preaching on those occasions. He was subsequently presented to the benefice of St Dunstan in the West in 1624 by the Earl of Dorset on the death of one of his chapter colleagues, Dr Thomas Whyte. His congregation at St Dunstan's, which would have been drawn in fair part from the legal community, represented a far more substantial undertaking on Donne's part, and he was diligent in his preaching, in his pastoral work, in his attendance at meetings of the vestry, and in seeing that renovations were carried out to the fabric of the church. Donne was a pluralist in an age of pluralists, but by the standards of his day – indeed, by comparison with some of his chapter colleagues – his clutch of ecclesiastical preferments was relatively modest.

It is impossible to identify all the public duties that would have inevitably come to Donne as Dean of St Paul's. His country parishes found some acknowledgement in the appearance of his name in the lists of Justices of the Peace for Kent and Bedfordshire in the 1620s. Donne's legal training would have stood him in good stead in his appointment on several occasions to hear appeals from the lower ecclesiastical courts and to sit in the Court of Delegates. He served also during his years at St Paul's as a member of the Court of High Commission – charged with the task of inquiring into and redressing ecclesiastical abuses – taking his place alongside senior churchmen, doctors of divinity and of civil law, judges and civilians. It is known that Donne became a governor of Charterhouse in 1621 and Prolocutor of the Lower House of the Convocation of Canterbury in 1626. He retained an interest in the affairs of the day – although there are few references in his sermons – and especially in so far as they impinged upon the religious settlements in England and Germany.

Donne had been dogged by periodic outbursts of ill health throughout his life, but none approached in severity the fever, the relapsing fever, with which he was struck down in the winter of 1623. It was an illness which might well have been fatal, having been occasioned by an epidemic which claimed many lives in the city. This period of illness and enforced convalescence possesses a peculiar interest because it led to the writing and the publication of Donne's most popular prose work, *Devotions Upon Emergent Occasions*, which appeared in three editions in the course of his lifetime and in two subsequent editions in 1634 and 1638.

What is revealed during this period of serious illness is the intensity and the urgency with which his mind continued to work. A probable timetable suggests that Donne was taken ill towards the end of November 1623, that the fever ran its course for six or seven days, that Donne was probably out of danger by 6 December, and that a period of convalescence followed in which he was denied access to books. It followed nonetheless that the *Devotions* was entered in the Stationers'

Register on 9 January 1624 and was actually published by 1 February.[19]

The book consists of twenty-three sections, which follow the successive stages of the illness and which are made up in turn of a meditation, an expostulation and a prayer. It may well be that Donne was able to draw upon all his intellectual and devotional resources in framing the meditations which addressed the familiar themes of sin, of the torments of this life, of the mercy and the judgement of God, of death, and of the Christian hope of resurrection; but nothing can detract from the extraordinary achievement – compulsive, even neurotic, though it might be – that is represented by the meditation, the writing and the publication.

Donne wrote with clarity and with great vividness concerning the onset of illness, the impotence of the human condition as the fever takes hold, and the ever-present fear of death.

> . . . this minute I was well, and am ill, this minute I am surpriz'd with a sodaine change, and alteration to worse, and can impute it to no cause, nor call it by any name.[20]

> In the twinkling of an eye, I can scarse see, instantly the tast is insipid, and fatuous; instantly the appetite is dull and desirelesse; instantly the knees are sinking and strengthlesse; and in an instant, sleepe, which is the *picture*, the *copie* of *death*, is taken away, that the *Originall, Death* it selfe may succeed.[21]

It is here also in the *Devotions* that we find Donne's incomparable statements of the catholicity of the church and of the interdependence of all people.

> The *Church* is *Catholike, universall,* so are all her *Actions*; *All* that she does, belongs to *all*. When she *baptizes a child,* that action concerns mee; for that child is thereby connected to that *Head* which is my *Head* too, and engraffed into that *body*, whereof I am a *member*. And when she *buries a Man,* that action concernes me; All *mankinde* is of one *Author*, and is one *volume*; when one Man dies, one *Chapter* is not *torne* out of the *booke*, but *translated* into a better *language* . . . but *God's* hand is in every *translation*; and his hand shall bind up all our scattered leaves againe, for that *Librarie* where every *booke* shall lie open to one another.[22]

> No man is an *Iland*, intire of it selfe, every man is a peece of the *Continent*, a part of the *maine*; if a *Clod* be washed away by the *Sea*, *Europe* is the lesse, as well as if a *Promontorie* were, as well as if a *Mannor* of thy *friends* or of *thine own* were; Any mans *death* diminishes *mee*, because I am involved in *Mankinde*; and therefore never send to know for whom the *bell* tolls; It tolls for *thee*.²³

The familiarity of these words does not detract from their genius, but the *Devotions* shows something more: a simplicity of faith which enables a complex and tortured soul to rest in God.

> How fully O my abundant God, how gently O my sweet and easy God, doest thou entangle me.²⁴

> *My God*, and *my Iesus, my Lord*, and my *Christ, My Strength*, and *my Saluation*, I heare thee, and I hearken to thee, when thou rebukest thy *Disciples*, for rebuking them, who brought children to thee; *Suffer little children to come to mee*, saiest thou. Is there a verier child then I am now? I cannot say with thy seruant *Ieremy, Lord, I am a child, and cannot speake*; but, *O Lord*, I am a sucking childe, and cannot eate, a creeping childe, and cannot goe; how shall I come to thee?²⁵

Donne's creativity did not confine itself to the writing of *Devotions* during this time of convalescence, but he wrote also the *Hymne to God the Father*²⁶ and probably also the *Hymne to God, my God, in my Sicknesse*.²⁷ It is the first of these two, perhaps the most evocative of all his religious poetry, which Donne caused to be set to music – 'a most grave and solemn tune' – and which was frequently sung by the choristers, and especially at Evening Prayer. Donne delighted in the words and the music:

> O the power of church-music! that harmony added to this hymn has raised the affections of my heart, and quickened my grace of zeal and gratitude; and I observe that I always return from paying this public duty of prayer and praise to God, with an unexpressible tranquility of mind, and a willingness to leave the world.²⁸

Donne's poem *A hymne to the Saints, and to Marquesse Hamylton* was written little more than a year later at the request of Sir Robert Ker. It was almost certainly the last poem Donne wrote. It was a eulogy, a tribute to the Marquess who had died at a relatively young age. Donne wrote with some reservation; and although the sentiments were entirely sincere and appropriate, the poem elicited the acerbic comment, 'though they be reasonable wittie and well don yet I could wish a man of his yeares and place to geve over versifieng'.[29] It may well be that Donne chose to distance himself from the poetry of his youth; but there were clearly others for whom the writing of verse was far too lacking in seriousness, far too frivolous a preoccupation, for someone of Donne's calling and eminence.

Donne's overriding priority was his preaching. It was the burden and the delight of his public ministry. It was his distinctive contribution to the life of the church. The long-established discipline of meticulous and wide-ranging study, coupled with all the artistic and rhetorical skills that he possessed, ensured that he established himself during his years at St Paul's as the foremost preacher of his day. Donne may not have preached with the frequency that Walton suggests, but he undoubtedly preached at St Paul's far more than the statutes required. The sermons at the great festivals of Christmas, Easter and Whitsun stand alongside his preaching on the Psalms assigned to the Prebend of Chiswick, and the sermons at Paul's Cross. As a chaplain to the King, he was required to preach on the first Friday in Lent, and he was also in attendance at Court during the month of April when he might also preach on one or two additional occasions. He would expect to preach in his country parishes during his summer visits, and he was diligent in his preaching at St Dunstan's in the West.

The sermons that have survived were probably written by Donne during two prolonged periods of absence from the City: the first at the time of plague in 1625, and the second at the onset of his final illness in 1630. The response of the Dean and Chapter to Archbishop Laud's Articles of Enquiry in 1636 makes it plain that 'in the long vacācon and times of dangerous infection wee all repaire to our benefices leaveing the ordering of the choir and divine service to the sub deane'.[30] Donne found refuge at Chelsea for five months during the summer and autumn of 1625 while the plague, described as 'more deadly than any experienced since the days of the Black Death',[31] ran its course. But Donne was fully occupied, writing out no less than eighty sermons, drawing freely upon whatever notes he had used in the pulpit, and giving them shape and form and style.[32] It was a phenomenal achievement; and, although it would not have been equalled – so far as the volume of work is concerned – by his activity in the autumn and winter months of 1630, it is clear that his time of retreat at Aldborough Hatch as he struggled once again with ill health was also used for writing out in full more of his sermons prior to their subsequent publication.[33]

Whatever the regard in which he was held by the congregations to whom he preached, it is clear that Donne's manner of preaching gave offence to some of the Puritan clergy of his day. His language, his style, his scholarship, his classical allusions, his appeal to the authority of the Fathers and the Schoolmen, his rhetoric would have been too complex, too convoluted, too ornate, for those who required a plain and unadorned preaching of the word. There may well have been more than a touch of envy on the part of some of his critics, but those who 'humm'd against' him did so largely on the grounds that his message was obscured by his 'fine words'.[34]

But Donne was clear in his own mind that, 'It is not the depth, nor the wit, nor the eloquence of the Preacher that pierces us, but his nearnesse; that hee speaks to my conscience, as though he had been behinde the hangings when I sinned, and as though he had read the book of the day of Judgement already'.[35] For Donne, 'Preaching is the thunder that clears the air, disperses all clouds of ignorance';[36] it is nothing less than 'Gods speaking to us'.[37]

Donne's appointment to St Paul's had given him a unique outlet for his gifts as a preacher, but it had provided also the recognition and the public office and – in due course – the income he had sought over so many years. It has been reckoned that his income from all sources probably exceeded £2,000 a year,[38] approximately £190,000 a year at today's values. Such an income enabled him to keep a large household, to dispense hospitality – 'my bondage of entertaining'[39] – and to be generous in his charitable giving.

Donne's generosity included gifts of money to those who had previously assisted him and who were now themselves in need of support, but it went far beyond small acts of personal kindness. Izaak Walton draws attention to two areas of special concern. He describes Donne as 'a continual giver to poor scholars, both of this and foreign nations'; and he speaks also of his being 'inquisitive after the wants of prisoners', paying small debts in some instances, and ensuring that 'his charity (was distributed) to all the prisons in *London* at all the festival times of the year', and especially at Christmas and Easter.[40]

There is little information concerning the later years of Donne's life. His health appears to have been largely unimpaired by earlier illnesses. His mind remains alert and vigorous. He continues to buy books and to read widely. His preaching continues to be his first priority. He is fully immersed in his public duties. His position at Court is well established and, having recovered from a brief loss of favour following upon a sermon in April 1627 when he referred obliquely to the Roman Catholic faith of Queen Henrietta Maria, it is clear that he was seen prior to the onset of his final illness as a man who might well be appointed to a bishopric when a suitable vacancy occurred.[41]

Donne shows throughout his years at St Paul's a familial concern for his children and for the marriage of his daughters. He had long since acknowledged the vicissitudes of his mother's life – 'a Sea, under a continuall Tempest, where one wave hath overtaken another'[42] – occasioned in fair measure by her Roman Catholic faith, and he brought her to live with him at the deanery during the final years of her life. The death of members of his family and of various friends must have weighed upon him: his daughter Lucy at the age of seventeen in January 1627, Sir Henry Goodyer in March 1627, Lady Bedford in May 1627, Lady Danvers in June 1627, Mr Christopher Brooke in February 1628, the Duke of Buckingham by assassination in August 1628, and his mother in January 1631 shortly before his own death.

Donne fell ill with a fever in August 1630, and he wrote ruefully but playfully of his condition. 'I am come now, not onely to pay a Feavour every half year, as a Rent for my life; but I am called upon before the day, and they come sooner in the year then heretofore.'[43] He had hoped that it might be nothing more than 'an exaltation of my damps and flashings, such as exercise me sometimes four or five daies, and passe away . . . But, I neglected this somewhat too long, which makes me . . . much weaker, then, perchance, otherwise I should have been.'[44] Donne approached ill health with resignation, and allowed himself to spend the winter at his daughter Constance's house in Essex. By November he was writing, 'I humbly thank God, I am only not worse; for, I should soon as look for Roses at this time of the year, as look for increase of strength'.[45] It is probable that Donne was dying of cancer, and by January 1631 – the month of his mother's death – he wrote, 'I am not alive because I have not had enough upon me to kill me, but because it pleases God to passe me through many infirmities before he take me'.[46] But Donne – stubborn, determined – refused to forgo his duty and returned to London to preach before the Court at Whitehall on the first Friday in Lent, 25 February 1631.

Donne had previously confessed his desire that 'I might die in the pulpit; if not that, yet that I might take my death in the Pulpit, that is, die the sooner by occasion of my former labours'.[47] His friends had failed to persuade him to abandon any thought of preaching before the Court; and Walton records that 'when to the amazement of some beholders he appeared in the pulpit, many of them thought he presented himself not to preach mortification by a living voice; but, mortality by a decayed body and a dying face'.[48]

The Psalms had been the starting point for so many of Donne's sermons, and he turned now to Psalm 68 for the text of what was to be his final sermon: 'And unto God the Lord belong the issues of Death'.[49] The sermon was published as *Death's Duel*, and it was subtitled, *A Consolation to the Soule, against the dying Life, and living Death of the Body*. Donne, who was undoubtedly speaking not only to the King and to the Court but to himself, returned to the familiar theme of our mortality.

> But whether the *gate* of *my prison* be *opened* with an *oyld* key (by a gentle and preparing sicknes) or the gate be *hewen downe* by a *violent* death, or the gate bee *burnt downe* by a *raging* and *frantique feaver, a gate into heaven* I *shall have*, for *from* the Lord is the *cause* of *my life* and *with God the Lord are* the *issues of death*.[50]

The sermon moved on to become a meditation on the death of Christ – 'There was nothing more free, more voluntary, more spontaneous then the death of Christ'[51] – and he proclaimed for the last time from the pulpit the Christian hope of resurrection. His final word – of resignation, of exhortation – was one of faith and trust.

> There wee leave you in that *blessed dependancy* to *hang* upon *him* that *hangs* upon the *Crosse*, there *bath* in his *teares*, there *suck* at his *woundes* and *lye downe in peace* in his *grave*, til hee vouchsafe you a *resurrection*, and an *ascension* into that *Kingdome*, which hee hath *purchas'd* for you, with the *inestimable price* of his *incorruptible blood*.[52]

Donne went to the deanery for the last five weeks of his life, attending to cathedral business and taking leave of various friends, until ten days before his death when Walton comments that 'now he was so happy as to have nothing to do but dye'.[53] His death on 31 March was followed three days later by his burial in the cathedral. The place of interment in the south quire aisle was one that Donne had long since chosen 'and by which he passed daily to pay his public devotions';[54] but 'he was not buried privately, though he desired it; for besides a number of others, many persons of nobility, and of eminency for learning, who did love and honour him in this life, did show it at his death'.[55] Walton adds that the place of his burial was strewn with 'an abundance of curious and costly flowers . . . (until) . . . the stones that were taken up in that church, to give his body admission into the cold earth . . . were again by the masons art so levelled and firmed as they had been formerly, and his place of burial indistinguishable to common view'.[56]

The effigy which was erected in due course was judged by Donne's contemporaries to be 'as lively a representation . . . as marble can express; a statue indeed, so like Dr. *Donne* that . . . *It seems to breathe faintly, and posterity shall look upon it as a kind of artificial miracle*'.[57] It is not the least of the ironies that surround this irrepressible servant of God that his effigy, which alone of all the effigies in Old St Paul's survived the Great Fire of 1666 and remains intact today, stands now 'as near as may be to its original position'.[58]

AN ANTHOLOGY

Part One

HUMANITY

"the frailty and the decay of his whole World"

THE HUMAN CONDITION

The Human Condition

THIS is *Natures nest of Boxes*; The Heavens containe the *Earth*, the *Earth*, *Cities*, *Cities*, *Men*. And all these are *Concentrique*; the common *center* to them all, is *decay, ruine*.[1]

And new Philosophy cals all in doubt,
  The Element of fire is quite put out;
The Sun is lost, and th'earth, and no mans wit
Can well direct him, where to looke for it.
And freely men confesse, that this world's spent,
When in the Planets, and the Firmament
They seeke so many new; they see that this
Is crumbled out again to his Atomis.
'Tis all in pieces, all cohaerence gone;
All just supply, and all Relation:
Prince, Subject, Father, Sonne, are things forgot,
For every man alone thinkes he hath got
To be a Phoenix, and that there can bee
None of that kinde, of which he is, but hee.
This is the worlds condition now.[2]

Shee, shee is dead; shee's dead: when thou knowst this,
  Thou knowst how lame a cripple this world is.
And learnst thus much by our Anatomy,
That this words generall sickenesse doth not lie
In any humour, or one certaine part;
But, as thou sawest it rotten at the hart,

Thou seest a Hectique fever hath got hold
Of the whole substance, not to be contrould,
And that thou hast but one way, not t'admit
The worlds infection, to be none of it.

Shee, shee is dead, she's dead; when thou knowst this,
Thou knowst how ugly a monster this world is:
And learnst thus much by our Anatomee,
That here is nothing to enamor thee:

Shee, shee, is dead; shee's dead: when thou knowst this,
Thou knowst how wan a Ghost this our world is:
And learnst thus much by our Anatomee,
That it should more affright, then pleasure thee.

Shee, shee is dead; shee's dead; when thou knowst this,
Thou knowst how drie a Cinder this world is.
And learnst thus much by our Anatomy,
That 'tis in vaine to dew, or mollifie
It with thy Teares, or Sweat, or Bloud: no thing
Is worth our travaile, griefe, or perishing,
But those rich joyes, which did possesse her hart,
Of which shee's now partaker, and a part.[3]

S hee, shee is gone; shee is gone; when thou knowest this,
What fragmentary rubbidge this world is
Thou knowest, and that it is not worth a thought;
He honors it too much that thinks it nought.[4]

A nd what essential joy can'st thou expect
Here upon earth? what permanent effect
Of transitory causes?[5]

N o more affoords this world, foundatione
To'erect true joye, were all the meanes in one.[6]

This World's Vice-Emperor

The soule with body, is a heaven combin'd
      With earth, and for mans ease, but nearer joyn'd.[7]

If all things be in all,
      As I thinke, since all, which were, are, and shall
Bee, be made of the same elements:
Each thing, each thing implyes or represents.
Then man is a world.[8]

Thus man, this worlds Vice-Emperor, in whom
      All faculties, all graces are at home;
And if in other Creatures they appeare,
They're but mans ministers, and Legats there,
To worke on their rebellions, and reduce
Them to Civility, and to mans use.
This man, whom God did wooe, and loth t'attend
Till man came up, did downe to man descend,
This man, so great, that all that is, is his,
Oh what a trifle, and poore thing he is![9]

What are wee then? How little more alas
      Is man now, then before he was? he was
Nothing; for us, wee are for nothing fit;
Chance, or our selves still disproportion it.
Wee have no power, no will, no sense; I lye
I should not then thus feele this miserie.[10]

Man is a lumpe, where all beasts kneaded bee,
      Wisdome makes him an Arke where all agree;
The foole, in whom these beasts do live at jarre,
      Is sport to others, and a Theater,
Nor scapes hee so, but is himselfe their prey;
      All which was man in him, is eate away,

And now his beasts on one another feed,
    Yet coupl'in anger, and new monsters breed;
How happy'is hee, which hath due place assign'd
    To'his beasts, and disaforested his minde!

Else, man not onely is the heard of swine,
    But he's those devills too, which did incline
Them to a headlong rage, and made them worse:
    For man can adde weight to heavens heaviest curse.

As Soules (they say) by our first touch, take in
    The poysonous tincture of Originall sinne,
So, to the punishments which God doth fling,
    Our apprehension contributes the sting.

Thus man, that might be'his pleasure, is his rod,
    And is his devill that might be his God.[11]

There is no health; Physitians say that we
    At best, enjoy, but a neutralitiee.
And can there be worse sicknesse, then to know
That we are never well, nor can be so?[12]

Her death hath taught us dearely, that thou art
    Corrupt and mortall in thy purest part.[13]

Shee, shee is dead; shee's dead: when thou knowest this,
    Thou knowest how poore a trifling thing man is.
And learn'st thus much by our Anatomee,
The heart being perish'd, no part can be free.[14]

Mankind decayes so soone,
    We're scarse our Fathers shadowes cast at noone.
Onely death addes t'our length: nor are we growne
In stature to be men, till we are none.[15]

The Human Condition

Old Grandsires talke of yesterday with sorrow,
  And for our children we reserve to morrow.
So short is life, that every peasant strives,
In a torne house, or field, to have three lives.
And as in lasting, so in length is man
Contracted to an inch, who was a span.[16]

Thinke in how poore a prison thou didst lie
  After, enabled but to suck, and crie.
Thinke, when t'was growne to most, t'was a poore Inne,
A Province pack'd up in two yards of skinne,
And that usurped, or threatned with the rage
Of sicknesses, or their true mother, Age.[17]

At birth, and death, our bodies naked are;
  And till our soules be unapparrelled
Of bodies, they from blisse are banished.[18]

Thou art too narrow, wretch, to comprehend
  Even thy selfe: yea though thou wouldst but bend[a]
To know thy body. Have not all soules thought
For many ages, that our body'is wrought
Of Ayre, and Fire, and other Elements?
And now they thinke of new ingredients.
And one soule thinkes one, and another way
Another thinkes, and ty's[b] an even lay.[c]
Knowest thou but how the stone doth enter in
The bladders Cave, and never breake the skin?
Knowst thou how blood, which to the hart doth flow,
Doth from one ventricle to th'other go?
And for the putrid stuffe, which thou dost spit,
Knowst thou how thy lungs have attracted it?

a. bend (condescend)
b. ty's (it is)
c. lay (wager)

[69]

There are no passages so that there is
(For ought thou knowst) piercing of substances.
And of those many opinions which men raise
Of Nailes and Hairs, dost thou know which to praise?
What hope have we to know our selves, when wee
Know not the least things, which for our use bee?[19]

We contemplate *man*, as the Receptacle, the Ocean of all misery. Fire and Aire, Water and Earth, are not the Elements of man; Inward decay, and outward violence, bodily pain, and sorrow of heart may be rather styled his Elements; And though he be destroyed by these, yet he consists of nothing but these.[20]

My body is my prison; and I would be so obedient to the Law, as not to break prison; I would not hasten my death by starving, or macerating this body: But if this prison be burnt down by continuall feavers, or blowen down with continuall vapours, would any man be so in love with that ground upon which that prison stood, as to desire rather to stay there, then go home? Our prisons are fallen, our bodies are dead to many former uses; Our palate dead in a tastlesnesse; Our stomach dead in an indigestiblenesse; our feete dead in a lamenesse, and our invention in a dulnesse, and our memory in a forgetfulnesse; and yet, as a man that should love the ground, where his prison stood, we love this clay, that was a body in the dayes of our youth, and but our prison then, when it was at best; wee abhorre the graves of our bodies; and the body, which, in the best vigour thereof, was but the grave of the soule, we over-love.[21]

I am the man which hath affliction seene,
    Under the rod of God's wrath having beene,
He hath led me to darknesse, not to light,
        And against me all day, his hand doth fight.[22]

L oth to goe up the hill, or labor thus
To goe to heaven, we make heaven come to us.
We spur, we raine[a] the stars, and in their race
They're diversly content t'obey our pace.[23]

T he World is but a Carkas; thou are fed
By it, but as a worme, that carcas bred;
And why shouldst thou, poore worme, consider more,
When this world will grow better then before.
Then those thy fellow-wormes doe thinke upone
That carkasses last resurrectione.
Forget this world, and scarse thinke of it so,
As of old cloaths, cast off a yeare agoe.[24]

a. raine (control)

THE WAY OF THE WORLD

The Human Scene: The Stage

Life is a voyage, and in our lifes wayes
Counties, Courts, Towns are Rockes, or Remoraes;[a]
They break or stop all ships, yet our state's such,
That though then pitch they staine worse, wee must touch.

Cities are worst of all three; of all three
(O knottie riddle) each is worst equally.
Cities are Sepulchers; they who dwell there
Are carcases, as if no such there were.
And Court are Theatres, where some men play
Princes, some slaves, all to one end, and of one clay.
The Country is a desert, where no good,
Gain'd, as habits, not borne is understood.
There men become beasts, and prone to more evils;
In cities blockes, and in a lewd court, devills.

Men are spunges, which to poure out, receive,
Who know false play, rather then lose, deceive.
For in best understandings, sinne beganne,
Angels sinn'd first, then Devills, and then man.
Onely perchance beasts sinne not; wretched wee
Are beasts in all, but white integritie.

I think if men, which in these places live
Durst look for themselves, and themselves retrive,
They would like strangers greet themselves, seeing then
Utopian youth, growne old Italian.

a. Remoraes (a sucking-fish)

Be thou thine owne home, and in thy selfe dwell;
Inne any where, continuance maketh hell,
And seeing the snaile, which every where doth rome,
Carrying his owne house still, still is at home.
Follow (for he is easie pac'd) this snaile,
Bee thine owne Palace, or the world's thy gaole.
And in the worlds sea, do not like corke sleepe
Upon the waters face; nor in the deepe
Sinke like a lead without a line: but as
Fishes glide, leaving no print where they passe,
Nor making sound; so, closely thy course goe,
Let men dispute, whether thou breathe, or no.[1]

S ince now, when all is withered, shrunke, and dri'd,
  All Vertues ebb'd out to a dead low tyde,
All the worlds frame being crumbled into sand,
Where every man thinks by himselfe to stand,
Integritie, friendship, and confidence,
(Ciments of greatnes) being vapor'd hence,
And narrow man being fill'd with little shares,
Court, Citie, Church, are all shops of small-wares,
All having blowne to sparkes their noble fire,
And drawne their sound gold-ingot into wyre;
All trying by a love of littlenesse
To make abridgments, and to draw to lesse,
Even that nothing, which at first we were.[2]

E ven as lame things thirst their perfection, so
  The slimy rimes bred in our vale below,
Bearing with them much of my love and hart,
Fly unto that Parnassus, where thou art.
There thou oreseest London: Here I have beene,
By staying in London, too much overseene.[a]
Now pleasures dirth our City doth posses,
Our Theatres are fill'd with emptiness.[b]

a. overseene (imprudent)
b. emptiness (because of the plague)

As lancke and thin is every street and way
As a woman deliver'd yesterday.
Nothing whereat to laugh my spleen espyes
But bearbaitings or Law exercise.
Therfore I'le leave it, and in the Country strive
Pleasure, now fled from London, to retrive.
Do thou so too: and fill not like a Bee
Thy thighs with hony, but as plenteously
As Russian Marchants, thy selfes whole vessel load,
And then at Winter retaile it here abroad.
Blesse us with Suffolks Sweets; and as it is
Thy garden, make thy hive and warehouse this.[3]

We are condemned to thys desart of London for all thys sommer, for yt ys company not houses which distinguishes between cityes and desarts.[4]

Suspitious boldnesse to this place belongs,
And to'have as many eares as all have tongues;
Tender to know, tough to acknowledge wrongs.

Beleeve mee Sir, in my youths giddiest dayes,
When to be like the Court, was a playes praise,
Playes were not so like Court, as Courts'are like playes.

Then let us at these mimicke antiques[a] jeast,
Whose deepest projects,[b] and egregious gests
Are but dull Moralls of a game at Chests.[5]

I which live in the Country without stupefying, am not in darknesse, but in shadow, which is not no light, but a pallid, waterish, and diluted one. As all shadows are of one colour, if you respect the body from which they are cast (for our shadows upon clay will be dirty, and in a garden green, and flowery) so all retirings into a shadowy life are alike from all causes, and alike subject to the barbarousnesse and insipid dulnesse of the Country.[6]

a. mimicke antiques (posturing antics)
b. projects (plots)

U nseasonable man, statue of ice,
　　What could to countries solitude entice[a]
Thee, in this yeares cold and decrepit time?
　　Natures instinct drawes to the warmer clime
Even small birds, who by that courage dare,
　　In numerous fleets, saile through their Sea, the aire.
What delicacie can in fields appeare,
　　Whil'st Flora'herselfe doth a freeze jerkin weare?
Whil'st windes do all the trees and hedges strip
　　Of leafes, to furnish roddes enough to whip
Thy madnesse from thee; and all springs by frost
　　Have taken cold, and their sweet murmure lost.[7]

The Human Scene: The Players

T he world containes
　　Princes for armes, and Counsailors for braines,
Lawyers for tongues. Divines for hearts, and more.
　　The Rich for stomachs, and for backes the Pore;
The Officers for hands, Merchants for feet
　　By which remote and distant Countries meet.
But those fine spirits, which doe tune and set
　　This Organ, are those peeces which beget
Wonder and love.[8]

S tatesmen purge vice with vice, and may corrode
　　The bad with bad, a spider with a toad:
For so, ill thralls not them, but they tame ill
　　And make her do much good against her will.[9]

W e see in Authors, too stiffe to recant,
　　A hundred controversies of an Ant.
And yet one watches, starves, freeses, and sweats,

a. entice (the line refers to Donne's absence in the country at the time of the wedding of Robert Carr, Earl of Somerset, to Lady Frances Howard, recently divorced from the Earl of Essex)

[75]

To know but Catechismes and Alphabets
Of unconcerning things, matters of fact;
How others on our stage their parts did Act;
What Caesar did, yea, and what Cicero said.
Why grasse is greene, or why our blood is red,
Are mysteries which none have reach'd unto.
In this low forme, poore soule what wilt thou doe?
When wilt thou shake off this Pedantery,
Of being taught by sense, and Fantasy?[10]

With whom wilt thou Converse? What station
Canst thou choose out, free from infection,
That wil nor give thee theirs, nor drinke in thine?
Shalt thou not finde a spungy slack Divine
Drinke and sucke in th'Instructions of Great men,
And for the word of God, vent them agen?
Are there not some Courts, (And then, no things bee
So like as Courts) which, in this let us see,
That wits and tongues of Libellars are weake,
Because they doe more ill, then these can speake?
The poyson'is gone through all, poysons affect
Chiefly the cheefest parts, but some effect
In Nailes, and Haires, ye excrements, will show;
So will the poyson of sinne, in the most low.[11]

Worldly Cares

The creeping serpent, the groveling Serpent, is Craft; the exalted
Serpent, the crucified Serpent, is Wisdome. All your worldly
cares, all your crafty bargaines, all your subtill matches, all your
diggings into other mens estates, all your hedgings in of debts, all
your planting of children in great allyances; all these diggings, and
hedgings and plantings savour of the earth, and of the craft of that
Serpent, that creeps upon the earth: But crucifie this craft of yours,
bring all your worldly subtilty under the Crosse of Christ Jesus,
husband your farmes so, as you may give a good account to him,
presse your debts so, as you would be pressed by him, market and

bargaine so, as that you would give all, to buy that field, in which his treasure, and his pearle is hid, and then you have changed the Serpent, from the Serpent of perdition creeping upon the earth, to the Serpent of salvation exalted in the wildernesse. Creeping wisedome, that still looks downward, is but craft; Crucified wisedome, that looks upward, is truly wisedome. Between you and that ground Serpent God hath kindled a war; and the nearer you come to a peace with him, the father ye go from God, and the more ye exasperate the Lord of Hosts, and you whet his sword against your own souls.[12]

Vanity

Nothing inflames, nor swels, nor puffes us up, more then that leaven of the soule, that empty, aery, frothy love of Names and Titles.[13]

Ambitious men never made more shift for places in Court, then dead men for graves in Churches.[14]

And as our pride begins in our Cradle, it continues in our graves and Monuments . . . O the earlinesse! O the latenesse! how early a Spring, and no Autumne! how fast a growth, and no declination, of this branch of this sin Pride . . . this love of place, and precedency, it rocks us in our Cradles, it lies down with us in our graves.[15]

The Deceits of Life

So then, when men of high degree doe not performe the duties of their places, then they are a lie of their owne making; And when I over-magnifie them in their place, flatter them, humor them, ascribe more to them, expect more from them, rely more upon them, then I should, then they are a lie of my making. But whether the lie be theirs, That they feare greater men then themselves, and so prevaricate in their duties; Or the lie be mine, that canonize them and make them my God, they, and I shall be disappointed.[16]

Others, whom wee call virtuous, are not so
   In theyr whole Substance, but theyr virtues grow
But in theyr Humors, and at Seasons show.

For when through tastles flatt Humilitee,
In Doe-bakd men, some Harmelesnes wee see,
Tis but hys Flegme that's vertuous, and not hee.

so ys the Blood sometymes; who ever ran
To Danger unimportund, hee was than
no better then a Sanguine vertuous man.

So Cloystrall Men who in pretence of fear,
All Contributions to thys Lyfe forbear,
Have vertu in Melancholy, and onley there.

spirituall Cholerique Critiqs, which in all
Religions, find faults, and forgive no fall,
Have, through thys Zeale, vertu, but in theyr Gall.

we'are thus but parcell-gilt;[a] To Gold we'are growen,
when vertu ys our Soules Complexione;
who knowes hys vertues Name, or Place, hath none.

vertu ys but Aguishe, when tis Severall;
By'Occasion wak'd, and Circumstantiall;
True vertu ys Soule, allways in all deeds all.[17]

The light of nature hath taught thee to *hide thy sinnes* from other
   men, and thou hast been so diligent in that, as that thou hast
hid them from thy self, and canst not finde them in thy owne *conscience.*[18]

It is . . . but an imperfect comfort for any man to say, I have overcome tentations to great sins, and my sins have beene but of
infirmity, not of malice. For herein, more then in any other contemplation appeares the greatnesse, both of thy danger, and of thy
transgression. For, consider what a dangerous, and slippery station

a. parcell-gilt (partly gilded)

thou art in, if after a victory over Giants, thou mayest be overcome by Pigmees; If after thy soule hath beene Canon proofe against strong tentations, she be slaine at last by a Pistoll; And, after she hath swom over a tempestuous sea, shee drowne at last, in a shallow and standing ditch. And as it showes the greatness of thy danger, so it aggravates the greatnesse of thy fault; That after thou hast had the experience, that by a good husbanding of those degrees of grace, which God hath afforded thee, thou hast beene able to stand out the great batteries of strong tentations, and seest by that, that thou art much more able to withstand tentations to lesser sins, if thou wilt, yet by disarming thy selfe, by devesting thy garisons, by discontinuing thy watches, merely by inconsideration, thou sellest thy soule for nothing, for little pleasure, little profit, thou frustratest thy Saviour of that purchase, which he bought with his precious blood, and thou enrichest the Devils treasure as much, with thy single money thy frequent small sins, as another hath done with his talent; for as God was well pleased with the widowes two farthings, so is the Devill well pleased, with the negligent mans lesser sins.[19]

Flattery

Y ou are that Alchimist which alwaies had
   Wit, whose one spark could make good things of bad.[20]

A Taper of his Torch, a copie writ
   From his Originall, and a faire beame
Of the same warme, and dazeling Sun, though it
   Must in another Sphere his vertue streame.[a][21]

S hould I say I liv'd darker then were true,
  Your radiation can all clouds subdue,
But one,[b] 'tis best light to contemplate you.

a. streame (these lines refer to the delegated authority of the newly appointed Ambassador to Venice in relation to the sovereign whom he represents)
  b. But one (except for God)

Humanity

You, for whose body God made better clay,
Or tooke Soules stuffe such as shall late decay,
Or such as needs small change at the last day.

This, as an Amber drop enwraps a Bee,
Covering discovers your quicke Soule; that we
May in your through-shine[a] front your hearts thoughts see.

You teach (though wee learne not) a thing unknowne
To our late times, the use of specular stone,[b]
Through which all things within without were shown.

Of such were Temples; so and such you are;
Beeing and *seeming* is your equall care,
And *vertues* whole *summe* is but *know* and *dare*.

But as our Soules of growth and Soules of sense
Have birthright from our reasons Soule, yet hence
They fly not from that, nor seeke presidence:

Natures first lesson, so discretion,
Must not grudge zeale a place, nor yet keepe none,
Not banish it selfe, nor religion.

Goe thither stil, goe the same way you went,
Who so would change, do cover or repent;
Neither can reach you, great and innocent.[22]

T his season as 'tis Easter, as 'tis spring,
        Must both to growth and to confession bring
My thoughts dispos'd unto your influence, so,
    These verses bud, so these confessions grow;
First I confesse I have to others lent
    Your stock, and over prodigally spent
Your treasure, for since I had never knowne
    Vertue or beautie, but as they are growne
In you, I should not think or say they shine,
    (So as I have) in any other Mine;
Next I confesse this my confession,

a. through-shine (translucent)
b. specular stone (an ancient building material as transparent as glass or crystal)

For, 'tis some fault thus much to touch upon
Your praise to you, where half rights seeme too much,
   And make your minds sincere complexion blush.
Next I confesse my'impenitence, for I
   Can scarce repent my first fault, since thereby
Remote low Spirits, which shall ne'r read you,
   May in lesse lessons find enough to doe,
By studying copies, not Originals.[23]

True vertu ys Soule, always in all deeds all.

Thys vertu, thinkinge to give Dignitee
To your Soule, found there no infirmitee;
for your Soule was as good vertu as shee.

shee therefore wrought upon that part of yow,
which ys scarse lesse then Soule, as shee could doe,
And soe hath made your Beauty vertue too;

Hence comes yt, that your Beauty wounds not harts
As others, with prophane and Sensuall darts,
But, as an Influence, vertuous thoughts imparts.

But if such frinds, by the'honor of your Sight
Grow capable of thys so great a light,
As to partake your vertues, and theyr might,

what must I think that Influence must doe,
where yt finds Simpathy, and Matter too,
vertu, and Beauty, of the same stuffe, as yow.[24]

Faire, great, and good, since seeing you, wee see
   What Heaven can doe, and what any Earth can be:
Since now your beauty shines, now when the Sunne
Growne stale, is to so low a value runne,
That his disshevel'd beames and scattered fires
Service but for Ladies Periwigs and Tyres[a]
In lovers Sonnets: you come to repaire
Gods booke of creatures, teaching what is faire.[25]

a. Tyres (attires)

[81]

B ut (madame) I now thinke on you; and here
Where we are at our hights, you but appeare,
We are but clouds, you rise from our noone-ray,
But a foule shadow, not your breake of day.
You are at first hand all that's faire and right,
And others good reflects but backe your light.
You are a perfectnesse, so curious hit,
That youngest flatteries doe scandall it.[26]

The Corruptions of Sin

A s long as there remains in thee one sin, or the sinfull gain of
that one sin, so long there is one enemy, and where there is one
enemy, there is no peace. Gardners that husband their ground to the
best advantage, sow all their seeds in such order, one under another,
that their Garden is always full of that which is then in season. If
thou sin with that providence, with that seasonablenesse, that all
thy spring, thy youth be spent in wantonnesse, all thy Summer, thy
middle-age in ambition, and the wayes of preferment, and thy
Autumne, thy Winter in indevotion and covetousnesse, though thou
have no farther taste of licentiousnesse, in thy middle-age, thou hast
thy satiety in that sin, nor of ambition in thy last yeares, thou hast
accumulated titles of honour, yet all the way thou hast had one
enemy, and therefore never any perfect peace.[27]

S in assisted by me, is now become a tyrant over me, and hath
established a government upon me.[28]

S olitude is not the scene of Pride; The danger of pride is in company, when we meet to looke upon another.[29]

O ur sinnes come to be reverenced in us, and by us; our sinnes
contract a majestie, and a state, and they grow *sacred* to us;
we dare not trouble a sinne, we dare not displace it, nor displease it;
we dare not dispute the prerogative of our sinne, but we come to

thinke it a kinde of sedition, a kinde of innovation, and a troubling of the state, if we begin to question our Conscience, or change that security of sine which we sleepe in, and we think it an easier Reformation to repent a sinne once a yeare, at *Easter*, when we must needs Receive, then to watch a sinne every Day.[30]

The Devil remembers from what height he is fallen, and therefore still clambers upward, and still directs all our sinnes, in his end, upon God: Our end, in a sin, may be pleasure, or profit, or satisfaction of affections, or passions; but the Devils end in all is, that God may be violated and dishonoured in that sinne.[31]

Thus sin is heavy in the *seed*, in the *grain*, in the *akorn*, how much more when it is a *field* of Corn, a *barn* of grain, a *forest* of Oaks, in the multiplication, and complication of sin in sin?[32]

As soone as *Adam* came to be ashamed of his nakednesse, he presently thought of some remedy; if one should come and tell thee, that he looked through the doore, that he stood in a window over against thine, and saw thee doe such or such a sin, this would put thee to a shame, and thou wouldest not doe that sin, till thou wert sure he could not see thee. O, if thou wouldest not sin, till thou couldst think that God saw thee not, this shame had wrought well upon thee. There are complexions that cannot blush; there growes a blacknesse, a sootinesse upon the soule, by custome in sin, which overcomes all blushing, all tendernesse.[33]

The Glory of this World

The light of the knowledge of the glory of this world, is a good, and a great peece of learning . . . To know how near nothing, how meer nothing, all the glory of this world is, is a good, a great degree of learning.[34]

THE LOVE OF MEN AND WOMEN

Sexual Desire

Come, Madam, come, all rest my powers defie,
Until I labour, I in labour[a] lie.
The foe oft-times having the foe in sight,
Is tir'd with standing though he never fight.
Off with that girdle, like heavens Zone glittering,
But a fair fairer world incompassing.
Unpin that spangled breastplate which you wear,
That th'eyes of busie fooles may be stopt there.
Unlace your self, for that harmonious chyme,
Tells me from you, that now it is bed time.
Off with that happy busk,[b] which I envie,
That still can be, and still can stand so nigh.
Your gown going off, such beautious state reveals,
As when from flowry meads th'hills shadowe steales.
Off with that wyerie Coronet and shew
The haiery Diademe which on you doth grow:
Now off with those shooes, and then softly tread
In this loves hallow'd temple, this soft bed.
In such white robes, heaven's Angels us'd to be
Receavd by men: thou Angel bringst with thee
A heaven like Mahomets Paradice, and though
Ill spirits walk in white, we easly know,
By this these Angels from an evil sprite,
Those set our hairs, but these our flesh upright.

a. in labour (in anxious anticipation)
b. busk (corset)

Licence my roaving hands, and let them go,
Before, behind, between, above, below.
O my America! My new-found-land,
My kingdome, safeliest when with one man man'd,
My Myne of precious stones: My Emperie,
How blest am I in this discovering thee!
To enter in these bonds, is to be free;
Then where my hand is set, my seal shall be.

Full nakedness! All joyes are due to thee,
As souls unbodied, bodies uncloth'd must be,
To taste whole joyes. Jems which you women use
Are like Atlanta's balls, cast in mens views,
That when a fools eye lighteth on a Jem,
His earthly soul may covet theirs, not them:
Like pictures, or like books gay coverings made
For lay-men, are all women thus array'd.
Themselves are mystick books, which only wee
(Whom their imputed grace will dignifie)
Must see reveal'd. Then since that I may know;
As liberally, as to a Midwife shew
Thy self: cast all, yea, this white lynnen hence,
There is no pennance, much less innocence:

To teach thee, I am naked first; why then
What needs thou have more covering then a man.[1]

Who ever loves, if he do not propose
    The right true end of love, he's one that goes
To sea for nothing but to make him sick:
Love is a bear-whelp born, if we o're lick
Our love, and force it new strange shapes to take,
We erre, and of a lump a monster make.

Can men more injure women then to say
They love them for that, by which they're not they?
Makes virtue woman? Must I coole my bloud
Till I both be, and find one wise and good?
May barren Angels love so. But if we
Make love to woman; virtue is not she.

[85]

Humanity

Although we see Celestial bodies move
Above the earth, the earth we Till and love:
So we her ayres contemplate, words and heart,
And virtues; but we love the Centrique part.

Nor is the soul more worthy, or more fit
For love, then this, as infinite as it.
But in attaining this desired place
How much they erre; that set out at the face?
The hair a Forest is of Ambushes,
Of springes, snares, fetters and manacles:
The brow becalms us when 'tis smooth and plain,
And when 'tis wrinckled, shipwracks us again.
Smooth, 'tis a Paradice, where we would have
Immortal stay, but wrinkled 'tis our grave.
The Nose (like to the first Meridian) runs
Not 'twixt an East and West, but 'twixt two suns;
It leaves a Cheek, a rosie Hemisphere
On either side, and then directs us where
Upon the Islands fortunate we fall,
Not faynte *Canaries*, but *Ambrosiall*,
Her swelling lips; To which when wee are come,
We anchor there, and think our selves at home,
For they seem all: there Syrens songs, and there
Wise Delphick Oracles do fill the ear;
There in a Creek where chosen pearls do swell,
The Rhemora[a] her cleaving tongue doth dwell.
These, and the glorious Promontory, her Chin
Ore past; and the straight *Hellespont* betweene
The *Sestos* and *Abydos* of her breasts,
(Not of two Lovers, but two Loves the neasts)
Succeeds a boundless sea, but yet thine eye
Some Island moles may scattered there descry;
And Sailing towards her *India*, in that way
Shall at her fair Atlantick Navell stay;
Though thence the Current be thy Pilot made,
Yet ere thou be where thou wouldst be embay'd,
Thou shalt upon another Forest set,

a. The Rhemora (sucking-fish)

Where many Shipwrack, and no further get.
When thou are there, consider what this chace
Mispent by thy beginning at the face.

Rather set out below; practice my Art,
Some Symetry the foot hath with that part
Which thou dost seek, and is thy Map for that
Lovely enough to stop, but not stay at:
Least subject to disguise and change it is;
Men say the Devil never can change his.
It is the Emblem that hath figured
Firmness; 'tis the first part that comes to bed.
Civilitie we see refin'd: the kiss
Which at the face began, transplanted is,
Since to the hand, since to the imperial knee,
Now at the Papal foot delights to be:
If Kings think that the nearer way, and do
Rise from the foot, Lovers may do so too.
For as free Spheres move faster far then can
Birds, whom the air resists, so may that man
Which goes this empty and Ætherial way,
Then it at beauties elements he stay.
Rich Nature hath in women wisely made
Two purses,[a] and their mouths aversely[b] laid:
They then, which to the lower tribute owe,
That way which that Exchequer looks, must go:
He which doth not, his error is as great,
As who by Clyster gave the Stomack meat.[2]

Marke but this flea, and marke in this,
How little that which thou deny'st me is;
It suck'd me first, and now sucks thee,
And in this flea, our two bloods mingled bee;
Thou know'st that this cannot be said
A sinne, nor shame, nor loss of maidenhead,
    Yet this enjoyes before it wooe,

a. Two purses (the mouth and the vulva)
b. aversely (lying at an angle to one another)

And pamper'd swells with one blood made of two
And this, alas, is more then wee would doe.[3]

For every houre that thou wilt spare mee now,
   I will allow,
Usurious God of Love, twenty to thee,
When with my browne, my gray haires equall bee;
Till then, Love, let my body raigne,[a] and let
Mee travell, sojourne, snatch, plot, have, forget,
Resume my last yeares relict: think that yet
   We'had never met.[4]

Till I have peace with thee, warr other men,
  And when I have peace, can I leave thee then?
Here let me warr; in these armes lett me lye;
Here lett me parlee, batter, bleede, and dye.
Thy armes imprison me and myne armes thee,
Thy hart thy ransome is: take myne for mee.
Other men war that they their rest may gayne:
But wee will rest that wee may fight agayne.
Those warrs the ignorant, these th'experience'd love,
There wee are always under, here above.
There Engins farr off breed a just true feare,
Neere thrusts, pikes, stabs, ye bullets hurt not here.
There lyes are wrongs; here safe uprightly[b] ly;
There men kill men, we'will make one by and by.
Thou nothing; I not halfe so much shall do
In these Warrs, as they may which from us two
Shall spring. Thousands wee see which travaile not
To warrs; But stay swords, armes, and shott
To make at home; And shall not I do then
More glorious service, staying to make men?[5]

a. raigne (range)
b. uprightly (flat on her back)

F or Godsake hold your tongue, and let me love,
　　Or chide my palsie, or my gout,
My five gray haires, or ruin'd fortune flout,
　　With wealth your state, your minde with Arts improve,
　　　　Take you a course, get you a place,
　　　　Observe his honour, or his grace,
Or the King's reall, or his stamped face[a]
　　Contemplate, what you will, approve,
　　So you will let me love.

Alas, alas, who's injur'd by my love?
　　What merchants ships have my sighs drown'd?
Who saies my teares have overflow'd his ground?
　　When did my colds a forward spring remove?
　　　　When did the heats which my veines fill
　　　　Adde one more to the plaguie Bill?[b]
Soldiers finde warres, and Lawyers finde out still
　　Litigious men, which quarrels move,
　　Though she and I do love.

Call us what you will, wee are made such by love;
　　Call her one, mee another flye,
We'are Tapers too, and at our owne cost die,
　　And wee in us finde the'Eagle and the dove,
　　　　The Phoenix ridle hath more wit
　　　　By us, we two being one, are it.
So, to one neutrall thing both sexes fit,
　　Wee dye and rise the same, and prove,
　　Mysterious by this love.[6]

I f yet I have not all thy love,
　　Deare, I shall never have it all,
I cannot breath one other sigh, to move;
Nor can intreat one other teare to fall.
And all my treasure, which should purchase thee,
Sighs, teares, and oathes, and letters I have spent,
Yet no more can be due to mee,

a. stamped face (that is, on coins)
b. plaguie Bill (weekly list of those dead of the plague)

Then at the bargaine made was ment,
If then thy gift of love were partiall,
That some to mee, some should to others fall,
    Deare, I shall never have Thee All.

Yet I would not have all yet,
Hee that hath all can have no more,
And since my love doth every day admit
New growth, thou shouldst have new rewards in store;
Thou canst not every day give me thy heart,
If thou canst give it, then thou never gavest it:
Loves riddles are, that though thy heart depart,
It stayes at home, and thou with losing savest it:
But wee will have a way more liberall,
Then changing hearts, to joyne them, so wee shall
    Be one, and one anothers All.[7]

The Love of Men and Women

I wonder by my troth, what thou, and I
Did, till we lov'd, were we not wean'd till then?
But suck'd on countrey pleasures, childishly?
Or snorted we in the seaven sleepers den?
T'was so; But this, all pleasures fancies bee
If ever any beauty I did see,
Which I desir'd, and got, t'was but a dreame of thee.

And now good morrow to our waking soules,
Which watch not one another out of feare;
For[a] love, all love of other sights controules,
And makes one little roome, an every where.
Let sea-discoverers to new world have gone,
Let Maps to other, worlds on worlds have showne,
Let us possesse one world, each hath one, and is one.

My face in thine eye, thine in mine appeares,
And true plaine hearts doe in the faces rest,
Where can we finde two better hemispheares
Without sharpe North, without declining West?

a. For (But)

What ever dyes, was not mixt equally;
If our two loves be one, or, thou and I
Love so alike, that none doe slacken, none can die.[8]

W here, like a pillow on a bed,
    A Pregnant banke swel'd up, to rest
The violets reclining[a] head,
   Sat we two, one anothers best;
Our hands were firmely cimented
   With a fast balme, which thence did spring,
Our eye-beames twisted, and did thred
   Our eyes, upon one double string,
So to'entergraft our hands, as yet
   Was all the meanes to make us one,
And pictures in our eyes to get
   Was all our propagation.

This Extasie doth unperplex
   (We said) and tell us what we love,
Wee see by this, it was not sexe
   We see, we saw not what did move:
But as all severall[b] soules containe
   Mixture of things, they know not what,
Love, these mixt soules, doth mixe againe,
   And makes both one, each this and that.[c]

Wee then, who are this new soule, know,
   Of what we are compos'd, and made,
For, th'Atomies of which we grow,
   Are soules, whom no change can invade.
But O alas, so long, so farre
   Our bodies why doe wee forbeare?
They are ours, though not wee, Wee are
   The intelligences, they the spheares.
We owe them thankes, because they thus,
   Did us, to us, at first convay,
Yeelded their senses force to us,
   Nor are drosse to us, but allay.

a. reclining (declining) b. severall (separate) c. each this and that (both he and she)

To'our bodies turne wee then, that so
    Weake men on love reveal'd may looke;
Loves mysteries in soules doe grow,
    But yet the body is his[a] booke.
And if some lover, such as wee,
    Have heard this dialogue of one,
Let him still marke us, he shall see
    Small change, when we'are to bodies gone.[9]

F irst, we lov'd well and faithfully,
    Yet knew not what wee lov'd, nor why,
Difference of sex no more wee knew,
    Then our Guardian Angells doe,
      Coming and going, wee,
Perchance might kisse, but not between those meales.[b]
      Our hands ne'r toucht the seales,[c]
Which nature, injur'd by late law, sets free,
These miracles wee did; but now alas,
All measure, and all language, I should passe,
Should I tell what a miracle shee was.[10]

C ome live with mee, and bee my love,[d]
    And we will some new pleasures prove
Of golden sands, and christall brookes;
With silken lines, and silver hookes.

Thee will the river whispering runne
Warm'd by thy eyes, more than the Sunne.
And there the'inamor'd fish will stay,
Begging themselves they may betray.

a. his (the)
b. meales (the agape or love feast or Eucharist of the early Christians)
c. seales (colloquially the sexual organs)
d. Come live with mee, and bee my love (see for the purposes of comparison *The Passionate Shepherd* by Christopher Marlowe and *The Nymph's Reply* by Sir Walter Ralegh)

When thou wilt swimme in that live bath,
Each fish, which every channel hath,
Will amorously to thee swimme,
Gladder to catch thee, than thou him.

If thou, to be so seene, beest loath,
By Sunne, or Moone, thou darknest both,
And if my selfe have leave to see,
I need not their light, having thee.

Let others freeze with angling reeds,
And cut their legges, with shells and weeds,
Or treacherously poore fish beset,
With strangling snare, or windowie net:

Let coarse bold hands, from slimy nest
The bedded fish in banks out-wrest,
Or curious traitors, sleavesilke flies[a]
Bewitch poore fishes wandring eyes.

For thee, thou needs no such deceit,
For thou thy self art thine owne bait,
That fish, that is not catch'd thereby,
Alas, is wiser farre than I.[11]

As the sweet sweat of Roses in a Still,[b]
As that which from chaf'd muskats[c] pores doth trill,[d]
As the Almighty Balme of th'early East,
Such are the sweat[e] drops of[f] my Mistris breast,
And on her necke her skin such lustre sets,
They seeme no sweat drops, but pearle coronets.[12]

a. sleavesilke flies (lures made of untwisted silk)
b. Still (distillery)
c. muskats (musk-cat's – i.e., the musk-deer's secretions used in the making of perfume)
d. trill (trickle)
e. sweat (sweet)
f. of (on)

Foulenesse is Lothsome: can that be so which helpes it? who forbids his Beloved to gird in her waste? to mend by shooing her uneven lamenesse? to burnish her teeth? or to perfume her breath? yet that the Face bee more precisely regarded, it concernes more:

Nor doth it onely draw the busie eyes, but it is subject to the divinest touch of all, to *kissing*, the strange and mysticall union of soules.

What thou lovest in her *face* is *colour*, and *painting* gives that, but thou hatest it, not because it is, but because thou knowest it.

If in *kissing* or *breathing* upon her, the *painting* fall off, thou art angry. Wilt thou be so, if it sticke on?

Bee constant in something, and love her who shewes her great *love* to thee, in taking this paines to seeme *lovely* to thee.[13]

Busie old foole, unruly Sunne,
    Why dost thou thus,
Through windowes, and through curtaines call on us?
Must to thy motions lovers seasons run?
      Sawcy pedantique wretch, goe chide
      Late schoole boyes and sowre prentices,
   Go tell Court-huntsmen, that the King will ride,
   Call countrey ants to harvest offices;
Love, all alike, no season knows, nor clyme,
Nor houres, dayes, moneths, which are the rags of time.

      Thy beames, so reverend, and strong
      Why shouldst thou thinke?
I could eclipse and cloud them with a winke,
But that I would not lose her sight so long:
      If her eyes have not blinded thine,
      Looke, and to morrow late, tell mee,
   Whether both the'Indias's of spice and Myne
   Be where thou lefts them, or lie here with mee.
Aske for those Kings whom thou saw'st yesterday,
And thou shalt heare, All here in one bed lay.

She'is all States, and all Princes, I,
    Nothing else is.
Princes doe but play us, compar'd to this,
All honor's mimique; All wealth alchimie;
    Thou sunne art halfe as happy'as wee
    In that the world's contracted thus.
  Thine age askes ease, and since they duties bee
  To warme the world, that's done in warming us.
Shine here to us, and thou art every where;
This bed thy center is, these walls, thy spheare.[14]

9 'Tis true, 'tis day, what though it be?
    O wilt thou therefore rise from me?
Why should we rise, because 'tis light?
Did we lie downe, because t'was night?
Love which in spight of darknesse brought us hether,
Should in despight of light keepe us together.

Must businesse thee from hence remove?
Oh, that's the worst disease of love,
The poore, the foule, the false, love can
Admit, but not the busied man.
He which hath businesse, and makes love, doth doe
Such wrong, as when a maryed man doth wooe.[15]

I scarce believe my love to be so pure
    As I had thought it was,
      Because it doth endure
Vicissitude, and season, as the grasse;
Me thinkes I lyed all winter, when I swore,
My love was infinite, if spring make'it more.
But if this medicine, love, which cures all sorrow
With more, not onely bee no quintessence,
But mixt of all stuffes, paining soule, or sense,
And of the Sunne his working vigour borrow,
Love's not so pure, and abstract, as they use
To say, which have no Mistresse but their Muse,

But as all else, being elemented too,
Love sometimes would contemplate, sometimes do.

And yet no greater, but more eminent,
    Love by the Spring is growne;
    As, in the firmament,
Starres by the Sunne are not inlarg'd, but showne,
Gentle love deeds, as blossomes on a bough,
From loves awakened root do but out now.
If, as in water stir'd more circles bee
Produc'd by one, love such additions take,
Those like so many spheares, but one heaven make,
For, they are all concentrique unto thee,
And though each spring doe adde to love new heate,
As princes doe in times of action get
New taxes, and remit them not in peace,
No winter shall abate the springs encrease.[16]

When thou and I first one another saw:
    All other things, to their destruction draw,
    Only our love hath no decay;
This, no to morrow hath, nor yesterday,
Running it never runs from us away,
But truly keepes his first, last, everlasting day.[17]

The Love of a Woman for a Woman

Thy body is a naturall Paradise,
    In whose selfe, unmanur'd, all pleasure lies,
Nor needs *perfection*; why shouldst thou than
    Admit the tillage of a harsh rough man?
Men leave behinde them that which their sin showes,
    And are, as theeves trac'd, which rob when it snowes.
But of our dallyance no more signes there are,
    Then *fishes* leave in streames, or *Birds* in aire.
And betweene us all sweetnesse may be had;
    All, all that *Nature* yields, or *Art* can adde.

My two lips, eyes, thighs, differ from thy two,
  But so, as thine from one another doe;
And, oh, no more; the likenesse being such,
  Why should they not alike in all parts touch?
Hand to strange hand, lippe to lippe none denies;
  Why should they brest to brest, or thighs to thighs?
Likenesse begets such strange selfe flatterie,
  That touching my selfe, all seemes done to thee.[18]

Delight and Desolation

As all things were one nothing, dull and weake,
Untill this raw disordered heape did breake,
And severall desires led parts away,
Water declin'd with earth, the ayre did stay,
Fire rose, and each from other but unty'd
Themselves unprison'd were and purified:

So was love, first in vast confusion hid,
An unripe willingnesse which nothing did,
A thirst, an Appetite which had no ease,
That found a want, but knew not what would please.

What pretty innocence in those dayes mov'd!
Man ignorantly walk'd by her he lov'd;
Both sigh'd and enterchang'd a speaking eye,
Both trembled and were sick, both knew not why.

It is not love that sueth, or doth contend;
Love either conquers, or but meets a friend.
Man's better part consists of purer fire,
And findes it selfe allow'd, ere it desire.

Love is wise here, keepes home, gives reason sway,
And journeys not till it finde summer-way.
A weather-beaten Lover but once knowne,
Is sport for every girle to practise on.

Who strives through womans scornes, women to know,
Is lost, and seekes his shadow to outgoe;
It must be sicknesse, after one disdaine,
Though he be call'd aloud, to looke againe.
Let others sigh, and grieve; one cunning sleight
Shall freeze my Love to Christall in a night.

I can love first, and (if I winne) love still;
And cannot be remov'd, unlesse she will.
It is her fault if I unsure remaine,
Shee onely can untie, and binde againe.

No more can impure man retaine[a] and move
In that pure region of a worthy love,
Then earthly substance can unforc'd[b] aspire,
And leave his nature to converse[c] with fire:
Such may have eye, and hand; may sigh, may speak;
But like swoln bubles, when they are high'st they break.

So able men, blest with a vertuous Love,
Remote or neare, or howso'er they move;
Their vertue breakes all clouds that might annoy,
There is no Emptinesse, but all is Joy.

He much profanes whom violent heats do move
To stile his wandring rage of passion, *Love.*
Love that imparts in every thing delight,
Is fain'd, which only tempts mans appetite.
Why love among the vertues is not knowne
Is, that love is them all contract in one.[19]

B ut oh, loves day is short, if love decay.

Love is a growing, or full constant light;
And his first minute, after noone, is night.[20]

L ove built on beauty, soone as beauty, dies.[21]

a. retaine (remain)   b. unforc'd (unrefined)   c. converse (mingle)

The Love of Men and Women

He is starke mad, who ever sayes,
    That he hath been in love an houre,
Yet not that love so soone decayes,
    But that it can tenne in lesse space devour;
Who will believe mee, if I sweare
That I have had the plague a yeare?
    Who would not laugh at mee, if I should say,
    I saw a flaske of *powder burne a day?*

Ah, what a trifle is a heart,
    If once into loves hands it come!
All other griefes allow a part
    To other griefes, and aske themselves but some,
They come to us, but as Love draws,
    Hee swallows us, and never chawes:[a]
By him, as by chain'd shot, whole rankes doe dye,
    He is the tyran Pike, our hearts the Frye.[b]

If 'twere not so, what did become
    Of my heart, when I first saw thee?
I brought a heart into the roome,
    But from the roome, I carried none with mee;
If it had gone to thee, I know
Mine would have taught thine heart to show
    More pitty unto mee; but Love, alas
    At one first[c] blow did shiver it as glasse.

Yet nothing can to nothing fall,
    Nor any place be empty quite,
Therefore I thinke my breast hath all
    Those peeces still, though they be not unite;
And now as broken glasses[d] show
A hundred lesser faces, so
    My ragges of heart can like, wish, and adore,
    But after one such love, can love no more.[22]

a. chawes (chews)
b. the Frye (small fish devoured by the Pike)
c. first (fierce)
d. glasses (mirrors)

Humanity

Strong is this love which ties our hearts in one,
  And strong that love pursu'd with amorous paine;
But though besides thy selfe I leave behind
  Heavens liberall and earths thrice-fairer Sunne,
  Going to where sterne winter aye doth wonne,[a]
Yet, loves hot fires, which martyr my sad minde,
  Doe send forth scalding sighes, which have the Art
  To melt all Ice, but that which walls her heart.[23]

Send home my long strayd eyes to mee,
  Which (Oh) too long have dwelt on thee,
Yet since there they have learn'd such ill,
    Such forc'd fashions,
    And false passions,
      That they be
      Made by thee
Fit for no good sight, keep them still.

Send home my harmlesse heart againe,
Which no unworthy thought could staine,
Which if it be taught by thine
    To make jestings
    Of protestings,
      And breake both
      Word and oath,
Keepe it, for then 'tis none of mine.

Yet send me back my heart and eyes,
That I may know, and see thy lyes,
And may laugh and joy, when thou
    Art in anguish
    And dost languish
      For some one
      That will none,
Or prove as false as thou art now.[24]

a. wonne (abide)

W hilst yet to prove,
　　I thought there was some Deitie in love
So did I reverence, and gave
Worship, As Atheists at their dying houre
Call, what they cannot name, an unknowne prower,
　　As ignorantly did I crave:
　　　　Thus when
Things not yet knowne are coveted by men,
　　Our desires give them fashion,[a] and so,
As they waxe lesser, fall,[b] as they sise, grow.

　　But, from late faire
His highnesse sitting in a golden Chaire,
　　Is not lesse cared for after three dayes
By children, then the thing[c] which lovers so
Blindly admire, and with such worship wooe;
　　Being had, enjoying it decayes:
　　　　And thence,
What before pleas'd them all,[d] takes[e] but one sense,
　　And that so lamely as it leaves behind
A kind of sorrowing dulnesse to the minde.

　　Ah cannot wee,
As well as Cocks and Lyons jocund be,
　　After such pleasures, unlesse wise
Nature decreed (since each such Act, they say,
Diminisheth the length of life a day)
　　This; as shee would man should despise
　　　　The sport,
Because that other curse of being short,
　　And onely for a minute made to be
Eager, desires to raise posterity.

　　Since so, my minde
Shall not desire what no man else can finde,
　　I'll no more dote and runne

a. fashion (form)
b. fall (abate)
c. the thing (love-making)
d. all (all the senses)
e. takes (affects)

To pursue things which had indammag'd me.
And when I come were moving beauties be,
   As men doe when the summers Sunne
           Growes great,
Though I admire their greatnesse, shun their heat;
   Each place can afford shadowes. If all faile,
'Tis but applying worme-seed[a] to the Taile.[b25]

How great love is, presence best tryall makes,
But absence tryes how long this love will bee.[26]

Since she must go, and I must mourn, come night,
Environ me with darkness, whilst I write:
Shadow that hell unto me, which alone
I am to suffer when my Love is gone.

Oh Love, that fire and darkness should be mixt,
Or to thy Triumphs soe strange torments fixt!
Is't because thou thy self art blind, that wee
Thy Martyrs must no more each other see!

Was't not enough that thou didst dart thy fires
Into our blouds, inflaming our desires,
And made'st us sigh and glow, and pant, and burn,
And then thy self into our flame did'st turn?
Was't not enough, that thou didst hazard us
To paths in love so dark, so dangerous:

Have we not kept our guards, like spie on spie?
Had correspondence whilst the foe stood by?
Stoln (more to sweeten them) our many blisses
Of meetings, conference, embracements, kisses?
Shadow'd with negligence our most respects?
Varied our language through all dialects,
Of becks,[c] winks, looks, and often under-boards[d]
Spoak dialogues with our feet far from our words?

a. worme-seed (used as an aphrodisiac)   b. the Taile (the penis)
c. becks (nods)   d. under-boards (under the table)

Rend us in sunder, thou canst not divide
Our bodies so, but that our souls are ty'd,
And we can love by letters still and gifts,
And thought and dreams; Love never wanteth shifts.

I will not look upon the quickning Sun,
But straight her beauty to my sense shall run;
The ayre shall note her soft, the fire most pure;
Water suggest her clear,[a] and the earth sure;
Time shall not lose our passages;[b] the Spring
How fresh our love was in the beginning;
The Summer how it ripened in the eare;
And Autumn, what our golden harvests were.
The Winter I'll not think on to spite thee,
But count it a lost season, so shall shee.
And dearest Friend, since we must part, drown night
With hope of Day, burthens well born are light.[27]

Temper, ô faire Love, loves impetuous rage,
  Be my true Mistris still, not my faign'd[c] Page;
I'll goe, and, by thy kinde leave, leave behinde
Thee, onely worthy to nurse in my minde,

Fall ill or good, 'tis madnesse to have prov'd
Dangers unurg'd; Feed on this flattery,
That absent Lovers one in th'other be.

When I am gone, dreame me some happinesse,
Nor let thy lookes our long hid love confesse,
Nor praise, nor dispraise me, nor blesse nor curse
Openly loves force, nor in bed fright thy Nurse
With midnights startings, crying out, oh, oh
Nurse, ô my love is slaine, I saw him goe
O'r the white Alpes alone; I saw him I,
Assail'd, fight, taken, stabb'd, bleed, fall, and die.
Augure me better chance, except dread *Jove*
Thinke it enough for me to'have had thy love.[28]

a. clear (innocent)
b. passages (acts of love)
c. faign'd (disguised)

D ull sublunary lovers love
  (Whose soule is sense) cannot admit
Absence, because it doth remove
  Those things which elemented it.

But we by a love, so much refin'd,
  That our selves know not what it is,
Inter-assured of the mind,
  Care lesse, eyes, lips, hands to misse.

Our two soules therefore, which are one,
  Though I must goe, endure not yet
A breach, but an expansion,
  Like gold to ayery thinnesse beate.[29]

O h doe not die, for I shall hate
  All women so, when thou art gone,
That thee I shall not celebrate,
  When I remember, thou wast one.

But yet thou canst not die, I know
  To leave this world behinde, is death,
But when thou from this world wilt goe,
  The whole world vapors with thy breath.

Or if, when thou, the worlds soule, goest,
  It stay, tis but thy carkasse then,
The fairest woman, but thy ghost,
  But corrupt wormes, the worthyest men.

O wrangling schooles, that search what fire
  Shall burne this world, had none the wit
Unto this knowledge to aspire,
  That this her feaver might be it?

And yet she cannot wast by this,
  Nor long beare this torturing wrong,
For much corruption needful is
  To fuell such a feaver long.

These burning fits but meteors bee,
Whose matter in thee is soone spent.
Thy beauty, 'and all parts, which are thee,
Are unchangeable firmament.[30]

So, so,[a] breake off this last lamenting kisse,
    Which sucks two soules, and vapors Both away,
Turne thou ghost that way, and let mee turne this,
    And let our selves benight our happiest day,
We aske none leave to love; nor will we owe
    Any, so cheape a death, as saying, Goe.[31]

Promiscuity

The heavens rejoyce in motion, why should I
    Abjure my so much lov'd variety,
And not with many youth and love divide?
Pleasure is none, if not diversifi'd:
The sun that sitting in the chaire of light
Sheds flame into what else soever doth seem bright,
Is not contented at one Signe to Inne,[b]
But ends his year and with a new beginnes.
All things doe willingly in change delight,
The fruitfull mother of our appetite:

Let no man tell me such a one is faire,
And worthy all alone my love to share.
Nature in her hath done the liberall part
Of a kinde Mistresse, and imploy'd her art
To make her loveable, and I aver
Him not humane that would turn back from her:
I love her well, and would, if need were, dye
To doe her service. But followes it that I
Must serve her onely, when I may have choice?
The law is hard, and shall not have my voice.

a. So, so (So, go)
b. to Inne (to Lodge)

How happy were our Syres in ancient times
Who held plurality of loves no crime!
With them it was accounted charity
To stirre up race of all indifferently;
Kindreds were not exempted from the bands:[a]
Which with the Persian still in usage stands.
Women were then no sooner asked then won,
And what they did was honest and well done.

Onely some few strong in themselves and free
Retain the seeds of antient liberty,
Following that part of love although deprest,
And make a throne for him within their brest,
In spight of modern censures him avowing
Their Soveraigne, all service him allowing.
Amongst which troop although I am the least,
Yet equall in perfection with the best,
I glory in subjection of his hand,
Nor ever did decline his least command:
For in whatever forme the message came
My heart did open and receive the same.[32]

V *enus* heard me sigh this song,
    And by Loves sweetest Part, Variety, she swore,
She heard not this till now; and that it should be so no more.
She went, examin'd, and return'd ere long,
And said, alas, Some two or three
Poore Heretiques in love there bee,
Which thinke to stablish dangerous constancie.
But I have told them, since you will be true,
You shall be true to them, who'are false to you.[33]

S ome man unworthy to be possessor
    Of old or new love, himselfe being false or weake,
    Thought his paine and shame would be lesser,

a. bands (sexual unions)

[106]

If on womankind he might his anger wreake,
     And thence a law did grow,
     One might but one man know;
     But are other creatures so?

   Are Sunne, Moone, or Starres by law forbidden,
To smile where they list, or lend away their light?
   Are birds divorc'd, or are they chidden
If they leave their mate, or lie abroad a night?
     Beasts doe no joyntures lose
     Though they new lovers choose,
     But we are made worse than those.

   Who e'r rigg'd faire ship to lie in harbors,
And not to seeke new lands, or not to deale withall?
   Or built faire houses, set trees, and arbors,
Only to lock up, or else to let them fall?
     Good is not good, unlesse
     A thousand it possesse,
     But doth wast with greedinesse.[34]

I can love both faire and browne,
  Her whom abundance melts, and her whom want betraies,
Her who loves lonenesse best, and her who maskes and plaies,
Her whom the country form'd, and whom the town,
Her who beleeves,[a] and her who tries,[b]
Her who still weepes with spungie eyes,
And her who is dry corke, and never cries;
I can love her, and her, and you and you,
I can love any, so she be not true.[35]

Women, are like the Arts, forc'd unto[c] none,
  Open to'all searchers, unpriz'd, if unknowne.
If I have caught a bird, and let him flie,

a. beleeves (trusts her lover)
b. tries (tests him)
c. forc'd unto (forbid to)

Another fouler using these meanes, as I,
May catch the same bird; and, as these things bee,
Women are made for men, not him, nor mee.
Foxes and goats; all beasts change when they please,
Shall women, more hot, wily, wild then these,
Be bound to one man, and did Nature then
Idly make them apter to'endure then men?

Likenesse glues love: and if that thou so doe,
To make us like and love, must I change too?
More then thy hate, I hate'it, rather let mee
Allow her change, then change as oft as shee,
And soe not teach, but force my'opinion
To love not any one, nor every one.
To live in one land, is captivitie,
To runne all countries, a wild roguery;
Waters stincke soone, if in one place they bide
And in the vast sea are more putrifi'd:
But when they kisse one banke, and leaving this
Never looke backe, but the next banke doe kisse,
Then are they purest; Change'is the nursery
Of musicke, joy, life and eternity.[36]

Thus I reclaim'd my buzard love, to flye
　At what, and when, and how, and where I chuse;
　　Now negligent of sports I lye,
　　And now as other Fawkners use,
I spring a mistresse, sweare, write, sigh and weepe:
And the game kill'd, or lost, goe talke, and sleepe.[37]

Cynicism

Goe, and catche a falling starre,
　Get with child a mandrake roote,
Tell me, where all past yeares are,
　Or who cleft the Divils foot,
Teach me to heare Mermaides singing,

[108]

Or to keep off envies stinging,
   And finde
   What winde
Serves to advance an honest minde.

If thou beest borne to strange sights,
  Things invisible to see,
Ride ten thousand daies and nights,
  Till age snow white haires on thee,
Thou, when thou retorn'st, wilt tell mee
All strange wonders that befell thee,
   And sweare
   No where
Lives a woman true, and faire.

If thou findst one, let mee know,
  Such a Pilgrimage were sweet,
Yet do not, I would not goe,
  Though at next doore wee might meet,
Though shee were true, when you met her,
And last, till you write your letter,
   Yet shee
   Will bee
False, ere I come, to two, or three.[38]

That Women are *Inconstant*, I with any man confesse, but that *Inconstancy* is a bad quality, I against any man will maintaine: For every thing as it is one better than another, so is it fuller of *change*; The *Heavens* themselves continually turne, the *Starres* move, the *Moone* changeth; *Fire* whirleth, *Ayre* flyeth, *Water* ebbs and flowes, the face of the *Earth* altereth her lookes, *time* stayes not; the Colour that is most light, will take most dyes: so in Men, they that have the most reason are the most alterable in their designes, and the darkest or most ignorant, do seldomest change; therefore Women changing more than Men, have also more *Reason*. They cannot be immutable like stockes, like stones, like the Earths dull Center; Gold that lyeth still, rusteth; Water, corrupteth; Aire that moveth not, poysoneth; then why should that which is the perfection of other things, be imputed to Women as greatest imperfection?

I would you had your *Mistresses* so constant, that they would never change, no not so much as their *smocks*, then should you see what sluttish vertue, *Constancy* were. *Inconstancy* is a most commendable and cleanely quality, and Women in this quality are farre more absolute than the Heavens, than the Starres, Moone, or any thing beneath it; for long observation hath pickt certainety out of their mutability.

Women are like *Flies*, which feed among us at our Table, or *Fleas* sucking our very blood, who leave not our most retired places free from their familiarity, yet for all their fellowship will they never bee tamed nor commanded by us. Women are like the *Sunne*, which is violently carryed one way, yet hath a proper course contrary: so though they, by the master of some over-ruling churlish Husbands, are forced to his Byas, yet have they a motion of their owne, which their Husbands never know of.

Philosophers write against them for spight, not desert, that having attained to some knowledge in all other things, in them onely they know nothing, but are meerely ignorant: *Active* and *Experienced* men raile against them, because they love in their livelesse and decrepit age, when all goodnesse leaves them. These envious *Libellers* ballad against them, because having nothing in themselves able to deserve their love, they maliciously discommend all they cannot obtaine, thinking to make men beleeve they know much, because they are able to dispraise much, and rage against *Inconstancy*, when they were never admitted into so much favour as to be forsaken. In mine Opinion such men are happy that Women are *Inconstant*, for so may they chance to bee beloved of some excellent Women (when it comes to their turne) out of their *Inconstancy* and mutability, though not out of their owne desert. And what reason is there to clog any Woman with one Man, bee hee never so singular? Women had rather, and it is farre better and more Judiciall to enjoy all the vertues in severall Men, than but some of them in one, for otherwise they lose their taste, like divers sorts of meat minced together in one dish: and to have all excellencies in one Man (if it were possible) is *Confusion* and *Diversity*.

To conclude therefore; this name of *Inconstancy*, which hath so much beene poysoned with slaunders, ought to bee changed into *variety*, for the which the world is so delightfull, *and a Woman for that the most delightfull thing in this world.*[39]

I am not of the feard *Impudence* that I dare defend *Women*, or pronounce them good; yet we see *Physitians* allow some *vertue* in every *poyson*. Alas! Why should we except *Women*? since certaine-ly, they are good for *Physicke* at least, so as some *wine* is good for a *feaver*. And though they be the *Occasioners* of many sinnes, they are also the *Punishers* and *Revengers* of the same sinnes: For I have seldome seene one which consumes his *substance* and *body* upon them, escape *diseases*, or *beggery*; and this is their *Justice.*[40]

Now thou hast lov'd me one whole day,
 To morrow when thou leav'st, what wilt thou say?
Wilt thou then Antedate some new made vow?
          Or say that now
We are not just those persons, which we were?
Or, that oathes made in reverentiall feare
Of Love, and his wrath, any may forsweare?
Or, as true deaths, true maryages untie,
So lovers contracts, images of those,
Binde but till sleep, deaths image, them unloose?

   Or, your owne end to Justifie,
For having purpos'd change, and falsehood; you
Can have no way but falsehood to be true?
Vaine lunatique, against these scapes[a] I could
   Dispute, and conquer, if I would,
      Which I abstaine to doe,
For by to morrow, I may thinke so too.[41]

Some that have deeper digg'd loves Myne then I,
 Say, where his centrique happinesse doth lie:
          I have lov'd, and got, and told,
But should I love, get, tell, till I were old,

a. scapes (subterfuges)

I should not finde that hidden mysterie;
    Oh, 'tis imposture all:
And as no chymique yet th'Elixar got,
    But glorifies his pregnant pot,
    If by the way to him befall
Some odoriforous thing, or medicinall,
  So, lovers dreame a rich and long delight,
  But get a winter-seeming summers night.

Our ease, our thrift, our honor, and our day,
Shall we, for this vaine Bubles shadow pay?
    Ends love in this, that my man,
Can be as happy'as I can; If he can
Endure the short scorne of a Bridegroomes play?
    That loving wretch that sweares,
'Tis not the bodies marry, but the mindes,
    Which he in her Angelique findes,
    Would sweare as justly, that he heares,
In that dayes rude hoarse minstralsey, the spheares.
  Hope not for minde in women; at their best,
  Sweetnesse, and wit they'are, but, *Mummy*,[a] possest.[42]

The Wedding Day : The Wedding Night

The sun-beames in the East are spred,
  Leave, leave, faire Bride, your solitary bed,
  No more shall you returne to it alone,
It nourseth sadnesse, and your bodies print,
Like to a grave, the yielding downe doth dint;
    You and your other you meet there anon;
    Put forth, put forth that warme balme-breathing thigh,
Which when next time you in these sheets will smother,
  There it must meet another,
    Which never was, but must be, oft, more nigh;
Come glad from thence, go gladder than you came,
To day put on perfection, and a womans name.

a. Mummy (body without mind)

The Love of Men and Women

Daughters of London, you which bee
Our Golden Mines, and furnish'd Treasurie,
 You which are Angels, yet still bring with you
Thousands of Angels on your mariage daies,
Help with your presence, and devise to praise
 These rites, which also unto you grow due;
 Conceitedly dresse her, and be assign'd.
By you, fit place for every flower and jewell,
 Make her for love fit fewell
 As gay as Flora, and as rich as Inde;
So may shee faire and rich, in nothing lame,
To day put on perfection, and a womans name.

Thy two-leav'd gates faire Temple unfold,
And these two in thy sacred bosome hold,
 Till, mystically joyn'd, but one they bee;
Then may thy leane and hunger-starved wombe
Long time expect their bodies and their tombe,
 Long after their owne parents fatten thee;
 All elder claimes, and all cold barrennesse,
All yeelding to new loves bee far for ever,
 Which might these two dissever,
 Alwaies, all th'other may each one possesse;
For, the best Bride, best worthy of praise and fame
To day puts on perfection, and a womans name.

Winter dayes bring much delight,
Not for themselves, but for they soon bring night;
 Other sweets wait thee then these diverse meats,
Other disports than dancing jollities,
Other love tricks than glancing with the eyes,
 But that the Sun still in our halfe Spheare sweates;
 Hee flies in winter, but he now stands still.
Yet shadowes turne; Noone point he hath attain'd,
 His steeds will be retrain'd.
 But gallop lively down the Westerne hill;
Thou shalt, when he hath runne the worlds half frame,
To night put on a perfection, and a womans name.

Humanity

The amorous evening starre is rose,
Why then should not our amorous starre inclose
   Her self in her wish'd bed? Release your strings
Musicians, and dancers take some truce
With these your pleasing labours, for great use
   As much weariness as perfection brings;
     You, and not only you, but all toyl'd beasts
Rest duly; at night all their toyles are dispensed;
But in their beds commenced
     Are other labours, and more dainty feasts;
She goes a maid, who, lest she turne the same
To night puts on perfection, and a womans name.

Thy virgins girdle now untie,
And in thy nuptiall bed (loves alter[a]) lye
   A pleasing sacrifice; now dispossesse
Thee of these chaines and robes which were put on
T'adorne the day, not thee; for thou, alone,
   Like vertue'and truth, are best in nakednesse;
     This bed is onely to virginitie
A grave, but, to a better state, a cradle;
Till now thou wast but able
   To be what now thou art; then that by thee
No more be said, *I may bee*, but, *I am*,
To night put on perfection, and a womans name.

Even like a faithful man content,
That this life for a better should be spent,
   So, shee a mothers rich stile doth preferre,
And at the Bridegroomes wish'd approach doth lye,
Like an appointed lambe, when tenderly
   The priest comes on his knees t'embowell her;
     Now sleep or watch with more joy; and O light
Of heaven, to morrow rise thou hot, and early;
This Sun[b] will love so dearely
   Her rest, that long, long we shall want[c] her sight;
Wonders are wrought, for shee which had no maime,
To night puts on perfection, and a womans name.[43]

a. alter (altar)   b. This Sun (The Bride)   c. want (lack)

Up then faire Phoenix, Bride, frustrate the Sunne,
      Thy selfe from thine affection
      Takest warmth enough, and from thine eye
All lesser birds will take their Jollitie.
      Up, up, faire Bride, and call,
Thy starres, from out their severall boxes, take
Thy Rubies, Pearles, and Diamonds forth, and make
Thy selfe a constellation, of them All,
      And by their blazing, signifie,
That a Great Princess falls, but doth not die;
Bee thou a new starre, that to us portends
Ends of much wonder; And be Thou those ends.
Since thou dost this day in new glory shine,
May all men date Records, from this thy Valentine.

Come forth, come forth, and as one glorious flame
      Meeting Another, growes the same,
      So meet thy Fredericke, and so
To an unseparable union growe.
      Since separation
Falls not on such things as are infinite,
Nor things which are but one, can disunite,
You'are twice inseparable, great, and one;
      Goe then to where the Bishop staies,
To make you one, his way, which divers waies
Must be effected; and when all is past,
And that you'are one, by hearts and hands made fast,
You two have one way left, your selves to'entwine,
Besides this Bishops knot, or Bishop Valentine.

But oh, what ailes the Sunne, that here he staies,
      Longer to day, then other daies?
      Staies he new light from these to get?
And finding here such store, is loth to set?
      And why doe you two walke
So slowly pac'd in this procession?
Is all your care but to be look'd upon,
And be to others spectacle, and talke?
      The feast, with gluttonous delaies,
Is eaten, and too long their meat they praise,

The masquers come too late, and'I thinke, will stay,
Like Fairies, till the Cock crow them away.
Alas, did not Antiquity assigne
A night, as well as day, to thee, O Valentine?

They did, and night is come; and yet wee see
        Formalities retarding thee.
        What meane these Ladies, which (as though
They were to take a clock in peeces,) goe
        So nicely about the Bride;
A Bride, before a good night could be said,
Should vanish from her cloathes, into her bed,
As Soules from bodies steale, and are not spy'd.
        But now she is laid; What though shee bee?
Yet there are more delayes, For, where is he?
He comes, and passes through Spheare after Spheare,
First her sheetes, then her Armes, then any where.
Let not this day, then, but this night be thine,
Thy day was but the eve to this, O Valentine.

Here lyes a shee Sunne, and a hee Moone here,
        She gives the best light to his Spheare,
        Or each is both, and all, and so
They unto one another nothing owe,
        And yet they doe, but are
So just and rich in that coyne^a which they pay,
That neither would, nor needs forbeare nor stay;
Neither desires to be spar'd, nor to spare,
        They quickly pay their debt, and then
Take no acquittances, but pay again;
They pay, they give, they lend, and so let fall
No such occasion to be liberall.
More truth, more courage in these two do shine,
Then all thy turtles have, and sparrows, Valentine.

And by this act of these two Phenixes
        Nature againe restored is,
        For since these two are two no more,
Ther's but one Phenix still, as was before.

a. coyne (i.e., their own sexual pleasure)

Rest now at last, and wee
As Satyres watch the Sunnes uprise, will stay
Waiting, when your eyes opened, let out day,
Onely desir'd, because your face wee see;
   Others neare you shall whispering speake,
And wagers lay, at which side day will breake,
And win by'observing, then, whose hand it is
That opens first a curtaine, hers or his;
This will be tryed to morrow after nine,
Till which houre, wee thy day enlarge, O Valentine.[44]

T hou are repriv'd old yeare, thou shalt not die,
 Though thou upon thy death bed lye,
  And should'st within five dayes[a] expire,
Yet thou art rescu'd by a mightier fire,
  Then thy old Soule, the Sunne,
When he doth in his largest circle runne.
The passage of the West or East would thaw,
And open wide their easie liquid jawe
To all our ships, could a Promethean art
Either unto the Northerne Pole impart
The fire of these inflaming eyes, or of this loving heart.

Blest payre of Swans, Oh may you interbring
  Daily new joyes, and never sing;
  Live, till all grounds of wishes faile,
Till honor, yea till wisedome grow so stale,
   That, new great heights to trie,
It must serve your ambition, to die;
Raise heires, and may here, to the worlds end, live
Heires from this King, to take thankes, you, to give,
Nature and grace doe all, and nothing Art.
May never age, or error overthwart
With any West, these radiant eyes, with any North, this heart.

a. within five dayes (the marriage was celebrated on 26 December)

What mean'st thou Bride, this companie to keep?
    To sit up, till thou faine wouldst sleep?
    Thou maist not, when thou art laid, doe so.
Thy selfe must to him a new banquet grow,
      And you must entertaine
And doe all this daies dances o'er again.
Know that if Sun and Moone together doe
Rise in one point, they doe not set so too.
Therefore thou maist, faire Bride, to bed depart,
Thou art not gone, being gone; where e'r thou art,
Thou leav'st in him thy watchfull eyes, in him thy loving heart.

As he that sees a starre fall, runs apace,
    And findes a gellie[a] in the place,
    So doth the Bridegoome haste as much,
Being told this starre is falne, and findes her such.
      And as friends may looke strange,
By a new fashion, or apparrells change,
Their soules, though long acquainted they had beene,
These clothes, their bodies, never yet had seene.
Therefore at first she modestly might start,
But must forthwith surrender every part,
As freely, as each to each before, gave either eye or heart.

Now as in Tullias tombe, one lampe burnt clear,
    Unchang'd for fifteene hundred yeare,
    May these love-lamps we here enshrine,
In warmth, light, lasting, equall the divine.
      Fire ever doth aspire,
And makes all like it self, turnes all to fire.
But ends in ashes, which these cannot doe,
For none of these is fuell, but fire too.
This is joyes bonfire, then, where loves strong Arts
Make of so noble individual parts
One fire of foure inflaming eye, and of two loving hearts.[45]

a. gellie (refers to a genus of algae which appears as a jelly-like mass on dry soil after rain and was believed to be the remains of a fallen star or meteor)

The Gift of Children

G od would not have the comelinesse, the handsomenesse of the
body defaced by incontinency, and intemperance, but he
would not have the care of that comelinesse, and handsomenesse
frustrate his purpose of children in mariage.[46]

M ariage without possibility of children, lacks one halfe of
Gods purpose in the institution of mariage.[47]

Maturity in Love

N o *Spring*, nor *Summer* Beauty hath such grace,
  As I have seen in one *Autumnall face*,
Yong *Beauties* force our love, and that's a *Rape*,
  This doth but *counsaile*, yet you cannot scape.
If t'were a *shame* to love, here t'were no *shame*,
  Affections here take *Reverences* name.
Were her first yeares the *Golden Age*; that's true,
  But now shee's *gold* oft tried, and ever new.
That was her torrid and inflaming time,
  This is her tolerable *Tropique clyme*.
Faire eyes, who askes more heate then comes from hence,
  He in a fever wishes pestilence.
Call not these wrinkles, *graves*; If *graves* they were,
  They were *Loves graves*; for else he is no where.
Yet lies not *dead* here, but here doth sit
  Vow'd to this trench, like an *Anachorit*.

Here, where still *Evening* is; not *noone*, nor *night*;
  Where no *voluptuousnesse*, yet all *delight*.
In all her words, unto all hearers fit,
You may at *Revels*, you at *counsaile*, sit.
This is loves timber, youth his under-wood,[a]
There he, as wine in *June*, enrages blood,
Which then comes seasonabliest, when our tast
And appetite to other things, is past.

a. under-wood (inflammable brushwood)

If we love things long sought, *Age* is a thing
Which we are fifty yeares in compassing.
If transitory things, which soone decay,
Age must be lovelyest at the latest day.

Since such loves motion natural is, may still
My love descend, and journey downe the hill,
Not panting after growing beauties, so,
I shall ebbe out with them, who home-ward goe.[48]

H ere take my Picture;[a] though I bid farewell;
Thine, in my heart, where my soule dwels, shall dwell.
'Tis like me now, but I dead, 'twill be more
When wee are shadowes both, than'twas before.
When weather-beaten I come backe; my hand,
Perhaps with rude oares torne, or Sun beams tann'd,
My face and brest of hairecloth, and my head
With cares rash sodaine stormes, being o'rspread,
My body'a sack of bones, broken within,
And powders[b] blew staines scatter'd on my skinne;
If rivall fooles taxe thee to'have lov'd a man,
So foule, and course,[c] as, Oh, I may seeme than,
This shall say what I was: and thou shalt say,
Doe his hurts reach mee? doth my worth decay?
Or doe they reach his judging minde, that hee
Should now love lesse, what hee did love to see?
That which in him was faire and delicate,
Was but the milke, which in loves childish state
Did nurse it: who now is growne strong enough
To feed on that, which to disus'd tasts seemes tough.[49]

a. Picture (miniature portrait)
b. powders (gunpowders)
c. course (coarse)

4

VIRTUOUS LIVING

Sparks of Virtue

If men be worlds, there is in everyone
Some thing to answere in some proportion
All the worlds riches: And in good men, this
Vertue, our formes forme and our soules soule is.[1]

There is no Vertue, but Religion:
Wise, valiant, sober, just, are names, which none
Want, which want not Vice-covering discretion.

Seeke wee then our selves in our selves; for as
Men force the Sunne with much more force to passe,
By gathering his beames with a christall glasse;

So wee, If wee into our selves will turne,
Blowing our sparkes of vertue, may outburne
The straw, which doth about our heart sojourne

So workes retirednesse in us; to rome
Giddily and be every where, but at home,
Such freedome doth a banishment become.

Wee are but farmers of our selves, yet may,
If we can stock our selves, and thrive, uplay
Much, much deare treasure for the great rent day.

Manure thy self then, to thy selfe be'approv'd,
And with vaine outward things be no more mov'd,
But to know, that I love thee; and would be lov'd.[2]

Let us therefore look first to that which is best in us naturally, that is, Reason; For if we lose that, our Reason, our Discourse, our Consideration, and sinke into an incapable and barren stupidity, there is no footing, no subsistence for grace. All the vertue of Corne is in the seed; but that will not grow in water, but onely in the earth: All the good of man, considered supernaturally, is in grace; but that will not growe in a washy soule, in a liquid, in a watery, and dissolute, and scattered man. Grace growes in reason; In that man, and in that minde, that considers the great treasure, what it is to have the Image of God in him, naturally; for even that is our earnest of supernaturall perfection.[3]

I have not been so pittifully tired with any *vanity*, as with silly *Old Mens* exclaiming against these times, and extrolling their owne: Alas! They betray themselves, for if the *times* be *changed*, their manners have changed them. But their senses are to *pleasures*, as *sick Mens* tastes are to *Liquors*; for indeed no *new thing* is done in the *world*, all things are what, and as they were, and *Good* is as ever it was, more plenteous, and must of necessity be *more common than evill*, because it hath this for *nature* and *perfection* to bee *common*.[4]

So the soule hath a naturall and untaught hatred, and detestation of that which is evill.[5]

Vertuous inclinations, and a disposition to morall goodnesse, is more naturall to the soule of man, and nearer of kin to the soule of man, then health is to the body.[6]

Business or Books

Onely the emploiments, and that upon which you cast and bestow your pleasure, businesse, or books, gives (the country) the tincture, and beauty. But truly wheresoever we are, if we can but tell our selves truly what and where we would be, we may make any state and place such; for we are so composed, that if abundance, or

glory scorch and melt us, we have an earthly cave, our bodies, to go
into by consideration, and cool our selves: and if we be frozen, and
contracted with lower and dark fortunes, we have within us a torch,
a soul, lighter and warmer than any without: we are therefore our
own umbrella's, and our own suns.7

A way thou fondling motley humorist,
  Leave mee, and in this standing woodden chest,[a]
Consorted with these few bookes, let me lye
In prison, and here be coffin'd, when I dye;
Here are Gods conduits, grave Divines; and here
Natures Secretary, the Philosopher;
And jolly[b] Statesmen, which teach how to tie
The sinews of a cities mistique bodie;
Here gathering Chroniclers, and by them stand
Giddie fantastique Poëts of each land.
Shall I leave all this constant company,
And follow headlong, wild uncertaine thee?[8]

O thou which to search out the secret parts
    Of the India, or rather Paradise
  Of knowledge, hast with courage and advise[c]
Lately launch'd into the vast Sea of Arts,
Disdaine not in thy constant travailing
    To doe as other Voyagers, and make
    Some turnes into lesse creekes, and wisely take
Fresh water at the Heliconian spring;
I sing not, Siren like, to tempt; for I
    Am harsh, nor as those Scismatiques with you,
    Which draw all wits of good hope to their crew;
But seeing in you bright sparkes of Poetry,
    I, though I brought noe fuell, had desire
With these Articulate blasts to blow the fire.[9]

a. chest (chamber for study)
b. jolly (presumptuous)
c. advise (judgement)

If thou unto thy Muse be marryed,
Embrace her ever, ever multiply,
   Be far from me that strange Adulterie
To tempt thee and procure her widowhed.
My Muse, (for I had one,) because I'am cold,
   Divorc'd her self, the cause being in me,
   That I can take no new in Bigamye,
Not my will only but power doth withhold.
Hence comes it, that the Rymes which never had
   Mother, want matter, and they only have
   A little forme, the which their Father gave;
They are prophane, imperfect, oh, too bad
   To be counted Children of Poetry
   Except confirm'd and Bishoped by thee.[10]

Muse not that by thy Mind thy body is led:
For by thy Mind, my Mind's distempered.
So thy Care lives long, for I bearing part
It eates not only thyne, but my swolne hart.
And when it gives us intermission
We take new harts for it to feede upon.
But as a Lay Mans Genius[a] doth controule
Body and mind; the muse being the Soules Soule
Of Poets, that methinks should ease our anguish,
Although our bodyes wither and minds languish.
Wright[b] then, that my griefes which thine got may bee
Cur'd by thy charming soveraigne melodee.[11]

Friendship : An Abundant Possession

You doe not duties of Societies,
   If from the'embrace of a lov'd wife you rise,
View your fat Beasts, stretch'ed Barnes, and labour'd fields,
   Eate, play, ryde, take all joyes which all day yeelds,
And then againe to your embracements goe:
   Some houres on us your friends, and some bestow

a. Genius (guardian angel)   b. Wright (Write)

Upon your Muse, else both wee shall repent,
I that my love, she that her guifts on you are spent.[12]

S ir, more then kisses, letters mingle Soules;
For, thus friends absent speake.[13]

I f, as mine is, thy life a slumber be,
    Seeme, when thou read'st these lines, to dreame of me,
Never did Morpheus nor his brother weare
    Shapes soe like those Shapes, whom they would appeare,
As this my letter is like me, for it
    Hath my name, words, hand, feet, heart, minde and wit:
It is my deed of gift of mee to thee,
    It is my Will, my selfe the Legacie.[14]

N either your Letters, nor silence, needs excuse; your friendship
is to me an abundant possession, though you remember me
but twice in a year: He that could have two harvests in that time
might justly value his land at a high rate; but, Sir, as we doe not
onely then thank our land, when we gather the fruit, but acknowledge that all the year she doth many motherly offices in preparing
it: so is not friendship then onely to be esteemed, when she is delivered of a Letter, or any other reall office, but in her continuall
propensnesse and inclination to do it.[15]

S o may thy pastures with their flowery feasts,
    As suddenly as Lard, fat thy leane beasts;
So may thy woods oft poll'd,[a] yet ever weare
    A greene, and when thee list, a golden haire;
So may all thy sheepe bring forth Twins; and so
    In chace and race may thy horse all out goe;
So may thy love and courage ne'r be cold,
    Thy Sonne ne'r Ward; Thy lov'd wife ne'r seem old;
But maist thou wish great things, and them attaine,
    As thou telst her and none but her my paine.[16]

a. poll'd (have their branches cut off)

Nothing returns oftner with more comfort to my memorie, than that you nor I ever asked any thing of one another, which we might not safelie grant; and we can ask nothing safelie, that implies an offence to God, nor injury to any other person.[17]

You that are shee and you, that's double shee,
    In her dead face, halfe of your selfe shall see;
Shee was the other part, for so they doe
    Which build them friendships, become one of two;
So two, that but themselves no third can fit,
    Which were to be so, when they were not yet
Twinnes, though their birth *Cusco*, and *Musco*[a] take,
    As divers starres one Constellation make,
Pair'd like two eyes, have equall motion, so
    Both but one meanes to see, one way to goe;

For, such a friendship who would not adore
    In you, who are all what both was before,
Not all, as if some perished by this,
    But so, as all in you contracted is;
As of this all, though many parts decay,
    The pure which elemented them shall stay;
And though diffus'd, and spread in infinite,
    Shall recollect, and in one All[b] unite.[18]

A Right Perspective

All our life is a continuall burden, yet we must not groane; A continuall squeasing, yet we must not pant; And as in the tendernesse of our childhood, we suffer, and yet are whipt if we cry, so we are complained of, if we complaine, and made delinquents if we call the times ill. And that which addes waight to waight, and multiplies the sadnesse of this consideration, is this, That still the best men have had most laid upon them.[19]

a. Cusco and Musco (Cuzco in Peru and Moscow)
b. All (the created order)

God made the Sun, and Moon, and Stars, glorious lights for man to see by; but mans infirmity requires *spectacles*; and affliction does that office. Gods meaning was, that by the sun-shine of prosperity, and by the beames of honour, and temporall blessings, a man should see farre into him; but I know not how he is come to need *spectacles*; scarce any man sees much in this matter, till affliction shew it him.[20]

So, reclus'd hermits often times do know
  More of heavens glory, then a worldling can.
 As man is of the world, the heart of man,
Is an epitome of Gods great booke
  Of creatures, and man need no father looke.[21]

Involved in Mankind

Perchance hee for whom this *Bell* tolles, may be so ill, as that he knows not it tolls for him; And perchance I may thinke my selfe so much better than I am, as that they who are about mee, and see my state, may have caused it to toll for mee, and I know not that.

As therefore the *Bell* that rings to a *Sermon*, calls not upon the *Preacher* onely, but upon the *Congregation* to come; so this *Bell* calls us all: but how much more mee, who am brought so neere the *doore* by this *sicknesse*.

The *Bell* doth toll for him that *thinkes* it doth; and though it *intermit* againe, yet from that *minute*, that that occasion wrought upon him, hee is united to God . . . Who bends not his *eare* to any *bell*, which upon any occasion rings? but who can remove it from that *bell*, which is passing a *peece of himselfe* out of this *world*? No man is an *Iland*, intire of it selfe; every man is a peece of the *Continent*, a part of the *maine*; if a *Clod* bee washed away by the *Sea*, *Europe* is the lesse, as well as if a *Promontorie* were, as well as if a *Mannor* of thy *friends* or of *thine owne* were; any mans *death* diminishes *me*, because I am involved in *Mankinde*; And therefore never send to know for whom the *bell* tolls; It tolls for *thee*.[22]

As we remember God, so for his sake, let us remember one another.[23]

Resolution

Who makes the Past, a patterne for next yeare,
  Turnes no new leafe, but still the same things reads,
Seene things, he sees againe, heard things doth heare,
  And make his life, but like a paire[a] of beads.

The noble Soule by age growes lustier,
  Her appetite, and her digestion mend,
Wee must not sterve, nor hope to pamper her
  With womens milke, and pappe unto the end.

Provide you manlier dyet; you have seene
  All libraries, which are Schools, Camps, and Courts;
But aske your Garners if you have not beene
  In harvests, too indulgent to your sports.[b]

Our Soule, whose country'is heaven, and God her father,
  Into this world, corruptions sinke, is sent,
Yet, so much in her travaile she doth gather,
  That she returnes home, wiser then she went;

However, keepe the lively tast you hold
  Of God, love him as now, but feare him more,
And in your afternoones thinke what you told
  And promis'd him, at morning prayer before.[24]

a. paire (string)
b. sports (diversions)

5

OUR MORTALITY

Torment of Sickness

This great consumption to a fever turn'd.
    And so the world had fits; it joy'd, it mourn'd.
And, as men thinke, that Agues physicke are,
And th'Ague being spent, give over care,
So thou, sicke world, mistak'st thy selfe to bee
Well, when alas, thou'rt in a Letargee.ᵃ¹

Variable, and therefore miserable condition of Man; this minute
    I was well, and am ill, this minute. I am surpriz'd with a
sodaine change, and alteration to worse, and can impute it to no
cause, nor call it by any name. We study *Health*, and we deliberate
upon our *meats*, and *drink*, and *ayre*, and *exercises*, and we hew,
and wee polish every stone, that goes to that building; and so our
Health is a long and a regular work; But in a minute a Canon
batters all, over-throwes all, demolishes all; a *Sicknes* unprevented
for all our diligence, unsuspected for all our curiositie; nay, un-
deserved, if we consider only *disorder*, summons us, seizes us,
possesses us, destroyes us in an instant. O miserable condition of
Man.²

O multiplied misery! We die, and cannot enjoy death, because
    wee die in this torment of sicknes; we are tormented with sick-
nes, and cannot stay till the torment come, but preapprehensions
and presages, prophecy those torments, which induce that *death*

a. in a Letargee (at the point of death)

before either come; and our dissolution is conceived in these *first changes*, *quickned* in the sicknes it selfe, and *borne* in *death*, which beares date from these first changes. Is this the honour which Man hath by being a *little world*, That he hath these *earthquakes* in him selfe, sodaine shakings, these *lightnings*, sodaine flashes; these thunders, sodaine noises; these *Eclypses*, sodain offuscations, and darknings of his senses; these *Blazing stars*, sodaine fiery exhalations; these *Rivers of blood*, sodaine red waters? Is he *world* to himselfe only therefore, that he hath inough in himself, not only to destroy, and execute himselfe, but to presage that execution upon himselfe; to assist the sicknes, to antidate the sicknes, to make the sicknes the more irremediable, by sad apprehensions, and as if he would make a fire the more vehement, by sprinkling water upon the coales, so to wrap a hote fever in cold Melancholy, least the fever alone should not destroy fast enough, without this contribution nor perfit the work (which is *destruction*) except we joynd an artificiall sicknes, of our owne *melancholy*, to our natural, our unnatural fever. O perplex'd discomposition, O ridling distemper, O miserable condition of Man.[3]

Self-Destruction

No law is so primary and simple, but it fore-imagines a reason upon which it was founded: and scarce any reason is so constant, but that circumstances alter it. In which case a private man is Emperor of himself . . . And he whose conscience well tempred and dispassion'd, assures him that the reason of selfe-preservation ceases in him, may also presume that the law ceases too, and may doe that then which otherwise were against that law.[4]

Death

O Soule, O circle, why so quickly bee
Thy ends, thy birth and death clos'd up in thee?[5]

D eath gets 'twixt soules and bodies such a place
    As sinne insinuates 'twixt just men and grace,
Both worke a separation, no divorce.[6]

D eath I recant, and say, unsaid by mee
    What ere hath slip'd, that might diminish thee.
Spirituall treason, atheisme 'tis, to say,
   That any can thy Summons disobey.
Th'earths face is but thy Table; there are set
   Plants, cattell, men, dishes for Death to eate.
In a rude hunger now hee millions drawes
   Into his bloody, or plaguy, or sterv'd jawes.
Now hee will seeme to spare, and doth more wast,
   Eating the best first, well preserv'd to last.
Now wantonly he spoiles, and eates us not,
   But breakes off friends, and lets us peecemeale rot.[7]

M an is the World, and death th'Ocean,
    To which God gives the lower parts of man.
This Sea invirons all, and though as yet
   God hath set markes, and bounds, twixt us and it,
Yet doth it rore, and gnaw, and still pretend,[a]
   And breaks our bankes, when ere it takes a friend.[8]

T eares are false Spectacles, we cannot see
    Through passions mist, what wee are, or what shee.
In her this sea of death hath made no breach,
   But as the tide doth wash the slimie beach,
And leaves embroder'd workes upon the sand,
   So is her flesh refin'd by deaths cold hand.[9]

N ow I grow sure, that if a man would have
    Good companie, his entry is a grave.
Mee thinkes all Cities now, but Anthills bee,

a. pretend (threaten)

Where, when the severall labourers I see,
For children, house, Provision, taking paine,
They'are all but Ants, carrying eggs, straw, and grain
And Church-yards are our cities, unto which
The most repaire, that are in goodnesse rich.
There is the best concourse, and confluence,
There are the holy suburbs, and from thence
Begins Gods City, New Jerusalem,
Which doth extend her utmost^a gates to them;
At that gate then Triumphant soule, dost thou
Begin thy Triumph; But since lawes allow
That at the Triumph day, the people may,
All that they will, 'gainst the Triumpher say,
Let me here use that freedome, and expresse
My griefe, though not to make thy Triumph lesse.[10]

O strong and long-liv'd death, how cam'st thou in?
 And how without Creation didst begin?
Thou hast, and shalt see dead, before thou dyest,
 All the foure Monarchies, and Antichrist.
How could I thinke thee nothing, that see now
 In all this All, nothing else is, but thou.
Our births and lives, vices, and vertues, bee
 Wastfull consumptions, and degrees of thee.
For, wee to live, our bellowes^b weare, and breath,
 Nor are wee mortall, dying, dead, but death,
And though thou beest, O mighty bird of prey,
 So much reclaim'd by God, that thou must lay
All that thou kill'st at his feet, yet both hee
 Reserve but few, and leaves the most to thee.[11]

D eath be not proud, though some have called thee
 Mighty and dreadfull, for, thou are not soe,
For, those, whom thou think'st, thou dost overthrow,
Die not, poore death, not yet canst thou kill mee;

a. utmost (outermost)
b. bellowes (lungs)

From rest and sleepe, which but thy pictures bee,
Much pleasure, then from thee, much more must flow,
And soonest our best men with thee doe goe,
Rest of their bones, and soules deliverie.
Thou art slave to Fate, chance, kings, and desperate men,
And dost with poyson, warre, and sicknesse dwell,
And poppie, or charmes can make us sleepe as well,
And better then thy stroake; why swell'st thou then?
One short sleepe past, wee wake eternally,
And death shall be no more, death, thou shalt die.[12]

Bereavement

A s aged men are glad
   Being tasteless growne, to joy in joyes they had,
So now the sick starv'd world must feed upone
   This joy, that we had her, who now is gone.[13]

H er death did wound, and tame thee than, and than[a]
   Thou mightst have better spar'd the Sunne, or Man;
That wound was deepe, but 'tis more misery,
That thou hast lost thy sense and memory.
T'was heavy then to heare thy voice of mone,
But this is worse, that thou are speechlesse growne.
Thou hast forgot thy name, thou hadst; thou wast
Nothing but she, and her thou hast o'rpast.[14]

S ome moneths she hath beene dead (but being dead,
   Measures of times are all determined)
But long shee'ath beene away, long, long, yet none
Offers to tell us who it is that's gone.

The Cyment which did faithfully compact
And glue all vertues, now resolv'd, and slack'd,
Thought it some blasphemy to say sh'was dead;
Or that our weakenes was discovered

a. than, and than (then, and then)

[133]

In that confession; therefore spoke no more
Then tongues, the soule being gone, the losse deplore.[15]

W hat ever order grow
 Greater by him in heaven, wee doe not so;
One of your orders growes by his accesse;
But, by his losse grow all our *orders* lesse;
The name of *Father, Master, Friend*, the name
Of *Subject* and of *Prince*, in one are lame;
Faire mirth is dampt, and conversation black,
The *household* widdow'd, and the *garter* slack;
The *Chappell* wants an eare, *Councell* a tongue;
Story, a theame; and *Musicke* lacks a song;
Blest *order* that hath him! The losse of him
Gangred all *Orders* here; all lost a limbe.[16]

N othing disproportions us, nor makes us so uncapable of being
 reunited to those whom we loved here, as murmuring, or not
advancing the goodness of him, who hath removed them from
hence. We would wonder, to see a man, who in a wood were left to
his liberty, to fell what trees he would, take onely the crooked, and
leave the streightest trees; but that man hath perchance a ship to
build, and not a house, and so hath use of that kinde of timber: let
not us, who know that in Gods house there are many Mansions,
but yet have no modell, no designe of the forme of that building,
wonder at his taking in of his materialls, why he takes the young,
and leaves the old, or why the sickly overlive those, that had
better health. We are not bound to think that souls departed have
devested all affections towards them whom they left here; but we
are bound to think, that for all their loves they would not be here
again: Then is the will of God done in Earth, as it is in Heaven, when
we neither pretermit his actions, nor resist them; neither pass them
over in an inconsideration, as though God had no hand in them, nor
go about to take them out of his hands, as though we could direct
him to do them better.[17]

B ut, above all, comfort your self in this, That it is the declared will of God. In sicknesses, and other worldlie crosses, there are anxieties, and perplexities; we wish one thing to day, in the behalf of a distressed child or friend, and another to morrow; because God hath not yet declared his will. But when he hath done that, in death, there is no room for anie anxietie, for anie perplexitie, no, not for a wish; for we may not so much as pray for the dead. You know, *David* made his child's Sicknesse his *Lent*, but his Death his *Easter*: he fasted till the Child's death, but then he returned to his repast, because then he had a declaration of God's will.[18]

The Influence of the Departed

L et no man say, the world it selfe being dead,
'Tis labour lost to have discovered
The worlds infirmities, since there is none
Alive to study this dissectione;
For there's a kind of world remaining still,
Though shee which did inanimate and fill
The world, be gone, yet in this last long night,
Her Ghost doth walke; that is, a glimmering light,
A faint weake love of vertue and of good
Reflects from her, on them which understood
Her worth; And though she have shut in all day,
The twi-light of her memory doth stay;
Which, from the carcasse of the old world, free,
Creates a new world; and new creatures be
Produc'd: The matter and the stuffe of this,
Her vertue, and the forme our practice is.[19]

T he art is lost, and correspondence too.
For heaven gives little, and the earth takes lesse,
And man least knows their trade, and purposes.
If this commerce twixt heaven and earth were not
Embarr'd,[a] and all this trafique quite forgot,

a. Embarr'd (Stopped)

Shee, for whose losse we have lamented thus,
Would work more fully'and pow'rfully on us.
Since herbes, and roots, by dying, lose not all,
But they, yea Ashes too, are medicinall,
Death could not quench her vertue so, but that
It would be (if not follow'd) wondred at:
And all the world would be one dying Swan,
To sing her funeral prayse, and vanish than.[20]

Shee did no more but die; if after her
    Any shall live, which dare true good prefer,
Every such person is her delegate,
    T'accomplish that which should have been her fate.
They shall make up that booke, and shall have thankes
    Of fate and her, for filling up their blanks.
For future vertuous deeds are Legacies,
    Which from the gift of her example rise.
And 'tis in heav'n part of spirituall mirth,
    To see how well, the good play[a] her, on earth.[21]

Seeing Beyond Ourselves

Beloved, we die in our delicacies, and revive not, but in afflictions: In abundancies, the blow of death meets us, and the breath of life, in misery, and tribulation.[22]

Gods first intention even when he destroyes is to preserve, as a physitians first intention, in the most distastfull physick, is health; even Gods demolitions are super-edifications, his Anatomies, his dissections are so many re-compactings, so many resurrections; God windes us off the Skein, that he may weave us up into the whole peece, and he cuts us out of the whole peece into peeces, that he may make us up into a whole garment.[23]

a. play (imitate)

I t is a lamentable perversenesse in us, that we are so contentiously
busie, in inquiring into the Nature, and Essence, and Attributes
of God, things which are reserved to our end, when we shall know
at once, and without study, all that, of which our lives study can
teach us nothing; And that here, where we are upon the way, we are
so negligent and lazy, in inquiring of things, which belong to the
way. Those things we learne in no Schoole so well as in adversity. As
the body of man, and consequently health, is best understood, and
best advanced by Dissections, and Anatomies, when the hand
and knife of the Surgeon hath passed upon every part of the body,
and laid it open: so when the hand and sword of God hath pierced
our soul, we are brought to a better knowledge of our selves, then
any degree of prosperity would have raised us to.[24]

A ll this life is but a *Preface*, or but an *Index* and *Repertory* to the
book of *life*: There, at that book beginnes thy study; To grow
perfect in that book, to be dayly conversant in that book, to find
what be the marks of them, whose names are written in that book,
and to finde those marks, ingenuously, and in a rectified conscience,
in thy selfe, To finde that no murmuring at Gods corrections, no
disappointing of thy hopes, no interrupting of thy expectations, no
frustrating of thy possibilities in the way, no *impatience in sicknesse*, and in the agony of death, can deface those marks, this is to
goe *forth*, and see thy self, beyond thy self, to see what thou shalt be
in the next world.[25]

The Christian Hope

B ut must we say shee's dead? May't not be said
    That as a sundred Clock is peece-meale laid,
Not to be lost but by the makers hand
   Repolish'd,[a] without error then to stand,
Or as the Affrique Niger streame enwombs
   It selfe into the earth, and after comes,

a. Repolish'd (reassembled and perfected)

(Having first made a naturall bridge, to passe
  For many leagues,) farre greater then it was,
May't not be said, that her grave shall restore
  Her, greater, purer, firmer, then before?
Heaven may say this, and joy in't; but can wee
  Who live, and lacke her, here this vantage see?[26]

We do but borrow Children of God, to lend them to the world. And when I lend the world a daughter in marriage, or lend the world a son in a profession, the world does not alwaies pay me well again; my hopes are not always answered in that daughter or that son. But, of all that I lend to, the Grave is my best pay-Master. The Grave shall restore me my child, where he and I shall have but one Father; and pay me my Earth, when that Earth shall be Amber, a sweet Perfume, in the nostrills of his and my Saviour. Since I am well content to send one sonne to the Church, the other to the Warrs; Why should I be loth to send one part of either sonne to Heaven, and the other to the Earth.[27]

No soule (whiles with the luggage of this clay
  It clogged is) can follow thee halfe way;
Or see thy flight; which doth our thoughts outgoe
So fast, that now the lightning moves but slow:
But now thou art as high in heaven flowne
As heav'ns from us; what soule besides thine owne
Can tell thy joyes, or say he can relate
Thy glorious Journals in that blessed state?
I envie thee (Rich soule) I envy thee,
Although I cannot yet thy glory see.[28]

What an Organe hath that man tuned, how hath be brought all things in the world to a Consort, and what a blessed Anthem doth he sing to that Organe, that is at peace with God? His Rye-bread is *Manna*, and his Beefe is *Quailes*, his day-labours are thrust-ings at the narrow gate into Heaven, and his night-watchings are extasies and evocations of his soule into the presence and communion of Saints, his sweat is *Pearls*, and his bloud is *Rubies*, it is at peace with God.[29]

If my span of life become a mile of life, my penny a pound, my pint a gallon, my acre a sheere; yet if there be nothing of the next world at the end, so much peace of conscience, so much joy, so much glory, still all is but *nothing* multiplied, and that is still nothing at all.[30]

Is your soule lesse then your body, because it is in it? How easily lies a letter in a Boxe, which if it were unfolded, would cover that Boxe? unfold your soule, and you shall see, that it reaches to heaven; from thence it came, and thither it should pretend; whereas the body is but *from* that earth, and *for* that earth, upon which it is now; which is but a short, and an inglorious progresse. To contract this, the soule is larger then the body, and the glory, and the joyes of heaven, larger then the honours, and the pleasures of this world: what are seventy yeares, to that latitude, of continuing as long as the Ancient of dayes?[31]

If I had fixt a Son in Court, or married a daughter into a plentifull Fortune, I were satisfied for that son and that daughter. Shall I not be so, when the King of Heaven hath taken that sone to him-selfe, and married himselfe to that daughter, for ever? I spend none of my Faith, I exercise none of my Hope, in this, that I shall have my dead raised to life againe. This is the faith that sustains me, when I lose by the death of others, or when I suffer by living in misery my selfe, That the dead, and we, are now all in one Church, and at the resurrection, shall be all in one Quire.[32]

The pure in heart are blessed already, not onely comparatively, that they are in a better way of Blessednesse, then others are, but actually in a present possession of it: for this world and the next world, are not, to the pure in heart, two houses, but two roomes, a Gallery to passe thorough, and a Lodging to rest in, in the same

House, which are both under one roofe, Christ Jesus; the Militant
and the Triumphant, are not two Churches, but this the Porch, and
that the Chancell of the same Church, which are under one Head,
Christ Jesus; so the Joy, and the sense of Salvation, which the pure
in heart have here, is not a joy severed from the Joy of Heaven, but
a Joy that begins in us here, and continues, and accompanies
us thither, and there flowes on, and dilates itselfe to an infinite
expansion.[33]

Part Two

DIVINITY

"all Divinity Is love or wonder"

6

ON DISCERNING GOD

The Desire to Know God

Every man, even in nature, hath that appetite, that desire, to know God.[1]

The soule of man brings with it, into the body, a sense and an acknowledgment of God; neither can all the abuses that the body puts upon the soule, whilest they dwell together, (which are infinite) devest that acknowledgement, or extinguish that sense of God in the soule.[2]

The world is the Theatre that represents God, and every where every man may, nay must see him.[3]

And when man is taught that which he desired to know, then the Soule is brought home, and laid to rest. Desire is the travaile, knowledge is the Inne; desire is the wheele, knowledge is the bed of the Soule.[4]

Now, in all our wayes, in all our journies, a moderate pace brings a man most surely to his journies end, and so doth a sober knowledge in matters of Divinity, and in the mysteries of Religion.[5]

God is best found, when we seeke him, and observe him in his operation upon us.[6]

The Light of Nature

To be a good Divine, requires humane knowledge; and so does it of all the Mysteries of Divinity too.[7]

We forbid no man the use of Reason in matters of Religion.[8]

The cleare light is in the Gospel, but there is light in Nature too.[9]

All things that are, are equally removed from being nothing; and whatsoever hath any being, is by that very beeing, a glasse in which we see God, who is the roote, and the fountaine of all beeing.[10]

The whole frame of the world is the Theatre, and every creature the stage, the *medium*, the glasse in which we may see God.[11]

Consider we alwaies the grace of God, to be the Sun it selfe, but the nature of man, and his naturall faculties to be the Sphear, in which that Sun, that Grace moves. Consider we the Grace of God to be the soule it self, but the naturall faculties of man, to be as a body, which ministers Organs for that soule, that Grace to worke by.[12]

Divers men may walke by the Sea side, and the same beames of the Sunne giving light to them all, one gathereth by the benefit of that light pebles, or speckled shells, for curious vanitie, and another gathers precious Pearle, or medicinall Ambar, by the same light. So the common light of reason illumins us all; but one imploves this light upon the searching of impertinent vanities, another by a better use of the same light, finds out the Mysteries of Religion; and when he hath found them, loves them, not for the lights sake, but for the naturall and true worth of the thing it self.[13]

K *nowledge* cannot save us, but we cannot be saved without Knowledge; Faith is not on this side Knowledge, but beyond it; we must necessarily come to *Knowledge* first, though we must not stay at it, when we are come thither.[14]

T he light of *nature* is far from being enough; but, as a *candle* may kindle a *torch*, so into the faculties of nature, well imployed, God infuses *faith*.[15]

The Necessity of Faith

H e that seeks proofe for every mystery of Religion, shall meet with much darknesse; but he that beleeves first, shall finde every thing to illustrate his faith.[16]

F aith most of all furthers and advances our salvation; but a man cannot believe that which he does not know.[17]

T he first step to faith, is to wonder, to stand, and consider with a holy admiration, the waies and proceedings of God with man.[18]

M en which seek God by reason and naturall strength . . . are like Mariners which voyaged before the invention of the Compass.[19]

L et not my minde be blinder by more light
Nor Faith by Reason added, lose her sight.[20]

A s faith without *fruit*, without *works*, is no faith; so faith without a *root*, without *reason*, is no faith, but an *opinion*.[21]

A s a stick bears up, and succours a vine, or any plant, more
precious then it selfe, but yet gave it not life at first, nor gives
any nourishment to the root now: so the assistance of reason, and
the voyce of the Creature, in the preaching of Nature, works upon
our faith, but the roote, and the life is in the faith it selfe; The light
of nature gives a glimmering before, and it gives a reflexion after
faith, but the meridianall noone is in faith.[22]

R eason is our Soules left hand, Faith her right,
By these wee reach divinity.[23]

On Seeing God

I must have the light of glory upon me, to see the glory of God,
and then by his glory I shall see his Essence.[24]

H e that searches too far into the secrets of God, shall be dazled,
confounded by that glory.[25]

W e look no further for *causes* or *reasons* in the *mysteries of
religion*, but to the *will* and pleasure of *God*.[26]

F or our sight of God here, our Theatre, the place where we sit
and see him, is the whole world, the whole house and frame of
nature, and our *medium*, our *glasse*, is the Booke of Creatures, and
our light, by which we see him, is the light of Naturall Reason. And

then, for our knowledge of God here, our Place, our Academy, our University is the Church, our *medium*, is the Ordinance of God in his Church, Preaching, and Sacraments; and our light is the light of faith. Thus we shall finde it to be, for our sight, and for our knowledge of God here. But for our sight of God in heaven, our place, our Spheare is heaven it selfe, our *medium* is the Patefaction,[a] the Manifestation, the Revelation of God himselfe, and our light is the light of Glory. And then, for our knowledge of God there, God himself is All; God himself is the place, we see Him, in Him; God is our *medium*, we see Him, by him; God is our light; not a light which is His, but a light which is He; not a light which flowes from him, no, nor a light which is in him, but that light which is He himself. *Lighten our darknesse, we beseech thee, O Lord, O Father of lights, that in thy light we may see light*, that now we see this through this thy *glasse*, thine Ordinance, and, by the good of this, hereafter *face to face*.[27]

M an hath a nobler light, an immortal, a discerning soul, the light of reason. Instead of the many stars, which this world hath, man hath had the light of the Law, and the succession of the Prophets: And instead of that Sun, which this world had, a Sun from God; man hath had the Son of God; God hath spoken to us by his Son; God hath shin'd upon us in his Son.[28]

R eligion is not a *sullen*, but a *cheerfull Philosophy*, and salvation not cast into a corner, but displayed as the Sunne, over all.[29]

T here is no Atheist; They that oppose the true, do yet worship a false god; and hee that sayes there is no God, doth for all that, set up some God to himselfe.[30]

W e can express God himselfe in no clearer termes, nor in termes expressing more Dignity, then in saying we cannot expresse him.[31]

a. Patefaction (disclosure)

That sight of God which we have . . . *in the Glasse,* that is, in nature, is . . . but the infancy, but the cradle of that knowledge which we have in faith, and yet that knowledge which we have in faith, is but . . . the infancy and cradle of that knowledge, which we shall have when we come to see God *face to face.*[32]

THE HOLY TRINITY

The Holy Trinity

The Doctrine of the Trinity, is the first foundation of our Religion, and no time is too early for our faith, The simplest may beleeve it; and all time is too early for our reason, The wisest cannot understand it.[1]

The subject of naturall philosophy, are the foure elements, which God made; the Subject of supernaturall philosophy, Divinity, are the three elements, which God is; and (if we may so speake) which make God, that is, constitute God, notifie God to us, Father, Sonne and holy Ghost.[2]

If we think to see this mystery of the Trinity, by the light of reason . . . we shall lose that hold which we had before, our naturall faculties, our reason will be perplext, and infeebled, and our super-naturall, our faith not strengthened that way.[3]

God, in the Trinity, is open to no other light, then the light of faith.[4]

And though (God) be in his nature incomprehensible, and in-accessible in his light, yet this is his infinite largenesse, that being thus infinitely One, he hath manifested himselfe to us in three Persons, to be the more easily discerned by us, and the more closely and effectually applied to us.[5]

[149]

The Father came neare me, when he breathed the breath of life into me, and gave me my flesh. The Son came neare me, when he took my flesh upon him, and laid downe his life for me. The Holy Ghost is alwaies neare me, alwaies with me.[6]

The root of all is God. But it is not the way to receive fruits, to dig to the root, but to reach to the boughs. I reach for my Creation to the Father, for my Redemption to the Sonne, for my sanctification to the holy Ghost: and so I make the knowledge of God, a Tree of life unto me.[7]

The Society of the Trinity

God, which is but *one*, would not appeare, nor bee presented so *alone*, but that hee would also manifest more persons.[8]

There is not only an Onely God in heaven; But a Father, a Son, a Holy Ghost in that God; which are names of a plurality, and sociable relations, conversable notions.[9]

There is but one God; but yet was that one God ever *alone*? There were more *generations* (infinitely infinite) before the world was made, then there have been *minutes*, since it was made: all that while, there were no *creatures*; but yet was God alone, any one minute of al this? was there not alwais a *Father* and a *Son*, and a *holy Ghost*? And had not they, always an acquiescence in one another, an exercise of *Affection*, (as we may so say) a love, a delight, and a complacency towards one another? So, as that the Father could not be without the *Son* and the *holy Ghost*, so as neither *Sonne*, nor *holy Ghost* could be without the *Father*, nor without one another; God was from all eternity collected into *one God*, yet from all eternity he derived himselfe into *three persons*: God could not be so alone, but that there have been three persons, as long as there hath been one God.[10]

The Persons of the Trinity

G OD, as hee is three persons, hath three Kingdomes; There is
. . . The Kingdome of power; and this wee attribute to the
Father; it is power and providence: There is . . . the Kingdome of
glorie; this we attribute to the *Sonn* and to his purchase; for he is *the
King* that shall say, *Come ye blessed of my Father, inherit the
Kingdome prepared for you, from the foundation of the World.*
And then betweene these there is . . . The kingdome of Grace, and
this we attribute to the *Holy Ghost*; he takes them, whom the king
of power, Almighty *God* hath rescued from the *Gentiles*, and as the
king of grace, *Hee gives them the knowledge of the misterie of the
kingdome of* GOD, that is, of *future glory*, by sanctifying them with
his grace, in his *Church*.[11]

N aturall apprehensions of God, though those naturall apprehensions may have much subtilty, Voluntary elections of a
Religion, though those voluntary elections may have much singularity, Morall directions for life, though those morall directions may
have much severity, are all frivolous and lost, if all determine not in
Christianity, in the Notion of God, so as God hath manifested and
conveyed himself to us; in God the Father, God the Son, and God
the Holy Ghost.[12]

N ow these notions that we have of God, as a Father, as a Son,
as a Holy Ghost, as a Spirit working in us, are so many
handles by which we may take hold of God, and so many breasts, by
which we may suck such a knowledge of God, as that by it wee may
grow up into him. And as wee cannot take hold of a torch by the
light, but by the staffe we may; so though we cannot take hold of
God, as God, who is incomprehensible, and inapprehensible, yet as
a Father, as a Son, as a Spirit, dwelling in us, we can.[13]

B y that impression of God, which is in the very beeing of every
creature, God, that is, the whole Trinity, is the Father of every
creature.[14]

G od is the Father of Christ, by that mysticall and eternal un-expressible generation, which never began nor ended.[15]

I f wee consider God; as a second Person in the Godhead, the Sonne of God, God of God, so God is *Logos, Sermo, Verbum, Oratio*; The Word, Saying, Speaking; But God considered primarily and in himself so, is *Actus purus*, all Action, all doing. In the Creation there is a *Dixit* in Gods mouth, still God sayes something; but evermore the *Dixit* is accompanied with a *Fiat*, Somthing was to be done, as well as said.[16]

G od Redeemed us not, by God alone, nor by man alone, but by him, who was both. He instructs us not, by the Holy Ghost alone, without the Ministery of man, nor by the Minister alone, without the assistance of the Holy Ghost.[17]

T he blessed Spirit of God then, the *Holy Ghost*, the third person in the Trinity, (and yet, not Third so, as that either Second or First, Son or Father, were one minute before him in that Co-eternity, that enwraps them all alike) . . .[18]

T his is that Spirit, who though hee were to be sent by the Father, and sent by the Son, yet he comes not as a Messenger from a Superiour, for hee was alwaies equall to Father and Son: But the Father sent him, and the Son sent him, as a tree sends forth blos-somes, and as those blossomes send forth a sweet smell, and as the Sun sends forth beames, by an emanation from it selfe.[19]

H ow great a God is he, that sends a God to comfort us? and how powerfull a Comforter hee, who is not onely sent by God, but is God?[20]

The Holy Ghost never comes to his owne but they receive him; for, onely by receiving him, they are his owne.[21]

Goodnesse is the Attribute of the Holy Ghost; If you have Greatness, you may seem to have some of the Father, for Power is his: If you have Wisdome, you may seeme to have some of the Son, for that is his: If you have Goodnesse, you have the Holy Ghost, who shall lead you into all truth. And Goodnesse is, To be good and easie in receiving his impressions, and good and constant in retaining them, and good and diffusive in deriving them upon others: To embrace the Gospel, to hold fast the Gospel, to propagate the Gospel, this is the goodnesse of the Holy Ghost.[22]

The holy Ghost moves, he is the first author; the holy Ghost perpetuates, settles, establishes, he is our rest, and acquiescence, and center; Beginning, Way, End.[23]

The *Sonne of* GOD did not abhorre the *Virgins* wombe, when hee would be made man; when he was man, he did not disdaine to ride upon an *Asse* into *Ierusalem*: the third person of the *Trinity*, the *Holy Ghost* is as humble as the second, hee refuses . . . no conveyance, no doore of entrance into you.[24]

Now all promises of God, are sealed in the *holy Ghost*; To whom soever any promise of God belongs, he hath the holy Ghost.[25]

This Spirit disposes, and dispenses, distributes, and disperses, and orders all the power of the Father, and all the wisdome of the Son, and all the graces of God. It is a Center to all.[26]

If I do but open my heart to my selfe, I may see the Holy Ghost there, and in him, all that the Father hath Thought and Decreed, all that the Son hath Said and Done, and Suffered for the whole World, made mine. Accustome your selves therefore to the Contemplation, to the Meditation of this Blessed Person of the glorious Trinity; Keep up that holy cheerefulnesse, which Christ makes the Ballast of a Christian, and his Fraight too, to give him a rich Returne in the Heavenly Jerusalem. Be always comforted; and always determine your comfort in the Holy Ghost.[27]

The manifestation of the mysterie of the Trinity was reserved for Christ. Some intimations in the Old, but the publication only in the New Testament; Some irradiations in the Law, but the illustration onely in the Gospell; Some emanation of beames, as of the Sun before it is got above the Horizon, in the Prophets, but the glorious proceeding thereof, and the attaining to a Meridianall height, only in the Euangelists. And then, the doctrine of the Trinity, thus reserved for the time of the Gospell, at that time was thus declared; So God loved the World, as that he sent his Son; So the Son loved the World, as that he would come into it, and die for it; So the Holy Ghost loved the World, as that he would dwell in it, and inable men, in his Ministery, and by his gifts, to apply this mercy of the Father, and this merit of the Son, to particular souls, and to whole congregations.[28]

Father of Heaven, and him, by whom
It, and us for it, and all else, for us
Thou madest, and govern'st ever, come
And re-create mee, now growne ruinous:
    My heart is by dejection, clay,
    And by selfe-murder, red.
From this red earth, O Father, purge away
All vicious tinctures, that new fashioned
I may rise up from death, before I'm dead.

    O Sonne of God, who seeing two things,
Sinne, and death crept in, which were never made,
    By bearing one, tryed'st with what stings
The other could thine heritage invade;

O be thou nail'd unto my heart,
And crucified againe,
Part not from it, though it from thee would part,
But let it be by applying so thy paine,
Drown'd in thy blood, and in thy passion slaine.

O Holy Ghost, whose temple I
Am, but of mudde walls, and condensed dust,
And being sacrilegiously
Halfe wasted with youths fires, of pride and lust,
Must with new stormes be weatherbeat;
Double in my heart thy flame,
Which let devout sad teares intend; and let
(Though this glasse lanthorne, flesh, do suffer maime)
Fire, Sacrifice, Priest, Altar be the same.

O Blessed glorious Trinity,
Bones to Philosophy, but milke to faith,
Which, as wise serpents, diversly
Most slipperinesse, yet most entanglings hath,
As you distinguish'd undistinct
By power, love, knowledge bee,
Give mee a such selfe different instinct
Of these let all mee elemented bee,
Of power, to love, to know, you unnumbred three.[29]

The Name of God

It is to God onely, and to God by name, and not in generall notions; for it implies a nearer, a more familiar, and more presentiall knowledge of God, a more cheerfull acquaintance, and a more assiduous conversation with God, when we know how to call God by a Name, a Creator, a Redeemer, a Comforter, then when we consider him onely as a diffused power, that spreads itselfe over all creatures; when we come to him in Affirmatives, and Confessions, This thou hast done for me, then when we come to him onely in Negatives, and say, That that is God, which is nothing els. God is come nearer to us then to others, when we know his Name.[30]

Y et certainly, we could not so much as say, God cannot be
named, except we could name God by some name; we could
not say, God hath no name, except God had a name; for that very
word, *God*, is his name. God calls upon us often in the Scriptures,
To call upon his Name; and in the Scriptures, he hath manifested to
us divers names, by which we may call upon him. Doest thou know
what name to call him by, when thou callest him to beare false
witnesse, to averre a falshood? Hath God a name to sweare by?
Doest thou know what name to call him by, when thou wouldest
make him thy servant, thy instrument, thy executioner, to plague
others, upon thy bitter curses and imprecations? Hath God a name
to curse by? Canst thou wound his body, exhaust his bloud, teare
off his flesh, breake his bones, excruciate his soule; and all this by his
right name? Hath God a name to blaspheme by? and hath God no
name to pray by? is he such a stranger to thee? Dost thou know
every faire house in thy way, as thou travellest, whose that is; and
doest thou not know, in whose house thou standest now?[31]

B eloved, to know God by name, and to come to him by name, is
to consider his particular blessings to thee; to consider him in
his power, and how he hath protected thee there; and in his wisedome, and how he hath directed thee there; and in his love, and how
he hath affected thee there; and exprest all, in particular mercies. He
is but a darke, but a narrow, a shallow, a lazy man in nature, that
knows no more, but that there is a heaven, and an earth, and a sea;
He that will be of use in this world, comes to know the influences of
the heavens, the vertue of the plants, and mines of the earth, the
course and divisions of the Sea. To the naturall man, God gives
generall notions of himselfe; a God that spreads over all as the
heavens; a God that sustaines all as the earth; a God that transports,
and communicates all to all as the sea: But to the Christian Church,
God applies himselfe in more particular notions; as a Father, as a
Son, as a holy Ghost; And to every Christian soule, as a Creator, a
Redeemer, a Benefactor; that I may say, This I was not born to, and
yet this I have from my God.[32]

G ods own name is *I am*: *Being*, is Gods name, and nothing is so
contrary to God as to be nothing.[33]

The Being of God

T hough God be our true glasse, through which we see
All, since the being of all things is hee.[34]

O nely God can comprehend God.[35]

G od alone is all; not onely all that is, but all that is not, all that
might be, if he would have it be.[36]

A cknowledg God to be the Author of thy Being; find him so at
the spring-head, and then thou shalt easily trace him, by the
branches, to all that belongs to thy well-being. The Lord of Hosts,
and the God of peace, the God of the mountaines, and the God of
the valleyes, the God of noone, and of midnight, of all times, the
God of East and West, of all places, the God of Princes, and of
Subjects, of all persons, is all one and the same God; and that which
we intend, when we say *Iehovah*, is all Hee.[37]

H ow often God admits into his owne Name, this addition of
Universality, *Omne*, *All*, as though he would be knowne by
that especially. He is Omnipotent, There he can doe All; He is
Omniscient, There he can know All; Hee is Omnipresent, There he
can direct All. Neither doth God extend himselfe to all, that he may
gather from all, but that he may gather all, and all might meet in
him, and enjoy him. So, God is all Center, as that hee looks to all,
and so, all circumference, as that hee embraces all. The Sunne works
upon things that he sees not, (as Mynes in the wombe of the earth)
and so works the lesse perfectly. God sees all, and works upon all,
and desires perfection in all.[38]

G od ever knewe all thinges that were, that are, and that shalbee, and that may be, and that may not be, because he will not have them be, for if he would, they should be. He knows them otherwise then they are, for he knows future thinges as present, and he knows contingent thinges as certaine and necessary.[39]

G od is not tyed to any *place*; not by essence . . . God fills every place, and fills it by containing that place in himselfe; but he is tyed *by his promise* to a manifestation of himselfe, by working in some certain places.[40]

The Character of God

F irst then, there is nothing good but God: neither can I conceive any thing in God, that concerns me so much as his goodnesse; for, by that I know him, and for that I love him.[41]

N othing supplies, nor fills, nor satisfies the desire of man, on this side of God; Every man hath something to love, and desire, till he determine it in God; because God only hath . . . an inexhaustible goodnesse; a sea that no land can suck in, a land that no sea can swallow up, a forrest that no fire can waste, a fire that no water can quench. He is so good, goodnesse so, as that he is . . . the cause of all good either received by us, or conceived in us; of all, either prepared externally for us, or produced internally in us . . . It is his goodnesse, that gilds and enamels all the good persons, or good actions in this world. There is none good but God.[42]

G od could no more meane ill, then doe ill; God can no more make me sin, then sin himself.[43]

T here is nothing good but God, there is nothing but goodnesse in God.[44]

There is nothing good in this life, nothing in the next, without God, that is, without sight and fruition of the face, and presence of God.[45]

GOD is *Love*, and the *Holy Ghost* is amorous in his *Metaphors*; everie where his *Scriptures* abound with the notions of *Love*, of *Spouse*, and *Husband*, and *Marriadge Songs*, and *Marriadge Supper*, and *Marriadge-Bedde*.[46]

I cannot name a time, when Gods love began, it is eternal, I cannot imagine a time, when his mercy will end, it is perpetual.[47]

Beloved, waigh Life and Death one against another, and the balance will be even; Throw the glory of God into either balance, and that turnes the scale.[48]

Never propose to thy self such a God, as thou wert not bound to imitate.[49]

The Activity of God

For all Gods works are intire, and done in him, at once, and perfect as soon as begun.[50]

Of God himselfe, it is safely resolved . . . that he never did any thing in any part of time, of which he had not an eternall pre-conception, an eternall Idea, in himselfe before.[51]

God himselfe made all that he made according to a pattern. God had deposited, and laid up in himselfe certain formes, patternes, *Ideas* of every thing that he made. He made nothing of which he had not preconceived the forme, and predetermined in himselfe, I will make it thus. And when he had made any thing, he saw it was good; good because it answered the pattern, the Image; good, because it was like to that.[52]

I n the act of Creation, the Will of GOD, was the Word of God; his Will that it should be, was his saying, Let it be.[53]

L ight out of darkness, is Musick out of silence.[54]

A Leviathan, a Whale, from a grain of Spawn; an Oke from a buried Akehorn, is a great; but a great world from nothing, is a strange improvement.[55]

G od is always so present, and so all-sufficient, that wee need not doubt of him, nor rely upon any other, otherwise then as an instrument of his.[56]

S ometimes God does the greater work, and yet leaves some lesser things undone. God chooses his Matter and his Measure, and his Means, and his Minutes.[57]

8

IN THE IMAGE OF GOD

A Child of God

God hath imparted a being, an essence, from himselfe, who is the roote, and the fountaine of all essence, and all being.[1]

God brought man into the world, as the King goes in state, Lords, and Earles, and persons of other ranks before him. So God sent out Light, and Firmament, and Earth, and Sea, and Sunne, and Moone, to give a dignity to mans procession; and onely Man himselfe disorders all, and that by displacing himselfe, by losing his place.[2]

In the great Ant-hill of the whole world, I am an Ant; I have my part in the Creation, I am a Creature; But there are ignoble Creatures. God comes nearer; In the Great field of clay, of red Earth, that man was made of, and mankind, I am a clod; I am a Man, I have my part in the Humanity.[3]

Take a flat Map . . . and here is East, and there is West, as far asunder as two points can be put: but reduce this flat Map to roundnesse, which is the true form, and then east and West touch one another, and are all one: So consider mans life aright, to be a Circle . . . In this, the circle, the two points meet, the womb and the grave are but one point, they make but one station, there is but a step from that to this.[4]

Man is but earth; Tis true; but earth is the center. That man who dwels upon himself, who is alwaies conversant in himself, rests in his true center. Man is a celestiall creature too, a heavenly creature; and that man that dwels upon himselfe, that hath his conversation in himselfe, hath his conversation in heaven.[5]

Simply, absolutely, unconditionally, we cannot say, Surely men, men altogether, high or low, or meane, all are lesse then vanity.[6]

Since God is so mindfull of him, since God hath set his minde upon him, What is not man? Man is all.[7]

He created thee, *ex nihilo*, he gave thee a being, there's matter of exaltation, and yet all this from nothing; thou wast worse then a worm, there's matter of humiliation; but he did not create thee *ad nihilum*, to return to nothing again, and there's matter for thy consideration, and study, how to make thine immortality profitable unto thee; for it is a deadly immortality, if thy immortality must serve thee for nothing but to hold thee in immortal torment.[8]

Since we consider men in the place that they hold, and value them according to those places, and aske not how they got thither, when we see Man made The Love of the Father, The Price of the Sonne, The Temple of the Holy Ghost, the Signet upon Gods hand, The Apple of Gods eye, Absolutely, unconditionally we cannot annihilate man, not evacuate, not evaporate . . . For, man is not onely a contributary Creature, but a totall Creature; He does not onely make one, but he is all; He is not a piece of the world, but the world it selfe; and next to the glory of God, the reason why there is a world.[9]

If I may pray, and say *Pater noster*, if I may call God Father, I may beleeve with a faithfull assurance, that I am the childe of God.[10]

An Eternal Election

God, in the Creation, had nothing at all: He called us when we were not, as though we had been.[11]

God hath elected certaine men, whom he intends to create, that he may elect them; that is, that he may declare his Election upon them. God had thee, before he made thee; He loved thee first, and then created thee, that thou loving him, he might continue his love to thee.[12]

Man had no power, no will, no not a faculty to wish that Christ would have come, till Christ did come, and call him . . . How should I pray at first, that God would come into me, whenas I could not onely not have the spirit of prayer, but not the spirit of life, and being, except God were in me already? Where was I, when Christ call'd me out of my Raggs, nay out of my Ordure, and wash'd me in the Sacramental water of Baptism, and made me a Christian so? Where was I, when in the loyns of my sinful parents, and in the unclean act of generation, Christ call'd me into the Covenant, and made me the childe of Christian parents? Could I call upon him, to do either of these for me? Or if I may seem to have made any step towards Baptism, because I was within the Covenant; or towards the Covenant, because I was of Christian parents: yet where was I, when God call'd me, when I was not, as though I had been, in the Eternal Decree of my Election? What said I for my self, or what said any other for me then, when neither I, nor they had any being?[13]

Onely he can raise a Tower, whose top shall reach to heaven: The Basis of the highest building is but the Earth; But though thou be but a Tabernacle of Earth, God shall raise thee peece by peece, into a spirituall building; And after one Story of Creation, and another of Vocation, and another of Sanctification, he shall bring thee up, to meet thy selfe, in the bosome of thy God, where thou wast at first, in an eternall election.[14]

When God gives me accesse into his *Library*, leave to consider his proceedings with man, I find the first book of Gods making to be the *Book of Life*. The Book where all their names are written that are elect to Glory. But I find no such *Book of Death*.[15]

Susceptible of Grace

Whatsoever God requires of man, man may finde imprinted in his own nature, written in his own heart.[16]

Man is that creature, who onely of all other creatures can answer the inspiration of God, when his grace comes, and exhibit acceptable service to him, and cooperate with him.[17]

If you carry a Line from the Circumference, to the Circumference againe, as a Diameter, it passes the Center, it flowes from the Center, it looks to the Center both wayes. God is the Center; The Lines above, and the Lines below, still respect and regard the Center; Whether I doe any action honest in the sight of men, or any action acceptable to God, whether I doe things belonging to this life, or to the next, still I must passe all through the Center, and direct all to the glory of God, and keepe my heart right, without variation towards him.[18]

In a Body that may, that must, that does, that did dye ever since it was made, I carry a Soul, nay, a Soul carries me, to such a perpetuity, as no Saint, no Angel, God himself shall not survive me, over-live me.[19]

Consider the dignitie of thy soule, which onely, of all other Creatures is capable, susceptible of Grace; If God would bestow grace any where els, no creature could receive it but thou. Thou art so necessary to God, as that God had no utterance, no exercise, no employment for his grace and mercy, but for thee. And if thou make thy selfe incapable of this mercy and this grace, of which nothing but thou is capable, then thou destroyest thy nature.[20]

There is a man, there is a soul in that man, there is a will in that soul; and God is in love with this man, and this soul, and this will, and would have it.[21]

God made man good, but in a *possibility* of being ill; Now, God findes man ill, but in a possibility of being good.[22]

Our dignity, and our greatest height, is in our interest in God, and in the world, and in our selves; and we fall from all . . . either by neglecting God, or by over-valuing the world.[23]

God hath made thee his own Image, and afforded thee meanes of salvation: Use them. God compels no man.[24]

God therefore having made man, that is *Mankinde*, in a state of love, and friendship, God having not by any purpose of his done any thing toward the violation of this friendship, in man, in any man, God continueth his everlasting goodnesse towards man, towards mankinde still, in inviting him to accept the means of Reconciliation, and a returne to the same state of friendship, which hee had at first, by our Ministery.[25]

Creatures of an inferiour nature are possest with the *present*; *Man* is a *future Creature*. In a holy and usefull sense, wee may say, that *God is a future God*; to man especially hee is so; Mans consideration of *God* is specially for the *future*.[26]

That man is something, a great thing, a noble Creature, if we refer to him to his end, to his interest in God, to his reversion in heaven.[27]

Man shall no more see an *end*, no more die, then *God* himselfe, that gave him life.[28]

9

THE HUMAN
PREDICAMENT

The Human Predicament

Thou know'st thy selfe so little, as thou know'st not,
How thou did'st die, nor how thou wast begot.
Thou neither knowst, how thou at first camest in,
Nor how thou took'st the poyson of mans sin.
Nor dost thou, (though thou knowst, that thou art so)
By what way thou art made immortall, know.[1]

The world is a Sea in many respects and assimilations. It is a Sea,
as it is subject to stormes, and tempests; Every man (and every
man is a world) feels that. And then, it is never the shallower for the
calmnesse, The Sea is as deepe, there is as much water in the Sea, in
a calme, as in a storme; we may be drowned in a calme and flattering fortune, in prosperity, as irrecoverably, as in a wrought Sea, in
adversity; So the world is a Sea. It is a Sea, as it is bottomlesse to any
line, which we can sound it with, and endlesse to any discovery that
we can make of it. The purposes of the world, the wayes of the
world, exceed our consideration; But yet we are sure the Sea hath a
bottome, and sure that it hath limits, that it cannot overpasse; The
power of the greatest in the world, the life of the happiest in the
world, cannot exceed those bounds, which God hath placed for
them; So the world is a Sea. It is a Sea, as it hath ebbs and floods, and
no man knowes the true reason of those floods and those ebbs. All
men have changes and vicissitudes in their bodies, (they fall sick)
And in their estates, (they grow poore) And in their minds, (they
become sad) at which changes, (sicknesse, poverty, sadnesse) them-

[167]

selves wonder, and the cause is wrapped up in the purpose and judgement of God onely, and hid even from them that have them; and so the world is a Sea. It is a Sea, as the Sea affords water enough for all the world to drinke, but such water as will not quench the thirst. The world affords conveniences enow to satisfie Nature, but these encrease our thirst with drinking, and our desire growes and enlarges it selfe with our abundance, and though we sayle in a full Sea, yet we lacke water; So the world is a Sea. It is a Sea, if we consider the Inhabitants. In the Sea, the greater fish devoure the lesse; and so doe the men of this world too. And as fish, when they mud themselves, have no hands to make themselves cleane, but the current of the waters must worke that; So have the men of this world no means to cleanse themselves from those sinnes which they have contracted in the world of themselves, till a new flood, waters of repentance, drawne up, and sanctified by the Holy Ghost, worke that blessed effect in them. All these wayes the world is a Sea, but especially it is a Sea in this respect, that the Sea is no place of habitation, but a passage to our habitations. So the Apostle expresses the world, *Here we have no continuing City, but we seeke one to come;* we seeke it not here, but we seeke it whilest we are here, els we shall never finde it.[2]

For spirituall things, the things of the next world, we have no roome, for temporall things, the things of this world, we have no bounds.[3]

When Man comes to be content with this world, God will take this world from him: when Man frames to himselfe imaginary pleasures, God will inflict reall punishments; when he would lie still, he shall not sleep; but God will take him and raise him, but to a farther vexation.[4]

All the qualities and properties of all other creatures, how remote and distant, how contrary soever in themselves, yet they all meet in man; In man, if he be a flatterer, you shall finde the groveling and crawling of a Snake; and in a man, if he be ambitious,

you shall finde the high flight and piercing of the Eagle; in a volup-
tuous sensual man, you shall finde [the] earthlinesse of the Hog; and
in a licentious man, the intemperance, and distemper of the Goate;
ever lustfull, and ever in a fever; ever in sicknesses contracted by
that sin, and yet ever in a desire to proceed in that sin; and so man is
every creature in that respect.[5]

A mongst *naturall Creatures*, because howsoever they differ in
bignesse, yet they have some proportion to one another, we
consider that some very little creatures, contemptible in themselves,
are yet called enemies to great creatures, as the Mouse is to the
Elephant. (For the greatest Creature is not *Infinite*, nor the least is
not *Nothing*.) But shall man, between whom and nothing, there
went but a word, *Let us make Man*, That Nothing, which is infinitely lesse then a Mathematicall point, then an imaginary Atome, shall
this Man, this yesterdayes Nothing, this to morrow worse then
Nothing, be capable of that honour, that *dishonourable honour*,
that confounding honour, to be the enemy of God, of God who is
not onely a multiplied Elephant, millions of Elephants, multiplied
into one, but a multiplied World, a multiplied All, All that can be
conceived by us, infinite many times over; Nay, (if we may dare to
say so,) a multiplyed God, a God that hath the Millions of the
Heathens gods in himselfe alone, shall this man be an enemy to this
God? . . . It is true, if we consider the infinite disproportion between
them, he cannot; but to many sad purposes, and in many heavy
applications Man is an enemy to God . . . And then to adhere to an
enemy, is to become an enemy; for Man to adhere to Man, to
ascribe any thing to the power of his *naturall faculties*, to thinke
of any beame of clearnesse in his own understanding, or any line
of rectitude in his owne will, this is to accumulate and multiply
enmities against God, and to assemble and muster up more, and
more man, to fight against God.[6]

A ll the world is under sin, and knows it not.[7]

We seeme ambitious, Gods whole worke t'undoe;
Of nothing he made us, and we strive too,
To bring ourselves to nothing backe; and we
Do what we can, to do't so soone as hee.[8]

I am thy sonne, made with thy selfe to shine,
Thy servant, whose paines thou hast still repaid,
Thy sheepe, thine Image, and till I betray'd
My selfe, a temple of thy Spirit divine;
Why doth the devill then usurpe on mee?[9]

The Fall

For wee
All reape consumption from one fruitfull tree.[10]

God made the first Marriage, and man made the first Divorce;
God married the Body and Soule in the Creation, and man
Divorced the Body and Soule by death through sinne, in his fall.[11]

God intended life and immortality for man; and man by sin
induc'd death upon himself at first.[12]

Man hath a reasonable soule capable of Gods grace, so hath no
creature but man; man hath naturall faculties, which may be
employed by God in his service, so hath no creature but man. Onely
man was made so, as that he might be better; whereas all other
creatures were but to consist in that degree of goodnesse, in which
they entred. Miserable fall! Only man was made to mend, and only
man does grow worse; Only man was made capable of a spirituall
soveraignty, and only man hath enthralled, and mancipated himselfe to a spirituall slavery.[13]

P rince of the orchard, faire as dawning morne,
    Fenc'd with the law, and ripe as soone as borne
That apple grew, which this Soule did enlive
Till the then climing serpent, that now creeps
For that offence, for which all mankinde weepes,
Tooke it, and t'her whom the first man did wive
(Whom and her race, only forbiddings drive)
He gave it, she, t'her husband, both did eate;
So perished the eaters, and the meate:
    And wee (for treason taints the blood) thence die and sweat.[14]

O riginall sinne . . . that snake in my bosome . . . that poyson in
    my blood . . . that leaven and tartar in all my actions, that casts
me into Relapses of those sins which I have repented.[15]

O riginall sinne, that ever smoakes up, and creates a soote in the
    soule.[16]

B efore our bones were hardned, the canker and rust of *Adams*
    sin was in our bones . . . before we were a minute old, we have
a sin in us that is six thousand years old.[17]

T hen, as mankinde, so is the worlds whole frame
    Quite out of joynt, almost created lame:
For, before God had made up all the rest,
Corruption entred, and deprav'd the best:
It seis'd the Angels, and then first of all
The world did in her Cradle take a fall,
And turn'd her braines, and tooke a generall maime.
Wronging each joynt of th'universall frame.
The noblest part, man, felt it first; and than
Both beasts and plants, curst in the curse of man.
So did the world from the first houre decay,
The evening was beginning of the day.[18]

This then is the miserable state of the world, It might know, and does not, that it is wholly under an inundation, a deluge of sin.[19]

Our will is poisoned in the fountaine; and, as soon as our will is able to exercise any election, we are willing to sin, as soone as we can, and sorry we can sin no sooner, and sorry no longer: we are willing before the Devil is willing, and willing after the Devill is weary, and seek occasions of tentation, when he presents none.[20]

For that first mariage was our funeral:
One woman at one blow, then kill'd us all,
And singly, one by one, they kill us now.
We doe delightfully our selves allow
To that consumption; and profusely blinde,
We kill our selves, to propagate our kinde.[21]

Man is so farre from being good of himselfe, as that he must forget himselfe, devest himselfe, forsake himselfe, before he can be capable of any good.[22]

There was a time when God and Man were friends, God did not hate man from all Eternitie, God forbid. And this friendship God meant not to breake; God had no purpose to fall out with man, for then hee could never have admitted him to a friendship . . . No man can love another as a friend this yeare, and meane to bee his enemy next. Gods foreknowledge that man and he should fall out, was not a foreknowledge of any thing that he meant to doe to that purpose, but onely that Man himselfe would become incapable of the continuation of this friendship.[23]

There is a Law of Nature that passes through all the World, a Law in the heart; and of the breach of this, no man can be alwayes ignorant. As every man hath a devil in himselfe . . . A Devill of his owne making, some particular sin that transports Him, so every man hath a kinde of God in himselfe, such a conscience, as sometimes reproves him.[24]

You see what you had, and how you lost it. If it might not bee recovered, God would not call you to it.[25]

A Continual Course of Sin

The sin that I have done, the sin that I *would* have done, is my sin.[26]

We sin constantly, and we sin continually, and we sin confidently; and we finde so much pleasure and profit in sin, as that we have made a league, and sworn a friendship with sin; and we keep that perverse, and irreligious promise over-religiously; and the sins of our youth flow into other sins, when age disables us for them.[27]

As the *eye* sees every thing but *it selfe*, so does *sinne*, too.[28]

All the foure changes of our life, Infancy, Youth, Middle Age, and Old, have been spent and worne out in a continuall, and uninterrupted course of sin.[29]

If thou have passed over the first heats of the day, the wantonnesses of youth, and the second heat, the fire of ambition, if these be quenched in thee, by preventing grace, or by repenting grace, be more and more holy, for thine age will meet another sin of covetousnesse, or of indevotion, that needs as much resistance.[30]

[173]

The Age that oppresses the sinner, is that when he is growne old in sin, he is growne weak in strength, and become less able to overcome that sin then, then he was at beginning. Blindnesse contracted by Age, doth not deliver him from objects of tentations; He sees them, though he be blind; Deafnesse doth not deliver him from discourses of tentation; he heares them, though he be deafe: Nor lamenesse doth not deliver him from pursuit of tentation; for in his owne memory he sees, and heares, and pursues all his former sinfull pleasures, and every night, every houre sins over all the sins of many years that are passed.[31]

You heare of one man that was drowned in a vessell of Wine; but how many thousands in ordinary water? . . . A gad of steele does no more choake a man, then a feather, then a haire; Men perish with whispering sins, nay with silent sins, sins that never tell the conscience they are sins, as often as with crying sins: And in hell there shall meet as many men, that never thought what was a sin, as that spent all their thoughts in the compassing of sin.[32]

Nothing can alienate God more from thee, then to think that any thing but sin can alienate him.[33]

Sin is so far from being nothing, as that there is nothing else but sin in us: sin hath not onely a place, but a Palace, a Throne, not onely a beeing, but a dominion, even in our best actions.[34]

No man falls lower, then he that falls into a course of sin; Sin is a fall; It is not onely a deviation, a turning out of the way, upon the right, or the left hand, but it is a sinking, a falling.[35]

Sins, which are but the Children of indifferent actions, become the Parents of great sins; which is the industry of sin, to exalt it selfe, and (as it were) ennoble it selfe, above the stocke, from which it was derived, The next sin will needs be a better sin then the last.[36]

E very sin leaves us worse, then it found us, and we rise poorer, ignobler, weaker, for every nights sin, then we lay down.[37]

M an all at once was there by woman slaine,
And one by one we'are here slaine o'er againe
By them. The mother poison'd the well-head,
The daughters here corrupt us. Rivolets,
No smalnesse scapes, no greatness breaks their nets,
She thrust us out, and by them we are led
Astray, from turning, to whence we are fled.
Were prisoners Judges, 'twould seeme rigorous,
Shee sinn'd, we beare; part of our paine is, thus
   To love them, whose fault to this painfull love yoak'd us.[38]

H e mocks God, that repents and sins over those sins every night, that every day he repents.[39]

B eloved, if we fear not the wetting of our foot in sin, it will be too late, when we are over head and ears.[40]

P erchance thou canst tell, when was the first time, or where was the first place, that thou didst commit such or such a sinne; but as a man can remember when he began to *spell*, but not when he began to *reade perfectly*, when he began to joyne his letters, but not when he began to write perfectly, so thou remembrest when thou wentest timorously and bashfully about sinne, at first, and now perchance art ashamed of that shamefastnesse, and sorry thou beganst no sooner. Poore bankrupt! that hast sinned out thy soule so profusely, so lavishly, that thou darest not cast up thine accounts, thou darest not aske thy selfe any whether thou have any soule left; how farre art thou, from giving any testimony to Christ, that darest not testifie to thy selfe, not heare thy conscience take knowledge of thy transgressions, but haddest rather sleepe out thy daies, or *drinke* out thy daies, then leave one minute for *compunction* to lay hold on; and doest not sinne alwaies for the love of that sinne, but for feare of a *holy sorrow*, if thou shouldest not fill up thy time, with that sinne.[41]

But beloved, sin is a serpent, and he that covers sin, does but keepe it warme, that it may sting the more fiercely, and disperse the venome and malignity thereof the more effectually.[42]

Whilst in our soules sinne bred and pamper'd is,
    Our soules become wormeaten carkases;
So we our selves miraculously destroy.[43]

Change of sin is not an overcomming of sin; He that passes from sin to sin without repentance . . . still leaves an enemy behind him; and though he have no present assault from his former enemie, no tentation to act any of his former sin, yet he is still in the midst of his enemies; under condemnation of his past, as well as of his present sins; as unworthy a receiver of the Sacrament, for the sins of his youth done forty yeares agoe, if those sins were never repented, though so long discontinued, as for his ambition, or covetousnesse, or indevotion of this present day.[44]

In the bloud-rednesse of sinne, God had no hand: but sinne, and destruction for sinne, was wholly from our selves.[45]

So fast in us doth this corruption grow,
    That now wee dare aske why wee should be so.
Would God (disputes the curious Rebell) make
A law, and would not have it kept? Or can
His creatures will, cross his?[46]

If a man of my blood, or allyance, doe a shamefull act, I am affected with it; If a man of my calling, or *profession*, doe a scandalous act, I feel my self concerned in his fault; God hath made all *mankinde* of *one blood*, and all *Christians* of *one calling*, and the sins of every man concern every man, both in that respect, that I, that is, *This nature*, is in that man that sins that sin; and I, that is, *This nature*, is in that Christ, who is wounded by that sin.[47]

S in is the roote of death . . . It is death because we shall dye for it. But it is death in it selfe, We are dead already, dead in it.[48]

Directing Temptations

W e can direct *tentations* upon our selves; If we were in a wildernesse, we could sin; and where we are, we tempt temptations.[49]

H e that runnes headlong into all wayes of wickednesse, and . . . precludes, or neglects all wayes of recovery: That is glad of a tentation, and afraid of a Sermon; that is dry wood, and tinder to Satans fire, if he doe but touch him, and is ashes it self to Gods Spirit, if he blow upon him; That from a love of sinne, at first, because it is pleasing, comes at last to a love of sinne, because it is sinne, because it is liberty, because it is a deliverance of himselfe from the bondage, as he thinks it, of the law of God, and from the remorse and anguish of considering sinne too particularly.[50]

I f we consider how early, how primarie a sinne Pride is, and how soone it possesses us. Scarce any man, but if he looke back seriously into himselfe, and into his former life, and revolve his owne history, but that the first act which he can remember in him-selfe, or can be remembred of by others, will bee some act of Pride. Before Ambition, or Covetousnesse, or Licentiousnesse is awake in us, Pride is working; Though but a childish pride, yet pride; and this Parents rejoyce at in their children, and call it spirit, and so it is, but not the best.[51]

This is the pride that is forbidden man; not that he think well of himselfe . . . That hee value aright the dignity of his nature, in the Creation thereof according to the Image of God, and the infinite improvement that that nature received, in being assumed by the Son of God; This is not pride, but not to acknowledge that all this dignity in nature, and all that it conduces to, that is, grace here, and glory hereafter, is not onely infused by God at first, but sustained by God still, and that nothing in the beginning, or way, or end, is of our selves, this is pride.[52]

God does not say of the proud man, I cannot worke upon him, I cannot mend him, I cannot pardon him, I cannot suffer him, I cannot stay with him, but meerly *I cannot*, and no more, I cannot tell what to say of him, what to doe for him; (*Him that hath a proud heart, I cannot*) Pride is so contrary to God, as that the proud man, and he can meet in nothing.[53]

How poore a *Clod* of Earth is a *Mannor*? How poore an *inch*, a *Shire*? How poore a *spanne*, a *Kingdome*? how poore a *pace*, the whole *World*? And yet how prodigally we sell *Paradise, Heaven, Soules, Consciences, Immortalitie, Eternitie*, for a *few Graines* of this *Dust*?[54]

Some sins we have done, because we are rich; but many more because we would be rich.[55]

Great sins are great possessions; but levities and vanities possesse us too; and men had rather part with Christ, then with any possessions.[56]

When a Man sees his small sins, there is not so much danger of great.[57]

W hen senses, which thy souldiers are,
  Wee arme against thee, and they fight for sinne,
When want, sent but to tame, doth warre
And worke despaire a breach to enter in,
    When plenty, Gods image, and scale
    Makes us Idolatrous,
And love it, not him, whom it should reveale,
When wee are mov'd to seeme religious
Only to vent wit, Lord deliver us.[58]

E very man may find in himself . . . sinne wrapped up in sinne, a
  body of sin. We bring Elements of our own; earth of Covetousnesse, water of unsteadfastnesse, ayre of putrefaction, and fire of
licentiousnesse; and of these elements we make a body of sinne . . .
so we may say of our sin, it hath a wanton eye, a griping hand, an
itching ear, an insatiable heart, and feet swift to shed blood, and yet
it is but one body of sin; It is all, and yet it is but One.[59]

H *illy ways* are wearisome ways, and tire the ambitious man;
  Carnall pleasures are *dirty ways*, and tire the licentious
man; Desires of gain, are *thorny ways*, and tire the covetous man;
Æmulations of higher men, are *dark* and *blinde ways*, and tire the
envious man; Every way, that is out of the way, wearies us . . . we
are wearied with our sins, and have no satisfaction in them; we
goe to bed to night, weary of our sinfull labours, and we will rise
freshly to morrow, to the same sinfull labours again; And when a
sinner does so little remember *yesterday*, how little does he consider
to morrow? He that forgets what he hath *done*, foresees not what he
shall suffer: so sin is a burden; it crookens us, it wearies us.[60]

H ow many men sinne over the sinnes of their youth again, in
  their age, by a sinfull *Delight* in remembring those sinnes, and
a sinfull *Desire*, that their Bodies were not past them? How many
men sin over some sins, but *imaginarily*, (and yet *Damnably*) a hundred times, which they *never sinned actually* at all, by filling their
Imaginations, with such thoughts as these, How would I be

revenged of such an Enemy, if I were in such a place of Authority? How easily could I overthrow such a wastfull young Man, and compasse his Land, if I had but Money, to feed his humours? Those sinnes which we have never been able to doe *actually*, to the harme of others, we doe as hurtfully to our owne Souls, by a sinful *Desire* of them, and a sinful *Delight* in them.⁶¹

Indifferent looking, equall and easie conversation, appliablenesse to wanton discourses, and notions, and motions, are the Devils single money, and many pieces of these make up an Adultery. As light a thing as a Spangle is, a Spangle is silver; and Leafe-gold, that is blowne away, is gold; and sand that hath no strength, no coherence, yet knits the building; so doe approaches to sin, become sin, and fixe sin.⁶²

Hee that thinkes all the world as one Jewell, and himselfe the Cabinet, that all was made for him, and hee for none, forgets his owne office, his Stewardship, by which he is enabled and bound to the necessities of others.⁶³

Vanity is nothing, but there is a condition worse then nothing. Confidence in the things, or persons of this world, but most of all, a confidence in our selves, will bring us at last to that state, wherein we would faine be nothing, and cannot.⁶⁴

Some of our sins do not offend God so much, as our inconsideration, a stupid passing him over, as though that we did, that which we had, that which we were, appertained not to him, had no emanation from him, no dependance upon him.⁶⁵

A soul may perish by a thoughtlessness, as well as by ill thoughts: God takes it as ill to be slighted, as to be injur'd.⁶⁶

A house is not clean, though all the Dust be swept together, if it lie still in a corner, within Dores; A Conscience is not clean, by having recollected all her sinnes in the *Memory*, for they may fester there, and *Gangreen* even to *Desperation*, till she have emptied them in the bottomlesse Sea of the bloud of Christ Jesus, and the mercy of his Father, by *this* way of *Confession*. But a house is not clean neither, though the Dust be thrown out, if there hang *Cobwebs* about theWalls, in how dark corners soever. A Conscience is not clean, though the sins, brought to our memory by this Examination, be cast upon Gods mercy, and the merits of his Sonne, by *Confession*, if there remaine in me, but a *Cobweb*, a little, but a sinfull delight in the *Memory* of those sins, which I had formerly committed.[67]

A n idle body, is a disease in a State; an idle soul, is a monster in a man.[68]

I mpenitence removes all sorrow for sins past, and hardness of heart all tendernesse towards future tentations.[69]

D evout men departed from their former fervor are the coldest and the most irreducible to true zeale, true holinesse.[70]

S ome man may be chaster in the Stews, then another in the Church; and some man will sin more in his dreams, then another in his discourse. Every man must know how much water his own vessell draws, and not to think to saile over, wheresoever he hath seen another (he knows not with how much labour) shove over.[71]

M iserable mistaking man that I am! I thinke my selfe able to overcome any tentation, and I am overcome even by that tentation of thinking so. I thinke my selfe conquerour, when I am captive, and am chained to the Chariot, when I think I sit in it.[72]

Judgement and Mercy

So no man falleth at first into any sinne, but he heares his own fall. There is a tendernesse in every Conscience at the beginning, at the entrance into a sinne, and he discerneth a while the degrees of sinking too: but at last he is out of his owne sight, till he meete this stone; (this stone is Christ) that is, till he meete some hard reprehension, some hard passage of a Sermon, some hard judgement in a Prophet, some crosse in the World, some thing from the mouth, or some thing from the hand of God, that breaks him: *He falls upon the stone and is broken.*[73]

So when this stone fals thus, when Christ comes to judgement, he shall not onely condemn him for his clay, his earthly and covetous sinnes, nor for his iron, his revengefull oppressing, and rusty sinnes, nor for his brasse, his shining, and glittering sinnes, which he hath filed and polished, but he shall fall upon his silver and gold, his religious and precious sinnes, his hypocriticall hearing of Sermons, his singular observing of Sabbaths, his Pharisaicall giving of almes, and as well his subtill counterfeiting of Religion, as his Atheistical opposing of religion, this stone, Christ himselfe, shall fall upon him, and a showre of other stones shall oppresse him too.[74]

It is true, that the justice of God is subtile, as searching, as unsearchable; and oftentimes punishes sins of Omission, with other sins, Actuall sins, and makes their lazinesse, who are slack in doing that they should, an occasion of doing that they should not.[75]

God is the universall Confessor, the generall Penitentiary of all the world, and all dye in the guilt of their sin, that goe not to Confession to him.[76]

All between God and man is conditionall, and where man will not be bound, God will not be bound neither; If man invest a habit and purpose of sinning, God will study a judgement against that man, and doe that, even in Israel, which shall make all our eares to tingle, and all our hearts to ake; Till that man repent, God will not, and when he does, God will repent too; For, though God be not Man, that he can repent, yet that God, who for Mans sake became Man, for our sakes, and his owne glory, will so farre become Man againe, as upon Mans true repentance, to repent the Judgements intended against that Man.[77]

B ut as in a River that is swelled, though the water do bring down sand and stones, and logs, yet the water is there still; and the purpose of Nature is to vent that water, not to pour down that sand, or those stones: so though God be put to mingle his Judgements with his mercies, yet his mercy is there still, and his purpose is, ever in those judgements, to manifest his mercy.[78]

A s when the spirit returns to him that gave it, there is a disso- lution of the man, So when God withdrawes his visitation, there is a dissolution of a Christian.[79]

W e call not Coyn, base Coyne, till the Allay be more then the pure Metall: Gods Judgements are not punishments, except there be more anger then love, more Justice then Mercy in them; and that is never.[80]

G od executes no judgement upon man in this life, but in mercy.[81]

A ll men were in *Adam*; because the whole nature, mankinde, was in him; and then, can any be without sin? All men were in Christ too, because the whole nature, mankinde, was in him; and then, can any man be excluded from a possibility of mercy?[82]

B ut proceed with thy self further, bring this dawning and breake of day to a full light, and this little sparke to a perfect acknow-ledgement of thy sinnes. Go home, with this spark of Gods Spirit in you.[83]

T hough . . . there are an infinite number of *Stars* more then we can distinguish, and so, by God's grace, there may be an infinite number of soules saved, more then those, of whose salva-tion, we discerne the *ways*, and the *meanes*.[84]

GOD AND MAN

God and Man

As it is a fearfull thing to fall into the hands of the living God, so it is an impossible thing to scape it.[1]

In me there is no merit, nor shadow or merit; In God there is no change, nor shadow of change. I am the same sinner, he is the same God; still the same desperate sinner, still the same terrible God.[2]

A troublesome spirit, and a quiet spirit, are farre asunder; But a troubled spirit, and a quiet spirit, are neare neighbours.[3]

Let the trouble of my soule be as great as it will, so it direct me upon God, and I have calme enough.[4]

As God, above whom there is nothing, lookes downewards to us; So except we, below whom there is nothing that belongs to us, looke upward toward him, we shall never meet.[5]

But the depth of the goodness of God, how much good God can do for man; yea the depth of the illness of man, how much ill man can do against God, are such seas, as, if it be not impossible, at least it is impertinent, to go about to sound them.[6]

As no man can deceive God, so God can deceive no man; God cannot live in the darke himselfe, neither can he leave those, who are his, in the darke: If he be with thee, he will make thee see, that he is with thee; and never goe out of thy sight, till he have brought thee, where thou canst never goe out of his.[7]

The Sun is not weary with sixe thousand yeares shining; God cannot be weary of doing good.[8]

God can, and sometimes doth effect his purposes by himselfe; intirely, immediatly, extraordinarily, miraculously by himselfe.[9]

And for the *next world*, though all that are borne into this world, doe not enter into the number of Gods Saints, in heaven, yet the Saints of heaven can be made out of no other materialls, but men borne into this world.[10]

God . . . desires to have his kingdome well peopled; he would have *many*, he would have *all*, he would have *every one* of them have all.[11]

Man speakes; and *God* speakes too; and first . . . *see that* you do heare him; for, as he that fears God, fears nothing else, so he that hears God hears nothing else, that can terrifie him.[12]

All the sunshine, all the glory of this life, though all these be testimonies of Gods love to us, yet all these bring but a winters day, a short day, and a cold day, and a dark day, for except we love too, God doth not love with an everlasting love: God will not suffer his love to be idle, and since it profits him nothing, if it profits us nothing neither, he will withdraw it.[13]

God shuts no man out of heaven, by a lock on the inside, except that man have clapped the doore after him, and never knocked to have it opened againe, that is, except he have sinned, and never repented.[14]

No man is so necessary to God, as that God cannot be without him.[15]

Batter my heart, three person'd God; for, you
As yet but knocke, breathe, shine, and seeke to mend;
That I may rise, and stand, o'erthrow mee, 'and bend
Your force, to breake, blowe, burn and make me new.
I, like an usurpt towne, to'another due,
Labour to'admit you, but Oh, to no end,
Reason your viceroy in mee, mee should defend,
But is captiv'd, and proves weake or untrue,
Yet dearely'I love you,'and would be lov'd faine,
But am betroth'd unto your enemie,
Divorce mee,'untie, or breake that knot againe,
Take mee to you, imprison mee, for I
Except you'enthrall mee, never shall be free,
Nor ever chast, except you ravish me.[16]

No man is so necessary to God, as that God cannot come to his ends without that man; God can lack, and leave out any man in his service.[17]

Christ saves no man against his will.[18]

Trust not to an irresistible grace, that at one time or other God will have thee, whether thou wilt or no.[19]

G od hath blessed me with that grace, that I trust in no helpe but his, and with this grace too, That I cannot looke for his helpe, except I helpe my selfe also.[20]

A s Grace could not worke upon man to Salvation, if man had not a faculty of will to worke upon, because without that will man were not man; so is this Salvation wrought in the will, by conforming this will of man to the will of God, not by extinguishing the will it selfe, by any force or constraint that God imprints in it by his Grace: God saves no man without, or against his will.[21]

G ive God sea-roome, give him his latitude . . . he that judges hastily, may soone mistake God's purpose.[22]

C hrist beats his Drum, but he does not Press men; Christ is serv'd with Voluntaries.[23]

G od cals, and he directs, and lightens our paths; never reproach God so impiously as to suspect, that when he cals, he does not meane that we should come.[24]

G od is a good *Husband*, a good *Steward* of Mans contributions, but contributions hee will have: hee will have a concurrence, a cooperation of *persons*.[25]

W hen man does any thing conducing to supernaturall ends, though the worke be Gods, the will of man is not meerly passive. The will of man is but Gods agent; but still an agent it is.[26]

W hen God bindes himselfe, he takes us into the band with him, and when God makes himselfe the debtor, he makes us stewards.[27]

God and Man

All that passes betweene God and man, from first to last, is blessings from God to man, and praises from man to God; and that the first degree of blessednesse is, to finde the print of the hand of God, even in his temporall blessednesse, and to praise and glorifie him for them, in the right use of them.[28]

Accustome thy selfe to find the presence of God in all thy gettings, in all thy preferments, in all thy studies, and he will be abundantly sufficient to thee for all.[29]

God is no in-accessible God, that he may not be come to; nor inexorable, that he will not be moved, if he be spoken to; nor dilatory, that he does not that he does, seasonably.[30]

It is a suspicious thing to doubt or distrust God in necessary things, and it is an unmannerly thing to presse him in superfluous things.[31]

As God sees the water in the spring in the veines of the earth, before it bubble upon the face of the earth; so God sees teares in the heart of a man, before they blubber his face; God heares the teares of that sorrowfull soule, which for sorrow cannot shed teares.[32]

Be but wormes and no more, in your owne eyes, and God shall make you men, bee but men and no more in your owne eyes, and God shall make you the men of his Israel.[33]

Whom God loves, hee loves to the end; and not onely to their own end, to their death, but to his end, and his end is, that he might love them still.[34]

Grace

O ur Creation ... our Vocation ... our Glorification. In the first, We, who were ... but nothing, were made Creatures; In the second, we, who were but Gentiles, were made Christians: In the third, we, who were but men, shall be made saints. In the first, God took us, when there was no world: In the second, God sustains us, in an ill world: In the third, God shall crown us, in a glorious and joyful world. In the first, God made us; in the second, God mends us; in the third, God shall perfect us.[35]

I n Nature wee have the capacity of Grace, but not Grace in possession, in Nature.[36]

A nd as Nature lookes for the season for ripening, and does not all before, so Grace lookes for the assent of the soule, and does not perfect the whole worke, till that come. It is Nature that brings the season, and it is Grace that brings the assent; but the season for the fruit, till the assent of the soule come, all is not done.[37]

A ll things desire to goe to *their owne place*, and that's but the effect of *Nature*; But if Man desires to goe the right way, that's an effect of *grace*, and of *Religion*. A *stone* will fall to the bottome naturally, and a *flame* will goe upwards naturally; but a stone cares not whether it fall through cleane water, or through Mud; a flame cares not whether it passe through pure aire, or cloudy; but a *Christian*, whose end is heaven, will put himselfe into a *faire way* towards it, and according to this measure, *be pure as his father in heaven is pure.*[38]

I nfinite sinnes call for infinite mercy; and *where sinne did abound, grace, and mercy shall much more.*[39]

God is always ready to build upon his owne foundations, and accomplish his owne beginnings.[40]

For me, as I am, I am altogether unfit; when thou shalt be pleased to work upon me, thou wilt finde me but stone, hard to receive thy holy impressions, and then but snow, easie to melt, and lose those holy formes again: There must be labour laid, and perchance labour lost upon me; but put the businesse into a safe hand, and under an infallible instrument and . . . *send him whom,* I know, *thou wilt send,* . . . send him, send Christ now.[41]

No man is born a Christian, but call'd into that state by regeneration.[42]

Our standing is meerely from the grace of God, and therefore let no man ascribe any thing to himselfe.[43]

No man can pray to God, to come, till God be come into him.[44]

How should I pray, that God would come into me, who not onely could not have the Spirit of praying, but not the Spirit of being, not life it selfe, if God were not in me already?[45]

No man can renew himselfe, regenerate himselfe; no man can prepare that worke, no man can begin it, no man can proceed in it of himselfe. The desire and the actual beginning is from the preventing grace of God, and the constant proceeding is from the concomitant, and subsequent, and continuall succeeding grace of God; for there is no conclusive, no consummative grace in this life; no such measure of grace given to any man, as that that man needs no more, or can lose or frustrate none of that.[46]

G od would have *all* men *saved*. And when we call Gods Grace
by other names then Preventing, whether *Assisting* Grace . . .
or *Concomitant* Grace . . . or his *Subsequent* Grace . . . when all is
done still it is the *Preventing Power*, and quality of that Grace, that
did all that in me.[47]

S o then, he comes in Nature, and he returnes in Grace; He comes
in preventing, and returnes in subsequent graces; He comes in
thine understanding, and returnes in thy will; He comes in rectifying
thine actions, and returns in establishing habits; He comes to thee in
zeale, and returnes in discretion; He comes to thee in fervour, and
returnes in perseverance; He comes to thee in thy peregrination, all
the way, and he returns in thy transmigration, at thy last gaspe. So
God comes, and so God returnes.[48]

I f Christ have not beene thus fully in thine heart, before, this is his
comming; entertaine him now: If he have been there, and gone
againe, this is his returning; blesse him for that: And meet him, and
love him, and embrace him, as often as he offers himselfe to thy
soule, in these his Ordinances: Wish every day a Sunday, and every
meale a Sacrament, and every discourse a Homily, and he shall shine
upon thee in all dark wayes, and rectifie thee in all ragged wayes,
and direct thee in all crosse wayes, and stop thee in all doubtfull
wayes, and returne to thee in every corner, and relieve thee in every
danger, and arme thee even against himselfe, by advancing thy
worke.[49]

I f the King come to thy house, thou wilt professe to take it for
an honour, and thou wilt entertaine him; and yet his comming
cannot be without removes, and troubles, and charges to thee. So
when God comes to thee, in his word, or in his actions, in a Sermon,
or in a sicknesse, though his comming dislodge thee, remove thee,
put thee to some inconvenience, in leaving thy bed of sinne, where
thou didst sleepe securely before, yet here is the progresse of the
Holy Ghost, intended to thy soule, that first he comes thus to thee,
and then if thou turne to him, he returnes to thee, and settles himselfe, and dwels in thee.[50]

Riches is the Metaphor, in which, the Holy Ghost hath delighted to expresse God and Heaven to us . . . Gods goodnesse towards us in generall, our Religion in the way, his Grace here, his Glory hereafter, are all represented to us in Riches.[51]

Truly to me, this consideration, That as his mercy is new every morning, so his grace is renewed to me every minute, That it is not by yesterdaies grace that I live now, but that I have . . . My daily bread, my hourely bread, in a continuall succession of his grace, That the eye of God is open upon me, though I winke at his light, and watches over me, though I sleep.[52]

If some King of the earth have so large an extent of Dominion, in North, and South, as that he hath Winter and Summer together in his Dominions, so large an extent East and West, as that he hath day and night together in his Dominions, much more hath God mercy and judgement together: He brought light out of darknesse, not out of a lesser light; he can bring thy Summer out of Winter, though thou have no Spring; though in wayes of fortune, or understanding, or conscience, thou have been benighted till now, wintred and frozen, clouded and eclypsed, damped and benummed, smothered and stupified till now, now God comes to thee, not as in the dawning of the day, not as in the bud of the spring, but as the Sun at noon to illustrate all shadowes, as the sheaves in harvest, to fill all penuries, all occasions invite his mercies, and all times are his seasons.[53]

Grace is the soule of the soule.[54]

Grace accepted, is the infallible earnest Glory.[55]

Repentance

He made us all of earth, and all of red earth. Our earth was red, even when it was in Gods hands: a rednesse that amounts to a shamefastnesse, to a blushing at our own infirmities, is imprinted in us, by Gods hand. For this rednesse, is but a conscience, a guiltinesse of needing a continuall supply, and succession of more, and more grace.[56]

In a word, then is a fit time of finding God, whensoever thy conscience tells thee he calls to thee; for, a rectified conscience is the word of God; If that speake to thee now this minute, now is thy time of finding God.[57]

There is a necessary sadness in this life, but even in this life necessary only so, as Physick is necessary . . . It is . . . a gift of God, a sadnes and sorrow infused by him, and not assumed by our selves upon the crosses of this world; And so it is physick, and it is . . . proper and peculiar physick for that disease, for sinne . . . Hath any man sinned against his God, and come to a true sorrow for that sinne? . . . he hath wash't away that sinne, from his soule; for sorrow is good for nothing else, intended for nothing else, but onely for our sinnes, out of which sadnesse first arose: And then, considered so, this sadnesse is not truly, not properly sadnesse, because it is not so intirely; There is health in the bitternesse of physique; There is joy in the depth of this sadnesse.[58]

Onely consider, that Comfort presumes Sadnesse. Sin does not make you incapable of comfort; but insensiblenesse of sin does. In great buildings, the Turrets are high in the Aire; but the Foundations are deep in the Earth. The Comforts of the Holy Ghost work so, as that only that soule is exalted, which was dejected. As in this place, where you stand, their bodies lie in the earth, whose soules are in heaven; so from this place, you carry away so much of the true comfort of the Holy Ghost, as you have true sorrow, and sadnesse for your sins here.[59]

We have no *warmth* in *our selves*; it is true, but Christ came even in the *winter*: we have *no light* in our selves; it is true, but he came even in the *night*. And now, I appeall to your own *Consciences*, and I aske you all . . . whether any man have made as good use of this light, as he might have done.[60]

It is a divine saying to thy soule, O what a savor of life, unto life, is the death of a beloved sin![61]

The *fruit* of the tree may be preserved and kept, after the tree it selfe is cut down and burnt; The fruit, and off-spring of our sin, calamity, may continue upon us, after God hath removed the guilti-nesse of the sin from us. In the course of civility, our parents goe out before us, in the course of Mortality, our parents die before us; In the course of Gods mercy, it is so too; The sin that begot the calamity, is dead, and gone, the calamity, the child, and off-spring of that sin, is alive and powerfull upon us. But for the most part, as if I would lift *an iron chain* from the ground, if I take but the first linke, and draw up that, the whole chain follows, so if by my repent-ance, I remove the uppermost weight of my load, *my sin*, all the rest, the declaration of the anger of God, and the calamities that I suffer, will follow my sin, and depart from me. But still our first care must be to take off the last weight, the last that comes to our sense, *The sin*.[62]

If thou feel now at this present a little tendernesse in thy heart, a little melting in thy bowels, a little dew in thine eyes, that if thou beest come to know, that thou art a sinner, thou dost therefore presently know thy sinnes . . . But proceed with thy self further, bring this dawning and breake of day to a full light, and this little sparke to a perfect acknowledgement of thy sinnes. Go home, with this spark of Gods Spirit in you, and there looke upon your *Rentalls*, and know your oppressions, and extorsions; looke upon your *shop-bookes*, and know your deceits and falsifications; looke upon your *ward-robes*, and know your excesses; looke upon your *childrens faces*, and know your fornications. Till then, till you come to this scrutiny, this survey, this sifting of the Conscience, if we should cry *peace, peace,* yet there were no peace.[63]

The *reformation* of manners, and bringing men to *repentance,* is a miracle. It is a lesse miracle to raise a man from a *sick bed,* then to hold a man from a *wanton bed,* a litentious bed; lesse to overcome and quench his fever, then to quench his lust. *Joseph* that refused his *mistris* was a greater *miracle* then *Lazarus* raised from the dead.[64]

Let us returne to God, so, as God may looke upon us, clothed in the righteousnesse of Christ; who will not be put on, as a fair gowne, to cover course clothes; but first put off your sinnes, and then put on him; sinnes of the *Time,* sinnes of your *Age,* sinnes of your *Sex,* sinnes of your *Complexion,* sinnes of your *Profession*; put off all; for your Time, your Age, your Sex, your Complexion, your Profession, shall not be damned; but you, you your selves shall. Doe not thinke that your *Sundayes zeale* once a weeke, can burn out all your extortions, and oppressions, and usury, and butchery, and simony, and chambering and wantonnesse practised from Monday to Saterday.[65]

Consider our debts to God, to be our sins, and so we dare not come to a reckoning with him, but we discharge our selves intirely upon our surety, our Saviour Christ Jesus; but yet of that debt we must pay an acknowledgement, an interest (as it were) of praise, for all that we have, and of prayer for all that we would have, and these are our debts to God.[66]

To weep for other things, and not to weep for sin, or if not to teares, yet not to come to that tendernesse, to that melting, to that thawing, that resolving of the bowels which good soules feele; this is a spunge . . . dried up into a Pumice stone; the lightnesse, the hollownesse of a spunge is there still but . . . dried in the Ætnaes of lust, of ambition, of other flames in this world.[67]

[196]

We fall every day, and every day need a new washing; for as from poore tenants, Landlords are not content to receive their rent at the years end, but *quarterly*, or in shorter termes, so from such beggerly and bankrupt soules as ours are, God is not content with an anniversary repentance once a yeare, at *Easter*; but we shall find our rent, our payment heavy enough, if we pay every day, and wash our feet every night for the uncleannesses of that one day.[68]

And we are all delivered from our Debts; for God hath given his word, his co-essentiall word, for us all. And though, (as in other prodigall debts, the Interest exceed the Principall) our Actuall sinnes exceede our Originall, yet God by giving his word for us, hath acquitted all.[69]

Repentance of sins past is nothing but an Audit, a casting up of our accounts, a consideration, a survey, how it stands between God and our soule. And yet, as many men run out of plentifull estates, onely because they are loath to see a list of their debts, to take knowledge how much they are behind hand, or to contract their expences: so we run out of a whole and rich inheritance, the Kingdome of heaven, we profuse and poure out even our own soule, rather then we will cast our eye upon that which is past, rather then we will present a list of our spirituall debts to God, or discover our disease to that Physician, who onely can *Purge us with hyssope, that we may be cleane, and wash us that wee may be whiter then snow.*[70]

This onely is true Repentance . . . To bewayle our sins, and forbeare the sins we have bewayled. Neither alone will serve; which deludes many. Many thinke they doe enough if they repent, and yet proceed in their sin; and many thinke they doe enough, if they forbeare their sin now, though they never repent that which is past; both are illusory, both deceitfull distempers.[71]

Though our sins have hardned us against God, and done a harder work then that, in hardning God against us, yet though we have turned God into a Rock, there is water in that rock, if we strike it, if we solicite it, affect it with our repentance. As in the stone font in the Church, there is water of Baptisme, so in the Corner stone of the Church, Christ Jesus, whom we have hardned against us, there is a tendernesse, there is a Well of water springing up into everlasting life.[72]

A s the *Needle* of a *Sea-compasse*, though it shake long, yet will rest at last, and though it do not look directly, exactly to the North Pole, but have some *variation*, yet, for all that variation, will rest, so, though thy heart have some variations, some deviations, some aberrations from that direct point, upon which it should be bent, which is an absolute conformity of thy will to the will of God, yet, though thou lack something of that, afford thy soul rest: settle thy soule in such an *infallibility*, as this present condition can admit, and beleeve, that God receives glory as well in thy *Repentance*, as in thine *Innocence*, and that the mercy of God in Christ, is as good a pillow to rest thy soule upon *after* a sinne, as the *grace* of God in Christ is a shield, and protection for thy soule, before.[73]

B ring every single sin, as soon as thou committest it, into the presence of thy God, upon those two legs, Confession, and Detestation, and thou shalt see, that as, though an intire Iland stand firm in the Sea, yet a single clod of earth cast into the Sea, is quickly washt into nothing; so, howsoever thine habituall, and customary, and concatenated sins, sin enwrapped and complicated in sin, sin entrenched and barricadoed in sin, sin screwed up, and riveted with sin, may stand out, and wrastle even with the mercies of God, in the blood of Christ Jesus; yet if thou bring every single sin into the sight of God, it will be but as a clod of earth, but as a graine of dust in the Ocean.[74]

A nd though the good opinion of good men, by good ways, be worth our study, yet popular applause, and the voice of inconsiderate men, is too cheape a price to set our selves at.[75]

And, who shall dare to aske then when I am
Dy'd scarlet in the blood of that pure Lambe,
Whether that colour, which is scarlet then,
Were black or white before in eyes of men?
When thou rememb'rest what sins thou didst finde
Amongst those many friends now left behinde,
And seest such sinners as they are, with thee
Got thither by repentance, Let it bee
Thy wish to wish all there, to wish them cleane;
Wish *him a David, her a Magdalen.*[76]

Sleep with cleane hands, either kept cleane all day, by integrity; or washed cleane, at night, by repentance.[77]

The Holy Ghost, suffers not me to impute to my selfe those sinnes, which I have truly repented. The over-tendernesse of a bruised and a faint conscience may impute sinne to it selfe, when it is discharged; And a seared and obdurate Conscience may impute none, when it abounds; If the Holy Ghost work, he rectifies both.[78]

In an obdurate conscience that feeles no sin, the Devill glories most, but in the over-tender conscience he practises most; That is his triumphant, but this is his militant Church; That is his Sabbath, but this is his six dayes labour; In the obdurate he hath induced a security, in the scrupulous and over-tender he is working for desperation.[79]

Thou must not rest upon the testimony and suggestions of thine owne conscience . . . thou must not rest in that vulgar saying . . . As long as mine owne Conscience stands right, I care not what all the world say. Thou must care what the world says, and study to have the approbation and testimony of good men. . . . Thine owne conscience is not enough, but thou must satisfie the world, and have . . . good men must thinke thee good.[80]

Many times we are better for (the Serpent's) tentations. My discerning a storm, makes me put on a cloak. My discerning a tentation, makes me see my weaknesse, and fly to my strength. Nay, I am somtimes the safer, and the readier for a victory, by having been overcome by him. The sense, and the remorse of a sin, after I have fallen into it, puts me into a better state, and establishes better conditions between God and me then were before, when I felt no tentations to sin.[81]

The Sun shall set, and have a to morrows resurrection; Herbs shall have a winter death, and a springs resurrection; Thy body shall have a long winters night, and then a resurrection; Onely thy sins buried in the wounds of thy Saviour, shall never have resurrection.[82]

Restoration

Mercy is Gods right hand, with that God gives all; Faith is mans right hand, with that man takes all.[83]

God made Sun and Moon to distinguish seasons, and day, and night, and we cannot have the fruits of the earth but in their seasons: But God hath made no decree to distinguish the seasons of his mercies; In paradise, the fruits were ripe, the first minute, and in heaven it is alwaies Autumne, his mercies are ever in their maturity.[84]

If I buy of the Kings land, I must pay for it in the Kings money; I have no Myne, nor Mint of mine owne; If I would have any thing from God, I must give him that which is his owne for it, that is, his mercy; And this is to give God his mercy, To give God thanks for his mercy, To give all to his mercy, And to acknowledge, that if my works be acceptable to him, nay if my very faith be acceptable to him, it is not because my works, no nor my faith hath any proportion of equivalencie in it, or is worth the least flash of joy, or the least spangle of glory in Heaven, in it self, but because God in his mercy, onely of his mercy, meerely for the glory of his mercy, hath past such a Covenant . . . Beleeve this, and doe this, and thou shalt live, not for thy deed sake, nor not for thy faith sake, but for my mercy sake.[85]

Nothing exalts Gods goodnesse towards us, more then this, that he multiplies the meanes of his mercy to us, so, as that no man can say, *once* I remember I might have been saved, *once* God called unto mee, *once* hee opened mee a doore, a passage into heaven, but I neglected *that*, went not in then, and God never came more. No doubt, God hath come often to that doore since, and knocked, and staid at that doore; And if I knew who it were that said this, I should not doubt to make that suspitious soule see, that God is at that doore *now*.[86]

To finde a languishing wretch in a sordid corner, not onely in a penurious fortune, but in an oppressed conscience, His eyes under a diverse suffocation, smothered with smoake, and smothered with teares, His eares estranged from all salutations, and visits, and all sounds, but his owne sighes, and the stormes and thunders and earthquakes of his owne despaire, To enable this man to open his eyes, and see that Christ Jesus stands before him, and sayes, *Behold and see, if ever there were any sorrow, like my sorrow*, and my sorrow is over-come, why is not thine? To open this mans eares, and make him heare that voyce that sayes, *I was dead, and am alive, and behold I live for evermore, Amen*; and so mayest thou; To bow downe those Heavens, and bring them into his sad Chamber, To set Christ Jesus before him, to out-sigh him, out-weepe him, out-bleed him, out-dye him, To transferre all the fasts, all the scornes, all the scourges, all the nailes, all the speares of Christ Jesus upon him, and so, making him the Crucified man in the sight of the Father, because all the actions, and passions of the Son, are appropriated to him, and made his so intirely, as if there were never a soule created but his, To enrich this poore soule, to comfort this sad soule so, as that he shall beleeve, and by beleeving finde all Christ to be his.[87]

Thou hast made me, And shall thy worke decay?
Repaire me now, for now mine end doth haste,
I runne to death, and death meets me as fast,
And all my pleasures are like yesterday,
I dare not move my dimme eyes any way,
Despaire behind, and death before doth cast
Such terrour, and my feeble flesh doth waste
By sinne in it, which it t'wards hell doth weigh;
Onely thou art above, and when towards thee
By thy leave I can looke, I rise againe
But our old subtle foe so tempteth me,
That not one houre my selfe I can sustaine,
Thy Grave may wing me to prevent his art,
And thou like Adamant draw mine iron heart.[88]

Oh my black Soule! Now thou are summoned
By sicknesse, deaths herald, and champion;

Yet grace, if thou repent, thou canst not lacke;
But who shall give thee that grace to beginne?
Oh make thy selfe with holy mourning blacke,
And red with blushing, as thou art with sinne;
Or wash thee in Christs blood, which hath this might
That being red, it dyes red soules to white.[89]

All Lent is *Easter Eve*; And though the *Eve* be a *Fasting Day*, yet the *Eve* is *halfe-holiday* too. *God*, by our *Ministery*, would so exercise you in a spirituall *Fast*, in a sober consideration of sinne, and the sad Consequences thereof, as that in the *Eve* you might see the *holy day*; in the *Lent*, your *Easter*; in the sight of your sinnes, the cheerefulnesse of his good will towards you.[90]

From how little a spark, how great a fire? From how little a beginning, how great a proceeding? She desired but the hem of his garment, and had all him.[91]

He that remembers Gods former blessings, concludes infallibly upon his future.[92]

As long as I consider that I have such a soule, capable of Grace and Glory, I cannot despaire.[93]

THE WORK OF CHRIST

Incarnation

⁹ T was much, that man was made like God before,
  But, that God should be made like man, much more.[1]

I *mmanuel* is God with us; it is not we with God: God seeks us, comes to us, before wee to him.[2]

S o *God loved the world that he gave his Son*: if he had not lov'd us first, we had never had his Son.[3]

C ould it ever have fallen into any mans heart, to have prayed to the Father, that his Son might take our Nature and dye, and rise again, and settle a course upon earth, for our salvation, if this had not first risen in the purpose of God himself? Would any man ever have solicited or prayed him to proceed thus? It was . . . out of (God's) owne goodnesse.[4]

W hen man was at worst, he was at a high price; man being fallen, yet then, in that undervalue, he cost God his own and onely Son, before he could have him. Neither became the Son of God capable of redeeming man, by any lesse, or any other way, then by becomming man. The Redeemer must be better then he whom he is to redeeme; and yet, he must abase himselfe to as low a nature as his; to his nature; else he could not redeeme him. God was aliened from man, and yet God must become man, to recover man.[5]

K ings pardon, but he bore our punishment.
And *Jacob* came cloth'd in vile harsh attire
But to supplant, and with gainfull intent:
God cloth'd himselfe in vile mans flesh, that so
Hee might be weake enough to suffer woe.[6]

T he obedience of the Son, was as large as the love of the Father,
Hee came to save all the world, and he did save all the world;
God would have all men, and Christ did save all men.[7]

S alvation to all that will is nigh,
That All, which alwayes is All every where,
Which cannot sinne, and yet all sinnes must beare,
Which cannot die, yet cannot chuse but die,
Loe, faithfull Virgin, yeelds himselfe to lye
In prison, in thy wombe; and though he there
Can take no sinne, nor thou give, yet he'will weare
Taken from thence, flesh, which deaths force may trie.
Ere by the spheares time was created, thou
Wast in his minde, who is thy Sonne, and Brother,
Whom thou conceiv'st, conceiv'd; yea thou art now
Thy Makers maker, and thy Fathers mother,
Thou'hast light in darke; and shutst in little roome,
Immensity cloysterd in thy deare wombe.[8]

A nd therefore he made *Christ*, God and Man, in one person,
Creature and Creator together; One greater than the *Sera-
phim*, and yet lesse then a worme; Soveraigne to all *nature*, and
yet subject to *naturall* infirmities; Lord *of life*, *life* it selfe, and yet
prisoner to *Death*; Before, and beyond all measures of *Time*, and yet
Born at so many *moneths*, *Circumcised* at so many *days*, *Crucified*
at so many *years*, *Rose* againe at so many *Houres*; How sure did
God make himselfe of a companion in Christ, who united himselfe,
in his godhead, so inseparably to him, as that that Godhead left not
that body, then when it lay dead in the grave, but staid with it then,
as closely, as when he wrought his greatest miracles.[9]

C hrist is so made of God and Man, as that he is Man still, for all the glory of the Deity, and God still, for all the infirmity of the manhood . . . The Godhead bursts out, as the Sun out of a cloud, and shines forth gloriously in miracles, even the raysing of the dead, and the humane nature is submitted to contempt and to torment, even to the admitting of death in his own bosome . . . but still, both he that rayses the dead, and he that dyes himself, is one Christ, his is the glory of the Miracles, and the contempt and torment is his too.[10]

G od comes to us without any purpose of departing from us againe; For the Spirit of life that God breathed into man, that departs from man in death; but when God had assumed the nature of man, the God-head never parted from that nature; no, not in death; When Christ lay dead in the grave, the God-head remained united to that body and that soule, which were dis-united in themselves; God was so united to man, as that he was with man, when man was not man, in the state of death. So when the Spirit of God hath invested, compassed thy soule, and made it his by those testimonies, that Spirit establishes it in a kinde of assurance that he will never leave it.[11]

T hat God and Man, are so met, is a signe to mee, that God, and I shall never bee parted.[12]

The Representative Man

A nd this is the mystery of the Incarnation. For since the devil has so surprized us all, as to take mankinde all in one lump, in a corner, in *Adams* loynes, and poysoned us all there in the fountain, in the roote, Christ, to deliver us as intirely, took all mankinde upon him, and so took every one of us, and the nature, and the infirmities, and the sins, and the punishment of every singular man. So that the same pretence which the devill hath against every one of us, you are mine, for you sinned in *Adam*, we have also for our discharge, we are delivered, for we paid our debt in Christ Jesus.[13]

God tooke into his mercie, all mankinde in one person: As intire-ly, as all mankinde was in *Adam*, all mankinde was in *Christ*; and as the *seale of the Serpent* is in all, by *originall sinne*, so the *seale* of God, *Christ Jesus*, is on us *all*, by his assuming our *nature*. Christ Jesus tooke our souls, and our bodies, our whole nature; and as no Leper, no person, how infectiously soever he be diseased in his body, can say, surely Christ never tooke this body, this Leprosie, this pestilence, this rottennesse, so no Leprous soule must say, Christ never tooke this pride, this adultery, this murder upon him-self; he sealed us all in *soule* and *body*, when he tooke *both*, and though both dye, the *soule in sin* daily, the *body in sicknesse*, per-chance this day, yet he shall afford a resurrection to both, to the *soule* here, to the *body* hereafter, for his seale is upon both. [14]

The Nativity

The manger-cradled infant, God below. [15]

*I*mmensitie cloysterd in thy deare wombe,
Now leaves his welbelov'd imprisonment,
There he hath made himselfe to his intent
Weake enough, now into our world to come;
But Oh, for thee, for him, hath th'Inne no roome?
Yet lay him in this stall, and from the Orient,
Starres, and wisemen will travell to prevent
Th'effect of *Herod*s jealous generall doome;
Seest thou, my Soule, with thy faiths eyes, how he
Which fils all place, yet none holds him, doth lye?
Was not his pity towards thee wondrous high,
That would have need to be pittied by thee?
Kisse him, and with him into Egypt goe,
With his kinde mother, who partakes thy woe. [16]

A ll times and all Generations before time was were Christs day; but yet he cals this coming in the flesh especially his day, because this day was a holy Equinoctial, and made the day of the Jews and the day of the Gentiles equal.[17]

F rom this day, in which, the first stone of that building, the Church, was laid, (for, though the foundations of the Church were laid in Eternity, yet, that was under ground, the first stone above ground, that is, the manifestation of Gods purpose to the world was laide this day, in Christs birth).[18]

T hough the Church doe now call Twelf-day Epiphany, because upon that day Christ was manifested to the Gentiles, in those Wise men who came then to worship him, yet the Ancient Church called this day, (the day of Christs birth) the Epiphany, because this day Christ was manifested to the world, by being born this day. Every manifestation of Christ to the world, to the Church, to a particular soule, is an Epiphany, a Christmas-day.[19]

O nely to Christ Jesus, *the fulnesse of time* was at his birth; not because he also had not a painfull life to passe through, but because the work of our redemption was an intire work, and all that Christ said, or did, or suffered, concurred to our salvation, as well his mothers swathing him in little clouts, as *Josephs* shrowding him in a funerall sheete; as well his cold lying in the Manger, as his cold dying upon the Crosse; as well the *puer natus*, as the *consummatum est*; as well his birth, as his death is said to have been *the fulnesse of time*.[20]

T he whole life of Christ was a continuall Passion; others die Martyrs, but Christ was born a Martyr. He found a *Golgotha*, (where he was crucified) even in Bethlem, where he was born; For, to his tendernesse then, the strawes were almost as sharp as the thornes after; and the Manger as uneasie at first, as his Crosse at last. His birth and his death were but one continuall act, and his

Christmas-day and his Good Friday, are but the evening and morning of one and the same day.[21]

The Sacrifice for Sin

That Crosse, our joy, and griefe, where nailes did tye
  That All, which alwayes was all, every where,
Which could not sinne, and yet all sinnes did beare;
Which could not die, yet could not chuse but die.[22]

God made all Mankinde of one blood, and with one blood, the blood of his Son, he bought all Mankinde again.[23]

His name of *Jesus*, a Saviour, he had by purchase, and that purchase cost him his bloud.[24]

Loe, where condemned hee
  Beares his owne crosse, with paine, yet by and by
When it beares him, he must beare more and die;
Now thou art lifted up, draw mee to thee,
And at thy death giving such liberall dole,
Moyst, with one drop of thy blood, my dry soule.[25]

Jesus is . . . not only a bringer, an applier, a worker of our salvation, but he is the author of the very decree of our salvation, as well as of the execution of that Decree: there was no salvation before him, there was no salvation intended in the book of Life, but in him . . . for it is not only his person, but it is his very righteousness that saves us.[26]

God found me nothing, and of that nothing made me; *Adam* left me worse then God found me, worse then nothing, the child of wrath, corrupted with the leaven of Originall sin; Christ Jesus found

[209]

me worse then *Adam* left me, not onely sowred with Originall, but spotted, and gangrened, and dead, and buried, and putrified in actual and habitual sins, and yet in that state redeemed me.[27]

As one cruell Emperour wished all mankinde in one man, that hee might have beheaded mankinde at one blow, so God gathered the whole nature of sinne into one Christ, that by one *action*, one *passion*, *sin*, all *sin*, the whole nature of sinne might bee overcome.[28]

What if this present were the worlds last night?
  Marke in my heart, O Soule, where thou dost dwell,
The picture of Christ crucified, and tell
Whether his countenance can thee affright,
Teares in his eyes quench the amasing light,
Blood fills his frownes, which from his pierc'd head fell
And can that tongue adjudge thee unto hell,
Which pray'd forgivenesse for his foes fierce spight?[29]

And for sin it self, I would not, I do not extenuate my sin, but let me have fallen, not seven times a day, but seventy seven times a minute, yet what are my sins, to all those sins that were upon Christ? The sins of all men, and all women, and all children, the sins of all Nations, all the East and West, and all the North and South, the sins of all times and ages, of Nature, of Law, of Grace, the sins of all natures, sins of the body, and sins of the mind, the sins of all growth, and all extentions, thoughts, and words, and acts, and habits, and delight, and glory, and contempt, and the very sin of boasting, nay of our belying our selves in sin; All these sins, past, present and future, were at once upon Christ, and in that depth of sin, mine are but a drop to his Ocean; In that treasure of sin, mine are but single money to his Talent.[30]

A ll sins, of all ages, all sexes, all places, al times, all callings, sins heavy in their substance, sins aggravated by their circumstances, all kinds of sins, and all particular sins of every kind, were upon him, upon Christ Jesus.[31]

A s my mortality, and my hunger, and thirst, and wearinesse, and all my *naturall infirmities* are his, so *my sins* are his sins.[32]

T hough any death had beene an incomprehensible ransome, for the Lord of life to have given, for the children of death, yet he refused not the death of the Crosse.[33]

I f the treasure of the blood of Christ Jesus be not sufficient, Lord what addition can I find, to match them, to piece out them! And if it be sufficient of it selfe, what addition need I seek? Other mens crosses are not mine, other mens merits cannot save me.[34]

T o have once been nothing, and now to be co-heires with the Son of God: That Son of God, who if there had been but one soule to have been saved, would have dyed for that; nay, if all soules had been to be saved, but one, and that that onely had sinned, he would not have contented himselfe with all the rest, but would have dyed for that. And there is the goodnesse, the liberality of our King, our God, our Christ, our Jesus.[35]

K now then, that Christ Jesus hath done enough for the salvation of all; but know too, that if there had been no other name written in the booke of life but thine, he would have dyed for Thee. Of those which were given him, he lost none; but if there had been none given him, but Thou, rather then have lost Thee, he would have given the same price for Thee, that he gave for the whole world.[36]

As Christ's merit, and satisfaction, is not too narrow for all the world, so is it not too large for any one Man; Infinite worlds might have been saved by it, if infinite worlds had been created; And, if there were no more Names in the book of life, but thine, all the Merit of Christ were but enough to save thy one sinfull soule, which could not have been redeemed, though alone, at any lesse price, then his death.[37]

And herein is the mercy of God, in the merits of Christ, a sea of mercie, that as the Sea retaines no impression of the Ships that passe in it, (for Navies make no path in the Sea) so when we put out into the boundlesse Sea of the blood of Christ Jesus, by which onely wee have reconciliation to God, there remaines no record against us; for God hath cancelled that record which he kept, and that which Satan kept God hath nailed to the Crosse of his Son.[38]

His death is delivered to us, as a *writing*, but not a writing onely in the nature of a peece of *Evidence*, to plead our inheritance by, but writing in the nature of a Copy, to learne by; It is not onely given us to reade, but to write over, and practise; Not onely to tell us *what he* did, but *how we* should do so too.[39]

To hate nothing in a sinner, but his sinne, is a great degree of perfection; God is that perfection; he hates nothing in thee but thy sinne; and that sinne he hath taken upon himself, and sees it not in thee.[40]

That day when Christ dyed, I, and you, and all that shall be saved, suffered, dyed, and were crucified, and in Christ Jesus satisfied God the Father, for those infinite sins which we had committed: And now, Second death, which is damnation, hath no more title to any of the true members of his mysticall body, then corruption upon naturall, or violent death, could have upon the members of his naturall body.[41]

We shall see the death of Death it self in the death of Christ. As we could not be cloathed at first, in Paradise, till some Creatures were dead, (for we were cloathed in beasts skins) so we cannot be cloathed in Heaven, but in his garment who dyed for us.[42]

All Heaven purchased by Death.[43]

For, if I could dye a thousand times for Christ, this were nothing, if Christ had not dyed for me before.[44]

Resurrection

Sleep sleep old Sun, thou canst not have repast
As yet, the wound thou took'st on friday last;
Sleepe then, and rest; The world may beare thy stay,
A better Sun rose before thee to day,
Who, not content to'enlighten all that dwell
On earths face, as thou, enlightned hell,
And made the darke fires languish in that vale,
As, at thy present here, our fires grow pale.[45]

There I should see a Sunne, by rising set,
And by that setting endlesse day beget;
But that Christ on this Crosse, did rise and fall,
Sinne had eternally benighted all.
Yet dare I'almost be glad, I do not see
That spectacle of too much weight for mee.
Who sees Gods face, that is selfe life, must dye;
What a death were it then to see God dye;
It made his owne Lieutenant Nature shrinke,
It made his footstoole crack, and the Sunne winke.
Could I behold those hands which span the Poles,
And tune all spheares at once peirc'd with those holes?[46]

First, the dignity of the Resurrection, marvaile at nothing so much, as at this, nothing is so marvailous, so wonderfull as this.[47]

The resurrection in it self, Christ's resurrection . . . even after it was actually accomplished, was still a mystery, out of the compasse of reason.[48]

For our resurrection shall not be like his . . . All we shall be raised from the dead, onely Christ arose from the dead. We shall be raised by a power working upon us, he rose by a power inherent, and resident in himselfe.[49]

We consider ordinarily three Resurrections: A spiritual Resurrection, a Resurrection from sinne, by Grace in the Church; A temporall Resurrection, a Resurrection from trouble, and calamity in the world; And an eternall Resurrection, a Resurrection after which no part of man shall die, or suffer againe, the Resurrection into Glory.[50]

When I beleeve God in Christ, dead, and risen againe according to the Scriptures, I have nothing else to beleeve.[51]

The Day of Salvation

O strong Ramme, which hast batter'd heaven for mee,
  Mild lambe, which with thy blood, hast mark'd the path;
Bright torch, which shin'st, that I the way may see,
Oh, with thy owne blood quench thy owne just wrath,
And if thy holy Spirit, my Muse did raise,
Deign at my hands this crown of prayer and praise.[52]

The time then of the Gospel is the time of finding.[53]

Christ is come to call sinners, onely sinners, all sinners.[54]

Mercy is his first-born. *His Mercy is new every morning*, saith the Prophet; not onely *every day*, but *as soon as it is day*. Trace God *in thy self*, and thou shalt find it so.[55]

His eternall birth in heaven is unexpressible, where he was born without a mother; His birth on earth is unexpressible too, where he was born without a father; but thou shalt feele the joy of his third birth in thy soul, most inexpressible this day, where he is born this day (if thou wilt) without father or mother; that is, without any former, or any other reason then his own meere goodnesse that should beget that love in him towards thee, and without any matter or merit in thee which should enable thee to conceive him. He had a heavenly birth, by which he was the eternall Son of God, and without that he had not been a person able to redeem thee; He had a humane birth, by which he was the Son of *Mary*, and without that he had not been sensible in himself of thine infirmities, and necessities; but, this day (if thou wilt) he hath a spirituall birth in thy soul, without which, both his divine, and his humane birth are utterly unprofitable to thee, and thou art no better then if there had never been Son of God in heaven, nor Son of *Mary* upon earth.[56]

We use to note three Advents, three commings of Christ. An Advent of Humiliation, when he came in the flesh; an Advent of glory, when he shall come to judgement; and between these an Advent of grace, in his gracious working in us, in this life; and this middlemost Advent of Christ, is the Advent of the Holy Ghost . . . when Christ works in us, the Holy Ghost comes to us.[57]

M oyst *with one drop of thy blood, my dry soule,*
  Shall (though she now be in extreme degree
Too stony hard, and yet too fleshly,) bee
Freed by that drop, from being starv'd, hard, or foule.
And life, by this death abled, shall controule
Death, whom thy death slue; nor shall to mee
Feare of first or last death, bring miserie,
If in thy little booke my name thou enroule,
Flesh in that long sleep is not putrified,
But, made that there, of which, and for which 'twas;
Nor can by other meanes be glorified.
May then sinnes sleep, and deaths soone from me passe,
That wak't from both, I againe risen may
Salute the last, and everlasting day.[58]

T he cheerefull feast of our Adoption, in which, the Holy Ghost
  convaying the Son of God to us, enables us to be the Sons of
God, and to cry Abba, Father.[59]

T herefore we consider againe, that as God came long agoe, six
  thousand years agoe, in nature, when we were created in
Adam, and then in nature returned to us, in the generation of our
Parents: so our Saviour Christ Jesus came to us long agoe, sixteene
hundred yeares agoe, in grace, and yet in grace returnes to us, as
often as he assembles us, in these holy Convocations. He came to us
then, as the Wisemen came to him, with treasure, and gifts, and
gold, and incense, and myrrhe; As having an ambition upon the
soules of men, he came with that abundant treasure to purchase us.
And as to them who live upon the Kings Pension, it is some comfort
to heare that the Exchequer is full, that the Kings moneyes are come
in: so is it to us, to know that there is enough in Gods hands, paid
by his Son, for the discharge of all our debts; He gave enough for us
all at that comming; But it is his returning to us, that applyes to us,
and derives upon us in particular, the benefit of this generall satisfaction. When he returns to us in the dispensation and distribution
of his graces, in his Word and Sacraments; When he calls upon us to
come to the receipt; When the greater the summe is, the gladder he

is of our comming, that where sinne abounds, grace might abound too.[60]

If you deale so with your soules, as with your bodies, and as you cloath your selves with your best habits to day, but returne againe to your ordinary apparell to morrow: so for this day, or this houre, you devest the thought of your sins, but returne after to your vomit . . . you have not beene truly in this place, for your hearts have been visiting your profits, or pleasures; you have not beene here with one accord, you have not truly and sincerely joyned with the Communion of Saints; Christ hath sent no Comforter to you this day, neither will he send any, till you be better prepared for him. But if you have brought your sins hither in your memory, and leave them here in the blood of your Saviour, alwaies flowing in his Church, and ready to receive them, if you be come to that heavenly knowledge, that there is no comfort but in him, and in him abundant consolation, then you are this day capable of this great Legacy, this knowledge, which is all the Christian Religion, *That Christ is in the Father, and you in him, and he in you.*[61]

To hinder the bloud of Christ Jesus, not to suffer that bloud to flow as far, as it will, to deny the mercy of God in Christ, to any sinner, whatsoever, upon any pretence, whatsoever, this is to be offended in Christ, to be scandalized with his Gospel . . . Deny no man the benefit of Christ; Blesse thou the Lord, praise him, and magnifie him, for that which hee hath done for thee, and beleeve, that he means as well to others, as to thee.[62]

Christ hath excommunicated no Nation, no shire, no house, no man: Hee gives none of his Ministers leave to say to any man, thou art not Redeemed, he gives no wounded nor afflicted conscience leave, to say it to selfe, I am not Redeemed.[63]

Salvation is a more extensive thing, and more communicable, then sullen cloystrall, that have walled salvation in a monastery, or in an ermitage, take it to be; or then the over-valuers of their own *purity*, and righteousnesse, which have determined salvation in themselves, take it to be . . . Salvation is the possession of such endowments, as *naturally* invite all, to the prosecution of that, which is exposed and offered to all; that we all labour here, that we may all stand hereafter, *before the Throne, and before the Lambe, clothed in white robes.*[64]

Till you come to Christ *you are without God*, as the Apostle says to the *Ephesians*: and when you goe beyond Christ, to Traditions of men, you are without God too.[65]

We dare not say, that any man is sav'd without Christ; we dare say, that none can be saved, that hath received that light, and hath not beleev'd in him.[66]

Let us embrace the way which God hath given us, which is, the knowledge of his Sonne, *Christ Jesus*: what other way God may take with others . . . let us not inquire too curiously, determine too peremptorily, pronounce too uncharitably: God be blessed, for his declaring his good-will towards *us*, and *his will be done* his way upon others.[67]

In a flat Map, there goes no more, to make West East, though they be distant in an extremity, but to paste that flat Map upon a round body, and then West and East are all one. In a flat soule, in a dejected conscience, in a troubled spirit, there goes no more to the making of that trouble, peace, then to apply that trouble to the body of the Merits, to the body of the Gospel of Christ Jesus, and conforme thee to him, and thy West is East, thy Trouble of spirit is Tranquillity of spirit.[68]

Never consider the judgement of God for sin alone, but in the company of the mercies of Christ. It is but the hissing of the Serpent, and the whispering of Satan, when he surprises thee in a melancholy midnight of dejection of spirit, and layes thy sins before thee then; Looke not upon thy sins so inseparably, that thou canst not see Christ too: Come not to a confession to God, without consideration of the promises of his Gospel.[69]

If a man in exchange of his heart receive Christ Jesus himselfe, he can no more die then Christ Jesus himselfe can die.[70]

To call him Lord, is to contemplate his Kingdome of power, to feele his Kingdome of grace, to wish his Kingdome of glory.[71]

Reconciliation is a redintegration, a renewing of a former friendship, that hath been interrupted and broken.[72]

We were contracted to Christ in our Election, married to him in our Baptism, in the Grave we are bedded with him, and in the Resurrection estated and put into possession of his Kingdom.[73]

THE BODY OF CHRIST

The Catholic Church

C hrist was never so alone, but that if he were not in the Church, the Church was in him; All Christians were in him, As all Men were in *Adam*.[1]

C hrist received no profit from the Church, and yet he gave him- selfe for it; and he stayes with it to the end of the world.[2]

T he office of the Holy Ghost is to gather, to establish, to illu- mine, to governe that Church which the Son of God, from whom together with the Father, the Holy Ghost proceeds, hath pur- chased with his blood.[3]

I n him who was truly Head of the Church, the whole Church was; Christ alone, was a Congregation, he was the Catholique Church.[4]

T he Holy Ghost is a Dove, and the Dove couples, paires, is not alone; Take heed of singular, of schismatical opinions; and what is more singular, more schismaticall, then when all Religion is confined in one mans breast? The Dove is . . . a sociable creature, and not singular; and the Holy Ghost is that; And Christ is a Sheep . . . they flock together: Embrace thou those truths, which the whole flock of Christ Jesus, the whole Christian Church, hath from the beginning acknowledged to be truths, and truths necessary to salva- tion.[5]

S how me dear Christ, thy Spouse, so bright and clear.
　What! is it she, which on the other shore
Goes richly painted? Or which rob'd and tore
Laments and mournes in Germany and here?
Sleepes she a thousand, then peepes up one year?
Is she selfe truth and errs? now new, now outwore?
Doth she, and did she, and shall she evermore
On one, on seaven, or on no hill appeare?
Dwells she with us, or like adventuring knights
First travaile we to seeke and then make Love?
Betray kind husband thy spouse to our sights,
And let myne amorous soule court thy mild Dove,
Who is most trew, and pleasing to thee, then
When she'is embrac'd and open to most men.[6]

The Church loves the name of Catholique; and it is a glorious, and an harmonious name; Love thou those things wherein she is Catholique, and wherein she is harmonious, that is . . . Those universall, and fundamentall doctrines, which in all Christian ages, and in all Christian Churches, have beene agreed by all to be necessary to salvation; and then thou art a true Catholique.[7]

God loves not singularity: God bindes us to nothing, that was never said but by one: As God loves Sympathy, God loves Symphony; God loves a compassion and fellow-feeling of others miseries, that is Sympathy, and God loves Harmony, and fellow-beleeving of others Doctrines, that is Symphony: No one man alone makes a Church; no one Church alone makes a Catholique Church.[8]

We may be sure, that whatsoever God hath promised to his Church . . . he will performe, re-performe, multiply performances thereof upon us.[9]

Beloved, there are some things in which all Religions agree; The worship of God, The holinesse of life; And therefore, if when I study this holinesse of life, and fast, and pray, and submit my selfe to discreet, and medicinall mortifications, for the subduing of my body, any man will say, this is Papisticall, Papists doe this, it is a blessed Protestation, and no man is the lesse a Protestant, nor the worse a Protestant for making it, Men and brethren, I am a Papist, that is, I will fast and pray as much as any Papist, and enable my selfe for the service of my God, as seriously, as sedulously, as laboriously as any Papist. So, if when I startle and am affected at a blasphemous oath, as at a wound upon my Saviour, if when I avoyd the conversation of those men, that prophane the Lords day, any other will say to me, This is Puritanicall, Puritans do this, It is a blessed Protestation, and no man is the lesse a Protestant, nor the worse a Protestant for making it, Men and Brethren, I am a Puritan, that is, I wil endeavour to be pure, as my Father in heaven is pure, as far as any Puritan.[10]

Beloved, it is a wanton thing for any Church, in spirituall matters, to play with small errors; to tolerate, or wink at small abuses, as though it should be always in her power to extinguish them when she would. It is Christs counsell to his Spouse, that is, the Church . . . Take us the little foxes, for they destroy the Vine; though they seeme but little, and able to doe little harme, yet they grow bigger and bigger every day; and therefore stop errors before they become heresies, and erroneous men before they become formall heretiques.[11]

For all this separation, Christ Jesus is amongst us all, and in his time, will break downe this wall too, these differences amongst Christians, and make us all glad of that name, the name of Christians, without affecting in our selves, or inflicting upon others, the other names of envy, and subdivision.[12]

God hath made all *mankinde* of one *blood* and all *Christians* of one *calling*.[13]

Christ gave the Apostles no Scriptures, but he gave them the holy Ghost in stead of Scriptures; But to us, who are weaker, hee hath given both, The holy Ghost in the Scriptures; and, if we neglect either, we have neither; If we trust to a private spirit, and call that the holy Ghost, without Scripture, or to the Scriptures without the holy Ghost, that is, without him, there, where he hath promised to be, in his Ordinance, in his Church, we have not the seale of that Promise, the holy Ghost.[14]

All ends in this; To fear God, is to adhere to him, in his way, as he hath dispensed and notified himself to us; that is, as God is manifested in Christ, in the Scriptures, and applied to us out of those Scriptures, by the Church: not to rest in Nature without God, nor in God without Christ, nor in Christ without the Scriptures, nor in our private interpretation of Scripture, without the Church.[15]

The Holy Ghost is sent to Teach; he teaches by speaking; he speaks by his Ordinance, and Institution in his Church. All knowledge, and all zeale, that is not kindled by him, by the Holy Ghost, and kindled here, at first is all smoke, and then all flame; Zeale without the Holy Ghost, is at first, cloudy ignorance, all smoke; and after, all crackling and clambering flame, Schismaticall rage, and distemper.[16]

If God wrought by a pattern, and writ by a copie, and proceeded by a precedent, doe thou so too. Never say, There is no Church without error: therefore I will be bound by none; but frame a Church of mine owne, or be a Church to my selfe. What greater injustice, then to propose no Image, no pattern to thy selfe to imitate; and yet propose thy selfe for a pattern, for an Image to be adored?[17]

If I come to extemporall prayer, and extemporall preaching, I shall come to an extemporall faith, and extemporall religion; and then I must looke for an extemporall Heaven, a Heaven to be made for me; for to that Heaven which belongs to the Catholique Church, I shall never come, except I go by the way of the Catholique Church, by former Idea's, former examples, former patterns, To beleeve according to ancient beliefes, to pray according to ancient formes, to preach according to former meditations. God does nothing, man does nothing well, without these Idea's, these retrospects, this recourse to pre-conceptions, pre-deliberations.[18]

That which Christ says to the Church it selfe, the Church says to every soule in the Church: *Goe thy way forth, by the footsteps of the flocke*; Associate thy selfe to the true shepheard, and true sheep of Christ Jesus, and stray not towards *Idolatrous Chappels*, nor towards *schismaticall Conventicles, but goe by the footsteps of the flock.*[19]

The *Church* is *Catholike, universall,* so are all her *Actions; All* that she does, belongs to *all.* When she *baptizes a child,* that action concernes mee; for that child is thereby connected to that *Head* which is my *Head* too, and engraffed into that *body,* wherefore I am a *member.* And when she *buries a Man,* that action concernes me: All *mankinde* is of one *Author,* and is one *volume;* when one Man Dies, one *Chapter* is not *torne* out of the *booke,* but *translated* into a better *language;* and every *Chapter* must be so *translated;* God emploies several *translators;* some peeces are translated by *age,* some by *sicknesse,* some by *warre,* some by *justice;* but *Gods* hand is in every *translation;* and his hand shall binde up all our scattered leaves againe, for that *Librarie* where every *booke* shall lie open to one another.[20]

The House of God

Religion is not a *melancholy;* the spirit of God is not a *dampe;* the Church is not a *grave:* it is a *fold,* it is an *Arke,* it is a *net,* it is a *city,* it is a *kingdome,* not onely a house, but a house that hath *many mansions* in it.[21]

These walles are holy, because the *Saints* of *God* meet here within these walls to glorifie him. But yet these places are not onely consecrated and sanctified by your comming; but to bee sanctified also for your comming; that so, as the Congregation sanctifies the place, the place may sanctifie the Congregation too. They must accompany one another; holy persons and holy places.[22]

The house of God, into which we enter by Baptisme, is the house of Prayer; And, as out of the Arke, whosoever swam best, was not saved by his swimming, no more is any morall man, out of the Church, by his praying: He that swomme in the flood, swomme but into more and more water; he that prayes out of the Church, prayes but into more and more sin, because he doth not establish his prayer in that, Grant this for our Lord and Saviour Christ Jesus sake. It is true then, that these holy ones, whose prayer is acceptable, are those of the Christian Church; Onely they.[23]

Gods House is the house of Prayer; It is his Court of Requests; There he receives petitions, there he gives Order upon them.[24]

He that hath a cause to be heard, will not goe to Smithfield, nor he that hath cattaile to buy or sell, to Westminster; He that hath bargaines to make, or newes to tell, should not come to doe that at Church; nor he that hath prayers to make, walke in the fields for his devotions. If I have a great friend, though in cases of necessity, as sicknesse, or any other restraints, hee will vouchsafe to visit me, yet I must make my suits to him at home, at his owne house. In cases of necessity, Christ in the Sacrament, vouchsafes to come home to me; And the Court is where the King is; his blessings are with his Ordinances, wheresoever: But the place to which he hath invited me, is his house.[25]

We know that God is alike in all places, but he does not worke in all places alike; God works otherwise in the Church, then in an Army; and diversly in his divers Ordinances in the Church;

God works otherwise in Prayer then in Preaching, and otherwise in the Sacraments then in either; and otherwise in the later, then in the first Sacrament. The power is the same, and the end is the same, but the way is not so.[26]

When we say, that God is tied to places, we must not meane, but that God is otherwise present, and workes otherwise, in places consecrated to his service, then in every prophane place. When I pray in my chamber, I build a Temple there, that houre; And, that minute, when I cast out a prayer, in the street, I build a Temple there; And when my soule prayes without any voyce, my very body is then a Temple: And God, who knowes what I am doing in these actions, erecting these Temples, he comes to them, and prospers, and blesses my devotions; and shall not I come to his Temple, where he is alwaies resident? My chamber were no Temple, my body were no Temple, except God came to it; but whether I come hither, or no, this will be Gods Temple: I may lose by my absence; He gaines nothing by my comming.[27]

Thou maist be a Sacrifice in thy chamber, but God receives a Sacrifice more cheerefully at Church . . . Only the Church hath the nature of a surety; Howsoever God may take thine own word at home, yet he accepts the Church in thy behalfe, as better security. Joyne therefore ever with the Communion of Saints.[28]

The Sabbath is the Holy Ghosts greatest working day: The Holy Ghost works more upon the Sunday, then all the week. In other dayes, he picks and chooses; but upon these days of holy Convocation, I am surer that God speakes to me, then at home, in any private inspiration. For, as the Congregation besieges God in publique prayers . . . so the Holy Ghost casts a net over the whole congregation, in this Ordinance of preaching, and catches all that break not out.[29]

Man being . . . subject naturally to manifold calamities, and spirituall calamities being incomparably heavier then temporall, and the greatest danger of falling into such spirituall calamities being in our absence from Gods Church, where onely the outward meanes of happinesse are ministred unto us, certainely there is much tendernesse and deliberation to be used, before the Church doores be shut against any man.[30]

Devotion is no Marginall note, no interlineary glosse, no Parenthesis that may be left out; It is no occasionall thing, no conditionall thing; I will goe, if I like the Preacher, if the place, if the company, if the weather; but it is of the body of the Text, and layes upon us an Obligation of fervour and of continuance.[31]

The Devill is no Recusant; he will come to Church, and he will lay his snares there.[32]

The English Reformation Settlement

God shin'd upon this Island early; early in the plantation of the Gospel, (for we had not our seed-Corn from *Rome*, howsoever we may have had some waterings from thence) and early in the Reformation of the Church: for we had not the model of any other Forreign Church for our pattern; we stript not the Church into a nakedness, nor into rags; we divested her not of her possessions, nor of her Ceremonies, but received such a Reformation at home, by their hands whom God enlightned, as left her neither in a Dropsie, nor in a Consumption; neither in a superfluous and cumbersome fatness, nor in an uncomely and faint leanness and attenuation.[33]

And nearer to (God), and to the institutions of his Christ, can no Church, no not of the *Reformation*, be said to have come, then ours does.[34]

For our Church, in the Reformation, proposed not that for her end, how shee might goe from Rome, but how she might come to the Truth; nor to cast away all such things as Rome had depraved, but to purge away those depravations, and conserve the things themselves, so restored to their first good use.[35]

Returne to God, with a joyfull thankfulnesse that he hath placed you in a Church, which withholds nothing from you, that is necessary to salvation, whereas in another Church they lack a great part of the Word, and halfe the Sacrament; And which obtrudes nothing to you, that is not necessary to salvation, whereas in another Church, the Additionall things exceed the Fundamentall; the Occasionall, the Originall; the Collaterall, the Direct; And the Traditions of men, the Commandements of God. [36]

You see then, what this Kingdome of God is; It is, when he comes, and is welcome, when he comes in his *Sacraments*, and speaks in his *Word*; when he speaks and is answered; knocks and is received, (he knocks in his *Ordinances*, and is received in our *Obedience* to them, he knocks in his *example*, and most holy conversation, and is received, in our *conformity*, and imitation.) So have you seen what the *Inheritance* of this Kingdome is, it is a Having, and Holding of the Gospel, a present, and a permanent possession, a holding fast, lest another (another Nation, another Church) take our Crown.[37]

The Church of God, is not so *beyond Sea*, as that we must needs seek it *there*, either in a *painted Church*, on one side, or in *a naked Church*, on another; a Church in a *Dropsie*, overflowne with *Ceremonies*, or a Church in a *Consumption*, for want of such Ceremonies, as the primitive Church found usefull, and beneficiall for the advancing of the glory of God, and the devotion of the Congregation.[38]

Trouble not thy selfe to know the formes and fashions of forraine particular Churches; neither of a Church in the lake, nor a Church upon seven hils; but since God hath planted thee in a Church, where all things necessary for salvation are administred to thee, and where no erronious doctrine . . . is affirmed and held, that is the Hill, and that is the Catholique Church.[39]

The Word of God is not above thee, says Moses, *nor beyond the Sea.* We need not clime up seven hills, nor wash our selves seven times in a Lake for it: God make the practise of our lives agreeable to the Doctrine of our Church; and all the world shall see that we have light enough.[40]

Princes are Gods Trumpet, and the Church is Gods Organ, but Christ Jesus is his voyce.[41]

If you can heare a good Organ at Church, and have the musique of a domestique peace at home, peace in thy walls, peace in thy bosome, never hearken after the musique of sphears, never hunt after the knowledge of higher secrets, then appertaine to thee; But since Christ hath made you . . . Kings and Priests, in your proportion, *Take heed what you hear,* in derogation of either the State, or the Church.[42]

The Law of the Prince is rooted in the power of God. The roote of all is Order, and the orderer of all is the King.[43]

Princes are sealed with the Crown; The Miter will not fit that seale. Powerfully, and gratiously they protect the Church, and are supreame heads of the Church; But they minister not the Sacraments of the Church. They give preferments; but they give not the capacity of preferment. They give order who shall have; but they give not orders, by which they are enabled to have, that have.[44]

Every man is the *Image* of God; every *Creature* is the *Ambassadour* of God; *The Heavens*, (and as well as the Heavens, the Earth) *declare the glory of God*; but the *Civill Magistrate*, and the *Spirituall Pastor*, who have married the *two Daughters of God*, The *State* and the *Church*, are the *Images* and *Ambassadours of God*, in a higher and more peculiar sense, and for that marriage are to be honoured.[45]

No Prince can have a better guard, then Subjects truly religious . . . What a wall to a City, what a Sea, what a Navy to an Iland, is a holy man?[46]

This then is the blessed state that wee pretend to, in the Kingdome of God in this life; Peace in the State, peace in the Church, peace in our Conscience: In this, that wee answer the motions of his blessed Spirit here in his Ordinance, and endeavour a conformity to him, in our life, and conversation; In this, hee is our King, and wee are his Subjects, and this is this Kingdome of God, the Kingdome of Grace.[47]

The Roman Church

The uncharitablenesse of the *Church* of *Rome* towards us all, is not a *Torrent*, nor it is not a *Sea*, but a *generall Flood*, an universall *Deluge*, that swallowes all the world, but that *Church*, and *Church-Yard*, that *Towne*, and *Suburbes*, themselves, and those that depend upon them; and will not allowe possibilitie of Salvation to the whole *Arke*, the whole *Christian Church*, but to one *Cabin* in that *Arke*, the *Church of Rome*; and then denie us this Salvation, not for any *Positive* Errour, that ever they charged us to affirme; not because wee affirme any thing, that they denie, but because wee denie some things, which they in their afternoone are come to affirme.[48]

O ur Adversaries of Rome charge us, that we have but a negative Religion; If that were true, it were a heavy charge, if we did onely deny, and establish nothing; But we deny all their new additions, so as that we affirme all the old foundations.[49]

T here is a man, the man of sin, at Rome, that pretends to be Christ, to all uses. And I would he would be content with that, and stop there, and not be a *Hyper-Christus*, Above Christ, more then Christ. I would he would no more trouble the peace of Christendome, no more occasion the assassinating of Christian Princes, no more binde the Christian liberty, in forbidding Meats, and Marriage, no more slacken and dissolve Christian bands, by Dispensations, and Indulgences, then Christ did. But if he will needs be more, if he will needs have an addition to the name of Christ, let him take heed of that addition, which some are apt enough to give him, however he deserve it, that he is *Antichrist*.[50]

The Communion of Saints

B e not apt to think heaven is an *Ermitage*, or a *Monastery*, or the way to heaven a sullen *melancholy*; Heaven, and the way to it, is a *Communion of Saints*, in a holy cheerfulnesse.[51]

F or they'are in Heaven on Earth, who Heavens workes do.[52]

A s there is a *Communion* of Saints, so there is a *Communication* of Saints. Think not heaven a Charter-house, where men, who onely of all creatures, are enabled by God to *speak*, must not speak to one another. The Lord of heaven is *Verbum*, The word, and his servants there talk of us here, and pray to him for us.[53]

L ittle knowest thou, what thou hast received at Gods hands, by the prayers of the Saints in heaven, that enwrap thee in their generall prayers for the Militant Church. Little knowest thou, what the publique prayers of the Congregation, what the private prayers of particular devout friends, that lament thy carelesnesse, and negligence in praying for thy selfe, have wrung and extorted out of Gods hand, in their charitable importunity for thee. And therefore, at last, make thy selfe fit to doe for others, that which others, when thou wast unfit to doe thy selfe that office, have done for thee, in assisting thee with their prayers.[54]

I *beleeve in the holy Ghost*, but doe not find him, if I seeke him onely in private prayer; But *in Ecclesia*, when I goe to meet him in the *Church*, when I seeke him where hee hath promised to bee found.[55]

T he mercy of Christ is not lesse active, not lesse industrious then the malice of his adversaries, He preaches in populous Cities, he preaches in the desart wildernesse, he preaches in the tempestuous Sea: and as his Power shall collect the severall dusts, and atomes, and Elements of our scattered bodies at the Resurrection, as materialls, members of his Triumphant Church; so he collects the materialls, the living stone, and timber, for his Militant Church, from all places, from Cities, from Desarts and . . . from the Sea.[56]

C ertainly he that loves not the *Militant Church*, hath but a faint faith in his interest in the *Triumphant*. He that cares not though the *materiall Church* fall, I am afraid is falling from the *spirituall*.[57]

A nd this is an inexpressible comfort to us, That our blessed Saviour thus mingles his Kingdomes, that he makes the Kingdome of Grace, and the Kingdome of Glory, all one; the Church, and Heaven all one; and assures us, That if we see him . . . in his Ordinance, in his Kingdome of Grace, we have already begun to see him . . . *face to face*, in his Kingdome of Glory; If we see him . . . as he looks in his Word, and Sacraments, in his Kingdome of Grace, we have begun to see him . . . As he is, in his Essence, in the Kingdome of Glory; And when we pray, *Thy kingdome come*, and mean but the Kingdome of Grace, he gives us more then we ask, an inchoative comprehension of the Kingdome of Glory, in this life. This is his inexpressible mercy, that he mingles his Kingdomes, and where he gives one, gives both.[58]

13

THE HOLY SCRIPTURES

The Old and New Testaments

As much as Paradise exceeded all the places of the earth, doe the Scriptures of God exceed Paradise. In the midst of Paradise grew the *Tree of knowledge*, and *the tree of life*: In this Paradise, the Scripture, every word is both those Trees; there is Life and Knowledge in every word of the Word of God . . . Knowledge and life growes upon every tree in this Paradise, upon every word in this Booke, because upon every Tree here, upon every word, grows Christ himselfe, in some relation.[1]

The two Volumes of the Scriptures are justly, and properly called two Testaments, for they are . . . The attestation, the declaration of the will and pleasure of God, how it pleased him to be served under the Law, and how in the state of the Gospell.[2]

This distinguishes the two Testaments, The Old is a Testament of *fear*, the New of *love*; yet in this they grow all one, That we determine the Old Testament, in the New, and that we prove the New Testament by the Old; for, but by the Old, we should not know, that there was to bee a New, nor, but for the New, that there was an Old; so the two Testaments grow *one Bible*: so in these two Affections, if there were not a *jealousie*, a fear of losing God, we could not love him; nor can we fear to lose him, except we doe love him.[3]

The *Judiciall* law of *Moses*, was certainly the most absolute, and perfect law of government, which could have been given *to that people*, for whom it was given; but yet to thinke, that all *States* are bound to observe those lawes, because God gave them, hath no more ground, then that all Men are bound to goe clothed in *beasts skinnes*, because God apparelled *Adam*, and *Eve* in that fashion. And for the *morall part* of that law, and the abridgement of that morall part, the *decalogue*, that begunne not to have force, and efficacy then, when God writ it in the tables, but was always, and always shall be written in the *hearts* of Men . . . So that he that will perfectly understand, what appertaines to his duty in any of the *ten Commandements*, he must not consider that law, with any limitation, as it was given to the *Jews*, but consider what he would have done if he had lived before the *Tables* had been written . . . For neither (the Commandment concerning the Sabbath) nor any other of the *ten*, began to bind then, when they were written, nor doth bind now, except it bound before that.[4]

The Psalmes are the Manna of the Church. As Manna tasted to every man like that that he liked best, so doe the Psalmes minister Instruction, and satisfaction, to every man, in every emergency and occasion.[5]

And as the whole booke of Psalmes is . . . an Oyntment powred out upon all sorts of sores, A Searcloth that souples all bruises, A Balme that searches all wounds; so are there some certain Psalmes, that are Imperiall Psalmes, that command over all affections, and spread themselves over all occasions, Catholique, universall Psalmes, that apply themselves to all necessities.[6]

*P*rophecy is but *antidated Gospell*, and *Gospell* but *postdated prophecy.*[7]

Let no man thinke that he hath heard enough, and needs no more; why did the Holy Ghost furnish his Church with foure Euangelists, if it were enough to reade one? And yet every one of the foure, hath enough for salvation, if Gods abundant care had not enriched the Church with more.[8]

For as an honest man, ever of the same thoughts, differs not from himself, though he do not ever say the same things, if he say not contraries; so the foure Evangelists observe the uniformity and samenesse of their guide, though all did not say all the same things, since none contradicts any. And as, when my soule which enables all my limbs to their functions, disposes my legs to go my whole body is truly said to go, because none stayes behinde; so when the holy Spirit, which had made himself as a common soule to their four soules, directed one of them to say any thing, all are well understood to have said it.[9]

The Authority of Scripture

The Scripture, *is a light*, it is the light, it is all light . . . God hath show'd enough, and said enough, and done enough, and suffer'd enough, for the salvation of his Church; he hath shin'd out upon all, and needs no supply of lesser lights.[10]

The Sun shining is not so good a proofe that it is day, as the Word of God, the Scripture is, that that which is commanded there, is a duty.[11]

The Scriptures are Gods Voyce; The Church is his Eccho; a redoubling, a repeating of some particular syllables, and accents of the same voice.[12]

Christ spoke Scripture; Christ was Scripture. As we say of great and universall Scholars, that they are . . . living, walking, speaking Libraries; so Christ was . . . living, speaking Scripture. Our Sermons are Text and Discourse; Christs Sermons were all Text: Christ was the *Word*.[13]

For all Christs promises are Scripture; They have all the Infallibility of Scripture.[14]

All the promises of his Scriptures belong to all.[15]

That this manifestation of his Will, must be permanent, it must be *written*, there must be a *Scripture*, which is his *Word* and his *Will*: And that therefore, from that Scripture, from that Word of God, all Articles of our Beliefe are to bee drawne.[16]

We lacked our redemption; we lacked all our direction; wee lacked the revealed will of God, the Scriptures; we have not God, if we have him not, as he hath delivered himselfe; and he hath done that in the Scriptures; and we imbrace him, as we finde him there; and we finde him there, to be one God in three persons, and the Holy Ghost to bee one of those three; and in them we rest.[17]

All those blessings by the *Sacraments of Baptism*, and all Gods other promises to his children, and all the mysteries of Christian Religion, are therefore beleeved by us, because they are grounded in the Scriptures of God; we beleeve them for that reason; and then it is not a worke of my *faith* primarily, but it is a worke of my *reason*, that assures me, that these are the Scriptures, that these Scriptures are the word of God.[18]

As in the heavens the stars were created at once, with one *Fiat*, and then being so made, stars doe not beget new stars, so the *Christian doctrine necessary* to salvation, was delivered at once, that is, intirely in one spheare, in the body of the Scriptures.[19]

All that the wit of Man adds to the Word of God, is all *quick-silver*, and it evaporates easily.[20]

Duties of this kinde, permanent and constant duties arising out of the evidence of Gods word, such as just and true dealing with men, such as keeping Gods Sabbaths, such as not blaspheming his name, have no latitude about them, no conditions in them; they have no circumstance, but are all substance, no apparell, but are all body, no body, but are all soule, no matter, but are all forme . . . they admit no deliberation, but require an immediate, and an exact execution. But then, for extraordinary things, things that have not their evidence in the word of *God* formerly revealed unto us, whether we consider matters of Doctrine, and new opinions, or matter of Practise, and new commands, from what depth of learning soever that new opinion seeme to us to rise, or from heighth of Power soever that new Command seeme to fall . . . still we are allowed, nay still wee are commanded to deliberate, to doubt, to consider, before we execute.[21]

The literall sense is alwayes to be preserved; but the literal sense is not alwayes to be discerned; for the literall sense is not alwayes that, which the very Letter and Grammer of the place presents, as where it is literally said, *That Christ is a Vine*, and literally, *That his flesh is bread* . . . But the literall sense of every place, is the principall intention of the Holy Ghost, in that place: And his principall intention in many places, is to expresse things by allegories, by figures; so that in many places of Scripture, a figurative sense is the literall sense.[22]

My *God*, my *God*, Thou are a *direct God*, may I not say a *literall God*, a *God* that wouldest bee understood *literally*, and according to the *plaine sense* of all that thou saiest? But thou art also (*Lord* I intend it to thy *glory*, and let no *prophane mis-interpreter* abuse it to thy *diminution*) thou are a *figurative*, a *metaphoricall God too*: A *God* in whose words there is such a height of *figures*, such *voyages*, such *peregrinations* to fetch remote and precious *metaphors*, such *extentions*, such *spreadings*, such *Curtaines* of Allegories, such *third Heavens* of Hyperboles, so *harmonious eloquutions*, so *retired* and so *reserved expressions*, so *commanding perswasions*, so *perswading commandements*, such *sinewes* even in thy *milke*, and such *things* in thy *words*, as all *prophane Authors*, seeme of the seed of the *Serpent*, that *creepes*, thou art the *Dove*, that flies. O, what words but thine, can expresse the inexpressible *texture*, and *composition* of thy *word*; in which, to one man, that *argument* that binds his faith to beleeve that to bee the Word of *God*, is *the reverent simplicity* of the Word, and to another, the *majesty* of the Word; and in which two men, equally pious, may meet, and one wonder, that all should not understand it, and the other, as much, that any man should.[23]

The Rivers of Paradise did not all run one way, and yet they flow'd from one head; the sentences of the Scripture flow all from one head, from the holy Ghost, and yet they seem to present divers senses, and to admit divers interpretations.[24]

The Reading of Scripture

It is the glory of Gods Word, not that it is come, but that it shall remain for ever: It is the glory of a Christian, not that he hath heard, but that he desires to heare still.[25]

All knowledge is ignorance, except it conduce to the knowledge of the Scriptures, and all the Scriptures lead us to Christ.[26]

Not to labour to understand the Scriptures, is to slight God; but not to believe them, is to give God the lye: he makes God a lyer, if he believe not the Record that God gave of his Son.[27]

Eloquence is not our net; Traditions of men are not our nets; onely the Gospel is. The Devill angles with hooks and bayts; he deceives, and he wounds in the catching; for every sin hath his sting. The Gospel of Christ Jesus is a net; It hath leads and corks; It hath leads, that is, the denouncing of Gods judgements, and a power to

sink down, and lay flat any stubborne and rebellious heart, And it
hath corks, that is, the power of absolution, and application of the
mercies of God, that swimme above all his works, means to erect an
humble and contrite spirit, above all the waters of tribulation, and
affliction. A net is . . . a knotty thing; and so is the Scripture, full of
knots, of scruple, and perplexity, and anxiety, and vexation, if thou
wilt goe about to entangle thy selfe in those things, which appertaine not to thy salvation; but knots of a fast union, and inseparable
alliance of thy soule to God, and to the fellowship of his Saints, if
thou take the Scriptures, as they were intended for thee, that is, if
thou beest content to rest in those places, which are cleare, and evident in things necessary. A net is a large thing, past thy fadoming, if
thou cast it from thee, but if thou draw it to thee, it will lie upon
thine arme. The Scriptures will be out of thy reach, and out of thy
use, if thou cast and scatter them upon Reason, upon Philosophy,
upon Morality, to try how the Scriptures will fit all them, and
beleeve them but so far as they agree with thy reason; But draw the
Scripture to thine own heart, and to thine own actions, and thou
shalt finde it made for that; all the promises of the old Testament
made, and all accomplished in the new Testament, for the salvation
of thy soul hereafter, and for thy consolation in the present application of them.[28]

If a man read the Scriptures a little, superficially, perfunctorily, his
eyes seem straightwaies enlightned, and he thinks he sees every
thing that he had preconceived, and fore-imagined in himselfe, as
cleare as the Sun, in the Scriptures . . . (But). . . as the Essentiall word
of God, the Son of God, is the Light of light, So the written Word of
God is light of light too, one place of Scripture takes light of another
. . . for the Scriptures are made to agree with one another, but not to
agree to thy particular tast and humour.[29]

As God gave his Children a bread of *Manna*, that tasted to every
man like that that he liked best, so hath God given us
Scriptures, in which the plain and simple man may heare God
speaking to him in his own plain and familiar language, and men of
larger capacity, and more curiosity, may heare God in that Musique

that they love best, in a curious, in an harmonious style, unparalleled by any.[30]

For the word of God is not the word of God in any other sense than literall, and that also is not the literall, which the letter seems to present, for so to diverse understandings there might be diverse literall senses; but it is called literall, to distinguish it from the Morall, Allegoricall, and the other senses; and is that which the Holy Ghost doth in that place principally intend . . . They which build, must take the solid stone, not the rubbish. Of which, though there be none in the word of God, yet often unsincere translations, to justifie our prejudices and foreconceived opinions, and the underminings and batteries of Hereticks, and the curious refinings of the Allegoricall Fathers, which have made the Scriptures, which are strong toyles, to catch and destroy the bore and bear which devast our Lords vineyard, fine cobwebs to catch flies.[31]

Let us use our liberty of reading Scriptures according to the Law of liberty; that is, charitably to leave others to their liberty, if they but differ from us, and not differ from Fundamentall Truths.[32]

This is . . . to *search the Scriptures*, not as though thou wouldest make a *concordance*, but an *application*; as thou wouldest search a *wardrobe*, not to make an *Inventory* of it, but to finde in it something fit for thy wearing.[33]

Come humbly to the reading and hearing of the Scriptures, and thou shalt have strength of understanding.[34]

Begin a *Lambe*, and thou will become a *Lion*; Reade the Scriptures modestly, humbly, and thou shalt understand them strongly, powerfully.[35]

THE LIFE OF THE CHURCH

Prayer, Preaching and Sacraments

It is the voice of the Archangell, (that is, the true and sincere word of God) that must raise thee from the death of sin, to the life of grace . . . Yet thou must heare this voice of the Archangell in the Trumpet of God. The Trumpet of God is his loudest Instrument; and his loudest Instrument is his publique Ordinance in the Church; Prayer, Preaching, and Sacraments; Heare him in these; In all these; come not to heare him in the Sermon alone, but come to him in Prayer, and in the Sacrament too. For, except the voyce come in the Trumpet of God, (that is, in the publique Ordinance of his Church) thou canst not know it to be the voyce of the Archangell.[1]

They are a powerful thunder, and lightning, that go together: Preaching is the thunder, that clears the air, disperses all clouds of ignorance; and then the *Sacrament* is the lightning, the glorious light, and presence of Christ Jesus himself.[2]

The aire is not so full of Moats, of Atomes, as the Church is of Mercies; and as we can suck in no part of aire, but we take in those Moats, those Atomes; so here in the Congregation we cannot suck in a word from the preacher, we cannot speak, we cannot sigh a prayer to God, but that that whole breath and aire is made of mercy.[3]

Petition God at prayers, and God shall answer all your petitions at the Sermon.[4]

You would scarce thank a man for an extemporall Elegy, or Epigram, or Panegyrique in your praise, if it cost the Poet, or the Orator no paines. God will scarce hearken to sudden, inconsidered, irreverent prayers. Men will study even for Complements; and Princes and Ambassadors will not speak to one another, without thinking what they will say. Let not us put God to speak to us so, (Preaching is Gods speaking to us) Let not us speak to God so, (Praying is our speaking to God) not extemporally, unadvisedly, inconsiderately.[5]

Prayer and Preaching may consist, nay they must meet in the Church of God. Now, he that will teach, must have *learnt* before, many yeers before; And he that will preach, must have *thought* of it before, many days before. *Extemporall Ministers*, that resolve in a day what they will *be*, *Extemporall Preachers*, that resolve in a minute what they will *say*, out-go Gods Spirit, and make too much hast.[6]

The sacraments exhibit and convey grace; and grace is such a light, such a torch, such a beacon, as where it is, it is easily seen. As there is a lustre in a precious stone, which no mans eye or finger can limit to a certain place or point in that stone, so though we do not assign in the sacrament, where, that is, in what circumstance or part of that holy action grace is; or when, or how it enters . . . yet whosoever receives this sacrament worthily, sees evidently an entrance, and a growth of grace in himself.[7]

Baptism

Baptisme is so necessary, as that God hath placed no other ordinary seale, nor conveyance of his graces in his Church, to them that have not received that, then baptisme.[8]

Baptisme doth truly, and without collusion, offer grace *to all*; and nothing but baptisme, by an ordinary institution, and as an ordinary meanes, doth so.[9]

To be born within the Covenant, that is, of Christian Parents, does not make us Christians, . . . the Covenant gives us a title to the Sacrament of Baptisme, and that Sacrament makes us Christians.[10]

No man hath seen God, and lives; but no man lives till he have *heard God*; for God spake to him, in his *Baptisme*, and called him by his *name*, then.[11]

To be baptized therefore *into the name* of Christ, is to be trans-lated into his *Family*, by this spirituall adoption . . . and there-fore to become truly *Christians*, to live Christianly, this is truly to be baptized into *his name*.[12]

The first, and principall duty of him, who hath ingrafted him-selfe into the body of the Christian Church, by Baptisme, is to informe himself of the Trinity, in whose name he is Baptized.[13]

Christ calls his *death a Baptisme*; So Saint *Augustine* calls our Baptisme a death . . . Because if we be so baptized into his *Name*, and into his *death*, we are thereby *dead to sinne*, and have dyed the *death of the righteous*.[14]

This is then the necessity of this Sacrament; not absolutely neces-sary, but necessary by Gods ordinary institution; and as it is always necessary, so it is always certaine; whosoever is baptized according to Christs institution, receives the Sacrament of baptisme; and the truth is always infallibly annexed with the signe.[15]

Doe I remember what I contracted with Christ Jesus, when I took the name of a Christian at my entrance into his Church by Baptism? Doe I find I have endevoured to perform those Conditions? Doe I find a remorse when I have not performed them? Doe I feel the remission of those sinnes applyed to me when I hear the gracious promises of the Gospel shed upon repentant sinners by the mouth of his Minister? Have I a true and solid consolation, (without shift, or disguise, or flattering of my conscience) when I receive the seal of his pardon in the Sacrament? Beloved, not in any morall integrity, not in keeping the conscience of an honest man, in generall, but in using well the meanes ordain'd by Christ in the Christian Church, am I justified.[16]

Holy Communion

When thou commest to this seale of thy peace, the Sacrament, pray that God will give thee that light, that may direct and establish thee, in necessary and fundamentall things; that is, the light of faith to see, that the Body and Bloud of Christ, is applied to thee, in that action; But for the manner, how the Body and Bloud of Christ is there, wait his leisure, if he have not yet manifested that to thee: Grieve not at that, wonder not at that, presse not for that; for hee hath not manfested that, not the way, not the manner of his presence in the Sacrament, to the Church.[17]

Christ is nearer us, when we behold him with the eyes of faith in Heaven, then when we seeke him in a piece of bread, or in a sacramentall box here. Drive him not away from thee, by wrangling and disputing how he is present with thee; unnecessary doubts of his presence may induce fearfull assurances of his absence: The best determination of the Reall presence is to be sure, that thou be really present with him, by an ascending faith: Make sure thine own Reall presence, and doubt not of his: Thou art not the farther from him, by his being gone thither before thee.[18]

As Christ was presented to God in the Temple, so is hee presented to God in the Sacrament; not sucking, but bleeding. And God gives him back again to thee. And at what price? upon this exchange; Take his first born, Christ Jesus, and give him thine. Who is thine? . . . The heart is the first part of the body that lives; Give him that.[19]

Confession

Gods Chancery is always open, and his seale works alwaies; at all times remission of sins may be sealed to a penitent soule in the Sacrament.[20]

True Confession is a mysterious Art. As there is a *Mystery of iniquity*, so there is a *Mystery of the Kingdome of heaven*. And the mystery of the Kingdome of heaven is this, That no man comes thither, but in a sort as he is a notorious sinner. One mystery of iniquity is, that in this world, though I multiply sins, yet the Judge cannot punish me, if I can hide them from other men, though he know them; but if I confesse them, he can, he will, he must. The mystery of the Kingdome of heaven, is, That onely the Declaring, the Publishing, the Notifying, and Confessing of my sins, possesses me of the Kingdome of heaven.[21]

Private Prayer

Prayer is our whole service to God.[22]

Pray personally, rely not upon dead nor living Saints; Thy Mother the Church prayes for thee, but pray for thy selfe too; Shee can open her bosome, and put the breast to thy mouth, but thou must draw, and suck for thy selfe. Pray personally, and pray frequently.[23]

Heare us, O heare us Lord; to thee
A sinner is more musique, when he prayes,
  Then spheares, or Angels praises been,
In Panegyrique Allelujaes,
    Hear us, for till thou heare us, Lord
    We know not what to say.
Thine eare to'our sighes, teares, thoughts gives voice and word.
    O Thou who Satan heard'st in Jobs sicke day,
    Heare thy selfe now, for thou in us dost pray.[24]

It is not enough to have prayed once; Christ does not onely excuse, but enjoine Importunity.[25]

As a Clock gives a warning before it strikes, and then there remains a sound, and a tingling of the bell after it hath stricken: so a precedent meditation, and a subsequent rumination, make the prayer a prayer; I must think before, what I will aske, and consider againe, what I have askt.[26]

All cleane beasts had both these marks, they divided the hoofe, and they chewed the cud: All good resolutions, which passe our prayer, must have these two marks too, they must divide the hoofe, they must make a double impression, they must be directed upon Gods glory, and upon our good, and they must passe a rumination, a chawing of the cud, a second examination, whether that prayer were so conditioned or no. We pray sometimes out of sudden and indigested apprehensions; we pray sometimes out of custome, and communion with others; we pray sometimes out of a present sense of paine, or imminent danger; and this prayer may divide the hoofe; It may looke towards Gods glory, and towards our good; but it does not chew the cud too; that is, if I have not considered, not examined, whether it doe so or no, it is not a prayer that God will call a sacrifice.[27]

But when we consider with a religious seriousnesse the manifold weaknesses of the strongest devotions in time of Prayer, it is a sad consideration. I throw my selfe downe in my Chamber, and I call in, and invite God, and his Angels thither, and when they are there, I neglect God and his Angels, for the noise of a Flie, for the ratling of a Coach, for the whining of a doore; I talke on, in the same posture of praying; Eyes lifted up; knees bowed downe; as though I prayed to God; and, if God, or his Angels should aske me, when I thought last of God in that prayer, I cannot tell; Sometimes I finde that I had forgot what I was about, but when I began to forget it, I cannot tell. A memory of yesterdays pleasures, a feare of to morrows dangers, a straw under my knee, a noise in mine eare, a light in mine eye, an any thing, a nothing, a fancy, a Chimera in my braine, troubles me in my prayer. So certainely is there nothing, nothing in spirituall things, perfect in this world.[28]

There is no forme of Building stronger then an Arch, and yet an Arch hath declinations, which even a flat-roofe hath not; The flat-roofe lies equall in all parts; the Arch declines downards in all parts, and yet the Arch is a firme supporter. Our Devotions doe not the lesse bear us upright, in the sight of God, because they have some declinations towards natural affections: God doth easilier pardon some neglectings of his grace, when it proceeds out of a tendernesse, or may be excused out of good nature, then any presuming upon his grace. If a man doe depart in some actions, from an exact obedience of Gods will, upon infirmity, or humane affections, and not a contempt, God passes it over oftentimes.[29]

Almost every meanes between God and man, suffers some adulteratings and disguises: But prayer least: And it hath most wayes and addresses. It may be mentall, for we may thinke prayers. It may be vocall, for we may speake prayers. It may be actuall, for we do prayers. For deeds have voyce.[30]

And whil'st this universall Quire,
That Church in triumph, this in warfare here,
  Warm'd with the one all-partaking fire
Of love, that none be lost, which cost thee deare,
    Prayes ceaslesly, 'and thou hearken too
    (Since to be gratious
Our taske is treble, to pray, beare, and doe)
Heare this prayer Lord, O Lord deliver us
From trusting in those prayers, though powr'd out thus.[31]

Let not thy prayer be lucrative, nor vindicative, pray not for temporall superfluities, pray not for the confusion of them that differ from thee in opinion, or in manners, but condition thy prayer, inanimate thy prayer with the glory of God, and thine own everlasting happinesse, and the edification of others.[32]

Prayer, when one Petition hath taken hold upon God, works upon God, moves God, prevailes with God, entirely for all.[33]

Public Prayer

A man may pray in the street, in the fields, in a fayre; but it is a more acceptable and more effectuall prayer, when we shut our doores, and observe our stationary houres for private prayer in our Chamber; and in our Chamber, when we pray upon our knees, then in our beds. But the greatest power of all, is in the publique prayer of the Congregation.[34]

Prayer consists as much of praise for the past, as of supplication for the future.[35]

The Church is the house of prayer, so, as that upon occasion, preaching may be left out, but never a house of preaching, so, as that Prayer may be left out. And for the debt of prayer, God will not be paid, with money of our owne coyning, (with sudden, extemporall, inconsiderate prayer) but with currant money, that beares the Kings Image, and inscription; The Church of God, by his Ordinance, hath set his stampe, upon a Liturgie and Service, for his house.[36]

They that undervalue, or neglect the prayers of the Church, have not that title to the benefit of the Sermon; for though God doe speake in the Sermon, yet hee answers, that is, applies himselfe, by his Spirit, onely to them, who have prayed to him before. If they have joyned in prayer, they have their interest, and shall feele their Consolation in all the promises of the Gospel, shed upon the Congregation, in the Sermon.[37]

As the Law of the Land is my Law, and I have an inheritance in it, so the prayers of the Church are my prayers, and I have an interest in them, because I am a Son of that family.[38]

Preaching

Preaching is in season to them who are willing to hear.[39]

Our mortality, and our immortality, which are the two reall Texts, and Subjects of all our Sermons.[40]

God makes nothing of nothing now; God eased himselfe of that incomprehensible worke, and ended it in the first Sabbath. But God makes great things of little still; And in that kinde hee works most upon the Sabbath; when by the foolishnesse of Preaching hee infatuates the wisedome of the world, and by the word, in the mouth of a weake man, he enfeebles the power of sinne, and Satan in the world . . . And this worke of his, to make much of little, and to doe much by little, is most properly a Miracle.[41]

All the Sermon is not Gods word, but all the Sermon is Gods Ordinance, and the Text is certainly his word. There is no salvation but by faith, nor faith but by hearing, nor hearing but by preaching; and they that thinke meanliest of the Keyes of the Church, and speak faintliest of the Absolution of the Church, will yet allow, That those Keyes lock, and unlock in Preaching; That Absolution is conferred, or withheld in Preaching, That the proposing of the promises of the Gospel in preaching, is that binding and loosing on earth, which bindes and looses in heaven.[42]

Not only we, we the Ministers of Gods Word, but you also the hearers thereof: for there is a knowledge, an art of hearing, as well as of speaking. Students make up the University, as well as Doctors: and Hearers make up the Congregation, as well as Preachers. A good hearer is as much a Doctor, as a Preacher: A Doctor to him that sits by him, in example, whilst he is here: a Doctor to all his Family, in his repetition, when he comes home: a Doctor, to that which is more then the whole world, to him, his own soul, all his life.[43]

How often is the Pulpit it selfe, made the shop, and the Theatre of praise upon present men, and God left out? How often is that called a Sermon, that speakes more of Great men, then of our great God?[44]

It is not the depth, nor the wit, nor the eloquence of the Preacher that pierces us, but his nearenesse; that hee speaks to my conscience, as though he had been behinde the hangings when I sinned, and as though he had read the book of the day of Judgement already.[45]

But at last, the habit of our sin hath seared us up, and we never find that it is we, that the Preacher means; we find that he touches others, but not us. Our wit, and our malice is awake, but our conscience is asleep; we can make a Sermon a libel against others, and cannot find a Sermon in a Sermon, to our selves. It is a sickness, and an evil sickness.[46]

O ur spirit beares witnesse sometimes when the Spirit does not; that is, Nature testifies some things, without addition of particular grace: And then the Spirit, the Holy Ghost oftentimes testifies, when ours does not: How often stands he at the doore, and knocks? How often spreads he his wings, to gather us, as a Hen her chickens? How often presents he to us the power of God in the mouth of the Preacher, and we beare witnesse to one another of the wit and of the eloquence of the Preacher, and no more? How often he bears witnesse, that such an action is odious in the sight of God, and our spirit beares witnesse, that it is acceptable, profitable, honourable in the sight of man? How often he beares witnesse, for Gods Judgements, and our spirit deposes for mercy, by presumption, and how often he testifies for mercy, and our spirit sweares for Judgement, in desperation?[47]

T o preach there where reprehension of growing sin is acceptable, is to preach in season; where it is not acceptable, it is out of season; but yet we must preach in season, and out of season too. And when men are so refractary, as that they forbeare to heare, or heare and resist our preaching, we must pray; and where they dispise or forbid our praying, we must lament them, we must weep.[48]

R emember thou thine own sins, first, and then every word that fals from the preachers lips shall be a drop of the *dew of heaven*, a dram of the *balme of Gilead*, a portion of the bloud of thy Saviour, to wash away that sinne, so presented by thee to be so sacrified by him.[49]

O ur errand hither then, is not to see; but much lesse not to be able to see, to sleep: It is not to talk, but much lesse to snort: It is to heare, and to heare all the words of the Preacher, but, to heare in those words, the Word, that Word which is the soule or all that is said, and is the true Physick of all their soules that heare.[50]

The People of God

God therefore hath shin'd in no mans heart, till he know the glory of GOD in the face of Jesus Christ, till he come to the manifestation of God, in the Gospel.[51]

Though there be in every Creature an Image of God; I have a livelier Image of God, Christ.[52]

The soule is that which inanimates the body, and enables the organs of the senses to see and heare; The spirit is that which enables the soule to see God, and to heare his Gospel.[53]

Every Christian is a state, a common-wealth to *himselfe*, and in him, the *Scripture* is his *law*, and the *conscience* is his *Iudge*.[54]

Thou art not a Christian, because thou wast borne in a Christian Kingdome, and borne within the Covenant, and borne of Christian Parents, but because thou hast dwelt in the Christian Church, and performed the duties presented to thee there.[55]

By the *Layetie* we intend the people glorifying *God* in their secular callings, and by the *Clergie*, persons seposed by his ordinance, for spiritual functions, The *Layetie* no farther remoov'd then the *Clergie*, The *Clergie* no farther entitled then the *Layetie*, in the blood of *Christ Jesus*, neither in the effusion of that blood upon the *Crosse*, nor in the participation of that blood in the *Sacrament*, and that an equall care in *Clergie*, and *Layetie*, of doing the duties of their severall callings, gives them an equall interest in the joyes, and glory of heaven.[56]

Yeoman, and *Labourer*, and *Spinster*, are distinctions upon Earth; in the Earth, in the grave there is no distinction. The *Angell* that shall call us out of that dust, will not stand to survay, who lyes naked, who in a Coffin, who in Wood, who in Lead, who in a fine, who in a courser Sheet; In that one day of the Resurrection, there is not a forenoone for Lords to rise first, and an afternoone for meaner persons to rise after. *Christ* was not whip'd to save Beggars, and crown'd with Thornes to save Kings: he dyed, he suffered all, for all; and we whose bearing witness of him, is to doe, as hee did, must conferre our labours upon all.[57]

In the Wildernesse, every man had one and the same measure of Manna; The same Gomer went through all; for Manna was a Meat, that would melt in their mouths, and of easie digestion. But then for their Quailes, birds of a higher flight, meat of a stronger digestion, it is not said, that every man had an equall number: some might have more, some lesse, and yet all their fulnesse. Catechisticall divinity, and instructions in fundamentall things, is our Manna: Every man is bound to take in his Gomer, his explicite knowledge of Articles absolutely necessary to salvation; The simplest man, as well as the greatest Doctor, is bound to know, that there is one God in three persons, That the second of those, the Sonne of God, tooke our nature, and dyed for mankinde; And that there is a Holy Ghost, which in the Communion of Saints, the Church established by Christ, applies to every particular soule the benefit of Christs universall redemption. But then for our Quails, birds of higher pitch, meat of a stronger digestion, which is the knowledge how to rectifie every straying conscience, how to extricate every entangled, and scrupulous, and perplexed soule, in all emergent doubts, how to defend our Church, and our Religion, from all the mines, and all the batteries of our Adversaries, and to deliver her from all imputations of Heresie, and Schisme, which they impute to us, this knowledge is not equally necessary in all; In many cases a Master of Servants, and a Father of children is bound to know more, then those children and servants, and the Pastor of the parish more then parishioners: They may have their fulnesse, though he have more, but he hath not his, except he be able to give them satisfaction.[58]

He that will dy with Christ upon Good-Friday, must hear his own bell toll all Lent; he that will be partaker of his passion at last, must conform himself to his discipline of prayer and fasting before. Is there any man, that in his chamber hears a bell toll for another man, and does not kneel down to pray for that dying man? and then when his charity breaths out upon another man, does he not also reflect upon himself, and dispose himself as if he were in the state of that dying man? We begin to hear Christs bell toll now, and is not our bell in the chime? We must be in his grave, before we come to his resurrection, and we must be in his death-bed before we come to his grave: we must do as he did, fast and pray, before we can say as he said . . . Into thy hands O Lord I commend my Spirit.[59]

Our *criticall* day is *not* the *very day* of our *death*: but the whole course of our life. I thank him that *prayes* for me when my bell tolles, but I thank him much more that *Catechises* mee, or *preaches* to mee, or *instructs mee how to live*.[60]

It is an unexpressible comfort to have beene Gods instrument, for the conversion of others, by the power of Preaching, or by a holy and exemplar life in any calling.[61]

The Office of a Priest

What a Coronation is our taking of Orders, by which God makes us a Royall Priesthood? And what an inthronization is the comming up into a Pulpit, where God invests his servants with his Ordinance, as with a Cloud . . . and then enables him to preach peace, mercy, consolation, to the whole Congregation.[62]

Thou, whose diviner soule hath caus'd thee now
    To put thy hand unto the holy Plough,
Making Lay-scornings of the Ministry,
Not an impediment, but victory.

Thou art the same materials, as before,
Onely the stampe is changed; but no more.
And as new crowned Kings alter the face,
But not the monies substance; so hath grace
Chang'd onely Gods old Image by Creation,
To Christs new stampe, at this thy Coronation;
Or, as we paint Angels with wings, because
They beare Gods message, and proclaime his lawes,
Since thou must doe the like, and so must move,
Art thou new feather'd with cœlestial love?

Let then the world thy calling disrespect,
But goe thou on, and pitty their neglect.
What function is so noble, as to bee
Embassadour to God and destinie?
To open life, to give kingdomes to more
Than Kings give dignities; to keepe heavens doore?
Maries prerogative was to beare Christ, so
'Tis preachers to convey him, for they doe
As Angels out of clouds, from Pulpits speake:
And blesse the poore beneath, the lame, the weake.

How brave are those, who with their Engine, can
Bring man to heaven, and heaven againe to man?
These are thy titles and preheminences,
In whom must meet Gods graces, mens offences,
And so the heavens which beget all things here,
And the earth our mother, which these things doth beare,
Both these in thee, are in thy Calling knit.
And make thee now a blest Hermaphrodite.[63]

U s, the Ministers of Gods Word and Sacraments. If we take Gods Word into our mouths, and pretend a Commission, a Calling, for the calling of others, we must be sure that God hath shin'd in our hearts.[64]

It must be a light; not a calling taken out of the darkness of melancholy, or darkness of discontent, or darkness of want and poverty, or darkness of a retir'd life, to avoid the mutual duties and offices of society: it must be a light, and a light that shines; it is not enough to have knowledge and learning; it must shine out, and appear in preaching; and it must shine in our hearts, in the private testimony of the Spirit there: but when it hath so shin'd there, it must not go out there, but shine still as a Candle in a Candlestick, or the Sun in his sphere; shine so, as it give light to others.[65]

The *first* of these *foure Creatures* hath the face of a *Lion*, the *second* of a *Calfe*, or an *Oxe*, the *third* of a *Man*, and the *fourth* of an *Eagle*. Now . . . These foure Creatures are the Preachers of the Gospell . . . But then . . . All these foure Creatures make up but one Creature; all their qualities concurre to the Qualification of a Minister; every Minister of God is to have all, that all foure had; the courage of a *Lion*, the laboriousness of an *Oxe*, the perspicuity and cleare sight of the *Eagle*, and the humanity, the discourse, the reason, the affability, the appliablenesse of a *Man*.[66]

God for his own glory promises . . . that his Prophet, his Minister shall be . . . a Trumpet, to awaken with terror. But then, he shall become . . . a musical and harmonious charmer, to settle and compose the soul again in a reposed confidence, and in a delight in God: he shall be . . . musick, harmony to the soul in his matter; he shall preach harmonious peace to the conscience: and he shall be . . . musick and harmony in his manner; he shall not present the messages of God rudely, barbarously, extemporally; but with such meditation and preparation as appertains to so great an imployment, from such a King as God, to such a State as his church.[67]

They who dwell in Gods house, whose livelihood growes out of the revenue of his Church, and whose service lies within the walls of his Church, are most inexcusable, if they have not a continuall Epiphany, a continuall Manifestation of Christ: All men should looke towards God, but the Priest should never looke off from God.[68]

As the sailes of a ship when they are spread and swolne, and the way that the ship makes, shewes me the winde, where it is, though the winde it selfe be an invisible thing; so thy actions to morrow, and the life that thou leadest all the yeare, will shew mee, with what minde thou camest to the Sacrament, to day, though onely God, and not I, can see thy minde.[69]

Through the ragged apparell of the afflictions of this life; through the scarres, and wounds, and palenesse, and mor-phews of sin, and corruption, we can look upon the soul it self, and there see that incorruptible beauty, that *white* and *red*, which the *innocency* and the *blood* of Christ hath given it, and we are mad for love of this soul, and ready to doe any act of danger, in the ways of persecution, any act of diminution of our selves in the ways of humiliation, to *stand at her doore*, and *pray*, and begge, that *she would be reconciled to God.*[70]

Good life it self is but a commentary, an exposition upon our preaching.[71]

How beautifull are the feet of them that preach the Gospel! Men look most to our feet, to our wayes: the power that makes men admire, may lie in our tongues; but the beauty that makes men love, lies in our feet, in our actions.[72]

Our actions, if they be good, speak louder then our Sermons; Our preaching is our speech, our good life is our eloquence. Preaching celebrates the Sabbath, but a good life makes the whole week a Sabbath.[73]

We have the light of Learning, and the light of other abilities to no purpose, if we have no good works to show, when we have drawn mens eyes upon us.[74]

God hath set our eyes in our foreheads, to look forward, not backward, not to be proud of that which we have done, but diligent in that which we are to doe.[75]

Every good Shepheard gives his life, that is, spends his life, weares out his life for his sheep.[76]

Since he bled, we may well sweat in his service, for the salvation of your souls.[77]

Christ will be fed in the poor that are hungry, and hee will be cloathed in the poore that are naked, so he would be enriched in those poor Ministers that serve at his Altar; when Christ would be so fed, he desires not feasts and banquets; when he would be so cloathed, hee desires not soft rayment fit for *Kings houses*, nor embroyderies, nor perfumes; when he would be enriched in the poor *Church-man*, he desires not that he should be a spunge, to drinke up the sweat of others, and live idly; but yet, as he would not be starved in the hungry, nor submitted to cold and unwholesome ayre in the naked, so neither would be he made contemptible, nor beggerly, in the Minister of his Church.[78]

Nothing shakes the Church more, then when Church-men are no better then other men are.[79]

Idle words, are but idle words in a secular mans mouth; but in a Churchmans mouth, they are blasphemies. So for our actions; it may become us, it may concern us to abstain from some indifferent things, which other men without any scandal may do.[80]

When Christ shall say, at the Judgement, *I was naked, and ye cloathed me not, sick, and ye visited me not*, it shall be no excuse to say, *When saw we thee naked, when saw we thee sick?* for wee might have seen it, wee should have seen it. When we shall come to our accompt, and see *them*, whose salvation was committed to *us*, perish, because they were uninstructed, and ignorant, dare we say then, *we never saw them* show their ignorance, wee never heard of it? That is the greatest part of our fault, the heaviest weight upon our condemnation, that we saw so little, heard so little, conversed so little amongst them, because we were made watchmen, and bound to see, and bound to hear, and bound to be heard: not by *others*, but by our *selves*; My sheep may be saved by others; but *I* save them not, that are saved so, nor shall *I* my self be saved by *their* labour, where *mine* was necessarily required.[81]

When at any midnight I heare a bell toll from this steeple, must not I say to my selfe, what have I done at any time for the instructing or rectifying of that mans Conscience, who lieth there now ready to deliver up his own account, and my account to Almighty God? If he be not able to make a good account, he and I are in danger, because I have not enabled him.[82]

What Sea could furnish mine eyes with teares enough, to poure out, if I should think, that of all this Congregation, which lookes me in the face now, I should not meet one, at the Resurrection, at the right hand of God![83]

The burden of the sinnes of the *whole world*, was a burden onely for *Christs* shoulders; but the sinnes of *this Parish*, will ly upon my shoulders, if I be *silent*, or if I be *indulgent*, and denounce not Gods Judgement upon those sinnes. It will be a burden to us, if we doe not, and God knowes it is a burden to us, when we do denounce those Judgements.[84]

For as there is no profit at all (none to me, none to God) if I get all the world and lose mine own soul, so there is no profit to me, if I win other mens soules to God, and lose mine owne.[85]

The Preacher

A sodain *light* brought into a room doth awaken some men; but yet a *noise* does it better, and a *shaking*, and a pinching. The exalting of *naturall faculties*, and good *morall life, inward inspirations*, and private *mediations, conferences, reading*, and the like, doe awaken some; but the testimony of the messenger of God, the *preacher*, crying according to Gods ordinance, shaking the soule, troubling the conscience, and pinching the bowels, by denouncing of Gods Judgements, these beare witness of the light, when otherwise men would sleep it out.[86]

Though a man can cut deeper with an Axe, then with a knife, with a heavy, then with a lighter instrument; yet God can pierce as far into a conscience, by a plain, as by an exquisite speaker.[87]

We must preach in the Mountaine, and preach in the plaine too; preach to the learned, and preach to the simple too; preach to the Court, and preach to the Country too. Onely when we preach in the mountaine, they in the plaine must not calumniate us, and say, This man goes up to Jerusalem, he will be heard by none but Princes, and great persons, as though it were out of affectation, and not in discharge of our duty, that we doe preach there: And when we preach on the plaine, they of the mountaine must not say, This man may serve for a meane Auditory, for a simple Congregation, for a Country Church, as though the fitting of our selves to the capacity, and the edification of such persons, were out of ignorance, or lazinesse, and not a performance of our duties, as well as the other. Christ preached on the mountaine, and he preached in the plaine; he hath his Church in both; and they that preach in both, or either, for his glory, and not their owne vain-glory, have his Example for their Action.[88]

B irds that are kept in cages may learne some Notes, which they should never have sung in the Woods or Fields; but yet they may forget their naturall Notes too. *Preachers* that binde themselves alwaies to *Cities* and *Courts*, and *great Auditories*, may learne new Notes; they may become *occasionall* Preachers, and make the emergent affaires of the time, their *Text*, and the humors of the hearers their *Bible*; but they may loose their Naturall Notes, both the *simplicitie*, and the *boldnesse* that belongs to the Preaching of the *Gospell*: both their power upon lowe understandings to raise them, and upon high affections to humble them. They may thinke that their errand is but to knocke at the doore, to delight the eare, and not to search the House, to ransacke the conscience.[89]

H ow much were we inexcuseable, if either out of fullness of fortunes, or emptiness of learning; if either out of state, or business, or laziness, or pretence of fear, where no fear is, we should smother this light, which if it have truly shin'd in our hearts, will shine in our tongues too?[90]

A preachers end is not a gathering of fame to himselfe, but a gathering of soules to God; and his way is not novelty, but edification.[91]

The Work of Evangelism

C hrist is given to us, that we might give him to others. So that in this kind of spirituall liberality, we can be liberall of no more but our owne; we can give nothing but Christ; we can minister comfort to none, farther then he is capable, and willing to receive and embrace Christ Jesus.[92]

T he love of God is not a contract, a bargaine, he looks for nothing againe, and yet he looks for thanks . . . God looks for nothing, nothing to be done in the way of exact recompence, but yet, as he that makes a Clock, bestowes all that labour upon the severall wheeles, that thereby the Bell might give a sound, and that thereby the hand might give knowledge to others how the time passes; so this is the principall part of that thankfulnesse, which God requires from us, that we make open declarations of his mercies, to the winning and confirming of others.[93]

I t is, I thinke, the greatest joy that the soule of man is capable of in this life . . . to assist the salvation of others.[94]

W hat action soever, hath in the first intention thereof, a purpose to propagate the Gospell of *Christ Iesus*, that is an *Apostolicall* action.[95]

A good hearer becomes a good Preacher, that is, able to edifie others.[96]

I f when we have begot you in Christ, by our preaching, you also beget others by your holy life and conversation, you have added another generation unto us, and you have preached over our Sermons again, as fruitfully as we our selves; you shall be our Crown, and they shall be your Crowns, and Christ Jesus a Crown of everlasting glory to us all.[97]

T o me, to whom God hath revealed his Son, in a Gospel, by a Church, there can be no way of salvation, but by applying that Son of God, by that Gospel, in that Church. Nor is there any other foundation for any, nor other name by which any can be saved, but the name of Jesus. But how this foundation is presented, and how this name of Jesus is notified to them, amongst whom there is no Gospel preached, no Church established, I am not curious in inquiring . . . And therefore humbly imbracing that manifestation of his Son, which he hath afforded me, I leave God, to his unsearchable waies of working upon other, without farther inquisition.[98]

Christ is come into the world; we will do little, if we will not ferry him over, and propagate his name, as well as our own to other Nations.[99]

CHRISTIAN OBEDIENCE

The Call to Discipleship

To be a good Morall man, and refer all to the law of Nature in our hearts, is but . . . The dawning of the day; To be a godly man, and refer all to God, is but . . . A Twylight; But the Meridionall brightnesse, the glorious noon, and heighth, is to be a Christian, to pretend to no spirituall, no temporall blessing, but for, and by, and through, and in our only Lord and Saviour Christ Jesus.[1]

To come to God there is a straight line for every man every where: But this we doe not, if we come not with our heart.[2]

God requires the heart, the whole man, all the faculties of that man; for onely that that is intire, and indivisible, is immovable.[3]

God asks nothing of man, but his heart; and nothing, but man, can give the heart to God.[4]

Seale then this bill of my Divorce to All,
On whom those fainter beames of love did fall;
Marry those loves, which in youth scattered bee
On Fame, Wit, Hopes (false mistresses) to thee.
Churches are best for Prayer, that have least light:
To see God only, I goe out of sight:
   And to scape stormy dayes, I chuse
     An Everlasting night.[5]

He must be crucified to the world, that will receive him, that was crucified for the world.[6]

Here's the election day; bring that which ye would have, into comparison with that which ye should have; that is, all that this world keeps from you, with that which God offers to you; and what will ye choose to prefer before him? for honor, and favor, and health, and riches, perchance you cannot have them though you choose them; but can you have more of them than they have had, to whom those very things have been occasions of ruin? The Market is open till the bell ring; till thy last bell ring the Church is open, grace is to had there: but trust not upon that rule, that men buy cheapest at the end of the market, that heaven may be had for a breath at last, when they that hear it cannot tel whether it be a sigh or a gasp, a religious breathing and anhelation after the next life, or natural breathing out, and exhalation of this; but find a spiritual good husbandry in that other rule, that the prime of the market is to be had at first: for howsoever, in thine age, there may be by Gods strong working . . . A day of youth, in making thee then a new creature . . . yet when age hath made a man impotent to sin, this is not . . . a day of choice; but remember God now, when thou hast a choice, that is, a power to advance thyself, or to oppress others by evil means; now . . . in those thy happy and sun-shine dayes, *remember him.*[7]

No solitude, no tempest, no bleaknesse, no inconvenience averts Christ, and his Spirit, from his sweet, and gracious, and comfortable visitations.[8]

At least be sure that he is so far come into the world, as that he be come into thee. Thou art but a little world, a world but of a few spanns in length; and yet Christ was sooner carried from east to west, from *Jerusalem* to these parts, then thou canst carry him over the faculties of thy Soul and Body; He hath been in a pilgrimage towards thee long, coming towards thee, perchance 50, perchance 60 years; and how far is he got into thee yet? . . . He may be come to the skirts, to the borders, to an outward show in thine actions, and yet not be come into the land, into thy heart. He entred into thee, at baptism; He hath crept farther and farther into thee, in catechisms and other infusions of his doctrine into thee; He hath pierced into thee deeper by the powerful threatnings of his Judgments, in the mouths of his messengers; He hath made some survey over thee, in bringing thee to call thy self to an account of some sinful actions; and yet Christ is not come into thee . . . He is not come into thee with that comfort which belongs to his coming . . . except he have over-shadowed thee all, and be in thee intirely.[9]

I t is good for a man that he beare his yoke in his youth, that he seek Christ early . . . Yet if we have omitted our first early, our youth, there is one early left for us; this minute; seek Christ early, now, now, as soon as his Spirit begins to shine upon your hearts. Now as soon as you begin your day of Regeneration, seek him the first minute of this day, for you know not whether this day shall have two minutes or no, that is, whether his Spirit, that descends upon you now, will tarry and rest upon you or not, as it did upon Christ at his baptisme.[10]

T hey are but hollow places that returne *Ecchoes*; last syllables: It is but a hollownesse of heart, to answer God *at last*.[11]

H umiliation is the beginning of sanctification; and as without this, without holinesse, no man shall see God, though he pore whole nights upon the Bible; so without that, without humility, no man shall heare God speake to his soule, though hee heare three twohoures Sermons every day. But if God bring thee to that humiliation of soule and body here, hee will emprove and advance thy sanctification . . . more abundantly, and when he hath brought it to the best perfection, that this life is capable of, he will provide . . . another maner of abundance in the life to come.[12]

Being in Christ

To him that is become a new creature, a true Christian, all old things are done away, and all things are made new: As he hath a new birth, as he hath put on a new man, as he is going towards a new *Jerusalem*, so hath he a new Philosophy, a new production, and generation of effects out of other causes, then before, he finds light out of darknesse, fire out of water, life out of death, joy out of afflictions.[13]

The Lord gives, and the Lord takes away, but the Lord never takes away himselfe from him that delights in blessing his name. Blesse, praise, speake; there is the duty.[14]

There is no love of God without feare, no Law of God, no God himselfe without feare; And . . . the feare of God is our whole Religion, the whole service of God; for . . . Feare him, includes Worship him, reverence him, obey him.[15]

There are many . . . outward badges and marks, by which others may judge, and pronounce mee to bee a true Christian; But the . . . inward badge and marke, by which I know this in my self, is joy.[16]

No man may take the frame of Christs merit in peeces; no Man may take his forty days *fasting* and put on that, and say, Christ hath fasted for me, and therefore I may surfeit; No man may take his *Agony*, and pensivenesse, and put on that, and say, Christ hath *been sad* for me, and therefore I may be merry. He that puts on Christ, must put him on *all*; and not onely find, that Christ hath dyed, nor onely that he hath died for *him*, but that he also hath died *in* Christ, and that whatsoever Christ suffered, *he* suffered *in* Christ.[17]

From this putting on Christ as a garment, we shall grow up to that perfection, as that we shall . . . put on *him*, his person; That is, we shall so appeare before the Father, as that he shall take us for his owne Christ; we shall beare his name and person; and we shall every one be so accepted, as if every one of us were *all Mankind*; yea, as if we were *he* himselfe. He shall find in all our bodies his *woundes*, in all our mindes, his *Agonies*: in all our hearts, and actions his *obedience*.[18]

Now this putting on of Christ, whereby we stand in his place at Gods Tribunall, implies . . . both our *Election*, and our *sanctification*; both the eternall purpose of God upon us, and his execution of that purpose in us. And because by the first (by our *Election*) we are members of Christ, in Gods purpose, before *baptisme*, and the second, (which is *sanctification*) is expressed after baptisme, in our lives, and conversation, therefore *Baptisme* intervenes, and comes *between both*, as a seal of the first, (of Election) and as an instrument, and conduit of the second, Sanctification.[19]

In Christ I can do all things; I need no more but him; without Christ, I can doe nothing; not onely not have him, but not know that I need him.[20]

Purity, Sincerity, Integrity, Holinesse, is a skirt of Christs garment; It is the very livery that he puts upon us; wee cannot serve him without it . . . we cannot see him without it.[21]

As they that build Arches, place centers under the Arch, to beare up the work, till it bee dried, and setled, but, after, all is Arch, and there is no more center, no more support; so to lie at the Lords feet a while, delivers us into his arms, to accustome our selves to his fear, establishes us in his love.[22]

L et nothing therefore that can fall upon thee, dispoyle thee of the dignity and constancy of a Christian; howsoever thou be severed from those things, which thou makest account do make thee up, severed from a wife by divorce, from a child by death, from goods by fire, or water, from an office by just, or by unjust displeasure, (which is the heavier but the happier case) yet never think thy self severed from thy Head Christ Jesus, nor from being a lively member of his body.[23]

W hen God hath made himselfe one body with me, by his assuming this *nature*, and made me *one spirit* with himselfe, and that by so high a way, as making me *partaker of the divine nature*, so that now, *in Christ Jesus*, he and I are one, this were . . . a tearing in peeces, a dissolving of Jesus, in the worst kinde that could be imagined, if I should teare my self from Jesus, or by any jealousie or suspicion of his mercy, or any horror in my own sinnes, come to thinke my selfe to be none of *his*, none of *him*.[24]

A n ungodly life in them that professe Christ, is a daily crucifying of Christ.[25]

N o descent in to hell, of what kinde soever you conceive that descent into hell to have been, put the Son of God out of heaven, by descending into hell . . . no Leave, no Commandement that God gives us, to doe the works of our calling here, excludes us from him; but as the Saints of God shall follow the Lamb, wheresoever he goes in heaven, so the Lamb of God shall follow his Saints, wheresoever they goe upon earth if they walk sincerely.[26]

Obstacles to Salvation

A *Christian* in profession, that is not a *Christian* in life, is so intestable, hee discredits *Christ*, and hardens others against him.[27]

B linde and implicite faith shall not save us in matter of Doctrine, nor blinde and implicite obedience, in matter of practice.[28]

W ho will beleeve that we know there is a ditch, and know the danger of falling into it, and drowning in it, if he see us run headlong towards it, and fall into it, and continue in it? Who can beleeve, that he that separates himself from Christ, by continuing in his sin, hath any knowledge, or sense, or evidence, or testimony of Christs being in him? As Christ proceeds by enlarging thy knowledge, and making thee wiser and wiser, so enlarge thy testimony of it, by growing better and better, and let him that is holy, bee more holy.[29]

L ive and die in such a sense of this plenteous Redemption of thy God, as though neither thou, nor any could lose salvation, except he doubted of it.[30]

T o pretend to doe good, and not meane it; To doe things, good in themselves, but not to good ends; to goe towards good ends, but not by good ways; to make the deceiving of men, thine end; or the praise of men, thine end: all this may have a whiteness, a colour of good: but all this, is a barking of the bough, and an indication of a mischievous leprosie. There is no good whiteness, but a reflection from Christ Jesus, in an humble acknowledgement that wee have none of our own, and in a confident assurance, that in our worst estate we may be made partakers of his.[31]

L et us, all us, cast off the works of darkness, and put on the armor of light; light it self is faith; but, the armor of light is knowledge; an ignorant man is a disarm'd man, a naked man.[32]

C urious men busie themselves so much upon speculative subtilties, as that they desert, and abandon the solid foundations of Religion, and that is a dangerous vomit; To search so farre into the nature, and unrevealed purposes of God, as to forget the nature, and duties of man, this is a shrewd surfet, though of hony, and a dangerous vomit.[33]

Even in spirituall things, there may be a fulnesse, and no satisfaction. And there may be a satisfaction, and no fulnesse; I may have as much knowledge, as is presently necessary for my salvation, and yet have a restlesse and unsatisfied desire, to search into unprofitable curiosities, unrevealed mysteries, and inextricable perplexities: And, on the other side, a man may be satisfied, and thinke he knowes all, when, God knowes, he knowes nothing at all; for, I know nothing, if I know not Christ crucified, And I know not that, if I know not how to apply him to my selfe, Nor doe I know that, if I embrace him not in those meanes, which he hath afforded me in his Church, in his Word, and Sacraments; If I neglect this meanes, this place, these exercises, howsoever I may satisfie my selfe, with an over-valuing mine own knowledge at home, I am so far from fulnesse, as that vanity it selfe is not more empty.[34]

Publish, declare, manifest your zeale. Christ is *Verbum*, *The Word*, and that excludes silence; but Christ is also λόγος, and that excludes rashnesse, and impertinence in our speech.[35]

To shake the constancy of a Christian, there will alwaies be *Scorners*, *Iesters*, *Scoffers*, and *Mockers* at *Religion*.[36]

They know, and pray, that wee may know,
  In every Christian
Hourly tempestuous persecutions grow,
Tentations martyr us alive; A man
Is to himselfe a Dioclesian.[37]

The naturall love of our naturall life is not *ill*: It is ill, in many cases, *not to love this life*: to expose it to unnecessary dangers, is alwayes ill; and there are overtures to as great sinnes, in *hating* this life, as in loving it.[38]

An idle word in a Church-mans mouth is sacriledge; so a wanton look in the Church, is an Adultery.[39]

That Christ should take my body, though defiled with fornication, and make it his, is strange; but that I, in fornication, should take Christs body, and make it hers, is more.[40]

They are not your works, if that that you give be not your owne. Nor is it your own, if it were ill gotten at first. How long soever it have been possessed, or how often soever it have beene transformed, from money to ware, from ware to land, from land to office, from office to honour, the money, the ware, the land, the office, the honour is none of thine, if, in thy knowledge, it were ill gotten at first.[41]

Make not too much haste to be rich: Even in spirituall riches, in spirituall health make not too much haste. Pray for it; for there is no other way to get it. Pray to the Lord for it: For, Saints and Angels have but enough for themselves. Make haste to begin to have these spirituall graces; To desire them, is to begin to have them: But make not too much haste in the way; Doe not think thy selfe purer then thou art, because thou seest another doe some such sins, as thou hast forborne. Beloved, at last, when Christ Jesus comes with his scales, thou shalt not be waighed with that man, but every man shall be waighed with God.[42]

Nothing hinders our own salvation more, then to deny salvation, to all but our selves.[43]

C all not light faults by heavie Names; Call not all sociablenesse, and Conversation, Disloyaltie in thy Wife; Nor all levitie, or pleasurablenesse, Incorrigiblenesse in thy Sonne; nor all negligence, or forgetfulnesse, Perfidiousnesse in thy Servant; Nor let every light disorder within doores, shut thee out of doores, or make thee a stranger in thine owne House. In a smoakie roome, it may be enough to open a Windowe, without leaving the place; In Domestique unkindnesses, and discontents, it may be wholesomer to give them a Concoction at home in a discreete patience, or to give them a vent at home, in a moderate rebuke, then to thinke to ease them, or put them off, with false divertions abroad.[44]

H eaven is alwayes so much worth, as thou art worth. A poore man may have heaven for a penny, that hath no greater store; and, God lookes, that he to whom he hath given thousands, should lay out thousands upon the purchase of heaven. The market changes, as the plenty of money changes; Heaven costs a rich man more then a poore, because he hath more to give. But in this, rich and poore are both equall, that both must leave themselves without nets, that is, without those things, which, in their own Consciences they know, retard the following of Christ. Whatsoever hinders my present following, that I cannot follow to day, whatsoever may hinder my constant following, that I cannot follow to morrow, and all my life, is a net, and I am bound to leave that.[45]

W ar is a fearfull state; but not so, if it be war of God, undertaken for his cause, or by his Word. Many times, a State suffers by the security of a Peace, and gains by the watchfulness of a War. Wo be to that man that is so at peace, as that the spirit fights not against the flesh in him; and wo to them too, who would make them friends, or reconcile them, between whom, God hath perpetuated an everlasting war.[46]

N one of us hath got the victory over flesh and blood, and yet we have greater enemies then flesh and blood are. Some disciplines, some mortifications we have against flesh and blood . . . for that we have some assistance; Even our enemies become our friends; poverty or sicknesse will fight for us against flesh and blood, against our carnall lusts; but for these powers and principalities, I know not where to watch them, how to encounter them. I passe my time sociably and merrily in cheerful conversation, in musique, in feasting, in Comedies, in wantonnesse; and I never heare all this while of any power or principality, my Conscience spies no such enemy in all this. And then alone, between God and me at midnight, some beam of his grace shines out upon me, and by that light I see this Prince of darknesse, and then I finde that I have been the subject, the slave of these powers and principalities, when I thought not of them. Well, I see them, and I try then to dispossesse my selfe of them, and I make my recourse to the powerfullest exorcisme that is, I turn to hearty and earnest prayer to God, and I fix my thoughts strongly (as I thinke) upon him, and before I have perfected one petition, one period of my prayer, a power and principality is got into me againe.[47]

God will have no *half-affections*, God will have no partners; He that fears God fears nothing else.[48]

If my feare of God fall, the word of God, so farre as it is a promise to me, falls to.[49]

Perseverance

Even Religion it self, must be looked upon, considered; not taken implicitely, nor occasionally, not advantageously, but seriously and deliberately, and then assuredly, and constantly.[50]

To sayle to heaven it is not enough to cast away the burdenous superfluities which we have long carried about us, but we must also take in a good frayte. It is not lightnesse, but an even-reposed stedfastnesse, which carries us thither.[51]

[275]

Our life is a warfare, our whole life; It is not onely with lusts in our youth, and ambitions in our middle yeares, and indevotions in our age, but with agonies in our body, and tentations in our spirit upon our death-bed, that we are to fight; and he cannot be said to overcome, that fights not out the whole battell. If he enter not the field in the morning, that is, apply not himselfe to Gods service in his youth, If hee continue not to the Evening, If hee faint in the way, and grow remisse in Gods service, for collaterall respects, God will overcome his cause, and his glory shall stand fast, but that man can scarce be said to have overcome.[52]

When therefore the Lord and his Spirit cals thee to this spirituall Circumcision, remember that *Abraham* did not say when he was call'd, Lord, I have followed thy voyce, in leaving my Country; Lord, I have built thee an Altar, what needs more demonstration of my obedience? Say not thou, Lord, I have built an *Hospitall*; Lord, I have *fed the poore* at *Christmas*; Lord, I have made peace amongst thy people at home; I have endowed an *Almeshouse*; but persevere in doing good *still*, for, God takes not the Tree, where it *growes*, but where it *fals*; for the most part, the death of a man is such, as his life was; but certainly the life of a man, that is, his everlasting life, is such as his death is.[53]

Our sanctification must goe through our *whole life* in a constant, and an even perseverance; we must not onely be *Hospitales*, and feed the poore at Christmas, be sober, and abstinent, the day that we *receive*, repent, and thinke of amendment of life, in the day of visitation, and *sicknesse*; but, as the garment, which Christ wore, was *seamlesse*, and intire, so this garment, which is *Christ Jesus*, that is, our sanctification, should be intire, and uninterrupted, in the whole course of our lives.[54]

Though thou *sit in darknesse*, and *in the shadow of death*, yet praise him for the light of his Countenance. Whatsoever *thy darknesse* be, put not out that candle, *The light of his Countenance.* Maintain that light, discerne that light, and whatsoever thy darknesse seemed, it shall prove to be but an *over shadowing of the Holy Ghost.*[55]

L imit not God therefore in his wayes or times, but yf you would be heard by him, heare him, yf you would have him graunt your prayers, doe his will. We pray you in Christs steed that you would be reconciled to God; and are you reconciled? durst you heare the trumpet nowe? Christ Jesus prayes for you nowe to his Father in heaven, that you might be converted and are you converted? If the prayers of the Church militant and the Church triumphant and the head of both Churches Christ Jesus, be not yet heard effectually on your behalfe, yet they shalbe in his time, his eternall election shall infallibly worke upon you. Soe if your owne prayers for your deliverance in any temporall or spirituall affliction be not presently heard, persevere for youre selves, as the Churches and the heade of them persevere in your behalfe, and God will certainly deliver you in his time, and strengthen you to fight out his battle all the way.[56]

I f thou canst take this light of reason that is in thee, this poore snuffe, that is almost out in thee, thy faint and dimme knowledge of God, that riseth out of this light of nature, if thou canst in those embers, those cold ashes, finde out one small coale, and wilt take the paines to kneell downe, and blow that coale with thy devout *Prayers*, and light thee a *little candle*, (a *desire* to read that Booke, which they call the Scriptures, and the Gospell, and the Word of God;) If with that little candle thou canst creep humbly into low and poore places, if thou canst finde thy Saviour in a *Manger*, and in his *swathing clouts*, in his humiliation, and blesse God for that beginning, if thou canst finde him flying into Egypt, and find in thy selfe a disposition to accompany him in a persecution, in a banishment, if not a bodily banishment, a locall banishment, yet a *reall, a spirituall banishment*, a banishment from those sinnes, and that sinnefull conversation, which thou hast loved more then thy *Parents*, or *Countrey*, or thine owne body, which perchance thou hast consumed, and destroyed with that sinne; if thou canst finde him contenting and containing himselfe at home in his fathers house, and not breaking out, no not about the worke of our salvation, till the due time was come, when it was to be done. And if according to that example, thou canst contain thy selfe in that station and vocation in which God hath planted thee, and not, through a hasty and precipitate *zeale*, breake out to an imaginary, and intempestive, and unseasonable *Reformation*, either in *Civill* or *Ecclesiasticall* businesse, which belong not to thee; if with this little poore light, these *first degrees of Knowledge* and *Faith*, thou canst follow him into the *Garden*, and gather up some of the droppes of his precious Bloud and sweat, which he shed for thy soule, if thou canst follow him to *Jerusalem*, and pick up some of those *teares*, which he shed upon that City, and upon thy soule; if thou canst follow him to the place of his scourging, and to his crucifying, and provide thee some of that balme, which must cure thy soule; if after all this, thou canst turne this little light inward, and canst thereby discerne where thy diseases, and thy wounds, and thy corruptions are, and canst apply those teares, and blood and balme to them . . . thou shalt never envy the lustre and glory of the great lights of worldly men, which are great by the infirmity of others, or by their own opinion, great because others think them great, or because they think themselves so, but thou shalt finde, that howsoever they magnifie their lights, their wit, their learning, their industry, their fortune, their favour, and *sacrifice to their owne nets*, yet thou shalt see, that thou by thy small light has gathered *Pearle* and *Amber*, and they by their great lights nothing but shels and pebles; they have determined the light of nature, upon the booke of nature, this world, and thou hast carried the light of nature higher, thy naturall reason, and even *humane arguments*, have brought thee to reade the Scriptures, and to that *love*, God hath set to the seale of *faith*. Their light shall set at noone; even in their heighth, some heavy crosse shall cast a damp upon their soule, and cut off all their succours, and devest them of all comforts, and thy light shall grow up, from a *faire hope*, to a modest assurance and *infallibility*, that that light shall never go out, nor the *works of darknesse*, nor the *Prince of darknesse* ever prevaile upon thee, but as thy light of *reason* is exalted by *faith* here, so thy light of *faith* shall be exalted into the light of *glory*, and fruition in the Kingdome of heaven.[57]

So since we are the generation and of-spring of God, since Grace is our Father, that Parent that begets all goodness in us . . . let us every day, every minute feele this new generation of spirituall children . . . Let us present our own will as a mother to the father of light, and the father of life, and the father of love, that we may be willing to conceive by the overshadowing of the Holy Ghost, and not resist his working upon our Soules . . . for, hearing is but the conception, meditation is but the quickning, purposing is but the birth, but practising is the growth of this blessed childe.[58]

God is the Rocke of our salvation; God is no Occasionall God, no Accidentall God; neither will God be served by Occasion, nor by Accident, but by a constant Devotion.[59]

Heaven is not to be had in exchange for an Hospital, or a Chantry, or a Colledge erected in thy last will: It is not onely the selling all we have, that must buy that pearl, which represents the kingdome of Heaven; The giving of all that we have to the poor, at our death, will not do it; the pearl must be sought, and found before, in an even, and constant course of Sanctification; we must be thrifty all our life, or we shall be too poor for that purchase.[60]

Growing up into Christ

Find thou a growth of the Gospel in thy faith, and let us finde it in thy life . . . If thou finde it not ascending, it descends; If thy comforts in the Gospel of Christ Jesus grow not, they decay; If thou profit not by the Gospel, thou losest by it; If thou live not by it, (nothing can redeeme thee) thou dyest by it.[61]

The kingdom of heaven is a feast; to get you a Stomach to that, we have preached abstinence. The kingdom of heaven is a treasure too, and to make you capable of that, we would bring you to a just valuation of this world. He that hath his hands full of dirt, cannot take up Amber; if they be full of Counters, he cannot take up gold.[62]

There is a spirituall fulnesse in this life . . . In which the more we eate, the more temperate we are, and the more we drinke, the more sober.[63]

Beloved, as it is a degree of superstition, and an effect of an undiscreet zeale, perchance, to be too forward in making indifferent things necessary, and so to imprint the nature, and sting of sin where naturally it is not so: certainly it is a more slippery and irreligious thing to be too apt to call things meerely indifferent, and to forget that even in eating and drinking, waking and sleeping, the glory of God is intermingled.[64]

It is not enough for you, to rest in an imaginary faith, and easinesse in beleeving, except you know also what, and why, and how you come to that beliefe. Implicite beleevers, ignorant beleevers, the adversary may swallow; but the understanding beleever, he must chaw, and pick bones, before he come to assimilate him, and make him like himself. The implicite beleever stands in an open field, and the enemy will ride over him easily; the understanding beleever, is in a fenced town, and he hath out-works to lose, before the town be pressed; that is, reasons to be answered, before his faith be shaked, and he will sell himself deare, and lose himself by inches, if he be sold or lost at last; and therefore . . . let all men know, that is, endeavour to informe themselves, to understand.[65]

How many in the world would have lived ten times more *christianly* then we do, if they had but halfe that knowledge of *Christ*, which we have?[66]

I would scarce ask more in any mans behalf, then that he would always be as good, as at some times he is; If he would never sink below himself, I would lesse care, though he did not exceed himself: If he would remember his own holy purposes at best, he would never forget God.[67]

Neither make so much haste to this spirituall riches, and health, as to think thy self whole before thou art: Neither murmure, nor despaire of thy recovery, if thou beest not whole so soone as thou desiredst. If thou wrastle with tentations, and canst not over-come them, If thou purpose to pray earnestly, and finde thy mind presently strayed from that purpose, If thou intend a good course, and meet with stops in the way, If thou seeke peace of conscience, and scruples out of zeale interrupt that, yet discomfort not thy selfe. God staid six daies in his first worke, in the Creation, before he came to make thee; yet all that while he wrought for thee. Thy Regeneration, to make thee a new creature, is a greater worke then that, and it cannot be done in an instant. God hath purposed a building in thee; he hath sat down, and considered, that he hath sufficient to accomplish that building, as it is in the Gospel, and therefore leave him to his leisure.[68]

God is a God of harmony, and consent, and in a musicall instru-ment, if some strings be out of tune, wee doe not presently breake all the strings, but reduce and tune those, which are out of tune.[69]

If the Lords arme bee not shortned, let no man impute weaknesse to his Instrument. But yet God will alwayes have so much weak-nesse appeare in the Instrument, as that their strength shall not be thought to be their owne.[70]

For, to take any one crosse patiently, is but to forgive God for once; but, to surrender one's self entirely to God, is to be ready for all that he shall be pleased to do.[71]

Since Christ embrac'd the Crosse it self, dare I
His image, th'image of his Crosse deny?
Would I have profit by the sacrifice,
And dare the chosen Altar to despise?
It bore all other sinnes, but is it fit
That it should beare the sinne of scorning it?

. . . the losse
Of this Crosse, were to mee another Crosse.
Better were worse, for, no affliction,
No Crosse is so extreme, as to have none.

Who can deny mee power, and liberty
To stretch mine armes, and mine owne Crosse to be?
Swimme, and at every stroake, thou art thy Crosse,
The Maste and yard make one, where seas do tosse.
Looke downe, thou spiest out Crosses in small things;
Looke up, thou seest birds rais'd on crossed wings;
All the Globes frame, and spheares, is nothing else
But the Meridians crossing Parallels.
Materiall Crosses then, good physicke bee,
But yet spirituall have chiefe dignity.

But most the eye needs crossing, that can rome,
And move, To th'other th'objects must come home.
And crosse thy heart: for that in man alone
Pants downewards, and hath palpitation.

Be covetous of Crosses, let none fall.
Crosse no man else, but crosse thy selfe in all.
Then doth the Crosse of Christ worke faithfully
Within our hearts.[72]

Christ needed not mans sufficiency, he took insufficient men; Christ excuses no mans insufficiency, he made them suffici-ent.[73]

Beloved, good dyet makes the best Complexion, and a good Conscience is a continuall feast; A cheerful heart makes the best blood and peace with God is the true cheerfulnesse of heart.[74]

Deceive not your selves, no man hath so much pleasure in this life, as he that is at peace with God.[75]

If I would not serve God, except I might be saved for serving him, I shall not be saved though I serve him; My first end in serving God, must not be my selfe, but he and his glory.[76]

Faith and Works

Every good work hath faith for the roote; but every faith hath not good works for the fruit thereof.[77]

He onely hath put on Christ, which hath Christ in himselfe by *faith*, and shewes him to others by his *works*, which is . . . *a burning lamp*, and a *shining lamp*, profitable to others, as well as to himselfe.[78]

Practice is the *Incarnation of Faith*, Faith is incorporated and manifested in a body, by works.[79]

All our moralities are but our outworks, our Christianity is our Citadel; a man who considers duty but the dignity of his being a man, is not easily beat from his outworks, but from his Christianity never.[80]

God requires the heart, *My sonne give me thy heart*; He will have it, but he will have it by gift; and those Deeds of Gift must be testified; and the testimony of the heart is in the hand, the testimony of faith is in works . . . God judges according to *the worke*, that is, Roote and fruit, faith and worke.[81]

The evidence that Christ produces, and presses, is good works; for, if a man offer me the roote of a tree to taste, I cannot say this is such a Pear, or Apple, or Plum; but if I see *the fruit*, I can.[82]

The works of a holy life, doe daily refresh the contract made with God . . . at our *Baptisme*, and testifie to the Church, that we doe carefully remember, what the *Church* promised in our behalfe, at that time.[83]

To will, as well as to doe, to beleeve, as well as to work, is all from God; but yet they are from God in a diverse manner, and a diverse respect; and certainly our works are more ours then our faith is, and man concurres otherwise in the acting and perpetration of a good work, then he doth in the reception and admission of faith.[84]

Never . . . take confidence in works, otherwise then as they are rooted in faith: For if thou shouldst see a man pull at an Oare, till his eye-strings, and sinews, and muscles broke, and thou shouldst aske him, whither he rowed; If thou shouldest see a man runne himself out of breath, and shouldst aske him whither he ranne; If thou shouldst see him dig till his backe broke, and shouldst aske him, what he sought, And any of these should answer thee, they could not tell, wouldst not thou thinke them mad? So are all Disciplines, all Mortifications, all whippings, all starvings, all works of Piety, and of Charity madnesse, if they have any other roote then faith, any other title or dignity, then effects and fruits of a preceding reconciliation to God.[85]

Neither faith, nor works bring us (to the Land of Rest) . . . but the *cause*, is onely, the free *election* of God. Nor ever shall we come thither, if we leave out either; we shall meet as many Men in heaven, that have lived without faith, as without works.[86]

One Body in Christ

Religion is no sullen thing, it is not a melancholly, there is not so sociable a thing as the love of Christ Jesus.[87]

A man is thy Neighbor, by his Humanity, not by his Divinity; by his Nature, not by his Religion: a Virginian is thy Neighbor, as well as a Londoner; and all men are in every good mans Diocess, and Parish.[88]

As in heaven, the joy of every soule shall be my joy, so the mercy of God to every soule here, is a mercy to my soule; By the extension of his mercies to others, I argue the application of his mercy to my selfe.[89]

Blessed are they who make haste to Christ, and publish their zeale to the encouragement of others: For, let no man promise himself a religious constancy in the time of his triall, that doth not his part in establishing the religious constancy of other men.[90]

Go thou to heaven, in an humble thankfulnesse to God, and holy cheerfulnesse, in that way that God hath manifested to thee; and do not pronounce too bitterly, too desperately, that every man is in an errour, that thinkes not just as thou thinkest, or in no way, that is not in thy way.[91]

So be thou a chearfull occasion of glorifying God by thy joy. *Declare his loving kindnesse unto the sons of men*; Tell them what he hath done for thy soule, thy body, thy state. Say, *With this staffe came I over Iordane*: Be content to tell whose Son thou wast, and how small thy beginning. Smother not Gods blessings, by making thy selfe poore, when he who is truly poore, begges of thee, for that Gods sake, who gave thee all that thou hast. Hold up a holy chearfulnesse in thy heart; Goe on in a chearfull conversation; and let the world see, that all this growes out of a peace, betwixt God and thee, testified in the blessings of this world; and then thou art that Person, and then thou hast that Portion, which growes out of this root . . . *Mercy shall compasse him about that trusteth in the Lord.*[92]

G od enables me to glorife him, to amplifie him, to encrease him, by my mercy, my almes.[93]

I f you touch a string below, the motion goes to the top: any good done to Christs poor members upon earth, affects him in heaven.[94]

Suffering for Christ

T ruly, if it were possible to feare any defect of joy in heaven, all that could fall into my feare would be but this, that in heaven I can no longer express my love by suffering for my God, for my Saviour. A greater joy cannot enter into my heart then this, To suffer for him that suffered for me.[95]

G ods suffering for man was the Nadir, the lowest point of Gods humiliation, mans suffering for God is the Zenith, the highest point of mans exaltation.[96]

S ince all his *life* was a *continuall passion*, all *our Lent* may well bee a *continuall good Fryday*.[97]

S ince I am bound to take up my crosse, there must be a crosse that is mine to take up; that is, a crosse prepared for me by God, and laid in my way, which is tentations or tribulations in my calling; and I must not go out of my way to seeke a crosse; for, so it is not mine, nor laid for my taking up.[98]

G od hath not made a week without a Sabbath; no tentation, without an issue; God inflicts no calamity, no cloud, no eclipse, without light, so see ease in it, if the patient will look upon that which God hath done to him, in other cases, or to that which God hath done to others, at other times . . . God brings us to humiliation, but not to desperation.[99]

God would not chuse *Cowards*: hee had rather we were valiant in the fighting of his battels; for battels, and exercise of valour, we are sure to have.[100]

But be ye reconciled to God . . . and this reconciliation shall work thus, it shall restore you to that state, that *Adam* had in Paradise . . . Go home, and if you finde an over-burden of children, negligence in servants, crosses in your tradings, narrownesse, penury in your estate, yet this penurious, and this encumbred house shall be your Paradise. Go forth, into the Country, and if you finde unseasonablenesse in the weather, rots in your sheep, murrains in your cattell, worms in your corn, backwardnesse in your rents, oppression in your Landlord, yet this field of thorns and brambles shall be your Paradise. Lock thy selfe up in thy selfe, in thine own bosome, and though thou finde every roome covered with the soot of former sins, and shaked with that Devill whose name is *Legion*, some such sin as many sins depend upon, and are induced by, yet this prison, this rack, this hell in thine own conscience shall be thy Paradise.[101]

We see the extent and latitude, and compass of Martyrdome . . . that not only loss of life, but loss of that which we love in this life; not only the suffering of death, but the suffering of Crosses in our life, contracts the Name, and entitles us to the reward of Martyrdome. All Martyrdome is not a *Smithfeild* Martyrdome, to burn for religion. To suffer injuries, and upon advantages offerd, not to revenge those injuries is a Court Martyrdome. To resist outward tentations from power, and inward tentations from affections, in matter of Judicature, between party and party, is a *Westminster* Martyrdome. To seem no richer then they are, not to make their states better, when they make their private bargains with one another, and to seem so rich, as they are, and not to make their states worse, when they are call'd upon to contribute to publick services, this is an Exchange-Martyrdome. And there is a Chamber-Martyrdome, a Bosome-Martyrdome too . . . Chastity is a dayly Martyrdome; and so all fighting of the Lords battails, all victory over the Lords Enemies, in our own bowels, all chearful bearing of

Gods Crosses, and all watchful crossing of our own immoderate desires is a Martyrdome acceptable to God.[102]

If I can fixe my self, with the strength of faith, upon that which God hath done for man, I cannot doubt of his mercy, in any distresse.[103]

For a sober life, and a Christian mortification, and discreet discipline, are crosses derived from the Crosse of Christ Jesus, and animated by it, and may be alwaies in a readiness to crosse . . . tentations.[104]

All the love, all the ambitions, all the losses of this world, are not worth a sigh; If they were, yet thou hast none to spare, for all thy sighs are due to thy sins; bestow them there.[105]

Teares are that usury, by which the joyes of Heaven are multiplied unto us; the preventing Grace, and the free mercy of God, is our stock, and principall; but the Acts of obedience, and mortification, fasting, and praying, and weeping are . . . the interest, and the increase of our holy joy.[106]

No man shall *suffer* like a *Christian*, that hath *done* nothing like a *Christian*: God shall thanke no man, for dying for him, and his glory, that contributed nothing to his glory, in the actions of his life.[107]

Woe be unto him that hath had no crosses. There cannot be so great a crosse as to have none. I lack one loaf of that dayly bread that I pray for, if I have no crosse; for afflictions are our spirituall nourishment; I lacke one limb of that body I must grow into, which is the body of Christ Jesus, if I have no crosses; for, my conformity to Christ, (and that's my being made up into his body) must be accomplished in my fulfilling his suffering in his flesh.[108]

Adversity

Affliction is truly a part of our patrimony, of our portion.[109]

No man is excused of future calamities, by former.[110]

Other mens crosses are not my crosses; no man hath suffered more then himselfe needed.[111]

As he that flings *a ball* to the ground, or to a wall, intends in that action, that that ball should returne back, so even now, when God does throw me down, it is the way that he hath chosen to returne me to himselfe.[112]

Mis-interprete not *Gods* former Corrections upon thee, how long, how sharpe soever: Call not his Phisicke, poison, nor his Fish, Scorpions, nor his Bread, Stone: Accuse not *God*, for that hee hath done, nor suspect not God, for that hee may doe, as though *God* had made thee, onely because hee lacked a man, to damne.[113]

Let me discerne that, that that is done upon mee, is done by the hand of God, and I care not what it be: I had rather have Gods Vinegar, then mans Oyle, Gods Wormewood, then mans Manna, Gods Justice, then any mans Mercy . . . Even afflictions are welcome, when we see them to be his.[114]

Hell is *darknesse*; and the way to it, to hell, is . . . blindnesse in our spirituall eyes. Eternal life hereafter is . . . the sight of God, and the way to that here, is to *see* God here: and the *eye-salve* for that is, to be crossed in our desires in this world, by the hand of God.[115]

Let no man be disheartned nor discouraged, if hee have brought a good conscience, and faithfull labour to the service of God. Let him not thinke his wages the worse paid, if God doe mingle bodily *sicknesse*, temporall *losses*, personal *disgraces*, with his labours; Let him not think that God should not doe thus to *them* that wear out themelves in his service; for the best part of our wages is *adversity*, because that gives us a true fast, and a right value of our prosperity.[116]

As a Cart that hath a full and plentifull load, and squeaks and whines the more for that abundance. Neither murmure that thou hast . . . not Goods enough, nor . . . Afflictions too many, but reckon how much more good God hath shewed thee, then thou hast deserved, and how much lesse ill.[117]

There is a feare of God too narrow, when we thinke every naturall crosse, every worldly accident to be a judgement of God, and a testimony of his indignation, which the Poet . . . calls a disease of the soule.[118]

That which you call the Day of the Lord is come upon you, beggary, and nakednesse, and hunger, contempt, and affliction, and imprisonment is come upon you . . . All this is *dies mundi*, and not *dies Domini*, it is the ordinary course of the world, and no extraordinary day of the Lord.[119]

Alas, that crosse of present bodily weaknesse, which the former wantonnesses of my youth have brought upon me, is not my crosse; That crosse of poverty which the wastfulnesse of youth hath brought upon me, is not my crosse; for these, weaknesse upon wantonnesse, want upon wastfulnesse, are Natures crosses, not Gods, and they would fall naturally, though there were (which is an impossible supposition) no God. Except God therefore take these crosses in the way, as they fall into his hands, and sanctifie them so, and then lay them upon me, they are not my crosses; but if God doe this, they are. And then this crosse thus prepared, I must *take up*.[120]

No study is so necessary as to know our selves; no Schoole-master is so diligent, so vigilant, so assiduous, as Adversity: And the end of knowing our selves, is to know how we are disposed for that which is our end, that is this Blessednesse.[121]

Let me wither and weare out mine age in a discomfortable, in an unwholesome, in a penurious prison, and so pay my debts with my bones, and recompence the wastfulnesse of my youth, with the beggery of mine age; Let me wither in a spittle under sharpe, and foule, and infamous diseases, and so recompence the wantonnesse of my youth, with that loathsomnesse in mine age; yet, if God with-draw not his spirituall blessings, his Grace, his Patience, If I can call my suffering his Doing, my passion his Action, All this that is temporall, is but a caterpiller got into one corner of my garden, but a mill-dew fallen upon one acre of my Corne; The body of all, the substance of all is safe, as long as the soule is safe.[122]

Beloved, whether Gods Rod, and his correction, shall have the *savour of life unto life,* or *of death unto death,* consists much in the *hand,* that is to receive it, and in the stomach that is to digest it.[123]

Our murmuring makes a *rod* a *staffe,* and a *staffe* a *sword,* and that which God presented for *physick, poyson.*[124]

For, as long as *God* punishes me, hee gives me *Phisick*; if he draw his knife, it is but to prune his Vine, and if hee draw blood, it is but to rectifie a distemper: If God breake my bones, it is but to set them strayter, And if hee bruse me in a Morter, it is but that I might exhale, and breath up a sweet savor, in his nosethrils: I am his *handy-worke,* and if one hand be under me, let the other lye as heavie, as he shall be pleased to lay it, upon me; let *God* handle me how he will, so hee *cast* mee not out of his hands: I had rather *God* frownd upon mee, then not looke upon me; and I had rather *God* pursued mee, then left mee to my selfe.[125]

The blood of Christ Jesus only is my cordiall; that restores me, repaires me; but affliction is my Physick; that purges, that cleanses me.[126]

As long as I have God by the hand, and feele his loving care of me, I can admit any waight of his hand; any fornace of his heating. Let God mould me, and then melt me againe, let God make mee, and then breake me againe, as long as he establishes and maintaines a rectified assurance in my soule, that at last he meanes to make me a Vessell of honour, to his Glory.[127]

Living in the World

The love of this life, which is *naturall* to us, and imprinted by God in us, is not *sinfull*.[128]

See God in every thing, and then thou needst not take off thine eye from Beauty, from Riches, from Honour, from any thing.[129]

From being anxious, or secure,
    Dead clods of sadnesse, or light squibs of mirth,
From thinking, that great courts immure
All, or no happinesse, or that this earth
        Is only for our prison fram'd,
        Or that thou art covetous
To them thou lovest, or that they are maim'd
From reaching this worlds sweet, who seek thee thus,
With all their might, Good Lord deliver us.[130]

And to seek (God) with a whole heart, is not by honest industry to seeke nothing else, (for God weares good cloathes, silk, and soft raiment, in his religious servants in Courts, as well as Cammels haire, in *John Baptist* in the Wildernesse; and God manifests himselfe to man, as well in the splendor of Princes in Courts, as in the and trade despise Armes; God in Christ may be had in every lawfull calling.[141]

Actions precious, or acceptable in Gods eye, must be *holy purposes* in their beginning, and then *done in season*; the *Dove* must lay the *egge*, and hatch the *bird*; the *holy Ghost* must infuse the purpose, and *sit* upon it, and *overshadow* it, and mature and ripen it, if it shall be precious in Gods eye.[142]

God will be loved *with the whole heart*, and God will have that love declared with our whole substance. I must not think I have done enough, if I have built an *Almes-house*; As long as I am able to doe more, I have done nothing.[143]

If yesterday, when I had lesse power, lesse grace, lesse help, all was but *Duty* and service that could be done, is it the lesse a service and a duty now, because God hath enlarged my capacity with more grace, and more helps then before? Doe I owe God the lesse, because he hath given me more?[144]

He that comes as neere uprightnesse, as infirmities admit, is an upright man.[145]

Upon this earth, a man cannot possibly make one step in a straight, and a direct line. The earth it selfe being round, every step wee make upon it, must necessarily bee a segment, an arch of a circle. But yet though no piece of a circle be a straight line, yet if we take any piece, nay if we take the whole circle, there is no corner, no angle in any piece, in any intire circle. A perfect rectitude we cannot have in any wayes in this world; In every Calling there are some inevitable tentations. But, though wee cannot make up our circle of a straight line (that is impossible to humane frailty) yet wee may passe on, without angles, and corners, that is, without disguises in our Religion, and without love of craft, and falsehood, and circumvention in our civill actions.[146]

[295]

The glory of God shines though godly men, and wee receive a beame and a tincture of that glory of God, when we have the approbation, and testimony, and good opinion, and good words of good men.[147]

Ease, and plenty in age, must not be looked for without Crosses and labour and industry in youth.[148]

The Wise-men of the East, by a lesse light, found a greater, by a Star, they found the Son of glory, Christ Jesus: But by darknesse, nothing; By the beames of comfort in this life, we come to the body of the Sun, by the Rivers, to the Ocean, by the cheerefulnesse of heart here, to the brightnesse, to the fulnesse of joy hereafter. For, beloved, Salvation it selfe being so often presented to us in the names of Glory, and of Joy, we cannot thinke that the way to that glory is a sordid life affected here, an obscure, a beggarly, a negligent abandoning of all wayes of preferment, or riches, or estimation in this World, for the glory of Heaven shines down in these beames hither; Neither can men thinke, that the way to the joyes of Heaven, is a joylesse severenesse, a rigid austerity; for as God loves a cheerefull giver, so he loves a cheerefull taker, that takes hold of his mercies and his comforts with a cheerefull heart, not onely without grudging, that they are no more, but without jealousie and suspition that they are not so much, or not enough.[149]

Goe chearfully, and joyfully forward, in the works of your callings. Rejoyce in the blessings of God without murmuring, or comparing with others. And establish thy joy so, in an honest, and religious manner of getting, that thy joy may descend to thine heire, as well as thy land. No land is so well fenced, no house so well furnished, as that, which hath this joy, this testimony of being well gotten.[150]

To have something to doe, to doe it, and then to Rejoyce in having done it, to embrace a calling, to performe the Duties of that calling, to joy and rest in the peacefull testimony of having done so; this is Christianly done, Christ did it; Angelically done, Angels doe it; Godly done, God does it.[151]

Looking Towards Our End

The love of the world, is but a smoke, there's the vanity; but such a one, as putts out our eyes, there's the vexation; we do not see God here, we shall not see God hereafter.[152]

The measure of our seeing of God is the measure of Joy. See him here in his Blessings, and you shall joy in those blessings here; and when you come to see him . . . in his Essence, then you shall have this Joy in Essence, and in fulnesse; of which, God of his goodnesse give us such an earnest here, as may binde to us that inheritance hereafter, which his Sonne our Saviour Christ Jesus hath purchased for us, with the inestimable price of his incorruptible blood.[153]

Our looking towards God, is the way to Blessednesse, but Blessednesse it self is only the sight of God himself.[154]

Blessednesse it self, is God himselfe; our blessednesse is our possession; our union with God.[155]

For though we be bound to rejoyce alwayes, it is not a blessed joy, if we do not know upon what it be grounded: or if it be not upon everlasting blessednesse.[156]

Here in this world, so far as I can enter into my Masters sight, I can enter into my Masters joy. I can see God in his Creatures, in his Church, in his Word and Sacraments, and Ordinances; Since I am not without this sight, I am not without this joy . . . I cannot put off mortality, but I can looke upon immortality; I cannot depart from this earth, but I can looke into heaven.[157]

The endowments of heaven are *Joy*, and *Glory*; joy and glory are the two Elements, the two Hemispheres of Heaven; And of this Joy, and this Glory of heaven, we have the best *earnest* that this world can give, if we have *rest*; satisfaction and acquiescence in our religion, for our beleefe, and for our life and actions, peace of Conscience.[158]

That . . . thou maist begin thy heaven here, put thy self in the sight of God, put God in thy sight, in every particular action.[159]

Here our best Wisedome is, but to goe towards our end, there it is to rest in our end; here it is to seek to bee Glorified by God, there it is, that God may be everlastingly glorified by mee.[160]

Peace in this world, is a pretious *Earnest*, and a faire and lovely *Type* of the everlasting peace of the world to come: And warre in this world, is a shrewd and fearefull *Embleme* of the everlasting discord and tumult, and torment of the world to come: And therefore, our *Blessed God*, blesse us with this externall, and this internall, and make that lead us to an eternall peace.[161]

As the sight of God is Heaven, and to be banisht from the sight of God, is Hell in the World to come, so the blessing of God, is Heaven, and the curse of God is Hell and damnation, even in this life.[162]

Hee that were to travell into a far country, would study before, somewhat the map, and the manners, and the language of the Country; Hee that looks for the fulnesse of the joyes of heaven hereafter, will have a taste, an insight in them before he goe.[163]

And as no man shall come to the joyes of Heaven, that hath no joy in this world . . . so no man shall come to the glory of Heaven, that hath not a holy ambition of this glory in this world.[164]

Man passes not from the miseries of this life, to the joyes of Heaven, but by joy in this life too; for he that feeles no joy here, shall finde none hereafter.[165]

How faire a beame of the joyes of Heaven is true comfort in this life?[166]

Make way to an everlasting Easter by a short Lent, to an undeterminable glory, by a temporary humiliation.[167]

Records of nobility are only from the book of Life, and your preferment is your interest in a place at the right hand of God.[168]

God doth not say, Live well and thou shalt dye well, that is an easie, a quiet death; But *live well here*, and thou shalt *live well for ever*.[169]

All the way to Heaven is Heaven.[170]

THE LAST THINGS

Death

Stay therefore patiently, stay chearfully Gods leasure till he call;
but not so over-chearfully, as to be loath to go when he cals.[1]

As he that travails weary, and late towards a great City, is glad
when he comes to a place of execution, becaus he knows that
is neer the town; so when thou comest to the gate of death, be glad
of that, for it is but one step from that to thy *Jerusalem*.[2]

Since I am comming to that Holy roome,
   Where, with thy Quire of Saints for evermore,
I shall be made thy Musique; As I come
   I tune the Instrument here at the dore,
    And what I must doe then, thinke here before.[3]

Death is nothing else, but a devesting of those defects, which
made us lesse fit for God.[4]

This is my playes last scene, here heavens appoint
   My pilgrimages last mile; and my race
Idly, yet quickly runne, hath this last pace,
My spans last inch, my minutes latest point,
And gluttonous death, will instantly unjoynt
My body, and soule, and I shall sleepe a space,

But my'ever-waking part shall see that face,
Whose feare already shakes my every joynt:
Then, as my soule, to heaven her first seate, takes flight,
And earth borne body, in the earth shall dwell,
So, fall my sinnes, that all may have their right,
To where they'are bred, and would presse me, to hell.
Impute me righteous, thus purg'd of evill,
For thus I leave the world, the flesh, the devill.[5]

When I consider what I was in my parents loynes (a substance unworthy of a word, unworthy of a thought) when I consider what I am now, (a Volume of diseases bound up together, a dry cynder, if I look for naturall, for radicall moisture, and yet a Spunge, a bottle of overflowing Rheumes, if I consider accidentall; an aged childe, a gray-headed Infant, and but the ghost of mine own youth) When I consider what I shall be at last, by the hand of death, in my grave, (first, but Putrifaction, and then, not so much as putrifaction, I shall not be able to send forth so much as an ill ayre, not any ayre at all, but shall be all insipid, tastlesse, savourlesse dust; for while, all wormes, and after a while, not so much as wormes, sordid, senslesse, namelesse dust) When I consider the past, and present, and future state of this body, in this world, I am able to conceive, able to expresse the worst that can befall it in nature, and the worst that can be inflicted upon it by man, or fortune; But the least degree of glory that God hath prepared for that body in heaven, I am not able to expresse, not able to conceive.[6]

Thinke then, My soule, that death is but a Groome,
Which brings a Taper to the outward roome,
Whence thou spiest first a little glimmering light,
And after brings it nearer to thy sight:
For such approches doth Heaven make in death.
Thinke thy selfe laboring now with broken breath,
And thinke those broken and soft Notes to bee
Division, and thy happiest Harmonee.
Thinke thee laid on thy death bed, loose and slacke;
And thinke that but unbinding of a packe,

To take one precious thing, thy soule, from thence.
Thinke thy self parch'd with fevers violence,
Anger thine Ague more, by calling it
Thy Physicke; chide the slacknesse of the fit.
Thinke that thou hearst thy knell, and think no more,
But that, as Bels cal'd thee to Church before,
So this, to the Triumphant Church, cals thee.
Thinke Satans Sergeants round about thee bee,
And thinke that but for Legacies they thrust;
Give one thy Pride, to'another give thy Lust:
Given them those sinnes which they gave thee before,
And trust th'immaculate blood to wash thy score.
Thinke thy frinds weeping round, and thinke that thay
Weepe but because they goe not yet thy way.[7]

Every fit of an Ague is an Earth-quake that swallows him, every fainting of the knee, is a step to Hell; every lying down at night is a funerall; and every quaking is a rising to judgment; every bell that distinguishes times, is a passing-bell, and every passing-bell, his own; every singing in the ear, is an Angels Trumpet; at every dimnesse of the candle, he heares that voice, *Fool, this night they will fetch away thy soul*; and in every judgement denounced against sin, he hears an *Ito maledicte* upon himselfe, *Go thou accursed into hell fire.*[8]

Death comes equally to us all, and makes us all equall when it comes. The ashes of an Oak in the Chimney, are no Epitaph of that Oak, to tell me how high or how large that was; It tels me not what flocks it sheltered while it stood, nor what men it hurt when it fell. The dust of great persons graves is speechlesse too, it sayes nothing, it distinguishes nothing: As soon the dust of a wretch whom thou wouldest not, as of a Prince whom thou couldest not look upon, will trouble thine eyes, if the winde blow it thither; and when a whirle-winde hath blowne the dust of the Church-yard into the Church, and the man sweeps out the dust of the Church into the Church-yard, who will undertake to sift those dusts again, and to pronounce, This is the Patrician, this is the noble flowre, and this the yeomanly, this the Plebeian bran?[9]

The poore of this world, are our poore; Gods poore are thy that lie in the dust, the dust of the grave, the dead; of whom, God hath a greater Congregation under ground, then of the living upon the face of the earth; And, God will not forget the congregation of his poore for ever.[10]

But think that Death hath now enfranchis'd thee,
Thou hast thy'expansion now and libertee;
Thinke that a rusty Peece, discharg'd, is flowen
In peeces, and the bullet is his owne,
And freely flies: This to thy soule allow,
Thinke thy sheell broke, thinke thy Soule hatch'd but now.[11]

No man is superannuated in the grave, that he is too old to enter into heaven, where the Master of the house is *The ancient of dayes*. No man is bed-rid with age in the grave, that he cannot rise. It is not with God, as it is with man; we doe, but God does not forget the dead: and, as long as God is with them, they are with him.[12]

Though a good man hath
Title to Heaven, and plead it by his Faith,

Yet Death must usher, and unlocke the doore.[13]

If the dead, and we, be not upon one floore, nor under one story, yet we are under one roofe. We think not a friend lost, because he is gone into another roome, nor because he is gone into another Land; And into another world, no man is gone; for that Heaven, which God created, and this world, is all one world.[14]

We must be in his grave, before we come to his resurrection, and we must be in his death-bed before we come to his grave: we must do as he did, fast and pray, before we can say as he said . . . Into thy hands O Lord I commend my Spirit.[15]

So by the soule doth death string Heaven and Earth,
For when our soule enjoyes this her third birth,
(Creation gave her one, a second, grace)
Heaven is as neare, and present to her face,
As colours are, and objects, in a roome
Where darknesse was before, when Tapers come.[16]

My hope *before* death is, that this life is the *way*; my hope *at* death is, that my death shall be *a doore* into a better state.[17]

Judgement

Wilt thou forgive that sinne where I begunne,
    Which was my sin, though it were done before?
Wilt thou forgive that sinne, through which I runne,
    And do run still: though still I do deplore?
        When thou hast done, thou hast not done,
            For, I have more.

Wilt thou forgive that sinne which I have wonne
    Others to sinne? and, made my sinne their doore?
Wilt thou forgive that sinne which I did shunne
    A yeare, or two: but wallowed in, a score?
        When thou hast done, thou hast not done,
            For I have more.

I have a sinne of feare, that when I have spunne
    My last thread, I shall perish on the shore;
But sweare by thy selfe, that at my death thy sonne
    Shall shine as he shines now, and heretofore:
        And, having done that, Thou haste done,
            I feare no more.[18]

Till Christ all was night; there was a beginning of day, in the beginning of the Gospel, and there was a full noon in the light and glory thereof; but such a day, as shall be always day, and over-taken with no night, no cloud, is onely the day of Judgement, the Resurrection.[19]

I know that he lives; I know that hee begunne not in his Incarnation, I know he ended not in his death, but it always was, and is now, and shall for ever be true . . . that he lives still. And then . . . I know hee shall stand at the last day to Judge me and all the world.[20]

At that last Judgement, we shall be arraigned for not cloathing, not visiting, not harbouring the poore; For, our not giving is a taking away; our withholding, is a withdrawing; our keeping to our selves, is a stealing from them.[21]

To what end is it for you? If your hypocriticall security could hold out to the last, if you could delude the world at the last gasp, if those that stand about you then could be brought to say, he went away like a Lambe, alas the Lambe of God went not away so, the Lamb of God had his colluctations,[a] disputations, expostulations, apprehensions of Gods indignation upon him then: This security, call it by a worse name, stupidity, is not a lying down like a Lamb, but a lying down like *Issaachers* Asse between two burdens, for two greater burdens cannot be, then sin, and the senslesnesse of sin.[22]

The dayes which God made for man were darknesse, and then light, still the evening and the morning made up the day. The day which the Lord shall bring upon secure and carnall men, is darknesse without light, judgements without any beames of mercy shining through them.[23]

a. colluctations (strivings)

For the Court of Heaven is not like other Courts, that after a surfet of pleasure or greatness, a man may retire; after a surfet of sin there's no such retiring, as a dissolving of the soul into nothing; but God is from the beginning the Creator, he gave all things their being, and he is still thy Creator, thou shalt evermore have that being, to be capable of his Judgments.[24]

When we come to stand naked before God, without that apparel which he made for us, without all righteousness, and without that apparell which we made for our selves; not a fig-leaf, not an excuse to cover us; if we think to deale upon his affections, he hath none; if we think to hide our sins, he was with us when we did them, and saw them: we shall see then by his examination, that he knowes them better then we our selves.[25]

When *you stand before the Throne*, you stand . . . *before the Lamb*: who having not opened his mouth, to save his owne *fleece*, when he was in the shearers hand, nor to save his own *life*, when he was in the slaughterers hand, will much lesse open his mouth to any repentant sinners condemnation, or upbrayd you with your former crucifyings of him, in this world, after he hath nailed those sinnes to that crosse, to which those sinnes nayled him.[26]

He that is my Witnesse, is my Judge, and the same person is my Jesus, my Saviour, my Redeemer; He that hath taken my nature, He that hath given me his blood. So that he is my Witnesse, in his owne cause, and my Judge, but of his ownc Title, and will, in me, preserve himselfe; He will not let that nature, that he hath invested, perish, nor that treasure, which he hath poured out for me, his blood, be ineffectuall. My Witnesse is in Heaven, my Judge is in Heaven, my Redeemer is in Heaven, and in them, who are but One, I have not onely a constant hope, that I shall be there too, but an evident assurance, that I am there already, in his Person.[27]

Acknowledge his first Judgment, thy election in him, cherish his second Judgment, thy justification by him, breath and pant after his third Judgement, thy Crown of glory for him.[28]

We think that *Paradise* and *Calvarie*,
  Christs Crosse, and *Adams* tree, stood in one place;
Looke Lord, and finde both *Adams* met in me;
As the first *Adams* sweat surrounds my face,
May the last *Adams* blood my soule embrace.

So, in his purple wrapp'd receive mee Lord,
By these his thornes give me his other Crowne;
And as to others soules I preach'd thy word,
Be this my Text, my Sermon to mine owne,
Therfore that he may raise the Lord throws down.[29]

Hell

Hell is darknesse; and the way to it, is the cloud of Ignorance; hell it self is but condensed Ignorance, multiplied Ignorance.[30]

Gods presence in anger, and in punishments, is a heavy, but Gods absence, and dereliction, a much heavyer burden; As (if extremes will admit comparison) the everlasting losse of the sight of God in hell, is a greater torment, then any lakes of inextinguishable Brimstone, then any gnawing of the incessant worme, then any gnashing of teeth can present unto us.[31]

The fires of hell, in their place, in hell, have no light; But any degrees of the fires of Hell, that can break out in this life, have, in Gods own purpose, so much light, as that through the darkest smother of obduration, or desperation, God would have us see him.[32]

B ut when we shall have given to those words, by which hell is expressed in the Scriptures, the heaviest significations, that either the nature of those words can admit, or as they are types and representations of hell, as *fire*, and *brimstone*, and *weeping*, and *gnashing*, and *darknesse*, and *the worme*, . . . when all is done, the hell of hels, the torment of torments is the everlasting absence of God, and the everlasting impossibility of returning to his presence.[33]

The Beatific Vision

F irst, *God commanded light out of darkness*, that man might see the Creature; then *he shin'd in our hearts*, that man might see himself; at last, he shall shine *so in the face of Christ Jesus*, that man may see God, and live; and live as long, as that God of light and life shall live himself.[34]

G od gave me the light of Nature, when I quickned in my mothers wombe by receiving a reasonable soule; and God gave me the light of faith, when I quickned in my second mothers womb, the Church, by receiving my baptisme; but in my third day, when my mortality shall put on immortality, he shall give me the light of glory, by which I shall see himself.[35]

T he heavens shall be open, and I shall see the Sonne of man, the Sonne of God.[36]

N o *man ever saw God and liv'd*; and yet, I shall not live till I see God; and when I have seen him I shall never dye.[37]

A s he that fears God, fears nothing else, so, he that sees God, sees every thing else: when we shall see God . . . as he is, we shall see all things . . . as they are; for that's their Essence, as they conduce to his glory.[38]

A ll our Beatification, and Glorification in our bodies consists in this, that we shall see him . . . *as he is,* in his Essence.[39]

T he endowments of the blessed . . . are ordinarily delivered to be these three . . . The sight of God, the love of God, and the fruition, the injoying, the possessing of God.[40]

The Glory of God

B efore, in the former acceptation, *the glory of God*, was our glorifying of God; here, the glory of God, is his glorifying of us: there it was his receiving, here it is his giving of glory.[41]

A nd as well, as I may know, that I am I; I may know, that He is He; for, I shall not know my selfe, nor that state of glory which I am then in, by any light of Nature which I brought thither, but by that light of Glory which I shall receive there.[42]

T he knowledge which I have by Nature, shall have no Clouds; here it hath: that which I have by Grace, shall have no reluctation, no resistance; here it hath: That which I have by Revelation, shall have no suspition, no jealousie; here it hath: sometimes it is hard to distinguish between a respiration from God, and a suggestion from the Devil. There our curiosity shall have this noble satisfaction, we shall know how the Angels know, by knowing as they know. We shall not pass from Author, to Author, as in a Grammar School, nor from Art to Art, as in an University; but, as that General which Knighted his whole Army, God shall Create us all Doctors in a minute. That great Library, those infinite Volumes of the Books of Creatures, shall be taken away, quite away, no more Nature; those reverend Manuscripts, written with Gods own hand, the Scriptures themselves, shall be taken away, quite away; no more preaching, no more reading of Scriptures, and that great School-Mistress, Experience, and Observation shall be remov'd, no new thing to be done, and in an instant, I shall know more, then they all could reveal unto me . . . all (shall be) as nothing, altogether nothing, less then nothing, infinitely less then nothing, to that which shall then be the subject of my knowledge, for, *it is the knowledge of the glory of God.*[43]

A nd that's the glory of God, which we shall know; know, by having it. We shall have a knowledge of the very glory, the Essential glory of God, because we shall see him . . . as God is, in himself; and . . . *I shall know, as I am known*: that glory shall dilate us, enlarge us, give us an inexpressible capacity, and then fill it; but we shall never comprehend that glory, the Essential glory; but that glory which Christ hath received in his humane Nature . . . we shall comprehend, we shall know, by having: we shall receive a Crown of glory, that fadeth not: It is a Crown that compasses round, no enterance of danger any way; and a crown that fadeth not, fears no winter: we shall have interest in all we see, and we shall see the treasure of all knowledge, *the face of Christ Jesus.*[44]

I f you looke upon this world in a Map, you find two Hemi-sphears, two half worlds. If you crush heaven into a Map, you may find two Hemisphears too, two half heavens; Halfe will be Joy, and halfe will be Glory; for in these two, the joy of heaven, and the glory of heaven, is all heaven often represented unto us.[45]

I n heaven we shall have Communion of Joy and Glory with all, alwaies . . . Where never any man shall come in that loves us not, nor go from us that does.[46]

G lory, and the seat and fountain of all glory, the face of Christ Jesus.[47]

An Infinite Eternity

W*e shall Bee*, we shall have a Beeing. There is nothing more contrary to God, and his proceedings, then annihilation, to Bee nothing, Do nothing, Think nothing. It is not so high a step, to raise the poore out of the dust, and to lift the needy from the dunghill and set him with Princes, To make a King of a Beggar is not so much, as to make a Worm of nothing.[48]

I shall rise from the dead, from the darke station . . . and never misse the sunne, which shall then be put out, for I shall see the Sonne of God, the Sunne of glory, and shine my self, as that sunne shines. I shall rise from the grave, and never misse this City, which shall be no where, for I shall see the City of God, the new *Jerusalem*. I shall looke up, and never wonder when it will be day, for, the Angell will tell me that *time shall be no more*, and I shall see, and see cheerefully that last day, the day of judgement, which shall have no *night*, never end, and be united to the *Antient of dayes*, to God himselfe, who had no *morning*, never began. There I shall beare witnesse for Christ, in ascribing the salvation of the whole world, to *him that sits upon the Throne, and to the Lamb*, and Christ shall bear witnesse for me, in ascribing his righteousnesse unto me, and in delivering me into his Fathers hands, with the same tendernesse, as he delivered up his owne soule, and in making me, who am a greater sinner, then they who crucified him on earth for me, as innocent, and as righteous as his glorious selfe, in the Kingdome of heaven.[49]

T*he upright in heart* shall have, whatsoever all Translations can enlarge and extend themselves unto; They shall *Rejoyce*, they shall *Glory*, they shall *Praise*, and they shall bee *praised*, and all these in an everlasting future, for ever. Which everlastingnesse is such a Terme, as God himselfe cannot enlarge; As God cannot make himselfe a better God then he is, because hee is infinitely good, infinite goodnesse, already; so God himselfe cannot make our Terme in heaven longer then it is; for it is infinite everlastingnesse, infinite eternity.[50]

Clocks and Sun-dials were but a late invention upon earth; but the Sun it self, and the earth it self, was but a late invention in heaven. God had been an infinite, a super-infinite, an unimaginable space, millions of millions of unimaginable spaces in heaven, before the Creation. And our afternoon shall be as long as Gods forenoon; for, as God never saw beginning, so we shall never see end.[51]

Heaven is called by many pretious names; *Life*, Simply and absolutely there is no life but that. And *Kingdome*; Simply, absolutely, there is no Kingdom, that is not subordinate to that. And *Sabbatum ex Sabbato*, A Sabbath flowing into a Sabbath, a perpetuall Sabbath: but the Name that should enamour us most, is that, that it is *Satietas gaudiorum*; fulnesse of Joy. Fulnesse that needeth no addition.[52]

We shall have . . . a life of one everlasting Sabbath hereafter, where to our Rest there shall be added *Joy*, and to our *Joy* *Glory*, and this *Rest*, and *Joy*, *and Glory* superinvested with that which crownes them all, Eternity.[53]

Partakers of the Divine Nature

The *field* is the *world*, and the *good seed* are the *Children* of the *kingdome*; And we are translated even into the nature of God, By his pretious promises we are made *partakers of the Divine nature*: yea we are discharged of all bodily, and earthly incombrances, and we are made *all spirit*, yea the spirit of God himselfe, *He that is joyned to the Lord, is one spirit with him*. All this we have, if we doe put on Christ: and we doe put on Christ, if we be baptized into him.[54]

Now we shall be made partakers of the Divine nature, and the Knowledge, and the Will, and the Power of God, shall be so far communicated to us there, as that we shall know all that belongs to our happiness, and we shall have a will to doe, and a power to execute, whatsoever conduces to that.[55]

So, if all the joyes, of all the men that have had all their hearts desires, were con-centred in one heart, all that would not be as a spark in his Chimney, to the generall conflagration of the whole world, in respect of the least joy, that that soule is made partaker of, that departs from this world, immediately after a pardon received, and reconciliation sealed to him, for all his sins.[56]

That God should be all in all, so as that at last, the whole nature of mankind, and indeed, all other natures and substances . . . should be swallowed up, and drowned in the very substance of God himself. But this transmutation is a glorious restoring of Gods image in us, and it is our conformity to him.[57]

The Life of Heaven

The ends crowne our workes, but thou crown'st our ends,
   For, at our end begins our endlesse rest,
The first last end, now zealously possest,
With a strong sober thirst, my soule attends.
'Tis time that heart and voice be lifted high,
Salvation to all that will is nigh.[58]

In heaven, where we shall *know* God, there may be no use of *faith*; In heaven, where we shall *see* God, there may be no use of *hope*; But in heaven, where *God* the Father, and the Son, love one another in the Holy Ghost, the bond of charity shall everlastingly unite us together.[59]

Beloved, Christ puts no man out of his way . . . to goe to heaven. Christ makes heaven all things to all men, that he might gaine all: To the mirthfull man he presents heaven, as all joy, and to the ambitious man, as all glory; To the Merchant it is a Pearle, and to the husbandman it is a rich field. Christ hath made heaven all things to all men, that he might gaine all, and he puts no man out of his way to come thither.[60]

I shall see all the beauty, and all the glory of all the Saints of God, and love them all, and know that the Lamb loves them too, without jealousie, on his part, or theirs, or mine, and so be maried *in aeternum*, for ever, without interruption, or diminution, or change of affections. I shall see the Sunne black as sackcloth of hair, and the Moon become as blood, and the Starres fall as a Figge-tree casts her untimely Figges, and the heaven roll'up together as a Scroll. I shall see a divorce between Princes and their Prerogatives, between nature and all her elements, between the spheres, and all their intelligences, between matter it self, and all her forms, and my mariage shall be, *in aeternum*, for ever. I shall see an end of faith, nothing to be beleeved that I doe not know; and an end of hope, nothing to be wisht that I doe not enjoy, but no end of that love in which I am maried to the Lamb for ever.[61]

Here then Salvation is eternall Salvation . . . where we shall be infinitely rich, and that without labor in getting, or care in keeping, or fear in loosing; and fully wise, and that without ignorance of necessary, or study of unnecessary knowledge, where we shal not measure our portion by acres, for all heaven shall be all ours; nor our term by yeers, for it is life and everlasting life; nor our assurance by precedent, for we shal be safer then the Angels themselves were in the creation; where our exaltation shal be to have a crown of righteousness, and our possession of that crown shal be, even the throwing it down at the feet of the Lamb; where we shal leave off all those petitions of . . . thy Kingdom come, for it shal be come in abundant power; and the . . . give us this day our dayly bread, for we shall have all that which we can desire now, and shal have a power to desire more, and then have that desire so enlarged, satisfied; And . . . we shall not pray to be delivered from evil, for no evil . . . either of sin to deserve punishment, or of punishmen for our former sins shal offer at us; where we shall see God face to face, for we shall have such notions and apprehensions, as shall enable us to see him, and he shall afford such an imparting, such a manifestation of himself, as he shall be seen by us; and where we shall be as inseparably united to our Saviour, as his humanity and divinity are united together: This unspeakable, this unimaginable happiness is this Salvation, and therefore let us be glad when this is brought neer us.[62]

But then in her Resurrection, (the) measure (of the life of the soule) is enlarged, and filled at once; There she reads without spelling, and knowes without thinking, and concludes without arguing; she is at the end of her race, without running; In her triumph, without fighting; In her Haven, without sayling: A freeman, without any prentiship; at full yeares, without any wardship; and a Doctor, without any proceeding: She knowes truly, and easily, and immediately, and entirely, and everlastingly; Nothing left out at first, nothing worne out at last, that conduces to her happinesse.[63]

Christ Jesus remember us all in his Kingdome, to which, though we must sail through a sea, it is the sea of his blood, where no soul suffers shipwrack; though we must be blown with strange winds, with sighs and groans for our sins, yet it is the Spirit of God that blows all this wind, and shall blow away all contrary winds of diffidence or distrust in Gods mercy; where we shall be all Souldiers of one Army, the Lord of Hostes, and Children of one Quire, the God of Harmony and consent: where all Clients shall retain but one Counsellor, our Advocate Christ Jesus, nor present him any other fee but his own blood, and yet every Client have a Judgment on his side, not only in a not guilty, in the remission of his sins, but in a *Venite benedicti*, in being called to the participation of an immortal Crown of glory: where there shall be no difference in affection, nor in mind, but we shall agree as fully and perfectly in our *Allelujah*, and *gloria in excelsis*, as God the Father, Son, and Holy Ghost agreed in the *faciamus hominem* at first; where we shall end, and yet begin but then; where we shall have continuall rest, and yet never grow lazie; where we shall be stronger to resist, and yet have no enemy; where we shall live and never die, where we shall meet and never part.[64]

Consider the joy of our society, and conversation in heaven . . . Where we shall be so far from being enemies to one another, as that we shall not be strangers to one another: And so far from envying one another, as that all that every one hath, shall be every others possession: where all soules shall be so intirely knit together, as if all were but one soule, and God so intirely knit to every soule, as if there were as many Gods as soules.[65]

Onely in Heaven joies strength is never spent;
   And accidentall things are permanent.
Joy of a soules arrivall neere decaies;
For that soule ever joyes, and ever staies.
Joy that their last great Consummation
Approaches in the resurrection;
When earthly bodies more celestiall
Shalbe, then Angels were, for they could fall;
This kind of joy doth every day admit
Degrees of grouth, but none of loosing it.[66]

And into that gate they shall enter, and in that house they shall dwell, where there shall be no Cloud nor Sun, no darkenesse nor dazling, but one equall light, no noyse nor silence, but one equall musick, no fears nor hopes, but one equal possession, no foes nor friends, but one equall communion and Identity, no ends nor beginnings, but one equall eternity.[67]

The glory of Gods Saints in Heaven, is not so much to have a Crown, as to lay down that Crown at the Feet of the Lamb.[68]

NOTES

Preface

1. Sermons II. 18. 485–6.
2. Sermons VIII. 7. 645–50.
3. A.J. Smith, 'New Bearings in Donne: "Air and Angels"', in Helen Gardner (ed.), *John Donne: A Collection of Critical Essays*, New Jersey: Prentice-Hall, 1962, p. 174.

An Introduction to John Donne

The Man and his Meaning

1. C.A. Patrides (ed.), *John Donne: Complete English Poems*, London: Everyman Library, 1991, p. 44.
2. As reported by William Drummond of Hawthornden (C.H. Herford and Percy Simpson (eds.), *Ben Jonson*, Oxford: Clarendon Press, 1925, Vol. I. p. 135).
3. Cited by David L. Edwards, *John Donne: Man of Flesh and Spirit*, London: Continuum, 2001, p. 18.
4. S.T. Coleridge, *Marginalia*.
5. Cited by Edwards, *John Donne*, p. 33.
6. Sir Richard Baker, *A Chronicle of the Kings of England – The Raigne of King James*. London 1643.
7. Cited by Edwards, *John Donne*, p. 45. R.C. Bald suggests that it may be taken for granted 'that the first two Satires, nearly all the Elegies, and an uncertain number of the "Songs & Sonnets" . . . (as well as verse letters addressed to friends) . . . belong to Donne's Lincoln's Inn days'. R.C. Bald, *John Donne: A Life*, Oxford: Clarendon Press, 1986, p. 77.
8. Helen Gardner, 'Donne the Preacher', in *A City Tribute to John Donne*, 1972.
9. 'Letter: John Donne to Sir Henry Wotton, (Probably c.1600)', cited by Evelyn M. Simpson, *A Study of the Prose Works of John Donne*, Oxford: Clarendon Press, 1948, p. 316.
10. 'Letter: John Donne to Sir George More (2 February 1602)', cited by Bald, *John Donne*, p. 134.
11. Izaak Walton, *The Life of John Donne*, published by Henry Kent, London, p. 27.

12. The exception is *Devotions upon Emergent Occasions*, written by Donne during his illness in the winter of 1623 and published first in 1624.

13. John Donne, *Letters to Severall Persons of Honour*, 1651.

14. 'John Donne to Sir Robert More, 28 July 1614' in E. Gosse (ed.), *The Life and Letters of John Donne*, London: William Heinemann, 1899, Vol. II. p. 46–7.

15. Patrides, *Donne's Poems*, p. 30.

16. *Biathanatos*. Probably written c.1609.

17. John Carey, *John Donne: Life, Mind and Art*, London: Faber & Faber, 1990. p. 37.

18. 'Letter: John Donne to Viscount Rochester' in *A Collection of Letters written by Sir Tobie Matthew*, London 1660, pp. 319–20.

19. John Carey, *John Donne*, p. 46. Paul Oliver, *Donne's Religious Writing*, Longman 1997.

20. Helen Gardner (ed.), *The Divine Poems*, Oxford: Clarendon Press, 1969, p. xviii.

21. Cited by Edwards, *John Donne*, p. 133.

22. Sermons III. 14. 395–6.

23. John Donne, *Essayes in Divinitie*, (Prayers 1), Evelyn M. Simpson (ed.), Oxford: Clarendon Press, 1952. p. 97.

24. 2 Cor. 4.7.

25. 'Letter: John Donne to Sir Robert More (10th August 1614)', in Gosse, *Life and Letters*, Vol. II. p. 48.

26. Bald, *John Donne*, p. 328. Edwards, *John Donne*, p. 267.

27. 'Letter: John Donne to Duke of Buckingham (8 August 1621)' in S.R. Gardiner (ed.), *Fortescue Papers*, London: Camden Society, 1871, New Series, Vol. I, pp. 157–8.

28. Edwards, *John Donne*, p. 299.

29. 'Letter: John Donne to Sir Robert Ker (c.1619)' in Donne, *Letters to Severall Persons of Honour*, 1651.

30. 'Letter: John Donne to Duke of Buckingham (1623)', Bodleian Library MS, 73.

31. Gardner, 'Donne the Preacher'.

32. Sermons II. 14. 547–8.

33. Sermons III. 3. 748–9.

34. Sermons VI. 8. 190–2.

35. Sermons VI. 2. 523–31.

36. 'Letter: John Donne to Mrs Cokayne (15 January 1631)', *Letters to Severall Persons of Honour*, 1651.

37. 'Letter: John Donne to Mr George Garrard', *Letters to Severall Persons of Honour*, 1651.

38. Walton, *Life of Donne*, p. 136.

39. Sermons X. 11. 429–31.

40. Bald, *John Donne*, p. 535.

41. Walton, *Life of Donne*, p. 146.

42. Cited by Geoffrey Keynes, 'The Donne Revival', in *A City Tribute to John Donne*, 1972.

43. Sermons VIII. 7. 646–50.

Poet, Propagandist, Preacher

1. C.M. Coffin, *John Donne and the New Philosophy*, New York: Columbia University Press, 1937, p. 284.
2. Gardner, 'Donne the Preacher'.
3. Poems: Letters to Severall Personages, To Mr. I.L. l. 9–10.
4. Poems: Songs and Sonnets, The Relique. l. 6.
5. Songs and Sonnets. Loves Usury. l. 5–6.
6. Songs and Sonnets. Breake of day. l. 1–4.
7. Poems: Epicedes and Obsequies. A hymne to the Saints, and to Marquesse Hamylton. l. 10–15.
8. Poems: The Anniversaries, The First Anniversary. An Anatomy of the World. l. 183–4, 237–8, 325–6, 369–370, 427–8.
9. Songs and Sonnets. The Canonization. l. 1.
10. Letters to Severall Personages. A letter to the Lady *Carey*, and Mrs *Essex Riche*, From *Amyens*, l. 20, 25, 28.
11. Songs and Sonnets. The broken heart. l. 1–8.
12. Letters to Severall Personages. To Sir Henry Wotton. l. 52–7.
13. Letters to Severall Personages. To Sir Edward Herbert at Julyers. l. 15–22.
14. Letters to Severall Personages. To Mr Rowland Woodward. l. 31–3.
15. Letters to Severall Personages. To Sir Henry Wotton. l. 7–10.
16. Poems: The Elegies. Elegie XVIII. Loves Progress. l. 47–54.
17. Elegie XX. Loves Warre. l. 29–32.
18. *Devotions upon Emergent Occasions*. I. Insultus Morbi Primus. I. Meditation.
19. Letters to Severall Personages. To Sir Henry Wotton. l. 21–6.
20. The Anniversaries. The Second Anniversarie. Of the Progres of the Soule. l. 173–6.
21. Letters to Severall Personages. To Mr. E.G. (Edward Gilpin). l. 9–10.
22. Songs and Sonnets. The Anniversarie. l. 5–10.
23. Songs and Sonnets. The good-morrow. l. 1–7.
24. Elegie XIX. To his Mistress Going to Bed. l. 25–6.
25. Elegie III. Change. l. 10–14.
26. Songs and Sonnets. Loves Alchymie. l. 23–4
27. Poems: Epithalamions. Epithalamion made at Lincolnes Inne. l. 88–90.
28. Elegie IX. The Autumnall. l. 1–2, 7–8.
29. Songs and Sonnets. The Sunne Rising. l. 9–10.
30. Patrides, *Donne's Poems*, p. 31.
31. *Devotions upon Emergent Occasions*: 5. ('Natures nest of boxes')
32. Epicedes and Obsequies. Elegie on M^{ris} Boulstred. l. 21.
33. Elegie on M^{ris} Boulstred. l. 5–6.
34. Elegie on M^{ris} Boulstred. l. 27–8.
35. Poems: Holy Sonnets. Divine Meditations. X. 13–14.

36. J.E.V. Crofts, 'John Donne: A Reconstruction', in Gardner (ed.), *Donne: Critical Essays*, p. 82.

37. E. Gosse, *Life and Letters*, Vol. II, p. 290.

38. *Pseudo-Martyr*. An Advertisement to the Reader. London 1610.

39. John Sparrow, 'Donne's Religious Development', *Theology*, Vol. XXII, March 1931.

40. Walton, *Life of Donne*, p. 16.

41. *Pseudo-Martyr*. Preface, Para. 4.

42. *Pseudo-Martyr*. Preface, Para. 4.

43. Poems: Satyres. Satyre III. l. 79–84.

44. Sparrow, 'Donne's Religious Development'.

45. Carey, *John Donne*.

46. Carey, *John Donne*, p. 1.

47. Carey, *John Donne*, p. 47.

48. Carey, *John Donne*, p. 37.

49. Carey, *John Donne*, p. 35.

50. Carey, *John Donne*, p. 118.

51. Carey, *John Donne*, p. 108.

52. Carey, *John Donne*, p. 110.

53. Edwards, *John Donne*, p. 158.

54. Gardner (ed.), *Divine Poems*, p. xx.

55. Gardner (ed.), *Divine Poems*, p. xviii.

56. Poems: Satyres. Satyre III. l. 89.

57. 'John Donne: John Donne to Sir Robert Ker (April 1627)', *Letters of John Donne*, 1651, p. 21.

58. Sparrow, 'Donne's Religious Development'.

59. Act in Restraint of Appeals (1533). 24 Henry VIII c. 1; Statutes of the Realm iii 247.

60. Cited by J.E. Neale, *Elizabeth I and Her Parliaments*, London: Jonathan Cape, 1953 and 1957, Vol. II, p. 198.

61. Sermons V. 14. 986–8.

62. Sermons VIII. 1. 49–51.

63. Sermons IV. 3. 655–7.

64. Sermons V. 13. 220–6.

65. Walton, *Life of Donne*, pp. 15–17.

66. R.C. Bald, *John Donne*, pp. 69–70.

67. 'An Apologie for the Oath of Allegiance', in C.H. McIlwaine (ed.), *The Political Works of James I*, Cambridge, Mass: Harvard University Press, 1918, p. 85.

68. Walton, *Life of Donne*, p. 48.

69. Evelyn M. Simpson, *A Study of the Prose Works of John Donne*, Oxford: Clarendon Press, 1948, pp. 179–80. Bald, *John Donne*, pp. 210–12.

70. A. Jessopp, *John Donne, Sometime Dean of St Paul's*, London 1897, p. 57.

71. Evelyn M. Simpson, *John Donne: Selected Prose*, Helen Gardner and Timothy Healy (eds), Oxford: Clarendon Press, 1967, p. 43.

72. Walton, *Life of Donne*, pp. 59–60.

73. Evelyn M. Simpson, *A Study of the Prose Works of John Donne*, Oxford: Clarendon Press, 1948, p. 190.

74. *Pseudo-Martyr*. Preface, para. 15.

75. *Pseudo-Martyr*. Preface, para. 3.

76. *Pseudo-Martyr*. Preface, para. 3.

77. *Pseudo-Martyr*. Preface, para. 3.

78. Walton, *Life of Donne*, p. 63.

79. Sermons IV. 13. 358.

80. Cited by William R. Mueller, *John Donne: Preacher*, Princeton, NJ: Princeton University Press, 1962, p. 29.

81. Sermons III. 4. 574–7.

82. Sermons VI. 14. 156–62.

83. Sermons VII. 16. 601–3.

84. Sermons VI. 12. 190–9.

85. Sermons VII. 18. 506–16.

86. Dominic Barker-Smith, 'John Donne's Critique of True Religion', in A.J. Smith (ed.), *John Donne: Essays in Celebration,* London: Methuen, 1972, p. 430.

87. Sermons IX. 6. 395–410.

88. Sermons II. 3. 615–19.

89. Anthony Quiller-Couch. *Studies in Literature*, New York: G. Putnam & Sons, 1918–30, Vol. I, p. 107.

90. Henry Alford, *The Works of John Donne*, 1839, Vol. I, p. v.

91. *In Memory of Doctor Donne.* An Elegy by Mr. R.B. *Poems by John Donne with Elegies on the Author's Death*, London 1633, p. 400–3.

92. H.H. Milman, *Annals of St Paul's Cathedral*, 2nd edition, London: John Murray, 1869, p. 328.

93. Walton, *Life of Donne*, p. 69.

94. Sermons VII. 11. 510–12.

95. Walton, *Life of Donne*, p. 34.

96. Walton, *Life of Donne*, p. 97.

97. Sermons IV. 3. 895–6.

98. Cited by L.P. Smith, *Donne's Sermons*, Oxford: Clarendon Press, 1932, p. xxxvi.

99. Sermons VII. 13. 168–70.

100. Sermons VII. 13. 155–7.

101. Cited by Gardner (ed.), *Divine Poems*, p. xix.

102. Simpson, *Study of Donne's Prose,* p. 111.

103. Sermons II. 2. 113–19.

104. Sermons II. 2. 124–7.

105. Gilbert Phelps, 'The Prose of Donne and Browne', in *A Guide to English Literature: Volume 3 – From Donne to Marvell,* Harmondsworth, Penguin Books, 1956, p. 120.

106. Phelps, 'The Prose of Donne and Browne', pp. 120–1.

107. *In Memory of Doctor Donne.* An Elegy by Mr. R.B. *Poems by Donne,* 1633.

108. Simpson. *Study of Donne's Prose,* p. 74.

109. Sermons III. 17. 791–4.
110. Sermons VI. 11. 5–7.
111. Sermons VII. 12. 720–8.
112. Sermons VII. 1. 427–31.
113. Sermons VII. 8. 39–41.
114. Sermons VII. 7. 385–7.
115. Sermons X. 5. 625–6.
116. Sermons VII. 11. 1–8.
117. Sermons VI. 2. 614–18.
118. Sermons VI. 16. 618–23.
119. Sermons VII. 3. 514–17.
120. Sermons II. 14. 35–6.
121. Sermons VIII. 15. 431–6.
122. Sermons VI. 1. 661–3.
123. Sermons VI. 7. 52–5.
124. Sermons X. 11. 422–5.
125. Sermons II. 14. 796–8.
126. Sermons III. 8. 627–9.
127. Sermons V. 13. 763–74.
128. Sermons I. 5. 367–8.
129. Sermons III. 3. 495–7.
130. Sermons III. 16. 250–4.
131. Sermons II. 10. 15–19.
132. Sermons III. 9. 652–4.
133. Walton, *Life of Donne*, p. 66–7.
134. Sermons V. 14. 480–4.
135. Phelps, 'The Prose of Donne and Browne', p. 125.
136. Sermons II. 16. 1–4.
137. Sermons VI. 2. 4–13.
138. Sermons IX. 3. 101–4.
139. Sermons VII. 14. 165–8.
140. Sermons V. 3. 322–6.
141. Sermons VI. 7. 414–17.
142. Sermons VI. 7. 418–424.
143. Sermons VIII. 16. 611–15.
144. Sermons VII. 5. 721.
145. Sermons VIII. 16. 595–9.

Deane of Paules

1. Walton, *Life of Donne*, pp. 87–8.
2. 'Letter: John Donne to Duke of Buckingham (8 August 1621)', cited by Bald, *John Donne*, p. 372.
3. Walton, *Life of Donne*, p. 88.
4. Walton, *Life of Donne*, p. 88.

5. H. Colvin (ed.), *The History of the King's Works*. London: HMSO, 1975, Vol. 3, 1485–1660. Part I, p. 148.

6. Colvin (ed.), *History of the King's Works*. Vol. 3, Part I, p. 148.

7. Colvin (ed.), *History of the King's Works*. Vol. 3, Part I, p. 148.

8. Colvin (ed.), *History of the King's Works*. Vol. 3, Part I, p. 148.

9. See also Carey, *John Donne*, p. 76.

10. Colvin (ed.), *History of the King's Works*. Vol. 3, Part I, p. 149.

11. *The Burnynge of Paules Church*, London 1561.

12. *Bishop Bancroft's Visitation (1598)*. Response of the Dean and Chapter and of the officers of the Cathedral to the Articles of Enquiry. *Registrum Statutorum et Consuetudinum Ecclesiae Cathedralis Sancti Pauli Londiniensis*. Edited from the original MSS. By W. Sparrow Simpson, London 1873.

13. *Bishop Bancroft's Visitation (1598)*.

14. *Archbishop Laud's Visitation (1636)*. Response of the Dean and Chapter and of officers of the Cathedral to the Articles of Enquiry. *Fourth Report of the Royal Commission on Historical MSS*. Part I. Report and Appendix, pp. 154–7.

15. See note 12.

16. Spur money was the fine that might be charged of any gentleman entering the Cathedral wearing spurs.

17. See note 12.

18. See note 14.

19. Bald, *John Donne*, pp. 450–1.

20. *Devotions upon Emergent Occasions*, John Sparrow (ed.), Cambridge: Cambridge University Press, 1923. Meditation 1.

21. *Devotions*. Meditation 2.

22. *Devotions*. 7. 'For whom the bell tolls'.

23. *Devotions*. Meditation 17.

24. *Devotions*. Expostulation 6.

25. *Devotions*. Expostulation 3.

26. Chapter 16, extract 18.

27. Chapter 16, extracts 3 (l. 1–5) and 18 (l. 21–30).

28. Walton, *Life of Donne*, p. 111.

29. 'Letter: John Chamberlain to Sir Dudley Carleton (23 April 1625)', in N.R. McClure (ed.), *The Letters of John Chamberlain*. Philadelphia, PA: American Philosophical Society, 1939. Vol. II, p. 613.

30. See note 14.

31. Bald, *John Donne*, p. 472.

32. Bald, *John Donne*, pp. 479–80.

33. Bald, *John Donne*, pp. 522–3.

34. *In Memory of Doctor Donne*. An Elegy by Mr. R.B. *Poems by Donne 1633*, pp. 400–3.

35. Sermons III. 5. 295–9.

36. Sermons IV. 3. 591–2.

37. Sermons IX. 9. 231–2.

38. Bald, *John Donne*, p. 426.

39. 'Letter: John Donne to Sir Robert Ker (4 January 1651)', *Letters to Severall Persons of Honour*, 1651.

40. Walton, *Life of Donne*, pp. 128–9.

41. Bald, *John Donne*, p. 515.

42. 'Letter: John Donne to Mrs Elizabeth Rainsford (c.1616)', cited by Gosse, *Life and Letters*, Vol.II. p. 86.

43. 'Letter: John Donne to Mrs Cokayne', *Tobie Mathew Collection*. pp. 349–50.

44. 'Letter: John Donne to Mrs Cokayne', *Tobie Mathew Collection*. pp. 349–50.

45. 'Letter: John Donne to Mr George Garrard (2 November 1630)', *Letters to Severall Persons of Honour*, 1651.

46. 'Letter: John Donne for Mrs Cokayne (15 January 1631)', *Letters to Severall Persons of Honour*, 1651.

47. 'Letter: John Donne to Mr George Garrard (? December 1630)', cited by Simpson, *John Donne: Selected Prose*, p. 170.

48. Walton, *Life of Donne*, p. 135.

49. Ps. 68.20.

50. Sermons X. 11. 435–440.

51. Sermons X. 11. 511–3.

52. Sermons X. 11. 668–673.

53. Walton, *Life of Donne*, p. 145.

54. Walton, *Life of Donne*, p. 147.

55. Walton, *Life of Donne*, p. 147.

56. Walton, *Life of Donne*, pp. 147–8.

57. Walton, *Life of Donne*, p. 149.

58. Geoffrey Keynes: Postscript to an edition of *Death's Duel*. Boston 1973. p. 43.

Part One. Humanity

Poems: The Aniversaries. The First Aniversarie. An Anatomy of the world. Dedicatory Note.

1. The Human Condition

The Human Condition

1. *Devotions upon Emergent Occasions*: 5. ('Natures nest of boxes'), cited by Simpson, *John Donne: Selected Prose*, p. 99.

2. Poems: The Anniversaries. The First Anniversary. An Anatomy of the World. l. 205–19.

3. An Anatomy of the World. l. 237–46, 325–8, 369–72, 427–34.

4. The Anniversaries. The Second Anniversary. Of the Progres of the Soule. l. 81–4.

5. Of the Progres of the Soule. l. 387–9.

6. Of the Progres of the Soule. l. 423–4.

This World's Vice-Emperor

    7. Poems: Letters to Severall Personages. To the Countesse of Huntingdon. l. 97–8.

    8. Poems: Satyres. Satyre V. l. 9–14.

    9. An Anatomy of the World. l. 161–70.

    10. Letters to Severall Personages. The Storme. To Mr Christopher Brooke. l. 51–6.

    11. Letters to Severall Personages. To Sir Edward Herbert at Julyers. l. 1–10, 15–18, 19–22, 31–2.

    12. An Anatomy of the World. l. 91–4.

    13. An Anatomy of the World. l. 61–2.

    14. An Anatomy of the World. l. 183–6.

    15. An Anatomy of the World. l. 143–6.

    16. An Anatomy of the World. l. 131–6.

    17. Of the Progres of the Soule. l. 173–8.

    18. Satyre I. l. 42–4.

    19. Of the Progres of the Soule. l. 261–80.

    20. Sermons II. 2. 229–33.

    21. Sermons VII. 11. 703–16.

    22. Poems: The Lamentations of Jeremy. l. 177–9.

    23. An Anatomy of the World. l. 281–4.

    24. Of the Progres of the Soule. l. 55–62.

2. The Way of the World

The Human Scene: The Stage

    1. Poems: Letters to Severall Personages. To Sir Henry Wotton. l. 7–10, 19–28, 37–42, 43–6, 47–58.

    2. Letters to Severall Personages. To the Countesse of Bedford. l. 1–8.

    3. Letters to Severall Personages. To Mr E.G. (Edward Guilpin). l. 1–20.

    4. 'Letter to Sir Robert More (10 August 1614)', cited by Simpson, *John Donne: Selected Prose*, p. 143.

    5. Letters to Severall Personages. To Sir Henry Wotton. l. 16–24.

    6. 'Letter to Sir Henry Goodyer (? 1608–9)', cited by Simpson, *John Donne: Selected Prose*, p. 134.

    7. Poems: Epithalamions. Ecclogue. 26 December 1613. l. 1–12.

The Human Scene: The Players

    8. Poems: The Anniversaries. The First Anniversary. A Funerall Elegie. l. 21–9.

    9. Letters to Severall Personages. To the Countesse of Bedford. l. 83–6.

    10. The Anniversaries. The Second Anniversary. Of the Progres of the Soule. l. 281–92.

    11. Of the Progres of the Soule. l. 325–38.

Worldly Cares

12. Sermons X. 8. 396–415.

Vanity

13. Sermons II. 14. 628–9.
14. Sermons VI. 18. 497–8.
15. Sermons II. 14. 321–48.

The Deceits of Life

16. Sermons VI. 15. 536–43.
17. Letters to Severall Personages. A Letter to the Lady *Carey*, and *Mrs Essex Riche*, From *Amyens*, l. 16–36.
18. Sermons IV. 5. 152–5.
19. Sermons V. 15. 156–78.

Flattery

20. Letters to Severall Personages. To E. of D. (Earl of Dorset) with six holy sonnets. l. 13–14.
21. Letters to Severall Personages. To Sir H.W. (Henry Wotton) at his going Ambassadour to *Venice*. l. 5–8.
22. Letters to Severall Personages. To the Countesse of Bedford. l. 19–39, 52–4.
23. Letters to Severall Personages. To the Countesse of Bedford. Begun in France but never perfected. l. 7–16.
24. Letters to Severall Personages. A Letter to the Lady *Carey* and *Mrs Essex Riche*, From *Amyens*. l. 36–51.
25. Letters to Severall Personages. To the Countesse of Salisbury. August 1614. l. 1–8.
26. Letters to Severall Personages. To the Countesse of Huntingdon. l. 77–84.

The Corruptions of Sin

27. Sermons IV. 1. 219–31.
28. Sermons VIII. 15. 447–8.
29. Sermons II. 14. 284–6.
30. Sermons VI. 9. 366–70.
31. Sermons VII. 16. 528–33.
32. Sermons II. 4. 90–2.
33. Sermons VI. 1. 653–63.

The Glory of this World

34. Sermons IV. 3. 1216–28.

3. *The Love of Men and Women*

Sexual Desire

   1. Poems: Elegies. Elegie XIX. To his Mistress Going to Bed. l. 1–48.
   2. Elegie XVIII. Loves Progress. l. 1–6, 19–24, 33–6, 37–72, 73–96.
   3. Poems: Songs and Sonnets. The Flea. l. 1–9.
   4. Songs and Sonnets. Loves Usury. l. 1–8.
   5. Elegie. XX. Loves Warre. l. 1–2, 29–46.
   6. Songs and Sonnets. The Canonization. l. 1–27.
   7. Songs and Sonnets. Lovers infinitenesse. l. 1–11, 23–33.

The Love of Men and Women

   8. Songs and Sonnets. The good-morrow. l. 1–21.
   9. Songs and Sonnets. The Extasie. l.1–12, 29–36, 45–56, 69–76.
 10. Songs and Sonnets. The Relique. l. 23–33.
 11. Songs and Sonnets. The Baite. l. 1–28.
 12. Elegie VIII. The Comparison. l. 1–16.
 13. *Paradoxes and Problems*. 2. That women ought to paint, cited by Simpson
John Donne: Selected Prose, pp. 7–8.
 14. Songs and Sonnets. The Sunne Rising. l. 1–30.
 15. Songs and Sonnets. Breake of day. l. 1–6, 13–18.
 16. Songs and Sonnets. Loves growth. l. 1–28.
 17. Songs and Sonnets. The Aniversarie. l. 5–10.

The Love of a Woman for a Woman

 18. Poems: Sapho to Philaemis. l. 35–52.

Delight and Desolation

 19. Poems: Letters to Severall Personages. To the Countesse of Huntingdon.
l. 37–42, 43–6, 47–50, 57–60, 61–4, 65–70, 71–4, 109–14, 121–4, 125–30.
 20. Songs and Sonnets. A Lecture upon the Shadow. l. 24–6.
 21. Elegie II. The Anagram. l. 27.
 22. Songs and Sonnets. The broken heart. l. 1–32.
 23. Letters to Severall Personages. To Mr. C.B. (Christopher Brooke). l. 7–14.
 24. Songs and Sonnets. The Message. l. 1–24.
 25. Songs and Sonnets. Farewell to love. l. 1–44.
 26. Songs and Sonnets. Valediction to his booke. l. 57–8.
 27. Elegie XII. His parting from her. l. 1–4, 13–16, 35–40, 45–52, 69–72, 73–84.
 28. Elegie XVI. On his Mistris. l. 13–16, 24–6, 47–56.
 29. Songs and Sonnets. A Valediction forbidding mourning. l. 13–24.
 30. Songs and Sonnets. A Feaver. l. 1–24.
 31. Songs and Sonnets. The Expiration. l. 1–6.

Promiscuity

32. Elegie XVII. l. 1–10, 15–24, 37–44, 61–72.
33. Songs and Sonnets. The Indifferent. l. 19–27.
34. Songs and Sonnets. Confined Love. l. 1–21.
35. Songs and Sonnets. The Indifferent. l. 1–9.
36. Elegie III. Change. l. 5–14, 23–36.
37. Songs and Sonnets. Loves diet. l. 25–30.

Cynicism

38. Songs and Sonnets. Song. l. 1–27.
39. *Paradoxes and Problems.* 1. A Defence of Womens Inconstancy, cited by Simpson, *John Donne: Selected Prose*, pp. 5–7.
40. *Paradoxes and Problems.* 6. That it is possible to find some vertue in Some Women, cited by Simpson, *John Donne: Selected Prose*, pp. 11–12.
41. Songs and Sonnets. Woman's Constancy. l. 1–17.
42. Songs and Sonnets. Loves Alchymie. l. 1–24.

The Wedding Day: The Wedding Night

43. Poems: Epithalamions. Epithalamion made at Lincolnes Inne. l. 1–12, 13–24, 37–48, 49–60, 61–72, 73–84, 85–96.
44. Epithalamions. An Epithalamion, or Marriage Song on the Lady Elizabeth, and Count Palatine. Stanzas III, IV, V, VI VII, VIII.
45. Epithalamions. Ecclogue. 26 December 1613. Stanzas I, VII, IX, X, XI.

The Gift of Children

46. Sermons VI. 13. 300–3.
47. Sermons VI. 13. 284–5.

Maturity in Love

48. Elegie IX. The Autumnall. l. 1–16, 21–8, 33–6, 47–50.
49. Elegie V. His Picture. l. 1–20.

4. *Virtuous Living*

Sparks of Virtue

1. Poems: Letters to Severall Personages. To Mr. R.W. (Rowland Woodward). l. 29–32.
2. Letters to Severall Personages. To Mr Rowland Woodward. l. 16–18, 19–21, 22–4, 28–30, 31–3, 34–6.
3. Sermons X. 1. 188–98.
4. *Paradoxes and Problems.* 4. That good is more common than evill, cited by Simpson. *John Donne: Selected Prose*, pp. 9–10.
5. Sermons V. 17. 367–8.
6. Sermons V. 17. 361–3.

Business or Books

7. 'Letter to Sir Henry Goodyer (1608–9)', cited by Simpson, *John Donne: Selected Prose*, p. 134.

8. Poems: Satyres. Satyre I. l. 1–12.

9. Letters to Severall Personages. To Mr. S.B. (Samuel Brooke). l. 1–14.

10. Letters to Severall Personages. To Mr. B.B. l. 15–28.

11. Letters to Several Personages. To Mr R.W. l. 1–12.

Friendship: An Abundant Possession

12. Letters to Severall Personages. To Mr. I.L. l. 7–14.

13. Letters to Severall Personages. To Sir Henry Wotton. l.1–2.

14. Letters to Severall Personages. To Mr. R.W. l. 1–8.

15. 'Letter to Mr George Gerrard. (14 April 1612)', cited by Simpson, *John Donne: Selected Prose*, pp. 141–2.

16. Letters to Severall Personages. To Mr. I.L. l. 13–22.

17. 'Letter to Mrs Cokayne. (August 1628)', cited by Simpson, *John Donne: Selected Prose*, p. 166.

18. Letters to Severall Personages. Elegie to the Lady Bedford (written as a consolation to the Countess on the death of a close friend). l. 1–10, 19–26.

A Right Perspective

19. Sermons VII. 1. 113–9.

20. Sermons IV. 6. 306–12.

21. Epithalamions. Ecclogue. 26 December 1613. l. 48–52.

Involved in Mankind

22. *Devotions upon Emergent Occasions.* 7. ('For whom the bell tolls'), cited by Simpson, *John Donne: Selected Prose*, p. 100–1.

23. Sermons II. 11. 476.

Resolution

24. Letters to Severall Personages. To Sir Henry Goodyere. l. 1–4, 13–16, 17–20, 29–32, 37–40.

5. Our Mortality

Torment of Sickness

1. Poems: The Anniversaries. The First Anniversary. An Anatomy of the World. l. 19–24.

2. *Devotions upon Emergent Occasions.* 1. *Insultus Morbi Primus.* Meditation. Cited by Simpson, *John Donne: Selected Prose*, p. 91.

3. *Devotions.* 1. *Insultus Morbi Primus.* Meditation. Cited by Simpson, *John Donne: Selected Prose*, pp. 91–2.

Self-Destruction

4. *Biathanatos*. 3. (The dispensing power of conscience). Cited by Simpson, *John Donne: Selected Prose*, p. 31.

Death

5. Poems: Epicedes and Obsequies. Obsequies to the Lord Harrington, brother to the Lady Lucy, Countess of Bedford. l. 105–6.

6. Epicedes and Obsequies. Elegie on M^ris Boulstred. l. 43–5.

7. Elegie on M^ris Boulstred. l. 1–12.

8. Epicedes and Obsequies. Elegie on the Lady *Marckham*. l. 1–6.

9. Elegie on the Lady *Marckham*. l. 15–20.

10. Epicedes and Obsequies. Obsequies to the Lord Harrington, brother to the Lady Lucy, Countess of Bedford. l. 165–82.

11. Elegie on M^ris Boulstred. l. 21–34.

12. Poems: Holy Sonnets. Divine Meditations X. l. 1–14.

Bereavement

13. Poems: The Anniversaries. The First Anniversary. A Funerall Elegie. l. 51–4.

14. The First Anniversary. An Anatomy of the World. l. 25–32.

15. An Anatomy of the World. l. 39–42, 49–54.

16. Epicedes and Obsequies. A hymne to the Saints, and to Marquesse Hamylton. To Sir Robert Carr. l. 7–18.

17. 'Letter to Lady Kingsmill (26 October 1624)', cited by Simpson, *John Donne: Selected Prose*, p. 158.

18. 'Letter to Mrs Cokayne (1629)', cited by Simpson, *John Donne: Selected Prose*, pp. 168–9.

The Influence of the Departed

19. An Anatomy of the World. l. 63–78.

20. An Anatomy of the World. l. 396–408.

21. The First Anniversary. A Funerall Elegie. l. 97–106.

Seeing Beyond Ourselves

22. Sermons VII. 15. 394–6.

23. Sermons IX. 9. 134–40.

24. Sermons IX. 11. 219–32.

25. Sermons VI. 14. 207–17.

The Christian Hope

26. The First Anniversary. A Funerall Elegie. l. 37–48.

27. 'Letter to Mrs Cokayne (1629)', cited by Simpson, *John Donne: Selected Prose*, p. 168.

28. The Anniversaries. The Second Anniversary. Of the Progres of the Soule. The Harbinger to the Progres (by Joseph Hall). l. 9–18.

29. Sermons X. 5. 450–2.
30. Sermons IV. 6. 297–301.
31. Sermons II. 17. 104–13.
32. Sermons VII. 15. 507–16.
33. Sermons VII. 13. 559–71.

Part Two. Divinity

Songs and Sonnets: Valediction to his booke, l. 28–9

6. On Discerning God

The Desire to Know God

1. Sermons VII. 12. 98–9.
2. Sermons VIII. 14. 578–82.
3. Sermons VIII. 9. 173–5.
4. Sermons VIII. 11. 188–91.
5. Sermons IX. 10. 430–3.
6. Sermons V. 15. 83–4.

The Light of Nature

7. Sermons IX. 11. 139–40.
8. Sermons I. 2. 41.
9. Sermons VII. 12. 111–12.
10. Sermons VIII. 9. 193–6.
11. Sermons VIII. 9. 176–7.
12. Sermons VII. 12. 179–83.
13. Sermons III. 17. 414–22.
14. Sermons III. 17. 404–7.
15. Sermons III. 17. 772–5.

The Necessity of Faith

16. Sermons VIII. 1. 103–5.
17. Sermons IV. 3. 1208–9.
18. Sermons VI. 13. 106–8.
19. *Essays in Divinity*. Section 1: of God.
20. Poems: Divine Poëms. The Litanie VII, l. 62–3.
21. Sermons V. 4. 213–15.
22. Sermons VI. 6. 403–9.
23. Poems: Letters to Severall Personnages. To the Countesse of Bedford. l. 1–2.

On Seeing God

24. Sermons VII. 9. 634–5.
25. Sermons IV. 3. 1250–2.
26. Sermons X. 11. 257–9.

27. Sermons VIII. 9. 42–60.
28. Sermons IV. 3. 567–73.
29. Sermons VI. 7. 543–5.
30. Sermons VI. 16. 511–13.
31. Sermons VIII. 3. 368–70.
32. Sermons VIII. 410–15.

7. The Holy Trinity

The Holy Trinity

1. Sermons VI. 6. 360–3.
2. Sermons IX. 1. 154–8.
3. Sermons VIII. 1. 649–53.
4. Sermons VIII. 1. 623–4.
5. Sermons III. 12. 270–4.
6. Sermons VII. 18. 199–203.
7. Sermons IX. 1. 200–4.

The Society of the Trinity

8. Sermons VI. 3. 5–6.
9. Sermons VIII. 16. 599–601.
10. Sermons VI. 7. 115–27.

The Persons of the Trinity

11. Sermons IV. 10. 112–24.
12. Sermons VIII. 1. 839–45.
13. Sermons III. 12. 275–82.
14. Sermons III. 12. 358–60.
15. Sermons V. 12. 124–6.
16. Sermons VIII. 7. 192–8.
17. Sermons V. 1. 177–81.
18. Sermons VII. 18. 33–6.
19. Sermons IX. 10. 308–14.
20. Sermons VI. 16. 150–2.
21. Sermons VI. 16. 625–7.
22. Sermons V. 3. 659–68.
23. Sermons IX. 3. 265–8.
24. Sermons IV. 10. 305–9.
25. Sermons V. 4. 475–7.
26. Sermons VI. 5. 543–5.
27. Sermons VII. 18. 213–22.
28. Sermons VII. 18. 78–90.
29. Divine Poëms: The Litanie I – IV, l. 1–36.

The Name of God

30. Sermons V. 16. 143–52.
31. Sermons V. 16. 171–87.
32. Sermons V. 16. 188–204.
33. Sermons VIII. 7. 130–1.

The Being of God

34. Poems: Epicedes and Obsequies. Obsequies to the Lord Harrington, brother to the Lady Lucy, Countesse of Bedford. l. 35–6.
35. Sermons VI. 8. 582.
36. Sermons IX. 5. 104–6.
37. Sermons V. 16. 275–82.
38. Sermons VII. 9. 380–90.
39. Sermons II. 6. 261–6.
40. Sermons II. 10. 138–41.

The Character of God

41. Sermons VI. 11. 321–3.
42. Sermons VI. 11. 338–50.
43. Sermons VI. 11. 370–1.
44. Sermons VI. 11. 390–1.
45. Sermons VI. 11. 457–9.
46. Sermons VII. 2. 524–7.
47. Sermons I. 1. 612–4.
48. Sermons V. 19. 111–13.
49. Sermons VII. 14. 425–6.

The Activity of God

50. Sermons IV. 2. 498–9.
51. Sermons VII. 1. 339–42.
52. Sermons IX. 2. 207–13.
53. Sermons IV. 3. 476–7.
54. Sermons IV. 3. 515–6.
55. Sermons IV. 3. 427–9.
56. Sermons VI. 15. 97–9.
57. Sermons IV. 4. 97–100.

8. In the Image of God

A Child of God

1. Sermons VIII. 12. 584–5.
2. Sermons IX. 17. 76–81.
3. Sermons V. 2. 447–51.
4. Sermons II. 9. 91–9.

5. Sermons VIII. 5. 392–7.
6. Sermons VI. 15. 257–9.
7. Sermons VI. 15. 192–4.
8. Sermons II. 11. 449–55.
9. Sermons VI. 15. 195–205.
10. Sermons V. 2. 525–6.

An Eternal Election

11. Sermons VIII. 12. 457–8.
12. Sermons VII. 1. 427–31.
13. Sermons VII. 5. 529–47.
14. Sermons VI. 8. 245–51.
15. Sermons VII. 14. 165–8.

Susceptible of Grace

16. Sermons IX. 7. 56–7.
17. Sermons I. 7. 127–9.
18. Sermons IX. 18. 567–75.
19. Sermons IV. 3. 1359–62.
20. Sermons IX. 17. 109–15.
21. Sermons IX. 3. 423–6.
22. Sermons VIII. 12. 135–7.
23. Sermons V. 10. 168–71.
24. Sermons X. 1. 818–20.
25. Sermons X. 5. 617–23.
26. Sermons VIII. 2. 458–61.
27. Sermons VI. 15. 206–8.
28. Sermons VIII. 2. 502–3.

9. The Human Predicament

The Human Predicament

1. Poems: The Anniversaries. The Second Anniversary. Of the Progres of the Soule. l. 254–60.
2. Sermons II. 14. 690–728.
3. Sermons III. 10. 397–9.
4. Sermons V. 9. 257–61.
5. Sermons V. 13. 322–31.
6. Sermons X. 5. 570–99.
7. Sermons VII. 8. 28–9.
8. The Anniversaries. The First Anniversary. An Anatomy of the World. l. 155–8.
9. Poems: Holy Sonnets. Divine Meditations II. l. 5–9.

The Fall

10. Poems: Epicedes and Obsequies. Elegie (upon the death of Mistress Bulstrode). l. 37–8.

  11. Sermons VII. 10. 1–4.

  12. Sermons VI. 18. 1–2.

  13. Sermons VII. 3. 526–34.

  14. Poems: Metempsycosis. The Progresse of the Soule. First Song IX. l. 81–90.

  15. Sermons II. 4. 59–62.

  16. Sermons III. 17. 279–80.

  17. Sermons VII. 7. 385–7.

  18. An Anatomy of the World. l. 191–202.

  19. Sermons VII. 8. 39–41.

  20. Sermons VII. 8. 107–12.

  21. An Anatomy of the World. l. 105–10.

  22. Sermons VIII. 12. 151–3.

  23. Sermons X. 5. 601–11.

  24. Sermons VII. 8. 69–75.

  25. Sermons X. 5. 625–6.

A Continual Course of Sin

  26. Sermons II. 3. 272–3.

  27. Sermons VIII. 15. 431–6.

  28. Sermons II. 4. 2–3.

  29. Sermons VII. 3. 514–17.

  30. Sermons IX. 10. 617–21.

  31. Sermons VIII. 8. 610–19.

  32. Sermons VI. 11. 88–96.

  33. Sermons VIII. 15. 397–9.

  34. Sermons II. 3. 174–6.

  35. Sermons VI. 2. 247–50.

  36. Sermons V. 15. 268–72.

  37. Sermons II. 3. 210–12.

  38. Metempsycosis. The Progresse of the Soul. First Song X. l. 91–100.

  39. Sermons IX. 14. 431–2.

  40. Sermons II. 3. 510–11.

  41. Sermons IV. 5. 158–73.

  42. Sermons IX. 11. 758–60.

  43. Epicedes and Obsequies. On himselfe. l. 15–17.

  44. Sermons VIII. 8. 579–88.

  45. Sermons IX. 2. 57–8.

  46. Metempsycosis. The Progresse of the Soule. First Song. XI. l. 101–5.

  47. Sermons II. 4. 111–17.

  48. Sermons VI. 2. 327–9.

Directing Temptations

49. Sermons II. 1. 289–91.
50. Sermons IX. 18. 347–55.
51. Sermons II. 14. 30–8.
52. Sermons IX. 17. 262–70.
53. Sermons II. 14. 231–7.
54. Sermons VII. 2. 163–7.
55. Sermons III. 1. 249–50.
56. Sermons VI. 11. 98–100.
57. Sermons III. 1. 382–3.
58. Divine Poëms. The Litanie. XXI. l. 181–9.
59. Sermons II. 2. 615–23.
60. Sermons II. 5. 126–38.
61. Sermons VI. 9. 493–504.
62. Sermons VI. 1. 673–9.
63. Sermons X. 10. 309–12.
64. Sermons VI. 15. 631–5.
65. Sermons IX. 10. 151–5.
66. Sermons IX. 7. 125–6.
67. Sermons VI. 9. 481–93.
68. Sermons IX. 7. 119–20.
69. Sermons V. 3. 614–6.
70. Sermons V. 15. 674–6.
71. Sermons IV. 13. 175–9.
72. Sermons IX. 15. 204–8.

Judgement and Mercy

73. Sermons II. 8. 421–9.
74. Sermons II. 8. 558–68.
75. Sermons V. 15. 201–5.
76. Sermons VI. 1. 683–5.
77. Sermons IX. 12. 783–92.
78. Sermons VI. 18. 155–60.
79. Sermons VII. 6. 875–7.
80. Sermons VIII. 8. 681–4.
81. Sermons VIII. 8. 691.
82. Sermons V. 3. 322–6.
83. Sermons IV. 5. 198–201.
84. Sermons VI. 7. 414–7.

10. God and Man

God and Man

1. Sermons X. 8. 65–6.
2. Sermons VIII. 4. 502–5.

3. Sermons VI. 1. 547–8.
4. Sermons VI. 1. 751–2.
5. Sermons IX. 17. 1–3.
6. Sermons I. 6. 140–4.
7. Sermons VI. 8. 619–24.
8. Sermons VI. 8. 226–7.
9. Sermons IV. 7. 81–3.
10. Sermons VI. 3. 114–17.
11. Sermons VI. 7. 52–5.
12. Sermons VII. 16. 675–7.
13. Sermons I. 5. 305–10.
14. Sermons X. 9. 316–17.
15. Sermons II. 14. 791–4.
16. Poems: Holy Sonnets. Divine Meditations XIV, l. 1–14.
17. Sermons X. 9. 237–9.
18. Sermons VII. 5. 551–2.
19. Sermons X. 1. 808–10.
20. Sermons VII. 1. 461–3.
21. Sermons V. 15. 766–72.
22. Sermons VIII. 14. 210–14.
23. Sermons VII. 5. 562–3.
24. Sermons VI. 6. 332–5.
25. Sermons IV. 7. 219–21.
26. Sermons IX. 2. 260–2.
27. Sermons VII. 9. 524–6.
28. Sermons III. 2. 203–8.
29. Sermons III. 2. 513–15.
30. Sermons VIII. 15. 216–18.
31. Sermons III. 2. 126–8.
32. Sermons VI. 1. 361–5.
33. Sermons VIII. 5. 453–6.
34. Sermons VI. 8. 190–2.

Grace

35. Sermons IV. 3. 127–35.
36. Sermons VII. 12. 243–4.
37. Sermons VI. 10. 285–90.
38. Sermons V. 8. 1–9.
39. Sermons III. 8. 382–3.
40. Sermons V. 17. 317–18.
41. Sermons VIII. 5. 44–51.
42. Sermons VII. 5. 607–8.
43. Sermons VIII. 16. 52–3.
44. Sermons V. 18. 66–7.
45. Sermons V. 18. 68–71.
46. Sermons II. 14. 670–8.

47. Sermons VII. 14. 138–44.
48. Sermons V. 18. 279–86.
49. Sermons V. 18. 315–25.
50. Sermons V. 18. 248–57.
51. Sermons VI. 15. 425–31.
52. Sermons VIII. 16. 480–5.
53. Sermons VI. 8. 140–52.
54. Sermons VI. 2. 357.
55. Sermons VII. 3. 859.

Repentance

56. Sermons IX. 1. 633–7.
57. Sermons IX. 14. 496–9.
58. Sermons III. 16. 316–43.
59. Sermons VII. 18. 612–20.
60. Sermons III. 17. 963–8.
61. Sermons IV. 1. 544–5.
62. Sermons II. 4. 273–87.
63. Sermons IV. 5. 191–206.
64. Sermons IV. 5. 246–51.
65. Sermons IV. 9. 894–904.
66. Sermons IV. 12. 28–33.
67. Sermons IV. 13. 554–61.
68. Sermons V. 8. 425–31.
69. Sermons V. 12. 193–7.
70. Sermons V. 15. 35–46.
71. Sermons IX. 14. 434–40.
72. Sermons VII. 7. 390–7.
73. Sermons IX. 4. 653–65.
74. Sermons IX. 6. 605–15.
75. Sermons IV. 8. 643–46.
76. Poems: Epicedes and Obsequies. An hymne to the Saints and to the Marquesse Hamylton. l. 33–42.
77. Sermons IX. 9. 168–70.
78. Sermons IX. 11. 480–5.
79. Sermons IX. 13. 345–50.
80. Sermons IV. 8. 415–27.
81. Sermons X. 8. 281–8.
82. Sermons IX. 11. 836–40.

Restoration

83. Sermons VII. 15. 1–2.
84. Sermons VI. 8. 132–6.
85. Sermons V. 19. 81–93.
86. Sermons X. 4. 201–9.

87. Sermons VIII. 10. 340–59.
88. Holy Sonnets. Divine Meditations I. l. 1–14.
89. Divine Meditations IV. l. 1–2, 9–14.
90. Sermons VII. 2. 1–6.
91. Sermons V.17. 189–91.
92. Sermons VIII. 11. 323–4.
93. Sermons VII. 12. 228–9.

11. The Work of Christ

Incarnation

1. Poems: Holy Sonnets. Divine Meditations XV. l. 13–14.
2. Sermons VI. 8. 589–90.
3. Sermons I. 5. 297–8.
4. Sermons V. 13. 243–8.
5. Sermons VI. 15. 154–62.
6. Divine Meditations XI. l. 9–14.
7. Sermons VI. 17. 464–7.
8. Holy Sonnets. Annunciation. l. 1–14.
9. Sermons VI. 7. 167–77.
10. Sermons III. 14. 268–78.
11. Sermons IX. 15. 499–508.
12. Sermons VI. 8. 421–2.

The Representative Man

13. Sermons IX. 10. 551–9.
14. Sermons VI. 7. 344–56.

The Nativity

15. Poems: Letters to Severall Personages. To the Countesse of Huntingdon. l. 14.
16. Holy Sonnets. La Corona: Nativitie. l. 1–14.
17. Sermons I. 9. 194–7.
18. Sermons IX. 5. 730–4.
19. Sermons VII. 11. 10–17.
20. Sermons VI. 17. 74–82.
21. Sermons VII. 11. 1–8.

The Sacrifice for Sin

22. Poems: Metempsycosis. The Progresse of the Soule. First Song. l. 73–6.
23. Sermons VII. 11. 95–7.
24. Sermons V. 16. 326–7.
25. La Corona: Crucifying. l. 9–14.
26. Sermons I. 9. 346–53.

27. Sermons VII. 4. 654–9.
28. Sermons II. 5. 237–41.
29. Divine Meditations XIII. l. 1–8.
30. Sermons VI. 13. 473–85.
31. Sermons VI. 2. 614–18.
32. Sermons II. 5. 254–6.
33. Sermons IV. 11. 489–91.
34. Sermons II. 14. 498–501.
35. Sermons VIII. 10. 508–14.
36. Sermons IX. 16. 316–21.
37. Sermons V. 7. 235–41.
38. Sermons V. 16. 15–21.
39. Sermons X. 9. 151–6.
40. Sermons IV. 8. 875–8.
41. Sermons IX. 10. 562–8.
42. Sermons II. 9. 208–11.
43. Sermons VI. 14. 306.
44. Sermons II. 14. 547–8.

Resurrection

45. Divine Poëms. Resurrection, imperfect. l. 1–8.
46. Divine Poëms. Good Friday, 1613. Riding Westward. l. 11–22.
47. Sermons VI. 13. 72–3.
48. Sermons VII. 3. 212–14.
49. Sermons VII. 3. 216–20.
50. Sermons VIII. 4. 36–40.
51. Sermons X. 6. 421–3.

The Day of Salvation

52. La Corona: Ascention. l. 9–14.
53. Sermons IX. 14. 457.
54. Sermons VII. 5. 721.
55. Sermons VII. 14. 236–9.
56. Sermons VI. 17. 150–65.
57. Sermons VI. 16. 618–23.
58. La Corona: Resurrection. l. 1–14.
59. Sermons IX. 10. 293–5.
60. Sermons V. 18. 288–307.
61. Sermons IX. 10. 350–66.
62. Sermons IX. 4. 396–404.
63. Sermons VI. 17. 479–83.
64. Sermons VI. 7. 41–50.
65. Sermons IV. 3. 1538–41.
66. Sermons IV. 3. 1535–7.
67. Sermons VI. 7. 418–24.

68. Sermons VI. 1. 726–33.
69. Sermons VIII. 8. 542–9.
70. Sermons VII. 11. 140–2.
71. Sermons VI. 5. 441–3.
72. Sermons X. 5. 565–6.
73. Sermons VI. 18. 320–2.

12. The Body of Christ

The Catholic Church

1. Sermons VII. 3. 410–2.
2. Sermons V. 5. 417–8.
3. Sermons IX. 3. 7–9.
4. Sermons IV. 12. 242–4.
5. Sermons IV. 14. 149–57.
6. Poems: Holy Sonnets. Divine Meditations XVIII. l. 1–14.
7. Sermons II. 13. 395–401.
8. Sermons VIII. 5. 911–17.
9. Sermons VII. 12. 490–5.
10. Sermons IX. 6. 395–410.
11. Sermons VII. 6. 326–34.
12. Sermons II. 3. 615–19.
13. Sermons II. 4. 113–14.
14. Sermons VIII. 11. 556–63.
15. Sermons I. 4. 455–61.
16. Sermons VIII. 11. 283–9.
17. Sermons IX. 2. 269–75.
18. Sermons VII. 1. 379–88.
19. Sermons VI. 14. 162–7.
20. *Devotions Upon Emergent Occasions*, 1624. Section 7: For whom the bell tolls.

The House of God

21. Sermons VI. 7. 72–5.
22. Sermons IV. 15. 16–22.
23. Sermons IX. 14. 107–16.
24. Sermons VII. 12. 643–4.
25. Sermons VII. 11. 469–79.
26. Sermons IX. 8. 718–24.
27. Sermons VII. 11. 456–69.
28. Sermons VII. 8. 649–54.
29. Sermons VI. 16. 647–54.
30. Sermons VII. 1. 280–6.
31. Sermons IX. 8. 198–202.
32. Sermons X. 1. 606–8.

The English Reformation Settlement

33. Sermons IV. 3. 639–48.
34. Sermons VII. 16. 601–3.
35. Sermons VIII. 1. 49–54.
36. Sermons V. 14. 981–8.
37. Sermons III. 4. 592–600.
38. Sermons VI. 14. 156–62.
39. Sermons V. 13. 220–26.
40. Sermons IV. 3. 654–9.
41. Sermons VI. 10. 456–7.
42. Sermons VII. 16. 508–14.
43. Sermons VIII. 4. 225–6.
44. Sermons IX. 2. 441–6.
45. Sermons VI. 3. 190–6.
46. Sermons IV. 9. 913–16.
47. Sermons III. 4. 494–9.

The Roman Church

48. Sermons VI. 12. 190–9.
49. Sermons IX. 18. 515–18.
50. Sermons VII. 18. 506–16.

The Communion of Saints

51. Sermons III. 4. 275–7.
52. Poems: The Anniversaries. The Second Anniversary. Of the Progres of the Soule. l. 154.
53. Sermons III. 4. 300–4.
54. Sermons X. 2. 271–80.
55. Sermons V. 13. 173–6.
56. Sermons II. 13. 13–21.
57. Sermons III. 17. 736–9.
58. Sermons IV. 2. 371–83.

13. The Holy Scriptures

The Old and New Testaments

1. Sermons VIII. 5. 131–2.
2. Sermons IX. 10. 1–5.
3. Sermons VI. 4. 643–51.
4. Sermons V. 7. 33–61.
5. Sermons VII. 1. 1–4.
6. Sermons VII. 1. 6–13.
7. Sermons IV. 6. 499–500.
8. Sermons V. 1. 719–24.
9. Sermons V. 12. 318–27.

The Authority of Scripture

10. Sermons IV. 3. 618–26.
11. Sermons III. 14. 75–6.
12. Sermons VI. 11. 5–7.
13. Sermons VII. 16. 253–7.
14. Sermons VII. 18. 5–6.
15. Sermons VIII. 4. 435–6.
16. Sermons III. 17. 374–8.
17. Sermons V. 2. 185–91.
18. Sermons V. 4. 215–21.
19. Sermons III. 17. 791–4.
20. Sermons V. 5. 397–8.
21. Sermons VIII. 5. 176–91.
22. Sermons VI. 2. 4–13.
23. *Devotions upon Emergent Occasions*. Section 8: The physicians, after a long and stormy voyage, see land.
24. Sermons II. 16. 1–4.

The Reading of Scripture

25. Sermons V. 1. 728–30.
26. Sermons IV. 3. 1280–2.
27. Sermons III. 9. 65–7.
28. Sermons II. 14. 755–80.
29. Sermons V. 1. 135–66.
30. Sermons X. 4. 8–14.
31. *Essays in Divinity*. Section 3: The True Sense of Scripture.
32. Sermons IX. 3. 101–4.
33. Sermons III. 17. 716–20.
34. Sermons IX. 4. 539–41.
35. Sermons IX. 4. 547–9.

14. The Life of the Church

Prayer, Preaching and Sacraments

1. Sermons IV. 2. 295–10.
2. Sermons IV. 3. 590–4.
3. Sermons VI. 8. 94–9.
4. Sermons VII. 12. 453–4.
5. Sermons IX. 9. 225–33.
6. Sermons VI. 4. 338–43.
7. Sermons II. 12. 290–301.

Baptism

8. Sermons V. 7. 403–5.
9. Sermons V. 7. 462–4.

10. Sermons VIII. 15. 618–22.
11. Sermons VI. 14. 33–5.
12. Sermons V. 7. 490–6.
13. Sermons VI. 6. 40–3.
14. Sermons V. 7. 531–7.
15. Sermons V. 7. 451–4.
16. Sermons II. 15. 470–81.

Holy Communion

17. Sermons VII. 11. 420–8.
18. Sermons VII. 4. 795–804.
19. Sermons VII. 11. 132–8.

Confession

20. Sermons II. 18. 492–4.
21. Sermons IX. 13. 2–12.

Private Prayer

22. Sermons V. 18. 1–2.
23. Sermons VII. 10. 431–5.
24. Poems: Divine Poëms. The Litanie. XXIII. l. 199–207.
25. Sermons VII. 10. 444–6.
26. Sermons VI. 1. 487–91.
27. Sermons VI. 1. 470–82.
28. Sermons VII. 10. 271–86.
29. Sermons VII. 10. 466–76.
30. Sermons V. 12. 43–7.
31. The Litanie XIV. l. 118–26.
32. Sermons IX. 9. 273–7.
33. Sermons V. 18. 30–1.

Public Prayer

34. Sermons VII. 12. 409–14.
35. Sermons V. 14. 171–2.
36. Sermons IV. 12. 247–54.
37. Sermons VII. 12. 431–7.
38. Sermons IX. 9. 221–3.

Preaching

39. Sermons IV. 3. 758–9.
40. Sermons II. 18. 485–6.
41. Sermons VII. 12. 1–11.
42. Sermons VII. 12. 720–8.
43. Sermons IV. 3. 1077–84.
44. Sermons IV. 12. 166–9.

45. Sermons III. 5. 295–9.
46. Sermons III. 1. 337–42.
47. Sermons V. 2. 415–28.
48. Sermons IV. 13. 403–9.
49. Sermons III. 17. 596–600.
50. Sermons V. 1. 760–4.

The People of God

51. Sermons IV. 3. 1305–7.
52. Sermons IV. 3. 1314–15.
53. Sermons V. 2. 266–8.
54. Sermons IV. 8. 229–30.
55. Sermons X. 2. 117–21.
56. Sermons IV. 15. 252–60.
57. Sermons IV. 10. 433–42.
58. Sermons V. 14. 303–28.
59. Sermons VIII. 7. 1–13.
60. Sermons X. 11. 422–5.
61. Sermons IX. 14. 94–6.

The Office of a Priest

62. Sermons VII. 4. 591–7.
63. Divine Poëms. To Mr *Tilman* after he had taken orders. l. 1–4, 13–22, 35–44, 47–54.
64. Sermons IV. 3. 732–5.
65. Sermons IV. 3. 746–55.
66. Sermons VIII. 1. 150–62.
67. Sermons II. 7. 92–102.
68. Sermons VII. 11. 248–53.
69. Sermons VII. 11. 290–5.
70. Sermons X. 5. 217–25.
71. Sermons VIII. 5. 576–7.
72. Sermons II. 7. 329–32.
73. Sermons IX. 6. 11–14.
74. Sermons IV. 3. 806–8.
75. Sermons VI. 3. 436–8.
76. Sermons IX. 5. 60–1.
77. Sermons X. 5. 101–3.
78. Sermons X. 6. 96–106.
79. Sermons IV. 3. 840–1.
80. Sermons IV. 3. 834–8.
81. Sermons VI. 3. 409–22.
82. Sermons VI. 3. 169–74.
83. Sermons VI. 3. 158–62.
84. Sermons VI. 3. 144–9.

85. Sermons VIII. 1. 489–92.

The Preacher

86. Sermons IV. 8. 40–9.
87. Sermons VI. 3. 403–6.
88. Sermons VII. 13. 330–1.
89. Sermons IV. 10. 419–30.
90. Sermons IV. 3. 795–9.
91. Sermons VII. 13. 155–7.

The Work of Evangelism

92. Sermons VIII. 10. 371–5.
93. Sermons VI. 1. 107–22.
94. Sermons V. 19. 148–50.
95. Sermons IV. 10. 550–2.
96. Sermons V. 1. 567–8.
97. Sermons III. 16. 548–53.
98. Sermons IV. 2. 570–81.
99. Sermons I. 9. 252–4.

15. Christian Obedience

The Call to Discipleship

1. Sermons VI. 2. 655–61.
2. Sermons VII. 9. 296–7.
3. Sermons IX. 7. 101–2.
4. Sermons IV. 3. 708–10.
5. Poems: Divine Poëms. A Hymn to Christ at the Authors last going into Germany. l. 25–32.
6. Sermons VII. 11. 216–17.
7. Sermons II. 11. 369–90.
8. Sermons II. 13. 110–12.
9. Sermons I. 9. 255–90.
10. Sermons I. 5. 517–32.
11. Sermons II. 17. 124–5.
12. Sermons IX. 5. 825–33.

Being in Christ

13. Sermons III. 16. 45–51.
14. Sermons III. 12. 150–2.
15. Sermons III. 13. 248–52.
16. Sermons III. 16. 250–4.
17. Sermons V. 7. 226–34.
18. Sermons V. 7. 318–25.
19. Sermons V. 7. 338–46.

20. Sermons VIII. 16. 517–19.
21. Sermons IX. 4. 384–8.
22. Sermons VI. 4. 604–8.
23. Sermons IX. 8. 681–7.
24. Sermons X. 4. 508–15.
25. Sermons IX. 4. 464–5.
26. Sermons VI. 1. 144–50.

Obstacles to Salvation

27. Sermons IV. 10. 374–5.
28. Sermons VIII. 5. 262–4.
29. Sermons IX. 10. 609–17.
30. Sermons VIII. 16. 593–5.
31. Sermons IX. 1. 747–55.
32. Sermons IV. 3. 1108–11.
33. Sermons IX. 5. 126–31.
34. Sermons V. 14. 290–303.
35. Sermons VIII. 4. 324–6.
36. Sermons VIII. 2. 65–6.
37. Divine Poëms. The Litanie XI. l. 95–9.
38. Sermons III. 8. 543–6.
39. Sermons IX. 16. 531–2.
40. Sermons VI. 13. 219–22.
41. Sermons X. 3. 425–30.
42. Sermons V. 17. 849–60.
43. Sermons VI. 7. 418–24.
44. Sermons VI. 12. 673–83.
45. Sermons II. 13. 601–13.
46. Sermons X. 8. 256–62.
47. Sermons X. 1. 532–53.
48. Sermons VI. 4. 590–1.
49. Sermons VII. 11. 348–9.

Perseverance

50. Sermons IV. 3. 1016–19.
51. *Biathanatos*. Section 4.
52. Sermons V. 14. 480–9.
53. Sermons VI. 9. 585–95.
54. Sermons V. 7. 182–9.
55. Sermons IX. 4. 565–70.
56. Sermons II. 6. 201–15.
57. Sermons III. 17. 458–516.
58. Sermons I. 8. 311–33.
59. Sermons IX. 13. 257–9.
60. Sermons I. 1. 199–206.

Growing up into Christ

61. Sermons X. 1. 416–22.
62. Sermons III. 1. 1–6.
63. Sermons V. 14. 269–73.
64. Sermons II. 15. 147–53.
65. Sermons IV. 14. 226–37.
66. Sermons V. 4. 399–401.
67. Sermons VIII. 11. 315–19.
68. Sermons V. 17. 866–80.
69. Sermons III. 5. 532–5.
70. Sermons II. 13. 196–9.
71. Letter: John Donne to Mrs Cokayne (1629).
72. Divine Poëms. The Crosse. l. 1–6, 11–14, 17–26, 49–52, 59–62.
73. Sermons II. 13. 167–8.
74. Sermons III. 3. 495–7.
75. Sermons X. 5. 450–2.
76. Sermons II. 14. 796–8.

Faith and Works

77. Sermons X. 3. 23–5.
78. Sermons V. 7. 169–73.
79. Sermons VI. 4. 255–6.
80. 'Letter: John Donne to Sir Henry Goodyer (4 October 1622)', cited by Simpson, *John Donne: Selected Prose*, p. 153.
81. Sermons III. 13. 452–60.
82. Sermons IX. 4. 450–2.
83. Sermons VI. 7. 371–4.
84. Sermons X. 3. 177–82.
85. Sermons IX. 17. 461–72.
86. Sermons V. 9. 423–30.

One Body in Christ

87. Sermons I. 5. 367–8.
88. Sermons IV. 3. 769–72.
89. Sermons IX. 11. 651–4.
90. Sermons VI. 11. 130–3.
91. Sermons VIII. 16. 611–5.
92. Sermons IX. 18. 734–45.
93. Sermons VIII. 12. 673–4.
94. Sermons III. 1. 425–7.

Suffering for Christ

95. Sermons VIII. 14. 288–92.
96. Sermons VIII. 7. 403–5.
97. Sermons X. 11. 475–7.

98. Sermons II. 14. 520–5.
99. Sermons VI. 10. 342–7.
100. Sermons VI. 4. 488–90.
101. Sermons X. 5. 724–42.
102. Sermons VIII. 7. 444–62.
103. Sermons VI. 8. 370–2.
104. Sermons VI. 1. 283–6.
105. Sermons VIII. 8. 220–2.
106. Sermons VI. 1. 324–9.
107. Sermons III. 8. 505–8.
108. Sermons III. 6. 375–82.

Adversity

109. Sermons X. 9. 288.
110. Sermons X. 9. 317.
111. Sermons II. 14. 492–3.
112. Sermons III. 8. 239–42.
113. Sermons VI. 12. 693–7.
114. Sermons V. 14. 589–96.
115. Sermons IV. 6. 373–7.
116. Sermons X. 9. 262–9.
117. Sermons IX. 12. 341–5.
118. Sermons III. 13. 189–92.
119. Sermons II. 18. 107–17.
120. Sermons II. 14. 508–17.
121. Sermons IX. 11. 255–9.
122. Sermons VII. 1. 182–92.
123. Sermons X. 9. 406–8.
124. Sermons X. 9. 418–20.
125. Sermons VII. 2. 339–48.
126. Sermons VI. 11. 537–9.
127. Sermons V. 16. 624–9.

Living in the World

128. Sermons III. 8. 529–30.
129. Sermons VIII. 9. 70–2.
130. Divine Poëms. The Litanie XV. l. 127–35.
131. Sermons IX. 14. 527–38.
132. Sermons VIII. 7. 253–5.
133. Sermons VI. 6. 47–9.
134. Sermons III. 6. 468–71.
135. Sermons III. 6. 499–501.
136. Sermons VII. 11. 166–7.
137. Sermons IV. 5. 150–60.
138. Sermons VIII. 7. 36–42.

139. Sermons IX. 1. 590–9.
140. Sermons IX. 2. 46–9.
141. Sermons VII. 11. 102–9.
142. Sermons III. 17. 918–22.
143. Sermons IX. 4. 492–5.
144. Sermons IX. 4. 427–32.
145. Sermons VII. 9. 289–90.
146. Sermons VII. 9. 272–83
147. Sermons VII. 9. 34–7.
148. Sermons IX. 2. 448–50.
149. Sermons III. 12. 516–31.
150. Sermons X. 18. 722–8.
151. Sermons X. 10. 102–6.

Looking Towards Our End

152. Sermons III. 1. 152–4.
153. Sermons X. 10. 576–83.
154. Sermons VI. 11. 461–2.
155. Sermons IX. 4. 685–6.
156. Sermons X. 10. 549–52.
157. Sermons V. 14. 706–13.
158. Sermons X. 6. 455–60.
159. Sermons VI. 11. 463–4.
160. Sermons IX. 2. 798–800.
161. Sermons IV. 7. 120–6.
162. Sermons VII. 14. 616–19.
163. Sermons III.16. 284–8.
164. Sermons VII. 9. 29–32.
165. Sermons X. 10. 28–30.
166. Sermons III. 12. 498–9.
167. Sermons IV. 1. 10–11.
168. Sermons VI. 11. 208–10.
169. Sermons X. 11. 429–31.
170. Sermons VII. 1. 729–30.

16. The Last Things

Death

1. Sermons VI. 2. 643–5.
2. Sermons II. 12. 603–6.
3. Poems: Divine Poëms. Hymne to God my God, in my sicknesse. l. 1–5.
4. Sermons III. 3. 373–4.
5. Poems: Holy Sonnets. Divine Meditations VI. l. 1–14.
6. Sermons VII. 15. 730–46.

7. Poems: The Anniversaries. The Second Anniversary. Of the Progres of the Soule. l. 85–108.
    8. Sermons II. 2. 459–66.
    9. Sermons IV. 1. 290–302.
    10. Sermons IV. 2. 147–51.
    11. Of the Progres of the Soule. l. 179–84.
    12. Sermons IV. 2. 92–7.
    13. Of the Progres of the Soule. l. 149–50, 156.
    14. Sermons VII. 15. 502–7.
    15. Sermons VIII. 7. 9–13.
    16. Of the Progres of the Soule. l. 213–18.
    17. Sermons III. 8. 627–9.

Judgement

    18. Divine Poëms. A Hymne to God the Father. l. 1–18.
    19. Sermons IV. 3. 1330–4.
    20. Sermons III. 3. 406–10.
    21. Sermons VIII. 1. 812–15.
    22. Sermons II. 18. 359–68.
    23. Sermons II. 18. 242–6.
    24. Sermons II. 11. 469–74.
    25. Sermons I. 6. 480–6.
    26. Sermons VI. 7. 571–8.
    27. Sermons IX. 9. 612–22.
    28. Sermons II. 16. 344–7.
    29. Hymne to God my God in my sicknesse. l. 21–30.

Hell

    30. Sermons VIII. 11. 99–100.
    31. Sermons II. 4. 359–64.
    32. Sermons II. 2. 554–7.
    33. Sermons V. 13. 763–74.

The Beatific Vision

    34. Sermons IV. 3. 135–9.
    35. Sermons VIII. 9. 494–9.
    36. Sermons IV. 5. 618–9.
    37. Sermons III. 3. 748–9.
    38. Sermons III. 3. 762–5.
    39. Sermons VII. 13. 623–5.
    40. Sermons IV. 2. 886–9.

The Glory of God

    41. Sermons IV. 3. 1452–4.
    42. Sermons III. 4. 206–10.

43. Sermons IV. 3. 1428–51.
44. Sermons IV. 3. 1469–81.
45. Sermons VII. 2. 654–8.
46. Sermons VI. 2. 541–4.
47. Sermons IV. 3. 40–2.

An Infinite Eternity

48. Sermons IV. 2. 818–23.
49. Sermons IV. 5. 620–38.
50. Sermons VII. 9. 699–707.
51. Sermons VI. 18. 538–44.
52. Sermons X. 10. 565–71.
53. Sermons X. 5. 756–60.

Partakers of the Divine Nature

54. Sermons V. 7. 75–81.
55. Sermons IV. 3. 1404–8.
56. Sermons VII. 15. 783–9.
57. Sermons I. 1. 490–5.

The Life of Heaven

58. Poems: Holy Sonnets. La Corona: l. 9–14.
59. Sermons II. 10. 15–19.
60. Sermons II. 14. 655–61.
61. Sermons III. 11. 490–504.
62. Sermons II. 12. 574–601.
63. Sermons VI. 2. 523–31.
64. Sermons II. 11. 506–25.
65. Sermons VII. 4. 774–8.
66. Of the Progres of the Soule. l. 487–96.
67. Sermons VIII. 7. 645–50.
68. Sermons III. 9. 652–4.

KOSTYA KENNEDY

56

Published by Sports Illustrated Books,
an imprint of Time Home Entertainment Inc.

Time Home Entertainment Inc.
135 West 50th Street
New York, New York 10020

Book design by Stephen Skalocky

Indexing by Marilyn J. Rowland

ISBN 10: 1-60320-177-7
ISBN 13: 978-1-60320-177-3
Library of Congress Control Number: 2010938186

Sports Illustrated Books is a trademark of Time Inc.

Cover photo: DiMaggio singles in the seventh inning,
June 29, 1941, keeping the streak alive at 42 games

56

JOE DIMAGGIO
and the
Last Magic Number
In Sports

KOSTYA KENNEDY

For Amy and Sonya and Maya,
the reason for it all.

And for Michael Goldstein, 1967–1989

Contents

PART III

Joe DiMaggio, 1941

Introduction

The most dramatic baseball event of the past three decades occurred on September 5, 1995, when Baltimore Orioles shortstop Cal Ripken Jr. completed 4½ innings against the California Angels. That was the night that he tied Lou Gehrig's record for consecutive games played. A few moments after the top of the fifth inning ended, making the game official, all of us in the packed and pulsing stands at Oriole Park at Camden Yards turned to look out beyond the right centerfield fence. Throughout that season the Orioles displayed Ripken Jr.'s consecutive game progress on spotlighted 10-foot-tall banners hung from the face of the old, brick B&O warehouse. When the fifth inning began the banners read 2,129. Now new sheets unfurled. The last two numbers changed: 2,130.

There it was. That impossible, ridiculous, extraworldy number that for nearly six decades had lived in our baseball books and in our imaginations. "That was something, wasn't it, to see it out there like that," the Angels infielder Rex Hudler said to me after the game. "I still have the goose bumps." We all did. The number spoke of a seemingly transcendent achievement—before Ripken Jr. no player had gotten to within even 800 games of Gehrig's total—and it hearkened to an old, true hero. Images of Gehrig, whose streak ended only when he was incapacitated by the ravages of ALS, the neuromuscular disease that killed him,

appeared on the screens at Camden Yards. The number, like few others of its kind, drew a line as well to a distinct and distant era in the continuum of baseball, and of America. Now 2,130 has been pushed aside, lesser known and far less luminous than before, and Ripken Jr.'s final consecutive-game total of 2,632, not yet gilded by the passage of time—and subsumed in the sea of figures and statistics that overwhelm today's game—has hardly replaced it in the baseball consciousness.

The game's other old and connotative numbers have since been passed too. Hank Aaron's 755 career home runs, which for three decades lived worthily alongside Babe Ruth's 714, was erased by a tainted player in a tainted era. Roger Maris's 61, the record for home runs in a 162-game season which also lived beside a Ruthian figure—the Babe's 60 homers in 1927—has been surpassed not once but six times by three players who are either admitted or deeply suspected users of steroids. The home run records, once hallowed, are hollow. Baseball's most resonant numbers keep falling. But Joe DiMaggio's is still there: 56 consecutive games with a hit. "And it feels pure," the former Giants' batting instructor Carney Lansford said to me one afternoon at the batting cage in San Francisco. "You can cheat and break the home run records. You can't do that with a hitting streak."

Other team sports have their records, and their streaks, yet few of those numbers resonate beyond the tightest circles of their game. LaDainian Tomlinson's NFL record for consecutive games scoring a touchdown (18); Dan Marino's 27-year old single-season passing mark (5,084); Kareem Abdul-Jabbar's NBA career point total (38,387); Punch Broadbent's NHL record for consecutive games with a goal (16)—none has left more than the faintest stamp. None has elevated the record-setter to a loftier place than where he might have resided anyway in the

public eye, and none of those records captured imaginations the way that Joe DiMaggio's did and still does.

DiMaggio was no baseball immortal, nor an American icon, when the spring of 1941 began. He was 26 years old and like all the young men around him conscious of the gathering heat of the war abroad and of the widening reach of the U.S. military draft. He was less than two years into his first and increasingly difficult marriage to a movie actress. He would soon become a father. DiMaggio's name had not yet been set to song. He had never appeared on television. He was more than a decade from meeting the love of his life, Marilyn Monroe, 14 years from induction into baseball's Hall of Fame and 32 years from his tenure as a pitchman for Mr. Coffee.

After the hitting streak DiMaggio's life, and his legacy, changed forever. And soon thereafter, on Dec. 7, 1941, America's way of life, and its legacy, changed too. Those two months of the streak, later preserved in so many memories, were unlike anything that DiMaggio or those around him had experienced, or would experience again.

PART I

Chapter 1
A Single Swing

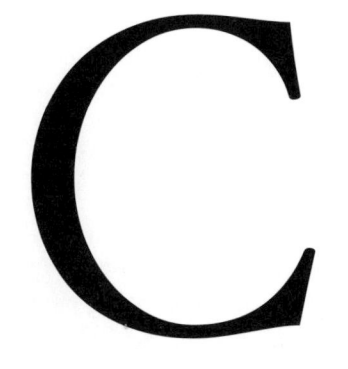

CLOUDS DRAPED OVER Yankee Stadium that afternoon, swept up from the warm Gulf Coast waters to render the sky a pale gray mass as far as Joe DiMaggio could see. He sat alone in the home team dugout, gazing out past the centerfield fence, squeezing the handle of his bat, now and then taking a gentle half-swing. And how warm it was—getting up on 80°, he'd guess. The Bronx air felt too heavy for the middle of spring. *Maybe it'll rain*, DiMaggio thought, *maybe we'll get a washout*. But rain was still a day away. It was May 15, 1941, and the Yankees and Joe DiMaggio were in a slump.

Four straight games the team had lost. What were the Yanks now, 5½ back of Cleveland? Fourth place? Twenty-eight games into the season and they'd lost just as many times as they'd won. A day earlier the team had gone down quietly to the Indians and DiMaggio had been hitless, again. He was down to .306, hadn't hit a lick since the first few games of the year. Up in Boston his brother Dom was outhitting him by 74 points; the Red

Sox player-manager, old Joe Cronin from back home in San Francisco, was batting better than .400. It wouldn't do.

The year before, the Yankees had fallen behind in the standings like this and never caught up, failing to win the American League pennant for the first time since 1935, for the first time since DiMaggio had arrived in '36. Maybe things had come a little too easy for him those first few seasons in the majors. He'd knocked in 125 runs as a rookie, smashed 46 homers in '37, hit .381 and won the American League's Most Valuable Player award in '39. Maybe he was due to slide some, maybe he couldn't expect to hit like that in the big leagues forever.

No. Things would turn around again. He'd start hitting. He always did. *Just get things rolling*, DiMaggio told himself. *Keep swinging and stay on the ball.* A hit here, a hit there. He'd be on his way.

The fans were not so sure. A little more than 9,000 had come out on this Thursday, game time 3 o'clock, and DiMaggio knew they weren't all sold on him. He was hardly the only struggling Yankee—rightfielder Tommy Henrich, stuck in the low .200s, had even been benched—but DiMaggio wasn't just another ballplayer. He was the franchise, the man who was meant to carry the Yankees, as Babe Ruth had done, and Lou Gehrig. Those guys didn't have bad years, not when they were young and healthy anyway. DiMaggio was the latest great one. And he sure was being paid that way. In the stands, the men took to their seats, adjusted their fedoras, rolled their necks. *What's he makin' again? Thirty-seven five? At 26 years old? And he wants more?*

Yes, DiMaggio liked his money. He had delayed even coming to the Yankees from his home in San Francisco in 1936, declining their mailed offer of $5,000 for the season, then nixing letter after letter that came in from New York with proposed raises until finally the Yankees general manager Ed Barrow wrote, "This is all!" and Joe accepted $8,500.

Fans had heard about that wrangling and they also knew that DiMaggio had missed the start of the 1938 season, demanding—just two years into his career!—a $40,000 salary. The team only wanted to pay him $25,000, and by late April, DiMaggio surrendered. Yankees owner Col. Jacob Ruppert had called him an "ungrateful young man," and many baseball fans, working for dimes to DiMaggio's dollars, were inclined to agree.

These weren't easy times, New Deal or not. The worst of the Depression still stung, too many hardworking lives were still in tatters, unemployment was still up near 10%. Those factory jobs, lost by the thousands in the early 1930s, hadn't come back in New York. The stock market sagged. And now, reverberating across the Atlantic, the war in Europe. *Isn't DiMaggio makin' enough? And he gets paid for those cigarette advertisements too. The guy was on a Wheaties box! What's he gonna do with all that dough?* Just a few years before, Babe Ruth himself had been taking pay cuts after every season. Hit 46 home runs one year, still agreed to lop 25% off his wage. *And that was the Babe!*

Now Ruth was retired, and the ailing Gehrig too. The Yankees just didn't seem the same anymore, seemed vulnerable like the rest of the world.

Booooo, shouted some among the Stadium crowd as DiMaggio loped out to centerfield to start the game that afternoon. *Booooooo.*

Joe McCarthy wasn't happy either. Not on a four-game losing streak. The manager would sometimes seethe even after the Yankees *won* a game if they looked sloppy doing it. You played the game the right way for McCarthy. You hustled. You threw the ball to the right base. You were smart. And you won. Nobody won more regularly as a manager than McCarthy did. He'd had winners in the minor leagues, and then in the National League with the Cubs, a pennant in 1929, and he'd really won with the Yankees, five world championships in 10 years. McCarthy's big league teams had won more than 60% of the games they were in. Missing the pennant in '40 was a sour blow and now there was this lackluster start in '41. If it kept up, his ballplayers knew, the Henrich benching would only be the first.

Before the game DiMaggio had seen that dark, dyspeptic look on McCarthy's face, watched him for a while as the manager stood surveying the field, shifting his weight on the dugout steps, working his chaw against his lower gum. The White Sox were in town and the Yankees were honoring Jimmy Dykes. *Of all people,* thought McCarthy, though he'd never complain out loud.

The media all loved Dykes, Chicago's ebullient, loose-tongued player-manager who enlivened every game he was part of. At 44 he was officially retiring as a player so as to clear space for a younger player on his roster. Dykes had been in the league for 22 years. He was 5' 9" and scrappy as junk metal, a sometimes .300 hitter who would grab his glove and play

wherever you put him. Usually, that was third base and now on the field the photographers were staging a picture: Dykes pretended to cling to the third base bag, as if refusing to go gently from his playing career, while a few of the White Sox players tried theatrically to tear him away.

McCarthy didn't go for that kind of horsing around—not by a manager, certainly. And he didn't go for Dykes, a man who would play cards in the clubhouse right up until game time, then later crack to the reporters that he'd come out late because he didn't want to have to look at "those bums, the umpires" for any longer than he had to. Dykes was always saying stuff, and the year before he'd gone too far, come right out and mocked McCarthy, declaring that anyone could manage the Yankees with the line-up they had, that all McCarthy had to do was "push buttons and watch his murderers' row win games for him."

What a thing to say. Petty. Bush. McCarthy would never diminish a man like that, not a peer, not in public. More irksome now was that this year manager Dykes had his undertalented White Sox ahead of the Yankees, and even challenging the Indians for first place. Everyone said Dykes was working miracles. During the last series between these teams, in Chicago about two weeks before, the White Sox had whupped the Yankees 8–1.

Dykes, thought McCarthy. His face darkened and he rubbed his mouth. He sent a thin brown line of saliva out of the dugout. *Damn Dykes*.

At home plate Dan Daniel, the dean of the New York baseball writers, was presenting Dykes with some kind of honorary scroll and talking into a microphone to the crowd. The Chicago manager took the scroll and then, his wit and loquaciousness blunted by the moment, by the real and present weight of his own retirement, could only lean into the micro-phone and say simply, "Thanks." Some of the Yankees players had gone out to join the White Sox, and stand along the foul line. Yanks pitcher Lefty Gomez even needled Dykes, lamenting that the one guy he could get out was hanging 'em up.

McCarthy wasn't out on the field for any of it, and neither was DiMaggio. They were in no mood. *This must be eating McCarthy alive*, DiMaggio thought on the bench, looking over at the only big league manager he'd ever had. And at that thought DiMaggio, in spite of him-self, couldn't help but smile.

Then the ceremony broke up and the players stood as the national anthem played, and DiMaggio ran out to his place in centerfield, hearing the boos that came down from the stands. And then the game began and the day got worse. The White Sox took a lead in the top of the first, going up 2–0, scoring their first run after DiMaggio's beeline throw to third base clipped the elbow of Chicago's Billy Knickerbocker, who'd headed there from first after a single. The ball bounded into the stands, Knickerbocker jogged home and the Yankees were trailing just two batters into the game. Listless, they would never even rally to tie the score.

At the end of the day it was Chicago 13, New York 1. And for those who missed it, the New York newspapers the next morning were unyielding: "The Yankees never looked worse," wrote Arthur Daley in *The New York Times*, "and derisive shouts greeted the final out of each inning." A wire report that went to newspapers across the country called it "one of the most humiliating defeats the Yanks have suffered in years. They did everything wrong."

So forgive the fans at Yankee Stadium if they did not, as they filed out of the park that early evening, look back fondly on, or even expressly recall, the fact that at shortly before 3:15 p.m., with two outs in the bottom of the first inning and the rookie Phil Rizzuto leading off second base, Joe DiMaggio drew a bead on a fastball from the White Sox's blond, 5' 10" 174-pound lefthander Edgar Smith and lined a hard, low single into left centerfield for his only base hit of the game.

Chapter 2
One Day In May

"I'M IN THE worst slump I've ever experienced in all my years in the game," DiMaggio had told reporters a week into May, and even now, 10 days later, his struggles showed little sign of letting up. "My timing is off," he said. "You come up saying to yourself, 'Here's one that's going out of the park.' The pitch comes in and it looks like a fat one and then instead of smashing it the way you want to, you only get a piece of it."

There had been other, lesser slumps, of course. Just the season before, in August 1940, DiMaggio had endured a nuisance of a spell when, swing as he might, he could not seem to drive the ball; he felt something strangely amiss. He hadn't been scuffling for long, though, when one evening at dinner Dorothy glanced at him from across the table and said—shyly, hesitantly—that she thought she could help. DiMaggio smirked, cocked his head, put down his fork and leaned back in his chair.

He looked back at his wife, and his eyes narrowed slightly. A faint, unbidden annoyance came over him. With his long fingers DiMaggio gathered up the napkin off his lap and wiped the corners of his mouth.

There was a tightness now in the room. *She thinks she can help.* He silently weighed the notion.

Dorothy attended just about every game at Yankee Stadium, always sat in the same seat behind home plate, a little over to the third base side, a few rows up. "I noticed something at the ballpark today," she said in her quiet voice.

When he'd met her, in 1937 on the set of a movie they both were in, she was a 19-year-old showgirl. Beautiful, blonde and smart, eyes wide and shining. She didn't even know who Joe DiMaggio was then, didn't care a whit for baseball. Three years later it was still a new game to Dorothy. Hitting, or anything else that went on at the place where Joe took care of business, was barely something she would ask him about, let alone offer advice on. But she was doing it now. DiMaggio looked over the table at Dorothy's broad, pretty face, saw the tentative way she held her hands, her nervousness. Steam rose up from the plates of ravioli that Dorothy had made. Their wedding had been nine months before, in San Francisco.

DiMaggio's smirk softened into a smile and the hardness faded from his eyes and he let the air out of his chest. "What did you notice?" he asked.

"Your hitting," she began. "The number five on your shirt is in a different position. I don't see it the same way anymore. You're not swinging the way you used to."

In an instant DiMaggio knew that Dorothy was right, that she was onto something about his form that he could fix. The next morning at Yankee Stadium DiMaggio worked on his stance, realized that he was striding just slightly too much, an involuntary, inchlong lunge that upset his balance. His body wasn't turning with its usual force, his follow-through was not quite complete, and the misstep had put an unwanted wrinkle in his smooth swing. DiMaggio shortened his step to the way it had been, the way he liked it, and after swinging for a while, after a good, long session of batting practice before the game, he felt natural again, comfortable. That afternoon he went 3 for 4. And he kept on hitting from there. With that—simply if improbably—that slump was over.

This one, though, he could not shake. For nearly four weeks he'd been hitting under .200. Only 14 hits in his last 73 at bats, one of the numbers guys around the clubhouse had informed him. *You're pressing, just relax,*

he had taken to telling himself before coming to the plate, reminding himself again and again to *keep on swinging, that's how you'll come out of it.* And yet every at bat felt like a wholly new start to DiMaggio, and every out a different kind of failure. Whenever he'd get things right for an at bat or two—his swing in sync, the barrel of his bat passing through the air just where it was meant to be—the next time up he'd again hit one off the handle or stub one off the end of the bat.

The day after that awful 13–1 loss to the White Sox, DiMaggio had smashed a home run deep over the Yankee bullpen and into the leftfield bleachers, a distant place where only two men alive, he and the Tigers' Hank Greenberg, had ever hit a baseball. Later, in the ninth inning of that game, DiMaggio tripled to the wall and the Yankees pulled out a 6–5 win.

But the next afternoon, against Chicago's tall, fastballing righthander Johnny Rigney, DiMaggio only singled harmlessly in the second inning, one hit in four times to the plate. It had rained earlier in the day, canceling batting practice and delaying the start of the game by more than 10 minutes. The weather kept the Saturday crowd to an undersized 10,272, among them New York City mayor Fiorello La Guardia sitting up front and rooting from his usual box. Twice in the closely contested game DiMaggio left two men on base, grounding out in the middle innings and then, in the eighth, popping a ball high into the dull gray sky to end a Yankee threat. When the 3–2 loss was complete, DiMaggio, the Yankees and even the mayor were happy just to have the White Sox leave town.

Now the St. Louis Browns were in for the first of three, and as the players did their fielding drills before the game and DiMaggio shagged his fly balls in the outfield he noticed that a stiff wind blew, snapping straight the U.S. flag above the monument to Miller Huggins in left centerfield. It was a Sunday, the 18th of May, and a pregame program was scheduled at Yankee Stadium to honor what the President had proclaimed as I Am An American Day across the nation. A few miles south in Central Park, a massive crowd of more than 750,000 had assembled on the Mall. On this day it didn't matter if you believed the United States should get more deeply involved in the war that was now thundering through Europe or if you felt it was better to just stay out of it. All that mattered was to be patriotic. It was a day of simple, essential affirmation that after all the country had

been through—those dark years when former bankers and businessmen sold apples on the streets, or found ditches to dig; when the long, cold sweep of joblessness and fear left no strata of society unharmed—and with all that the country now faced, the American people had something they could hold on to: each other.

A few days before, 2,000 children had shown up at City Hall, given Mayor La Guardia a petition upon which citizens had pledged their allegiance to America. The staggering volume of the signatures, some four and a half million collected in a matter of days, moved the mayor's voice to crack as he stood on the steps thumbing through a sheaf of pages, and wishing, he said, that "the entire country" could see what these children had done.

The mayor was among those on the Mall now as the mass of New Yorkers literally pledged allegiance, rhythmically and in determined unison, saying the words, ". . . one nation, indivisible. . ." Speakers and entertainers followed—comedian Eddie Cantor who said, looking out from the rise at the rows upon rows upon rows of faces, that the crowd was so large it reminded him of his wife Ida's relatives coming for dinner; and the beloved tap dancer Bill (Bojangles) Robinson, who between his frisky shuffles went to the microphone and vowed that if Hitler ever dared to come to Harlem that he, Bojangles Bill himself, would personally make sure that the Führer never got past Yankee Stadium.

Cheers kept going up all afternoon. There were songs and there were serious speeches. La Guardia said some words as did President Roosevelt's Secretary of the Interior, Harold Ickes, who wasn't shy about his view on the war. "We must give the British everything we have," he said. "Everything needed to beat the life out of the common enemy." Ickes added: "We must know our will."

Scenes like this played out all across the country. In Chicago 125,000 came together at Soldier Field to hear speeches and to see the great actress Helen Hayes read some patriotic passages; in Boston 100,000 flooded onto the Common. Tens of thousands more assembled in Los Angeles, Detroit, Milwaukee. Church sermons in hamlets from coast to coast took as their theme the importance and righteousness of American values, preaching, most assuredly, to the choir.

In Washington D.C., there was a ball game to be played, the Senators

hosting the White Sox, and soldiers came out in uniform to Griffith Stadium. The Senators afforded old Jimmy Dykes an honor there too, allowing him to be the one to walk out into the outfield before the game and raise the U.S. flag. Then everyone, the people in the stands, and the two teams of ballplayers and the long rows of soldiers side-by-side on the field, quieted for the singing of *God Bless America*.

At Yankee Stadium a brass band played as Phil Rizzuto fielded the last of his pregame ground balls at shortstop then jogged in and clicked down the steps into the dugout. He was now part of the second-string practice unit that included another rookie, Jerry Priddy, at second base, Buddy Rosar catching and the Yankee bat boy, Timmy Sullivan, helping out at first. None of them left their gloves on the field, as the starting players would. The beginning of the game was maybe half an hour away. A Bronx politician, with a few men in suits around him, stepped out and prepared to address the crowd, to talk about the "advantages of the American way."

Rizzuto, a shy wisp of a kid, ambled over to take his new spot in the dugout beside McCarthy. DiMaggio felt for the rookie, now relegated to the bench. McCarthy had indeed not stopped at the Henrich benching. Rizzuto, whose batting average was down to .246, and Priddy, overmatched from the beginning of the season and hitting just .204, had both been relieved of the starting jobs they'd won in the spring. "We'll let the kids look around, sit and observe things," McCarthy said, explaining his decision. "They're better than they have been so far, but the heaviest type of pressure has been on them." So veteran Frankie Crosetti was back in at shortstop, and Joe Gordon back at second base after a trial at first.

Priddy's benching DiMaggio could understand. His poor hitting seemed to be affecting him in the field too, and at 21, loud and cocky, he had some learning to do about the Yankee way. In late March, Priddy had boasted that he was already better than Gordon, who'd been a 100-RBI man and an All-Star two years running. Priddy's résumé—40 homers and a .319 batting average over two years in the farms with Kansas City, smooth on the double-play turn—had inspired the Yankees to move Gordon to first base at the start of the season to make room for the heady kid. A month later that decision seemed rash. Priddy just wasn't working out.

Rizzuto, though, he was special, had something the older players liked. Scrawny and determined, he'd been the MVP of the American Association the year before, hit .347, stole 35 bases, wound up on the cover of *The Sporting News*. But for all the stories that were written to praise him, all the hullabaloo when he arrived in New York, Rizzuto never flaunted the hype, never called attention to himself—until you saw him play. He gathered ground balls as gently as if scooping up a baby into his skinny arms. He battled at the plate, fouling off the nastiest pitches and, until his recent struggles, finding some way to get on base. In the minors Rizzuto had been nicknamed Scooter for the way he glided about on the ballfield. He ran the bases with an alertness and an edge that DiMaggio—who covered the basepaths more determinedly and efficiently than anyone, anywhere—approved of. Rizzuto honored the veterans, and sought their counsel, respectfully probing Crosetti for bits of game-day wisdom.

He took everything in stride that first March day in the locker room in Florida, when, before practice, Lefty Gomez seized upon Rizzuto's diminutive stature, his baby face and, loud enough for everyone to hear, told Rizzuto to "grab your scooter and let's go!" He took the ribbing naturally and at barely 5' 6" he was used to jokes about his size. Rizzuto was not much surprised when Gomez, at it again on a different day, rushed in carrying a footstool while Rizzuto was showering in the clubhouse. Gomez was concerned, he told Rizzuto, that the "water doesn't get ice cold by the time it reaches you."

During the early days around the batting cage Rizzuto scarcely got the chance to hit. The veterans, guys like George Selkirk, Charlie Keller, squeezed him out, running through the batting order again and again and indifferently skipping Rizzuto who stood away from the pack, timid and helpless and bat in hand until DiMaggio, having had enough, said quietly between batters that he wondered how well the rookie could hit. And that was it. The sea of pinstripes parted. Rizzuto came up next.

He adored DiMaggio, followed him shyly around, stared at him doing the simplest things, the cool way he would pull out his locker-room stool, and sit down on it, legs crossed at the ankles, take a cigarette from the clubhouse guy and smoke. DiMaggio wasn't only the best ballplayer Rizzuto had ever played with, DiMaggio had class, he could see that. There

was an elusiveness about him, a kind of majesty in all that he did. Rizzuto even liked to watch DiMaggio shave.

Rizzuto cried when McCarthy benched him, the sharp news, after his sudden rise, simply too much to bear. When he stood at his locker that day, working and reworking the belt around his waist, keeping himself busy and trying to look down, his pain seemed true and sincere and his teammates let him alone, held back on the teasing. Other Yankees had been subject to McCarthy's rookie benchings in seasons past. Nine years earlier, Crosetti had cried too.

On the bench, Rizzuto would spend the games beside the manager listening as McCarthy dinned into him the nuances of the game, pointing out the poise that Crosetti showed whatever the situation, and just as importantly in McCarthy's mind, showing Rizzuto that even big league opposition wasn't without flaws, thus assuring the rookie that he belonged. "I've learned a lot already," Rizzuto said a couple of days into his ordered rest. He added hopefully: "They've told me to keep my ears and eyes open and my chin up." Rizzuto did as he was told and at night, when sleep wouldn't come, he thought about just how he would go about things in the games when he got back in there.

The pregame pageantry marched on and clusters of clouds passed through the sky, but the rain of recent days had not returned. A fine spring sunshine bathed the murmuring crowd, listening now, along with the Yankees and Browns, to the patriotic songs. What a voice Lucy Monroe had! High-pitched and clear and layered with the sense of deeply felt emotion, so that you just wanted to shush your neighbor and close your eyes to try to listen more intently, to climb deeper inside the voice and the words.

She had already sung for the masses at Central Park, then come up to the Stadium and now, standing behind home plate, gripping gently the microphone in its stand, Monroe had both of the teams, and the more than 30,000 who had come out for the game, in her thrall. "Keep the Home Fires Burning" she sang, the old, heart-wrenching number from the first World War, and it was impossible then for the fans and the players not to think about the current war, and what might become of any or all of them.

The Tigers' Greenberg had already gone into the service, and Rizzuto

had been among the big leaguers summoned to a local draft board. No wife, no children, good health. Only because he was supporting his aging parents did Rizzuto get a deferment, a ruling of 3-A. He would last the summer, it seemed, but Rizzuto was acutely aware that when the armed forces came calling in earnest, it would not be long before they were calling him. Hundreds of thousands of young men had been brought in and rated and hundreds of thousands had been conscripted; U.S. soldiers weren't yet dispatched anywhere en masse, though there was a sense that, inevitably, they would be.

"Keep the home fires burning/While your hearts are yearning/Though your lads are far away/They dream of home." The song, especially as Monroe sang it, demanded optimism—"there's a silver lining . . . turn the dark cloud inside-out"—and coming as it did on this particular afternoon, the music sent goose bumps fluttering across the necks and shoulders in the crowd, so that when Monroe finished, the stadium burst into wild applause and cheers that didn't wane until she tossed her brown hair back behind her shoulders and again took hold of the microphone to begin the song that everyone wanted to hear. "On the street, in the home/In a crowd, or a-lone . . . Shout! Wherever you may be/I am an American, I am from the heart of me."

And nearly everyone knew the words, and nearly everyone did shout upon the lyrics' command, so that the stadium seemed to sway and a feeling of togetherness and purpose touched the crowd. Lucy Monroe delivered the final chorus, lingering—"I am an American/I am . . . every part of me"—then she bowed and waved to all sides and walked off as a boy ran out and carried away the microphone. Gomez threw his last warmup pitches to Bill Dickey, and the Browns shortstop, Johnny Lucadello, took his stance.

The Yankees had their way in this game—St. Louis was again a bad team this season, outclassed. DiMaggio had three base hits in the 12–2 thrashing, though in truth they were softly gained. On one slow-moving ground ball, third baseman Harlond Clift might have done a cleaner job of fielding and thrown DiMaggio out; another hit was more a pop fly than the hard-hit double it would look like in the newspaper box score, a ball that the Browns' rightfielder really could have had. DiMaggio got on base

on a catcher's interference too. The batting average ticked upward, but the slump was hardly over.

In the field DiMaggio's attention to the wind was rewarded. Twice he took off and caught balls on the dead run, erasing certain extra-base hits by Don Heffner in the second inning and Chet Laabs in the fifth, and each time bringing the crowd to its feet. The men clapped or punched a fist into their opposite palm. *Whoa, how does he get to balls like that? Every time!* DiMaggio and the other outfielders could run without caution again now that the grass was no longer wet from the rain. Even the sometimes-muddy edges of the ball field, the stretches of dirt by the stands in foul grounds, were all but dry, the afternoon sun having baked away the mire.

Chapter 3
Perfect, Imperfect

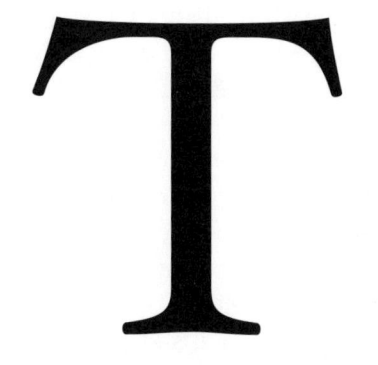HE TIGERS WERE pitching to him. That was a surprise. Winning run on second—Henrich—no outs in the bottom of the ninth and the righthanded reliever Al Benton looking in for the sign. Usually in this spot they'd be walking DiMaggio intentionally. *It'll be the slider, I'll bet,* DiMaggio thought. Benton, 6' 4" and 215 pounds, threw hard, and lately he'd honed his slider into one of the league's toughest pitches; even good hitters couldn't help but drive it into the ground. Benton's slider was all the more reason to put DiMaggio on and set up the next guy, Charlie Keller, for a double play. But no. Tigers' manager Del Baker wanted DiMaggio, thought Benton could get him out with the game on the line. The Stadium crowd was alive—two Yankee runs had already come across in the inning, tying the game at 4–4.

Benton threw and DiMaggio swung, and the result, the far too familiar result these days, was a softly struck roller to the left side. Eric McNair, playing third base for Detroit, picked up the ball and threw out DiMag-

gio, who'd hustled to make it close. Henrich couldn't move off second.

DiMaggio turned and jogged quickly back to the dugout. When he was feeling right he would knock that pitch right back through the box. When he was really right he'd put it into the gap or over the wall. Still, there was just one out, and maybe Keller could get the winning hit, or Gordon after him. *At least maybe I helped Tommy get on track today*, DiMaggio thought passingly; earlier that afternoon he had loaned Henrich one of his bats. DiMaggio clacked down the dugout and strode to his place on the bench. When he turned to look toward home plate the Tigers catcher, Birdie Tebbetts, was standing up.

What? They're walking Keller? DiMaggio felt stunned. *Pitched to me and now they're walking Charlie Keller! What, now he's the hitter that scares them?*

This never happened to DiMaggio. He was always the batter the other team avoided. Teams had even put him on base to get to Gehrig—though that was in the final, quixotic stage of Gehrig's career when he had gradually and then seemingly all at once lost his strength. In one game, Opening Day of 1939, the Red Sox had twice walked DiMaggio in order to face Gehrig, and both times Lou had hit into double plays. Gehrig kept his head straight up, refusing to look beaten, knowing that before this weakness had come on he would never have let a pitcher get away with that. You were not supposed to walk guys in front of Lou Gehrig. And in 1941 you certainly were not supposed to pitch to Joe DiMaggio and then put the fine but mortal slugger Charlie Keller on base.

Ball one.

Baker was a smart manager, though. DiMaggio knew that. Crafty, and unrelenting in his search for an edge. He was about as good a sign-stealer as there was in baseball; they said Baker got his guys five extra hits a year by telling them what was coming. So what did he see in going against the book, in risking victory to take on DiMaggio, who'd already knocked a couple of singles in the game? Baker had seen DiMaggio slumping in Detroit a couple of weeks back, grounding the ball weakly time and again in the Tigers' three-game sweep. Maybe too, Baker had talked with Fred Haney, the Browns manager who'd just left town. Haney could have told him that DiMaggio wasn't out of it yet, that his 3 for 3 the other day wasn't as good as it looked on paper and that after-

ward DiMaggio hadn't done much in the rest of the series, just a double in one game, a single in the next.

Haney would have been happy to share information if it would help the Tigers beat the Yanks. Any manager would have. "I'm in favor of kicking the Yankees in the teeth when they're down," Dykes had said not long before—giving voice to a feeling his peers all shared. The Yanks were too good, too advantaged, to be liked. After New York had won its fourth straight World Series in 1939 the American League had proposed a rule stating that the league's "championship club may not make any trades" for an entire season except for picking up a player off waivers. The idea was to stop the rich from getting richer. More precisely the idea was to slow the Yanks. When the league's eight teams voted on the rule it passed 7–0. The Yankees abstained.

Yes, the Tigers were themselves the defending American League champions now, having lost to the Reds in the 1940 Series. But nobody expected them to repeat, and far less so now that Hank Greenberg was gone, the first big-name ballplayer drafted into the service. (The less formidable Hugh Mulcahy, a Phillies pitcher, had entered in March.) Greenberg had clubbed two home runs in his last game, May 6 against New York, then hung up his jersey on the hook of his locker-room stall and headed to Michigan's Fort Custer for a new uniform, Army issue. Since then the Tigers were a shell of themselves, sliding in the standings and destined, it seemed, to slide further still. But that didn't mean that Del Baker wasn't trying to win every game he could. And apparently he'd thought the best way to win this game was to take his chances and pitch to DiMaggio. For the Tigers, so far, so good.

Ball two.

DiMaggio looked out past the outfield, past the half-empty bleachers to the Burma-Shave billboard, and another for Philip Morris tobacco. Soon, he thought, he'd have a smoke. There were about 10,000 fans in Yankee Stadium. How many of them understood that this walk to Keller was a slight to him? He hated the thought of that, hated the idea of being anything less than perfect in the public's eye. That's why he took things so hard when the crowd booed him over the money. "I only want to get what I'm worth," he had said during one salary standoff,

thinking that might help people understand. "I only want what's fair."

The holdout in 1938 had led to the worst of the jeers, and if the Yankees' championships and the brilliance of DiMaggio's play in the seasons that followed had surely eased that hostility there were still those who wouldn't forget, especially when he was struggling at the plate, and especially because he'd fought again for better pay, though less stridently, in '39 and '40. Missing the start of training camp had become an annual ritual, but it wasn't as if DiMaggio didn't want to be with the team; really, that's all that he wanted—just for the right price.

By the time he and the Yankees' general manager Ed Barrow had settled on his 1941 salary in March—$37,500, nearly triple the big league average but less than Greenberg or Indians' ace Bob Feller were set to make—the rest of the Yankees had already reported to spring training. Joe and Dorothy drove off from San Francisco and headed for Florida that very day and so hurriedly that he'd gotten a speeding ticket before they were out of California, stopped by a state patrolman for going 70 miles an hour on the Golden State Highway.

When he'd arrived in St. Petersburg, DiMaggio played with a determination unlike anyone else's. Even in the exhibition season. Before the Yankees broke camp he had hit safely in 19 straight games, a run that would continue for eight more after the regular season began. There was never a question, then or ever, of DiMaggio's effort, his self-imposed insistence on doing whatever it took to win. That intractable drive could at times seem almost cruel—no one slid harder into a base—but over time revealed itself as a simple, cold judgment: that on the baseball field the need to win subjugated all else. That's how DiMaggio would always play and how he always had, since his sandlot days. He just wanted to be paid fairly for bringing home those Yankee titles, for helping to put people in the seats.

He knew well how hard times had been. His father made a living catching fish off a little boat in San Francisco Bay. Try feeding nine children that way, even when the country was flush. The DiMaggios always had to count pennies back home. And in the '30s, even as he was beginning to make good money playing ball, Joe had seen the people on the streets hocking their things. He'd seen baseball players come home as teams folded on the West Coast, and he'd heard about pro leagues where

pitchers were getting paid by the inning, 30 cents for every three outs.

Still, what did that have to do with his own contract? Get whatever you can get. Isn't that what every worker wanted, DiMaggio reasoned, whether you were cutting metal parts in a factory, or running a barber-shop, or making house calls with a doctor's kit in your hand?

No one else seemed to see things quite that way. Not even McCarthy. DiMaggio had never quite forgiven his manager for siding with the Yankees brass in '38, for saying that the team could get along without DiMaggio and that the $25,000 offered to him by the club seemed fair. "Well maybe McCarthy knows what he's talking about, maybe he doesn't," DiMaggio retorted before he'd given in. He was in a spot when it came to money, and he knew it. Guys in the service were making $21 a month. And to the fans, baseball wasn't really a job, wasn't really work. Nothing was being built or farmed or produced. No one was being healed. These were grown men playing a game. The people in Yankee Stadium didn't care about how much profit team owners might be making on ticket sales or on bags of peanuts, they only knew that they would do anything just to wear pinstriped flannel for a day. *Why, I'd play for free if I could*, they thought.

Ball three.

And yet baseball mattered. The day's games were splashed on the front page of the newspaper. A headline would read YANKEES BEAT SOX, 6–5 and then below that—in larger type, but still, *below*—ROOSEVELT DEFIES NAZI BRIGADE. You'd see the box score from the Yankees' game, or from the Giants' or the Dodgers' right beside news of a looming subway strike. So you couldn't say that baseball was irrelevant, that the players' work didn't have impact. President Roosevelt believed that the game was vital for the country's morale. DiMaggio never forgot that every day millions of people were watching and judging: baseball, the Yankees, him.

Ball four. Keller was on.

This DiMaggio slump, and these Yankees' troubles, gave fodder to many of those judging millions, the baseball fans who in precincts across the country—a soda shop in Cleveland, a newsstand in Philadelphia, a hotel bar in St. Louis—debated the issues of the game. Would you rather have a great shortstop or a great catcher? Was the White Sox' Thornton Lee now the best lefthanded pitcher in the game? Did Feller throw harder

than Walter Johnson had? Were the Brooklyn Dodgers at long last for real? Discussion would inevitably turn to determining the greatest player in the game, and DiMaggio's name would always emerge, his virtues enumerated and extolled until, "Mize is better" someone would blurt out, and the argument would ensue.

Cardinals slugger Johnny Mize had broken in the same year as DiMaggio, had led National Leaguers in batting in 1939, in home runs and RBIs in '40. If his batting averages over the years, typically about .340, were less than DiMaggio's, well, Mize played in the National League where all the hitters' averages were down compared to the American League. And Mize, who would stand on deck swinging three bats in hand, who crushed low pitches better than anyone alive, never had a lineup around him like DiMaggio did.

DiMaggio could drive the ball, sure, but not, someone would invariably point out, as majestically as Jimmie Foxx, the Beast, a man so big and burly that he had to turn sideways to get through a doorway. Foxx had a vicious, compact swing and, at 33, he still hit home runs so far that his Red Sox teammates knew even as they were watching the ball soar to incomprehensible heights that they would be called liars when they retold the tale. Four times Foxx had led the AL in home runs; three times he'd won MVP; in 1938 he'd knocked in 175 runs. And in his eight full seasons with the Athletics, and through his five in Boston, Foxx never had much of a lineup around him either.

This kind of baseball talk provided daily sustenance for the teams at the Bellefair, the brightly lit ice cream and sandwich shop on Junction Boulevard in Queens where Commie Villante and several other members of the Jackson Heights Hornets now sat in booths, pulling on their malteds. The school day was done and dusk was coming on. Saturday, and a big ballgame against the Corona Hawks over at Aces Field, was a couple of days away. Now Richie Cassata was talking. "I still say Mel Ott."

Commie rolled his eyes. Cassata was the one nutso Giants fan in the group. Commie and the rest of the DiMaggio guys, among them Squeaks Tito who could and would recite more Joe DiMaggio statistics and trivia than anyone else would care to remember ("Didja know he hit .398 his last year in the Pacific Coast League but still missed the batting title?")

pointed out that Ott, at 32, had been fading some, and that anyway the short rightfield fence at the Polo Grounds, a playground-like 258 feet down the line, was the real reason why he'd been the National League's best home run hitter in five different seasons. "That's where he always hits 'em," said Commie, "and they'd just be fly outs anywhere else."

Commie and Squeaks didn't protest against Cassata too much, though, not really wanting to change Richie's stance. His mom was the one who took the raffle money and got the Hornets' uniforms every year, which meant that Richie had first crack at whatever number he wanted. Like his idol, Richie was a lefthanded hitter and an outfielder, so he always took Ott's number 4, leaving in play the digits of all the Yankee heroes: number 15 for pitcher Red Ruffing, say, or number 8 for catcher Bill Dickey; number 6 for Gordon, or the most coveted, DiMaggio's number 5.

If Cassata's Ott argument fell somewhere between cute and specious, Commie knew that Gimpy Moskowitz at least had a case when he said he believed that Greenberg was the best player in the game. Gimpy, whose sprained ankle years before had secured his nickname in perpetuity, played ball for the Hawks, and lived on the other side of Roosevelt Avenue. But he was a Bellefair regular, munching now his tuna salad on white. Gimpy made Commie laugh with the jokes he told and all the Hornets liked him fine. Gimpy wasn't the only Greenberg booster around either. There were reasons that Greenberg earned baseball's highest salary—$55,000 a year—and his 183 RBIs in 1937 was one of them. His 58 homers in '38, tied with Foxx for the most ever by a righthanded hitter, was another. His 1940 MVP trophy was a third. And just look at how the Tigers had fallen apart this season without him. In New York, a city of two million Jews where Greenberg's following was as strong as anywhere but Detroit, the newspapers occasionally floated, even advocated, the potential benefits of a DiMaggio-for-Greenberg trade, just to get folks talking.

The glass door at the front of the Bellefair swung open and a few of the Bettes came in, walked toward the rear of the seating area, waved and took a booth of their own. Commie and Squeaks waved back and called out greetings—Commie was sweet on a Bette named Janette—and in that pause Harry the Hawk jumped in. "Fine, Gimpy, but what about his field-

ing? Joe's out there pulling down balls better than anyone in centerfield. Greenberg's just bumbling around at first."

For his part Harry the Hawk manned the outfield, or the second sewer in the stickball games, like a statue; he'd gotten his nickname not for any swiftness or sharp eye but because of a strange sound he sometimes made when calling for a ball. But Harry had a point. The allusion to defense was valid enough to dismiss not just Greenberg but first basemen Mize and Foxx as well.

DiMaggio covered the vast meadow of the Yankee Stadium outfield with long easy strides, a gorgeous gallop that on any day might lead to a game-changing play. Once, with Spud Chandler on the hill in a lopsided late-season game against Detroit at Yankee Stadium, DiMaggio took off after a high, colossal drive from Greenberg himself, racing on and on, out past the centerfield monuments and the flagpole, and deep into the grave-yard, as the players called it, before catching the baseball more than 450 feet from home plate, two strides before the wall. DiMaggio had never even turned around, just looked up once, then flicked out his glove and snared the ball. Greenberg, envisioning an inside-the-park home run, was already at second base when DiMaggio made the catch, that's how high and far the ball was hit; Greenberg just put his hands akimbo and stared mutely into the outfield.

The crowd wouldn't shush for five full minutes after that ball came down. The play immediately became The Greatest Catch I Ever Saw for all of the Yankees and all of the Tigers and for the 13,000 more who were at the Stadium that day, and for the tens of thousands of others who were not at the Stadium that day but who later said they were. "I couldn't make a better one," DiMaggio said afterward. Joe would have doubled the Tigers' Earl Averill off of first base too on the play if only DiMaggio hadn't paused a moment before throwing the ball in, almost surprised himself, and even then if Crosetti's relay throw hadn't hit Averill in the back as he hurried to return to first base.

There were other DiMaggio catches, many, many others, improbable essays to render the uncatchable caught. Whenever a ball was hit deep, Gordon at second base or Crosetti at short would turn from the infield and see DiMaggio already with his back to the plate, already in full stride,

his number 5 smoothly and swiftly receding. Then, though they'd seen it before, the infielders would nonetheless let out a soft and awestruck gasp, right along with the roar of the crowd, as DiMaggio turned and raised his weathered glove and casually plucked the baseball from mid-air like some upstate schoolboy taking an apple off a tree.

Yet even that defense was not above reproach. Late in the summer of 1939, Tris Speaker, the peerless centerfielder who'd gone into radio after ending his 21-year playing career in 1928 and whose spot in baseball's alltime greatest outfield was secure between Ruth and Cobb, got ornery, saying that "Joe DiMaggio is good. Understand that, please. But he is not great...and he plays too deep." DiMaggio, after all, had had a season in which he'd made 17 errors, another in which he'd made 15. Speaker alleged that he could name 15 outfielders better than DiMaggio—though that was a claim he would retract. Later, when Speaker was asked to choose between DiMaggio or the gap-hitting Cardinals leftfielder Ducky Medwick as the finer all-around player, Speaker's response was curt: "I'd take Medwick."

Other players got support too—lately people were saying that the skinny young kid with the big bat in Boston, Ted Williams, could one day wind up the greatest hitter of all. But deep down everyone, and certainly all the guys in Jackson Heights, even Gimpy, now putting on their club jackets and leaving their nickels on the table and getting up to walk out of the Bellefair and wend along the yellow-lit city streets to their boyhood rooms, knew that if they had to pick one player for their team, it would be DiMaggio. Finally, the numbers game fell his way: 691 RBIs in his first 686 big league games, two straight batting titles, and although he played in a ballpark so phenomenally spacious as to emasculate a righthanded batter, a season in which he hit 46 home runs. DiMaggio struck out a total of 71 times from 1938 through 1940. That was half of Mize's total in that time, a third of Foxx's. Greenberg typically struck out about 100 times *in a single season.*

The Yankees won one World Series in the seven seasons before DiMaggio arrived. Then they won it in each of his first four years. DiMaggio played every element of the game with a controlled and beautiful ferocity, a fullness that Cleveland's Feller called "inspirational."

If some fans were quick to detract, to say "Yeah, but. . . ." and bring up Mize or Foxx or Greenberg or any of the rest, maybe it was because they still resented DiMaggio's complaints about his contract. Maybe it was because people outside of New York were sick of the Yankees' dominance. Maybe it was because DiMaggio didn't yet have that single irrefutable achievement, something akin to Babe Ruth's 60-home run season or Lou Gehrig's 2,130 consecutive games played or Ty Cobb's 4,191 career hits, to firmly exalt him. Maybe it was because DiMaggio could be shy and even aloof when the fans descended. Maybe there was also something else.

Chapter 4
The Italian

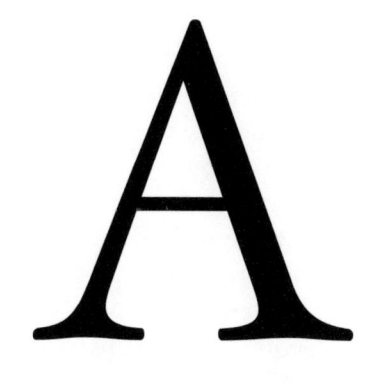LL OF THE Italian players got called Dago, not just Joe. When he'd first come up there were three of them on the Yankees: Tony Lazzeri, Big Dago; Crosetti, Little Dago; and DiMaggio just Dago. Now Lazzeri was gone, Rizzuto had come in, and he was Little Dago too. Sometimes the guys on the team—Gomez, McCarthy, Bill Dickey, any of them—got it mixed up: which Dago was which? Half the time even the Italian ballplayers called each other Dago, or Daig, bantering the word among themselves, diluting any sense of negativity with their own nonchalance. Some other nicknames, though, they were less likely to use.

In opposing stadiums and from out of opponents' dugouts, all sorts of epithets came Joe's way. Even as the Yankees went on to beat the Tigers 5–4 at the Stadium that afternoon—on Red Rolfe's triple in the 10th inning (Del Baker's strategy of pitching to DiMaggio and walking Keller had worked to help Detroit get out of the ninth)—and then beat them again the next day with DiMaggio singling in the seventh, Joe, as ever, heard it from the

Tigers' bench each time he came to bat: "You big Guinea, DiMaggio!" Or one chirper's particular favorite: "Hey Spaghetti Bender!"

This was common jockeying and everyone was a target, especially if you could play. Guys would scream anything that they thought might distract a hitter, rile him up, get him thinking about something other than the pitch coming in. McCarthy always ordered a couple of Yankees backups to lean out of the dugout and ride the Tigers' Greenberg—"Heeb" or "Jewboy" they'd hurl toward him—to try to push him off his game. Ted Williams heard it for being so damn skinny and for the way he fidgeted around in the batter's box. Williams let it show when the jockeying rankled him, yelled right back sometimes.

DiMaggio, though, never looked over at the catcallers, not even the smallest glance. He just dug into his stance and stood waiting for the pitch, still as a photograph.

He'd been hearing the coarse names and letting them roll off for years. That's what you did. Yet the needling felt different now, the words somehow sharper and full of implication. It wasn't easy to be an Italian in America in the spring of 1941. Not with Italy and its fascist dictator Benito Mussolini allied alongside Hitler's Nazis, and not with the U.S. invested in beating down the Italians in the war. Just a week earlier, mid-May, more than 80 Italian men had been rounded up in New York City, taken out to Ellis Island and held there before being deported. They were waiters and busboys, dishwashers and cooks (and even a lawyer too) seized at the Ritz-Carlton Hotel and the Pierre and the Caviar Restaurant right there on 49th Street two blocks from Toots Shor's where DiMaggio liked to go for a steak. They were young guys trying to make the start of a life, not wanting to go back to Italy, guys who had come to work at the Italian Pavilion at the World's Fair and never left, illegally overstaying their permits. These men were not U.S. citizens—any more than DiMaggio's father and mother were—and in these times America did not want them.[1]

More than one and a half million Italian-born immigrants lived in the

---

[1] Ten months later, with the U.S. officially engaged in the war, non-citizen Italians were classified as enemy aliens and placed under a nightly curfew that rendered the streets of the San Francisco neighborhoods where DiMaggio grew up desolate after 9 p.m. His father, Giuseppe, was barred from coming near Fisherman's Wharf, from where he had set out on his boat each workday for more than two decades.

United States, more than half a million in New York, packed closely in neighborhoods in each of the city's five boroughs. Those numbers quadrupled when you added in the next generation, all those—like DiMaggio and his brothers—who had been born on U.S. soil to one of the millions who had left Italy in the first 15 years of the century.

For years, through the 1920s and '30s, many Italian-Americans, especially among the older generation, had approved of Mussolini and of fascism. From afar, Il Duce gave to some of them feelings of pride and dignity. Italy, long seen as inept and bumbling, suddenly had a strong and seemingly competent government that was regarded seriously, if warily, by other nations. Italy wasn't going to be a pushover anymore.

And if that affection for the new Italy had dissipated in recent years as many thousands of Italians began to flee their home country expressly to get away from Mussolini's brutal intolerance and heavy fist, and if for many Italian-Americans Il Duce's embracing of Nazism and anti-Semitism was now not a source of pride but rather of shame and anger—a betrayal that led them to enlist in the U.S. Army and prove their Americanism by joining the fight against their homeland—well, even still some of the old sentiments, along with that strange begrudging sense of respect that a bully like Il Duce can inspire, lingered on. Now, a flood of antifascist Italians might rally in New York City one day, but a gathering of profascist Italians might parade on the streets in New Jersey the next. The scores of Italian-language newspapers across the U.S. split themselves by necessity for their readers: A paper was either in support of fascism or against it. Black and white.

Being an Italian in America meant having to "overcome more handicaps than a pure Anglo-Saxon. Therefore he has to run twice as fast, or else he will be treated forever as a Wop...an alien," wrote an Italian immigrant in *The Atlantic Monthly* in 1940. And yes, that prejudice was there, evident in the things people said, and read and did. An editorial in *Collier's* decried the discrimination and mocked it: "You would think that from some of the talk in circulation that our Italians were getting ready to carve up our government and hand it to Mussolini on a spaghetti-with-meatballs platter." In this climate many Italians changed their names to hide, as the writer Giuseppe Fappiano had done upon

taking a job in sports at *The New York Times* some years before. He went by Joseph Nichols now.

In the *World-Telegram*, the same newspaper in which Dan Daniel tirelessly, passionately and sometimes eloquently covered DiMaggio and the Yankees, the popular news columnist Westbrook Pegler went on a kind of crusade, chastising not only those Italian immigrants who would congregate loudly in the city and cheer for the fascist cause, but also those who simply felt a fondness for their heritage, who dared to look homeward. Their country was a scourge, Pegler declared, and he wrote indignantly, "The Americans of Italian birth or blood have no reason to love Italy."

Yet no break could ever be that clean. There was an affinity for the homeland and a kinship among Italian-Americans that crossed political lines; their bonds were sustained in part by the way Italians were so often lumped together in the jaundiced public eye, lampooned in songs and cartoons as good-for-nothing wine swillers and macaroni eaters. And now the Italian military, even under the tough-talking Mussolini, was being roasted anew for its ineptitude in battle, which had been made plain by Italy's botched attempt to take Greece in late 1940 and early '41. The invading Italian troops were summarily beaten back and tied down, helpless until the Nazi war machine arrived to save them. Earlier Italy had taken over powerless Ethiopia in '35—causing riots in Harlem, to the south of Yankee Stadium, where African-Americans and Italians lived cheek by jowl—and had declared war against a badly weakened France in the summer of '40.

For many Italians in America, whatever their thoughts on Mussolini, however virulently they might oppose Il Duce and the fascist ideal, there was still this: Someone back home was fighting on the Italian side. A brother or a cousin or a friend, or the brother of a friend, or someone else whose life could not be subsumed in a statistic—530,000 Italian troops trudging through Albania—but was valued and precious. Back home in Italy the men had to fight for Il Duce whether they believed in him or not. Soldiers died. For an Italian in America, the knowledge that on any day a letter might arrive, bearing news of a loved one's peril or injury or death, complicated the allegiance to the United States even at the very moment the Italian immigrant planted an American flag in his front yard. When you prayed, what exactly did you pray for?

Little Gay Talese, nine years old and the son of an Italian-born and antifascist tailor in Ocean City, N.J., had uncles and cousins in Mussolini's army. Whenever Talese, conspicuously olive-skinned in a schoolyard of fair classmates, saw pictures of the southern land where his father was from, or heard of some fine accomplishment by a famous Italian, he felt his own vicarious pride. Too many times, though, the news that filtered down through the papers and adult conversations to his young awareness was of Italian gangsters in America like Al Capone or the New York crime boss Frank Costello, men whom his parents reviled. The more palatable stories came from the boxing rings and the ballparks where Italians were staking a claim, and where now, above all else, lorded DiMaggio.

His father was no baseball fan, but Gay was falling in love with the game, and with a ballplayer, that spring. Though the Taleses lived just a short afternoon's drive from the heart of Philadelphia where both Connie Mack's Athletics and the woebegone Phillies played at Shibe Park, and though it was the Dodgers, alone among the New York teams, whose live-game broadcasts would sometimes float out over the radio waves and into the center of Ocean City, there was only one baseball team, the Yankees who played some 150 miles away, that Gay cared for and followed.

He waited on the news and sometimes, as a way to gain slightly better reception, Gay would steal downstairs and dim the spotlights in the dress department of his parents' shop, then clamber back up to his room and the radio beside his bed, to listen through the crackling static for the voice of Mel Allen or some other New York announcer giving a report of that day's game: which team won and, most importantly to Talese, what DiMaggio had done.

DiMaggio had that hold on legions of boys like Talese, and like Mario Cuomo, the son of two Italian-born parents who was himself about to turn nine. Mario lived in an apartment in South Jamaica, Queens, among multiethnic neighborhoods so tough that you gave people your whereabouts by police precinct—"I'm over in the 113th, how 'bout you?"—rather than by street name or school district. Looking out from Queens, standing outside his father's grocery shop with his baseball glove seemingly permanently affixed to his left hand, young Mario might have followed any of the three New York teams. He had his justifications

for rejecting both the neighboring Dodgers (essentially Mario held to a provincial disgust for Brooklyn, where people seemed haughty, more privileged. "They think who they are" is how South Jamaicans slangily put it) and the Giants (forget it; they played in a stadium with a name—the Polo Grounds—that sounded like it was made for the wealthy). But the real reason that Mario chose to rise and fall with the Yankees was because they in effect picked him, on the day that he learned about Joe DiMaggio, the greatest Italian ballplayer of them all.

When DiMaggio himself was nine years old he had never even thought of himself as Italian, or more accurately, he had never fully realized that there was anything different or unusual about that. Everybody in his San Francisco neighborhood of North Beach was Italian. Everyone's mother cooked the sauce on Sunday, and made some version of *cioppino*, that dreadful fish stew. The men and women might get a piece of focaccia at the Liguria Bakery over on Washington Square and then sit beneath the willows and talk to one another in the old language. Joe and all the boys on the block had to go over and sit with the swarthy Italian Catholic priests at Saints Peter and Paul now and then. Everybody's last name ended in a vowel.

It was only later, during his brief time as a student in the gray lockered hallways of Galileo High, where kids of many backgrounds mixed outside the classrooms, that DiMaggio had first really understood that being Italian was not a given, but that it was a badge—of one kind or another—that made you part of a group not everyone was part of.

When DiMaggio first reached the Yankees, the photographers wasted little time lining him up next to Lazzeri and Crosetti, each player posed on one knee with a bat in hand. "McCarthy's Italian Battalion" read the photo caption a few days later. Even now, five years into his career, the newspapers often referred to Joe as Giuseppe—why he didn't know. That was his father's name, not his. Joe didn't even speak Italian! But such details didn't matter. Every Italian Joe was a Giuseppe.

For all of his gradually broadening appeal, DiMaggio was, in the eyes of many, still first an Italian star. In the spring of 1939 *Life* magazine published a long story about DiMaggio, delving into his life back in San Francisco; his new restaurant on Fisherman's Wharf, Joe DiMaggio's Grotto; the way he was raised and how during his rookie season his mother Ro-

salie had traveled across the country to see him, bearing an "armful of Italian sausages." In the story, Joe's heritage was not underplayed. The author, Noel Busch, described him as emblematic of Italians who, "bad at war, are well suited to milder competition." DiMaggio, Busch wrote, wasn't what you'd expect from a black-haired, dark-eyed 24-year old Italian kid: "Instead of olive oil or smelly bear grease he keeps his hair slick with water. He never reeks of garlic and prefers chicken chow mein to spaghetti." Busch was wrong about the chow mein. Joe loved spaghetti— he whirled the long strands up off his plate in the same careful manner now that he had adopted as a kid, his fork tines pressed for stability into the spoon he held lightly in his left hand.

If DiMaggio had not been Italian, and famously so, he would never have met Jerry Spatola and all the guys from Newark. Spatola had read newspaper stories about DiMaggio during Joe's early time in New York, read that he was shy and on his own without any nearby family. That was all it took. Spatola got over to Yankee Stadium, waited outside the players' gate after a game and introduced himself to DiMaggio. Spatola could be that way, forthright and confident and then a breeze to talk to. He brought Joe to Newark and into his home.

Spatola's wife Rose cooked alltime Italian dinners, heaping plates of manicotti or lasagna that the Spatola daughters, Geta and Bina, would bring out and set before Joe. The girls adored DiMaggio and Bina began to keep a scrapbook of Joe's newspaper clippings, a book that she could later pore over and show off to friends or to Joe himself the next time he came by. The Spatola cousins would come over for those dinners, along with any number of friends, and around the busy dining table plates were passed and red wine was poured. Amid the happy commotion, all those voices going and laughing at once, Joe would sit silently and eat, keeping to himself. He was relaxed. The dinners at the Spatolas reminded him of the best days as a kid back home with the family in San Francisco.

So, in some ways, did life in Newark's First Ward remind Joe of North Beach. Every coffee shop and fruit stand in the First Ward, every candy store and bakery, had stenciled on its window an Italian family's name. The peddlers walking down Garside Street or Seventh Avenue pushed carts filled with special meats or carried covered trays of warm pizza, and

they would advertise their wares in loud voices using the Italian names. Spatola knew everyone in town it seemed. He ran the local funeral parlor below the family's home on Mount Prospect Avenue, and he would organize Italian Catholic burials with all the right touches. It was the funeral parlor that led Spatola to get in with Richie the Boot. Richie all but owned that part of Newark, controlled its crime patterns, decreed who owed money to whom, and decided, often, what the local politicians would say. Richie was the guy that all the liquor and the numbers ran through. He wore a diamond as big as a baseball on his belt buckle.

The story was that Richie the Boot—Boiardo was his surname—wanted the store owners in the First Ward to "unionize," that is to pay a little something on the side just to keep things nice and orderly, make sure that nobody somehow accidentally and unfortunately got hurt. But Spatola wouldn't do it. The funeral parlor was his business, passed down from his father, and he wasn't about to give chunks of it away for the privilege of being allowed to keep running it the way that he always ran it. Sometimes a couple of guys would stop by Spatola's office and suggest to him again why getting in the union might make a lot of sense for a guy like him, with a young family and all. Spatola still said no.

One night Spatola was outside the place when he was confronted by an especially neckless man he'd seen around plenty of times and who was carrying something that seemed sure to make Spatola change his mind. "No," Jerry said. "I'm not giving you money. I won't pay."

The bullet, it turned out, went down through the side of Spatola's cheek and out the underside of his jaw; when he came upstairs and into the house that night, he was bloody and in a bad way. He had to go to the hospital, of course, and when the police heard about the injury and caught up to Jerry, to find out just what had happened in a neighborhood they were hoping somehow to get clean, he did not have much to offer. Spatola said it was just plain dumb luck that he had run into a mugger or whoever that was. He said that he had no idea who had shot him nor why. Unfortunately, Spatola said, he had just never gotten a real good look at the guy. The police gave up the case.

With that, Spatola won Richie the Boot's respect. All the boys now knew to let Jerry Spats alone, and, more than that, to take care of him when he

needed anything. That's how Spatola became a regular at Richie's restaurant, the splendid Vittorio Castle on Eighth Avenue, with its high ceilings and its heavy curtains in the doorways, street scenes of Italy painted on the walls. Spatola would bring DiMaggio here—or sometimes across the street to Vesuvius, another old-world Italian place—and Richie and his son Tony Boy and whoever else was hanging around that night made sure that Joe got treated right. In his immaculate suits and with his way of sitting quietly while others buzzed around him, DiMaggio fit right in. Even before they were married, he began taking Dorothy to the Castle sometimes too, for a meal with Jerry and Rose, and once for the party celebrating their engagement. Dorothy's diamond engagement ring, four carats and emerald cut, had come to DiMaggio as a gift from Richie the Boot.

Spats did more than that for Joe. He lined him up a driver, a guy who could watch out for DiMaggio in the city or in Newark or wherever Joe needed him. In 1939 Spatola cooked up a testimonial dinner for DiMaggio, held at Newark's upscale Essex House on the eve of the Yankees' World Series opener against the Cincinnati Reds. More than 1,000 people turned out, all the local big shots, assorted New Jersey mayors and a dozen Yankees including Dickey, Gehrig, Henrich, Red Rolfe and even bat boy Timmy Sullivan. The Yankees sat flanking Joe at a long table set up at the head of the ballroom beneath a nearly life-size photo of Joe that hung luminously from a beam above. Dorothy sat with Rose and the Spatola girls at one of the big round tables nearby.

At the end of the night the people of Newark, it was announced, had given Joe a brand new convertible to drive off in. He deserved it, they all felt. This was *their* Joe DiMaggio. Whenever news spread that he was in town people came out of their homes and gathered near the rounded brick facade at the front of Vittorio Castle, or, depending on the hour, swung by Vincent's barbershop at Eighth and Boyden to see if they could catch a glimpse of DiMaggio getting a trim, perhaps they could even say hello. A Yankees farm team, the powerful Newark Bears, played in town and everybody was a Yankees fan.

Joe helped out Spatola here and there, got him tickets to the games whenever he asked for them or went over to the Hospital and Home for Crippled Children on Clifton Avenue, one of Spatola's causes, to sign

balls and hospital gowns and brighten up the kids' lives for an hour or two. Mainly DiMaggio's presence leant a priceless cachet, his friendship a proof that Jerry Spats, gregarious and all about town, was truly someone special, someone to pay attention to. Richie the Boot and all the rest in Newark knew that it was mainly because of Spatola's initiative that DiMaggio so often came around, baseball's conquering Italian giving blessing to the neighborhood.

There had been Italians in the major leagues for years, and not just Lazzeri and Crosetti. Ernie Lombardi began his career as a .300-hitting catcher for the Reds in 1932. The next season first baseman Dolph Camilli broke in, and he had since become a power-hitting star for the Dodgers. DiMaggio's old pal from North Beach, Dario Lodigiani was doing okay as a third baseman for the White Sox. None of those players, though, mattered much in Newark. Or in Ocean City, N.J., or in South Jamaica, Queens, or anywhere in the Italian diaspora. Joe was the show.

"DiMaggio has attracted a new type of fan to our game," declared the Philadelphia Athletics' manager and sage, Connie Mack. "He has made the Italian population baseball conscious."

They came to see him on the road, and they came to see him at Yankee Stadium, up from the densely packed streets of East Harlem or Mulberry Bend, from Brooklyn and from the Bronx. They brought with them Italian flags of various sizes, small hand-held ones to be shaken back and forth, and others so large that four people had to get together to hold it properly aloft. They sat in the bleacher seats or in the upper deck at the Stadium and waved flags and cheered for Joe DiMaggio. To hell with Westbrook Pegler, or anyone else who might try to tell them which country was really their own. These were Americans, at a baseball game drinking Coca-Cola and still proud of their homeland. They loved Italy and they loved DiMaggio.

At this moment, early in 1941, DiMaggio still belonged to the Italians. He still belonged to the people of North Beach, who proudly watched him from afar—"That's our Joe!"—and who each winter gathered by the thousands to greet him and welcome him back home to San Francisco. Not yet did DiMaggio belong to all of America, everywhere.

The newspaper guys called him Giuseppe, or sometimes, in reference to his prowess at the plate, the Wallopin' Wop.

Chapter 5
Big Brother

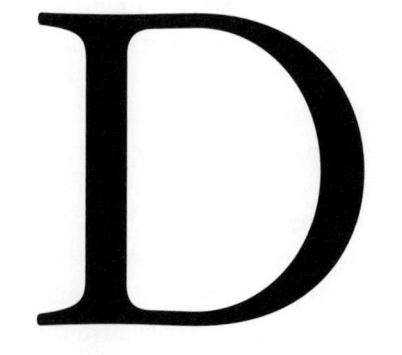D OM DIMAGGIO LIKED coming to New York. He liked the bustle of the city, the swift pulse that beat through Grand Central Terminal and the Hotel Commodore, where the Red Sox always stayed when they came to town. And you knew there was a ballgame on when you played at Yankee Stadium, just like you knew it at Fenway. The noisy crowds, intense and savvy—they'd let you hear it on every pitch.

Dominic always felt a little something extra facing the Yankees, and not only because it meant playing against his older brother Joe. A couple of years earlier, before Dom got to the majors, the Yankees and Red Sox had brawled spectacularly at the Stadium, a fracas that started when Sox player-manager Joe Cronin and the Yankees' Jake Powell grappled on the field (Powell took exception to the Boston pitcher, Archie McKain, throwing too close), then continued their disagreement as they both left through the exit in the Yankees' dugout. The argument carried on in the tunnel beneath the stands and, to the thrill of a large and roaring crowd,

players left the benches to join in while the umpires followed in hopes of keeping peace. When Cronin finally emerged, his face, along with those of several other players, was reddened and badly scratched.

Since that day, the stakes in the Yanks-Sox games had gone up, it seemed, and it often felt like the crowd was hoping something like that melee might happen again. The teams were closely bound; Boston had finished one slot behind the Yankees in the standings for three years running. And who knew, the way New York was struggling, maybe this was the year the Red Sox, close on their heels, would come out ahead.

True, Dominic didn't enjoy it much when some Yankee fans would yell from the bleachers, "Hey little Dommy, go on home will ya! You're just in the big leagues because of Joe." But he was used to hearing that. It had been that way when he started playing pro ball with the San Francisco Seals, Joe's old team. He was so much smaller than Joe, by five inches and 25 pounds, and he wore wire-rimmed eyeglasses.

"You don't look like a ballplayer," a fan or an opposing player would dig at him when the Seals went across San Francisco Bay to play the rival Oakland Oaks. "You look like somebody did your big brother a favor." Then Dominic hit .360, ran the bases like someone was chasing him, and that shut everybody up.

Whatever the barbs in Yankee Stadium, real baseball fans knew by now that Dom wasn't simply riding Joe's reputation. Some coaches in the league thought he was an even better fielder than Joe—or just as good, anyway—and as a Red Sox rookie in 1940 Dominic had batted .301. Cronin told the press that except for Joe's power, he didn't see much difference between these two DiMaggios at all.[1]

The Red Sox and Yankees played a strange game that Friday afternoon, a 3 p.m. start that unfurled into a long, unsatisfying battle, threatened continuously by rain, and finally suspended by the umpires after more than three hours and nine innings of play with the score tied at 9–9 and the cloud-covered sky having darkened so deeply that the hitters could no

---

[1] Vince DiMaggio, playing for the Pirates in Pittsburgh, covered centerfield brilliantly too, and could hit home runs. But he never put up much of a batting average and he struck out way too often, becoming the butt of running jokes among sportswriters. For Vince, the eldest of the three younger DiMaggio boys and the brother who'd first paved the way into pro baseball, Joe's shadow was long and dark.

longer see the ball. Joe knocked a single that helped the Yankees go briefly ahead in the bottom of the eighth. Dominic had two hits in the game. If the DiMaggio brothers didn't compare themselves to one another—and they did, of course they did—the newspapers would do it for them.

Joe and Dom didn't talk about how they had played, or much of anything, on the ride to Joe's apartment after the game. Just being together like this was a rarity; the brothers almost never saw each other off the field during the season. But Joe wanted to show Dom his penthouse, 20 floors up on the West Side of Manhattan and newly leased. Dorothy was making dinner for both of them that night.

The radio played softly in the car on the way downtown, and Joe's driver chatted about the weather and the news of the war. Joe would make a noise here and there to acknowledge that he'd been listening. The driver was one of Spatola's friends from Newark, Jimmy Ceres, an amiable, meaty guy—the size of his hands!—who always had something to say. Ceres did more than just drive. He worked things out for Joe, made sure that the people whom Joe wanted to see he saw, and that the people whom Joe didn't want to see were kept away. He'd done some boxing as a young guy coming up in Newark, which to look at him wouldn't surprise you.

Ceres must have been about 34 years old and even before he started this part-time work for Joe, even when no one knew just what his job was, he somehow always had money in his pocket. Jimmy Ceres came from a large Italian family and he knew a lot of people in Newark. He put on a clean, full suit each morning. Everyone called him Peanuts.

"See you tomorrow, Joe," Peanuts said as they pulled up in front of the building. "Regular time?"

"Game starts at 2:30," DiMaggio said. "Come early."

"Right," said Peanuts. "Dominic, we gotta get you out to Newark sometime and really feed you."

Dom laughed and waved goodbye, and the doorman at 400 West End Avenue nodded in greeting as he held open the thick front door and let the two DiMaggios inside. The elevator operator took them straight up to the penthouse, where Dorothy met them as they stepped out.

Dom liked her. Smart, worldly and beautiful. She could be a little brassy too, crack a joke, especially when Joe was in the next room. Doro-

thy had seemed at ease on her visits to San Francisco. At Christmas and at other family occasions she would fuss around happily with the four DiMaggio sisters, even as she remained deferential, tacitly conceding her place on the outskirts of the big DiMaggio clan, never helping to cook until Ma asked her to, and then doing things just as Ma showed her, crushing cloves of garlic or cutting tomatoes into hearty wedges. Pa thought Dorothy was great.

It was still a kick that Joe was married to her at all. An actress! Dorothy was good in the serials, especially that strange, suspenseful one with Bela Lugosi, *The Phantom Creeps*. Shapely and slender, her bob of curly hair cut just so, Dorothy often delivered her lines with the hint of a smile, and her characters possessed that same coyness and allure that she had in real life. She moved nimbly on the screen. There was a richness in her voice, like thick honey.

The irony in Joe being with a woman like this—or really, the boys at home might crack, being with any woman at all—was that as a teenager he wouldn't even talk to girls. He'd disappear when one of his sisters brought home a friend for dinner, then come back and eat later on his own. When Joe showed up to the parish dances at Garibaldi Hall, he would stand off by himself, looking at everything and no one, never once asking one of the girls to dance. And now he was married to a showgirl.

Dorothy, Dominic felt, was good for Joe. She was four months pregnant, her belly ever so slightly swollen beneath her dress.

The apartment tour began, and Dom spent a lot of time shaking his head and grinning as Joe showed him the living room with its weighty, dark wood paneling and the recessed shelves; a fireplace with a few birch logs lying in a low iron rack set up just for show; a heavy polished lintel above the archway that led into the hall. The guest bedroom, furnished with two pristinely dressed beds, had room enough for four; the linen closet was itself big enough for a grown man to sleep in. The view from Joe and Dorothy's master suite looked south, and on clear days, they told Dominic, you could see for miles, out past the foot of Manhattan and to the Statue of Liberty. The windows in their bathroom, indeed in all three of the apartment bathrooms, were

fitted with stained glass so that someone out on the terrace could not see in. At the far end of the apartment, behind the kitchen and through a few small hallways, Joe had his study. This, said Dorothy, chuckling when they finally got there, was Joe's sanctuary; there were a few newspapers arranged on the writing desk, which had before it a sturdy, high-backed chair.

They all agreed that this was not a night for eating outside, too wet and too windy, but Joe and Dorothy took Dom out onto the brick terrace that wrapped around three sides of the place, and they walked the full length of it. From the north end, the widest area of the terrace where the tables and chairs were arranged, you could see in three directions: across the Hudson River to New Jersey, over the treetops in Central Park and, most impressively at night, straight ahead to the bright lights festooned upon the George Washington Bridge, now twinkling and blurred in the moist sky. They were a long, long way from Taylor Street, from the crowded flat where Joe and Dominic were raised.

Seeing Joe away from the ballpark like this reminded Dom of home, and of the early years, of stepping out of that first-floor apartment to a world of games and youth. He and Joe, the two youngest of the nine children, would listen in the predawn darkness as their father, Giuseppe, pulled on his old boots and crept outside to walk the half mile downhill to the wharf where he would clamber into his boat, the *Rosalie D* (named for Ma) for another day on the water in San Francisco Bay, baitfishing with Tom or more likely Mike or sometimes both of his older boys along to help him out.

Giuseppe imagined that one day they'd have a fleet of DiMaggio boats, more fish, more money and the old family tradition living proudly on for another generation. But later, when the youngest boys Joe and Dominic were old enough to help fish or clean the boat, they rarely did. Joe especially. He would mend the nets that had torn along the reef. He was good at that, his long fingers working swiftly and nimbly, a cigarette hanging from his mouth. But he did the mending on the dock. As for fishing, Joe said he couldn't take the smell, and that riding in Pa's little boat made him seasick.

As boys they ate what they could find in the house for breakfast, on

lucky days the butt end—the *culo* as Tom called it, laughing—of a loaf of Italian bread, brushed with a little olive oil. When the bread was stale, as it often was because it came cheaper that way, Ma put it in the oven and made it good as new.

After the day at the Hancock School, which took up the corner at Taylor and Filbert, practically right next door to home, Dom and Joe and maybe their neighbor Dante or one of the other kids from the block would devise a game using a ball and a branch, or perhaps the DiMaggios' well-worn family bat, to play on Valparaiso Street, a flat, narrow alley off of Taylor's precipitous drop. That was safer; miss a ball on Taylor and it might roll down five blocks or more. Joe was in the fourth grade. Dom was in the second. When enough boys were around they'd sometimes head down to the dusty horse lot by the wharf, play baseball with a beat-up ball. There were never enough gloves to go around and piles of manure dotted their makeshift field.

The real games, especially in the years when Joe had begun at Francisco Junior High, took place a dogleg away from home, a block-and-a-half scamper on the coarsely paved streets to North Beach playground. Here's where people began to take more serious notice of the way Joe played ball. Vince, two years older, was good too, very good, but no one hit the ball farther than Joe, and no one played more intently. Joe never spoke much, and if his team lost, he wouldn't speak at all.

Even the kids who weren't playing, guys like Paul Maniscalco, the Crab King's son, who went to the school at the church, liked to gather to watch the games. They'd sit in clusters in the shade of the evergreens or stand near the concrete wall, flipping baseball cards they'd gotten out of Cracker Jack boxes.

Sometimes there would be betting on the ball games, a dime here or there, a nickel, and nothing got Joe's attention more than when there was a little money to be won. Then he'd really bear in, hit with a ferocity that flat-out frightened the infielders, even after they'd taken their three steps back when he came to the plate. Joe could intimidate on defense too. If a guy tried to score on him he'd throw the ball in from the outfield so hard it might knock the catcher right off his feet.

In the spring and summer, when the light lasted, they would come home

late, miss dinner, and their father, old Giuseppe who never had the time—or the desire—to come down to the playground and watch the games himself, would complain that the boys were wasting their young lives, that all baseball was good for was wearing out the clothes that the DiMaggios could barely afford. Giuseppe and Rosalie spoke only Italian at home.

Joe and Dom got jobs for a while, selling afternoon newspapers—Joe the *Call-Bulletin,* Dominic the *News*—on the busy streets over in the financial district. But Joe didn't last long at that; he was too shy, too reserved to bellow out the headlines to entice buyers. Perky Dom would sell all of his batch then come help Joe sell his too, so they could go back and play ball for nickels again, or mooch a cigarette, or head to La Rocca's Corner Tavern on Columbus and try to wangle free plays out of the pinball machine—Joe had a trick—until the bartender ran them out. Later they would sometimes come back to La Rocca's and listen to Vince sing opera songs. People passed the hat and said that Vince, 15 or 16 then, had the voice to be a star if he only got the chance.

There wasn't much money in those days—Joe and Dom wore shirts that had first been passed down from Tom to Mike to Vince, and most of the money they made from selling the newspapers went straight to the family—but that didn't matter so much to Dom.

There was always the smell of something Italian cooking in the neighborhood. As a goof some of the boys liked to hop onto the back of the grape truck that rode up and down the North Beach streets, maybe the only car that they'd see on the block all day, bringing the fruit to all the families for wine-making in their cellars. Giuseppe and Rosalie made wine too. Even in the prohibition years the law allowed wine for medicinal or religious reasons. In North Beach the grown-ups used to joke, "We have a lot of sick people, and we have a lot of devout people."

Those early years, before they'd started playing ball with the Seals—first Vince, then Joe, then Dom—were the times that lingered richest for Dom. Joe, 27 months older, was bigger and better than he was at everything. Everything physical, that is. Of course Joe was pretty much better than everybody in everything athletic, proving deft and resilient even in the games of touch football the boys played on the horse lot. (In tennis, good lord! Joe could have gone professional if there had been any money in that.) Dom

might tease Joe for never learning Italian, or for hating to go out on the boat, but none of that diminished the awe in which he silently held him.

By now, in 1941, the family had left the house on Taylor Street. Ma and Pa were living in the Marina District in the new home Joe had bought for them; a bigger place and a better address. Mike was out fishing in his blue-and-white boat, also a gift from Joe. And Tom ran the restaurant, Joe DiMaggio's Grotto, on the wharf. Marie and Mamie were married. Things were different for the DiMaggios—better, to be sure. Though for Dom nothing would replace those childhood years with Joe, before they started to drift, when the days stretched long and he felt like he had his big brother all to himself.

The three of them ate that evening in the dining room of the penthouse, not saying much beyond the small talk that Dorothy facilitated. Dom knew not to point out the improbable fact of their current respective batting averages—when the daily DiMag-o-Log came out in *The San Francisco Chronicle* the next morning it would have Dominic on top at .339, Joe at .319 and Vince at .266. It was Joe, though, who brought up baseball during the meal, saying: "You're playing a little shallow in centerfield, you know, just a couple of strides."

Dom stiffened. "I'm just fine playing where I do, Joe," he said.

Joe paused and looked impassively at his brother, as if to say "suit yourself." But he didn't say anything. He just let the moment pass and turned back to his plate.

After dinner Dom said goodbye, took the elevator down and stepped out onto the street below the ginkgo trees. Before he could even ask, the doorman had hailed him a cab and Dom rode back to the Hotel Commodore to get some rest for the next day's game.

Anyone would have to say that the brothers played to a draw that weekend, which for Dom was an achievement in itself. Joe's two-run single helped ensure a 7–6 Yankee win on Saturday—that was four wins in a row, plus the tie—but on Sunday, Dom doubled and scored three times as Boston's old Lefty Grove, appearing in very good, if not vintage form, won his 296th career game, 10–3. Joe produced an inconsequential first inning single. That afternoon, May 25, Bill (Bojangles) Robinson attended and celebrated his birthday by dancing on the dugout roof. Near the end of the

game, in what one newspaper the next day would call "a reminder of serious things," an announcement came over the loudspeaker that the personnel of the U.S.S. *George E. Badger*, a destroyer docked nearby, needed to get back to their ship.

For these last two games of the series, Dom made a small change. Upon getting out to centerfield on Saturday afternoon he surveyed again the huge expanse of Yankee Stadium grass, an area he had played on often before. Then, during the first inning, sometime before the number 2 batter, Red Rolfe, strode to the plate, Dom quietly took two long steps back toward the fence just as Joe had suggested he should.

Chapter 6
America's Voice

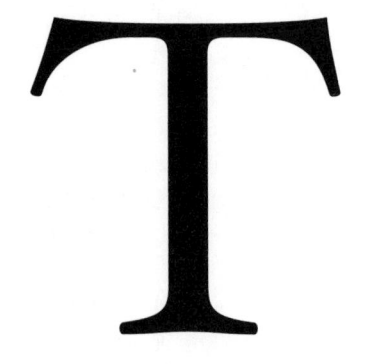HINGS WERE GOING badly in England. During the past two years the Nazis had taken the better part of Europe, run over nation after nation with astonishing and terrifying force. After overwhelming France, the Axis powers—Germany, Italy, Japan—had turned their sights and the German war machine on Great Britain, the gateway to the Atlantic Ocean. The Luftwaffe's ongoing blitz upon England, which by May of 1941 had been unleashed off and mostly on for 10 months, had taken an audacious turn. Having already bombed the Port of London and many of England's other harbors—Bristol, Liverpool, Manchester and more—the Nazis now let fly upon London's most sacred sites.

Bombs fell on the Houses of Parliament, destroying the House of Commons. The British Museum was hit, as was the centuries-old St. James's Palace and then Westminster Hall itself. When the smoke at Westminster lifted, the very site where kings and queens had been coronated for more than 600 years lay under a mountain of bricks and ashes and shards of blackened debris.

To many Americans this news, and the photographs of the wreckage, was somehow more galling than even the tragic raids that had earlier leveled scores of London's small storefronts, put craters in Charing Cross, wiped out hospitals and sent up in flames the factories, railway lines and slums of London's benighted East End. In the view of a late-May editorial in New York's *Journal American*, these latest bombings widened the fight: "Long since, Westminster ceased to be a part of London and became a symbol beloved by all the world."

The Allies, which in effect meant Great Britain, battled gamely. Its Navy had just sunk the *Bismarck*, one of Germany's most lethal ships. The British Army was making gains in Baghdad, having overturned a pro-Nazi coup that had seized control of Iraq. The slender silver lining in that most recent raid on London was that the German bombers had then been shot down. But these were small victories that scarcely stanched the relentless onslaught of the Nazis, the Italians, the Japanese. Germany had an iron grip on the continent, was staging the ground for an attack on Russia and was taking territory at every instance. Now German paratroopers were alighting with clear intentions on the shores of Crete. It had become evident that the Allies were not going to be able to sustain the fight without America's help.

Nor was the U.S. standing idly by. America's cloak of neutrality, publicly donned in 1939 two days after Britain (and Australia) had declared war on Germany and less than 12 months after the last of the New Deal programs had gone into effect, had since been plainly shucked off. If there was concern over what the U.S. government could reasonably afford, having been tapped by the years of assistance spending during the Depression, any reluctance was gradually being overwhelmed by fear of what the country stood to lose. In March of 1941 President Roosevelt signed the Lend-Lease Act, an agreement by which the U.S. would send war materials to the Allies in exchange for the lease of military bases in the West Indies, Newfoundland and elsewhere. Already 50 of the U.S.'s largest naval destroyers had been dispatched to aid Britain and Canada. Roosevelt had then gotten workers at tool factories and defense plants across the nation to agree to keep operations active seven days a week and around the clock, hoping to ensure that military supplies would be delivered at a rate nearer to meeting the demand.

Even with the war's engagements far from home soil, the U.S. Army began playing what it billed as war games crucial to the nation's safety. Foot soldiers had been scattered along the coast of New Jersey to prepare in case of an unexpected attack. The government had twice ordered trial blackouts: for 15 minutes one night in Newark—lights out in the Vittorio Castle—and on another night for several hours across Oahu and the whole of the Hawaiian Islands. In late May, some 700 miles from a British port on the coast of Sierra Leone, the Nazis sank a U.S. merchant ship.

Major league baseball players knew that a rifle might soon replace the bat in their hands. Greenberg and Hugh Mulcahy had been called to service and other players appeared on the verge, those who were unmarried and classified as I-A by their draft board. The All-Star quality outfielder Buddy Lewis and the .381-hitting shortstop Cecil Travis were among them, both players integral to the Washington Senators who, on the afternoon of May 27, were hosting the Yankees at Griffith Stadium.

It was here in Washington six weeks earlier that the 1941 season had begun for DiMaggio and the Yanks, an Opening Day memorable not for New York's 3–0 win but for the presence of the popular Roosevelt. He was determined, he'd said, to keep baseball going through the war and, with a happy overhand toss from his box behind home plate, threw out the season's ceremonial first pitch. Senators owner Clark Griffith had presented the President with a golden card that granted him access to every major league stadium—as if Roosevelt wouldn't have been let in without it!—and had given another to the First Lady, Eleanor. Roosevelt adored baseball, valued its intrinsic joys and believed in the importance of its wider societal reach, seeing the sport as a connective thread among American citizens even, or perhaps especially, in a time of troubling uncertainty.

The red-white-and-blue Opening Day bunting was gone from Griffith Stadium now, as was the April chill. On this sun-filled afternoon, DiMaggio had his finest game in weeks: four hits, among them a three-run homer beyond the 402-foot sign in leftfield, in a 10–8 Yankees win. The game, though, slipped quickly from the thoughts of the fans making their way from the stadium and up to Georgia Avenue after the final out.

One of President Roosevelt's fireside chats, this one designed to make

clear America's policy of defense, was to air live that night at 9:30 p.m. Nearly 70 million people would tune in across the U.S.—about 75% of the population aged nine and above—and millions more would listen overseas. In Washington D.C., hardly a radio anywhere was turned off that night. Radios were certainly playing in the chandeliered lobby and in the polished rooms of the Shoreham Hotel on Calvert Street, where a day earlier the nation's Secretary of the Interior, Harold Ickes, had given a lecture on the danger of the Nazi threat, and where DiMaggio and the rest of the Yankees were now spending the night, two miles from Roosevelt's broadcast microphone in the White House.

The President had relied heavily and successfully on the increasing power of radio during his eight years in office and by now, in the first stages of his third term, his chats were deeply anticipated and cherished. Issues of pressing importance seemed to have shaped every moment of FDR's Presidency and he addressed each with a firmness of content and a mastery of tone. He spoke with a fatherly eloquence, a confidence revealed subtly in his pauses and emphases. The language that he used was strong and unambiguous; Roosevelt's talks inspired people, gave them faith. Some said that he sounded the way Moses must have. Newspapers sometimes referred to him as "the Voice."

At about 9:35 p.m., just a few moments into this night's speech, Roosevelt went to the heart of the matter. "It is unmistakably apparent," he said, "that unless the advance of Hitlerism is forcibly checked now, the Western Hemisphere will be within range of the Nazi weapons of destruction." He spoke proudly of America's expanding military and he reaffirmed that the Lend-Lease Act was not an act of generosity to the Allies but was "based on hardheaded concern for our own security." Then Roosevelt lauded the way that "Britain still fights gallantly, on a far-flung battle line" and cheers went up in living rooms all over London. It was 3:40 in the morning there.

They were listening too under the lights at Sportsman's Park in St. Louis, delaying the start of the Cubs-Cardinals game. The public address system broadcast Roosevelt's words as a crowd of nearly 16,000 sat quietly in the stands on the warm, moonless night. Inside the clubhouse, some of the Chicago players, among them outfielders Augie Galan and Bill Nicholson, and some of the Cardinals, including catcher Gus Man-

cuso and the old sidearming righthander Lon Warneke, mustered around a small radio that had been set up between the locker rooms.

Roosevelt's speech came over the loudspeakers at the Polo Grounds in New York as well, the gathering of 17,009 fans fairly fixed in their seats, the players in the dugouts, the 1–1 game between the hometown Giants and the Boston Braves halted after the seventh inning and set to resume when the President was finished.

People listened in restaurants and nightspots in Chicago, Philadelphia, San Francisco. At the Stork Club and the Versailles in Manhattan not a drink was served, spirits temporarily on hold. Taxis with radios in them pulled to the sides of the lamplit city streets. The drivers turned off their meters, rolled down their windows, and strangers came and stood close to hear. Others lingered next to newsstands at Times Square and Grand Central Terminal.

In Queens, the Bellefair and the other ice cream shops stayed open late, radios brought forth and set down onto the countertops as the customers leaned in. Even now, despite the late hour and the darkness of the sky, neighbors in Queens convened around portable radios on building stoops, just as they did in Brooklyn and the Bronx. It was not unlike the way many of these same listeners often gathered round for an afternoon ball game, to hear the Dodgers' Red Barber, the best announcer going, unfurl a game in all its savory details, people as attentive to Barber's syrupy Southern lilt—"They're tearin' up the pea patch!"—as they were now to Roosevelt's raspy baritone.

"In the Nazi book of world conquest . . ." the Voice continued, ". . . they plan to strangle the United States of America and the Dominion of Canada." Lose this fight, Roosevelt went on to say, and lose your way of life. The American laborer would have his wages and hours fixed by Hitler, his right to worship decided by Hitler. Roosevelt reminded people that in Africa the Germans were occupying Tripoli and Libya and threatening to claim Egypt. Again and again he came back to his essential point: "The war is approaching the brink of the Western Hemisphere. It is coming very close to home."

The President reached far back into history, recalling the U.S.'s success in beating back the Barbary Pirates, in helping to expel Napoleon from Mexico. He cited the Battle of Bunker Hill and spoke of the dedi-

cation and effectiveness of U.S. convoys in the first World War. "In this Second World War, however, the problem is greater," Roosevelt said, his tone deeper now, foreboding. The enemy, he explained, had far more dangerous weapons these days, more lethal submarines and a "bombing airplane, which is capable of destroying merchant ships seven or eight hundred miles from its nearest base." In other words, the President was saying, this was no time to flinch.

Now Roosevelt's speech entered its coda and with it a series of emphatic vows:

"We shall actively resist...every attempt by Hitler to extend his Nazi domination.

"We shall give every possible assistance to Britain and to all who, with Britain, are resisting Hitlerism or its equivalent.

"We are placing our armed forces in strategic military positions."

Then Roosevelt announced that he had issued a proclamation declaring that in America a state of "unlimited national emergency exists and requires the strengthening of our defense to the extreme limit of our national power and authority."

In a suburban tavern north of New York City, a man drained the last of his beer, slapped his hand on the bar and announced, "We're in, boys!" In Washington, D.C., a crowd standing outside a Ninth Street restaurant soberly applauded. On a sidewalk in midtown Manhattan, a woman said: "It frightens me. But what else can we do?"

Who wasn't frightened, even as Roosevelt's words roused in his listeners a sense of resolution and solidarity? Who wasn't afraid of war? There were those who simply opposed America's involvement, isolationists or anticommunists such as the aviator turned public speaker Charles Lindbergh, who whipped up thousands as he toured the country decrying the Allies, saying that he'd prefer even an alliance with the Nazis than with any side that might soon include the Soviet Union. Or New York congressman Hamilton Fish who a few hours before Roosevelt's fireside chat had addressed a crowd in a high school auditorium and warned that if the U.S entered the war "we would have chaos and revolution at home and Communism abroad."

Trepidation, though, wasn't limited to the fear-mongers and alarmists.

Even among the greater part of the American whole, those who believed in Roosevelt, those who nodded in approval when a Marine at a Times Square bar bellowed near the end of the President's speech: "Let's go! We've taken enough dirt from those guys," even those who were outraged at the impudence of the Nazi onslaught, who were appalled and angered by the treatment of the Jews, even many of those people were wary and reluctant when it came to engaging in war.

So many families had been weakened, some torn asunder, by the effects of the Depression. Futures had been wiped out, dreams destroyed. Now, barely free of that awful economic time, they were going to be asked to send their young men to war? Mothers wrote letters to the White House begging President Roosevelt not to do anything that might take away their boys.

Whippoorwills flitted noisily in the air above Sportsman's Park as the crowd sat rapt and the President's speech wound down. The teams' respective batteries—the Cubs' catcher Clyde McCullough and pitcher Jake Mooty; the Cardinals' Mancuso and lefthander Max Lanier—came out to loosen up, the four players alone on the bright and otherwise empty field.

At the Polo Grounds the 1–1 game was soon to begin again. Murmurs coursed through the stands, the people trying to sort through all they had just heard. *We're going to war I bet. . . . Maybe we'll just send convoys again this time. . . . Wonder how long 'til Hitler hears that speech. . . . How old is your son again?*

"Old Long Pants" Carl Hubbell was on the mound for the Giants, throwing the last of his warmup pitches into Harry Danning's glove. A pinch hitter, Lloyd (Little Poison) Waner, squeezed his bat handle in front of the Braves dugout, began to stride toward the plate. Mel Ott looked in from rightfield, Jo-Jo Moore from left. Then, even as the ringing of Roosevelt's final words echoed through the Polo Grounds—a trenchant line from the Declaration of Independence: "we mutually pledge to each other our lives, our fortunes, and our sacred honor"—the rookie umpire Jocko Conlan pointed with both index fingers out to Old Long Pants Hubbell and shouted, "Play ball!"

Chapter 7
A Pair Of Sox

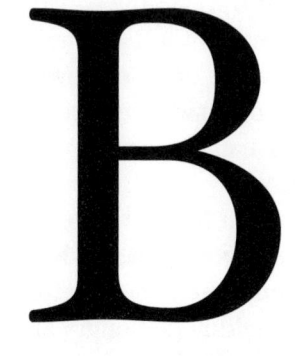UGS WERE EVERYWHERE, dancing around the hot rectangular banks of lights that shone down upon Griffith Stadium. In quiet moments you could hear them, a gleeful swarm of gnats, moths and mosquitoes who seemed to believe that all this gorgeous brightness had suddenly appeared—oh sweet mystery of life!—for their pleasure, rather than to illuminate the first night game in Washington Senators' history, a game now in its middle innings with the Senators up a few runs on the Yankees. From centerfield, DiMaggio glanced up at the insects. He felt sluggish. Maybe it was the heat, still clinging after a stifling afternoon in which the thermometer had reached 97°—a record for D.C. in May. At times the Yankee players had sought refuge in the air-conditioned ballroom at the hotel.

The day had seemed strange and surreal. The newspapers and the radio shows were chock-a-block with the politicians' reactions to the President's address the night before—"A ringing call to duty and service for all Americans," proclaimed one senator; "Roosevelt has turned the Atlantic

Ocean into a Pan-American lake" said another. DiMaggio had a dull, stiffening pain in his neck.

He didn't go for night games. Seeing the ball wasn't the problem, the way it was for some guys. Under the kind of lights that big-league teams sprung for—the Senators had spent $120,000 on theirs—he could pick up pitches better than he sometimes could when he was at bat in the half shadows of a late afternoon. The trouble was that night games upset his routine. Typically, he liked to finish breakfast by 11 o'clock or so, for a 3 p.m. start. Black coffee, a couple of eggs, toast. Sometimes at home he'd get up a little earlier and Dorothy would make him an omelet and he'd lounge a while, let her talk about her parents or her sisters, or something funny that Lou Costello—she just called him Lou—had said in the news. He'd have a third cup of coffee, another smoke, read through the papers and then step out onto the balcony and look uptown toward Gomez's apartment 20 blocks away. DiMaggio would wave a white or yellow towel and if Lefty saw it from his window he would wave a towel wildly too, and that was signal enough. The two of them would drive up to the ballpark together. DiMaggio liked to get there early.

He wouldn't eat again until later, a nice dinner an hour or two after the game. Same thing when the Yankees were on the road, a late breakfast in the room, sometimes his postgame dinner there too. But for night games, DiMaggio had to eat differently. He couldn't go hungry all afternoon. Today he'd gotten something light at the Shoreham at about 4 o'clock, but he still felt off, and his throat was swollen, when at 8:30 p.m. the retired Walter Johnson, the greatest Senator of all, strode out to the mound and with his long right arm threw a fastball through a narrow beam of light to trigger the stadium floodlights and the dawn of night baseball in Washington.

At 53 years old and 14 seasons removed from his last game in uniform, the Big Train still put some zip on the ball. The old-timers said he'd been the fastest pitcher ever, faster than Grove, faster than Feller. In Johnson's day the umpires didn't change the game balls so much and if something got stuck onto the stitches or the hide of a ball—a little swatch of mud, say—batters could actually hear the baseball buzz past when Johnson let go of a high hard one. Really, the old-timers said. No bull.

After Johnson's ceremonial pitch, there were now only three American League teams remaining that did not play night games in their home park: the Red Sox, the Tigers and the Yankees. New York's position on the matter was set by their hidebound president and general manager, 73-year-old Edward G. Barrow. "I do not believe in night baseball," Barrow would sniff when the subject came up, just as he dismissed the idea of allowing Yankee home games to be broadcast over the radio. Elsewhere in the league, teams embraced playing at night and club governors in cities such as Cleveland were pushing the commissioner's office to add to the limit of seven night games that each team was allowed to host per season. Barrow was among those on the league board who voted that proposal down. He didn't give a damn that night games lifted attendance for many clubs that needed it; the Yankees, when it came to ticket revenue, were doing fine.

In Washington, D.C., the nighttime novelty had lured about 25,000 to Griffith Stadium, not the sellout that team owner Clark Griffith had hoped for but three times as many fans as had shown up the previous afternoon. The Yankees were having trouble with the Senators' tall right-hander Sid Hudson, who kept dropping his hard curveball over the plate, knee-high. McCarthy had sent out the rookie Steve Peek, himself a curve-baller, believing the curve was the pitch that would be toughest to read in the artificial light.

Washington held a 3–1 lead with one out in the top of the eighth inning when DiMaggio, hitless until then, drove a triple against the high rightfield wall, shaking the torpor from his own body and from the Yankees. The next three men reached base and then George Selkirk—most often called Twinkletoes for his running style, heels-up in a kind of prance—lofted a convincing grand slam, the white ball disappearing past the mist of insects and into the night, all but sealing the Senators' 10th consecutive loss.

Throughout the three days in Washington, including the afternoon after the night game when he singled in the fourth inning of what would be a rain-shortened 2–2 tie, DiMaggio endured that swollen throat, as well as the rigidity in his neck that traveled down through his trapezius and into his shoulders. He could barely turn to the side to talk to

someone. Looking up for a fly ball required uncommon effort. At night, Gomez grinned and cracked an off-color joke when he saw DiMaggio wrapping heat pads on his neck as he got into bed. DiMaggio didn't want to tell the reporters about his pains, didn't want to tell McCarthy either. This would pass. Whatever it was, he'd had it before. He always had something; for DiMaggio injuries were a curse. Back in 1934 he'd torn up his left knee in the Pacific Coast League, delaying his Yankees' debut by a full year. Then in his rookie season, '36, a left foot injury and a burn from a heat lamp kept him out until early May. DiMaggio had tonsillitis in '37. In '39 he'd torn muscles in his legs. In '40 he had problems with his right knee and his ankles.

Now DiMaggio just wanted to ignore his wretched neck and stay in the lineup. Especially because he'd been hitting a little better lately, and because the Yankees, still in third place, needed him, and because the team was now going into Boston to play a doubleheader against the Red Sox, Dominic and Ted Williams.

Williams. What a fuss everyone made over that kid, a hero in his third season. They all talked about his power, the way the ball flew off his lefthanded swing with a force that belied Williams's beanpole frame. Power, sure, but still DiMaggio would look enviously out at that bullpen in Fenway Park. The Red Sox had added it before the 1940 season especially to benefit Williams. In effect the bullpen had moved the fence closer to the plate by 23 feet, smack in Williams's rightfield power alley—and it was a low fence at that. When DiMaggio drove a ball into his sweet spot in left center at Yankee Stadium he had to hit it 80 feet farther, at least, to have a chance at a home run. During batting practice at the Stadium sometimes, Henrich and Keller would set up cones in left centerfield, mimicking the distance of a more normal ball field—like Comiskey Park in Chicago, or Briggs Stadium in Detroit—to see how many homers Joe could hit. The answer was that he could hit a lot of them. The other Yankees tended to stop and watch when DiMaggio was taking his licks before a game.

DiMaggio couldn't understand why Williams drew so many walks. A hitter with his talent? What, did Williams *like* giving up a chance to hit? DiMaggio himself would gladly swing at a pitch off the plate to try to

drive in a run or move a base runner. "I go after everything I think I can hit," he said. Not Williams. If the pitch wasn't just about perfect he let it go. They said he had the eyesight of an eagle. He made the pitcher give in. Right now, 37 games into the Red Sox season, Williams was hitting .421, easily the best average in either league.

Williams was just different from DiMaggio, more outgoing, always yapping, sparring with opponents and needling the umps. DiMaggio rarely said a thing. To DiMaggio hitting was principally, as he framed it in his mind, a "God-given gift," an ability akin to running speed or arm strength that might be tinkered with and honed but not significantly improved. He never wasted a turn at the plate, but his approach was by and large intuitive; often, he didn't know who the other team's pitcher would be until shortly before the game began. For Williams, it seemed, hitting was like a science to be studied and explored with every at bat, his or someone else's. His teammates had come to expect to be grilled by Williams each time they got back to the dugout after a turn at the plate—"What's he got on that fastball?" "Was that third pitch a sinker or a slider?" When an opposing pitcher came out to warm up for a game, Williams would break off from playing pepper and just stare at him. "When I walk down the street I'd like for them to say, 'There goes Ted Williams, the best hitter who ever lived,'" he told people. Old-timers had begun comparing him with Babe Ruth.

Before the start of the doubleheader Dominic and Ted stood near one another in the outfield, bantering while catching flies and occasionally pointing up into the Fenway stands that were rapidly filling in. It was a holiday Friday, Memorial Day. Now Dominic shouted something out and Ted laughed and pointed back at him, then threw a gentle air punch Dom's way.

Dominic always made friends easily. Growing up, he was the DiMaggio that the other kids came by the three-step stoop to see. Dom was easy to talk to, small and unthreatening, lively and open to frivolity in a way that Joe could never bring himself to be. Like the cheese-rolling, for example. One of Dominic's friends was the son of a cheese maker and Dom and his guys would get together and roll wheels of cheese, competing for distance, on a flat stretch of Bay Street near the wharf. The winner took

a pot of change. Everyone cheered and laughed the day little Dom set the record for a Bay Street cheese roll: nearly three full blocks.

Dominic was Ma's favorite, or so it seemed to Joe. She and the older sisters doted on him, the baby of the nine kids. Marie called Dom "a little doll." Ma referred to him as her "angel." And Dom played the part, helping voluntarily around the house, complimenting his sisters on their looks, once devoting himself to try to teach Ma to speak better English. (Not that it had helped much, Joe thought with a smile.) When Dom used to tease Joe about his lousy grasp of Italian, no one at home scolded Dom but rather chuckled right along.

Mainly, Dominic was smart—the best checkers player at the North Beach Playground for one thing. He used to say that he wanted to be a chemical engineer. And six years after Joe had walked in the front entrance of Galileo High, strolled through the inner courtyard and then out a side door onto Polk Street without even staying long enough to get a grade, Dominic left the building with a diploma in his hand. Class of 1934. Ma and Pa were proud. Around the ballfield Dominic, in his spectacles, was called the Little Professor.

You wouldn't even know they were brothers, Red Sox second baseman Bobby Doerr thought when he saw the DiMaggios pass each other wordlessly on the field. *It's like they don't even know the other exists.*

They knew. By the start of the doubleheader Joe had gotten his batting average up to .329. Dom was at .345.

In the first game Joe's ninth-inning single came in the middle of a three-run rally and the Yankees went into the clubhouse with a 4–3 win. Earlier in the game, though, he had dropped Joe Cronin's easy fly ball. Now, between games, DiMaggio was trying to get some movement into his neck. *I'll throw it out,* he thought. *I'll throw the ball as hard as I can, break right through this tightness.*

Not once but twice in the second game did DiMaggio, throwing home to try to get a base runner, heave the baseball over Yankees catcher Buddy Rosar and into the stands, a performance which, combined with a misplay of a ball hit by Williams, gave him four errors on the day. The Yankees were on their way to a 13–0 loss and Joe's pop-fly double in the fifth inning did nothing to stop the fans from chanting "Meatball Joe" when

he came to bat, or from shouting out "Dommy's better" when Joe took the field. (A day later, after Gomez let slip to the writers about Joe's injured neck, DiMaggio wouldn't lean on it to explain his errors. "I just had a bad day," he snapped.)

The shutout was the first of the season inflicted upon the Yankees. Dominic had three hits in the two games. Williams went 3 for 5 (naturally, he also walked a few times); he was now hitting .429.

The Red Sox and Yankees headed west on the same chartered Pullman late that afternoon, the Sox bound for Detroit, the Yankees to Cleveland for three games. And though Dominic and Joe were but a few hundred feet apart, though they might have met and chatted in one of the dining cars as some of the other Red Sox and Yankees players did, the brothers did not meet. Anyway, after a 13–0 game there was not a lot to say.

Chapter 8
The Loss

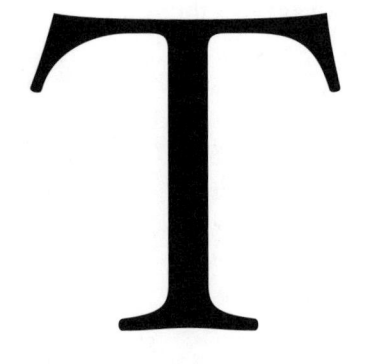HE INDIANS WERE now the favorites in the American League, all the experts said. They had Bobby Feller, the most dominant and thrilling pitcher in base-ball, and they had other starting pitch-ers who could shut a team down too. Cleveland had a powerful first baseman in Hal Trosky and a good-hitting outfielder in Jeff Heath. The infield, with Ken Keltner at third base, Lou Boudreau at shortstop and Ray Mack at second, included some of the finest defensive players in the game. Keltner, who often batted third and was a home run threat, stole a hit per game with his glove, it seemed. Boudreau, so quick afield despite his sluggardly pace on the bases, and Mack, brilliant on the pivot, went by the nickname Murder Inc. for the many double plays, the 6-4-3 rally killers, that they turned. Cleveland won 11 straight games in late April and early May, and four weeks later the team was still in front of Jimmy Dykes's overachieving White Sox. The Yankees had come into Cleve-land's Municipal Stadium at the start of June in third place, four games

behind. When they departed, they were a game closer in the standings.

Those few days in Cleveland now seemed a blur to DiMaggio, though the Yankees had just left the city that afternoon. At the beginning of the series, heavy rains had given the teams a day off, allowing DiMaggio to rest at the Hotel Cleveland, helping his neck to heal. The Yankees doubleheader sweep the next day in front of more than 50,000 fans was achieved on the strength of fine pitching by Red Ruffing in the first game and by Gomez in the second. DiMaggio's single against the lefthander Al Milnar helped make the difference in the opener. In game two he scratched a ground ball hit off the tough breaking-ball pitcher Mel Harder. And though Cleveland, with Feller on the mound, had responded with a 7–5 win in the third game, the Yankees were pleased to have won twice in the series, and pleased that even in their final-game loss they'd hit well against the Indians' ace.

DiMaggio had knocked a single and a double against Feller, his first multihit game since the opener against the Senators. He usually handled Feller. At the plate, DiMaggio would prepare himself for Feller's fastball— really, you had to do that or you'd have no chance to hit it when it came— and though the ball would zip in at near to 100 miles per hour, DiMaggio had the bat speed to meet it. If Feller threw his curve, DiMaggio would wait stock still until the last instant and then lash at the pitch.

It's as if he waits and waits so that he can watch my curveball break and only then swings, Feller thought. *Is it possible he can do that and still hit it? Not even Williams can do that.*

On the train trip from Cleveland to Detroit, Joe Gordon had sung gaily in the aisle, entertaining the team. Henrich had talked about the two home runs he'd hit off Feller. Rizzuto was teased for the stiff new suit he'd just bought; in response he stood and sang along with Gordon. The Yankees players made jokes and were happy, and McCarthy did not seem to mind.

But now, just a few hours later, that train ride was forgotten, irrelevant. DiMaggio stood silently in the splendid lobby of the Book-Cadillac Hotel in Detroit. He shifted his weight and then smoothed his tie. It was 10:30 at night. The glinting marble walls and the gilded latticework of the hotel seemed out of place, unreal. There was a tremulous hush all through the big lobby. Gomez stared somberly, seeing nothing. Selkirk tore a piece of

paper once and then again and kept tearing it until the paper was in tiny strips. McCarthy sat on one of the pinkish upholstered couches, alone and away from everyone else. Some players clustered by the room clerk's desk and collected a piece of mail or the key to their room. Other players stood with their hands in their pants pockets quietly murmuring to one another. Nothing that anyone did seemed to matter.

Catcher Bill Dickey, Lou Gehrig's old roommate, came in through the front door. He had been out for a malted. One of the bellmen told him the news. "My God!" said Dickey. "I only spoke to Lou a few days before we left New York. He told me he felt fine."

The Yankees had been expecting this, of course. They had seen the hard, awful signs over the past years. The end result was inevitable. Even so, the news landed like a blow from behind: sudden and harsh. For DiMaggio, in the first moments of knowing, it almost seemed impossible. Lou Gehrig was dead.

They had met for the first time in the Yankees clubhouse in St. Petersburg, spring training 1936. DiMaggio was the young Italian rookie with the big reputation. He wasn't sure how people would take to him. He remembered feeling Gehrig's strong hand against his back and then hearing Gehrig say, "Nice to have you with us, Joe."

DiMaggio had never been as struck by a ballplayer as he was by Gehrig. His strength—the bands of muscles that ran across and up and down his broad back—was extraordinary. At bat Gehrig gave an impression of power greater than any DiMaggio had ever seen. Gehrig hit the ball with a straightforward authority, like a skilled carpenter addressing a nail. Over DiMaggio's first two seasons Gehrig batted .353 and drove in 311 runs and the older players kept assuring Joe that Gehrig had been even better a few years back.

They lockered directly beside one another at Yankee Stadium, in the corner by the window, and though their conversations tended to be brief they exchanged words often. "Gee, that was a bad ball I hit at," DiMaggio might say quietly, and Gehrig would tell him not to worry, he'd have another chance the next day. That simple optimism was reassuring to the young player.

DiMaggio was moved by the courtesy and graciousness with which

Gehrig spoke to the writers who covered the team. Gehrig had been the second star to Babe Ruth for most of his career; now DiMaggio, from the other side of the country and wrapped in intrigue, had arrived and begun socking the ball, and the attention on Gehrig was diluted again. That did not seem to matter to him. Gehrig remained cheerful and patient and uncomplaining. He rarely spoke about other ballplayers to the press but he did speak to them about DiMaggio. "He has a marvelous disposition for a ballplayer," Gehrig said once, early in DiMaggio's career. "His expression never changes. You mark my words. He is going to be the greatest right-hand hitter in baseball."

At another time, in DiMaggio's second season, Gehrig said: "Joe is the best defensive outfielder in the game. Once he is told where to shift for a certain batsman, he never has to be reminded."

Such superlatives were uncommon from Gehrig, the writers and DiMaggio knew, and so they carried all the more weight.

Sometimes, when both of these quiet players were in the right mood and the Yankees were winning, they would horse around before a game, point their bats like rifles maybe, and, for the cameras, DiMaggio would reach out and muss the top of Gehrig's hair. They would laugh together.

They laughed too on the morning after Gehrig made his gaffe on the radio. He'd gone on an interview program, hired to speak a few words in praise of the breakfast cereal Huskies. But at the crucial moment when the radio host asked him to name his cereal of choice Gehrig had said, in a slip-up, "Wheaties." The flub made some news and the next day a reporter came by the lockers at the Stadium and asked Gehrig "What did you eat for breakfast?" And Lou, not yet catching on, had said frankly and in innocence, "Two eggs, a little toast." Then DiMaggio, playing along with the writer, began to grin and said, "What about the things you put in a bowl, with sugar on top? Dandelions! Don't you eat those?" DiMaggio was not often silly in this way, but around Gehrig it felt okay.

Now Gehrig's locker was empty, had been for many months, day after day after day, and no one would ever use it or wear Gehrig's number 4 for the Yankees again.

It had been right here in the Hotel Book-Cadillac, two years and one month earlier, that Gehrig had taken himself out of the lineup 2,130 con-

secutive games after he'd first stepped in. He had visited McCarthy in his room and said that he could no longer play well enough to stay in there, that his coming out of the lineup was for the good of the team. In the moments that followed McCarthy said to him kindly and with love in his voice, "Lou, fellows like you come along once in a hundred years."

The manager had called the baseball writers into his room then to tell them the news that would be the next day's headlines. "I'm sorry to see it happen," said McCarthy, adding, in a notion that Gehrig would echo when he spoke to the writers himself: "Maybe the warm weather will bring him around."

No one, not McCarthy nor Gehrig nor the men who followed the team, believed that.

Gehrig had been failing for some time. He had seemed empty in that spring training of '39—*Something is wrong*, DiMaggio remembered thinking from the moment he saw him—and still emptier after the season began. His power had dramatically and inexplicably vanished. Even when Gehrig would strike the ball squarely on the sweet round flesh of the bat, it would not go anywhere. By early May, he was batting .143. Gehrig ran as if he had weights tied to his ankles. He was not yet 36 years old. Nobody had ever seen a player decline so shockingly fast.

Later Gehrig told DiMaggio why he had decided to quit when he did. In a game against the Senators, Gehrig had fielded a ground ball and thrown it over to the pitcher, Johnny Murphy, who stepped on first base. "Murph, Gordon and Dickey all gathered around me and patted me on the back," Gehrig told DiMaggio. " 'Great stop,' they all said together, and then I knew I was washed-up. They meant to be kind, but if I was getting wholesale congratulations for making an ordinary stop, I knew it was time to fold."

All through the early part of the 1939 season the Yankees had been worried that Gehrig might get hurt on the field. Even after Gehrig's trip to the Mayo Clinic soon afterward, after learning there that he had what the doctors diagnosed as a form of infantile paralysis, and even after his July 4, 1939, speech before the big crowd at Yankee Stadium, when Gehrig had called himself "the luckiest man on the face of the earth" to have the kind of teammates he had and to have the love of the fans the way he

did—and Babe Ruth standing there had put his arms around Gehrig and wept, genuinely forgetting, it seemed, the rift between them—even after that, Gehrig had stayed and traveled with the team all season.

DiMaggio could never bring himself to watch Gehrig getting dressed in his uniform. He would look away rather than see the great man fumble with his buttons and his belt, rather than see the look of confusion that time and again passed over Gehrig's face. Gehrig played bridge and DiMaggio remembered the day when Lou for the first time could no longer shuffle the cards. Gehrig began trailing his left foot when he walked. The next season, 1940, he stopped coming regularly to the park. He would sometimes appear in the Yankee dugout before a game to watch batting and fielding practice but then when DiMaggio glanced over again, Gehrig, ghostlike, had disappeared.

Gehrig's demise was still, for all the evidence, impossible to fully accept; in the recesses of many Yankee minds there lingered a small hope— "hope even against hope" as Ruth put it—that if anyone could overcome this insidious thing it would be Gehrig. No one else had his resolve or his resiliency. He had taken the field every single day for more than 13 seasons without respite. Long before his final at bat, back when he had played in "only" 1,800 of those 2,130 consecutive games, he had been commended by the league with a notice that lauded the qualities his teammates saw game after game and year after year: "Eighteen hundred games in spite of broken fingers, ribs, toes, sprained ankles, severe spike wounds, concussions of the skull as a result of being hit with a pitched ball, severe colds and bruises. No wonder the baseball world hails Lou Gehrig as the 'Iron Man.' "

So now in the saddened lobby of the Book-Cadillac Hotel—as the Yankee players each took a few moments to organize a simple sincere message and went to the clerk's desk to send telegrams to Eleanor, Lou's wife— there remained a sense of disbelief. "I just can't express my thoughts. I can't realize Lou is gone," said McCarthy. Dickey said that Gehrig was like a brother to him. Art Fletcher, the Yankees' third base coach, said: "It is the most painful news that I have ever heard."

The next morning DiMaggio and Dickey and Gomez were called over to Briggs Stadium to speak on a radio program that was honoring Lou and being aired across the country. When it was DiMaggio's turn, he

moved near the microphone and said: "I lost a very fine friend in Gehrig. Lou helped me more, just about as much as, anybody connected with baseball. I too, like Lefty, would like to join and offer my sympathy to his wife, mother and dad."

DiMaggio listened to the others, like the Tigers' president Walter Briggs and then the manager Del Baker, who talked about "what a grand hustler Lou Gehrig was. He should live as an inspiration to all ballplayers." Then the radio show went to Cleveland where the Red Sox were playing the Indians, and Jimmie Foxx said, "I am deeply grieved. He was the greatest hitter I ever saw." Feller spoke too. Then the show went to New York where the Giants' Carl Hubbell said some words and so did Mel Ott. The Babe came on the radio, and so too did the president of the National League, Ford Frick, who talked of the "emptiness that you feel in your heart." When the show signed off, the host, the former big leaguer Ty Tyson, said simply, "Lou Gehrig has left us a heritage. May we do it proud."

It was decided that McCarthy and Dickey would leave the team to attend the funeral, McCarthy right away, and Dickey after that afternoon's game— a dreary one at which the flags flapped at half-staff and the outcome, a 4–2 Yankee loss despite DiMaggio's fourth-inning home run, scarcely had meaning. There was none of the usual bench jockeying that day. When the Yankees players passed through the Detroit dugout on the way to their own, the Tigers just nodded solemnly and said "Tough about Lou" or "What a man Lou was, really." Rudy York, the Tigers' slugging first baseman whom Lou had taken time to mentor here and there, felt especially low.

The sky was a blackish gray and some rain had fallen, and the crowd of barely 3,500 was smaller than any for a Yankee game at Briggs Stadium in five years. Before Dizzy Trout's first pitch of the game both teams and all those hardy fans stood in silence, hands or caps over their hearts, for a full minute. The flags hung at half-staff in every ballpark in the major leagues.

Gehrig had died in the Bronx, at home and in his bed, with Eleanor and his parents and his mother-in-law and a doctor beside him. Ed Barrow had been the last Yankee to visit him, three days before. They had sat together by the window and watched the Hudson River rippling by. As the Yankees president prepared to leave the house that afternoon, he kissed Gehrig on the head in farewell and Lou looked up at him the best

he could and said in the voice that had gotten thick and raspy in the last few months: "I'll beat it, Boss. Keep those Yankees up."

The night before the funeral more than 5,000 people stood on the streets outside the tiny Christ Episcopal Church, just two blocks from Gehrig's home, waiting to see his body as it lay in state. Children and oil-stained truck drivers and men in business suits and women in long dresses all filed heavily past the bier. Gehrig lay in a mahogany coffin with roses all around.

In the morning, Dorothy attended the funeral with Lefty's wife, June. The women were good friends, both of them actresses of some stature before they'd married into baseball. On this day they shared a single umbrella. They wore dark clothes and simple hats, and before Dorothy and June even got to the Christ Church on that soggy morning to join the group of friends—a small, intimate group as the Gehrig family wished—Dorothy had wept. She knew what Joe thought of Lou, the respect that Gehrig had earned from everybody. Dorothy had heard that when the telegrams arrived at Gehrig's house from the Yankee players, each man having sent his own, the stack of them as thick as a drugstore novel, Eleanor had finally collapsed. She had lived for two years knowing that Lou would die. Now Eleanor sat bereft and stoic, her topcoat still on, holding her handbag tightly to her side.

Oh, poor Eleanor, Dorothy thought. *To go through that and now the loneliness. Poor Eleanor.* Dorothy stayed near June all day. She was four and a half months pregnant now.

Among the honorary pallbearers were McCarthy and Dickey and members of the New York Parole Commission—where Gehrig had worked, appointed by Mayor La Guardia, for the last years of his life—and Bill (Bojangles) Robinson. Timmy Sullivan, the Yankees' bat boy who played first base at practice, sat in a pew. "We need no eulogy because you all knew him," said Reverend Gerald V. Barry, and soon the service was over and a phalanx of 20 cars drove out to a crematory in Queens beneath a steady, pelting rain. It had rained all morning on the vine-cloaked church, just as it had rained steadily in Detroit, washing out the Yankees-Tigers game. The Yankee players sat joyless in the big hotel and remarked at how fitting the downpour and the cancellation were. "They're burying

Lou along about now," someone said. And it was hard, even if you didn't go much for sentiment, not to look outside into the grayness and imagine that the sky was weeping too.

So it was in early June of 1941. Lou Gehrig was dead, and the United States stood on the precipice of war. A few days before, many millions of people had turned out for Memorial Day parades across the country, more than 500,000 in the heart of Manhattan alone, a showing unlike any since the first World War. President Roosevelt had just announced a call for a second mandatory draft registration, for those men who had turned 21 since the first registration, eight months before. That call-up had enlisted nearly 17 million potential soldiers. Now another 750,000 or more would soon be signing up.

On the day of Gehrig's funeral, in Washington D.C., a congressman from New York City's East Side, M. Michael Edelstein, stood up in the House and rebutted, passionately and angrily, the argument by the Mississippi congressman John Rankin that a "group of our international Jewish brethren are attempting to harass the President and Congress into plunging into the European war." Edelstein responded swiftly and to the point, dismissing Rankin's charge, chastising him for his ignorance and for using Jews as a scapegoat just as Hitler would do, and closing tersely with a reminder to that gentleman from Mississippi that "all men are created equal regardless of race, creed or color." Then, even as the applause for his response still echoed through the House, M. Michael Edelstein walked out of the chamber and into the corridor and fell straight down, dead from a heart attack at age 53. Some 15,000 New Yorkers would come out for his funeral two days later. The reverend at Gramercy Park Memorial Chapel called Edelstein a "martyr at the altar of democracy and true Americanism."

That was all part of the biting strangeness that hung over New York in those late spring days. A strangeness hung over the third-place Yankees too, an unquestionable void. And an uncertain feeling was settling upon all of America, upon Ocean City, N.J., where volunteers with binoculars patrolled the boardwalk looking out for suspicious boats; upon the smacks in San Francisco Bay, where state police had now begun to guard the waterfront, and upon so many other places in between.

Buffeted by the portentous Saturday newsreels ("In California, U.S.

soldiers test the world's largest war plane. . .") and the sober newspaper headlines (ARE WE READY FOR WAR?) and the radio bulletins from home and abroad, the country still sought to maintain the rhythms of life. Millions of people listened on Sunday nights to Jack Benny and his whimsical comedy skits. They tuned in to Martin Block's *Make Believe Ballroom* and danced along. Teenagers, the Hornets and Dukes and Best Bettes of Jackson Heights among them, hummed the radio hit, *I Dream of Jeanie with the Light Brown Hair* on their way to school. Grown-ups packed into the movie theaters to see *Citizen Kane*, gripping and ingenious—a masterpiece, the critics agreed. In the daily comic strips, from Los Angeles to St. Louis to Cleveland and New York, people followed Popeye and Blondie, Flash Gordon and the Lone Ranger.

Some people followed the horse races and the great thoroughbred Whirlaway, who was galloping out to win the Triple Crown. Many followed boxing and the much anticipated Joe Louis-Billy Conn heavyweight title fight that was now just a couple of weeks off. Many, many people followed baseball, attendance having ticked upward again after the worst of the Depression years and more radio stations than ever were broadcasting the sport.

It was good to have all of those things, Benny's wisecracks, Block's frisky tunes, ballplayers like Feller and Williams and Joe DiMaggio and the suddenly surprisingly competent Brooklyn Dodgers; it was good to think about those things when you didn't want to think more about the heavier matters at hand.

Many newspaper readers, on the same morning they had read about Gehrig's death and learned about a bomber boat that had crashed, killing four in a test outside San Diego Bay, also read about the Yankees and their 7–5 loss in Cleveland. In *The New York Times*, coverage of that game appeared in a narrow single-column article by James P. Dawson. The story was succeeded by a series of brief and random notes about the team, including, at the very end of the piece, just above the box score, a blurb that many readers surely missed or scarcely registered, which read in its entirety: "DiMaggio, incidentally, has hit safely in nineteen straight games."

Thinking Can Be Dangerous

I n its earliest stages, a hitting streak—Joe DiMaggio's or anyone else's—is not really a hitting streak at all. A batter has simply hit safely for a handful of games in a row. Only after a streak has reached a certain length (in DiMaggio's case about 20 games) does the hitter really start to think about it—and that, as those in the game can tell you, will almost certainly work against him.

"If a player didn't know that he had a hitting streak going on, he'd be able keep it up longer, no doubt," Colorado Rockies hitting instructor Don Baylor said when I visited with him during a Rockies series against the Diamondbacks. Baylor was sitting in full uniform at a desk in the coaches' office. He leaned back in his swivel chair, crossed his cleated feet and smiled slowly, in thought. At 61, he is an avid student of the game. "The problem comes when you start thinking about it too much."

Baylor, a powerful righthanded hitter who was the Most Valuable Player in the American League in 1979, has worked as a major league coach and manager since he retired as a player after the '88 season. He is relaxed and insightful in discussion and his teaching method draws in part on the styles and techniques of successful hitters throughout baseball history. After Baylor and I spent some time together, I agreed to swap him some footage I had of DiMaggio hitting in exchange for one of

his Ted Williams' discs. He planned to show the DiMaggio clips to his righty batters; he likes Joe's follow-through and the consistency of his swing. Baylor told me that DiMaggio's currency in the minds of today's young hitters comes in large part from his hitting streak, "a record that has stood out there so far in front for so long it's almost holy," he said. Baylor himself never had a streak longer than 14 games.

"You just want your guys to be hitting, and hitting with the right form," Baylor went on. "A big part of it is for guys to just hit the way they can, naturally, without thinking about what they're doing when they're in the box. A hitting streak makes you worry about things that you shouldn't be worrying about."

Many of the players I spoke with agreed. Keith Hernandez, the former Cardinals and Mets first baseman and a perennial .300 hitter, said, "I never knew when I was in a hitting streak until I picked up the newspaper in the morning. I'd read a note that said: 'Hernandez has hit in 13 straight games.' Then that night I'd be sure to go 0 for 4." (Hernandez's career-high streak: 17 games in 1987.)

Rockies second baseman Clint Barmes, a career .254 big league hitter who once hit safely in 30 consecutive games while playing at Indiana State, says he now starts noticing that he's on a streak when he's gotten a hit in "10 or 12 games in a row; for me that's pretty good. But then you start thinking about it and you have to keep yourself from going outside your hitting zone to try to get a knock to keep it going. That's exactly how you get yourself out. I expand my zone too much anyway, and if I have a hitting streak going I may *really* expand it. It's not good."

Sports psychologists hear that kind of talk all the time.

"We don't want you out there thinking consciously, but rather *operating* unconsciously," says Alan Goldberg, a former sports psychology consultant for the University of Connecticut athletics department who has worked with hundreds of athletes through his Massachusetts-based practice Competitive Advantage. Think of the brain as having three parts, Goldberg says, simplifying to help make his point: the forebrain, which processes information consciously and uses words and logic; the midbrain which is involved with emotional states; and the hindbrain which is more about knowing than about thinking. The hindbrain handles involuntary actions and works outside of conscious thought; you understand things in the hindbrain through your experience.

"When you're hitting a baseball you want to be operating as much as possible from the hindbrain," says Goldberg. "The forebrain is analytical and slow and judgmental—it will tell you 'you should really keep your elbow back, you know' or 'you can't get a hit in yet another game, that's crazy.' The forebrain will have you thinking about the speed of the pitcher's fastball and your own statistics and so on as if it's putting together a 100-piece puzzle piece-by-piece. The hindbrain uses muscle memory and it's instantaneous. It coordinates the whole so that you're seeing the 100-piece puzzle at once, all put together. At the beginning of a hitting streak you can be working from the hindbrain but once you've become aware of the streak, the forebrain inevitably comes more and more into play.

"The actual doing is in the hindbrain," Goldberg added. "The potential outcome is fodder for the forebrain."

Or as Rockies All-Star Todd Helton—a potent slugger whose career longest hitting streak is just 17 games despite his .324

batting average—suggested: "When you know that you're on a hitting streak, you might start to think about the result rather than the process, and that's the wrong way around."

———◆———

ATHLETES OFTEN DESCRIBE themselves as being "in the zone," which is the same sensation that analysts in numerous disciplines call having "flow." The psychologist Mihaly Csikszentmihalyi, now a professor at Claremont Graduate University in California, conceived the term and popularized it in his 1990 book, *Flow: the Psychology of Optimal Experience.* "Flow" describes a mental state marked by a diminishment of self-consciousness along with a heightened sense of involvement with an environment or task. You become extremely focused on doing something without realizing it.

The subconscious and one's learned, automatic responses are central to flow, as is the idea that gratuitous or "irrelevant" information is prevented from entering your mind. (The thought that you need a base hit to extend a consecutive-games hitting streak, for example, is irrelevant to the information you need to strike the baseball well.) In a state of flow, Csikszentmihalyi believed, experience is intensified and performance is maximized.

"The idea of flow is applicable to hitting a baseball," says Gordon Bower, a cognitive psychologist and professor emeritus at Stanford who also pitched for Case Western University and in semipro leagues during the early 1950s. "You want the hitting skill to be automated, so that you are responding to a particular cue, or to a small set of cues, without necessarily being aware of what you are responding to. You're just subconsciously remembering what to do. If you start bringing in an

extra cue, such as needing to perform the task in a particular way, that interrupts the response.

"We see this on memory-retrieval tests. If you get subjects to think about something negative—'Oh this test is so hard' or 'My parents will kill me if I mess up this test after what they're paying for me to go here'—they'll probably perform poorly on the test. The same thing holds true if you get them thinking about something good, such as 'After this test, I'm going on a vacation with my fiancée' or 'My professor is about to give me the assistant teaching position I've been trying to get.' They're more likely to screw up the test under those circumstances too. The crucial point is that getting them to think about something else gets in the way of their normal performance, and that is clearly applicable to muscle memory and to hitting a baseball."

George Brett, one of the game's great hitters, had a 30-game streak with the Royals in 1980, the same season he batted .390. He likens the feeling you get during a hitting streak to being at basketball practice and having the coach say to you as he heads to the locker room: "O.K., just hit 10 straight free throws and you can quit."

"You'll drain the first four or five no problem," says Brett, "but then you start thinking about it, thinking 'I can't miss.' And that's when shooting suddenly gets tricky. A hitting streak is like that because until you get your hit that day you're thinking 'I need to get one. I need to get one.' "

To see how an automated, hindbrain process can be interfered with by the forebrain, try this: take a few moments and make yourself intentionally conscious of your breathing. Pay close attention to how you bring the air in, then let it out; invariably the breathing becomes less fluid, awkward even— a shallow breath here, a deeper one there. You breathe most

naturally when you don't think about breathing. Self-awareness has not simply influenced the process, it has weakened it.

This is the same kind of thing that cuts to the heart of one of the oldest tricks on the links. The buddy you're playing against for a case of Pabst is pulling away late in the round when you suddenly say, "Wow, man, you're playing great today! Are you doing something new with your grip?" Or you point out cheerily, "You know if you can just keep it to two over par on the next three holes, you'll beat my best score on this course." Then watch him fade.

In 1986 Roy Baumeister and Carolin Showers published a paper in the *European Journal of Social Psychology* titled, "A review of paradoxical performance effects: Choking under pressure in sports and mental tests." The notion of choking has received a fair amount of attention among social psychologists, virtually all of whom agree with Baumeister's and Showers's suggestion that an athlete failing to perform in a pressurized environment (in this case that would mean going hitless for a game and thus killing the streak) "may result from distraction or from the interference of self-focused attention with the execution of automatic responses." That's the forebrain getting in the way of the hindbrain again.

So, there's that. In addition to the inherent difficulty of getting a hit off a major league pitcher, there is the simple but inescapable matter of being overly aware of what you are trying to do. That little piece, cited by ballplayers like Baylor and Brett, by behaviorists like Bower, and by psychologists like Goldberg, has been enough to derail the barely formed hitting streaks of many, many players, including some of the best hitters in the game.

At 20 games, or thereabouts, news of Joe DiMaggio's hitting streak had yet to make it back to San Francisco, was hardly a

topic of talk in New York City, was barely noticed in the Yankee clubhouse, was little more than the stuff of sidenotes for the herd of daily writers. And yet it had already firmly attached itself to the man himself. DiMaggio knew that with a hitless day he'd be back at zero, starting over again. Or, looking at it the other way and perhaps more significantly, he knew that with another handful of successful games, maybe a good week or so, he could have something truly powerful in the works. A long hitting streak is the most captivating and dramatic of all baseball events—then, now and always—and DiMaggio, by dint of his own experience, knew that as well as just about anyone.

"All the other stuff—the media being on top of you and people asking you about it and all the outside reminders—that all works against you when you're in a hitting streak," says Goldberg. "But to mess things up with too much conscious thinking? For that, all you really need is yourself."

Joe and his father Giuseppe, San Francisco, 1937

Joe with older brother Vince (left) and younger brother Dominic

DiMaggio and Lou Gehrig, 1936

PART II

Chapter 9
Like A Bullet

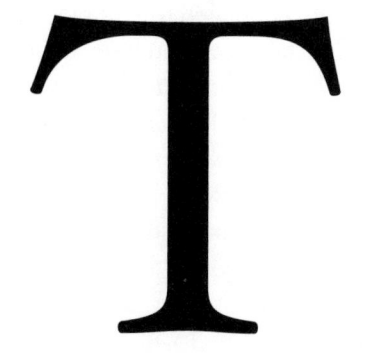HE CROWD WAS sparse at Sportsman's
Park, as usual. Even on a comfortable Sat-
urday afternoon in St. Louis; even now
with the Browns on an improbable three-
game winning streak (the best of the year
for the ever-lousy club) and with their exuberant, newly installed manager Luke Sewell vowing better days ahead; even on this Ladies' Day at
the ballpark, and even with so many kids being allowed in for free (all you
had to be was nine years old, breathing and enrolled in a school somewhere and you could get a pass that let you into any Browns game anytime); even now with a chance to come and watch the mighty Yankees,
Lefty Gomez on the bump; even so, only 2,300 people had paid their way
to see the game. The St. Louis Browns had won 16 and lost 29 on the
season and they were 12 games out of first place. Sometimes it felt like the
Cardinals played in a one-team town.

DiMaggio didn't mind the emptiness of the ballpark. Nor had he ever
minded the unusual, jerry-rigged look to the old place, with its roofed,

double-deck grandstand. He'd always hit well here. The dimensions were fair and the Browns' pitching was generally unthreatening. Today too it felt good to be anywhere but in Detroit where, for three days, heavy clouds had sat dark and unmoving. In the second of the two games at Briggs Stadium, despite DiMaggio's RBI triple in the sixth and then a dramatic Henrich homer in the ninth, the Tigers had won 5–4, in 10 innings, to complete a rain-shortened sweep.

Now in St. Louis, out of the Book-Cadillac and into the Chase Hotel, Gehrig's death had become more a hard fact and less an emotional shock. McCarthy and Dickey were back with the team and the Yankees were up against a tall, righthanded rookie named Bob Muncrief. The young pitcher, though, did not last long. Four relievers were needed to follow him in the Yankees' eventual 11–7 win. Keller hit a grand slam, DiMaggio three singles. His hitting streak was now at 22 games; one more, he knew, and he'd equal the 23 straight he'd run off the season before. *I could get past that in the doubleheader tomorrow.* DiMaggio's neck and shoulder no longer ached. He was leading the American League with 65 base hits. *I'm beginning to feel it now. I'm beginning to feel like I can smash that ball to pieces.*

And the next day in the doubleheader, DiMaggio all but did that, belting three home runs, two in the 9–3 rout by the Yankees in the first game and another in the second game that clattered onto the roof of the hokey rightfield pavilion and closed the scoring in an 8–3 win cut short after seven innings by approaching darkness. DiMaggio had seven RBIs that afternoon and almost had a fourth home run; he drove a double in the second game that crashed into the screen above the rightfield wall. It was not only DiMaggio who carried the Yanks in their series in St. Louis; Keller, back from a pointed four-game McCarthy benching, homered twice; Red Rolfe had five base hits and scored five times in the three games. But it was DiMaggio that every Yankee moved to. "The boys are just waiting for Joe to show 'em how to do it," McCarthy had told the writers a few days earlier. The 1941 Yankees were Joe DiMaggio's to lift and to bear; McCarthy knew it, they all did. And so it was DiMaggio's hits—seven of them in the three games—that sent the real electricity through the bench, that had his New York teammates nodding and squeezing their hands into happy fists, their emotions hot but reserved,

as McCarthy demanded. *The Big Dago's stirring, boys, the Dago's coming alive!* They could feel it, they all could.

The rookie Rizzuto, still tethered to the bench day after day, absorbed it all, his eyes following DiMaggio as he strode up to bat, as he swung, and then as he charged out of the batter's box. *He's outdoing himself,* Rizzuto thought. *Everything he hits is like a bullet.* If DiMaggio hit a home run, Rizzuto watched him as he rounded the bases, his gait slow and even but never without intensity, a firm and unchanging pace that delivered DiMaggio on stride to the plate. Rizzuto watched. He watched DiMaggio's silence, for in DiMaggio silence could be seen. Often it was a literal silence: He would remain wordless for long stretches, and his body moved soundlessly. Then too there was an underlying silence to DiMaggio, even as he came down the dugout steps and accepted the congratulations of his teammates with a short deep laugh and a few words of thanks—even then there was something unspoken, unreckoned, silent. He would stand at the fountain and fill a Dixie cup with water and drink it there, not spilling a drop, and then he would sit down. Rizzuto watched. After games he would hang around late, just as DiMaggio did, and maybe get to leave the ballpark with him.

Jeez, how Rizzuto wanted back in the lineup. But it was Crosetti's job now and the old stalwart was playing okay, fielding better in fact than he had in years. Besides, McCarthy had his plan. The major league education of a young shortstop, he now felt, was best begun sitting by his side. As talented as Rizzuto was, there was no need, not yet, to make any change.

The ancient showerheads sputtered in the Sportsman's Park locker room and an odorous, unidentifiable film covered the old floor and old walls. The Yankees got dressed in cramped aisles in front of their stalls, inevitably and sometimes awkwardly bumping into a teammate. That's just how it was at Sportsman's Park, and none of those nuisances could bother the Yankees much now. They had come to St. Louis and at the expense of the poor Browns had righted things again. The Yanks left town, bound for an exhibition game in Kansas City and then on to Chicago, tied with the Red Sox and the White Sox for second place. Keller was suddenly hot, and so was Henrich, still swinging that bat Joe had given him. DiMaggio's batting average was up to .340, not exactly Williams territory but high enough to

push his slumping brother Dom in the DiMag-O-Log back home. Joe's hitting streak, so extravagantly extended, was now appreciably long enough that some of the other players—though this was not something that they would talk about directly with him—had begun to take notice.

———————

SO JOE HAD a hitting streak. Twenty-four games. Dario Lodigiani had been around one of these streaks before, back when Joe was playing in the PCL in San Francisco and Lodi and the others used to go out after their day at Galileo High to Seals Stadium to watch Joe, just 18 years old, and see if he could keep it alive another day. Now here they were, eight years later, Joe the magnificent Yankee, Lodi sticking as a third baseman for the White Sox. Would've been nice to talk to Joe a little bit on the field, catch up. But that was against the rules—no fraternizing!—and besides it wasn't Joe's way. All business. There was a coolness to the way Joe played, a ruthlessness. As if he saw everyone on the other team in the same impersonal way.

The game was in the seventh inning now and some of the spectators at Comiskey Park noticed that DiMaggio was without a hit in three times up. Lodigiani had thrown him out at first base in the sixth. *It'd be nice to get him again here*, Lodi thought, chuckling to himself. That would burn Joe just right, give Lodi something to tell the boys about next winter: how he'd stopped Joe's streak.

Poor Johnny Rigney though. The White Sox starter sure was having a tough go on the mound all of a sudden. Falling apart. Worst start of the season, no doubt. Rigney wasn't a half-bad righthander. He'd gone 15–8 in 1939 and so far in '41 he'd been pitching like an ace, just into his usual hard luck. Two starts before Rigs had thrown a three-hitter and still took the loss. After that game Rigney's luck went harder still: His draft board called and gave him a reporting date less than three weeks away. Tough blow to Rigney, and to the White Sox. He asked to defer for 60 days, so he could stay on the team long enough for his contract bonus to kick in—and wouldn't you know, the draft board said okay!

That didn't end the headaches though. Now Johnny heard the carping, the complaints about a ballplayer getting preferential treatment. The

Illinois director of the selected service—apologetically, while professing to be a White Sox fan—had even filed an appeal straight to President Roosevelt to reverse Rigney's deferment, to make an example out of the $12,000 a year pitcher and to set a standard. The director just didn't think the deferment was right: What about the clerks, the accountants, the salesmen and proofreaders and waiters who were supporting their wives and children or their aging parents, or both? Hadn't they had their deferments denied? There were hundreds of folks like that. It didn't seem fair to give a pass to a big leaguer, and especially not this one. Rigney was engaged to marry Dorothy Comiskey—yes, of those Comiskeys, the family who owned the team, who had the ballpark named after them. Dorothy was the White Sox treasurer and an heir to the team. And Rigney needed the extra cash from his bonus?

So Rigney, and guys like Buddy Lewis in Washington, and several other players who were looking to defer, heard it from the fans in the stands, and sometimes loudly. *Hey Rigney, Greenberg went in. What makes you so special?* In the game against the Yankees, Rigney had been getting by all right until he gave up five runs in the sixth.

Draft talk was all over the ballparks then—the latest had it that Bobby Feller would get called up in August—and some people around the majors feared that as the war thickened, baseball might get shut down altogether. Everyone knew how Roosevelt loved the game, honored its place, respected its might. The President and Eleanor had sent a wreath to the Gehrig home when they'd heard about Lou. Yet just the other day there was National League president Ford Frick fanning the fears, announcing loudly his dread that a "government official might try to do away with baseball . . . during this time of stress and turmoil." The way things were leaning then—lately Mussolini had taken to taunting the U.S., baiting them to officially get into the fight, labeling Roosevelt a dictator—could set Frick or anybody else on edge.

Seventh inning, one out, nobody on, the Yankees up five-zip. Rigney was ready to throw. *This could be my last time up,* DiMaggio thought stepping in. *One more chance at it.* He didn't have any kind of book on pitchers but he knew something about Rigney: if he got you out once with a pitch, he'd like to throw it again the next time around. Fastball, usu-

ally. You could look for it. Rigney reared and pitched. DiMaggio swung.

Damn, it's coming right at me! Even though Lodigiani was playing DiMaggio deep and tight against the third-base line—just the way he used to play him on the scuffed macadam at North Beach playground—the low whistling drive arrived so fast that he had scarcely moved his hands when the ball kicked off the dirt and into his chest. Six inches higher on the hop and there'd have been teeth scattered on the infield. Lodigiani, though, was going to stay with this one; make Joe earn his way on. Lodi snatched up the ball and heaved it hard and accurately to first. But he was too late, by barely a blink it seemed. BASE HIT, read the scoreboard, and of course it was—not even Keltner could have come up clean on a ball hit like that. At first base, DiMaggio took his lead and glanced toward second. The thought, *that's 25 in a row*, had already been through his mind and gone. DiMaggio would come around to score. The Yanks would win 8–3

A cool rain fell the next afternoon, game canceled, but on the third day in Chicago the Yankees and White Sox played at Comiskey Park beneath the lights, some 37,000 on hand. The Yankees' 3–2 win was secured in the 10th inning on DiMaggio's two-out home run (he had also singled in the fourth) and the satisfaction that McCarthy felt came not just from the team's now five-game winning streak, nor that the Yankees had moved into second place. The sweep and the beating back of the upstart White Sox came amid all the more ballyhoo for Dykes, a front-page story in *The Sporting News* marveling at how he was turning other teams' castoffs into Chicago stars. As if Dykes's hot brand of bristle and bounce made up some kind of magic fairy dust. *I know what I think,* McCarthy said to himself. *I think if any team is going to run away with the pennant, it's gonna be the Yankees.*

The minor miracle of the visit to Chicago was that Dykes had been around to see every out of the two Yankee wins, even with umpire George Pipgras calling things from behind the plate for the first game, manning first base in the next. No one loved to run a guy more than Pipgras did—legend was that he'd once tossed 17 players from a single game—and no one could rankle an umpire quite as expertly as Dykes.

In the ninth inning of that 3–2 win, the Yankees had been down 2–1 to Chicago's sharp lefthander Thornton Lee when Red Ruffing, in as a pinch

hitter, knocked a two-out double to bring in Gordon from first. Dykes came hurtling out of the dugout, arguing that a fan had interfered with the play by getting in the way of Chicago leftfielder Myril Hoag as he tried to catch the ball. At the very least Dykes wanted Gordon put back on third. He appealed to the second base umpire. He appealed to the third base umpire. Nothing doing. Then Dykes went to home plate and told that night's head ump, Steve Basil, that he was playing the damn game under protest. Dykes steamed off, never bothering to confront Pipgras, avoiding an altercation. From inside the Yankees dugout McCarthy had quietly reveled in Dykes's futile stomparound.

An inning later, when a long fly ball landed in the upper deck in leftfield, it wasn't the first time that DiMaggio had changed the game that night. In the third inning he had twice made excellent running catches, once to steal a hit from Lodigiani. In the fifth, when Lodi tried to score from second base on a single, DiMaggio let go a wire from deep centerfield to catch him dead at home. There would be no question, the next time that DiMaggio and Lodi's eyes met, about who had gotten the better of whom.

The Yankees' train left Chicago around midnight, an eastbound charter that would deliver the team to New York City well into the morning light. It was close to 1 o'clock by the time the players got their dinners in the Pullman dining car. They ate with care as the train rumbled along, hoping not to splatter their good clothes—jacket and tie wherever you went as a Yankee, another McCarthy rule. Joe was looking forward to getting home, to seeing Dorothy and to touching her skin, to the solitude of his study, to smokes on the terrace, to getting back to a routine. He supposed, sighing softly, that Dorothy would want to spend some time talking about the funeral and Eleanor and Lou.

Maybe he would take her to Toots Shor's for dinner that week. Or maybe he'd go alone. He'd wait and see. But it was time to get back there, into the New York night. He would pick his way through the bustle under the awning out in front of Toots's place, then whisk through the revolving front door, a path suddenly clearing through the crowd inside, and come up near to that spectacular round bar in the center of the room that always seemed layered thick with athletes and politicians and writers, as well as just about every guy in midtown who'd gotten off work and

wanted a belt. Showgirls came around, and the crime guys in their hats. This was the center of everything. DiMaggio had a table in the back.

A month earlier, when he wasn't hitting and the Yankees weren't winning, DiMaggio hadn't wanted to go to the saloon at all. Sometimes he would call and arrange to meet Toots outside on 51st Street and the two of them would take a long walk through the city, DiMaggio quiet and brooding. They would exchange a few words about Toots's kids or whether J. Edgar Hoover had come by the place lately and just get away from things for a while. But that was it. Then Joe would go back home. DiMaggio couldn't stand the way that he felt in Toots's place when things were going badly on the field. Then, in every friendly greeting and salute, every "Hey Joe, how ya doin'?" he would hear an admonition. As if maybe he wasn't doing enough. Why wasn't he hitting? Why had the team lost the game that day? When was he going to turn it around? In the tough times, DiMaggio was certain that these were the thoughts people had when they said hello to him through the smoke and conviviality of Toots Shor's. These were the thoughts he could not push from his mind, even when Toots came up, grinning through his rubbery cheeks, and wrapped DiMaggio in an ursine hug—boy, only Toots could do that—and blurted out his "Hiya crumb bum!" After the Yankees had lost a couple of games, DiMaggio did not want to talk with anyone who might say something about baseball. He did not want to answer any question about anything at all.

But now things were going just fine, and the greetings at Toots's— those same "How ya doin' Joes?"—would feel joyous and celebratory. DiMaggio had gotten a hit in 26 games running, after all, and was returning as the hero of the Yankees' winning trip out West. Toots could lead Joe and Dorothy back to DiMaggio's table to eat dinner in relative quiet, and for something close to free. He would let come around only the people that Joe and Dorothy wanted to come around. DiMaggio could feel the people's eyes upon them (and Dorothy adored this, he knew) and not worry that someone would barge over and ask for an autograph the moment he sliced into his steak.

Toots controlled things, just the way that he did for Jack Dempsey or Babe Ruth or Jackie Gleason or any of the other saloon regulars that everyone wanted to touch. Toots knew just how to do it. He would let a few of

the autograph seekers come to Joe of course, would bring over a football player or an actor or someone else to say hello. Toots understood the way Joe was. DiMaggio had two fears when he went out in public. One was that everybody would pay attention to him. The other was that nobody would.

The Yankees would be home for nearly two weeks now. Maybe Joe would give Jerry Spats a call and see about having dinner with him and Rose and Dorothy at the Castle. Maybe, and this was a good idea, he would take Dorothy to the movies one hot evening. *In the Navy* was out now, the new Abbott and Costello, their first since that hilarious war movie they'd done, *Buck Privates.* Joe and Dorothy had gone to the set of that one in Hollywood the winter before, had a meal there, watched Bud and Lou carry on. Abbott: *Suppose you had five dollars in this pants pocket and 10 dollars in this pants pocket, what would you have?* Costello: *The captain's pants on.*

Those boys were real movie stars now. DiMaggio had met them years back through Dorothy and had hit it off, especially with Lou. He'd even brought Lou out to Newark to visit the crippled children's hospital as a favor to Spatola. A few minutes inside and Lou would be breaking everybody up.

So he and Dorothy could go to the movies one evening, have Jimmy drive them down to a theater on Broadway and get them in the back way. They'd sit in the air-conditioned cool, have some laughs. He'd get out at night with Lefty here and there too. The Joe Louis-Billy Conn fight was at the Polo Grounds next week. On Thursday, Dorothy would make him spaghetti and meatballs, more than even he could eat.

A gibbous moon glowed above the Yankees' Pullman as it rolled along: Ohio, Pennsylvania, New York. For DiMaggio it felt good to be going home.

Chapter 10
Seeing Rapid Robert

"ONE MORE AND he ties his own record, longest streak he's had in the big leagues." Squeaks had gotten it from somewhere, from one of the newspapers the others hadn't seen or from one of "his guys" he was always talking to about DiMaggio. Joe's previous 27-game run wasn't really official, Squeaks explained, because 19 were spring training games. "But this one counts fellas. And if he gets a few more in a row he'll have the longest ever for a Yankee."

Following the Yankees, and Joe, was a rite for all of the Hornets. News and opinion were currency—you had to be up to speed. But no one, even among all the boys in Jackson Heights who imitated Joe's batting stance, his haircut, the deepness of his voice and the plainness of his speech, no one had it for DiMaggio quite so much as Squeaks Tito. DiMaggio was everything. Once when the Hornets had picked out their latest uniforms, Squeaks made off gleefully with number 9. "What are you so hot about getting Charlie Keller's number for?" Commie asked. "You're a third baseman."

"Keller? Nah, nine's the number Joe D wore when he came up in '36," Squeaks had sniffed. Now it was a Friday night and he was talking about DiMaggio and this new streak. "You know if I ever saw DiMaggio walking down the street and he didn't say 'Hi' to me I think I might go over and punch him in the nose," Squeaks said to Commie.

"Why?" Commie was laughing now, along with his big brother Sal. "You think that because you spend so much time thinking about him, he should somehow know you?"

"Yes!" said Squeaks and his voice, tinnier and tighter than any other that any of the Hornets had ever heard, pinched higher still. "That's exactly how I see it."

Sometimes Commie and Sal called Squeaks the mystery man. No one seemed to know just where he lived or what his parents did. He wouldn't answer questions. He'd simply appear for games, or to hang out. He was always around until he wasn't. Squeaks had quick hands—he was becoming a Golden Gloves boxer—and a barrel chest that he willingly used to knock down the hot ones at third, and he had a good arm for someone his size. He went with a girl that everyone knew as The Moose.

Some of the guys had bought loosies from the news dealer and they were standing in front smoking them: Camels. The El train rattled and creaked into its stop above Roosevelt Avenue and the latest herd of commuters clattered down the steel steps to the street. A cool, light rain fell and on the sidewalk among the pack of green Hornets jackets mingled a few blue-and-white ones too; some of the Dukes were hanging around. There was talk about a dance that night over at the Knights of Columbus. The Bettes were going: Eileen, the two Marys, maybe Janette. "Let's meet at Bickford's in an hour," Joe Party Time said. And Gigilo announced he was going home first to get dressed. About a week left of school before summer break was all, and a weekend of ball in front of them if the rain held off, under the lights on Saturday night, then a couple of games at Hornets Field on Sunday. "I hear Panza's going to see the Yankees tomorrow," Commie said. "If he can get off work." Panza was a few years older, Janette's big brother. They all called him Iceman because he and his father delivered blocks of ice.

"That'll be Feller pitching for Cleveland, right?" Sal said.

"Yep."

"He'd *better* get off work," Squeaks said. "For a game like that. . . ."

Everyone wanted to see the Yankees, and Joe, meet up against Bobby Feller. There wasn't a pitcher anywhere that stirred the fans like Feller did—still just 22 years old, but already in his sixth major league season. At 17 he'd come off the Iowa plains, from a homespun ballyard on his daddy's dusty farm—hogs, corn, a few cows—and struck out Cardinal after Cardinal after Cardinal, eight of them in three innings of an exhibition game. That was July of 1936. In early September, Feller struck out 17 Philadelphia A's. In October he went back for his senior year at Van Meter High. At the same time DiMaggio was making his first mark in the majors, and like DiMaggio, Feller hadn't let up since. Every year he struck out more batters than anyone. He'd gone 24–9 in '39, 27–11 in '40, and now, two months into the '41 season Feller already had 13 wins, the most in the majors and more than a third of the games the Indians had won in all. Cleveland was holding on to first place, four games up on New York, and when Feller was on the mound, every fourth day as steady as the milkman, they were the best team in baseball. During one stretch already this season he had pitched 30 consecutive innings without allowing a run.

He was dubbed Rapid Robert and you knew about his famous fastball, the heir to Walter Johnson's. Brother, the way that fastball juddered and juked as it sped in. It was the pitch that people turned out to see. Or maybe just to hear as it thudded into the catcher's mitt loud enough, in some ballparks, to make an echo. Feller had a curveball that killed too; it came in hard and still broke two feet, a pitch that many hitters dreaded even more than the heat. Feller would throw the curve anytime—behind in the count, runners on, didn't matter. Some overthinking scientists were suggesting that the curveball, anyone's curveball, was merely an optical illusion. None of them had ever come to bat against Bob Feller. The Yanks' Charlie Keller said Feller's curve "behaved like an epileptic snake."

Feller was the big draw in baseball, a reason to come see the game even when the Indians weren't in a pennant race. With Feller, you never knew what you might see. He was like Babe Ruth in that way, ever given to the spectacular. Like on the last day of the 1938 season, when the Tigers came into Cleveland along with Hank Greenberg and his 58 home runs. Thirty

thousand fans turned out to see if Greenberg could get up to Ruth's home run record, 60 in a season, or whether Feller could keep him down. (Five hundred miles away most Yankee fans were Feller fans for the day: *Protect our Babe.*) The crowd did see a record in Municipal Stadium that afternoon, they saw Rapid Robert Feller strike out 18 men—including Greenberg twice—surpassing himself for the most ever in an American League game.

Then there was Opening Day of 1940, gray and bitter and barely 40° in Chicago, when Feller looked around him in the ninth inning and realized he had not allowed a base hit. His parents and his sister had come in from Iowa for the game. Three outs later Feller was striding off the field at Comiskey Park a 1–0 winner, the no-hit feat complete, his Indians teammates backslapping and cheering while every Chicago player returned to the clubhouse with exactly the same batting average—.000—that he had when the game began. White Sox manager Dykes, because of the chill in the air or because of the outcome of the game, or both, applied a hot water bottle to the side of his head.

When the Yankees and DiMaggio faced Feller, though, the crowd learned it might see something else. Sure Feller could beat New York—he'd done it twice already in '41—but Joe gave him trouble. People still talked about the game in Cleveland in 1937 when DiMaggio tripled against Feller (who was just 18 years old at the time) and then later doubled against him and then, with the Yankees and Indians tied at 1–1 in the ninth and DiMaggio down 0 and 2 in the count and the bases loaded, how Feller had come with the curveball, just a little too high and DiMaggio had driven it into the leftfield stands. The grand slam silenced the big crowd and made winners of the Yanks. DiMaggio had hit Feller pretty well ever since.

The Yankees didn't need to have the nation's ace visiting in order to lure a crowd to the Stadium on a Saturday in June, not with the team and DiMaggio streaking. Still, Feller made for something special, something rich. It was the third inning now and more than 44,000 looked on. The Yankees had a 1–0 lead after another home run by Henrich—that made seven homers in two weeks for Tommy; DiMaggio's old bat was serving Henrich well. Two on, two out and up came DiMaggio for the second time. He'd walked in the first. Now he was digging in, like always, his back foot clawing a rugged patch into the dirt, making the batter's box his own.

A lot of righthand hitters wouldn't stand in so firmly against Feller, on account of the fact, they said only half-joking, that they didn't want to get maimed. In addition to everything else, Feller could be plenty wild, more than wild enough to keep most hitters in a state of unease, literally on their toes. Joe was not that way. And though he would never admit to it, his teammates believed that DiMaggio eyed the mound with a little extra purpose when Bob Feller was standing upon it. *So, let's see who's the best.* Keller said that he could see the veins in DiMaggio's neck bulge out as he waited for Feller's pitch.

Whoever the pitcher, DiMaggio always dug right in. His stance was unvarying, powerful and mute. He was six feet, two inches tall and he weighed 193 pounds. He stood at bat as if something were coiled inside. He stood stiller than it seemed possible a hitter could stand. *Why waste energy moving around until you have to? Get set and hit.*

His cleats were always wide apart, four feet or so between them, and his stride was improbably slight. His back leg bent gently at the knee, his front leg held straight as a stanchion. He stood as deep as he could in the batter's box, right foot on the chalk. He held his bat back, the barrel a few inches off his shoulder and he did not choke up on the bat handle at all. "I have always taken that stance since I have been playing ball," DiMaggio said. "And I keep my head steady all the way through. Nobody ever told me to do it that way. It just seemed the natural thing to me."

The baseball men thought it unusual for a hitter to stand and stride in this fashion, particularly for a hitter who generated such power. Babe Ruth had been pigeon-toed, his front foot curled back and pointing toward the catcher before he unwound. Hank Greenberg took a healthy stride to meet the ball. Mel Ott wound up for his swing with a kick that was like stepping over a fence. What Joe conveyed in his sheer flat-footed stillness—what he had always conveyed, even on his semipro teams and in the Pacific Coast League back home—was the feeling of complete and unyielding control. From his unblinking stance DiMaggio rarely flinched or checked his swing. *If Joe wants to swing at a pitch he goes and gets it,* noticed the young hitter Bill Rigney, who was a few years behind Joe in the PCL. *If he doesn't want it, nothing moves.*

When DiMaggio swung, his whole body leaned in and his fingers rif-

fled quickly as he began to move the bat. His front foot rose maybe two inches, moved maybe two inches forward before setting back down. Then with a sharp swivel, DiMaggio's bat came whipping around. He had very strong wrists. "This is the source of my power," he said.

Gehrig had had a wide stance and Dickey too. But no stance in the major leagues was quite so wide or so motionless as Joe DiMaggio's, except, that is, the stance of his brother Dominic in Boston. "No, I didn't teach him to do it," Joe said, and Dom preferred not to talk about this coincidence at all.

DiMaggio stood in now against Feller, with a chance to lengthen the Yankees lead. Feller ran the count to 3 and 0, but DiMaggio did not want to take a walk. Not with Rolfe leading off of second base, Henrich off of first. When the next pitch got enough of the plate, DiMaggio lashed into it, sending the ball hard into right centerfield. Rolfe came around to score, Henrich held at third. The Yankees had a 2–0 lead and DiMaggio pulled in at second base.

That night at Aces Field in Jackson Heights the boys would talk about the Yankees' 4–1 win ("Forget Feller, Atley Donald pitched sharp dint he?") and about the team moving closer to first place and about DiMaggio now hitting in 27 straight. The girls would come out to watch the game, the Hornets versus the Dukes, and so would some of the moms and dads, and the little brothers and a few other folks in the neighborhood. When the players passed the hat in the middle innings, people dropped in a coin or two, money to be spent on new balls or bats or bases, with enough sometimes to get ice cream for both teams after the game. When the boys came up to hit in the chalky artificial light, some of them—Commie and Squeaks, Harry the Hawk, Eddie (Flip) Coyne, the Hornets centerfielder—would get into a stance that you wouldn't have seen so often a few years back. They stood flat-footed, feet spread wide, bat handle back, front elbow just in front of the top of their ribs, quiet and still, and waited for the pitch.

Chapter 11
Just That Way

SCHOOL DAYS COULD feel never-ending in the spare classrooms at Newark's Saint Vincent Academy, especially with summer vacation so near. By the late afternoon Bina would get distracted, feel her eyes drifting away from the nattering nun at the head of the class to gaze instead out the window at the slender trees bending gently in the wind. She thought about getting home. Maybe she could catch Dad at the funeral home before he went out for the night, sit with him a while and hear the latest bits of neighborhood news, or any new stories he had to tell. Dad knew everyone: the mayor, the police captains, the ministers, the men in the suits with the new cars. Also the bakers, tailors, butchers, restaurant owners and everybody else, it seemed, who worked anywhere around the blocks. Every guy in Newark had something to see Jerry Spats about.

And, of course, there was Joe DiMaggio. Ever since Dad had started bringing Joe around, and the girls had realized exactly what a big deal he was, Bina had begun keeping a DiMaggio scrapbook, pasting

in newspaper stories and photographs of events like the time Dad went on the field at Yankee Stadium before a game to present DiMaggio with a diamond-studded wristwatch. The watch was given on behalf of the Crippled Children's Welfare Committee, in thanks to Joe for coming around to visit, and during the little ceremony McCarthy and a lot of the Yankees players gathered on the field. Jerry, with Peanuts right beside him, stood in the middle of it all. The scrapbook made Bina feel closer to DiMaggio. She looked for him in the newspaper every day. That the Spatolas knew Joe DiMaggio made Bina feel special among the girls in her class.

The Yankees were back in New York now and Bina was sure that she would see Joe soon, even if he just stopped by the house before going out to dinner. Maybe this time he would bring Dorothy with him. Bina had never been around a more glamorous woman. No one could wear a hat the way Dorothy could, completely without airs, as if she'd forgotten it was there—as if this gorgeous, flamboyant, frilly, red or white or yellow thing belonged naturally on the top of her head.

Dorothy would hug Bina and her big sister Geta when she greeted them and she'd ask what was going on at school. Dorothy asked as if she really wanted to know, maybe not about schoolwork exactly, but she wanted to hear something, a little story about one of the teachers maybe, or some gossip from the neighborhood. They would chat and Dorothy would tease. *She's not so much older than us*, Bina would think, and then she would think again that, really, Dorothy was a world away. She was beautiful and kind and whenever the Spatolas did something for the DiMaggios—not just a favor for Joe, but after Rose had cooked a meal for the two of them, say, or after the family had sent their engagement gifts— an envelope would soon arrive at 240 Mount Prospect Avenue, and inside it would be Dorothy's tidily penned note of thanks.

Bina understood that for Dorothy things weren't always quite as charmed as they seemed—Mom had let her and Geta know about that. Dorothy felt pressures, Rose said, and told the girls about how when they were all out to dinner, Dorothy would eat and eat, voraciously, unselfconsciously, until everything was gone from her plate. And then, soon after, Dorothy would slip off to the ladies' room. Once, Rose told them, she had

gone into the bathroom after Dorothy and found her there, over the toilet, a finger in her own throat, throwing up the meal she had just finished. Maybe that's what you did if you were a Hollywood actress, Rose said, and shrugged, leaving it at that.

Still, to see them together, Dorothy was the perfect girl for Joe, Bina decided. They *looked* perfect. Joe always cut so fine a figure in his tailored pinstriped suit, his crisp white shirt clasped through the wide cuffs by gold or bejeweled links, the handkerchief in his left breast pocket setting off his tie just so. His black hair lay shiny and unruffled, parted sharply through the right side, cropped above the ear. *Bella figura*, the Italians said of a man like this. Seeing Joe beside Dorothy, she in a long dress, black gloves on her slender hands, and the way they walked, tall and just that close, they seemed like royalty.

The Italians in Newark, the people all around the Spatolas, didn't agree on everything then, certainly not on the right way to do "business"—Jerry could vouch for that—and not always about the war. Just then, some Italian shipmen were on trial in the federal courthouse for having intentionally damaged a boat as it lay docked in Port Newark. The charge was sabotage. During the trial they gave the fascist salute right there in the courtroom. Maybe these were traitors, lock them up for 20 years, or maybe they were just countrymen confused about their loyalty who'd done something dumb. You could see it different ways, just as you could feel different ways about being an Italian-American in this difficult time.

When it came to Joe DiMaggio though, well, there was only one way to look at him if you were Italian: he made you feel proud when you watched him play ball, and he made you feel especially proud if you knew him. Jerry had told Bina that Joe was on a hitting streak, to look out for fresh news for her scrapbook.

———

AT THE STADIUM the day after defeating Feller, the Yankees won again, and once again with close to 44,000 people in the stands. DiMaggio hit a giant home run into the upper leftfield bleachers to make the difference, the 3–2 final score achieved as well on the strength of Red Ruffing pinpointing his fastball and his hard sinker. ("I don't throw curves,"

Ruffing said plainly.) The Indians finished with just six hits in the game, the Yankees but five, and one hour and 45 minutes after Ruffing threw his first pitch, he threw his last. It was as fast a game as there had been at the Stadium all year.

Joe was jogging in after the final out, nearing the Yankees dugout and wending through a small grove of fans that had spilled onto the field. He sensed the boy an instant before it happened, glimpsed him reaching up awkwardly and then, faster than DiMaggio could duck away, plucking the cap clumsily off DiMaggio's head. The physical contact was the most unsettling part. And the cap, worn-in for a while, had fit fine. DiMaggio chased straight after the boy, barely went a few strides before he was hard upon him and the kid stopped in fear. DiMaggio glared coldly and took his baseball cap back.

It wasn't the first time he'd had fans get so close to him like this. It had happened when he first burst into the major leagues and again at some of the World Series games. He hated the feeling of strangers' fingers poking at him, or their hands on his back. The past couple of years, though, the fans had been letting him alone, as if they'd gotten used to him or some of the excitement had worn off. Why, just a few weeks ago they'd been booing him! *No one tried to grab my cap then, did they?* Now the Yankees had won seven games in a row and DiMaggio, his streak at 28 games, was providing a reason to cheer every single day. At Yankee Stadium the announcement of DiMaggio's name again brought loud applause. Things had changed.

In the mornings at home, and sometimes after the games, DiMaggio liked to read the newspapers, sitting outside on one of the wicker chairs or splaying the pages out upon his desk. He sifted as best he could through all the news. Now U.S. divers were planting mines in the waters around the city to protect the harbor; now Roosevelt had ordered the closing of the Italian and German consulates. There was talk of a subway strike.

In the *Daily News* DiMaggio came across an article about George Sisler, the great retired first baseman of the St. Louis Browns who in 1922 had batted an audacious .420. That was also the year in which Sisler had hit safely in 41 consecutive games, and that streak was the real subject of the article, pegged to the idea that DiMaggio, although he was still nearly

two weeks of daily hitting away, might be able to reach it. *A little ahead of themselves aren't they?* DiMaggio thought. Sisler, in the story, was asked to remember those weeks of '22. "Sure I'm proud of it," he said. "I went through an awful lot to make it. You'd be surprised at the strain a hitter is under. . . . I tried to forget about the streak but it can't be done. It's in your head every time you step to the plate."

George Sisler's streak. Could you imagine? It seemed far away and from a different time. DiMaggio was seven years old then. *Nobody hits .420 anymore.* After finishing with the newspapers DiMaggio sat a while and smoked, thinking about what he'd read.

The hitting streak record for a Yankee—beckoning now—was 29 games, set in 1919 by the shortstop Roger Peckinpaugh, matched 12 years later by centerfielder Earle Combs.[1] Both would be in the ballpark for the next game, Monday afternoon against Cleveland in the finale of the three-game series, to see DiMaggio try to tie it: Combs as the quiet but razor-sharp Yankees' first base coach, Peckinpaugh as the Indians' manager. The two men were links to Yankee history. Combs had batted leadoff on the Yanks' great 1927 World Series team and Pecks had been a Yankee captain for years before Ruth even arrived.

These days you could almost feel bad for Pecks with all the heat that was on him. The previous season, 1940, the Indians had disintegrated under manager Ossie Vitt, relinquishing a September grip on first place and finishing behind the Tigers by a single game. Vitt had by then alienated the team with his harsh, often gratuitous criticisms. He would chastise players in front of the rest of the team, even belittling Feller on those rare occasions when he proved fallible. *If Vitt doesn't respect us, why should we respect him?* the Indians players reasoned. Then they stopped letting him lead. Vitt once came out to the mound to make a pitching change only to have the first baseman Hal Trosky talk him out of it, leaving the just-arrived reliever to trudge into the dugout without having thrown a pitch.

It became known that some of the Cleveland players had gone directly to the Indians owner, Alva Bradley, to sound off about Vitt. After that the team was often mocked by fans, derided as prima donnas and called by

---

[1] Years later research revealed that in 1907 Yankees first baseman Hal Chase had actually hit safely in 33 straight games, a fact unmentioned and unknown in '41.

many the Cleveland Crybabies; during a series in Detroit, people threw baby bottles onto the field. This was Peckinpaugh's inheritance (Vitt, as expected, was fired at season's end), but he had also inherited a highly talented team, still the team to beat some said. Already in 1941, the Indians had led the American League by as many as five games, but now that lead was down to two. It had not taken long for the hollering to begin: "Here go the Indians, folding again!" A third straight loss to the Yankees and the first-place cushion would be just one game. The problem, some of the writers who covered the Indians decided, was that Peckinpaugh, the anti-Vitt, was simply too nice a guy.

At the end of the fourth inning, with the score tied and DiMaggio still without a hit, a steady rain began to fall. The umpires stopped the game and the teams went back inside to wait. In the clubhouse DiMaggio set down his cap and loosened the laces on his cleats and sat on the stool in front of his locker. He smoked cigarettes and drank black coffee—half a cup at a time so that it would stay hot until he finished it. "Cup of coffee, Pete," Joe would say, and in a moment Pete Sheehy, the clubhouse guy, would have a half-filled cup in DiMaggio's hands. During a delay like this Sheehy might answer a knock on the clubhouse door to find Ed Barrow there, then go and lean into McCarthy's office to tell him that Barrow wanted to see him. The manager and the general manager would sit quietly together at the little table at the Harry M. Stevens serving area outside the locker room, have coffee and maybe a slab of pound cake, and talk about the team. Which players were really pulling the weight of their salary and which were not?

The league deadline for making a trade had just passed and the Yankees, after stalking a first baseman—the White Sox's power-hitting Joe Kuhel had been in the offing—had chosen instead to stick with the rookie Johnny Sturm, who could certainly pick it around the bag, and who was also getting on base enough that McCarthy had him hitting first in the order. Sturm's lack of power, Barrow and McCarthy now felt, could be overcome by the lineup behind him: Rolfe, Henrich, DiMaggio, Gordon, Dickey and Keller. Crosetti batted eighth, though today that was suddenly, if perhaps temporarily, Rizzuto's spot. Before the rain arrived that afternoon, Cro had been spiked at second base on a slide by Trosky and taken

a slash across his right middle finger that sent him from the game to get stitches and a splint. The doctor said he'd be out five days. Within an inning after replacing Crosetti, Rizzuto had already singled and scored. McCarthy had a good feeling about the kid.

It was not uncommon for Barrow and McCarthy to meet this way, or for the players to see them there, Barrow listening intently beneath his thick eyebrows or suggesting something to the manager in his stern and serious tone. Barrow, and this can be said for him, never came into the clubhouse itself. The team in its nest, he agreed, belonged to McCarthy.

Inside now some of the Yankees players went over and got change from the old wooden chest where they'd stowed their valuables before the game and called over to Pop Logan for something to eat. Logan sometimes went by a nickname—"Nickelhamsandwich"—and on this nickname he now delivered. The guess was, one of the umpires had said, that they would be sitting around the clubhouse for an hour or more waiting for the rain to pass.

Beside DiMaggio's locker, Gehrig's flannel number 4 hung in his empty stall; around the corner hung Ruth's number 3. Tying the Yankee hitting streak record, if the game ever started up again, would mean something. DiMaggio figured he had two more times at bat, three if the Yankees opened things up. At the Feller game Ruth had been in the stands, and been showered with such applause and such unceasing adoration that a policeman had to stay near the Babe all game to keep the fans away. Ruth was 46 years old, retired six seasons, and still it seemed the game of baseball, and certainly Yankee Stadium, belonged to him. Still he loomed large, larger than life. The rumor was that Ruth would star as himself, alongside Gary Cooper, in a movie based on Gehrig's life.

DiMaggio had so narrowly missed playing alongside the Babe—just one season between Ruth's last game as a Yankee and DiMaggio's first— that they were forever linked. "Here is the replacement for Babe Ruth," Dan Daniel had written in the *New York World-Telegram* when DiMaggio joined the Yanks, and in some sense he was exactly that. Going into his rookie year, before DiMaggio had really comprehended the size of Ruth's singular feat, and also before he had grasped just how vast left center-field was at Yankee Stadium, he said to reporters, "Naturally I would like

to break Babe Ruth's record, 60 home runs." Some writers referred to DiMaggio as the Little Bambino.

The first time DiMaggio had met the Babe—it must have been 1937 or '38—Ruth had come into the Yankees' locker room and walked over to gather DiMaggio's long hand into his own warm, fleshy paw. "Hello, Joe," the Babe said, pumping hard on the handshake. Gomez's eyes opened wide. The brief meeting was remarkable, Gomez assured DiMaggio later. Ruth had two names for a ballplayer: "Doc" if you'd been around a bit and "Kid" if you were new. "That's the first time I ever heard him call anybody by name," Gomez said. DiMaggio grinned and said that he felt honored. Lefty was always looking out for Joe.

You could feel the glow around Ruth when you stood beside him, as DiMaggio sometimes did at the baseball writers' dinner, the two players turned out in their tuxedos. They posed together for photos. The writers would sometimes ask Ruth what he thought about Joe, or about Joe's swing, being as it was so much more level than the Babe's. Ruth would chuckle and backslap and maunder genially through a noncommittal reply. Ruth would be aware of DiMaggio's hitting streak by now. He knew what it meant to set records, what they could do for you—in the moment and for years afterward. Numbers and statistics were baseball's most sacred currency. Nobody got that better than the Babe.

DiMaggio put out his cigarette and took up his glove. The game would soon begin again. In the bottom of the fifth inning, the score still knotted at 3–3, he stepped in against the large and lanky lefthander Al Milnar, still in the game despite the long break, and on a 3–1 pitch DiMaggio lined a double into leftfield. The crowd exulted and DiMaggio stood impassive at second base. The Yankees would later win the game, erasing a 4–3 deficit by coming back on Milnar to score three in the eighth after two were out. Peckinpaugh's Indians were stunned, and their lead in the standings trimmed to a whisker.

WHEN IT WAS at last time to leave Saint Vincent Academy for the day, Bina would stand and smooth out her navy blue dress—part of a uniform that she would soon pack away for the summer months—and make her

way quickly through the halls. She had books in her arms and she was nearly at the double doors up front when she saw one of the men who worked at the school coming out of an office. They must have had a radio in there. The man saw Bina and grinned. "You know your friend Joe DiMaggio got another hit today," he said. "Thank you!" Bina blurted. And then she hurried happily out of the school and all but ran the eight long blocks back home.

Chapter 12
The Fight

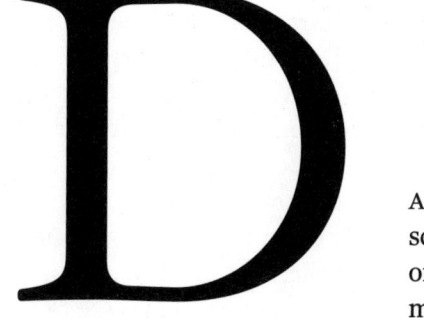AN DANIEL ADJUSTED his tie. He squeezed the tight knot at the center of the bow and stared for a lingering moment at the field. The others in the press box all watched him, waiting.

Joe DiMaggio was standing on first base, and it was the bottom of the seventh inning. Daniel was not only covering the game for the *World-Telegram*, he was also the game's official scorer. *Tough call. That ball DiMaggio hit sure took a vicious bad bounce,* Daniel told himself. *Routine grounder until it kicked up and smacked Appling on the shoulder, maybe caught the side of his face. Tough play. Tough dang play. But would a niftier shortstop than good ol' Luke Appling have put it away? Might another guy have handled it and thrown DiMaggio out?* Ordinarily, Daniel might have quickly signaled for a hit on a play like this, but now, with the streak on the line. . . .

Still the other writers looked at Daniel, and now some of the Yankee players had stepped out of the dugout and were turned toward him, looking up. What'll it be, Daniel? *Maybe I should call it an error,* Daniel

thought. *Demand a little more of Joe, make sure no one says he got one easy.* As much as Daniel cherished moments like this—the sense of real power that he felt with an outcome hanging on his word—the weight of this one lay upon him. *Make the right call,* he told himself, *just make the right call.* DiMaggio still needed a hit to extend his streak to 30 consecutive games. John Drebinger of *The New York Times* sat beside Daniel. "Looked like a hit to me," Drebinger said. "Dumb luck. That thing took a terrible hop."

There was nobody out and the Yankees were trailing the White Sox 7–2. Whatever happened it appeared almost certain that DiMaggio would get another crack at it in the ninth. And even as well as Johnny Rigney had been pitching for Chicago in this game, there was always the chance he would unravel. This start for Rigney now really did look to be his last before the Army took him; because of that determined state director, Rigney had withdrawn his request for a deferral. He was headed back to Chicago after the game, his military physical set for three days hence.

Maybe the Yankees would rattle Rigney now. The way the Yanks were hitting home runs these days—"The window breakers are back!" was the cry from the stands whenever a ball sailed out—maybe they'd tie this thing up, give DiMaggio even more than one other at bat.

Rizzuto looked at DiMaggio, as ever. While some Yankees found it natural to stare up into the press box, awaiting Daniel's ruling, DiMaggio just wiped his hands on his thighs at first base and never turned his gaze from the field. He watched Rigney, and then Keller walking toward the batter's box, and he did not appear to be anything but calm and unconcerned.

Why can't I be like that? Rizzuto thought. All those weeks when he wasn't playing, he had fretted spectacularly, pottering gloomily around the clubhouse, nervous and easily startled once the game began. The veterans tried to tease him out of it, joking, just as they did about the beat-up jalopy he drove into the Stadium lot. Gomez in particular razzed Scooter and reminded him that he needed to look the part—that being a Yankee did not just begin when you walked through Gate 4 in the Bronx but was a defining and everpresent condition. Rizzuto would laugh along at the ribbing. But at night he lay awake in bed in the hotel room he shared with the other benched rookie, Jerry Priddy, and curled his little body into itself. "You think there's a chance we'll get back into the lineup tomorrow?" Rizzuto would say into the darkness.

McCarthy's mentoring, Scooter knew, had helped. Nearly every game the manager would point to the field after some opposing infielder had kicked a ground ball or, more sinfully, had thrown to second base when he should have thrown to first or thrown to first when the play was at second. McCarthy would let out a sharp breath through his nose. "Look at that," he'd say to Rizzuto "He's supposed to be a major leaguer. You'd never make a mistake like that." The manager's aim was clear: to cut everyone down to Rizzuto's size, to make the majors seem like just another league to the rookie.

Teammates helped him too. Gordon reminded Rizzuto that he himself had endured a benching early in his career and had come out the better for it. Henrich offered encouragement. Rolfe pointed out the proper way to shade this or that opposing hitter. Even Crosetti, the idol that Rizzuto had once worshipped from afar on the pickup fields of Brooklyn, gave advice. "When you get to first base scoop up dirt in both hands and make a fist," he said. "Then when you go sliding into second you'll be protecting your fingers."

Crosetti, now 30 years old and in his 10th season, was always onto details like that, little ways to try to get the better of the game. For McCarthy it was like having another coach around. During infield practice, especially on the road, Crosetti would inspect the grass, determine whether it was playing fast or slow. He would roll baseballs gently down the foul lines in front of home plate to see which way a bunt might break, fair or foul. During long innings in the field Crosetti knew the right moment to walk over from shortstop and hand the struggling pitcher the rosin bag, try to break his failing rhythm. Crosetti always seemed to do this just at the moment that McCarthy thought he should; it was as if he could read McCarthy's mind.

And from the bench, to which he was now relegated with his stitched-up hand, there were few better jockeys, few shrewder at unnerving opponents, than Crosetti. Rizzuto had always seemed due to get back in the lineup at some point in 1941, but Crosetti's injury had brought that day sooner than expected. Crosetti had had just one hit in his last 18 times up when he suffered Trosky's slash, but even slumping, Frankie was an asset in the game.

Rizzuto listened to them all. He had learned more about the major

leagues in the few months since the start of spring training than he'd ever imagined it was possible to learn. Maybe he really did belong here, in pinstripes and covering the same swatch of infield dirt as players like Chicago's Luke Appling, an All-Star year after year. When Appling batted .388 in 1936 he'd nearly edged out Gehrig for the MVP award. When he hit .348 in 1940 he had pushed DiMaggio to the final day in their battle for the batting title, finally bowing to Joe by less than four percentage points. Luke Appling was the one player that Jimmy Dykes and the White Sox would never trade. Appling did make errors—Kid Boots was one of his early nicknames—but he also got to more balls than anyone in the game, leading the league in assists and turning double plays almost as deftly as Lou Boudreau in Cleveland.

So what about this play right here, this nasty bounce that had knocked Appling back on his heels? A hit would put DiMaggio alone in the Yankees record book, 30 straight games. Daniel glanced at Drebinger, and sat on the decision for a few seconds more. Keller was about ready to step in. Daniel leaned forward from his press box seat, out over the railing of the mezzanine so that the Yankee players could see him, and thrust out an index finger. Base hit.

Through the innings that followed, as the Yankees' indeed routed Rigney to tie the score, with Keller homering again, Daniel hoped that DiMaggio would get another hit, to remove any doubt at all. "If you think the hitting streak is tough for you," he would tell DiMaggio later, "you should be in the press box." With one out in the eighth inning DiMaggio drove a pitch from Rigney deep and on a line into rightfield, the ball seemingly sure to clear the short wall, or at the very least crash safely against it. In the last instant, though, White Sox rightfielder Taft Wright leaped and with one hand snared the baseball, before colliding into the fence himself and holding on. When the Yankees came to bat in the bottom of the ninth, now trailing yet again, 8–7, their final rally ended with two men on base and DiMaggio waiting on deck. Daniel straightened his vest. In the box score the verdict was simple and clear: DiMaggio had gone 1 for 4.

———

IN THE 12TH round of the fight, Billy Conn really rattled Joe Louis. He drove a left uppercut into Louis's stomach, sent another left to the side of his face, splashed a short right across the nose and then, rearing back, the

challenger unleashed a searing left hook that crashed, unimpeded, into the right side of Louis's head. Had Conn in his exuberance not left his feet while delivering that last punch, it would surely have dropped the champion. And now Louis, looking to clinch, had grabbed onto Conn; it was all that kept him from falling to the floor.

More than 30 seconds remained in the round. DiMaggio sat fully upright in his seat, raised his chin toward the ring. The static of the crowd behind him had become a voluminous roar. Men stood up spontaneously, waving their hats. Billy Conn, against the odds—Louis had gone off as a 3–1 favorite in some houses, as high as 4–1 in others—was winning the fight, having battered the champion impudently and courageously all night long, all the while feinting to defray so many of Louis's blows. Even after Louis had opened him up in Round 5 Conn had not quit, but rather had come back harder still. By now all of the judges had seven or eight rounds going to Conn; none gave more than five rounds to Louis. The fight fans at the Polo Grounds leaned in and shouted. Radio listeners all over reached to turn up the volume on their sets. Billy Conn, the Pittsburgh Kid, a light heavyweight who had moved up in class for the chance at Louis's title and who at the opening bell was giving away 25 pounds or more, really was winning the fight.

Toots Shor could feel that good and giddy surge, his eyes and cheeks aglow. He had bet $100,000 on Conn. Toots shifted comfortably in his seat, anticipating, and joined the growl of the crowd. He held a drink in his right hand. "C'mon Billy, finish the crumb-bum!" This was the biggest bet that Toots had ever made in his life. It was much, much more money than he could afford to lose.

DiMaggio sat beside Toots, soaked in. He loved the big-time fights, the hugeness and the heat of it, the absence of ambiguity. Two men each with the same simple and straightforward assignment: to beat the other. DiMaggio was a Joe Louis man, and had been since before the summer of 1937 when he went to Pompton Lakes, N.J., and dropped in on Louis, then barely two months into his heavyweight champion reign and training to fight Welshman Tommy Farr. Louis had stopped what he was doing that afternoon, put away his jump rope, and he and DiMaggio had spent better than two hours together, talking baseball mostly. Louis was

a Tigers fan from Detroit but after that day he said he would always be rooting for DiMaggio too.

"I hope you win your bout against Farr," DiMaggio said in farewell. DiMaggio, Louis later told the press, had "class, plenty of class." If he were a ballplayer, Louis said, he'd want to be a ballplayer like Joe DiMaggio.

The promoters had expected 40,000 at the Polo Grounds for Louis's fight against Conn, but by the time DiMaggio walked into the noisy stadium in his double-breasted suit many more than that had already arrived. People were crammed back into the $2.50 seats, or settling in closer up at $11.50, or right near the ropes in the most coveted and costly spots, the seats that DiMaggio's friend and ticket broker George Solotaire preferred to traffic in: $25 a pop. The ring was set up in the middle of the ball field where the New York Giants played and hot bright lights were strung above it. A half moon hung in the black sky. When the last receipts were counted, 54,487 people had made their way inside.

Louis was guaranteed 40% of the purse, Conn 20%. But in truth it was the impish challenger as much as the beloved champion who caused the excitement. At last Louis, even favored as he was in this his 18th title defense, faced a serious test; Conn had won 19 fights in a row, the last four by knockout. He could not be thought of as just another entry in the bum of the month club. And he was handsome as a movie star. The betting commissioners on 49th Street said there had not been this much wagering on a fight since the second Louis–Max Schmeling match in 1938.

You still couldn't think of Louis without Schmeling coming to mind. His defeat of Louis in 1936 drew praise and the predictable, poisonous propaganda from Adolf Hitler himself: *See? No black man could beat a German fighter.* And then, two years later, again in sold-out Yankee Stadium, Louis had responded with a pure and beautiful vengeance, burying Schmeling with three knockdowns in Round 1, a victory for every black man, a victory for all of America. A victory for everyone, everywhere. After one particular punch Schmeling had yelped audibly in pain.

Now Schmeling was in the news again, engaged in a more serious fight as one of the first German paratroopers who a few weeks before had landed in Crete through a buzz of gunfire. The subsequent rumors of

Schmeling's death that made it into U.S. newspapers had been exaggerated; he was ill and in a hospital in Athens.

Under the hot lights in the Polo Grounds, Louis staggered and held on. He somehow ducked beneath another wild Conn left, then avoided another and another as the 12th round ticked down. Flashbulbs popped. Both boxers wore dark purple trunks. There were some women in the crowd and even a few children, allowed out late. DiMaggio, the walls of sound around him, sat rapt, his long day and the Yankees 3–2 loss to the White Sox for the moment forgotten.

After breakfast that morning, the sunlight fair upon the terrace, he had left the apartment earlier than he usually did. Peanuts had driven DiMaggio over the bridge to a hospital in Jersey City. He had agreed to visit a kid over there. The boy was 12 years old and named James Licata, and he told DiMaggio that he was a ballplayer too, on the sandlots. But now, after the accident had taken three fingers off his right hand, he wondered if he would ever play again. DiMaggio sat with him for awhile in the hospital room and when he left he gave the boy an autographed baseball and tickets to a game.

Later at the Stadium the White Sox had walked DiMaggio intentionally in the first inning of the game, the correct thing to do with one out and runners on second and third. When DiMaggio came up in the fifth, 0 for 1 after grounding into a double play, short to second to first, he again hit one Appling's way, a knuckling bloop of a ball that bounded onto the infield dirt and sent the shortstop to the edge of his long range to smother it with his glove. Appling didn't even try to throw to first. With DiMaggio churning down the line and smelling a hit, there was no reason to. "The guy runs as fast as he needs to run to get there," Bill Dickey sometimes said. Earle Combs gave DiMaggio a pat on the rump when he got back to the first base bag; players slapped hands in the Yankee dugout.

If DiMaggio had had a little luck to keep his streak going the past two days, he wasn't about to give a hit back. Especially not the way he was stinging the ball now, punishing pitches high and low, on every part of the plate. Getting on base with an infield single, or because of a bad hop, seemed only fair considering all the rotten luck balls—like that smoker that Taft Wright had caught against the wall. DiMaggio felt as if he could

hit anything. Once, a year or two earlier when DiMaggio had been in a very good stretch at the plate, he had asked Gomez in their room, "Do you think that a guy could hit .500 in this league." Gomez chuckled loudly—*Yeh, and McCarthy might come to work in a tutu*—but DiMaggio wasn't joking.

Gomez was at the Conn fight too, and so was McCarthy somewhere. The manager felt partial to Conn, and not, he said with a grin, just because he was Irish. For many people Conn had the underdog's charm. "Louis has been a great champion, but it's time for someone else to begin getting the gravy," McCarthy said.

Louis made it through the 12th and even after the bell the crowd scarcely quieted. The outcome of the match, the changing of the belt, felt inevitable. When the 13th round began all Conn had to do was to jab a little and dodge, stay away from Louis, just as the men in his corner were telling him to. Three rounds of staying upright and the heavyweight title would be his. But Conn instead brought the fight straight to the champ, wanting a knockout and believing, after the way he had just shaken Louis, that he had the power to get one. For Billy Conn this was a matter of pride. He stood in there and traded punch after punch with Louis. The 13th round was like a brawl. Conn was full of energy and completely unbowed; Louis, the great champion, fought back. DiMaggio could not take his eyes off what was happening.

And then in the final stages of the round Louis delivered: suddenly, precisely and brutally. He hit Conn with a hard right to the jaw. He caught him once on the ear. Conn grew unsteady on his feet and his body angled forward into Louis. That quickly, the fight had changed. Now it was Louis who was zeroing in. It was almost like seeing a man rise from the dead. Toots grew suddenly quiet and unusually stiff and the smile ran away from his heavy face. Now Louis connected once and then again, to Conn's belly and to his chest, and then came the short hard righthand blow that landed on the back of Conn's skull and sent him to the ground. Louis went to his corner. Conn was unable to get to his feet quickly enough. When he was counted out there were two seconds left in the 13th round and Joe Louis was still the heavyweight champion of the world.

Louis walked past Conn at his stool. "I knew you'd screw it up, you crazy Mick," said Louis. "The title was yours." He was saying it with a

kind of sympathy and bewilderment; Louis liked Billy Conn. Later Conn, still his endearing self, would say of his failed strategy, "What's the use of being Irish if you can't be thick?"

The fight stayed with DiMaggio, as it did with McCarthy, powerful and rankling; the result did not seem in any way amusing to them. How could anyone be so daft as to do what Conn had done? How could anyone take a certain victory and throw it away? DiMaggio thought too about Louis and how when the match had been the hardest, Louis had been his best. That was a thing that great men, great athletes, did.

But in his apartment that night as he uncuffed his sleeves and slipped off his belt in the yellow light of the hallway outside the bedroom, and as he glanced in at Dorothy, five months pregnant and asleep on her side, something else came into DiMaggio's mind. When he had entered the Polo Grounds, and first been noticed, the people around him had broken into sustained and exuberant cheers, all 54,486 standing and applauding it seemed. Then there were suddenly police officers surrounding him, helping him move through the crowd, keeping the groping fans away. He had not anticipated this. It had never crossed DiMaggio's mind that he would inspire such a reaction, or anything beyond the usual and moderate fuss. DiMaggio had at once felt the blood rush to his face and a little flip in his stomach and then the stoniness rise inside him. He wondered if anything were now expected of him. He raised his hands in acknowledgment and the noise of the people in the Polo Grounds grew louder still. It was as if DiMaggio were at Yankee Stadium having just hit a home run to win a game. But all he was doing was walking to his seat, a spectator on a night that belonged to other men.

It was only later, here now in the narrow apartment hall, at about the same time that Louis was being mobbed at his Harlem hotel and that Conn was making off with his sweet colleen, that the realizations came to DiMaggio. That in these times, doing what he was doing at the ballpark, he was a man on the minds of others, and that for a charged-up crowd at a boxing match, the joy of the moment was plain: Joe DiMaggio, with his 31-game hitting streak, was among them.

The View From Here

Everybody Needs A Little Luck

Over the decades, as DiMaggio's streak has gone unbroken and unassailed, some fidgety historians have sought to explain away, or at least to bring into more natural order, an accomplishment so phenomenally singular that the eminent evolutionary biologist and baseball fan Stephen Jay Gould called it "the most extraordinary thing that ever happened in American sports." How could anyone unfurl a hitting streak that extends so extravagantly past all others?

There is, however, meager grist for the skeptics, and scant rationale to insert the "Yeah, but. . ." that often attaches itself to monumental statistical achievement. And so it is that the flukishness and the minor ambiguity of the base hit that DiMaggio got in Game 30 of the streak—that bad-hop ground ball to Luke Appling that Dan Daniel fretted over before officially ruling it a single—has been occasionally brought into question. Did DiMaggio really deserve a hit in that game? Or should Appling have been given an error and the streak potentially stopped? One relatively recent and nicely synthesized version of the argument that Appling may have committed an error appeared in the October, 2007, issue of the Canadian magazine, *The Walrus,* and was written by David Robbeson. The issues raised in that essay were subsequently picked up and debated in various news outlets—the topic earned a spot

on ABC news for one—and a few of the baseball wonks I talked with made mention of the piece. People will always gather to watch a building torn down.

The case for an Appling error essentially boils down to two separate but related questions: Did the baseball truly take a bad hop or was it simply, as Robbeson writes, "adjudged bad by Dan Daniel"? More intriguingly: Was Daniel consciously generous in awarding DiMaggio a hit—that is, was the official scorer a willing and crucial conspirator in keeping the streak alive?

To the first point: Let's look at some of the accounts of the play as written by eyewitnesses other than Daniel that appeared on the evening or morning after the game. The New York *Daily News* called it, "a lucky, bad hop single." *The New York Times* wrote that "a ground ball that was labeled an easy out in the seventh suddenly took a bad hop [and] hit Luke Appling on the shoulder." The *New York Post* observed that DiMaggio "kept his hitting streak alive on a grounder that took a bad bounce in front of Appling." The *Journal American* said that DiMaggio, "led off the seventh with a ground ball that took a bad hop over Appling's shoulder." And, the paper added: "If DiMag has a sense of gratitude he will search out the pebble that caused that hop and have it stuffed and mounted."

Other, independent accounts describe the play in much the same way and at least one observed that the bounce was so sharp and unexpected that the baseball hit Appling in the face.

No one who was at the game and reported on it suggested that the ball took anything but an unusual and difficult-to-handle hop. Is it possible that after the game Daniel—whose piece in the *World-Telegram* said that the ball, "took a bad hop over Luke Appling's left shoulder"—went around the press

area and as his competitors on the Yankees beat banged out their stories on deadline cajoled each one of them to say that there was a bad hop when there was not? Sure, it's *possible*. But highly implausible.

The more titillating suggestion is that Daniel was biased toward DiMaggio and thus awarded a hit where an objective observer would have determined that the play was an error. Like many reporters at the time Daniel got treated well—"taken care of"—by the Yankees who, in the custom of the day, paid for many of his and other writers' expenses. He was also on friendly terms with DiMaggio, just as most reporters were with many players. Daniel, though, was not a DiMaggio chum or a night-out-at-Toots's pal, as was a writer such as Jimmy Cannon (who was not among those who covered the Appling game). It is not at all evident that Daniel was any closer to DiMaggio than he was to other Yankee players or even, say, to Earle Combs the Yankees first base coach whose record DiMaggio was chasing. Yet the question is: Are those relationships, with the Yankees and with DiMaggio, enough to suspect Daniel of some complicity?

Daniel was 51 years old in the summer of 1941 and he had been covering baseball for more than three decades. He typically worked games dressed to the hilt—full suit, vest buttoned snugly, handkerchief in his breast pocket, the most meticulously shined shoes in the house. He wore, as the writer Ray Robinson recalled for me, "everything but a homburg." Daniel was then the president of the New York chapter of the Baseball Writers' Association and he regarded baseball and his role in it with a kind of sanctimoniousness. He took his assignment as an official scorer very, very seriously. For Daniel the history of the Yankees and of baseball, with all its

gorgeous numbers, was very much a history of his own life; the integrity of the game occupied a central place in Daniel's sense of self. He had covered Ruth and Gehrig and the hallowed manager Miller Huggins, and had relationships with them all. He had also covered and known for many years Combs and Roger Peckinpaugh, the venerated former Yankee players whose streaks DiMaggio would break by hitting in a 30th consecutive game. Is it possible that Daniel would choose to at once undermine the Yankee tradition he held in such august light, and to also diminish his own authority at the ballpark, the very thing that defined him, by making an intentionally bogus call at a high-profile moment? Sure, it's *possible*. But not at all likely.[1]

Indeed, rather than being eager to award barely deserved

---

[1] One strange tactic used to advance the theory that Daniel may have covered up for an Appling miscue draws on fielding statistics. Appling committed 672 errors over the course of his 2,359 career games, an average of one error every 3.51 games. Thus, some among the short-sighted suggest that the fact that Appling was charged with but a single error in the 12 games that the White Sox and Yankees played during the streak implies that something was up—that Daniel, with the hitting streak on his brain, was disposed to award hits over errors. ("Appling's defence during the streak was adjudged three times more efficient than over the course of his career," the *Walrus* essay intoned.) This argument, either willfully or naively, ignores a fundamental rule of probability: the decreased reliability of a small (in this case minuscule) sample size. Twelve games out of 2,359 mean nothing; they are statistically insignificant. Actually, over the course of that many games, there are hundreds of one-error-in-12-games samples, just as if you tossed a coin 2,359 times you would get many, many 12-toss sequences in which only two heads rather than the expected six came up. That's no conspiracy, that's randomness. Should we ascribe to dark forces the fact that in 1940 and '41 Appling played 35 errorless games against the Detroit Tigers, 25% more than the 28 errorless games he played against the St. Louis Browns? Is some sorcerer behind the fact that Appling closed the '41 season with just one error in his final 23 games (only one of which, for the record, was played against the Yankees)? Silly. Finally, even citing 12 games as a basis is a gross misrepresentation. Three of those games were played in New York at the very start of the streak when it was not a streak at all, that is, when there would be no reason to lean DiMaggio's way on a close call. Six of the other nine games were played in Chicago where neither Daniel nor any other New Yorker worked as the official scorer. So in fact there were just three mid-streak games in which Appling played and that Daniel scored. To use these fielding statistics as evidence of Daniel's reluctance to charge an error, or for that matter as evidence of anything at all, is simply false. Herrings have rarely been redder.

hits, Daniel at times appeared reluctant to call hits on questionable plays during the streak. About a week after the Appling grounder, Daniel ruled an error on a DiMaggio ground ball to Browns' shortstop Johnny Berardino that might have been judged a hit, thus incurring gestures of displeasure from several Yankees and forcing DiMaggio to go to his final at bat to keep the streak alive. In a piece that appeared in the *1942 Baseball Record Book*, Daniel maintained that he and all "scorers leaned backward in their determination to make the streaker earn every hit—and then some."

Even if we accept that the hop was indeed untrue and that Daniel's motives were pure, a third question still arises: Did Daniel simply blow the call? Despite the wicked bounce should Appling have been able to recover and make the play? Other reporters didn't seem to think so. This was at a time when baseball writers frequently took an official scorer to task if they disagreed with a judgment. Then, as now, such second-guessing was part of the sports pages' regular fare. Yet no one attacked Daniel's ruling in print. The nearest thing to a quibble came from the *New York Sun* which said that the play was a "close decision." Not a wrong decision. Just a close one.[2]

Was Daniel's call consistent with what another scorer might have ruled? The sections of the *1941 Baseball Rule Book* that relate to official scoring are full of vague, ambiguous and at times contradictory guidance, but one passage, a subsection of Rule 70, section 5, dictates that a base hit should be scored, "When a fair hit ball is partially or wholly stopped by a fielder in motion, but such player cannot recover himself in time to field the ball to first before the batsman

---

[2] Two people who spoke to Daniel about the play years later told me that his ruling was influenced in part by the *Times'* John Drebinger whose immediate conviction was that the ball was a hit.

reaches that base. . . ." Accounts of the play say that Appling was moving when he attempted to field the ball; that would call for a ruling of "hit."

The rule book has been made steadily more specific and explicit as it relates to official scoring and in 1955 a note was added that sets clearer parameters. Rule 10.05c instructs the scorer to rule a base hit, "When a batter reaches first base safely on a fair ball which takes an unnatural bounce so that a fielder cannot handle it with ordinary effort." A note at the end of entry 10.05 decrees that, "In applying the above rules, always give the batter the benefit of the doubt." Again, by both of those standards the Appling ball would have been ruled inarguably a hit.

Would that ball be a base hit today? In an effort to get further clarity on what might go through a scorer's mind, I spoke to Ivy McLemore, who has been an official scorer for more than 1,000 major league games, beginning in 1975. He works out of Houston. I did not tell McLemore that I was inquiring about a play that occurred during Joe DiMaggio's hitting streak, but merely described a hypothetical event, based on the numerous descriptions of the play. I said, "If a routine ground ball were hit to the shortstop and then took a bad hop that hit him in the shoulder, does that sound to you like a hit or an error?"

McLemore did not hesitate. "That would be a hit," he said, "because that play had an X factor and that has to be weighed in your decision. Funny plays like that must be accounted for."

"Would it matter to you who was fielding?" I asked. "Would it have any impact on your decision whether the shortstop were a Gold Glover as opposed to the league's most stone-handed oaf?"

"No," said McLemore. "I just ask myself: 'Was that a play that an average major leaguer would make with ordinary effort.' If the answer is no, I score it a hit."

I also queried Michael Duca, a veteran scorer at San Francisco Giants' and Oakland A's games, and I described the play in exactly the same way. Duca also said that the ball "sounds like a hit." While he agreed with McLemore that the skill level of the fielder would not impact how he scored the play, he said that the speed of the batter might. "A runner who can get down the line would be more likely to beat that long throw even if the shortstop was able to recover from the bad hop," Duca said. "With a fast-moving runner I'd almost definitely have to rule it a hit." DiMaggio had well-above-average speed. He was known for running as hard as he could on every play, regardless of the score or circumstances. In this case, in a close game and with his hitting streak on the line, it is hard to imagine that DiMaggio was coming down the first base line giving anything less than all he had.

IT IS THE stature of DiMaggio's achievement that has made the events of Game 30 worthy of inquiry. Imagine how often a highlight of the Appling play would be aired today. Upon closest inspection the ball seems to have been irrefutably a hit. But of course there is no way to know for sure. Certainly DiMaggio got a lucky break in that game, just as he did with his infield hit a day later—and just as he got an unlucky break when the White Sox's Taffy Wright made the one-handed catch of his near home run in the eighth inning. But to view that good luck as any kind of diminishment or qualification of the validity of the streak is misguided, a captious complaint. As Stephen

Jay Gould points out, "long streaks always are, and must be, a matter of extraordinary luck imposed upon great skill."

There's scarcely a long streak that does not have points of minor controversy or luck. Pete Rose's 44-game run in 1978 was sustained when he dropped down a bunt in Game 32 with two outs in the ninth inning and his team leading 7–2. George Sisler was awarded a hit (by his hometown scorer) in Game 40 of his 41-game streak on a ball that bounced off the shin of the Yankees' second baseman. The Florida Marlins' Luis Castillo had 18 infield hits during his 35-game streak in 2002. In Game 34 of Chase Utley's 35-game streak with the Phillies in 2006 Utley was 0 for 4 in the eighth inning against St. Louis when he got on base on a slow roller to the Cardinals pitcher. The play was ruled a fielder's choice before Phillies p.r. man Greg Casterioto, as he recalls, "went crazy yelling at the official scorer." The ruling was then changed to a hit.

In a more sweeping sort of "Yeah, but. . ." the Brewers' Paul Molitor achieved his 39-game streak in 1987 entirely as a designated hitter and less than halfway through the streak was put permanently into the leadoff spot to help ensure more at bats. Wee Willie Keeler's 44-game run in 1897? Forget it. Keeler played at a time when foul balls (except foul bunts and foul tips) were not counted as strikes, an incalculable advantage for the hitter. Even Lou Gehrig's great consecutive-games-played streak was propped up in 1934 when, suffering from lumbago, Gehrig batted once as the leadoff batter—he singled, of course, being Lou Gehrig—and then came out of the game.

And so on, and so on, and so on. The *Mona Lisa* has no eyebrows.

To put what DiMaggio achieved in 1941 into further perspective, let's imagine for the moment that he was indeed stopped in

Game 30. Let's also imagine—and this, as we'll see, is far less of a stretch—that he got a base hit in the game in which the streak actually ended. DiMaggio went on to hit safely in 16 straight games after that streak-snapping night. So if as a lark we apply those two "what ifs," DiMaggio in '41 would have wound up with a 29-game hitting streak and then, immediately afterward, a 43-game streak, the latter still longer than any other hitting streak in the 109-year history of the American League.

Chapter 13
Something Inside

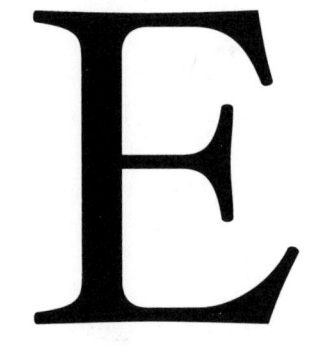EVEN NOW THE sight of Joe in the newspaper quickened Marie and gave her a fleeting feeling of surprise. *That's our Joe!* When she thought of him—and, too, when she thought of Vince or of Dommy—Joe was still a little brother, hardly older than her own darling Betty was now. She could remember playing games of catch with Joe when he was not yet six years old and how effortlessly, even then, he caught the ball in his little hands. Later he had lengthened, his teenaged legs and arms extending like slender stems. The boys at the playground called him *gambi*.

Joe was the gangliest of the DiMaggio sons but there had never been any awkwardness when he moved. Once, when Marie had been downtown, near the corner of Sansome and Market Street, she had come upon Joe and Dommy after they'd just finished selling their newspapers for the afternoon. They were throwing the wadded-up wrapper from one of their bundles of papers back and forth across the wide street, 30 feet maybe. The makeshift ball was the size of a small melon—although it was

buoyant in the air—and the boys darted about the busy sidewalks making improbable catches. It was almost like a dance. Some people stopped to watch. Who would have thought that now, years later, both Joe and Dom would be playing centerfield in the major leagues, and that the newspapers being sold on that corner would carry articles about them.

The afternoon light came in through the big bay windows of her parents' house on Beach Street, rays of orange sun slanting in above the rooftops across the way. The palm trees outside stood still. Marie was the fourth eldest of the DiMaggio children, the third girl. She had long, black hair and plenty of forehead and her face was round like their ma's. She was eight years older than Joe.

Marie took out the scissors and the paste and opened her scrapbook on the table. There were years of clippings of all the ballplaying brothers in the book, of Vince and of Dom, but of course now mostly of Joe. Even after all that had happened for him, with the Seals and then the Yankees, all the many articles—and that family portrait in *Life* magazine, Marie standing right behind Joe, little Betty wedged in upon his lap—and the World Series victories and Joe's massive wedding and the hero's welcome that he got when he came back home from a triumphant season in New York, Marie had never entirely gotten used to it all.

Finding a sketched cartoon of Joe in the *San Francisco Call-Bulletin* seemed to Marie almost surreal. Her Joe. She remembered the shock of the first time she had seen him as a kid with a cigarette in his mouth. She remembered the way Joe would move silently and seriously around at the North Beach playground, or through the Taylor Street apartment, almost unapproachable, a distance imposed between him and all others that Marie somehow understood. It was something different than shyness. At times she thought of him and Dom as like sons to her. When Joe first left San Francisco to join the Yankees, Marie gave him a signet ring.

The *Call-Bulletin* caricature showed Joe with overlarge teeth and his mouth stretched into an exaggerated smile. He was in a pole vaulter's milieu, using a bat to leverage himself over a bar labeled "32." Above that, nine notches on the wooden frame, hung a tag that read: "George Sisler's 1922 Major League Record—41." The sketch was labeled, JOE DIMAGGIO'S RACE FOR THE CONSECUTIVE GAME HITTING RECORD

and the headline at the top of the page inquired: *Will Di Mag Make It?*

People in the neighborhood often asked about Joe, asking not only Marie, of course, but all the family, including Giuseppe when he went down to the wharf to help Mike mend nets or to watch him scrub down the bow of the boat, or just to kill a little time. Giuseppe would look out into the bay, his old fingers still nimble as he tied the becket knots, and would talk to Mike or to one of the men standing on the dock. He would feel at once wistful and grateful that now all those predawn mornings and the long days and the unceasing roll of the tide, and the coarseness of the crabs and fish in his calloused hands, that all of that was over. One of the other fishermen, Maniscalco maybe or one of the younger guys, would ask in Italian "How are the boys? How's Joe?" And Giuseppe would tell them something about what Joe had said when he'd called that week. Then somebody would remark again for the thousandth time how Joe had never taken to the boats, how much he hated to fish. Mike laughed easily. He had a handsome smile and thick hair and he was broader across the chest than any of the other DiMaggio boys.

Sometimes a guy from one of the papers would come around and ask about Joe too, in English. Giuseppe would stiffen and respond as if the question were naive and the answer obvious, "Joe justa good. He's like alla my boys."

That wasn't quite true though. Joe wasn't like the rest. Joe's success was the reason why Giuseppe and Rosalie had the house up in the Marina District on Beach Street. And if they still weren't quite at home there, even a couple years after moving in, that was O.K. Maybe Giuseppe would never feel as comfortable on those whitewashed sidewalks as he had felt in their shack across the bay in Martinez or then in the flat on Taylor Street, but that was no matter. The Marina was one of the finest neighborhoods in San Francisco. The house had four bedrooms and two bathrooms and a big garage with more than enough room to make the wine. It was a white house with rococo designs beneath the eaves. Rosalie cleaned every day, sweeping the steps that led up to the front door and rubbing down the satinwood furniture inside.

The DiMaggio household was smaller now, with the younger boys away and the older girls married. Still the home was often bustling with

Giuseppe and Rosalie's children and their children's children. Marie and Betty were around, and Tom in the mornings and Mike at mealtimes. Rosalie always seemed to be ironing something.

From the front door Giuseppe and Rosalie had to walk little more than a block to get to the Presidio with the fountain there in the pretty little lake, and the wide green flower-specked lawns and the benches to sit on. The park wasn't full of old country Italians the way Washington Square in North Beach was, but Giuseppe did not go in much for small talk anyway. Living on Beach Street was a better and more respected place to be, and really that was what Giuseppe's dream was all about. He had made the journey here alone at age 26 from their Sicilian home on the Isola delle Femmine, and he had lived the four frugal years missing Rosalie and their little one, Nell, and then all the hours and hours and days and days and years and years on the boat, all of the time thinking about making a better and more prosperous life.

Now he had that life by way of the sons he and Rosalie had raised. Giuseppe had imagined each of his boys becoming fishermen just as he had followed his father and his grandfather in Sicily, but only Mike had done so. Giuseppe accepted now that Vince and Joe and Dom had created far richer careers on the baseball diamond. Joe's money had altered all of their lives and taken the worry out of Giuseppe's nights. Sometimes a reporter would ask Giuseppe (as if, in fact, there were some doubt) who was the best baseball player among his sons. The brothers all said Tom— what an arm he had before he got hurt!—but for Giuseppe the answer was simpler. "Joe. He makes-a the most money. So he is the best."

When he grew tired of standing out at the docks, Giuseppe went across Jefferson Street and climbed the stairs to the restaurant for a glass of dark red wine. He leaned into the kitchen and asked Ugo to put him up a bowl of spaghetti. Giuseppe still couldn't read in Italian or in English but years ago when Joe had had his hitting streak in the Coast League, Giuseppe had taught himself to understand the box scores and the standings well enough to follow along. Now the sports pages, lately carrying the DiMag-O-Log, were a source of pride. He sat at a table near the Grotto bar and drank his inky wine and twirled the spaghetti onto his fork and looked at the different newspapers and the scores, and stopped to linger for a while

when he came to a sketch or a photo of Joe. Tom would appear and go behind the bar to put on the radio and they would listen to the news and wait for the baseball scores.

There were only a few customers around now in the late afternoon but soon the tourists would start to come in and sit by the windows overlooking the boats and eat seafood and then at some point get up and walk to the bar against the back wall to look at the trophies there—Joe's various MVP and player of the year awards and even a small trophy that Dominic got while with the Seals. Always some dimwit would ask if Joe himself was around, and Tom would say politely, "No, he's in New York, with the Yankees." Later the band would play and people would dance on the dark inlaid floor. Tom looked slightly worried when he was on the job; he treated the responsibility of managing the staff and operations of Joe DiMaggio's Grotto (the swankest place on the wharf, no question) with the seriousness that it deserved. It was Tom, too, who handled Joe's contract negotiations with the Yanks.

Giuseppe would listen to the radio at home as well, the heavy wood-encased machine another gift from Joe. This was a way to follow all three of their sons in the major leagues. Rosalie also listened to the sports reports. And so did fans all over San Francisco, many of them with an ear cocked for the DiMaggio name, especially Joe's and especially now as his hitting streak stretched into the 30s and moved nearer to the alltime record. In North Beach, Joe was the native son and the teenage boys could not get enough news about him. "Did he get a hit today?" they'd ask one another at the playground, though that information alone wasn't nearly enough. What kind of hit? More than one? What else had he done?

Alessandro Baccari Jr. was 16 years old and he had been an altar boy at Joe's wedding. Less than a week before that big day Joe had taken Al and the Salesian Panthers baseball team to the Athens Creamery for milkshakes. (Though after Joe ordered his two scoops of pistachio ice cream many of the boys canceled their shakes and ordered pistachio scoops instead.) Alessandro loved Joe. Loved him. The way he played ball, the way he carried himself. Like a king. Al had been 10 when he'd first met DiMaggio. Joe and the Seals manager Lefty O'Doul had come

by the Baccari's house one evening after a game—Lefty and Al's dad were good friends—and helped shell the peas for the pasta they would all eat together. Alessandro saw that his mother Edith felt happy to have Joe and Lefty in the house; she sang softly in Italian and the bottom of her skirt bounced as she moved about tending to the table or the stove.

Al and his friends were now big-dreaming local league ballplayers themselves and they were deeply into DiMaggio's hitting streak. They would call the newspapers, the *Chronicle*, the *Call-Bulletin*, the *News*. "We want more information about Joe DiMaggio," they would say. "Do more stories on Joe." The boys got to know all the sports editors and the guys on the AP desk. They'd call anyone to plead. "Let's try Prescott Sullivan," Al said one afternoon as the hitting streak swelled. He phoned the *Examiner* and got Sullivan's line. "Hello Mr. Sullivan, Alessandro Baccari Jr. here. We want some news about Joe DiMaggio. What's the very latest on Joe?"

And Sullivan said: "Huh? I'm a *columnist*."

"Yes, Mr. Sullivan, the very best there is. Now what's going on with our Joe?"

Before long, the San Francisco papers were indeed running more stories about DiMaggio and featuring those stories ever more prominently, and Al and his friends joked to one another that it was really their persistent pestering—not Joe's ascent toward the major league's longest hitting streak—that had made the difference.

THERE WAS NO way to ignore this thing now that all the writers were hot upon it. On the day that DiMaggio extended his streak to 32 straight games, he hit two singles, drew a walk and lined a home run into the lower leftfield stands. In the fourth inning he was on first base when Buddy Rosar singled to left. DiMaggio, sensing he might catch White Sox leftfielder Myril Hoag a step slow, cut a sharp angle as he rounded second base and kept going to third, sliding in powerfully ahead of the ball. An inning later, DiMaggio's single into left-center sent Red Rolfe from first to third, drawing a throw, and DiMaggio, never pausing as he trailed the play, hustled safely into second. *If there's an extra base to take, Big Dago takes it*, thought Tommy Henrich in the dugout. In the Yankees' 7–2 win

Charlie Keller homered again, a grand slam in the fourth, to make it 15 straight games that the Yanks had hit a long ball.

"Would you ever bunt to keep your streak going Joe?" one of the reporters asked DiMaggio after the game. "The third basemen sure play you deep."

DiMaggio was quiet for a while. He looked over at Lefty. Then he turned slowly back to the reporter and after a moment he said: "It just would not do for me to go up there and lay one down deliberately for a bunt to keep a streak going. . . . Sure I like to keep the streak going but to drive in runs is my first and only thought when I step up to the plate."

It was after that 32nd game, too, that a poem appeared in the *New York World-Telegram*, written by the columnist Tim Cohane:

Our Joe Di Maggio has hit
  in thirty-two straight games.
A batting streak that calls for cheers
  from Yankee guys and dames.
If there's a mental strain in this
  our Joseph doesn't show it.
He merely takes his batting stance
  and dares the bums to throw it.

The writers—and the sports cartoonists—weren't alone in taking notice. DiMaggio now was on the verge of Rogers Hornsby's 33-game streak, the record for a righty batter.[1] That streak had stood for 19 years, just as long as Sisler's, and everyone in the game regarded Hornsby as the greatest righthanded hitter who'd ever lived. He'd batted over .400 three times, including an astonishing .424 one year, and he'd done it without choking up on the bat handle the way other high-average guys like Ty Cobb or Wee Willie Keeler or Nap Lajoie had done it in the early days. Hornsby gripped his bat right down at the knob, stood far from the plate and swung hard; he hit more than 300 home runs in his career. He once

---

[1] Bill Dahlen, a righthanded hitter with the Chicago Colts (now the Cubs), hit in 42 straight games in 1894. This streak was either overlooked or dismissed by those covering the game in 1941. Hornsby's 33 games was uniformly regarded as the righthanded and National League record; Sisler's 41 games as the overall modern mark.

said that he couldn't care less if he faced a righthanded or a lefthanded pitcher, that the guy could "throw with his foot as long as the ball came in the strike zone."

Hornsby could be a cuss. Yankees' third base coach Art Fletcher told of how, when he was managing the Phillies in 1925 and Hornsby was player-manager of the Cardinals, they'd gotten into an argument at home plate and Hornsby had hauled off and slugged him in the face. Just like that. Gomez's memory was of getting beaten by Hornsby, then 37 years old and winding down his playing career as a St. Louis Brown, with a game-winning three-run homer with two outs in the ninth inning and Hornsby rounding the bases and calling out to any Yankee who could hear him that he was "still good enough to beat you sons-a-bitches." And yet Hornsby was beautiful to watch. When he stepped in to take batting practice, some older players recalled, everyone on the field stopped to watch his silky swing. Nobody but Cobb had ever finished with a higher career batting average than Hornsby's .358. DiMaggio knew all about him.

The White Sox were gone and the Tigers were in New York now and they were sending out their ace, the hefty righthander Bobo Newsom. Bobo—they'd called him Buck in the minors back on the West Coast—threw about as hard as anyone south of Feller. He'd gone 21–5 in 1940 and won two more games in the Series. Newsom was 6' 3", 220 pounds and sometimes it looked like he had a couple of chins. He earned a star's salary, $35,000, and Ol' Bobo Newsom from Hartsville, S.C., was this kind of pitcher: During the third inning of a game in 1935, a line drive off the bat of the Indians' Earl Averill broke his knee cap. Newsom finished the game, winning it, then wound up in a cast for five weeks. Another time, in 1936, he was on the mound for Washington when a throw to first by the third baseman caught Newsom in the face and broke his jaw. He pitched six more innings and finished that game too.

Ol' Bobo, as he liked to call himself, would sure be pleased to put an end to DiMaggio's streak before Joe could get his name next to Hornsby's. No doubt about that. Back in 1933 in the PCL, before pitching against a streaking DiMaggio (Joe was 30 some odd games into that streak too), Newsom had proclaimed. "I'm gonna stop him tomorrow." He hadn't, though. Nor had he stopped Joe when he faced him again during that same streak two

weeks later. Nor had Newsom lived up to his boasts during DiMaggio's first season with the Yankees when Newsom vowed that he would cool off the rookie. "I know Joe's weakness," the pitcher said. Against Ol' Bobo that day Joe had a weakness for doubles; he hit three of them.

Today it was Newsom, tomorrow somebody else would want to be the guy to try to stop the streak and get his name in the headlines. It was June 20, and the Bronx sky was thick with white-gray clouds. DiMaggio tested the firmness of the ground in centerfield, gauging how ground balls might play. He was shagging flies, maybe an hour before the game. Over in rightfield Henrich was climbing the wall again. Every so often Henrich had Earle Combs hit him fly balls just to that spot, so that he had to climb up the short rightfield fence and stand on top of it for an instant, to catch the ball and take away a woulda-been home run. When rookies first saw Henrich at it they thought he was just goofing around. But he wasn't. "I need to practice this," Henrich said. "One of these days I'm going to have to go up and catch a ball like that in a game."

That was the kind of thinking and devotion to detail that McCarthy loved. Any edge you could get was worth taking. Before games McCarthy and the head groundskeeper, Walter Owen, would tailor the field. When the banjo-hitting Senators came in with their swift outfielder George Case, for example, McCarthy would have Owen cut the grass short so that bunts or soft-hit grounders would reach the Yankee fielders more quickly. Then again he might have the grass along one edge of the first baseline left a little long so that a visiting runner like Case might be slowed even just the slightest bit.

Such subtleties were the stuff of McCarthy's every-day machinations—*there are so many ways to win a ballgame besides pitching and hitting,* he felt—and part of why his players revered him. Yet with these power-hitting 1941 Yankees, the finer points were often little more than salt sprinkled on the deep wounds they inflicted upon their opponents. The Yankees rocked Newsom that day: four runs in the first inning when Henrich hit his 11th home run of the year and "King Kong" Keller clubbed his 14th, on the way to a 14–4 win. DiMaggio was in it from the start, singling hard in the first inning against Ol' Bobo and getting three additional hits. He went 4 for 5 with a run batted in. His batting average was up to .354, fifth

in the league—if still nearly 70 points behind the amazing Williams. Over the past two weeks DiMaggio had batted .468. He needed one more day of hitting to leave Rogers Hornsby behind.

That evening a photographer from the *Daily News* came by the apartment to shoot Joe and Dorothy together after his big and record-tying game. For the photo, Joe wore a crisp white shirt, suspenders and a tie, and he sat in his desk chair reading the newspaper. He wore his wedding ring.

The headlines in the papers now were about the more than 50,000 New Yorkers who were expected to volunteer to become local air raid wardens, just as citizens had done in London; they would be taught what procedures to follow when an alarm sounded or, heaven forbid, if bombs fell on New York City. The Nazi barrage had not slowed, and that day the Italian high command released a statement declaring that it was "battering British troops in North Africa." The German and Italian consuls across the U.S., per Roosevelt's order, knew they now had less than a month to officially close up. The President had dispatched a terse note to Italy demanding "the removal of all Italian nationals in any way connected with organizations of the Italian government in the U.S." Lines were being clearly drawn.

When Joe spoke to Rosalie and Giuseppe by telephone now—broken English on their side, scraps of Italian on his—they talked often about the nearness of the war, and whether the waterfront in San Francisco might be at risk. Rosalie fretted. What would war mean for an Italian alien? She and Giuseppe had been thinking about finally trying to become U.S. citizens after all these years, if only they could learn to read English well enough to pass the test. Joe was all for that, he said. Then Giuseppe told Joe about how the fish were running for Mike, and Joe said that he would call Tom to ask about business at the Grotto, and Giuseppe said that they were all following his hitting streak, of course.

Dorothy dressed fine for the newspaper photograph too, a print dress and flowers in her hair, just a little bit of powder on her cheeks. At the photographer's bidding she stood and rested her arm on the back of Joe's chair, and then as he tilted his head upward and to the side, smiling all white teeth, Dorothy leaned down and put her lips to the side of his face. On the front page of the *Daily News* the next day, beneath a photo of a

woman filling out a form to be an air raid warden at a police station on East 67th Street (she was one of 64,000 who would sign up in all), that picture of the DiMaggios appeared. "Joe DiMaggio got himself four hits out of five chances yesterday making it the 33rd straight game in which he hit safely," the photo caption read. "The Missus was so pleased she gave him this kiss."

After the photographer left and the two of them were standing close in the living room, Dorothy brought up to Joe how important this hitting streak seemed to be, how from what she was hearing in the stands, and starting to read in some of the fan mail, it felt to her like the streak could be something that really set him apart. She said this in a light and encouraging tone. Still, Joe found himself irritated by Dorothy's words. As if he didn't know. As if he could possibly be unaware that people were now attaching such significance to what he was doing. As if, because he didn't talk to her about the streak, that meant it was never on his mind. Joe looked unsmilingly at Dorothy and walked silently out of the room. Dorothy's eyes fell, and her hands dropped to her sides. She had only wanted to talk.

When Joe was away from Dorothy he sometimes missed her so much that a melancholy came upon him. He felt it most deeply in the night, and when he awoke in the morning. No hotel room, not even with Lefty or some gal in it, ever felt like home. He missed the way that Dorothy looked at him when he walked through the door and the way that her arms wrapped around him. He missed falling asleep beside her, and opening his eyes in the early morning and moving his body close to hers. He called her from the road and sometimes they lingered on the phone for a long time.

Joe was always happy to hear something from home, news about the doorman, say, or whether figs—DiMaggio adored them, a treat growing up—had come in to the market, or that June, Lefty's wife, had stopped by for lunch. Joe and Dorothy would talk about the baby and about the things they would do together when he got home, how they would spend his off day and their evenings and nights. When Joe was away he preferred that Dorothy stay at home. And especially now that she was pregnant, she usually did. The first few days of Joe's homecoming were always happy and busy. Dorothy cooked and came early to the games and they were constantly

together. But gradually Joe would be reminded of the things that bothered him about Dorothy: that she laughed too loud; that she still thought about restarting her acting career when the baby grew old enough; and, mainly, that she always wanted to talk and talk. About whatever.

There could at times be a kind of tone deafness to Dorothy, Joe felt—like when she had started in on the significance of his batting streak—and often she said things that Joe wished she hadn't said. She asked him questions that he felt too tired or uninterested to answer. *Who do you talk with in the locker room?* Or, *How come we haven't heard from your brother Vince in so long?* Dorothy always wanted to learn more about Joe. She was always trying to get closer to him, closer than he could let anyone get—even his wife who was bearing his child. Joe would then need some time on his own or with a pal who didn't care whether he said anything about anything. He might call Lefty, or have Peanuts bring the car around, or just go down and see Toots on his own.

At other times, on the good nights between them, Joe and Dorothy would come out of the shower together and get dressed at the same time, she finally tightening his tie just a last little bit, he fastening her necklace behind her neck, so that they both looked impeccable and ready to go out together into the night. Sometimes they went to one of the spots that she favored, El Morocco or the Copacabana, where the show business and Hollywood people would turn out. June and Lefty sometimes made it a foursome.

But on this night Joe didn't feel like any of that. Impatience and irritation had taken hold of him and something chewed at his stomach. That newspaper poem by Cohane was true: DiMaggio didn't betray any mental strain on the field. No situation on the baseball diamond, no matter how large, changed the way he played, not when he was a rookie, not when he was in the World Series and not now. As a teenager in the Pacific Coast League he had been tagged with the nickname Dead Pan Joe for his unflinching stoicism, and the name still stuck. Before DiMaggio's first year with the Yankees, Ed Barrow had cautioned him about the heavy attention he might receive in New York and warned him not to get overanxious; DiMaggio, then 21, said, "Don't worry. I never get excited." And he never did, not on the outside. The things that mattered to him—winning, surpassing expectations, making money, pleasing his father, never look-

ing foolish or beaten—he thought about in his own quiet way. But often these days his stomach hurt.

DiMaggio was glad the next afternoon against the Tigers when his base hit came early. That meant that nothing hung over him for the rest of the game, neither the pressure of needing a hit to keep the streak alive nor the nagging thoughts that came with it—that taking a base on balls might help the team but would undermine his chances, say; or that the innings were drawing late.

He came to bat with two outs in the first inning and Red Rolfe on third base. Sweat already soaked through the uniform of Detroit pitcher Dizzy Trout. Henrich had just hit a ground ball to second base that had gone Gehringer to Croucher to York for a double play, dampening the Yankees' rally and hushing the crowd. But when DiMaggio lined a single to right-field, the more than 20,000 fans at the Stadium, among them groups of uniformed soldiers that the Yankees (just like the Dodgers and the Giants and all the major league clubs) now let into games for free, rose in loud ovation. *Way to keep it going Joe! That's 34!* Combs came over and put a hand on DiMaggio's back.

The news that he had extended his streak to 34 games was sent immediately to press boxes in Philadelphia, D.C., Chicago, Brooklyn and everywhere else a major league game was being played that day. The crowd kept cheering and the players in the Yankees dugout applauded, and DiMaggio stood at first base, arms akimbo, placid and accomplished, knowing he had done something no righthanded batter had ever done before.

Chapter 14

Mrs. Joe

HERE WAS JOE?

Dorothy stood by the bedroom window, looking downtown over the building tops. There was still some daylight left and there would be for an hour or two more. A warm breeze came into the room. Dorothy put her hand on her belly and rubbed the back of her neck. Joe had left without saying goodbye.

She wondered what would happen when Joe came home, whether he would he speak to her or not. At times after they had fought, or after she had merely done or said something that had struck Joe as bothersome or wrong, he could go without saying anything to her for a long time. Hours. Days even. It felt like forever. Early on in their time together, she had teased him when it happened. *You're like a clam!* But even then the teasing hadn't changed anything; Joe would meet it only with a remote look. Now when Joe stopped speaking to her, Dorothy just stayed quiet too. She too had pride. Dorothy might break the silence to ask Joe about

something that, practically, needed to be asked, or to tell him if somebody had phoned. And Joe, if the situation demanded, might say, "yes" or "no" or "later" but that was the whole of it. Joe would go about the house, his movements terse, looking away when he passed her, going out the front door without a word. The argument was in the silence itself, and the silence itself was a weapon, remorseless and blunt.

Until at some point—over breakfast or as they lay in bed or if he was looking for his tie with the gray-blue squares and needed Dorothy's help in finding it—Joe would speak to her and they would begin to talk again just like that, as if nothing had happened, joking lightly to define the new mood. But for Dorothy something *had* happened and had not gone away. Joe's silence could sit inside her for days after it ended, like something cold.

This was not always how it was, no, no, no. Sometimes, and maybe this would be one of them, Dorothy thought, Joe's anger and annoyance would pass quickly, the silence would be brief. When things were good with Joe, they held hands at the movies. At home he might suddenly reach out and pull her onto his lap; at Toots's or one of the other places, they might raise a glass together and smile broadly for a camera. He preferred, as a rule, that she not speak much to other men, and as the night grew louder around them Joe at some point would give her a look, knowing, warm even, that said, *let's get out of here, you and me.* At times there arose between Dorothy and Joe a sudden intimacy that was entirely unplanned, their eyes locking and something passing between them that said *that's the way I feel too.* Joe would lean in and kiss her neck. Dorothy wanted those to be the moments that lasted forever. Then everything would make sense, being Mrs. DiMaggio and having given up the things she'd given up and now embracing the things she had. These days Joe sometimes liked to lounge with his hand upon her belly, feeling the baby kick.

Maybe he'll have forgotten all about being angry by the time he comes home, Dorothy thought. Joe was happiest, of course, when things were going well on the field.

Dorothy had her own friends, many of them actors and show people. Lou and Anne Costello, June, and the agent Mort Millman, who had first taken her to Hollywood, and who still believed she could be a star. She was 5' 4½", with blue-gray eyes and honey-blonde hair that she had taken

to pinning back. Before getting pregnant she had weighed 115 pounds. She went 34-24-35½, like an hourglass, with hips that made men weak. People noticed when she walked into a room. She could still have a career ahead of her, she thought. Maybe she'd start up again if Joe had to go into the service. Dorothy read a lot to help her stay up on things, and she went to the pictures whenever she could. The talk was that the latest Hemingway, *For Whom the Bell Tolls*, was going to be made into a movie, Ingrid Bergman and Gary Cooper starring. That was the best-selling book with the strange first quote: "No man is an Iland, intire of itself; every man is a piece of the Continent, a part of the Maine. . . ." That was as much of it as Dorothy remembered. Those words couldn't help but remind her of Joe. *He is like an island sometimes,* she thought, and she shivered.

Dorothy sat down on the edge of the bed and pulled the shoes off her swollen feet. Then she got up again, unsettled, and walked into the living room. Windows stood open at either end of the long apartment and a light wind blew comfortably through. She went and stood in the narrow doorway leading onto the terrace and from there, looking West, she could see a coal barge silently splitting the waters of the Hudson, traveling upstream. Starlings and wrens darted among the treetops that crowded together on the riverbank. From above the birds looked like insects. Then a hawk came into view, gliding above the water.

It was DiMaggio's bearing, his confidence, and—yes, sure—that silent, almost mysterious manner, that first drew Dorothy in. He carried himself as if he were what mattered in the world. He wasn't particularly good-looking, not like so many of the show business men she knew. Teeth set too far forward. A faint jowliness around his narrow jaw. Too much nose.

He had fallen for her hard. She was 19 years old and working as an extra on the set of the movie *Manhattan Merry-Go-Round* when a man shuffled over and said, "Joe DiMaggio would like to meet you." And Dorothy said: "Who's that?" DiMaggio was playing himself in the film, a brief appearance in which he sang, badly, in his deep voice, "Have you ever been in heaven, well I was last night. . . ."

It was the summer of 1937, and Dorothy was not being coy—it was still quite possible for someone to live in New York and to never have heard of Joe DiMaggio. "I fell in love with him before I knew he was a

celebrity," she told the newspapers later. Now the idea of that seemed almost absurd to Dorothy.

Her given name was Dorothy Arnoldine Olson, though she'd changed it to Dorothy Arnold even before she left Duluth to try to make it in the business. They lived on a steep hill on the west end of town, and they went to church on Sundays. Dorothy was the third of four girls and by the time she came along her father, Victor Arnold Olson, had his heart set on a boy. He'd been a local ski jumping champion, soaring on the long, narrow wooden skis his own father had made for him. Now he worked the rails for Northern Pacific, a conductor mainly, and he wanted to pass on his love of sports to someone. So he taught Dorothy to ski and to skate, and he helped to coach her as she took up tennis, basketball and swimming at school. Dorothy won a city championship in the pool and another on the tennis court, and Victor let her know how proud of her he was. Her sisters called her a tomboy, affectionately though. Dorothy's mother, Clara, sewed all the girls' dresses on a treadle machine and cooked meals passed down from the old folks in Norway—roast pork and cabbage on a Sunday, maybe—and kept the house as clean as October snow.

Dorothy was the most talented of the Olson girls. Besides the sports, she also sang and danced, for the family and neighbors at first, then at local gatherings (where folks passed a hat!) and then in children's revues across Minnesota and even into Wisconsin. Victor's job meant that they rode the trains for free. In the summers between her school years at Denfeld High, Dorothy sang at parties with a college band and picked up gigs dancing a set show with another girl named Dorothy. "Dot and Dot with a Little Bit of Dash," they were billed and people came out and paid good money in tough times to see them. Dorothy Arnold, as she was now known on the marquee, started to think that maybe she was on her way.

And maybe she was. While she was still a senior at Denfeld she won a spot in the Band Box Revue, a solid pro outfit that traveled the Midwest out of Chicago. She graduated early to take the job and soon thereafter, at a stop in Madison, Wis., impressed a visiting movie executive so much that at the age of 18 the girl from Duluth was brought to New York to screen test for Paramount. Even after they'd told her no thanks—her voice was "too low for talking pictures," the man said—Dorothy stayed on in the

city, getting modeling assignments for magazines, singing in nightclubs, doing radio spots for NBC. She took whatever work she could find and if the life was hard at times, living cheap in the Chesterfield Hotel with just enough money for food (she had discovered the pleasures of ketchup soup), it was also the life she wanted.

Dorothy was not afraid. She felt that success and fame were all around her, right outside her window in the winking Broadway night, and that one day soon she would have them both.

She met DiMaggio while doing that bit part on location in the Bronx, and even as their relationship quietly warmed—somehow, from the start, she felt worldly next to Joe—Mort Millman took notice of Dorothy over at NBC. Dorothy, Millman decided, had remarkable talent. He was sure she could make it big in no time if she'd take another run at a movie house. At Universal Studios the decision-makers *liked* her deep voice—alluring and rich—and liked the oomph-girl curves of her body and that honey-blonde hair. She signed her name to a contract that was to last for seven years. When her film *The Storm* opened at the Lyric theater in downtown Duluth, the locals poured out to see the homegrown girl made good, never mind that Dorothy's role was so small. Victor sat through the movie twice, making him late for work on the railroad for the first time in many years.

And how excited her father and all the family had been that Dorothy was dating Joe DiMaggio. Dorothy now lived in Hollywood and DiMaggio in New York but she came to see him on occasion during the season, and they had spent that winter in California together. Once again Dorothy was sure that the next, grander step was near. "I haven't a ring or anything," she told one of the gossip writers, "it's just understood."

The film work was steady and very good now for Dorothy: a featured part in the movie *The House of Fear* and then a recurring role, the female lead, in the serial *The Phantom Creeps*. In *Phantom* she played a determined ("and beautiful," reviewers said) reporter chasing after the evil Dr. Zorka, a mad scientist portrayed by Bela Lugosi. "My editor hired me because I move fast and I'm not easy to scare," Dorothy's character, Jean Drew, tells a detective at one point. And after unearthing an important detail of Zorka's nefarious plan (at times a giant silver robot would get involved on Dr. Zorka's behalf) she would say to the police things like, "not

bad for a nosy reporter, huh?" Each episode ended with Jean Drew in a terrible and uncertain fix—flung into the sea after a boat crash, say—and you had to wait until the next episode to see it resolved. Dorothy wore high heels and lace hats in almost every scene and she never let go of her purse. She could handle her own stunts. Week after week she appeared on screens all across the country. In Minnesota the newspapers called Dorothy "Duluth's No. 1 glamour girl."

He gave her a diamond ring in the summer of 1939 and he told her he would hit a home run for her in the next day's All-Star game. And then he had done it. She went home to tell her parents—*lord, Clara, that diamond looks like an ice cube on her hand*—and when word got around Duluth, the newspaper reporters came to the Olsons' house and from that moment the watch was on. Everyone in town wondered when the wedding would be, and where. *Here? In our Duluth?*

Even Walter Winchell called the Olson house looking for the latest scoop, and in the months that followed, writers everywhere took more of an interest in Dorothy. One paper did a story recounting her diet secrets ("only fruit for dessert, but she eats all the spaghetti and meat she wants!") and others asked whether she planned to stay in pictures even after she wed. "I don't intend to let marriage interfere with my career," Dorothy said, though she knew that wasn't true. Wishful thinking. Before DiMaggio had slid the ring onto her finger he had told her that he wanted her to give up acting. She could not keep living in Hollywood, for one thing, and he needed her around and unencumbered. (Biddable, he meant by this, and there for him to lean on.)

Dorothy had resisted the urge to argue with him. This was Joe DiMaggio she was getting ready to marry! "A good marriage like our parents have," she told her sister Joyce, was more important than even a movie career. The wedding, it was finally announced, would take place in San Francisco, some time after the World Series that fall.

NOW DUSK WAS beginning to settle over the Hudson. Occasionally a car horn sounded or someone shouted on the street below. The soft sun slipped behind the trees across the water in New Jersey. Maybe she would sit on the terrace for a while and read; or maybe she'd stay in and put the

radio on. First, Dorothy went into the kitchen to see about getting something to eat. She couldn't go an hour without feeling hungry these days. It had been a few weeks now since she'd first felt the baby move.

No matter what happened between Dorothy and Joe in the years ahead, they would always have that wonderful, on-top-of-the world time of 1939 and '40: the months leading up to the wedding; the great, surreal day itself; and then the enchanted period afterward. Never had Dorothy been happier. Joe was happy then too, looser and more comfortable somehow, and, in the summer of 1939, on his way to batting .381. Dorothy came and stayed with DiMaggio in his rooms at the Hotel New Yorker that season and when she wasn't filming the last episodes of *The Phantom Creeps*, she sometimes met him on the road. They were the handsomest couple around, and full of one another. Once, at the Shoreham Hotel in D.C., they had gone down to the bar and Joe had sat at the piano and, jokingly, banged on the keys (literally banged, he couldn't play at all) and then Dorothy sang a little something for the people there.

She went with him to the World Series in Cincinnati where the Yankees finished a sweep of the Reds (Vince's team, although he had joined the club too late in the season to be allowed to play in the Series games) and then, stopping in Chicago along the way, Dorothy and Joe had traveled to San Francisco. There a crowd of well-wishers from North Beach, and DiMaggio's family, as well as, most thrillingly, a wedding date, four weeks hence, awaited them.

The days were happy and light. She modeled her dress for Marie and the other DiMaggio sisters, and bantered sometimes with Dominic, and played cards in the sitting room with Joe. One afternoon Rosalie took Dorothy into the kitchen and taught her how to make the spaghetti and the sauce and the meatballs just the way Joe liked them. (Eighteen months later, in the apartment in New York, Dorothy still fixed that meal for Joe once a week.) On a day in early November, Joe received a telegram addressed to him at the wharf, at Joe DiMaggio's Grotto, and Dorothy was beside him when he opened it to see that he had won the American League's Most Valuable Player award.

The church of Saints Peter and Paul, covered in scaffolding for repairs, rose majestically upward from the block alongside Washington Square in

Joe's old neighborhood. It was here that Dorothy took daily instruction from Father Parolin—the same pastor who had tutored little Joe and the rest of the boys in the church's clubroom many years before—and on the Thursday before the Sunday wedding she stood at the high altar and was accepted into the Catholic faith. She and Joe had signed their marriage license together at the county clerk's by then and Dorothy's parents and sisters and grandfather had arrived from Duluth. On Saturday night Joe had a bachelor's dinner at the Grotto.

The day of the wedding, Nov. 19, 1939, was like a dream fulfilled for Dorothy: She was like a princess and Joe like a prince. The police said that they had never seen such a crowd in North Beach, 10,000 people or more, they guessed, packed into the streets around Saints Peter and Paul. There was absolutely no place to park. Across the way in Washington Square, people stood on benches and young men climbed up the boughs of the willow trees or to the tops of the stout pines along the sidewalks, going wherever they could for a better glimpse. Even the bronze fireman statue had people draped upon it. This was the scene that Dorothy saw from the back seat of the limousine as it inched carefully through the thick crowd trying to get to the front of the church. The wedding was set for 2 p.m. but many people, the vast majority of them entirely uninvited, had arrived inside Peter and Paul early that morning and sat through not one but two services to make sure that when the wedding began they would be in a good spot to see. In two days Dorothy would turn 22 years old; Joe would turn 25 in six.

In the limousine Dorothy realized that she, and her parents sitting beside her, were late. This hardly mattered to her. The scene around them was like something from a movie. People cheered as the car rolled slowly along, and some banged happily on the hood and called out her name, or Joe's. Dorothy understood that this mass of people, in their homburgs and Sunday bests, were there first to see the marriage of their Joe, the Yankee hero from the playground down the block. But she knew they were there for her too. Nothing could have convinced Dorothy otherwise. Just look at all the women in the crowd, straining and craning for a look as the car passed by. This was no ordinary girl that Joe was marrying. They wanted to see what a Hollywood starlet looked like on her wedding day, what she

wore and how she held her hands. By now it was half an hour past when the ceremony had been scheduled to begin. The sky was clear and the sun shone warmly down. An ambulance idled along a side street, just in case. Already a woman had fainted by the doors of the church.

The car stopped and police officers came to help Dorothy and her parents push through the crowd and through the front doors of Saints Peter and Paul. No longer did the grand space with its high, vaulted ceilings seem cavernous, as it had to Dorothy during her days of instruction. Now there were 2,000 people inside. Every pew was packed beyond capacity and people stood shoulder-to-shoulder in the aisles and the naves. Boys and girls balanced on top of the confessional boxes. "I beseech you to be calm," Father Parolin had begged the noisy crowd just before Dorothy came in. "Remember that you are in the house of the Lord. I ask you in His name to be silent." Nonetheless, when they saw her they stood and cheered. Dorothy recognized hardly a single face.

A moment passed and then she was starting down the bridal aisle on her father's arm. The church organ played *Ave Maria*. Dorothy wore a white, satin dress, V-necked and sculpted to fit. Five feet of train trailed behind her. Orange blossoms on her veil, orchids in her arms. Later a reporter would write that she was so "utterly beautiful that it just hurt to look at her." Dorothy moved past the candlelit stands of pom-poms and gladioli. The crowd had quieted to a buzz. Ahead of her on the altar she saw Joe, tall, confident and dashing—yes, dashing was the word—in his cutaway tuxedo, wing collar and polka-dotted ascot tie. His brother Tom stood beside him as the best man. The four DiMaggio daughters were the bridesmaids, Dorothy's sister Irene the matron of honor. The altar looked wintry and magical, its white Carrara marble seemingly covered in white chrysanthemums. Father Parolin stood in his snowy robe. On the ceiling of one of the side altars smiling white-winged cherubs frolicked among white clouds against a light blue sky. "Be happy, Dottie. We love you," whispered Victor as he let her go. Their families and their friends sat in the first 10 rows, along with the dignitaries. San Francisco mayor Angelo Rossi had a spot up front with his wife. It was he who had given the chrysanthemums.

The fairy-tale day had only just begun. After the blur of the ceremo-

ny, and the kiss that the women would say laughingly was too brief for their liking, Dorothy and Joe walked down the long aisle together and out through the wide, open doors. Just above them two boys lay inside the scaffolding, like stowaways, peering impishly down. (*I know that guy,* Joe thought, chuckling to himself. *The kid from Taylor Street, Dino Restelli.*) Again policemen, sweaty by now, helped clear the way through the crush and to the DiMaggios' car.

Dorothy and Joe had their portraits taken a few blocks away and then went for a celebrative family meal—just the 60 of them—at the Grotto. That night, 400 people turned out to the reception there, to drink bottles of gin and get merry, swing-dancing to a three-piece band. On the tables, amid a magnificent feast of turkey and sides of beef, hams, roasted capons and caviar, stood ice sculptures of ballplayers at the bat. It was all like a happy dream to Dorothy, almost preposterous. She cut the white wedding cake and fed the first piece to her husband by hand, and Joe, by way of a speech, said, "Well, I've had many a thrill in my days as a ballplayer and everything else, but I just want to say this is one of my happiest and best thrills I've ever had." They stayed at the reception for only a short time, laughing and chatting and stealing kisses, before leaving into the salt-aired night to begin the rest of their lives.

The glow of that day lasted long inside Dorothy, and inside both of them. They honeymooned in California: a night at the Pine Lake Lodge near Fresno, where a little brook ran beside the candlelit dinner tables, and a stay down south at the Hotel Del Coronado, where they lunched in their bathing suits on the beach.

When Dorothy went home to Duluth the following month the papers asked her again about her career and this time she told them the truth— that she was putting it on hold. She had canceled her contract with Universal. She planned to devote herself to "being a good wife."

As winter drew to a close and Tom hammered out Joe's contract with the Yankees for the 1940 season, Joe insisted on a specific add-on to go with his salary of thirty-two five. "The New York Club further agrees to pay transportation for Mrs. DiMaggio from San Francisco to New York, and return to San Francisco," the contract read. Dorothy, in other words, was part of the package. That summer in New York she hired an Italian

tutor, four times a week, so that she could surprise Rosalie and Giuseppe and, speaking their language, get to know them better the next time Joe brought her home.

WAS SHE WRONG to be disappointed? Was she wrong to want more?

She couldn't say that she didn't miss it, the charge she had felt each time she stepped onto a soundstage, the way she could sense the eyes of everyone upon her, the feeling, after delivering her lines, that people had liked what she had done. She had loved seeing WITH DOROTHY ARNOLD in a newspaper display's thick, bold print. Her parents kept a scrapbook of her clippings. Since the marriage, though, the only work Dorothy had done was barely work at all—a magazine ad for Swift Premium Tender Frankfurts. AS A DINNER MEAT THEY'RE A REAL WINNER! SAYS MRS. JOE DIMAGGIO, read the big type. In the photograph she held up a platter of frankfurters and little toasts. She wore a black-and-white striped shirt buttoned to her neck and a look of amused endurance on her face. "Both in the movies (she was Dorothy Arnold before her marriage) and in big league sports, Mrs. Di Maggio has had a lot of experience recognizing 'winners,' " the words beside her picture continued. " 'I'm not surprised that those new frankfurts are so popular,' says Mrs. Di Maggio. 'Their grand mild flavor makes a real hit with hearty outdoor appetites.' "

It had been a payday at least, and the allusion to her past life in the movies—well, at least there was that. Everywhere now she was only Mrs. Joe DiMaggio, or equally often, "Mrs. Joe." That's what the doormen called her as she went out, "How are you, Mrs. Joe? Think Mr. DiMaggio will get another hit today?" She would smile and say that she hoped so. Joe was receiving more fan mail than ever these days; he seemed to be on everybody's mind.

It got too hot in the apartment! When the afternoon sun beat down through the big west-facing windows the living and dining rooms filled with luminous heat. It got hotter with each pregnant week. Sometimes Dorothy had to draw the shades to block out the sun, giving the rooms a gray gloominess.

She wondered if she and June would even be friends if not for Lefty

and Joe. She wondered which friends were really hers. These days even her actor pals like George Raft and Virginia Pine seemed more interested in getting tickets to the Yankees game than in seeing her. They knew that Joe was on a real run. At the ballpark each day the reporters and the photographers and the people sitting near her box on the third base side noticed when Dorothy walked in.

Was she wrong to feel unhappy sometimes? Was she wrong to be sad?

She had money and new clothes, and places to wear them to, and circles of famous people to move in at night. Isn't this how it was supposed to be? Their penthouse apartment cost $300 a month in rent alone. It overlooked the Apthorp, for goodness sake, the block-long luxury building with the huge inner courtyard, and one of Manhattan's most coveted addresses. Literally, they looked down upon it, and upon all of this great city, thirteen hundred miles from the two-story wood frame house where Dorothy was born. Joe loved her, she knew that. He loved her deeply in his way. Her belly was growing larger each day, though when she lay down on her back on top of the bedcovers she could look downward and still see her feet.

The truth was she wouldn't have minded any of it, giving up her career, the trading in of "Dorothy Arnold" for "Mrs. Joe," being the woman by the hero's side, if not for the distance that often came between them. She wouldn't have minded toning down her own natural gabbiness and residing in Joe's surrounding stillness, or going with him to the nightspots that he most liked to go, or even spending some nights at home by herself. She wouldn't have minded any of that if not for the feeling she so often had. The feeling of. . .being *tolerated*. That was it. She felt that she was being tolerated and not adored, and that Joe's good humor with her might in an unforeseen moment disappear.

The baby will change things, she thought. The baby would make them whole again, restore their unity. She remembered the January night when their child may have been conceived, a beautiful bright memory that shone through the days they had spent together in Duluth that winter. They had made love in the bed at Joyce's apartment, intensely and noisily—her parents in the next room had heard!—and then a day later all of them had gone bowling. Joe hadn't seemed to mind at all when she got the better score. Joe loved her, she was sure of that. And he was good

with kids, goofing around with his nieces Betty and Joan in San Francisco, taking them upon his lap or letting them comb his hair and tug on his tie. He was good to Jerry Spatola's girls too, and Joe, playing the same game now for a rich living that he had once played on the days he was skipping school, still had a boyishness in him. He liked to sit on their living room floor, even in his tie and suspenders, and operate his train set. When the baby came, she told herself, the sad feelings would go away and they would be happy, a real family at last, and Joe would love her the way she wanted and needed to be loved.

That was what Dorothy believed. That, along with thoughts of the happy times, carried her through. When the photographers came to the apartment she put on an apron and served Joe a plate of food or lit a cigarette for him or leaned down and kissed him on the side of his face as he read the newspaper. "On edge and tense," she said in solidarity with Joe when the reporters asked how she felt during her husband's hitting streak.

And on game days, in the late morning or early afternoon, Dorothy did her hair and plucked her fine eyebrows and dabbed on makeup in front of the bedroom mirror until she looked just right. She slipped on the pale blue organdy, maybe, or something yellow and short-sleeved. Then she went to Yankee Stadium. Joe would be trying to get another hit, to keep his streak alive, and whenever he got it, Dorothy would stand right up at her seat and clap her hands together and cheer.

Chapter 15
Next To Lefty

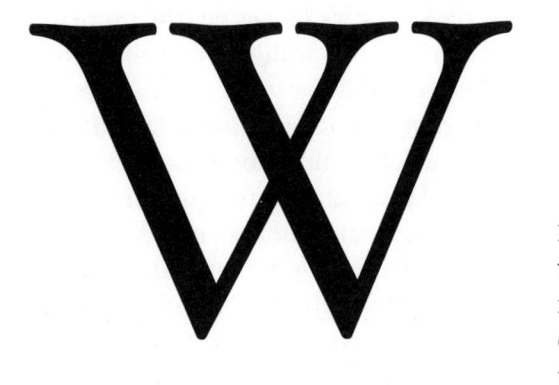HEN DIMAGGIO GOT to thinking about things too much, about all that was expected of him and all that he expected of himself, he wanted a cigarette. He smoked whatever his mood, but especially in times of stress. Smoking gave him something to do with his hands, and lent a sense of purpose to idle moments. The way DiMaggio smoked—the way that he nonchalantly held the cigarette, then took those long, languorous drags—made him appear at ease and comfortable in a way that he might not have otherwise appeared.

He had been smoking since grade school (at first because he wanted to look grown-up) and these days he always smoked Camels; as part of his agreement with the company they sent him carton upon carton for free. He was an ideal spokesman, epitomizing the Camel brand of "extra coolness" and "extra mildness." One magazine ad showed DiMaggio in silhouette, taking his unmistakable swing of the bat, and below that a

photo of him seated, in a suit, grinning, with an unlit Camel between the forefinger and middle finger of his right hand. "Experts call him one of the greatest natural hitters in the game," the ad type read. "How he gets all that extra power into his bat even Joe DiMaggio himself can't say. But you can easily see below how he gets the extras in his cigarette. 'I smoke Camels for extra mildness and extra flavor,' says Joe."

Now, as his hitting streak pushed forward, DiMaggio had taken to smoking two packs a day. He was drinking coffee in outlandish quantity, too—an oceanful before each game, always black and always a half a cup at a time. "He could drink 23 half-cups in a day," said Pete Sheehy, the clubhouse guy.

The daily watch of the streak brought a new kind of focused and unceasing attention on DiMaggio. His sixth-inning home run off the Tigers' long lefthander Hal Newhouser, late in the hot afternoon of June 22, contributed to a different streak: a major-league-record 18th consecutive game in which the Yankees had hit at least one home run. (That streak had been kept alive a day earlier in the 7th inning when Rizzuto lofted a fly ball into the front of the leftfield stands—an improbable display of power from a shortstop who stood smaller than batboy Timmy Sullivan, who greeted him with a handshake at home plate.) The Yankees would go on to win the Newhouser game by rallying for two runs in the ninth inning off the beleaguered and heavily perspiring Bobo Newsom who had entered in relief and who eventually walked in the winning run.

The Yankees were now two games behind the Indians, in second place, and smacking all those home runs. Yet it was Joe's hitting streak that had swaggered to center stage. BIG QUESTION IS "WHO WILL STOP DIMAGGIO?" asked a headline in the New York Post. HE'S NEAR A RECORD, read another. A strange cartoon in one paper showed a squadron of fighter planes—some with propellers on the nose and wings, much like the F4F Wildcats the U.S had been building in such earnest—buzzing through the sky. The planes were inscribed with the words BRONX BOMBERS and they fired upon a gigantic globelike baseball, the ammunition labeled with both "Yanks' Homer Mark of 18 straight games" and "DiMaggio Hits in 35 Straight Games." Elsewhere DiMaggio's photo appeared on a page among images of baseball's other great hit-streakers: Hornsby, whom he'd just recently passed; Cobb who'd

hit in 40 straight games in 1911; and of course Sisler with his record 41.

DiMaggio knew Cobb from back home in California, where Cobb was living in retirement. It was he more than anyone who had encouraged DiMaggio to defy Barrow and hold out for more money in his first Yankees contract—Cobb's tenacity clearly not limited to the ballfield. Now, in the summer of his 55th year, Cobb was playing a few rounds of charity golf alongside Babe Ruth to raise money for the USO. And if DiMaggio had any doubt that the game's greats were now paying attention to his run at Sisler's mark, that doubt was dispelled when Cobb, en route to the links, said to reporters, "A better fellow couldn't do it. DiMaggio is wonderful. I like to see records broken." But Tyrus Raymond Cobb would never be a man to lavish unqualified praise. "DiMaggio is a hell of a ballplayer, but I'm disappointed in him," Cobb went on. "I know he could be greater. . . . If he only conditioned himself in the winter by walking or hunting to keep his legs in shape, he'd be so far ahead of the others that it wouldn't even be close."

It was true that DiMaggio didn't exercise much. To what end? He played ball. He practiced his swing. He practiced running down flies in centerfield, then throwing the ball in on a line to second or third or home. DiMaggio might run the bases here and there to make sure he was cutting the angles just right. But exercise in the off-season? *Hunt?*

Cobb was destined to stay disappointed. DiMaggio, in the shape he was in, was about a week shy of Sisler's number.

———

JOE'S SISTER MARIE and young Bina Spatola certainly were not the only ones keeping scrapbook chronicles of DiMaggio. All over New York City and San Francisco kids kept scrapbooks, and in other places too: Kansas City, St. Louis, Philadelphia, D.C., wherever fans had baseball on the brain. In Jackson Heights, Squeaks Tito could get beside himself with excitement over DiMaggio's streak; he'd get so worked up you worried he'd spit on you when he talked. In South Jamaica, Mario Cuomo left the family grocery store, grabbed a pal, Willie or Artie, and went for the box scores every evening. Down in Ocean City, Gay Talese, upstairs and out of any adult's earshot, fiddled with his radio. And in Bensonhurst, N.Y., an

enclave of Italians and Jews near the western reach of Brooklyn—Dodger country, full-bore—nine-year-old Maury Allen kept a scrapbook of his own. Dodgers or not, this was another neighborhood where the boys told the barbers to cut their hair and slick it back, like DiMaggio's, and where kids would grip a broom handle, stand astride the sewer top that was home plate and pretend that they too were on a hitting streak.

Maury was crazy for baseball, a gift handed down from his father and older brother Sheldon—but from his mother not so much. When the Allens went to ball games they usually went to Ebbets Field, but early in the 1941 season, just before DiMaggio's streak began as it happened, someone had given them tickets to see the Yankees and the Indians up in the Bronx. They were told to pick up the tickets at a booth outside Yankee Stadium, near third base. To which Frances, Maury's mom, replied: "Where's third base?"

At about seven o'clock each night, Maury got his newspapers down the block at Joe's Candy Store, and even if he turned first to the sports pages like all his friends did, he could not miss the headlines in the news. You might see the score of the Yankees game or the Dodgers game on Page One, or a picture of DiMaggio, and you might see a headline like this, in big type, an inch and a half high: GERMANY DECLARES WAR ON RUSSIA; TROOPS MOVE.

Maury knew about the Nazis, and about how Hitler hated the Jews. His parents talked about this sometimes in their low adults-only voices. But Maury was Jewish! And so were a lot of his friends! It was a strange thing to be nine years old and learn that the leader of a big, famous country, a man who has never met you, hates you, and might want to kill you even. The word *Hitler* cut through any whispering or any conversation like a line of barbed wire. There were photos in the paper of Nazi soldiers with their guns pointed at the backs of Russian people, forcing them to march.

Still, the war seemed far away. "This doesn't really affect us," his parents told the kids. Jews may not have been allowed to hold good jobs in Germany, but Maury's dad, Harry, sure had one, selling coffee and tea to hotels and restaurants. The Allens rented a comfortable five-room apartment that Frances kept in fine order. Bensonhurst, Brooklyn, was a safe, happy place and to Maury the war was a distant malevolence. It got scary only when he let himself think about it too long. He might see that headline, the Nazis on the move or the Luftwaffe dropping bombs,

but then he could turn back to the sports pages and see that DiMaggio, his hero, had hit in another game, a home run this time on a line into the right centerfield seats. The hitting streak was alive and Maury read all about it and then clipped out his favorite articles and the best of the photographs, to save, he imagined, forever.

WHENEVER DIMAGGIO NEEDED a haircut—and in summertime, when the humid air curled the ends of his dark locks, it seemed he needed one every two weeks—he liked to go to Vincent's. The three-chair barbershop on 8th Avenue in Newark, around the corner from St. Lucy's Church and just a few blocks from the Spatolas, had no name on the window, no fancy storefront display. Just a couple of guys with shears, a place to tarry and read the city papers or the Italian press and, quite often, breathe the scent of something cooking in the back. Vincent cut Joe's hair for free.

"Don't say anything about the streak!" uncle Jimmy had warned the kids before Joe came to the barbershop that day. "Don't ask him about it, don't tell him you know about it, just don't say anything at all. You understand me?" When Jimmy Ceres gave an order like that, boys like his 16-year-old nephew Larry Chiaravallo knew well enough to listen. Jimmy's hands looked like two-pound rib-eyes. None of the boys would have dared to call him Peanuts to his face.

Peanuts picked up DiMaggio in Manhattan and drove him to Newark, over the river, past the long stretches of green parkland and then into and through the bustling daytime streets of the first ward. The Cadillac, as always, turned heads. How could you miss it? Gun-metal gray, red leather seats, a license plate that read JOE D-5 and you-know-who riding inside. A crowd gathered as soon as the car eased to a stop on 8th Avenue. "Who wants to wash Joe's car?" uncle Jimmy asked, stepping out into the late-morning light. They all did, of course, and Jimmy tossed one of the older boys the keys. Soon the Cadillac was in the care of a dozen loving hands, being soaped up, rubbed down, Simonized until it shone. The kids knew that DiMaggio wouldn't pay them a nickel for the work but none of them minded. They only hoped that when DiMaggio came out of Vincent's and saw the gleaming car, he might stop and autograph a baseball or two, or

grab one of their playground bats and show them just how he liked to grip it.

Peanuts's nephew Larry swept the barbershop floor and tried to look casual. In a few moments Larry would put the hot towel on Joe's face, apply the soap, get him ready for his shave. It was all that Larry could do not to ask, "So how long do you think you'll keep this streak going, Mr. DiMaggio?" or something like that, something to tell his pals from the McKinley School, but he kept quiet.

Peanuts took a seat near the window, DiMaggio the chair nearest the back. Everyone in the barbershop was in a good mood; the men chatted and laughed easily together. The radio played. As Joe was attended to, first the shave and then Vincent's meticulous trim, the shop gradually began to get crowded with people who, they said, had just happened by. *Oh, Joe, what a surprise. I didn't know you were around today.*

Everyone in the place was Italian. Sometimes during the haircut Jerry Spatola would swing in, on his way to this or that, and greet DiMaggio and see if he wanted to come to the Vittorio Castle that night *(Richie would love to see you, Joe)*, or whether there was anything else DiMaggio needed. The year before, on Joe DiMaggio Night at a Bears game in Newark, Joe and Dorothy had hung around and smoked at Vincent's before going over to the Stadium. It was like family at the barbershop, and after getting his haircut Joe would wander back into the kitchen and say hello to Vincent's pretty wife Carmelina who would put a plate of manicotti before him.

They all fussed over Joe here. And he knew that no matter how many times he offered, no one would take a dime for anything. He could relax. Around Vincent's everyone understood the importance of things left unsaid. No one asked him a lot of questions—not even when his name came over the radio in the sports news. Out here, Joe never had to think too hard or worry about what he said.

DiMaggio and Peanuts stepped out of the barbershop and the kids gathered around. DiMaggio signed a baseball, a glove, someone's scrapbook. The heat had broken from recent days and the high sun fell through the fluttering leaves of the ginkgo trees, casting shadows onto the street and reflecting off the polished Cadillac. An old horse-drawn ice truck clomped and rattled by.

Across the Hudson the struggling St. Louis Browns were arriving in

New York for three games and DiMaggio knew that the newspaper guys would soon be asking him about his hitting streak. He did not look forward to it. Sometimes writers phrased things in such a way that DiMaggio didn't understand at first what was being said. He would take a few moments to be absolutely sure of the meaning of a question before he answered it. Teammates could see DiMaggio pause, his face stiff and the faintest look of uncertainty, even suspicion, in his eyes. The crucial thing to DiMaggio was to not have what he said come out wrong, to not have it betray any sense that he was somehow confused, or overmatched. He often feared that his words might make him seem like a rube—or worse, dumb. He hated the thought of being embarrassed in this way.

It was the same reason he'd never even taken a chance on making it through Galileo High; surely the other students would have laughed at him when they saw him struggling to understand. And how would he have looked next to Dom, for whom the reading and the studies came easy?

At Yankee Stadium, the writers sometimes spoke quickly, back and forth, bantering. Lefty or Henrich or Crosetti, or even the rookie Rizzuto seemed to have no trouble bantering back. For Joe, the words were sometimes unfamiliar, or he recognized them but wasn't sure what they meant. He was getting better though. DiMaggio read the newspapers— headlines and parts of the stories anyway—and tried to make sense of the way the language was being used, tried to make mental notes to carry with him. His goal was to learn two new words from the dictionary each day, a practice he had begun while with the Seals in San Francisco. He preferred to learn big words for the most part. They sounded smarter. "Hey Joe, where've you been?" one of his Seals teammates might ask in those days. And Joe would reply, "Oh, I've been nonchalantly meandering down the pike."

He envied Dorothy that she had no troubles with such things. Just like Dom, Dorothy always seemed to know just what to say and how to say it. For Joe, when he was asked to speak to a group or at any other formal gathering, he became nervous. He brought Lefty along to banquets.

He had decided that the best thing to do before speaking to reporters was to prepare and rehearse. It was good, he felt, to appear completely cool and unbothered by the hitting streak. As ever, Dead Pan Joe. On the day

before the first of the three Browns games, he was asked whether chasing Sisler's record was causing him concern; DiMaggio said, "Why should I worry? The only time to worry is when you're not hitting. I'm not worried now—I'm happy. It's no strain to keep on hitting, it's a strain not to be hitting." DiMaggio did not mention to the reporters that sometimes his stomach hurt; it was better to keep emotions to yourself. He was sure of that.

The Yankees clubhouse, before games and certainly after a loss, could be quiet and serious. There was work to be done. If DiMaggio had an exceptional fluidity on the baseball field, a grace that made it seem as if playing baseball was the reason he was put on earth, he could in the game's social circles be inartful and stiff. In the locker room, he preferred less conversation, less repartee. This was fine with McCarthy. The raucousness and joviality that had characterized the Yankee clubhouse when Babe Ruth was at the center of it had long since faded. Sometimes guys would complain among themselves that the place had grown as quiet as a church. But that was the tone DiMaggio set, and no one wanted to behave in a way that would lead him to cast his fish-eye upon them, that look of displeasure that might mean he was shutting you out. The players by and large kept the joking and the banter to small groups and to appropriate times.

Of course none of this applied to Lefty Vernon Gomez—Goofy, El Goofo, the Gay Caballero—who could break any silence, liven any mood, cut through DiMaggio's shield with a simple quip. Lefty was willing and eager to lampoon anyone, to put humor into any situation, to talk an endless stream, and in 1941 he was probably the best friend that Joe DiMaggio had.

When DiMaggio first came to New York in '36, Gomez was the Yankees' ace, one season removed from a record of 26–5 and as effective as just about any pitcher alive. McCarthy instinctively put the two of them together to room on the road, the silent rookie and the garrulous lefthander. Jack Sprat and his wife, the manager figured, and he figured right. The pitcher had a lightness and an ease about him that held DiMaggio in thrall. "I wish I could be like Lefty," Joe would say, watching his friend hold court at the end of a bar. "But I can't."

Lefty loved to go out at night, but the next day he came to the ballpark and won his game. He had been with the Yankees for six full seasons, had

beaten the Cubs in the '32 World Series, had roomed, for a while, with the Babe. Gomez, McCarthy made clear, was to look out for DiMaggio in the Big City. He made DiMaggio laugh and protected him as best he could from the favor-seekers and the hangers-on. When DiMaggio returned to the Yankees clubhouse early in the 1937 season wearing a suit, still sidelined after having had his tonsils and adenoids removed, Gomez hammered it up for the cameras, performing an impromptu "examination" and peering soberly down into DiMaggio's throat. Nothing ever seemed dire when Lefty was around.

The reporters adored him, everyone did. One year, after signing a contract, Gomez pledged to donate part of his salary to an "asylum for southpaws," or, better yet, "to a home for astigmatic writers." It was Gomez who said of the stocky Charlie Keller, with his squarish head and dark eyes, that no scout had discovered him but rather that the famous exotic animal collector Frank Buck "had brought him back alive." (For the rest of his career, Keller never shook the nickname King Kong.) Gomez had been known to stop, mid-windup, to gaze at an airplane flying overhead. He scooped up caps that fans tossed onto the field and kept them to wear himself. He needled Lou Gehrig even into Gehrig's awful, final months, and Gehrig, you could tell by his smile, was grateful for it. Vernon Gomez, born in Rodeo, Calif., the son of an Irishwoman and a Spanish cowhand, married a movie starlet—the former June O'Dea before she gave up her career for married life. He named their first daughter Vernona.

Gomez, besides being nimble with a joke, was also exceptionally handy. One day near the end of the 1940 season DiMaggio found something wrong with his sunglasses. He brought them to Gomez in the dugout. "Think you can fix 'em, Lefty?" Sure enough after some fiddling Gomez had straightened them out. "That's baseball for you," Lefty griped good-naturedly as he handed the sunglasses back to Joe. "You start out being a great lefthanded pitcher and wind up your career being a valet to a lousy outfielder."

OVER THE YEARS a change came gradually and naturally to the friendship of Lefty and Joe, even as their relationship deepened to include their wives and occasional day-trips into the country. DiMaggio began flowering as a superstar while Gomez's career began to wilt. Gomez took to re-

ferring to DiMaggio as "the captain" of their hotel room, the one who set the night's agenda. Lefty realized that now he needed Joe even more than Joe needed him. In 1940, bothered by injuries to his wrist and arm as well as a chronically aching back, Gomez won just three games and for the first time in the eight-year history of the All-Star game was not chosen for the American League team. The Yankees believed they had younger and better pitchers to take his place, and when the season ended they let it be known that they planned to trade Gomez or sell him to another club. But on a late December day, Christmas in the air, Lefty showed up at Ed Barrow's office at Yankee Stadium and wheedled and cajoled and charmed and vowed and got himself a reprieve: one more year.

Gomez and DiMaggio knew that another lousy season would end the pitcher's Yankees career and it seemed to their teammates that DiMaggio played with an added intensity on the days that Gomez pitched in 1941— and that Gomez recognized that effort and responded. *DiMaggio is good for Gomez*, is how the rookie first baseman Johnny Sturm saw it. Gomez began warming up earlier and more deliberately before his starts. He no longer threw near to 100 mph, but he pitched more purposefully, more carefully. Still, at 32, he had not shed his affection for whimsy. In one of Rizzuto's first games—an exhibition against the Dodgers at a packed Ebbets Field—Lefty suddenly called the rookie shortstop to the mound in the middle of an inning. "How do you like being with the Yankees?" Gomez asked.

"Fine, I think it's great," Rizzuto said.

"Are your mother and father here today?"

"Yes, they're here," said Rizzuto, quizzically.

"Well just stand here," Lefty said. "I want to talk to you a little while. Just think: Your parents can go home tonight and say that 40,000 people saw their little boy talking to the great Gomez."

In Gomez's five starts over the course of DiMaggio's hitting streak the Yankees had not lost. Lefty was beginning a resurgence that would lead him to go 15–5, his best record in seven years. Like all of his teammates, and more than most of them, Gomez felt the excitement of the hitting streak. Now, with Joe trying to make it 36 in a row, Lefty was pitching against the Browns' Bob Muncrief, a 6' 2" 190-pound righthander in his first full season in the major leagues. Muncrief was 25 years old and re-

lied on a sharp, biting curveball—a kind of slider, really—as his out pitch.

DiMaggio grounded harmlessly to third base in the first inning and popped up a ball backward and into the glove of the St. Louis catcher Rick Ferrell in the third. It was a Tuesday afternoon and each time that DiMaggio came to the plate the Yankee Stadium crowd leaned forward and called out to him. *All right Joe! Let's get one off this bum.* Before the game DiMaggio had been summoned onto the field and given a good luck gift—a small, smiling Buddha—from the Young Yankees, a team of Chinese boys who played in downtown Manhattan. The boys had stood around DiMaggio, seven of them, in their button-up uniforms and striped socks and looked at him in awe.

He thought he had his hit in the fifth inning, and so did just about everyone in the park. The high drive off DiMaggio's bat flew to the deepest part of the Stadium, into left centerfield and more than 450 feet from home plate, a triple by the looks of it. But after a long and frenzied gallop, the fine fielding St. Louis leftfielder Roy Cullenbine got to the ball and reached over his shoulder to glove it. Henrich, on first base at the beginning of the play, was around third when Cullenbine made the catch. The Browns easily doubled him up.

Now, two innings later, DiMaggio stood in centerfield. Before each pitch he raised his right hand and shielded his eyes as he looked toward home plate. The sun was falling and DiMaggio knew that the time of the game was approaching when hitting became more difficult. Shadows would cloak the batters while the pitcher remained in light. He would have one more crack at Muncrief, he thought.

In the outfield DiMaggio repositioned himself before each batter and his doing so served as an unspoken cue. Henrich would look over from rightfield and Keller from left and by seeing where DiMaggio stood, they understood how to position themselves too. He felt fidgety. In six innings just one fly ball had come his way. Chances were he wouldn't be up at bat again for a while. Mainly, he wanted a cigarette. He wanted Gomez to wrap up another inning so that he could put down his glove and go into the dugout and then disappear into the tunnel to that cavernous underbelly of the stadium and smoke there, out of sight of anyone. A few moments to himself. This wasn't the first time during the hitting streak that

DiMaggio had stood in the outfield and thought about having a smoke.

Gomez was pitching well—the Yanks led 4–0 after six—and then with the Yankees batting in the seventh inning an unlikely event occurred. Lefty hit a single. ("I have only one weakness: a pitched ball," he liked to say of his batting prowess. Or, "I'm a good .150 hitter in any league, and I don't care who's pitching.") So delighted was Gomez with his base hit that when he reached first base he put out his hand to umpire Harry Geisel and Geisel shook it, sending ripples of laughter through the crowd and the Yankees dugout. Even McCarthy had to laugh at that. And Joe.

Now it was the eighth inning and the game seemed salted away. Henrich had just hit a two-run home run and the Yankees were ahead 6–0. There was nobody on base. As DiMaggio came to the plate the fans in the crowd began to chant, "We want a hit! We want a hit!" They knew that this would almost certainly be DiMaggio's last at bat of the game.

Muncrief looked over and saw Browns manager Luke Sewell emerging from the first base dugout. Was he coming to take Muncrief out of the game? Sewell had been on the St. Louis job for just a couple of weeks and he had an ornery side. "Walk him," Sewell said when he got out to Muncrief. The pitcher looked at his manager in surprise. "But, why?" Muncrief said.

"Because I don't want this son of a bitch to get a base hit."

"Skip, I'm not walking him," said Muncrief.

"You don't walk him, I'm going to take you out of the game."

Bob Muncrief was the child of sharecroppers—the family had gotten through the Depression picking cotton on other people's land for pennies a day. They lived in Madill, Okla., and they kept a couple of cows and a couple of pigs. When Bob had a chance out of high school to go to college on a basketball scholarship, he instead accepted an offer of $60 a month to play in the Texas League. That was more money than he or his parents had ever seen. Each month he sent $45 home and lived off the rest. Bob Muncrief was not someone to take an opportunity for granted. He had once pitched against the great Dizzy Dean in an exhibition game down in San Antonio. Not just pitched against him, he beat him 2–1. Winning that game may have been what really got Muncrief noticed, got him called up to the big leagues. Now Muncrief wanted to be the pitcher who

stopped DiMaggio's streak—there was nothing in that moment that Muncrief wanted more—but he wanted to earn it, to set DiMaggio down fair and square one more time. *Not* to end things with a walk.

"You take me out of the game and I'll go up there in front of everyone and apologize to DiMaggio. He doesn't deserve this. Let me get him out, Skip."

Sewell looked out to the bullpen. He didn't have much there. A righty named Jack Kramer was ready to go, but he'd been getting knocked around. And who knew if Kramer would listen to Sewell either?

"Get him out then," said Sewell, rankled, and went back to the dugout.

Muncrief looked in to the plate. Ferrell set up inside. Some pitchers said that this was the best way to pitch to DiMaggio. Others said to go low and away. Either one struck the other Yankees as hilarious; DiMaggio crushed inside pitches, pulling them into leftfield. Outside pitches he drilled to right center. The only safe way to pitch to DiMaggio, especially going the way that he was going now, was to not throw the ball at all.

Muncrief's fastball did come inside, so far inside that it nicked DiMaggio's bat. Foul ball. 0 and 1. *Better not get hit with a pitch.* DiMaggio thought. *Then it'll be over.* The second pitch came inside too and DiMaggio let it go by. 1 and 1.

The crowd's chanting had not stopped. "We want a hit! We want a hit!" DiMaggio stepped back and wiped sweat from his right eye. He adjusted his cap and shook his bat once and then he stood in, ready. Muncrief raised his leg—he used a high and powerful kick—and let the ball go. Again the pitch came onto the inside part of the plate, a curveball this time, and DiMaggio ripped into it, whistling the ball over the head of shortstop Johnny Berardino and into the outfield. Base hit. The crowd rose and cheered and clapped as if the Yankees had just turned a defeat into victory. On the top step of the dugout the Yankee players rattled the bats in the rack and thwacked one another on the back. DiMaggio, again, simply stood at first base. *This guy,* thought Rizzuto. *I cannot believe this guy.*

After the game, a 9–1 final, Sewell again spoke to young Bob Muncrief. "So why wouldn't you walk him like I told you to?" the manager demanded.

And Muncrief said, "That would not have been fair to him, or to me. He is the greatest player I have ever seen."

Chapter 16

Not His Alone

IN THE SHADE-COVERED seats behind the Yankees dugout the men had taken off their jackets, laid their hats upon their laps and rolled their shirtsleeves elbow high. The afternoon was warm and windless and a vendor called out, "Peanuts here, *peee-nuts!* Last chance for peanuts!" He was a teenaged boy in a white hat and a white shirt and white pants. This was to be his final walk through the weekday crowd, a last soliciting of the men in their ties and the women up front in their collared dresses and their brimmed hats—the players' girlfriends and wives, DiMaggio's Dorothy among them and leaning in.

Tommy Henrich, standing on the trodden grass before the dugout, could hear from the crowd a restless, anticipatory rumble. He looked at the bat in his hands. It was one of DiMaggio's, still the same bat he'd borrowed a few weeks back, 36 ounces and 36 inches long, and still serving him so well. Already Henrich had homered in the game, his second long one in three days. He always could hit Elden Auker, the Browns starter today, a righthander with a submarine pitching style—his knuckles all but

scraped the mound—that got so many of the other Yankee hitters out of sorts. *I must be batting .600 against this guy*, Henrich thought. There was one out in the bottom of the eighth inning and Red Rolfe stood on first base; the Yankees had a 3–1 lead. Henrich was coming up and DiMaggio, due to bat behind him, still did not have a hit in the game. His streak was at 37 in a row, and this seemed sure to be the Yankees last turn at bat.

What if I rip a line drive to Heffner or McQuinn, Henrich thought looking over the infield. *What if they double Red off of first base?* No one sized up situations on the field more instinctively than Henrich did. He was like Crosetti in that sense: smart, ceaselessly attentive and always deep into the game. A good and reliable Yankee, a McCarthy type. *They turn a double play here and that's it, Henrich thought. The Big Dago's streak is done.*

He admired DiMaggio, cherished him almost. It didn't matter that DiMaggio barely ever spoke to Tommy beyond the few clipped and necessary exchanges; that was just the Dago's immutable way. It didn't matter to Henrich that not once in more than four seasons as teammates had he and Joe eaten a meal together. Henrich had never been around a ballplayer like DiMaggio, and what he admired went beyond the majesty of DiMaggio's great and conspicuous moments at the bat or in the far regions of centerfield.

Henrich saw the way that DiMaggio grinded through the game each day, a foot soldier engaged. DiMaggio would slide ferociously into a base, tearing his flesh so that the blood ran down his thigh and then moments later if the play called for it, slide into a base again with the same pure and unhesitant violence, tearing the flesh anew. All that mattered was being called safe. Henrich had seen DiMaggio win games by racing to cut off a ball in the gap to keep a runner from rounding third, or by beating out a slowly hit ground ball in an early, seemingly innocuous at bat and then a batter or two later coming in to score what would turn out to be the deciding run. It was those things Henrich prized, on top of DiMaggio"s long hits into the wide leftfield alley or over the rightfield fence just when the Yankees most needed them. No one, Henrich felt, found more ways to beat a team than the Big Dago did. "DiMaggio *is* the Yankees," he would say to his friends.

Of course Henrich had never said anything to DiMaggio about this ad-

miration and respect, and DiMaggio had never said anything of the sort to Henrich. DiMaggio's own conviction that Henrich was the smartest ballplayer he had ever played with went unsaid. And yet these feelings were sensed between them. They covered ground side-by-side in the outfield, and they batted one after the other in the lineup. Henrich understood that DiMaggio respected the way that he played the game too. It had been Joe's idea, seeing Henrich slumping, to lend him the bat.

"Give me a second, will you?" Henrich called out to umpire Art Passarella behind home plate. Then he turned and took a few strides back toward the dugout and caught McCarthy's eye. "Be all right if I bunted here, Joe?" he asked. Immediately McCarthy saw it too. A bunt would keep them out of the double play, ensure DiMaggio another at bat. A slugger like Henrich did not normally put down a sacrifice bunt in a spot like this—not ever, actually. It didn't make much sense, especially with one out. But it wouldn't hurt them really, would it? To just move the runner along? A dugout full of Yankees, McCarthy among them, wanted to see DiMaggio get a chance to push his hitting streak another day. McCarthy nodded at Henrich. "That'll be all right," he said.

The Yankees were in first place now, just atop Cleveland. They had won 13 of their last 16 games; their early season struggles were distant and forgotten. The winning, though, had not taken hold of the people who followed the game in the way DiMaggio's streak had. The day before, after he'd hit in his 37th straight, lining a fourth-inning home run into the leftfield seats, a photographer from the Associated Press had come to DiMaggio following the game and asked him to strike the double biceps pose—shirtless. DiMaggio's picture was taken from the front and then from behind, so that newspaper readers all over could see in full flex the pale, defined muscles that, as the photograph's caption read, powered the streak. It was as if DiMaggio were some kind of superhero.

The Stadium crowd barely noticed now that the Yankees, with their two-run lead, were on the verge of beating the badawful Browns again, or even that Marius Russo, the New York lefthander who some said was on his way to being one of the best in the game, was pitching the masterpiece of his young career. Russo hadn't given up a hit until the seventh inning when, with one out, the power-hitting St. Louis first baseman George McQuinn

homered past Henrich's wall-climbing reach and seven rows back into the rightfield stands to end the no-hitter and the shutout. Through eight innings Russo had faced just 25 batters. The Browns couldn't touch him.

It was DiMaggio, though, that the people had left work early to see. He had struggled against Auker as he usually did, flying out to leftfield in the second inning and then in the fourth rapping a brisk ground ball that the St. Louis shortstop Johnny Berardino could not handle. The Yankee players came out of the dugout then, just as they had a week before, and turned to stare up at Dan Daniel in the press box, hoping that they might influence him, intimidate him even, into calling the play a hit. Daniel felt hot in his seat. In the still air, sweat had formed on his brow and along the sides of his face. He knew once again that his decision might determine the outcome of DiMaggio's hitting streak, and he felt the many eyes upon him—the Yankees', the other writers', and the eyes of those keener fans who knew just where to look. Berardino had muffed it, Daniel felt. Sharply hit or not, Johnny should have made the play. Daniel put his forefinger and thumb in the shape of an O and leaned forward out of his chair. Error. The Yankee players shook their heads in disapproval and Joe Gordon gave to Daniel a curt and dismissive wave. DiMaggio was 0 for 2.

He grounded out weakly in the sixth, and when the bottom of the eighth inning began he was due to be the fourth man up. The Yankees needed a base runner for DiMaggio to even have a chance. So after Johnny Sturm led off with a pop-up to second baseman Don Heffner for the first out, an uneasiness settled onto the Stadium. "Hey, streak-killer," one of the writers called over to Daniel. The Yankees' dugout was quiet and unanimated and the fans around the infield shifted in their seats. Dorothy sat with her hands tightly clasped. And so it followed that after the next batter, Red Rolfe, worked Auker deep into the count and finally drew a walk, the fans rose and cheered as mightily as if Rolfe had clubbed a grand slam. *DiMaggio's gonna get up!* It was now that Henrich saw the danger of a double play before him and chose to lay down a bunt. On his second attempt the bunt stayed fair and Henrich was thrown out at first base; Rolfe made it safely to second and with two outs in the Yankees' final turn at bat, Joe DiMaggio began striding to the plate.

Maybe Auker will walk him, Marius Russo thought in the dugout. He

always took the game apart with a pitcher's mind now, after more than two years of McCarthy being on him. "Are you in the game? Are you in it?" the manager would ask inning after inning, game after game. He'd remind Russo to think about the batters who were coming up, to think about what he would do if one of them got on base, to consider not just the batter but the inning and the score and the game as a whole. *This whole sacrifice bunt thing is a little crazy,* Russo thought. *I bet Auker walks him.*

Auker had gone to 3 and 0 on DiMaggio in the second inning, had run the count full in the fourth, but walking him intentionally now, or even pitching around him, was not a thought that came into the righthander's mind. He'd always handled DiMaggio well; he knew Joe didn't like his submarine style. Get him out and the inning's over and the Browns come up with one more chance to make up the two runs, maybe steal him a win. Walk DiMaggio instead? So that another power hitter, the lefthanded-batting King Kong Keller could come up with two men on? That was not Auker's kind of thinking.

The crowd rumbled and the players came to the front of the dugout to watch. All of the infield was in shadow. Elden Auker—bringing that sneaky underhanded stuff for nine major league seasons now, and for 11 years since he'd fatefully separated his shoulder playing college football in Kansas—had a chance to make headlines, to be the streak-stopper. DiMaggio stood in, motionless, and a hush fell on the Stadium. The peanut vendors and the Cracker Jack vendors stopped in their routes. Auker brought his glove forward and then swung it back below his waist and then he threw his curveball to the plate.

The line drive was past third base, a white blur six inches above Harlond Clift's head, before Auker could even turn. The ball rolled deep into the leftfield corner as the fans hollered and whooped, realizing they would have this to tell when they got home, and then again the next morning—*I was there!* The Yankees players applauded and rattled the bats in the bat-rack and Rolfe stepped emphatically on home plate and Gomez, capless, danced a little jig in the dugout. Auker looked over to see DiMaggio pulling in at second base, implacable, imperious, cool.

The thrill never left the crowd that day, not after the eighth inning ended nor as Russo set the Browns down, in order once again, in the

ninth. After the final out some of the fans came down onto the field and ran to slap Joe on the back as he jogged in from centerfield—*Way to go Joe! You're the best!* It was their last chance to have him in their midst before the Yanks went down to Philadelphia and Washington for a weekend on the road. DiMaggio kept one hand on his cap.

Thirty-eight games in a row, and now George Sisler's record was right there before him. DiMaggio clattered through the tunnel and up the few, steep steps to the Yankees' locker room, hearing his teammates' happy voices echoing through the belly of the Stadium. The streak was not his alone, DiMaggio realized, and it wasn't just something that enthralled the fans. The streak belonged to his Yankees teammates too. Henrich had laid down that bunt just for him. And though the players had steered wide of DiMaggio as his hitless game went along, he had seen them standing to glare at Dan Daniel, and he had felt his teammates at his back when they gathered at the top step of the dugout, expectant and engaged, as he stood at the plate his last time up. *They're all on my side,* he thought.

A ballplayer might have picked up some superstitions during a streak like this, but not DiMaggio. Nothing to add to the little kick he always gave to the back of his left heel with his right toe before settling into his batting stance, or to his habit of stepping squarely on second base each time he ran in from centerfield at the end of an inning. "Hoodoos aren't going to stop me, a pitcher will," DiMaggio had declared a few days before. Some of his teammates, though, had lately adopted superstitions on his behalf. A few of them wore the same pregame shirt day after day. The kid Rizzuto kept the same stale and sugar-spent wad of gum stuck beneath the bill of his cap. Nobody wanted to be the one to turn DiMaggio's luck.

They came around him in the clubhouse to grip his hand and pound his back, the coaches Fletcher and Combs and the players one by one or in small groups. Everything was bubbly and the solemn quiet that so often attended the clubhouse was gone. DiMaggio shook their hands, grinned wide and boyishly and said, "Thank you, fellas" in his deep voice. And guys went off to the showers, loose and snapping towels. For Joe, this was perfect. *It's like I'm one of them,* he thought. And he was, even as he remained the player around whom the Yankees sun revolved. *Everybody is on my side.*

DiMaggio did not want these sweet, clear and happy times after the games to end. He lingered in the clubhouse, the last man out of the shower, the last one to get his watch and cufflinks and wallet from his box in the old valuables chest by the locker room's front door. He was in no rush to go, to meet Dorothy and Jimmy and step into the Cadillac and leave the ball field behind. For all the tension the streak sometimes caused DiMaggio—the stomach, the sensation, as he would say, that he was "dying inside"—these moments with the other Yankees in the clubhouse, when he was at once the favored hero and one of the guys, were precious and rare. He was warmed by a feeling he would not forget even long after the streak ended. Years and decades later, after so many fine and defining events—the birth of his son that fall, the big contract in '49, even then the golden courtship of Marilyn before things went bad—he would still remember the feeling he had now, and he would say to people that these moments in the locker room, the streak freshly extended for yet another day and his teammates all abuzz, were the very best moments of his life.

The View From Here

The Way Of All Streaks

Nine players in major league history have run off hitting streaks of more than 35 games in a season. Four of them—the Boston Braves' Tommy Holmes in 1945; the Reds' Pete Rose in '78; the Brewers' Paul Molitor in '87 and the Phillies' Jimmy Rollins in 2005—have done it in the 70 years since DiMaggio set his mark. Rollins, who hit in 36 consecutive games to end the '05 season then added two more at the start of '06, broke into the majors in 2000. For years he abided by an annual springtime ritual in which he would tell his younger brother Antwon: "This is the season I'm going to break Joe DiMaggio's hitting streak." I asked Rollins recently why he set his sights on that particular outsized achievement—why didn't he vow to hit .400, say? Or steal 100 bases? Or get 250 hits? Or score 150 runs? Rollins replied, "Because people say that those things can be done. Why not go for the Golden Grail?"

DiMaggio's record retains a deep resonance for ballplayers today in part because of its remarkable endurance and also because any time that anyone gets on a hitting streak of even moderate length, DiMaggio's name and the enormousness of the accomplishment come up. As Mets third baseman David Wright put it, "How big of a deal is DiMaggio's streak? Ryan Zimmerman got halfway there [in May of 2009] and it was on the front page of every sports section and led every sports

highlight show. He was halfway. Halfway! Think about that."

Mention DiMaggio's streak in a modern baseball locker room and a look of reverence often passes over players' faces. It's a bit like saying "Harding's ascent" to a group of rock climbers at Yosemite, or "Escoffier's soufflé" among young chefs at a culinary institute. There is something sacred to it, and something surreal. "Pfffft, that's one of those Bugs Bunny numbers," Ken Griffey Jr. said to me, shaking his head. "People do that in cartoons, not in real life."[1]

"It is huge and it is humbling," Yankees captain Derek Jeter said of DiMaggio's streak. "Get a hit for two straight months? It's hard to get a hit for two straight days."

But really, is it *that* hard? Couldn't it be done by a player today? In its simplest breakdown, all that a batter needs to do is go 1 for 4 or even 1 for 5 each day. DiMaggio's feat feels tantalizingly attainable, unlike some of the old and now hard to fathom pitching accomplishments such as Cy Young's 511 career wins, or Jack Chesbro's 41 victories in 1904. In the past 35 years only the retired knuckleballer Phil Niekro has even *started* 41 games in a season, but today's hitters have essentially the same opportunities and same limitations in pursuing a consecutive-games hitting streak that DiMaggio had in 1941, that George Sisler had

---

[1] While most players I spoke with were very familiar with DiMaggio's streak, there were a few exceptions. A few days after the veteran outfielder Gary Sheffield hit his 500th career home run I met with him in the New York Mets' clubhouse. As we talked Sheffield stood in front of his locker and pounded his right fist rhythmically into the glove on his left hand. I sought to engage him, in a general sense, on the meaning and weight of milestones and statistical achievement in baseball. During our conversation it became evident that Sheffield did not know what the record was for the longest major league hitting streak, nor who held it. He pointed out that as a power hitter he wasn't likely to run off a hitting streak himself, and so, said Sheffield, "I'm not someone who follows that. Now someone who follows that, they would know. . . . But anyway," and here he raised an eyebrow with interest, "what is that hitting streak record?" I told him. Sheffield stopped pounding his fist into his glove and stared directly at me. He didn't say anything for several seconds. Then he said, "Man, that is a frickin' long hitting streak."

in '22, that Rose had in '78. "Same game, same challenge," said Giants outfielder Aaron Rowand. "Though today you might face three or four pitchers in a game—that's one thing that could make it harder now."

In comparing the game as it was in 1941 to the game as it is today, baseball people often echo Rowand's thought—that the current use of fresh and often specialized relief pitchers can work against a hitter putting together a long streak.[2] It might be pointed out, for example, that over the course of DiMaggio's streak he faced a total of 55 different pitchers. In what wound up as a 30-game hitting streak in 2009, Zimmerman faced 66.[3] Zimmerman, a third baseman for the Nationals, was less likely than DiMaggio to see a pitcher three or four times a game, and Zimmerman was much more likely to have to contend with a live and unfamiliar arm out of the bullpen. (Still, as Zimmerman said, "Getting a hit off the *same* pitcher for that many days in a row would be tough.") Intuitively, the idea that pitching variety makes a streak more difficult seems clearly correct. And yet there is no evidence at all to support that notion. In fact there is evidence to the contrary—the highest preponderance of long streaks have occurred in the era of pitcher specialization. Of the 44 hitting streaks of 30 games or more in the past 135 years of the major leagues, 12 of them, or 27%, have come since 1997, just 13 seasons.

---

[2] Other comparisons tend to be minor and nondefinitive. Today's travel is more extensive, but in 1941 the trips were less luxurious and took place on trains not on team planes. There were more day games then, arguably a benefit to a hitter's sight, but then again most '41 parks were without the blacked-out "batter's eye" in centerfield that today yields an ideal background for picking up the pitched ball. And so on.

[3] This is not purely a function of the trend in pitcher usage, of course, but also a result of expansion; DiMaggio's Yankees played against only seven different teams in 1941; Zimmerman's Nationals played against 19 in 2009.

The implication of the impact of pitching specialization is not simply that it is more difficult to maintain a hitting streak these days but that it is more difficult to hit, period. Yet again, on a comparative basis, this does not appear to be true. In 1941, hitters were statistically just as likely to get hits as they are today. The major league batting average of .262 in '41 is consistent with the National League averages over the past five seasons that have ranged from .259 to .266. (I use the NL—rather than the AL or the entire MLB—as the point of modern reference because National League numbers have not, with the exception of a handful of interleague games, been distorted by the designated hitter.) And it's worth noting that for every stingy closer such as Mariano Rivera or Joe Nathan, or even a nasty lefty specialist such as Darren Oliver, you have today many lesser known and highly ineffective bullpen guys who might surrender an average of 12, 13 or even 14 hits per nine innings.

Whatever the baseball era, the players who reel off long hitting streaks are almost always extraordinarily talented. These are not random or lightning-in-a-bottle events. An average ballplayer does not simply get lucky and put together a long streak the way that, say, journeyman outfielder Mark Whiten tied a standard with four home runs in a game for the Cardinals in 1993, or that Rennie Stennett went a record 7 for 7 one day for the Pirates in 1975. Ordinary hitters may chance upon any number of other streaks: The thoroughly mediocre Dale Long has the National League record of hitting a home run in eight consecutive games, while in 2009 the Florida Marlins' Jorge Cantu, a career .274 hitter, had an RBI in 14 straight games to challenge Ray Grimes's major-league record of 17 in a row.

Consecutive-game hitting streakers, however, are a breed apart. Of the nine over-35-game streaks, six were achieved not

just by Hall of Famers but by elite Hall of Famers—DiMaggio, Wee Willie Keeler, Sisler, Ty Cobb, Molitor and Rose. (Yes, I include the banished Hit King as a Hall of Famer; in my book he is certainly that.) Then there's Rollins, a three-time All-Star and the 2007 NL MVP and Tommy Holmes, who hit .302 over the course of 11 seasons. Of the nine, only former Chicago player Bill Dahlen, a .272 career hitter who ran off 42 straight games, appears to have been a fluke—and he did it in 1894, when foul ball rules made hitting success easier to come by.

No active player seems more likely to mount a seriously long hitting streak than the Mariners' Ichiro Suzuki, who in 2004 broke Sisler's 84-year-old record of 257 hits in a season.[4] With a total of 2,244 hits over 10 major league seasons and a .331 career batting average, Suzuki has been by far the most prolific and consistent hit producer of his time. He batted .372 in 2004 and he has had seven hitting streaks of 20 games or more, one shy of the record held by Cobb, Keeler and Rose. In 2009 Ichiro hit in 27 straight games, a personal best. After setting the Mariners franchise record and drawing a standing ovation with a hit in Game 26, Ichiro was clearly moved. "I wish that I would have asked my wife, Yumiko, and my dog, Ikkyu, to come to the game today," he told reporters in the postgame press conference.

Throughout his major league career Ichiro has been asked to rate the difficulty of putting together a streak the length of DiMaggio's as compared to baseball's other famously elusive offensive hallmark, batting .400 in a season, which also has not been done in 70 years. "Hitting in that many games in a row is definitely tougher than hitting .400," Ichiro said. "That hitting streak is the toughest of all the records."

---

[4] Sisler did it in a 154-game season; Ichiro passed the mark in his 160th game and wound up with 262 hits while playing in 161 games on the year.

Almost every hitter that I asked agreed with Ichiro's assessment. "Hitting .400 would be very, very, very hard but you could have some days when you went 0 for 2 with a couple of walks or a sac fly and then you could make it up with a couple of hits in your next game," reasoned the Rockies' Todd Helton, who in 2000 batted .372. And from former Royals third baseman George Brett, whose .390 batting average in 1980 is the highest since Ted Williams's .406 in 1941: "There is no question that DiMaggio's hitting streak is harder than hitting .400—for a lot of reasons. One thing is that while pitchers pitch around you when you're going for .400 that doesn't necessarily hurt you; it could even help to draw the occasional walk. Pitchers tend to pitch around you when you're on a hitting streak too, even in the early innings, and that can be enough to finish you off."

A STREAK IS by nature unrelenting, a quality that sets it apart from so many other pursuits in sports. As Helton suggested, you never get a game off. Not physically, and not mentally. On the night in 2002 that Marlins second baseman Luis Castillo extended his hitting streak to 35 games—a record for a Latin-born player—he reached first base on an infield single. Two batters later Castillo made it around to third, where he looked at coach Ozzie Guillen and said, "My God, I've got to do this shit again tomorrow night."

By then Castillo was no longer watching sports highlights on TV. After games he would return home to his family and sit quietly sipping beer. He had trouble sleeping. He fretted about the weather. ("It rained a lot in Florida that year," he recalled. "And I was afraid that if I didn't get my hit early in the game we could get rained out and I'd lose my chance.") A speedy

and pesky player, Castillo plotted and schemed. Each time up he considered bunting. "Every day I would think about the situation," he said.

For some batters being on a streak leads inevitably to superstitious behavior, or at least to forming habits that they're unwilling, for the duration of the streak, to change. As *Bull Durham* catcher Crash Davis put it: "A player on a streak has to respect the streak." When Phillies' second baseman Chase Utley got deep into the throes of what would end up a 35-game run in 2006—he and Rollins are the only teammates ever to have streaks of 35-plus games—he became increasingly withdrawn and enigmatic. Reporters would ask him after a game about one of his at bats and Utley would respond, "I think Jon Lieber pitched well for us and we played some good defense," deflecting with non sequiturs any talk that might touch even incidentally upon his batting streak. He kept that up for weeks. Utley refused to change his cleats throughout the streak and, although temperatures ranged above 90° for some July and early August games, he came to the ballpark each day wearing the same stocking cap that he wore when the streak began in late June. "My way of dealing," Utley explained years later. "The things I was doing worked so I stuck with them."

Rollins, who admits that he had mixed feelings when Utley was closing in on his Phillies record—"You want to be first in an organization," Rollins told me—casually mentioned the streak to Utley when Utley was somewhere in the high-20s. "Big eyes, that's all you get from him," Rollins told the New York *Daily News* a few days later. "I don't even try to talk to him any more."

During his own streak in 2005, Rollins spoke openly about his daily quest, volunteering that he "hoped to get the record" and then during the spring of 2006, when he was at 36 straight

games and counting, repeatedly addressing the niggling question of whether his streak would even "count" if he did pass DiMaggio, given that he would have done it over the course of two seasons.[5]

Eighteen years earlier Molitor had taken quite a different public stance while in the latter stages of his 39-game run, adopting a sort of middle ground between Utley's hermetic responses and Rollins's effusiveness. Molitor went out of his way to downplay what he was doing—in effect respecting his own streak by respecting DiMaggio's. "You talk about 38 in comparison to what the record is," he said then, "and it's not that significant. . . . If you're realistic, you realize that each day your chances of it continuing are less and less."

THE PRECARIOUSNESS OF a streak, along with the uncommon attention it receives, can impact not only the hitter himself but also his teammates, his manager and even the players and managers on opposing teams. When, if ever, should the pursuit of extending the streak alter the way that a game situation is played? On June 22, 2002, with one out and a runner on second base in the bottom of the ninth inning of a 4–4 game against the Tigers, veteran outfielder Tim Raines was called upon to pinch hit for the Marlins. Castillo, 0 for 4 with his 35-game hitting streak on the line, stood on deck. Raines felt unsure what to do; a hit would win, but also end, the game. "Should I bunt?" Raines asked manager Jeff Torborg. Said Torborg: "No, win the

---

5 Dominic DiMaggio, whose 34-game streak in 1949 ended when he lined out to Joe in center-field, was among those who spoke up then. He said that a Rollins streak over two seasons, were it to extend past Joe's record, should not be considered equal to what Joe had done, a touching—and to some surprising, given the history of the two DiMaggios—defense of his late brother's legacy.

game. The team comes first." Castillo was a very well-liked and extremely hardworking teammate—"We are all pulling for him so hard," first baseman Kevin Millar had said a few days earlier—and on the bench the Marlins players felt torn. "I was hoping Raines would walk," third baseman Mike Lowell said. But a wild pitch advanced the runner, Andy Fox, to third base, and then, on a 2-and-2 count, Raines hit a fly ball to centerfield deep enough that Fox tagged up and scored. The Marlins had won, but Castillo's streak was over. As the Florida players celebrated at home plate, Torborg took a moment to put an arm around Castillo. "We had to play it that way, Luis," he explained, and Castillo said that he understood.

In the stands, boos of disappointment mixed with cheers for the Marlins dramatic win, which is more that can be said for the reaction of the Milwaukee crowd on the night of Aug. 26, 1987. Similarly to Castillo, Paul Molitor was 0 for 4 and waiting on deck with his 39-game hitting streak when Rick Manning singled home the winning and game-ending run to beat Cleveland in the bottom of the 10th inning. It was a thrilling and crucial victory for a team chasing the pennant but the hometown crowd was not at all pleased. The boos were loud and forceful, "and then," recalled third base coach Tony Muser, "everyone was silent... as if somebody had passed away." Rather than being able to bask in a hero's postgame glow, Manning joked that he would have to wear a bulletproof vest to the next day's game. Molitor quipped that, as soon as Manning's ball went into centerfield, he'd started waving the runner, Mike Felder, back to third base so that Felder wouldn't score and the game would go on.

Earlier in that same game, Molitor's streak had already exerted a clear influence on events; he had been granted what some observers deemed an extra at bat. The game was score-

less with two outs and a runner on second in the eighth inning when Molitor stepped up. On deck was Robin Yount, a fine hitter but not close to being the threat that Molitor was at that point. (Yount's season batting average was then more than 50 points lower than Molitor's.) The smart, by-the-book move was to intentionally walk Molitor and set up a force play. But Indians manager Doc Edwards, who had said publicly that he appreciated the class with which Molitor handled himself during the streak, did not want to deprive Molitor of a chance to hit in what was potentially (and, it turned out, actually) his last time up. "I had a gut feeling the percentages were running out on Paul," Edwards said later. Damning the odds out of deference to the streak, the Indians pitched to Molitor. He grounded out.

A similar act of kindness—or respect, or sportsmanship, call it what you will—did not go unpunished in 1969 when the Dodgers' Willie Davis came up hitless and on a 30-game streak in the bottom of the ninth inning against the Mets. There was one out and the score was tied and the potential winning run had just been sacrificed to second base. Davis's run meant nothing to the outcome of the game and walking him would have set up a double play. Even casual fans at Dodger Stadium were so sure that an intentional walk was coming that they began to boo before Davis even got to the plate. But Mets manager Gil Hodges, aware that the streak was on the line, elected to go ahead and give Davis the chance to hit. On the first pitch, Davis doubled to win the game. His streak was stopped the next night at 31 games.

Those events, which dealt the Mets a painful—though ultimately not costly—loss in their improbable run to the 1969 pennant, made a deep impression on Steve Hirdt, now an executive vice president at the Elias Sports Bureau and then an 18-year-old Mets fan living in New York. "I just couldn't under-

stand how they could have pitched to him," says Hirdt. "When Davis came up I was screaming 'Walk him! Walk him!'"

As Hirdt went on to devote his professional life to sifting through and analyzing sports' magnificent minutiae, the Davis game stayed with him. He thought of it years later when he was asked about the 38th game of DiMaggio's streak, and the possibility that Elden Auker might have chosen to intentionally walk DiMaggio his last time up, as Yankees' pitcher Marius Russo and some others in the ballpark that day thought he would. "It wasn't quite the same," said Hirdt. "The game wasn't on the line"—indeed the Yankees led 3–1 with two outs in the eighth inning, rendering the case for an intentional walk far less compelling than it was in Davis's case—"but there was a sacrifice bunt that set things up, and DiMaggio *might* have been intentionally walked but wasn't. The pressures that a hitting streak applies can give you a little window into the way baseball people think. If I had been alive and a Browns fan in 1941, I wonder if I would have been yelling, 'Walk him! Walk him!' then too."

Chapter 17
The Street

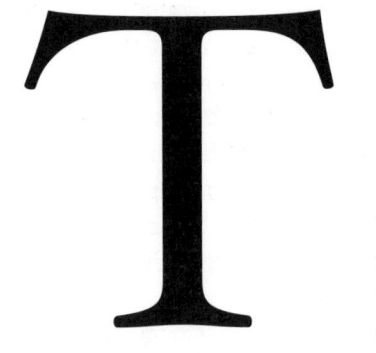

HEY ALL HAD summer jobs now, shelving items at the grocer's or sweeping up at the drugstore, or stacking boxes and packages in the musty back room at the post office. Iceman Al Panza still helped his dad bring around the blocks of ice and Itsy had begun taking shifts behind the counter at his parents' candy store a few blocks from the el. Some of the Hornets and Dukes worked in construction—there was plenty of that going on in Jackson Heights—and some threw morning paper routes on their bikes. Commie delivered local orders for the fish market, toting ice-wrapped sacks of striper filets, tuna steaks, clams by the dozen.

On the evenings and weekends, they sometimes rode around in Frankie's rumble seat, calling out to the girls they passed, or they'd clamber into Itsy's old Chevy. No one cared how loudly the Chevy rattled along, or that the gas pedal kept getting stuck—Itsy had tied a string to it so that he could yank it back up. It was a car, and that's all that mattered. They could have driven anywhere, to the Long Island beach-

es, say, or to the heart of Manhattan, but they rarely went far. Everything that the boys wanted that hot summer was close to home: the ball games and the meeting spots and the dances that were never more than a mile or two away. Their spending money went to the ice-cream shops (12 cents for a banana split, a nickel for an egg cream) and to burger binges at the White Castle. They'd take the Bettes to the movies at the Polk Theater (Clark Gable and Rosalind Russell starring in *They Met in Bombay*) and now and again the Hornets and Dukes might chip in with the older guys for a keg of weekend beer, to be drunk only after they'd played the league game or doubleheader, never before.

"Hey, Petey's at it again!" Commie cackled. Petey Morrell was the Hornets catcher—short, stocky, could throw from his knees—and during batting practice now he always did the same thing: whip it out and pee right there on home plate. Marking his territory as it were. He'd done it once many weeks before and the Hornets had won that game. And so Petey had peed there the next time out, against the 34th Avenue Boys, and the Hornets had won again. They were winning a lot this summer, on top of the standings, and Petey Morrell's pregame ritual was, they all agreed, a good luck charm. "DiMaggio may have a 39-game hitting streak," Itsy called out, "but Petey, you've got a streak just as long for pissing on home plate."

Often now there was talk of DiMaggio and the streak he was on. For Commie, it was the one thing that *everybody* he knew talked about, more than anything else. The boys were always talking to each other about Joe D, and they would scramble to get the evening paper when it came off the truck—"Good photo of his swing today," the delivery guy would call out before the bundle even hit the ground. Mr. Ratner brought up DiMaggio when he sold the boys their frozen Pepsis. So did the old German guy who made the tuna salad sandwiches at the Bellefair. Commie's father said that at his barbershop, there on the south side of 14th Street in Manhattan, DiMaggio was the "Number 1 topic of conversation," bigger even than the weather and the war. You couldn't give a guy a trim or a shave without him piping up something like "DiMaggio had a close call yesterday, didn't he?" Even Commie's mother would ask about the streak. Back from a day of work as a seamstress in the garment district

she suddenly wanted to know. "Did he get one? Did DiMaggio do it again today?" Commie reasoned that if his mother was paying attention to the hitting streak—she wasn't exactly one for baseball—that really meant it was big news.

All around them that summer they could see Jackson Heights changing, expanding by the week it seemed. The garden apartments and the leafy streets, the "unhurried, congenial living" that the realtors touted, had made the neighborhood a popular destination point for families just moving to New York. You could get to Manhattan in 15 minutes by subway or through the Midtown Tunnel, so Jackson Heights was just right for commuters.

Some of the men now climbing the steps to the train on Roosevelt Avenue wore military issue, the Army and Navy having dispatched thousands of deskmen to New York as the U.S. defense corps swelled. The men in uniform, greeting one another with salutes, were a regular reminder of the war. Some of the older guys the Hornets knew—Ponzo, Danny the Greek—had already been drafted. Billy'd gone into the Marines. Another round of draft registration was just a few days away, for anyone who had turned 21 since October. "Yeh, Charlie's a 1-A," Itsy would say, "He's going in." Or, "Maybe Rizos will get a 4-F with that limp he's got." They would talk standing outside the candy store in the late afternoon sun, or sitting on the stoop nursing their icy Pepsis and waiting for a little more of the day's high heat to fall off.

They played three-on-three stickball on 94th Street, maybe put a quarter each on the game. Some of the guys would take their position in the outfield, two sewers back from home plate, with a cigarette dangling from their mouths. Squeaks had learned that DiMaggio sometimes smoked while he was out shagging balls on an off day. Car fenders marked first and third base, a sewer cover was second base and they would chalk in a box for home plate. You stood with the broom handle held high and tried to hit the pink rubber ball on one bounce. The game's progress was peppered with discussion about whether or not a batted ball had gone foul, or what to do when the ball got caught up in a fire escape, or whether to demand a do-over when some passer-by unknowingly walked onto the "field" and disrupted a play. After a while

Mrs. McCarthy, Jack's mom, would call out from her first floor window and then there would be fresh cookies for the taking on her sill, warm and with the fresh-baked smell. Just one was never enough. Neither, really, were the two that they each got.

They would play for hours, switching around the teams here and there; their parents, or other adults, coming home from work carrying bags of groceries or just out on a walk, would stop and watch, pleased to see the boys and to see how much the games mattered to them and how happy they were in these moments. For the parents the stickball games played against the backdrop of darker things. They understood that there was more than just this week's draft registration ahead of them, that there would certainly be other drafts and that the war, by the looks of it, would be long and that some or most or even all of these boys might have their numbers called one day too. *Where will the war lead us? What will it cost?* Watching the teenagers chasing after a bouncing pink ball in the bronze evening light, gay and unburdened, the adults would feel a sudden bolt of sadness and loss. It was, in the way one might feel upon seeing a row of red tulips in their plumpest April bloom, a realization of just how fleeting the sweet scene before them was. They were grateful for the boys' stickball games, and for their weekend baseball league, and grateful too for the Yankees and the Dodgers and for the boxing matches and all the diversions. And of course for DiMaggio, a simple hero engaged in a simple if daunting feat that in this summer seemed to them so extraordinary and so important. Knowing rationally that what DiMaggio did or didn't do in a baseball game was, in the deeper sense, inconsequential—would another hit matter, really, to any of their lives?—did nothing to dull the opposite sensation: that the hitting streak did matter and that there was something tangible and far-reaching at stake when DiMaggio came to bat. Everyone, it seemed, put some small measure of hope upon DiMaggio each day and then later scurried to find out if he had fulfilled it.

The boys would look for him in the newsreels before the main feature at the movies. (And to the boys, if not to the Bettes, these newsreels were a lot more interesting than seeing Clark Gable and Rosalind Russell in a clinch.) A chronicling of Joe D's hits might unfold among accounts of

the latest Army buildup or of the old submarine, the O–9, that had gone down during a test in the waters off New Hampshire and had not come back up. There were images of soldiers firing guns on a practice range somewhere and then moments later of DiMaggio swinging his bat. For the Hornets and the Dukes it was all a sea of energy and experience, excitement, power, uncertainty and hope. For them, "Did he get one?" seemed as important as any question that anyone could ask.

Chapter 18
An Ornery Offering

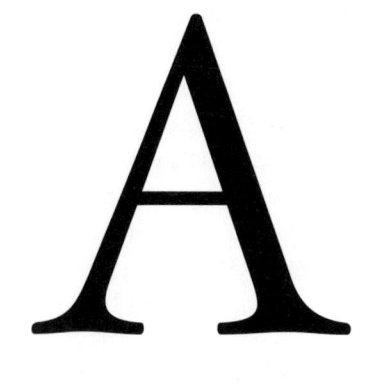TERRACED IRON HOME RUN wall towered 34 feet above rightfield in Philadelphia's Shibe Park, running from the foul line to centerfield. It was now more than six seasons old. The Athletics' owners had built it to block the view of fans who for decades had gathered by the hundreds to watch ballgames from the flat rooftops and second-story bay windows of the row houses along North 20th Street. Some homeowners had constructed bleachers upon those roofs and on game days charged admission and sold hot dogs and Coca-Cola, angering the Athletics who saw this only as a skimming of their profits. The homeowners chafed bitterly against the building of the fence and the moment it went up—a forbidding expanse of unpainted corrugated metal that stung the neighborhood like a slap with the back of a hand—everyone in Philadelphia, and around the major leagues, called it the Spite Wall.

The Spite Wall was a strange, ugly and, for outfielders, unpredictable thing. Fly balls that struck off those ribbed terraces might fall straight

down or might bounce 100 feet back toward second base. When a ball was driven high and far over his head in rightfield Henrich would turn his back to home plate and face the wall, tense with uncertainty. Sometimes the ball hit the fence and bounded right to Henrich. Sometimes it ricocheted out near DiMaggio in centerfield. Sometimes Gordon or Rizzuto ended up with the baseball near the infield. A fly ball that soared toward the Spite Wall, some 330 feet from home plate at the rightfield edge, close to 450 feet away in center, caused all of the Yankee fielders to prepare for any crazy bounce.

Shibe Park had other peculiarities as well. The tiny visitors' locker room was dim and spartan, and one of the two showerheads invariably sputtered. There were just 20 steel lockers, not enough to accommodate a full team. Some of the newest Yankees, like Jerry Priddy and the pitcher Charley Stanceu, had to hang their clothes on nails driven crudely into a wall. The deep concrete dugouts flooded badly in heavy rains and pools of water collected inside the players' tunnel that ran beneath the stands. But the field itself was always immaculately groomed, the grass a vibrant and unvarying green. The infield and the outfield produced the truest hops in the league. Perhaps because of that high wall, the sharp *pock* of a fastball arriving into a catcher's mitt echoed uniquely in Shibe Park and could be heard even on the radio broadcasts that originated from a small balcony extending off the bottom of the upper deck.

By now the Tall Tactician, Connie Mack, was nearing 80 years old— *80!*—and in his 41st season as the Athletics manager. He still wore his long thin neckties and his white, high-collared shirts and throughout each game he clutched the lineup sheet in his narrow hands. Much like Shibe Park itself, built of steel and concrete to great fanfare and excitement in 1909, Mack seemed a treasure from another era, a relic to be revered. Despite the stadium's mild nuisances and cramped quarters and despite the ungodly heckling of the Philadelphia fans, Shibe Park was not, DiMaggio felt, a bad place to play. Its idiosyncrasies created a distinct atmosphere, a personality almost, that was more than just tolerable, it was interesting— at least for 11 games each year. The home run fences were well within reach (the concrete wall in leftfield stood a more standard 12 feet high), and the Athletics were often quite easily beaten. Once in 1939, over the

course of a doubleheader in which DiMaggio hit three home runs, the Yankees outscored Philadelphia 33–2.

Whatever the charms at Shibe Park—its façade looked more like a temple built during the French Renaissance than the entrance to a ballfield—facing the Athletics' righthanded pitcher Johnny Babich was not among them. He had defeated the Yankees five times in six games during the 1940 season, almost single-handedly preventing them from reaching the World Series. On the final Friday of the season in Philadelphia, Babich and the last-place A's had stopped the Yankees 6–2, at once ending their pennant hopes and forcing them to settle for third-place money. Less than a year before, Babich had himself been property of the Yankees, winning 17 games and losing just six for their minor league team in Kansas City in 1939. But instead of bringing him up and into the big league fold, Ed Barrow had let him go to Philadelphia.

Babich maintained that he "didn't bear down any harder against the Yanks than against any other club," but DiMaggio didn't believe it. He knew about Babich from back home. Johnny had grown up in Albion, 150 miles north of San Francisco, and had played with Vince on a team in Tucson for a while and then played for the Seals just before Joe arrived. After the Seals had let Babich go, he hooked on with the crosstown Missions and then set about beating his old team time and again. Since breaking into the majors with the Dodgers in 1934, Babich had been traded three times and had spent three full seasons ('37, '38, '39) in the minor leagues after having surgery on his pitching elbow. With such a fragile arm, who knew how long his career would last. When Babich got a chance to pitch in a big game—in 1940 he'd acquitted himself splendidly in matchups against Feller—he seized the chance with conviction.

DiMaggio was familiar with Babich's long-legged windup and with the muscular width of chest that Babich turned toward the plate as he brought his long right arm straight down to release the ball. He made his living with a pitch they called "the slideball" or "the sailer," an ornery offering that all at once dropped and veered to the right. To righthanded batters he would work the pitch off the outside corner. It could be deadly.

Babich was 28 years old and lived with his wife, Francine, and a white-haired fox terrier they called Stinky, and he bore a chip on his shoulder.

He would rather be playing for a World Series contender than for the Philadelphia A's. He *deserved* to play for a contender. In that pennant-determining 1940 game against the Yankees (the team that had given up on him and that he'd already defeated four times), Babich had allowed just five base hits. Now, facing the Yankees for the first time since that game, Babich had let it be known to his teammates—and in turn word had come to the Yankees and to DiMaggio—that he intended to stop Joe's hitting streak right where it was at 39 straight games. He had a simple plan to do it too. If he could get DiMaggio out once, then he would walk him the rest of the game. In this way the Yankee-slayer would make his most dramatic kill.

More than 13,600 fans were in the stands this Saturday, better than twice the A's typical weekend-game crowd. It was an extremely hot afternoon and in the city people sought relief in places like Gimbels department store, which boasted of being "the largest air-cooled area in Philadelphia." The Athletics were a sixth-place club; it was not their sluggers—the outfielders Sam Chapman and Bob Johnson and the second baseman Benny McCoy could all drive the ball—that the people sweating in the Shibe Park seats had come to see. The day before, the newspaper headline JOE DIMAGGIO AND HIT STREAK HERE TO FACE A'S had run across the top of a page. The teams themselves, readying for a two-game set, were an afterthought.

DiMaggio had been grateful in the first of the two games, the previous afternoon, when he singled off the A's Chubby Dean on the first pitch of his first at bat to run the streak to 39 games, easing his mind at once. (Later he smacked a home run more than 450 feet.) This was the first time since the streak had really taken hold of everyone's attention that DiMaggio was playing on the road. Although he was always closely watched as a player, he had never felt such particular and elevated attention in the major leagues. He had come under focus as a rookie, of course, and again after his contract disputes when he would be regularly booed. In those times DiMaggio would wake in the middle of the night, the boos still sounding in his mind, and leave his bed and smoke cigarettes, pacing the floor until the light of day. Now there was a similar feeling. He realized that he was again being judged on a standard beyond whether

the Yankees won or lost; this was something else: Get a hit and succeed. Don't, and fail. The streak was now completely defining him. And with that, DiMaggio knew, came a chance to leave an imprint that could last even after he was gone. Like Ruth's home runs and Cobb's batting average and Gehrig's impossible string of games played. With the streak, DiMaggio was after something larger than the day's final score; larger, even, than the Yankees run to the pennant. Larger, maybe, than the game itself.

In the evening at the Benjamin Franklin Hotel in Philadelphia he listened to the radio, first the quiz show and then the news in which he played a principal part. "Tomorrow, Joe DiMaggio will try to hit in his 40th straight game and get one step closer to George Sisler's record," the radio man said. Then followed more dispatches about the Nazis' advance and the British dropping bombs in France, about the Philadelphia racketeers who were shorting folks on coal deliveries across the city and about a local teenager with a flourishing turkey farm. Mrs. Roosevelt, in other news, had advanced the notion of implementing a national service program for girls.

DIMAGGIO DID NOT care for Johnny Babich, nor for the bases-on-balls plan that Babich had devised. In the first inning against Babich, DiMaggio pulled the ball hard down the leftfield line where it landed a few inches on the wrong side of the foul line, a few inches from a streak-extending double. On his next swing Joe lifted a high pop fly that the shortstop Al Brancato settled under and caught. Babich had his out.

Now, as DiMaggio came up to lead off the third inning, Brancato moved a couple of strides to his right, toward third base, playing him to pull. This was Connie Mack's instruction, communicated from the dugout with a casual wave.

At second base Benny McCoy held his usual position. In truth you could never predict where DiMaggio would drive a pitch. McCoy deeply admired DiMaggio although he didn't know him much, certainly not in the way that he'd already gotten so friendly with Dominic just in passing around the league. Benny liked to banter but Joe was never open to him in that way. Still, McCoy felt an affinity with Joe. A few months before the 1940 sea-

son McCoy and some other players in the Detroit Tigers' system had been declared "free agents" by commissioner Kenesaw Mountain Landis; the Tigers, Landis ruled, had willfully mishandled the players' contracts and blocked their financial progress. In the bidding war that followed, McCoy, with only half a season of big league baseball behind him, drew a guarantee of $65,000 over two years to sign with the A's. That was superstar money. And so when Benny had a bad game, which he often had that first season, the crowd heckled and booed. *There goes the $65,000 beauty. Oh cripes. You know, I could strike out like that for half the dough he's getting paid!* McCoy had heard of, and then heard for himself, the booing that DiMaggio sometimes got because of the money he made. Players who bargained for big contracts did not fare well in the public's mind. *Why, I'm the Joe DiMaggio of the Philadelphia A's*, McCoy sometimes thought to himself with a smile.

McCoy was playing better this season, fielding well and driving in runs. But lately he was in another pickle. His draft number had been called that spring and his repeated requests for deferment on the grounds that he had parents and siblings to support—most recently he'd been granted a respite until late July—did not sit easily with every fan. Again McCoy heard some heckling from the stands. He had talked about the draft situation with Dom DiMaggio when the Athletics were up in Boston, and so the news that arrived just that day, with the Yankees in town, that Dom had been spared military induction on account of his poor eyesight was encouraging to McCoy. So was the fact that the White Sox's Johnny Rigney had been spared conscription at the 11th hour by what the Army doctors were calling a perforated ear drum. Maybe if it came down to it the draft board would find a way to exempt McCoy, too. *Maybe I'll get to play out this whole season after all,* he thought.

McCoy looked in from second base. The sun was hot upon the infield. He was not pleased with Babich's plan either. McCoy wanted to beat the Yankees, of course, and who better than Johnny to do that, but he couldn't help but root for DiMaggio to get his hit. The streak was exciting; they all felt it. At the very least Joe should get his fair cracks and not be walked. In the first inning many in the crowd had actually risen to watch as DiMaggio's pop-up fell into Brancato's glove. DiMaggio was now standing in the batter's box again.

Babich's first pitch came in well outside and the second one did too, and perhaps that was the pitch that truly sounded the tocsin in DiMaggio's mind. *Babich really could do this. He could just walk me.* Ball three arrived, once again well off the plate.

DiMaggio stepped out and looked down to Art Fletcher at third base to see if he would be asked to take a pitch on the 3–0 count. From the dugout McCarthy gave Fletcher the sign to let Joe swing away and then DiMaggio turned back toward the plate to take his stance again. Through the shadows McCarthy could see Joe's features harden and contract and a darkness encroach upon his eyes. It was a look of hot resentment, fierce but controlled. Seething. It was not a look that McCarthy recalled ever seeing on a ballplayer's face.

The fourth pitch from Babich came in, high and again decidedly off the plate, but this time not quite far enough. *I can reach it,* DiMaggio thought. His bat was suddenly in motion and the baseball violently struck, on a line, a blistering missile right back through the box and into centerfield. Babich, nearly hit by the whistling ball, toppled off balance and the blood drained from his face. "He was as white as a sheet," DiMaggio would later recall. The ball skipped deeper onto the outfield grass and centerfielder Bob Johnson gathered it before it rolled into the gap. DiMaggio never slowed as he ran down the line and with coach Earle Combs urging him on, he took the turn at first base on a hard angle and hurtled to second, sliding in safely, a single having become a double by DiMaggio's determination that it be so. Though DiMaggio would later call this blow off the insolent Babich "the most satisfying hit of the streak," he did not let that satisfaction show as he stood on second base. He simply watched Babich get the ball back and he prepared to take his lead. McCoy wanted to greet DiMaggio, even just a quick hello, but shyness would not let him. *He has other things on his mind than saying hello to me,* McCoy thought. The streak was now at 40 games.

The Yankees won the game 7–4. Charlie Keller's home run extended the team's streak to 23 straight with a homer, and fans spilled onto the field after the final out in the ninth, hoping as ever to get near Joe. Later in the victorious locker room—the odors of sweat and breath mixing with soap and cigarettes—as the team prepared to catch its chartered bus for

the train station, DiMaggio received a telegram from Jefferson Hospital downtown requesting that he come there right away. A flagging and incurably ill 10-year-old boy wanted to meet DiMaggio; perhaps the baseball star would bring joy in the final hours. Lefty went with Joe of course. Now he was always at DiMaggio's side, there to deflect the increasing attention, to steer people away, to handle the inquiring press. "You nervous about the streak?" a reporter would call out and it would be Lefty who would turn and reply, "Joe? Nah, he's fine. Me? I threw up my breakfast."

A spleen disease afflicted the boy, Tony, and in the hospital room Joe sat and talked with him for awhile. Tony was terribly thin but DiMaggio found him bright and cheerful. Because the boy had listened to the radio and knew all about the streak, and because this was the sort of thing a baseball hero was supposed to do, DiMaggio assured Tony that the next day he would have him in mind when he played a doubleheader against the Senators. DiMaggio said that he would break the hitting streak record and that doing so would be his way of communicating his thoughts and well wishes to Tony. Then Joe and Lefty went from the hospital and took a cab to the 30th Street Station and got on board the evening train to Washington, D.C.

Chapter 19

Bedlam

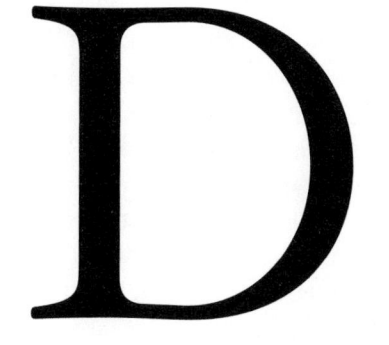IMAGGIO SAT READING *Superman* and smoking in his room at the Shoreham Hotel. Joe adored the *Superman* comics, although he did not want many people to know this. If the newspapers picked up on it, and he felt they surely would, who knew what people might think? What if they made fun of him for the *Superman* thing? Lefty had the assignment of discreetly buying the weekly comic book for Joe; whenever DiMaggio himself carried a copy he tucked it away and out of sight. He read the daily *Superman* strips in the newspaper too.

Superman was a story of simple and unambiguous heroism in which the seemingly impossible was routinely achieved. Something important was always at stake. Everybody loved Superman and unfailingly he saved the day. There was also in the story the everpresent element of secrecy, of Clark Kent's disguising a completely other identity that no one, not even Lois Lane, could ever know.

"Why, Joe, you're just like him," Lefty would kid. "He puts on his uni-

form and all of a sudden no one can stop him! He's everyone's hero." Sometimes when buying the comic—and DiMaggio always had Lefty get it on the very day it came out—Gomez would goof around and call out loudly to DiMaggio, hovering off to the side: "You mean *this* comic book, Joe? Or this one, the *Superman*?" DiMaggio would scowl and turn his back and walk off a few paces. Only Lefty could get away with tweaking him like this.

Tonight, with the doubleheader and Sisler's record waiting in the balance at Griffith Stadium the next day, Joe and Lefty would stay in the room. As DiMaggio had realized, over the last days in New York and then again staying at the Ben Franklin in Philadelphia, being out in public now meant being subject to an almost relentless pestering.

Even in ordinary times when DiMaggio went out someone invariably wanted a piece of him—and wanted his autograph. Fans interrupted his meals at restaurants and surrounded him when he left Yankee Stadium. At the movies DiMaggio found it best to sit near the back, to limit the number of people who might see him and come over to greet him even as the picture rolled. The fawning and the people's eagerness to approach him had become far greater now; it seemed that each day his celebrity grew.

Now, even a simple stroll or an attempt to sit quietly in the hotel lobby was a sure invitation to be bothered. That was too bad. DiMaggio liked the hotel lobbies, saw them as a comfortable place to relax. He liked to sit in the plush armchairs beneath the fancy chandeliers and, with one or two of the guys in the chairs beside him, watch the hotel guests come and go. They'd sit without speaking. A few years back in St. Louis a reporter had seen DiMaggio, Frankie Crosetti and Tony Lazzeri together in the lobby of the Chase Hotel. The teammates sat for nearly an hour and a half without exchanging a single word. Then DiMaggio cleared his throat. "What did you say?" Crosetti asked. And Lazzeri said, "Shut up. He didn't say anything." And then the three men fell back into silence. They sat and watched and were left to do so in peace.

That would not be possible in this time of the hitting streak and so DiMaggio would stay in the room, and he and Lefty would put the radio on and order up steak. Even on a night like this some enterprising fans would come and knock on the door claiming to be a bellhop or a maid. Gomez would tell them to bug off, and that DiMaggio wasn't even there.

At times, though, a pretty woman would arrive to the room, and if Joe had invited her or if he wanted her to stay (he had a fondness then for redheads), Gomez would let the woman inside and then leave the two of them alone for a while. Rarely did Joe ever see any of these women again. He expected nothing of them and he made it clear that they should expect nothing of him. DiMaggio did not offer to take any of the women out for a meal, nor did he suggest that they spend any additional time together. To none of the women did he play the cavalier. The dalliances may have briefly pleased DiMaggio but they did not satisfy him, and they did not lessen the loneliness he felt for Dorothy when he was away. When he was apart from Dorothy she seemed in every aspect ideal. His annoyances with her seemed small and unimportant and were far from his thoughts; she became in his mind the missing ingredient he needed to feel at ease. No other woman changed that. DiMaggio still, or even more so, looked forward to returning home to Dorothy's arms and to their first moments together; he still wanted her to be at the ballpark for every game and to be on his arm when the photographers came. Out in the nightlife, DiMaggio's moments of gallantry were reserved only for his wife. There may have been other women sometimes, but really there were none. Joe was always true to Dorothy, in his fashion.

And now Superman is foiling the enemy again, withstanding the blast from a death-ray gun, snaring a falling bomb just before it lands on the innocents below, flying above the tall city buildings carrying Lois safely in his arms. The wordy language of the comic strip was pleasing to DiMaggio, too—"Forward battles Superman against the insidious force of the ray!"— and over time the comic book would become creased and dog-eared, its margins foxed. DiMaggio lingered on the pages, reading and rereading, and smoked his Camels and ate his steak with Lefty, and then he tried to put the next day's assignment out of his mind, to see whether he could fall asleep.

———◆———

HAD IT EVER been so hot in Griffith Stadium? DiMaggio reached up and wiped his brow. Ninety-five degrees and still nearly an hour before game time; the ballpark was a cauldron. The crowd made everything hotter and steamier still. Even in these conditions fans had mobbed their way to the

Stadium. They had come down from New York, Baltimore, Philadelphia and up from the South. And from who knows where else. When DiMaggio and Lefty had arrived at the park and stepped out of their cab, people had shouted and whooped and pushed near. Finally, there would be 31,000 fans packed in the stands shoulder-to-shoulder, sweaty shirtsleeve to sweaty shirtsleeve—more people even than the 30,600 that Griffith Stadium was officially supposed to hold. Many others were turned away at the entrance gate. The last time the two teams had played here, a day game in the middle of the week with DiMaggio's hitting streak at an unnoticed 14 straight, 1,500 people had turned out.

"We couldn't draw flies before this," the Senators manager Bucky Harris said to reporters, peering up into the sea of hats. "The capacity crowd we have here is due to Joe and to nobody and nothing else."

Nor were these fans reserved in their affection. As DiMaggio made his way to home plate for batting practice, groups of boys and young men spilled from the aisles and pushed past the ushers onto the field and came right up against Joe, tugging on his uniform, pulling on his arm, begging for his autograph. *Over here, Joe!* A kid held a baseball and a pen. *Joe, over here!* Another had a program in his hands. At this outpouring DiMaggio did not quite know what to do. He smiled and quickly signed his name on a couple of things as he walked, and then demurred and went to take his batting practice swings. Soon afterward DiMaggio moved to get away from the boys and to go back into the dugout and up into the shaded tunnel for a few moments of respite. A last half-cup of coffee. A Camel. Christ it was hot. DiMaggio just wanted the game to begin.

So did McCarthy. Aside from the DiMaggio hoopla there was still a game to be won—two games actually—and a chance for the Yankees to break away from the persistent Indians and move firmly into first place. The Senators, even at well under .500, were scrappy, with good speed and a couple of All-Star hitters. Their two best pitchers, the knuckleballer Dutch Leonard and the young righthander Sid Hudson, would be starting in the doubleheader.

Washington had won nine of its last 13 games and Bucky Harris, McCarthy knew, was always up to something. Whenever the Yanks played in Griffith Stadium, McCarthy had to keep an eye on their bat bags or else the bags would wind up stashed in the shower room. (Innocently enough,

the clubhouse boy would say.) The Senators believed that the moisture from the showers might make the Yankee bats a little heavier, sap a little of their zing. The Senators did not win much anymore—"Washington: first in war, first in peace, last in the American League" as the vaudeville routine went—but under Harris they did not lie down.

Sisler had played here in 1928, acquired from the Browns for a forgettable, six-week stint near the end of his career. After appearing in just 20 games as a Senator, he'd been traded again, to the Boston Braves, but it was not those days the old-timers remembered when they thought about Gentleman George. With the Browns in St. Louis he had been the best first baseman in baseball for years, bar none; the predecessor to Lou Gehrig. As a rookie in 1915, fresh off the diamonds at the University of Michigan where Browns manager Branch Rickey had found him, the lefthanded Sisler had pitched too; in his first major league start he had gotten the better of Walter Johnson, the Big Train himself. As a hitter Sisler was most often compared to Ty Cobb.

Sisler batted .407 in 1920, hit .371 a year later, and then came 1922. It was said that no ballplayer—not Cobb, not the Babe—ever had a better all-around season than Sisler had that year. He batted .420 and hit in 41 consecutive games. He led the American League with 246 hits, 51 stolen bases and 18 triples. He dominated on defense too, fielding his position with a range and agility unlike any first baseman before or since. Sisler could deflate a rally all by himself. Once, on an opponents' squeeze play, he had raced in, scooped the bunt into his glove, tagged out the batter and dived to the far side of home plate to tag out the runner trying to score from third. A 3-3-3 double play you could say.

At 5' 11" and 170 pounds Sisler swung an oversized 42-ounce bat, and he swung it wisely. Branch Rickey called Sisler "the smartest hitter I've ever seen," and added that he wasn't surprised given that Sisler had graduated from Michigan in four years with a degree in mechanical engineering. For Gentleman George—he did not smoke, drink or cuss— baseball came naturally. "I always could hit even against bigger boys," he explained, almost sheepishly. "And I always could field. I never had to learn. I just seemed to do everything right instinctively."

And then, just after that brilliant 1922 season, something terrible hap-

pened. Sisler was 29 and entering his peak when, that off-season, he contracted a strange sinus infection. Before long the infection started to put pressure on his optic nerve, blurring his sight. Sisler was out driving one day when he thought he saw two cars approaching him, though really there was only one. The doctors had him sit out all of the 1923 season. He would appear sometimes in the St. Louis stands wearing dark glasses to protect against the sun. Slowly his eyes began to heal, though never completely. When Sisler made his comeback with the Browns in 1924 he batted just .305. He became a symbol of an athlete dying young. One newspaper columnist wrote that watching Sisler with his diminished sight was like it would be to watch the great thoroughbred Man o' War trying to race without his forelegs.

Even so Sisler played six more seasons and four times he batted better than .325, impressive figures for many players, though for Sisler so much lower than his heights. He wound up with 2,812 hits and a .340 lifetime batting average and who knows what records he would have set if not for the trouble with his eyes. In 1939, Sisler was elected to the Baseball Hall of Fame. He was regarded throughout the game as one of the greats.

The attention on DiMaggio at this doubleheader in D.C. was not limited to the sweltering mass at Griffith Stadium—nor to the room in St. Louis where Sisler, now a sporting goods salesman, tuned in. Radios played on the stoops in Jackson Heights and on the fire escapes of East Harlem where Italian was still commonly the language of the street; in another Italian enclave, upstate, a radio was rigged to an outdoor loudspeaker. Guests at a lakeside resort in New Hampshire asked to receive updates on DiMaggio throughout the afternoon. The streak was being followed in Kansas City by Rugger Ardizoia and Bud Metheny and the rest of the would-be Yankees playing for the minor league Blues. Radios were on in Newark, of course— big Sunday crowd at the Vittorio Castle—and in small Connecticut towns. The play-by-play broadcast by the Senators' guy, Arch McDonald, would carry on the powerful airwaves of WMAL through Washington, D.C., and out the many miles east to the coasts of Maryland, Delaware, New Jersey— the seaside hamlets that lay an entire country's width from Joe DiMaggio's Grotto on Fisherman's Wharf in San Francisco.

Business was thriving at the Grotto, income having spiked terrifically as

compared with the summer before, and the explanation for this was clear. Tom estimated that in the days since the streak had caught fire the restaurant's daily take had doubled. Tourists wanted to be around Joe's name, to see the newspaper clippings of him on the wall and his trophies in the back, to chat a bit with his brothers and to imagine the hit-streaking DiMaggio returning to this place when his season was done. "Any wonder that I'm trying to keep this streak going?" DiMaggio, grinning, had told reporters after getting Tom's report on the Grotto. "It's cash in the register, boy."

All week long DiMaggio's father, Giuseppe, had paced the front rooms of the house on Beach Street waiting each day for news of Joe's fate. The old man understood that Joe had something special at stake. Tom couldn't remember ever having seen their father so preoccupied, had never known Giuseppe to be so concerned with any of his sons' baseball accomplishments. The radio that Joe had bought his parents played throughout the afternoons and evenings—you never knew when you would hear some talk of the streak—and sometimes Giuseppe would ask his granddaughter Betty to call the newspapers to see if anything new had come in. Such fussing, though, was not Rosalie's way. Each night she quietly lit a candle for Joe and changed the flowers in the icon, hoping to help bring good fortune to her son.

Now at the busy, bustling Grotto, Tom hustled about stroking his mustache and tidying things and making sure that the customers were comfortable and pleased. Soon, Mike came in off the docks. Wine was being poured in the middle of the day. People ordered cioppino—*it's authentic at DiMag's place*, they reasoned. The radio had been turned on and set atop the bar, where it had been stationed throughout the week. No one knew just when the bulletins would come. Several times, Tom had to scold the waiters and the bus boys to keep their minds on their work.

They were listening too over in the Mission District, at the Double Play lounge and in the smokeshop outside Seals Stadium. And they were listening, as ever, in North Beach, on the church square and at the taverns and in the kitchens of their homes. Still all afternoon Alessandro and his buddies wore out the line phoning the *Call-Bulletin* and the *Chronicle*, hoping that a ticker tape had just delivered some news and that they would have it even a moment or two before others in the city. Getting

the news first mattered to them. This was their Joe, *their* hometown hero, even if he had now captured the nation's gaze. The boys who came from the playgrounds of North Beach clung to Joe's roots and to the memories they had of him as a teenager and as a younger man. They would remind anyone in San Francisco then, just as they would go on reminding people all over for many, many years, that Joe was their Joe first.

PHOTOGRAPHERS KNELT ALONG both foul lines at Griffith Stadium as if it were a World Series game and saved their film for when DiMaggio came to bat. Motion picture cameras were also trained upon Joe, there to capture him and his historic at bats for the newsreels. DiMaggio remembered to give a casual smile into the lens, a short wave, a friendly salute. When he prepared to hit, swinging two bats before tossing one aside upon his approach the plate, DiMaggio moved easily and with a seeming nonchalance. His face revealed nothing. Inside, though, he churned. It had been like that for some days now, as Sisler's record had come nearer, and at times this stress affected DiMaggio's behavior. A couple of games back he'd done something he could not remember ever having done before. A pitch came in that he believed was off the plate for a ball and when the umpire disagreed, barking out "strike!" DiMaggio turned back sharply to look at him. Every strike mattered; every hitless at bat could hasten the end of the streak. Yet even in the moment that he turned his head, DiMaggio regretted doing so. Looking at an umpire this way was a sign of disrespect. More than that, it was an act of self-insubordination, a self-inflicted blemish upon his polished image. DiMaggio simply did not question umpires nor ever betray disapproval of a call. He played the game as well and as intently as he could; the rest, he felt, was not his business. So uncharacteristic was DiMaggio's backward look that the umpire was himself taken aback. "Honest to god, Joe, it was right down the middle," he said through his mask. DiMaggio, chiding himself, wondering what had gotten into him, just swiveled back to face the pitcher and did not say a word.

Washington's first-game starter, Dutch Leonard, was a coal miner's son from Illinois. At 32 he had the look of a man well into middle age, flabby with a moon-face and a hairline in full retreat. The guys called him "butch-

er boy" and "big blubber" when they razzed him from the dugout. Leonard threw a knuckleball, an extravagantly slow curve and a fastball that on its own was nothing to remark on. But it was no accident that he had won 20 games in 1939 and was having another strong season. His big, jerky windup could throw a hitter off, and sometimes that sandlot fastball, when it came just after one of Leonard's butterfly balls had danced by, seemed the size of a pea. For this reason, DiMaggio had recently described Leonard as having one of the trickiest fastballs in the league.

As DiMaggio dug in his first time up, the temperature had climbed to 98 degrees. The cameras clicked as he took his stance, and when he swung hard at the very first pitch—as if to say, *Let's go, let's get this done with*—and drove the ball into the outfield the people rose in the stands, only to see the able Doc Cramer glide over from centerfield, reach up and squeeze the ball into his glove.

In the fourth inning Leonard nibbled around the plate, coming in too high with his first pitch, missing off the outside corner on his second, putting a knuckleball too far inside on his third. With the count 3 and 0, DiMaggio again looked to Fletcher for the sign. Again McCarthy was allowing DiMaggio to swing away—even now with one out and a runner on first base and no score in the game; even though with Keller, the team's leading RBI man, on deck, a walk might have done the Yankees good. In came a pitch that DiMaggio should have taken, but he swung at it nonetheless and as his pop fly landed in the glove of the third baseman George Archie, groans of disappointment came from the crowd.

Leonard was still in the game, trying to keep the Yankees' lead to 3–0 and fighting the mid-afternoon heat, when DiMaggio stepped up for the third time, in the sixth. Again Joe swung at the first pitch and this time he missed. An errant curveball set the count at 1 and 1. Leonard looked in. *If I can get a fastball past him I bet I could finish him off with the knuckler,* he thought. And so it was the fastball that Leonard threw, knee high and on the outer half of the plate. The barrel of DiMaggio's bat caught the baseball flush and in a moment it was bounding on the outfield grass toward the 422-foot sign in left centerfield. *Forty-one!* There was suddenly reason for the fans—now cheering and slapping backs—to weather the heat and stay around for the second game. They watched DiMaggio turn

hard around first base and bear down toward second, his cleats kicking up the dun earth, slowing as he reached the bag with a stand-up double. The cheering continued in the stands and the Yankees dugout throbbed with excitement. Though DiMaggio did not clap, or clench his fist or raise his arms, he felt inside him a release and a momentary ease.

Sweat soaked through DiMaggio's flannel uniform—up and down his pantlegs as well as across his chest and back. He was sweatier even than most of his teammates, though this seemed paradoxical. That quality of DiMaggio's game, which other ballplayers often called gracefulness and fluidity, was at its core simply an economy of movement. Just as all of DiMaggio's swing was captured completely inside the batting stroke itself—nothing extra before or after—so was he equally efficient when running the bases or making his swift, yawless errands to chase down balls in centerfield. There was nothing superfluous about DiMaggio in the things that he did. Still he sweated heavily in the heat. And when that first game ended—Yankees 9, Senators 4—DiMaggio felt very much in need of a shower.

Fans had already jumped onto the field by the time he reached the dugout for the break between games; again pens and scorecards were thrust upon him. A longtime U.S. Senator from California, Hiram Johnson, had also come around. His aides and some photographers wanted DiMaggio to come over so that the two could pose together. Johnson had been California's governor the year DiMaggio was born. But there were so many people, everywhere, and more coming over the rail. His teammates were disappearing into the tunnel toward the clubhouse. With the second game still to play DiMaggio felt tired and sticky-wet all over. He could come back for the senator, he thought, and so he asked the photographers if they wouldn't mind waiting, and then he pushed through the swarm of bodies to the clubhouse.

DiMaggio showered and pulled on a fresh uniform and said a few words to the newspaper reporters about the low pitch that he had hit for the record-tying double. When he slipped back out to the field where autograph seekers still milled around, and looked for Senator Johnson and the cameramen they were gone. *Don't they still want me to pose?* DiMaggio wondered. *Are they sore with me now?* Maybe the Senator felt

slighted. DiMaggio hoped this wasn't so and hoped the incident would not put him in a poor light. It wasn't his fault! He'd needed to cool his body and get away from the frenzy on the field. It really had been a hectic scene. So great was the commotion between games, in fact, that someone among the busying crowd had slipped into the Yankees dugout and stolen DiMaggio's bat.

"TOM!" HENRICH TURNED back to the dugout to see who had called his name. "Tommy, you got my ball bat?" It was DiMaggio. Henrich, out on the grass and preparing to hit in the first inning of the second game of the doubleheader, did have a DiMaggio model—the same one he'd borrowed and been swinging for weeks. But he did not have the bat that DiMaggio was using in the games, the one Joe had sanded down just so. The bat was not with the others in the rack. Nor could it be found leaning against a dugout wall, or lying beneath the bench. The bat was gone.

So when DiMaggio, facing Sid Hudson in the first inning, swung at a waist-high fastball and looped a fly ball that the rightfielder Buddy Lewis came forward to catch, DiMaggio did so using a reserve piece of wood. Who knows? Had he been swinging his usual ball bat maybe that fly ball would've dropped in safely. DiMaggio entertained this thought himself. Baseball is a subtle game.

He used that same bat his second time up, in the third inning, and when Hudson dropped down to whip in a sidearm curve, DiMaggio was not fooled. His line drive reached the shortstop Cecil Travis before DiMaggio had gotten out of the batter's box and Travis, without moving his feet, caught the ball at shoulder height. 0 for 2. The game wore on and the heat did not wane. DiMaggio sat by himself on the bench, and the Senators brought in Arnold Anderson to pitch. Anderson weighed 210 pounds and stood 6' 3", an Iowa farm boy with auburn hair and a freckled face. His best pitch was the heater. Everybody called him Red.

In the fifth inning against DiMaggio, Red came inside with the fastball on the first pitch, then missed away with the curve. When he came back inside with the fastball one more time DiMaggio could only get the handle of his bat on the pitch and the ball never really had a chance, dy-

ing in Cramer's glove in short centerfield. The fans in Griffith Stadium sat back down. The sun had fallen lower in the sky.

The score was tied at 4–4 when the Yankees scored twice in the top of the sixth to take the lead, but if ever a game-turning rally seemed beside the point, it was this one. The fans and many of the players had one thought on their minds: DiMaggio was 0 for 3. Joe never did the things that some ballplayers do when they're nervous on the bench. He did not scratch the side of his face, or finger his lower lip, or rub his hands together. DiMaggio only sat and looked in front of him. Unless something happened that called for his attention, he did not turn to the left or to the right. He stared straight ahead.

No one in the Yankees dugout would speak to Joe at all. But when the seventh inning arrived and with it, perhaps, DiMaggio's final turn at bat, Henrich came over. He suggested that DiMaggio try using the bat that Henrich was using—it too was DiMag's bat after all, and the other one Joe had used today hadn't had much luck in it. DiMaggio agreed and took the Henrich bat with him to the plate. Again Red Anderson started off high and close with his fastball, this time forcing DiMaggio to jerk back out of its way. Maybe Red, in his first full major league season, got cocky. Or maybe the fastball was the only pitch that he trusted. Whatever the reason, on 1 and 0 he threw it again—this time over the plate.

You could have heard the crowd's roar on Georgia Avenue, past the trolley tracks and way up the hill, when DiMaggio hit that ball, a hard, clean single into leftfield. At first base Earle Combs slapped DiMaggio on the back and first baseman Mickey Vernon shook his hand and DiMaggio gave Vernon a pat on the rump. There would be no enforcing of the league's antifraternization rule today. When the first base umpire, Bill McGowan, strolled over he gave DiMaggio a tap on the behind himself. The joyful scenes repeated themselves in the Yankee dugout—caps tossed in the air, players dancing. And now DiMaggio did smile, broadly and without reservation. He looked around and hitched his pants. Suddenly children—"the urchins" as the Yankee players laughingly called them—ran onto the field and toward DiMaggio. In the crowd, the bedlam (and this was the word that the newspaper writers would use) did not quickly subside. Joe touched the bill of his cap, once and then a

second time. Several minutes passed before the game could start again.

And when Keller tripled, bringing DiMaggio home to score, the crowd stood and hollered anew as he arrived at the dugout, greeted before the first step by Johnny Sturm, and then by Lefty and Twink, and Dickey and Henrich and Rolfe and then by all of his teammates as he stepped down among them, all of them wanting to envelop their Joe. McCarthy grinned and Rizzuto hopped about and DiMaggio was filled with relief and happiness.

The euphoric mood continued in the locker room after the game as the reporters came rushing in. DiMaggio sat naked on a trunk, laughing and unabashed. Players tossed towels at him and even tousled his sweating black locks. All of this was O.K. to do now. When McCarthy came over and shook DiMaggio's hand the manager would not let go. His smile was unrestrained as he looked at Joe and an understanding passed between them. DiMaggio knew that McCarthy had compromised his game strategy more than once in deference to the streak. This was no small thing for a manager like McCarthy. The divide that had existed between the two men ever since McCarthy had toed the Yankee line over DiMaggio's contract, now seemed forgotten and closed. "I don't deserve the credit all alone," DiMaggio told the writers first thing that day. "You have to give Mr. McCarthy some of it. He allowed me to hit that 3 and 0 pitch and it brought me many a good ball to swing at."

Before long a 10-word telegram arrived at the clubhouse from Sisler in St. Louis: "Congratulations," it read. "I'm glad a real hitter broke it. Keep going."

DiMaggio spoke as expansively as he could to the writers. "Sure I'm tickled, who wouldn't be," he said. "It's a great thing." It was impossible for him to measure every word. There were many questions and they came fast. "When I got so close to Sisler's mark I didn't want to stop," DiMaggio said. "I never felt so much on the spot before. . . . It is the most excitement I guess I've known since I came into the majors."

By then the news had traveled to all the ballparks in baseball. And in New York, New England and California, and across the middle states, some version of this news report burst through the radio broadcasts: "The Nazis, continuing their march, are now said to be just 225 miles from Moscow." Then a pause. "And this has just come in from our na-

tion's capital: Joe DiMaggio has done it! The Yankee slugger has hit in 42 consecutive games, a new record."

In San Francisco customers ordered Scotch highballs at the Grotto and Giuseppe felt relieved and all aglow. And who said he couldn't joke around in English? A reporter from the *Chronicle* spoke to Papa DiMaggio and transcribed his words this way: "Joe, he waited too long. He waits until da seexth inning before he ties da record of Seesler. Then he waits until da seventh inning before he breaks Seesler's record in da second game. He makes his papa worry too long. Why cannot my son Joe do it in da first inning?"

In Jackson Heights on the bench outside the White Castle on Northern Boulevard—the joint where big Eddie Einsidler once knocked back 35 of those little burgers in a sitting, putting the rest of the Dukes and Hornets to shame—Squeaks Tito was keening, his voice now at a pitch, as Commie and the rest of the guys joked, that only a dog could hear. The radio sung the words from Washington: His Joe DiMaggio had come through.

Twenty-one-year-old Ray Robinson was a summer morning clerk at the Lake Stafford Hotel in Keene, N.H.—afternoons off, tennis, swimming, tanned young women up for a lark. Truly, Robinson wondered, could a guy have a better job? When he got the news, he hurried to spread it around.

A shout went out in Bensonhurst where Maury Allen and the rest of the young stickballers stopped their game and ran to the first radio they could find.

The main street buzzed in Ocean City, N.J., and little Gay Talese, his parents scarcely aware, felt thrilled, empowered even, by what DiMaggio had done.

In South Jamaica, Queens, the radio hummed on the grocery store counter and Mario Cuomo sat on the milk box, fiddling with his pea shooter, and all ready to go. It was a hot Sunday night, and often on hot Sunday nights Mario and his parents and his brother and sister would all get into the wood-paneled station wagon and drive out to Rockaway Beach. They would park right on the sand and put the tailgate down and sit together in the back of the car listening to the water lapping in, and talking, perhaps, about the things that had happened in the ball games that day. The sun

slipped to the horizon and you could hear the voices from the boardwalk. There was not the hubbub here of a place like Coney Island with its roller coasters and the Wonder Wheel, and the air-rifle shooting galleries where now, in a nod to the times, the tin ducks had been replaced as targets by little models of Nazi paratroopers. At Rockaway Beach the night was quieter; there was just noise enough. Mario could fall asleep under the blankets, the sea breeze upon him, full of sweet anticipatory giddiness, knowing that the next day his ballplaying hero Joe DiMaggio would be all over the newspapers. The hitting feat would be there for Mario to feast upon just as soon as dawn arrived and they awoke to the sounds of the seabirds and rubbed the salt from their eyes and drove back into South Jamaica to open up the store.

Chapter 20
Now, Wee Willie

T FIRST DOMINIC thought the newspaper story was a joke. Wee Willie Keeler? In 1897? Where did they come up with this stuff? For a couple of weeks now the news he'd been getting in Boston or on the road was about Joe's trying to catch George Sisler at 41 straight. Now Joe had done that and, it seemed to Dominic, a longer record had suddenly materialized. Sisler, they were now saying, only held the "modern" record. Keeler had run off 44 consecutive games for the Baltimore Orioles more than four decades earlier, before the turn of century. Dominic hadn't spoken to Joe in many weeks and was thinking about what he could say by way of congratulations when, soon after he and the Red Sox had arrived at the Hotel Commodore in New York for a doubleheader, with Joe's streak at 42 games, Dom saw the headline: DIMAGGIO WILL AIM FOR ALL-TIME HITTING RECORD. *So it's true,* Dom thought. *Joe still has a few games to go. It isn't a put-on.*

Dom paid attention to the streak, of course, as did Vince, with the Pirates. In fact Dom could not have avoided it if he'd tried: On the radio and in the bars and restaurants, the streak was on everybody's lips. Even in the Red Sox dugout these days, when someone said "DiMaggio" they were often referring not to Dom but to Joe. When Dominic called home it was Joe's streak that his father always got around to before long. Sometimes Dominic would be out somewhere, at a grocery shop or by a newsstand, and hear for the umpteenth time a lady ask some guy, "What did DiMaggio do today?" It was all Dom could do not to lean over and say, "Oh, I got 2 for 4 and thanks for asking."

At away games word of Joe's getting a hit was sometimes announced between innings over the stadium loudspeaker. At home in Fenway Park Dominic received information more intimately, as he stood in centerfield. Ted Williams had asked the scoreboard operator inside Fenway's big green monster of a leftfield wall to alert him whenever there was an update on Joe. Suddenly Dominic would hear Williams's booming voice: "Dommy! Dommy! Joe got a hit. The streak's alive."

No one on the Red Sox kept a closer eye on what Joe DiMaggio was doing than Williams did. He would check on DiMaggio's daily statistics in the box scores, and then he would talk about what he'd read. *You would guess that Ted was the brother,* thought the Red Sox second baseman Bobby Doerr. By this time Williams was batting .404, easily the best average in baseball and a full 55 points better than DiMaggio's. For a stretch of nearly a month from mid-May to mid-June, Williams had hit .517. Hardly anyone noticed. Some writers lamented how Williams's run at a historic season—nobody had hit better than .400 since Hornsby in '24—was being "obscured" and "submerged" by DiMaggio's streak. Yet obscured and submerged it remained. While the crowds swelled to see DiMaggio, Williams's gaudy average appeared to have no effect on the turnstiles. When comparisons were drawn between the two players the argument that DiMaggio was the better fielder and the more intimidating base runner inevitably won out. When Williams was asked for his own evaluation, he spoke respectfully of DiMaggio. "Joe is stronger," Williams said. At 22, Williams was remarkably thin. He earned about a third of DiMaggio's salary.

Still, the fact that he could be hitting over .400 and with power too—his 15 home runs and 56 RBI barely trailed DiMaggio in those categories—and nonetheless be rendered an afterthought was not always easy for Williams to take. "I had a 23-game hit streak this season," he pointed out during an interview just before Boston came to New York, and even as DiMaggio's streak rose upward Williams spoke undaunted. "I'd like to break every hitting record in the book," he declared.

Joe wasn't spending much time thinking about Williams, or about any other rival player. He thought about his own play and about what he still needed to do. There had certainly been a sense of achievement after passing Sisler's record, the beacon that for so long had shone brightly before him. The Yankees had celebrated DiMaggio as a conqueror when he reached 42—on the train ride up from D.C. he had bought every teammate a bottle of beer—and the public celebrated too. A story headlined, DIMAGGIO SETS CONSECUTIVE HITTING MARK, ran on the front page of *The Washington Post*.

Yet Keeler lurked in DiMaggio's mind. Dominic's surprise notwithstanding, newspapers had been mentioning Keeler's streak for the better part of a week. While the Yankees were in Philadelphia, DiMaggio had gotten a call from a reporter friend in San Francisco confirming that Keeler's record, set way back then, was indeed the official major league mark. Even in the exultant locker room shortly after he had eclipsed Sisler, DiMaggio had allowed that he was still looking ahead. "Now I'm going after that 44 game mark," he said. Keeler was the new goal. *Imagine getting this close and then not breaking it.* To DiMaggio this was an unsettling thought.

———

THE FACT THAT DiMaggio could tie Keeler with a hit in each game of the doubleheader against the Red Sox was something neither the Yankees nor the New York reporters were shy about advertising. The hitting streak sold: newspapers, tickets, score books. Rarely had a baseball plotline had legs like this. Thus Keeler, a .341 career hitter who had died too young of heart disease in 1923, was resurrected. Some old-timers argued that Wee Willie had it tougher than current hitters, given the way that in his day

baseballs could be kept in play for entire games, becoming filthy with soil and tobacco juice, becoming too soft for a batter to really drive. The ball was "dead" in that era, they said, and players swung smaller bats. Keeler's was 30½ inches long and 30½ ounces in weight, the smallest piece of lumber the folks at the Louisville Slugger factory had ever turned for a major leaguer. Even so, Keeler choked up six inches on the handle. When he first stepped into the batter's box he looked like a sandlot novice, a kid. He stood less than 5' 5" and he weighed 140 pounds.

Keeler grew up (if you could call it that) in Brooklyn and baseball gripped him from the start. He would come to the Gates Avenue School carrying a bat in his hands, and with a weathered ball stuffed into each of his coat pockets. The hips of his trousers were worn from sliding, his palms were rough and callused. Sometimes Wee Willie had about him the faint smell of horses; his father drove a streetcar on the DeKalb Avenue line.

Wee Willie had a schoolteacher, Miss Emma Keeler. "I am very sorry to acknowledge that you are a namesake of mine," she said to him, "but I am thankful that you are not of my kin." Miss Keeler never appreciated the love that Willie felt for America's young and growling game. As a baseball player Wee Willie was the best in the school. As a student he couldn't tell fowl from fish or from anything else. "You ought to be ashamed of yourself!" Miss Keeler said as she returned a test paper to Willie. "You should be ashamed to say that the rhinoceros, an animal the hide of which cannot be pierced by a bullet, is noted for its fine feathers. A boy who pays no more attention to his studies than you do will never amount to much when he gets to be a man." Then Miss Keeler paused: "I also wish to add that I shall no longer tolerate the bringing of baseball bats into this schoolroom."

So Wee Willie wasn't long for the schoolroom. He could box, tenacious in the ring despite his tiny stature, and when he wrestled he could toss a guy twice his size. But nothing else mattered if there was a ball game going on. Willie pitched, played the infield—who cared if he was lefthanded—and would even fill in at catcher, anything to earn money in the semipro leagues. Everyone in Brooklyn got to know Willie's name but when he made it big, he made it big in Baltimore, as the

rightfielder on a team with the formidable likes of Hughie Jennings and John J. McGraw. Those three led the Orioles to the championship of the National League in 1894, '95 and '96. In '97 Keeler started the season by getting a hit in 44 straight games, and finished it with a batting average of .424.

Opponents stuck Willie with the nickname Little Boy, yet even as they cursed his pesky style, the little boy was transforming the game. He could place a base hit as accurately as another guy could throw a baseball. He'd bunt his way on base—daring and happy to do it even with a runner on third—and when the infielders came in close to try to take that bunt away, he would just chop the ball over their heads or slap it hard past their gloves. If Keeler saw a fielder moving to cover a base, he hit the ball right to the spot where the fielder had been. It was Wee Willie who brought the hit-and-run play to the major leagues.

They called him a "scientific hitter" and around the time that he was averaging better than .370 in each of six seasons in a row, people begged him for a treatise on the art. "Keep your eyes clear and hit 'em where they ain't. That's all," he said. Over the years "hit 'em where they ain't" had found purchase in the lexicon, attached to Keeler, and was a philosophical truth in dugouts across the land.

Some said that in those years of the late 1890s and the early aughts Wee Willie was the best player in baseball—better even than Nap Lajoie. Keeler ran the bases with great speed and he covered wide ground in the outfield. Some of that was the ground that sloped sharply down and out of sight in Baltimore's old Union Park. It was there that crafty Willie would secretly stow baseballs in the grass. When a batter hit one out past the slope in rightfield Keeler would race back, vanish from view, and then, miraculously, come up throwing a moment later. In this way the Orioles often got startled runners out. Then came the day that both Keeler and the Baltimore centerfielder disappeared chasing a ball over the brow. A moment later not one but two baseballs came hurtling toward second base. From then on the umpires checked the grass.

Keeler returned to Brooklyn to play for the Superbas and twice helped that team win the National League. Folks called Keeler the pride of Wil-

liamsburg for the neighborhood where he was raised. Out in front of the Superbas' Washington Park a boy would sometimes wave a score card before games, shouting "you can't tell the players without one!" But the fans were interested in one player in particular. And when they looked out to see Wee Willie Keeler standing beside a teammate, perhaps the 6' 1" Duke Farrell, well, the fact was you could tell *that* player without any help from the score card at all.

Keeler went on to play for the Giants and for the Highlanders too, retiring finally in 1910 at the age of 38 with 2,932 hits, two batting titles, and an unmatched eight seasons of 200 base hits or more. "Records don't mean much to me," he said, but of one even Wee Willie was proud. In a span of more than a full season in the 1890s Keeler had come to bat 700 times without striking out.

He would have been great in any era—everyone chewing it over at Yankee Stadium that day agreed. But could you really compare Wee Willie's time to 1941? Foul balls did not even count as strikes then. Poking with his little club, Keeler would knock foul after foul, wearing a pitcher down in body and in mind until he threw just the pitch that Keeler wanted. *What about that?* went the argument in the Stadium bleachers. *A good hitter could be up forever! No wonder they got wise and changed the rule. That deck was stacked.*

It was the first of July, a Tuesday afternoon, and nearly 53,000 fans had jammed into Yankee Stadium for the doubleheader with the Red Sox. The size of the crowd was astonishing, the largest of the year. Not even the Yankees had expected this many fans to show up, not in the middle of the week and certainly not with the heat being what it was. There had been no letup. Temperatures remained in the mid 90s and the air had become even heavier and more stifling. A 54-year-old man in Brooklyn died of prostration. A 39-year-old news reporter from the *Journal-American* became so overheated that his heart gave out. Many people throughout the area were hospitalized. The papers offered advice about what to do— put a cold compress on the neck; lie in cool bathwater in the middle of the day. Around the city the air-conditioned movie theaters were packed regardless of what they were showing on their screens. On a day like this you did not pay to sit in the open sun at Yankee Stadium, with the body

heat of thousands around you, unless something special was going on.

They are here to see me, DiMaggio thought as he jogged out to stand in centerfield. He could hear the people calling out his name. *They're here to see me get a base hit in both games.*

In the bottom of the first inning of Game 1 against the second-year lefthander Mickey Harris, DiMaggio fell behind 0 and 2. Then he hit a foul pop-up that was caught by the Boston first baseman Lou Finney.

DiMaggio had still not recovered the stolen bat, a fact that Bina Spatola, sitting in the first row right behind the Yankees dugout and right in front of Jerry Spatola, her dad, was well aware of. She still couldn't quite believe that she was here at the game, on this day in the heart of the streak. She and Geta were in Joe's good seats, the same seats where actors like George Raft and Virginia Pine sometimes sat. Or Lou Costello and his wife. Bina had her hair pulled back and she was wearing a sundress. Geta had sunglasses on.

Jerry had been working to get Joe D his bat back. The word on the street had revealed some news, a few suspects. The bat was apparently in Newark somewhere—that much even Bina had heard. An usher had seen a guy leaving Griffith Stadium carrying the bat, but by now it had changed hands who knew how many times. Jerry Spats, with the help of the broad-knuckled Peanuts (and probably, though Bina would never have been able to say for sure, with the help of some of Richie's guys), was making sure the bat got back to Joe where it belonged. *If Dad has to pay somebody for it that's what he'll do,* Bina thought. *He'll get it back.* She liked to put her hands on the top of the warm dugout roof. Home plate was right there in front of her.

In truth losing the bat didn't matter all that much to DiMaggio. Certainly he was sorry not to have it—he was sorry for anything that forced a change in his habit, and he had liked that bat fine. But DiMaggio was not finicky about bats. When he was first breaking in, tall tales were written of how Joe had grown up in San Francisco hitting with oar handles. Those stories may as well have been true. DiMaggio had been ordering from Louisville Slugger since 1933, and just in the past couple of years the company had sent him 36-inch bats that weighed 33, 34, 35, 36 and 37 ounces. When Fritz Bickel turned a bat for DiMaggio he

was as assiduous as ever, working his calipers and gauges, bent intently over the lathe. But Bickel knew that he would never hear about it if he didn't get the weight exactly right. It wasn't like turning a bat for Williams. The Splinter demanded the best wood, with a long narrow grain. Eight grains per inch or he might send it back. And you had better not miss on the weight. It was said that Williams could pick through a batch of 10 bats and just by hefting each one know which was two-tenths of an ounce lighter than the rest. DiMaggio? Not quite. Once in a rare while if he thought a bat felt funny he'd take it to the butcher and have him put it on a hanging scale.

Sometimes DiMaggio switched to lighter bats in the summer months, a trick that Cobb swore by. Go down a couple of ounces and your swing would keep its zip through the season's most draining slog. But some seasons DiMaggio didn't go down in weight at all. When he ordered a half-dozen new bats after the theft in Washington they were the same 36 by 35½ as the batch he'd ordered in April. He swung a Y4 model, named for the Tigers' Rudy York and made of white Northern ash. Joe thought nothing of lending his bats to other players.

DiMaggio sometimes dipped his bat in olive oil—another Cobbism—but other times he did not. Sometimes he applied resin to the handle. Sometimes he left the handle clean. When a photographer asked DiMaggio to rub the bat with a beef bone for a funny picture, he'd do that too. He did like to sand the handles, carefully and repeatedly, so that over time, as with the bat that was stolen, the handle became smooth, and thinner than the way it arrived. Truly, though, these were not matters of high concern to DiMaggio. A couple years back the Yankees had floated the idea of using bats made of yew. The experiment never materialized but all along DiMaggio had been game. Why not? He could hit a baseball with anything.

Anyway, the boys in Newark would get his bat back—for pride as much as anything. You didn't steal a bat from Joe DiMaggio and get away with it. If that bat was still in one piece (or even if it wasn't) Spats and Peanuts would find it and bring it in. But it wasn't back yet today, with Keeler's 44-game streak on the table and DiMaggio already 0 for 1.

———

ITALIAN FLAGS WAVED in the grandstands and men used handkerchiefs to wipe their foreheads and the backs of their necks. People fanned themselves with their score cards; everybody had one it seemed. By the fifth inning a thick, bluish haze of cigarette smoke had gathered in the sultry air and sat upon the field. The mass of white shirts shimmering beyond the centerfield fence made it difficult for the batter to pick up the ball. *Of all the ballparks in the league this is the hardest place to hit,* Doerr thought. Still, when he looked around at the massive crowd and heard the heckling as the Red Sox came in and out of the dugout—*G'wan home Dominic, this is your big brother's turf!* and, *You're nothin' but a bum, Williams!*—Doerr knew that this was a hell of a good place to be playing a ball game.

The Yanks had a 4–0 lead and DiMaggio, after grounding out to the third baseman Jim Tabor in the third inning, was 0 for 2 as he prepared to hit against the righty reliever Mike Ryba in the fifth. Ryba hadn't made it to the majors until he was into his 30s. Now he was 38 and had a pair of gold teeth. He could play catcher too, and sometimes did. The heat drained some of the players—Williams said that a day like this made him lose his snap—and at times a torpor came over the crowd. But this was never the case just before, during, or after one of DiMaggio's at bats. The murmur began each time he stepped onto the on-deck circle, while Henrich was still in the batter's box. Then as DiMaggio strode to the plate that murmur swelled to a steady and determined clamor that drowned out the announcement of his name. Sometimes on the field a player could hear the first shouts of encouragement (*This is the time, Joe, give it a real knock!*) but then the different voices and the different, clapping hands all merged into one larger noise, static and imprecise, the ocean very loud in a conch shell, until DiMaggio took his stance and the pitcher looked in. Then the noise quieted to a low, reverberant hush, a lingering sound like a phrase of music just played.

Ryba threw DiMaggio two screwballs, both of them for strikes. The fans reacted to each pitch and when Ryba missed with the next three, running the count full, they began to boo, fearing a walk. DiMaggio also feared this and though he was fooled by the next pitch, a slow curveball too far inside, he swung hard, catching the top half of the baseball with the handle of his bat. The ball took a high bounce in front of the plate

and landed just 30 feet down the third base line. Tabor got to it, and with DiMaggio running hard toward first, threw hurriedly and wildly over the head of the first baseman Finney. In the press area Daniel needed no time to make his judgment: A hit. Not even a strong and accurate throw could have caught DiMaggio, Daniel decided. But many of the fans—most of them—were not aware of Daniel's call. Wasn't it an error? Tabor's throw was way off and DiMaggio had looked so out of character in his swing, flailing at the ball. That's not what a streak-extending hit looks like. That's not what DiMaggio looks like.

He's pressing thought Moe Berg, one of the Red Sox coaches. So unusual was it to see DiMaggio like that, to see him lunging and off-balance, that a photograph of the swing was later passed around among players and coaches in other ballparks. His right knee nearly touched the ground. His left foot was too far extended and it was awkwardly turned. "Why, that's not the way Joe bats," said Connie Mack in Philadelphia. "I never saw anything like it."

It was the impression of DiMaggio's awkwardness, and the poor throw that allowed him to go down to second base, that led so many fans to believe that the Tabor play had been an error and thus that DiMaggio was still hitless when he came to bat in the sixth. Again there was the murmuring and the noise—*It's as if they're very close but also far away,* Dominic thought—only this time it was followed by an explosion of happy shouts: DiMaggio lined a 1 and 0 pitch into leftfield for a single. The hit streak, at 43, was now secure and definite in everybody's mind.

As soon as the Yankees' 7–2 win was complete—Dom had homered for one of Boston's runs—Joe went straight off the field and into the locker room. Word that he had continued the streak had long since made its way onto the airwaves. At Ebbets Field in Brooklyn, Red Barber gave the DiMaggio news on WOR as he worked the Dodgers game against the Phillies. The Dodgers, at long last, were challenging for the pennant. The team was drawing fans and six Brooklyn players were bound for the upcoming All-Star Game. Still, on these early July days the Dodgers could not get top billing in the newspapers, not even in *The Brooklyn Eagle*. Thought Dodgers catcher Herman Franks, *I suppose that's as it should be. DiMaggio is all of that and more.*

Joe showered quickly, relishing the cool water and the clean medicinal smell of the red Lifebuoy soap, and came out to sit by his locker. His black cleats had been buffed and aired out for him and a fresh uniform hung on its hook. "Half-cup, Pete," DiMaggio said, and Sheehy brought it to him. DiMaggio had room to extend his long legs while he drank the coffee and smoked. Over by the trainer's room sweat-soaked jerseys hung on a drying cabinet and soon Doc Painter came around to all the stalls giving out the salt pills. The heat could not even briefly be ignored. One of the writers mentioned that the Yankees' home run streak had just ended at 25 games, but none of the players cared.

DiMaggio dressed, pulling his black laces tight through the eyes of his cleats, and then he was down the steep steps out of the clubhouse and across the wooden plank beneath the stands and out into the dugout and then jogging briskly out to centerfield, hearing the cheers of the fans once again. *DiMaggio earned his year's salary today,* a man said to another. *Look at this crowd.* Although black clouds were now visible near the stadium and the scent of rain was heavy in the air, no one had left for home.

Black Jack Wilson, with his fine fastball, took the mound in the bottom of the first for the Red Sox. The suspense, this time, was brief. In the first inning, on a 1-and-0 count, DiMaggio rapped a single over shortstop Joe Cronin's head. Just like that. Forty-four. The Yankees dugout became like a beehive and the fans, tossing score books and hats in the air, would not quiet down. *There he is,* Doerr thought, watching Joe stand placidly at first base. *There's the great Joe DiMaggio.* The Red Sox seemed tired and deflated. In that first inning, the Yankees scored three runs.

Then, slowly, the crowd did begin to thin. Looking across the field Bina could see people getting up and walking out through the aisles. She was not going anywhere, not from these seats so close to the Yankees and to Joe. Maybe Dad would take them to see him after the game. Once, coming in from the outfield an inning or two after getting that record-tying hit, DiMaggio had looked over at the Spatolas and touched his cap.

The score was 9–2 at the end of the fifth and the clouds had become so thick as to greatly darken the field. The fans that remained had surely

gotten their money's worth—their DiMaggio had done it and the Yankees were on the way to a sweep—and so the umpire behind the plate,
the former big league knuckleballer Eddie Rommel, called over McCarthy and Cronin and they all agreed that given how bad the light was, it
made sense to call the game. With that, the fans spilled onto the field.

Soon after in the Yankees' happy locker room, amid the handshakes
and the kidding around, DiMaggio was asked to pose for some photographs, first leaning against and then holding on his lap a large rectangu-
lar chalkboard on which was written in block letters, 44 EQUALS RECORD.
There would be another game against the Red Sox the next afternoon.

Chapter 21
Aglow

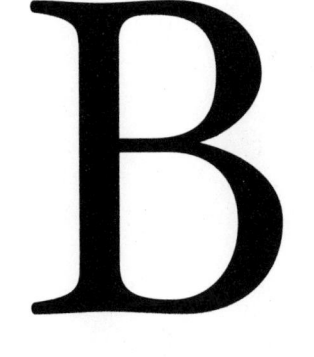EFORE OR AFTER one of his big band's spritzy, feel-good numbers, Les Brown liked to take the microphone at the head of the bandstand and say a few words. Lately he had been talking every night about DiMaggio. "And look at our Joe D! Two more hits today and now he's got that batting streak up to 44 games." One of the drummers would rip off a celebratory roll and a trumpeter would blow a few bright ascending notes and someone in the audience would whistle through his fingers as everyone huzzahed. Brown's intent was not to deliver the news to people—anyone anxious to know would have heard it by then on an evening sports report with Mel Allen or Stan Lomax or Jimmy Powers—but rather to add to the good feeling and the togetherness in the house. Acknowledging DiMaggio's streak made people feel like participants, as if they somehow had a stake in what was being achieved.

Brown and his orchestra were finishing a two-week stage show at the Strand Theatre in Manhattan, among the nightspots near the Broadway

plays, not far from Toots Shor's. In a few days they would pack up for a run at the Log Cabin in Armonk. It was a roadside dance hall, much smaller than the Strand and an hour or so north of the city, just past the Kensico Dam. Brown and his band were happy to be on their way, and not simply to get out of the city and into the cooler wilds during this hot summer stretch. This was a real opportunity. On many nights the owners of the Log Cabin invited a radio station to set up at the shows and broadcast the music live. WEAF was there now, meaning that soon the songs of Les Brown and his Band of Renown, as they sometimes called themselves, might be heard in homes for many miles around.

Things were going well for Brown; you didn't get a gig at the Strand for nothing. The orchestra had been touring successfully for several years and he had recently brought on a dark-haired, apple-faced young singer with a sweet and jaunty voice, Betty Bonney. All that the big band needed was its first real hit.

"What do you think of doing a song about DiMaggio?" Alan Courtney was a disc jockey and sometimes songwriter who liked to hang around with Les and the guys. Courtney had gone so far as to write out some words: "He started baseball's famous streak that's got us all aglow/He's just a man and not a freak, Joltin' Joe DiMaggio."

Brown had Courtney sit down with an arranger, a fellow named Ben Homer. They wanted a melody that was simple and accessible, popcorn to the ears. It should be something you could dance to. Homer noodled on the piano. The refrain, Courtney figured, might go something like this: "Joe, Joe DiMaggio, we want you on our side."

The song needed work. More lyrics had to be written, the tune wasn't nailed down. But there was something there. Maybe they could ham it up a little when they performed the song, put on baseball caps, maybe have Betty or one of the side-singers swing a bat. Maybe Les Brown and his Band of Renown could get this song together and try it up at the Log Cabin, on the radio and all. Maybe, if DiMaggio stayed even half as prominent in the public mind as he was right then, a song called *Joltin' Joe DiMaggio* could really take off.

———◆———

THOSE STORM CLOUDS around Yankee Stadium had never dropped any rain and the heat had risen higher still, well into the 90s and on its way to set a high for the year. The beaches at Coney Island and the Rockaways teemed with people seeking relief. Five more had died in New York City and many others had taken ill. The animals at the Bronx Zoo were brought into the shade. The great Lefty Grove, set to pitch for the Red Sox at the Stadium, decided that at his age, 41, he'd better not.

All along it was a strange and unusual day for DiMaggio. Dorothy's family was in town. He had left the apartment and come to the park early with Gomez. The weather had finally beaten back the crowd—8,682, still a nice midweek showing, had braved the brutal heat—yet the attention upon DiMaggio seemed closer still. Motion picture cameras had been set up in the stands and a man from *Life* magazine was hovering around eyeing things; he was planning to do an oil painting of DiMaggio, and the Yankee Stadium scene.

Joe had also agreed to meet with a *New York Times* writer, not one of the regular guys but some big shot from the magazine. That's why he'd come in early. DiMaggio sat with the writer for a while in the clubhouse before the game and answered his questions about the hitting streak. "Trying to be natural is a bit of a strain," DiMaggio allowed at one point. Gomez came and sat beside DiMaggio, to make sure everything was going okay and to see if he could help Joe out. He'd crack a joke here and there to make things easier.

Gomez picked at his spikes. He was getting ready to pitch that day. The Yankees lead on Cleveland was now at 2½ games and the locker room was in the pregame quiet that DiMaggio preferred. Doc Painter appeared with the salt pills again and McCarthy said it would be okay for the team to skip infield. The players walked around bare-chested, their faces, necks and arms well-browned, their torsos pale as the belly of a fish.

In place of Grove, the Red Sox sent out Heber Newsome, a rookie at 31. Boston loved Newsome, and with his assortment of pitches he was the team's biggest winner. The first time Newsome faced DiMaggio on this afternoon he got ahead with a curveball just above the knees. If the crowd was far smaller than it had been the day before, its principals were hardly more contained. These were the people who, heat-be-damned, wouldn't

have missed this game for anything. Newsome could not win: Throw a strike and the crowd shouted out, annoyed at anything that went against DiMaggio. Throw a ball and they booed him for playing the coward.

Now there were three photographers kneeling along the first base line to shoot DiMaggio, and two more behind him. One of them kept his lens trained on the Yankees dugout, ready to catch the players in their lively leaps should DiMaggio make his hit. On a 1–1 pitch DiMaggio drove an outside curveball deep into right centerfield, a double for sure. The players jumped up in the dugout, the fans rose from their seats. But the Boston rightfielder, Stan Spence, closed hard on the ball and at the last instant jumped and made a one-handed catch.

Before the game DiMaggio had agreed to a few photographs with Williams. The two of them were posed holding a bat, handle-up, between them and going hand over hand as if choosing up sides for a game in the yard. Joe had not talked with Dom though, not about the streak nor about Dom's having been excused from the draft. The two DiMaggios had not talked together about anything during Boston's stay in New York. *Joe's caught up in the hitting streak, that's why,* Dom thought. *And maybe not talking is just as well right now, both of us preparing for the games and all.*

In the third inning DiMaggio again swung at a curveball on 1 and 1. This time he pulled it down the third-base line, where Tabor, who'd looked so clumsy the day before, snagged the ball backhanded behind the bag, straightened and threw out DiMaggio with a stride to spare.

It must have been 100 degrees on the field that day. In the dugout, when he wasn't hitting or about to hit, DiMaggio sat by himself with his eyes half-closed, silent and still. Gomez had a shutout through five.

Photographers worked in the stands too and there they were especially attendant to Dorothy, sitting gamely in her unshaded box seat, in her pretty patterned dress and her hat, and her handbag held against her pregnant belly. Her mother and father sat beside her. Each time Joe came to bat a photographer waited with Dorothy in his sights, hoping to capture that first reactive smile if her man came through.

When Newsome missed twice to fall behind DiMaggio in the fifth inning the booing that arose seemed to the writers on hand to be far louder than a crowd this size should rightfully produce. People hissed angrily.

Pitch to him, ya bum! Pitch to him! Then DiMaggio hit a long foul ball into the leftfield stands and it was 2 and 1. Now Newsome threw again, and DiMaggio swung. And now the ball was in the air above the outfield, very high and very deep. The leftfielder Williams could only turn and watch it go. Home run.

People said they saw DiMaggio smiling as he trotted briskly around the bases. He kept no recollection of this himself. Dorothy was standing, her round face radiant and her hands held high as she clapped. Her parents stood and cheered along with her. Elsewhere the cameras caught fans in the bleachers who moments before the 2-and-1 pitch had sat tensely, score cards gripped, but who now were jubilant and waving their arms. At home plate Red Rolfe shook DiMaggio's hand and then Timmy Sullivan did and then, again, he was back among the rest of his teammates. DiMaggio felt as if he were in a trance. Everything felt wonderful. He had done it. No other major leaguer, not even back in the dusty days of the last century, had ever hit in 45 straight games. DiMaggio's name stood alone above the rest. "You have got to do the best that you can while you last in this game" he had said to the magazine writer before the game.

In the dugout his mind wandered. His home run had been part of a six-run rally that would yet again make a winner of Gomez. At one point, perhaps because he'd seen Dorothy and June in the stands, or perhaps because of something reminiscent in the sunlight on the grass, or perhaps for some other reason he really couldn't say, DiMaggio asked Gomez when the four of them could go on a trip to Bear Mountain again. It was an odd time to ask, but DiMaggio adored those trips. Lefty would drive them up along route 9W, more than 90 minutes into the countryside, and at the park they would find a spot in the sun and unpack the food. Gomez and DiMaggio would horse around by the water's edge. Once on such a trip, in a moment of uncharacteristic unrestrained glee, Joe had beat with his palms a little rhythm on Gomez's bare back. They'd go in the water and then come out and lie next to the girls and snack on something while their swimming trunks dried in the sun. They would recall for their wives funny times with the team, like when Lefty had once asked Joe to carry a suitcase for him back to the hotel. The suitcase had been so heavy and Joe's shoulder had so ached that back at the room he couldn't wait

to open the bag and see what weighed it down. Inside was a thick, solid wooden log, there only for the purpose of Gomez's prank. The two men had laughed then at the hotel, and now they laughed again in the retelling. Joe loved Lefty.

The final innings passed dreamily and the game ended, another easy Yankees win. Again Joe was besieged by oncoming fans as he ran off the field and he could not stop a boy from snatching his cap and racing off with it toward the centerfield exit. DiMaggio, floating, would have just let it go. But the Red Sox' Mike Ryba, coming out of the bullpen, saw the boy and knocked him down and then the ushers came and got Joe's cap.

In the Yankees clubhouse there was great excitement and commotion. McCarthy spoke about the strain that the streak had put not just on DiMaggio but on all the team, about how nervous they all had often been and how pleased they all now were. "I don't believe anyone but a ballplayer is in a position to appreciate what it is to hit in 45 straight games," McCarthy said. He said that he did not think DiMaggio's record would be beaten. DiMaggio again thanked McCarthy for letting him swing at those 3 and 0s. Henrich and the pitcher Tiny Bonham hoisted DiMaggio onto their shoulders and he grinned and held on. The chalkboard was back, this time inscribed: 45 CRACKS RECORD. No one wanted to go home, neither the players nor the fans; when Joe finally did leave he would need a police escort to get through the throng that was waiting for him outside the stadium.

In the meantime he smoked in the clubhouse and sifted through the latest stack of fan mail. He said to the reporters, "I don't know how far I can go but I'm not going to worry about it now." Then it was Gomez, ever japing, who gave the writers their line for the next day. In clubbing that record-breaking home run Big Joe had used Wee Willie's own formula, Gomez reasoned. "Fact is," he said, "Joe hit 'em where they ain't."

The View From Here
The Challenger, Pete Rose

Peter *Edward Rose is sitting at a small, cordoned-off*
table near the front entrance of the Field of Dreams
sports memorabilia store at the Caesars Forum
shopping mall in Las Vegas. It is a Thursday in April.
Rose, nearly 70, is wearing a long-sleeved gray cotton T-shirt, tight designer blue jeans and a pair of heeled, narrow-toed pale leather boots. Cowboy chic. He has a square head and short, unfortunately dyed red hair, roughly the color of a rooster's wattle. He is affable, at ease and often ebullient.

Shoppers who've come here to get with Rose have a few options. They may purchase a baseball, a bat, a photograph or one of numerous other items (a bobblehead doll of Rose sliding headfirst; a rooster-red second-baseman's mitt that's a replica of the one he wore in Cincinnati; a copy of his 2004 book, *My Prison Without Bars*) and take it to Rose to sign. Prices range from $79 for a 6-inch-by-9-inch photo of Rose in his playing days to $400 for a suite of items including an authentic number 14 Reds, Phillies or Expos jersey. For their fee, buyers also get a few minutes with Rose. They are allowed behind the red velvet ropes to sit beside him as he signs, to make small talk and to have their picture taken while shaking his hand. In addition to his signature, Rose adorns items with inscriptions such as HIT KING and CHARLIE HUSTLE or sometimes NL CHAMPS 1980 if he's signing a Philadelphia jersey.

He'll also write just about anything else a customer asks him to write, working from a quiver of Sharpie pens of various colors and widths. He uses a thick blue pen to sign jerseys; a pencil-thin black one for autographing a baseball card. One customer came forward with Rose's 1963 Topps rookie card, a coveted collectible worth more than $1,000, and had Rose write on it MOVE OVER TY! an allusion to Ty Cobb, whom Rose eclipsed in 1985 as baseball's alltime hits leader. Rose always signs neatly and deliberately.

During the signing session Rose is a terrific banterer and raconteur. He likes to ask people where they're from and then make some geographic inquiry ("Isn't that the town from where you can really *smell* Cleveland?") or offer up pronouncements of sports trivia. "You're from Pittsburgh?" Rose asks a guy in a Steelers cap. "Do you know that your quarterback, Ben Roethlisberger, won more games in his first five years in the NFL than anyone ever?" When a couple of middle-aged men from Chicago settle in to have a bat autographed, Rose launches into a brief but well-reasoned polemic about the omission of Ron Santo, the beloved Cubs third baseman from 1960 through '73, from the Hall of Fame. "He has more home runs and a higher batting average than [former Orioles third baseman] Brooks Robinson, and Robinson's in!" Rose declares. The Chicagoans are delighted. "Amen, Pete!" says one. "You're the best."

Rose will crack short, prefab jokes as he signs ("You want this to read 'to Bob'? O.K., but do you mind if I spell Bob backward?") and he'll tell stories about old colleagues such as Willie Mays. "One time, and this is a true story," Rose begins, addressing a clutch of rapt, thirtysomething Minnesotans. "I'm out to dinner with Willie. We're in town for an All-Star

Game. Willie was always a sharp dresser and he's wearing this dark, sharkskin suit. Well, he goes to the bathroom and when he comes back he has water all over the outside of his leg. I said, 'What happened?' And he says," (now Rose begins to mimic Mays's comically falsetto voice) "'Pete, I was standing there taking a pee and suddenly the guy next to me just turns himself toward me,'—Rose is up out of his seat now, standing and swiveling his entire body to illustrate the approaching mishap—'and he says to me, 'Hey aren't you Willie Mays?'... 'He pissed on me!'" The crowd around the table, those signing, those waiting their turn, customers and store employees just pausing to listen in, all burst into laughter. "So," Rose finishes off, "there's someone out there who pissed on Willie Mays. And it wasn't me."

Rose is generous with his time and patient with his visitors. When he finishes with the autograph session, Rose himself packs up the signed items for the customers, sliding a photo carefully into a plastic sheath or folding a newly signed jersey just so and covering it with a clear wrap. Then he encourages an extra free photograph or two—"Don't you want to get your son in here with us for one?"—and, as the shoppers finally start to inch away, Rose invariably adds a parting zinger. "You know, the whole time your wife was sitting next to me, she had her hand on my ass...."

The customers love it, of course. And in a few hours of work Rose has sold nearly $10,000 worth of merchandise. On a weekday. On weekend afternoons that number can double. In 2007, his third year working about 15 days a month at the Field of Dreams store, Rose sold, among other items, 5,000 jerseys and 17,000 baseballs. Rose says that a representative from Rawlings, the ball maker, told him he was the company's

31st biggest customer that year, trailing only Major League Baseball's 30 franchises.

"Pete, you are the greatest," says a woman named Harriet who isn't buying anything but has just stopped to say hello, "In our house you are already in the Hall of Fame."[1]

Rose nods at this. "Thank you, sweetheart," he says. Rose doesn't quite look his age; his body, fleshier, naturally, than it was during the playing career from which he is now a quarter century removed, nonetheless remains similar in character: chesty, compact. He has substantial shoulders, thick wrists and small, wide hands. No neck. Legs that are slightly bowed. He is 5' 11" or so, and has a pot belly that's hidden on this day beneath the loosely fitting shirt. Rose's eyes flicker with an eager restlessness and—in the firmness of his handshake, in the way he might turn his head sharply to attention or absently roll his shoulders—he recalls that same intractable energy, that superball quality he possessed more than three decades ago, in the summer of 1978 when, at age 37, he hit in 44 consecutive games and became the only player since Joe DiMaggio to have a streak of even 40 in a row.

That 44-game run is another thing that customers like to talk to him about. "I was there in New York when you tied the National League hitting streak record, Pete!" someone will say. Some fans even bring Rose faded game programs from one of the games late in his streak, just to show him.

"That was the hardest thing I ever did in baseball," says Rose of the feat that would win him, among numerous other

---

[1] Dozens of people say things like this to Rose every day. His banishment from baseball in 1989 for having bet on the sport while managing the Reds rendered him, according to Hall of Fame bylaw, ineligible for induction. For millions of fans, Rose's continued exclusion from Cooperstown is keenly felt as an injustice.

benefits and accolades, an extended audience with President Jimmy Carter at the White House. "That really was the only time in my career that I felt pressure. When I was going after Ty Cobb's hit record [in 1985] I had all of September to pass him. I did it on September 11th, but if I hadn't I would have done it on September 12th. In a streak when it is June 23rd, you've got to get a hit. When it's June 24th, you've got to get another fucking hit. No rest. That's what made it hard, and that's what made it fun. As much as that streak was the most challenging thing for me as a player, it was also the most fun, just great. I felt like I was helping baseball, like it was good for the game.

"I tried to stay focused by just setting close-term goals for myself when it was going on—beat the Reds team record, beat the National League record, get to 40 in a row," Rose goes on. "But sure, I thought about getting to Joe DiMaggio. Once I reached 40, somewhere in the back of my mind I thought that maybe I could do it, break that record. Even though I knew that I was still really a long way off."

THE THIRD CHILD and first son of Harry and LaVerne Rose was born on April 14, 1941—"The year of DiMaggio's streak," Pete tells people today—the same afternoon that President Franklin Roosevelt tossed out the baseball season's ceremonial first pitch in Washington, D.C. It's fitting. "Pete plays every day like it's Opening Day," Reds teammate Joe Morgan would say more than 35 years later.

Raised in Anderson Ferry, a bare-knuckled, blue-collar section of Cincinnati, hard by the Ohio River, Pete, like his father before him, was an undersized and enormously driven athlete.

Harry played semipro football, and was known as both a hard man to bring down and as a ferocious defender; one time, as Pete tells it, Harry suffered a broken hip on a play, but still got up to tackle the ball-carrier.

Pete also played football, and also relentlessly. But even before he made the varsity team at Western Hills High he realized that this was a game, in the long run, better left to larger men. In baseball, where size hardly mattered, he could improve his performance and get ahead of the others through sheer repetition in practice. Rose likes to say that he played baseball for the opportunity to succeed the way his father, "the only man who ever truly influenced me," never had. At age nine, at Harry's bidding, Pete, a natural righthanded batter, became a switch hitter. From that day forward, Pete says, "I never went two days of my life without swinging a bat. Really. Most days, whenever I could, I would hit for hours."

That dedication, and the fact that Rose was a hometown boy, attracted the Reds far more than did his natural ability. Rose was smart and intense on the field and he had a knack for making contact with the ball. In 1961, during Rose's first pro assignment, to the Florida State League, another Cincinnati prospect named Chico Ruiz said after watching Rose, "That guy has a base-hit bat."

He won the National League Rookie of the Year award at age 22 in 1963 and the old-timers said that they'd never seen a ballplayer quite like him. Rose played every moment as if it were his first, and last, on the ball field, hurtling headfirst through the air to slide into third or even into home, crashing into railings to catch pop-ups and famously bolting to first base after drawing a walk. His joy was unceasingly apparent, the way he would fairly yelp and clap his hands after getting a hit, mak-

ing the turn at first base and then hungrily eyeing second. To Rose, playing baseball was a privilege and opponents calling him "hot dog" or "Hollywood" didn't diminish his zeal. When veterans chided him for racing to first base after ball four ("It's called a walk for a reason, bush-leaguer," they'd call out), Rose just kept right on doing it. He wanted to get to first as fast as possible, he told reporters, flashing his gap-toothed grin, "Because I'm afraid the ump might change his mind."

He batted leadoff, came to the plate 700 times a season and was good for more than 200 hits. "The only thing I don't like about baseball," Rose said during those early years, "is that they don't play enough games."

Watching Rose play was certainly nothing like watching Joe DiMaggio. Rose, forever churning, never looked graceful on the field. Where DiMaggio's effort was fluid and concealed, Rose's was ever obvious. DiMaggio, long and angular, always knew just how hard to run—to glide, really—to get to where he needed to go and always, it seemed, got there safely. Rose, burly and broad, played like a bull just let into the ring, his romps around the basepaths ending, inevitably, in a spray of dust.

Yet Rose felt a clear and certain kinship to DiMaggio, his boyhood idol. Far more than most players around him Rose studied, and felt a connection to, the history of the game. He read baseball biographies, and he would ask coaches and veterans for information, for small but salient details he might apply to his own career, about the players who came before him. What impressed Rose most about DiMaggio—what made him leap when he was offered the chance, before the 1968 season, to go with DiMaggio on a goodwill trip to visit U.S. troops in Vietnam—was a single element of the DiMaggio

legacy: Late in his career, his body aching and breaking down, DiMaggio still ran out every hopeless pop-up, every routine ground ball, even in the final throes of a blowout game. "It's because there may be someone in the crowd who has never seen me play before," DiMaggio said memorably, explaining his hustle. Those were words that Rose heard about as a young ballplayer, words that never left him.

"I still don't know why they invited me to go to Vietnam with him," says Rose. "I wasn't really famous yet, just in Cincinnati. When they said, 'Do you want to go to see the troops, to lift morale?' I said, 'not necessarily.' It was 1967 in Vietnam! Kind of scary. Then they said Joe DiMaggio was going and I said put me down. If it was good enough for Joe DiMaggio, it was good enough for me.

"We got over there and it was a jungle. Hot as hell. They gave us these 'GS 15' identification cards and we always had to have them with us to show we were part of the military. GS 15 made us honorary colonels! I must have been the youngest colonel ever. You needed those cards so that in case you got captured you'd be treated like a prisoner of war. Otherwise if they got you they could do whatever they wanted to you.

"We were in Vietnam for 19 days, just going from barracks to barracks in different spots. It was hot, man. And it was pretty hairy sometimes. You heard mortar shells going off pretty much wherever you were. We'd sometimes travel in a helicopter and we'd fly low, practically skimming the treetops, going very fast, 140 miles an hour. I thought it was the pilot playing with us, giving us a little joyride, but then we found out it was because of ground fire. We had to move fast so no one could shoot us. In one place that we were, a U.S. helicopter came in and they started bringing out body bags—

I counted them. Nineteen. All dead marines. I swear to God. I just kept telling myself, Hey if Joe DiMaggio can be here and do this, then I can too.

"The soldiers all couldn't wait to meet him, they'd come up and gather around. But then all they wanted to ask him about was Marilyn Monroe! He never talked about her. I couldn't have cared less, I just wanted to talk to Joe about hitting, about baseball, about how to stay out of a slump—I hated slumping. He didn't say much, but if he did tell me an old story, I would eat it up. I was just thrilled because I knew that after that trip Joe DiMaggio would always know me. I figured he'd be watching me."

———

BY THEN, AND on into the 1970s, most major leaguers couldn't help but to appreciate, even admire, Rose as much as the fans did. Sure, he still irked some players, guys who wished he'd just pipe down, but there was no dismissing the sincerity of Rose's style. Even if he was brassy, barreling about, embracing the press, ready to talk baseball, anytime, anywhere, with anyone; even if he had a certain hubris, declaring his intention to be the best hitter and highest paid player in the game; well, even so, he never lost his innocent affection for the game, never betrayed a moment of guile, never shed the aw-shucks aura that had marked him when he strode into the major leagues as a big-eared, buzz-cut rookie. He won a batting title in 1968, another in '69, and between those years he was visited in spring training by Ted Williams, who said to him, with everyone listening, that if there was anyone out there who could hit .400 in a season and be the first to do it since Williams himself had hit .406 in that long-ago and

gilded summer of '41, if anyone could do it, it would be "you Pete, you've got the goods."

Rose coveted statistics, cited them unbidden in postgame interviews (in 1964 after ending a modest 11-game hitting streak he'd volunteered to a reporter, "I never did think Joe DiMaggio's streak was in danger") and this was just another part of his strange charm. The numbers were carrots to a plow horse. "Pete Rose is the most statistics-conscious ballplayer I've ever known," the great Reds catcher Johnny Bench said once. "And I wish we had eight more guys like him."

Rose turned 37 in 1978, his hair long and shaggy now, his muttonchop sideburns running deep along his jawline. Pete Rose was now nearly as often called Charlie Hustle, a nickname first bestowed with a mild sense of derision when Rose was an exuberant minor leaguer, but now imbued with respect. A *Cincinnati Enquirer* poll that season—published, coincidentally, just a few days after Rose's hitting streak had begun—reported to no one's surprise that his peers around the National League considered Rose the "best competitor in the game." A total of 30 players were surveyed. Rose received 14 votes. No one else got as many as four.

The oldest player on the Reds, Rose should have been in his twilight. He'd played in nearly 2,400 career games, come to bat some 11,000 times, worn down more cleats than all but a tiny handful of major leaguers will wear down in a lifetime. And yet it was impossible to view Rose, on the heels of yet another 200-hit, .300 season as in anything but full bloom. "Rose ignores birthdays," said Cincinnati manager Sparky Anderson that spring. "In his mind he's a 17-year-old, with the same enthusiasms and desires of a kid that age."

He began that '78 season 34 hits shy of 3,000 in his career,

and just before Opening Day he predicted, correctly as it turned out, that he would pass the milestone in a May series against the Expos. After that? "Four thousand hits is impossible," said Rose, "but 3,631 is possible—that would top Stan Musial's National League record. I'd like that."

The nation now knew well who Pete Rose was, and not just from his amusing Aqua Velva TV commercials. In the ads, Rose, in his Reds uniform, was shown at the plate, rapping pitch after pitch; a moment later he was holding up a flask of the blue aftershave lotion, grinning his toothsome grin, his bangs low on his forehead, and singing—yes, singing!—that there was something about an Aqua Velva man. The irony that the irrepressible Rose, the sweatiest ballplayer alive, would rely not on nature's salty funk but on a store-bought tonic to make him "smell like a man," was lost on no one. He had become a household name with the Reds' four trips to the World Series between 1970 and '76, and with his 1973 National League MVP Award. He'd batted .370 in Cincinnati's win over Boston in the entrancing, seven-game Series of 1975; stepping up to bat in the 10th inning of the epic Game 6, Rose had turned to Boston catcher Carlton Fisk and said, "This is some kind of game, isn't it?" At the end of that season SPORTS ILLUSTRATED had named Pete Rose its Sportsman of the Year.

"You have to think first of what Rose has meant to baseball," said Reds second baseman and two-time MVP Joe Morgan a few days after Rose had lashed an opposite-field single off Expos' ace Steve Rogers for hit number 3,000 in '78. "Pete has everyone's respect. And he'd have it if he hit only .220."

Rose did hit .220, practically, for more than a month after getting that 3,000th hit against Rogers, slipping into an extended slump that reached a nadir of 5 hits in 43 at bats. When

the Cubs came to town to play the Reds on June 14, Rose was hitting .267. "Geez, it looks like even the umpires are wearing gloves out there," he said. That day, with Dave Roberts on the hill for Chicago, Rose got two hits. He had it in his mind that he needed to raise that batting average quickly, to get it up over .300 before the All-Star game, when his treasured numbers would be posted up on the scoreboard and flashed on TV screens for all the country to see.

In the beginning, naturally, the streak was barely notable; Rose was just shaking his slump and returning to his consistent ways. In game number 2, Tom Seaver, the Reds ace who had been wrenched dramatically from the Mets in a 1977 trade and was already vaunted in Cincinnati, threw a no-hitter. After game number 9, in which Rose had four hits, the papers first made note of Rose's fledgling streak and noted it again at game 14. The Reds were scuffling—on July 2 they'd lost six straight—but Rose was beginning to feed off his own success: three hits in game 19, three more in game 22, and then the All-Star break did come, the players bound for San Diego. Rose was up to .303, just as he'd wanted, and his hitting streak stood at 25 games, tying the longest of his career, inching upward into rare air for any ballplayer. He volunteered after that 25th game that he was just 12 games shy of the modern National League record, 37 games, set in 1945 by Tommy Holmes. And then reporters asked Rose for the first time about DiMaggio, about where Rose thought he might take this streak of his. Rose shrugged and let his grin open up. "I might go on forever," he said.

Rose had received 2,980,377 All-Star votes, a record for a third baseman, and he got a hit in that game too, doubling during the seventh inning of the NL's 7–3 win. When the reg-

ular season resumed, Rose passed the Reds modern-era club record for a hitting streak (27 games), then broke Red Schoendienst's major league record for a switch hitter (28). After Rose hit in his 31st straight, oddsmakers in Las Vegas put him on the board. He was 5-to-1 to pass Holmes. ("If anyone can do it, Rose can," said Bob Martin, who set the betting line for the Union Plaza Hotel.) To pass DiMaggio? Those odds were 1,000-to-1.

There was not a ballplayer in the game better suited to the attention and excitement that began to follow Rose. He embraced the horde of media, and as the crush grew with each game, as Reds shortstop Dave Concepción, who—wearing No. 13 and thus lockering next to No. 14 Rose—grumbled that he could hardly get dressed at his locker for all the reporters hovering around, new provisions were made. Rose would meet the press in a separate conference room, home or away, before every game and then once again, triumphantly, after it. The national media was drawn not just by the length of the streak, but by the magnetism of the man who was on it.

When it came to the media and to social presence, Rose could not have been more unlike DiMaggio—Pete exceptionally garrulous, Joe exceptionally demure. (Later in Rose's career he and DiMaggio sometimes appeared together at charity golf tournaments. "Joe could be stiff; he was uncomfortable around people," Rose recalls. "I loosened him up.") So too was Rose a much different man than DiMaggio in the batter's box. In game 32, against Philadelphia reliever Ron Reed, Rose bunted his way on in his final at bat—with two outs in the top of the ninth inning and Cincinnati leading the Phillies 7–2. By baseball etiquette this was certainly no bunting situation and Reed recalls that, "I must have been screaming at Pete all the

way down the first base line." It was one of six times that Rose kept his streak alive with a bunt, something DiMaggio had never done. (Once, in the late 1930s, manager Joe McCarthy was asked whether DiMaggio was an able bunter. He replied, "I'll never know.") DiMaggio homered 15 times in his streak, Rose not once. Rather, Rose proved Keeleresque—time and again placing balls just outside a fielder's reach. Rose joked that if baseball teams added a fourth outfielder for short centerfield, "I'd bat .260."

No one was more a victim of Rose's precision than Mike Schmidt, the Phillies third baseman—a prodigious hitter and a 10-time gold glove winner of whom Rose would say, "He was the best player I've ever been on a baseball field with." Schmidt couldn't scoop that surprise bunt that Rose laid down in game 32 of the streak, nor come up with another perfectly placed one in game 41. Then in game 43, moments after Philadelphia manager Danny Ozark had motioned Schmidt to come several strides closer to the plate, Rose, batting lefthanded, drove a hot, low line-drive past Schmidt's left side and into the outfield. If Schmidt were playing back, in his normal spot, he would have snagged the ball easily. "Rose is my hero," Schmidt said later. "He makes me look in the mirror and if what I see is 100%, then I'm coming up short."

Opponents couldn't help but root for Rose, an elder statesman who always had time to talk about hitting, to give a restaurant tip, to offer some pithy advice on women. On the field he was electrifying, his helmet flying off, a hit machine, and, in that summer of '78, he was elevating the game. Crowds came out on the road to see him: an extra 11,000 people per night for a three-game series in Philadelphia; an added 8,000 per game during a visit to Montreal. When Rose came to New

York, on the cusp of Holmes's National League record, aiming to extend his streak to 37, 38, and 39 games, the Mets were averaging 14,503 fans a night. For that three-game set more than 94,000 turned out to Shea Stadium.

The New York crowds wanted their cellar-dwelling Mets to win, but just as ardently wanted Rose to get his hit. The media all but ignored Seaver in this return to Shea, scarcely dwelled on the Reds' tight position in the pennant race. Rose was the story and the fans adored him, even here at Shea Stadium, where in the 1973 playoffs he had memorably fought with Mets shortstop Bud Harrelson—trading violent blows right in the open at second base—and thus incurred the wrath of fans who for seasons afterward hurled obscenities and vicious boos and even bottles and batteries at Rose whenever he came to town. Now they had a different view of the man. When Rose stepped up in the seventh inning of the first game of the series and swung at an outside pitch, lining a 1-and-1 sinker from Pat Zachry into leftfield for the single that brought the streak to a record-tying 37 straight games, that Shea Stadium crowd stood en masse, cheering and clapping for more than three minutes, and shouting in adoration, "Pete, Pete, Pete, Pete."

They roared like that the next night too, when Rose, again with a single to left, in the third inning this time, made the record all his own. The fans hollered louder still as Rose raised his helmet in acknowledgment, and some waved pennants or puffed out their chests, flaunting the T-shirts that they'd bought, full of hope, outside the Stadium: I SAW PETE ROSE DO IT, the shirts and pennants read. The game was stopped and the Reds players stood clapping at the edge of their dugout and the photographers descended onto the field.

Mets pitcher Craig Swan walked back to the dugout and put on a warmup jacket to wait it out. To first base came the now-former record holder Tommy Holmes, who was then, as fate had it, working in the Mets front office. He shook Rose's hand, refused Rose's offer to keep the historic baseball and then, as cameras flashed, Tommy Holmes, four months past his 61st birthday, leaned in and said, "Thanks for making me famous again, Pete."

When the inning ended, and Rose was stranded at first, the Reds refused to bring out his glove to him, refused to take the field, waiting for Rose to come back to the dugout, to come home as it were, to get his glove himself and to be hugged and back-slapped and cheered again before the game could go on.

Not that the Mets players had wanted this to happen. As much as they may have revered him—before the middle game of the series, Mets shortstop Tim Foli and his wife hit up Rose for an autograph—they wanted to foil him too. The night after the record-breaker the Mets put on a defensive shift, plugging up the left side of the infield and successfully denying Rose a would-be hit in the first inning before his double into the right centerfield gap in the fifth beat the shift and extended the streak to 39 games.

"Sure, there was a part of each of us that wanted to see him do well," recalls Zachry, who had come over from Cincinnati in the Seaver trade the year before. "But mainly we wanted to be the ones to stop that streak. Every pitcher wanted to be the one to end it. Our whole team, we'd get together and talk about how best to stop the guy." After giving up the record-tying single in game 37, and then coming out of the game, Zachry says, "I was so ticked off, just so disappointed. I had to let it out." Boiling, Zachry tried to kick a helmet in the

Mets dugout. He missed, connected instead with the dugout step, and broke his foot. Zachry had won 10 games already that year, had made the All-Star team, was an early Cy Young contender; the foot injury ended his season.

Rose got to the ballpark even earlier than usual during his streak, and now he had purpose beyond his extra batting practice. He was doing radio and television interviews with every local outlet that asked; he appeared on *Good Morning America*, on *Donahue*, on *The Today Show*; he landed new commercials—Swanson's Hungry Man pizza, for one—with each passing day. Mail poured in now, shoeboxes full, fans encouraging Rose to keep on hitting and thanking him for his spirit, his hustle, for the way he played the game. When 30-year-old Johnny Bench was asked around this time what he thought he would be doing at age 50, the catcher responded with a quizzical look, as if the answer were obvious: "Why, I'll be at the ballpark watching Pete play," he said.

With Holmes now passed, congratulatory missives also arrived from the governors of Ohio and New York. Baseball commissioner Bowie Kuhn wrote to Rose; NFL commissioner Pete Rozelle sent a bottle of champagne. The comedian Bill Cosby wrote Rose a fan letter, as did the singer Toni Tennille from the hit TV show *The Captain & Tennille*. And Morganna, the mononymical, bleached-blonde and mammoth-breasted lounge stripper known as the Kissing Bandit—her singular skill was to run onto a major league field in the middle of a game and plant her lips on a player's mouth, and in 1971 Rose had been her first victim—well, she too sent her fondest wishes.

The streak was making Rose whole in every way. In early June, Pete and his wife, Karolyn, had separated after 14 years

of marriage. Pete took the blame, saying he had neglected his wife because of his obsession with baseball, but both Roses hoped to reconcile. When, with the streak in the 30s, Karolyn was contacted by a reporter, she spoke of how closely she and their two children, Fawn and Pete Jr., were following what Pete was doing. She talked about what an "amazing man" Pete was, about what strength he had. Later that summer, the Roses got back together.

He worked exhaustively at the plate, never taking a day off, adjusting his stroke. Rose was choking up more now, the slightest concession to age. Before games he would wipe his bat clean with rubbing alcohol so that later he could see what marks had been left, see exactly how he had hit the ball, and learn something from it—the bat barrel a palimpsest of horsehide smudge. Even on off days when most Reds were taking a rest from it all, Rose was at the ballpark. He'd bring eight-year-old Petey with him sometimes, and they would pitch to each other and shag fly balls, just the two of them along with a Reds coach or two that Rose had enlisted to throw BP. And after a few buckets of baseballs had been hit, sprayed all over the field, Pete and Petey would each take an empty bucket in their hands and bustle into the outfield, where together they would gather baseballs off the grass.

Dom DiMaggio had sent Rose a telegram after Rose passed Dom's mark of hitting in 34 straight games, at the time the ninth longest streak in history. Joe DiMaggio's record, though, was still too far off to warrant any note from the record holder himself. (After Rose had reached 36 straight, against the Expos, Montreal's Tony Perez had called out cheerily that Rose had "only 20 more games to go" to reach Joe DiMaggio. The comment broke everybody up; it was the "only" that got

them.) When Rose reached 42 games a reporter from the Associated Press got in touch with Joe DiMaggio and asked him whether he was rooting for Rose to break his streak. DiMaggio did not feint. "Does a fish like to be out of water?" he said. The answer, 37 years after the defining act, was no.

———

ON THE NIGHT of July 31, the Braves drew 45,007 fans to their home game against the Reds, nearly quadruple Atlanta's average crowd. In the sixth inning Rose, hitless in two at bats, grounded a single into rightfield off knuckleballer Phil Niekro, tying Wee Willie Keeler at 44 games.[2] This was the mark that mattered to Rose even more than Holmes's had. Fireworks went off. Rose was presented with an arrangement of roses in the shape of the number 44. (The Braves, appreciative of the excitement that brightened an otherwise dull, losing year, and also hoping against hope to sign Rose when he became a free agent after the 1978 season, would later engage a horticulturist to make a new strain of flower called the "Pete" rose.)

The next night yielded Rose a challenge far different from the one he'd just faced in the veteran and future Hall of Famer Niekro, against whom Rose had batted scores of times. Atlanta sent out Larry McWilliams, a tall rookie lefthander with an irregular, almost spasmodic motion. McWilliams had a record of 2–0 and before the game, Rose watched him closely as he warmed up, determining that McWilliams had three pitches—fastball, curveball, forkball. Rose was ready to go to work.

"I was more nervous in that game that I ever had been

---

[2] Subsequent research has given Keeler a 45-game, two-season streak, crediting him with one game at the end of the 1896 season to go with 44 straight at the start of 1897.

or ever would be pitching in the major leagues," McWilliams remembers. "That was just the fourth start of my career and ever since I'd seen Pete get that ball through against Niekro the night before I knew that I'd be pitching against him with the streak intact. The atmosphere at the park was just amazing, electric, the crowd was so alive. This was the kind of game, you know, that if I hadn't been on the team, I would have wanted to buy a ticket to see it.

"I really did not want to walk Pete—the people hadn't come out to see that," McWilliams continues. "But his first time up he ran the count to 3 and 2. I threw a fastball and he hit a rocket just foul by the bullpen down the rightfield line. I mean he hit that ball really hard. So then I got shy and threw a curveball and walked him. I was a little disgusted by that. The next time Pete came up I wanted to get ahead of him in the count so I threw a fastball on the first pitch and he hit a line shot right back at me that I just reached behind and was able to catch. It was a reaction-type play; I didn't think about it before I caught it. That ball was a base hit most nights. And if I remember right Pete applauded the catch, literally clapped a few times and nodded his head, before he went back to the dugout.

"I faced Pete once more and he hit a pretty routine ground ball to shortstop. Jerry Royster was playing there and he threw him out. We had a big lead by then and after the fifth inning the manager, Bobby Cox, took me out of the game and told me to go shower up."

Rose's fourth at bat came in the seventh inning against the sidearming righthander Gene Garber and for the third time Rose hit the baseball on the nose, lining it chest high and into the glove of third baseman Bob Horner. The ball got there so

fast that Horner threw across the diamond and doubled off the runner, Dave Collins, at first base.

By the time Rose came to the plate in the ninth inning, with two outs and nobody on, Atlanta led 16–4. But none of the more than 31,000 fans had left Atlanta-Fulton County Stadium, nor was there any doubt about what they wanted to see. The crowd booed loudly when Garber, who had petitioned Cox to stay in the game so that he could face Rose again, fell behind 2 and 0. Still Garber wouldn't give in, throwing a changeup off the plate that Rose fouled back. Garber got another strike, and then, on 2–2, went back to the changeup— his out pitch. The ball came in four inches outside, but Rose, fearing a walk, swung. And missed. The game was over. The streak was over. Forty-four. And now Garber leapt into the air, his arms outstretched, and catcher Joe Nolan rushed out to embrace him. Rose shot Garber a look, blew a bubble with his gum and went inside.

The scoreboard urged the crowd to chant "Ge-no, Ge-no," to celebrate the victorious reliever, but the Atlanta fans weren't having it. "Pete, Pete, Pete," they called, until Rose, now stripped down to a red T-shirt adorned with the words HUSTLE MADE IT HAPPEN, came out and waved.

"I was in the clubhouse in my regular clothes by then," says McWilliams, "And someone told me to go into the pressroom. So I did and I was just sitting there at the end of a table. The room was crammed with media but no one asked me a thing. After a few minutes Pete came in and asked me to scoot over, and he sat down beside me. He was kind of ticked off that Garber had thrown him a changeup. He said Garber had been pitching that at bat like it was Game 7 of the World Series.

"Then Pete was just rolling along with the reporters, rip-

ping off one-liners, cracking people up, it was neat to see," says McWilliams.[3] "He said some complimentary things about my pitching, which was really nice. I was just sitting there quietly in a sport jacket. I had bushy hair that you wouldn't have seen on the field under my cap and after a while one of the people in the media picked up on the fact that Pete had no idea who I was. He said, 'Hey, Pete, would you know Larry McWilliams if he were sitting right next to you?' Well, there was a pause and you could just see the wheels start to turn in Pete's head real fast. Then he turned to me and said, 'Oh, is that *you*?' "

McWilliams, who would end up pitching 13 seasons and winning 78 games, recalls that as a "pinnacle moment for me, this was the night I had the most impact on the game of baseball." Garber, now running a chicken farm in Lancaster, Pa., gets calls from reporters every August, around the anniversary of the day he stopped the streak. "People don't let me forget it," Garber says, and adds that he has no regrets about the changeup that he chose to throw, nor the location where he chose to throw it. Rose doesn't complain about that anymore either.

Though DiMaggio's record had been so visible, shimmering in the distance and dropped into nearly every mention of Rose as the streak of 1978 wore on, the record had not really been threatened. When Rose passed the 40-game mark, the president of Dartmouth College, the renowned philosopher and mathematician John G. Kemeny, did some computing and proclaimed that DiMaggio's streak was safe for "at least another 500 years."

Even Rose, who in the aftermath of the 45th game finally

---

[3] When Rose was asked by *The Washington Post* that night whether all the interviews and media obligations he'd handled in recent weeks had made him lose sleep, he replied, "Those aren't interviews, they're conversations. [And] reporters don't make me lose sleep. I'm not sleepin' with any of them."

admitted to having "been under strain" and to feeling the daily pressure mount along with the size of the streak, never regard-ed DiMaggio's achievement as quite in his sights. On the night he hit in his 43rd straight, Rose declared that after catching Keeler he would turn his attention to Sidney Stonestreet. "He played for the Rhode Island Reds in the Chickenbleep League," Rose explained. "He hit in 48 straight games way back when. You probably never heard of him. I just invented him." Staring out at DiMaggio's record, two weeks of ball games away, was too much even for Rose. He had needed to create another goal for himself, something more plausible that could push him and sustain him along the way.

DiMaggio during Game 41 of the streak, after tying Sisler's mark

DiMaggio with pal Lefty Gomez (left) and manager Joe McCarthy.

The bride Dorothy, with Rosalie DiMaggio (far right) looking on

DiMaggio and the rookie Phil Rizzuto

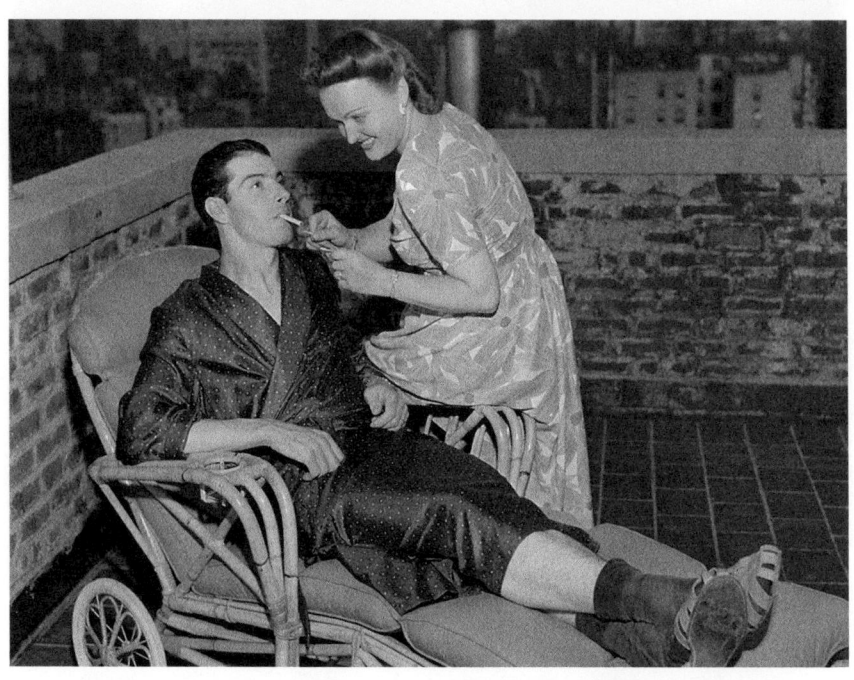

Dorothy and Joe on the terrace of the West Side apartment

DiMaggio reaches the Wee Willie Keeler milestone

PART III

Chapter 22
American Beauty

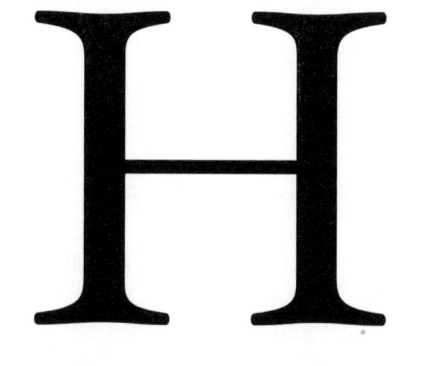OW LIGHT AND easy DiMaggio felt after breaking Keeler's record! That night after the game a photographer from the Associated Press came to the penthouse to shoot Joe and Dorothy sitting close together on the living room couch, he holding up a baseball with "45" printed in black ink between the wide stitches. DiMaggio's eyes were warmly set on Dorothy and hers warmly upon him. She wore her hair brushed back, fresh lipstick and hoop earrings. Something about Joe, though, was different. A rare casualness. Although he looked sharp as ever—hair slick and neat, suspenders over a crisp white shirt—he had not shaved for the photo nor had he put on a tie. He smiled gently, his eyebrows raised.

A flood of calls came in for Joe, from his friends in and around New York—Toots and George Solotaire—and from Lefty O'Doul in San Francisco. He spoke with Giuseppe and Rosalie, of course, and when Tom called, Joe could hear the buzz of the Grotto customers in the back-

ground. Other calls came in from people DiMaggio hadn't talked with in some time. Again and again he described to the different callers the game, and the home run that he had hit and the reaction of the fans. The phone calls were short and breezy and DiMaggio did not tire of them. He would pour himself something to drink and move around the apartment in a happy and untroubled way.

For Dorothy, everything was relaxed. The things she said and did that at other times might have bothered Joe, he now brooked and kept his easy mood. Dorothy's parents and her sister were made to feel at home. They talked about the baby and about how the pregnancy had straightened Dorothy's hair. There would be no autumn trip to Minnesota or San Francisco this year, with the little one due.

The baby's name was chosen, Joseph Paul, and DiMaggio thought the timing of the birth was fortuitous. "He'll always be able to say he was born the year I set the record," Joe said. "That'll make it easier for folks to remember his birthday."

"Suppose it's a girl," Dorothy said.

"Then," said Joe, smiling, "that'll make it easier for folks to remember the birthday of Josephine Pauline DiMaggio."

To the Olsons every moment spent in the lofty apartment felt luxurious. DiMaggio worked his train set for Dorothy's little nephew Orin. The boy must have been no more than two, playful and engaged, and when at some point during his stay Orin rolled the "45" ball off the edge of the terrace so that it hurtled down nearly 200 feet to West End Avenue below, even that caused no trouble. A doorman saw the ball land and went after it. A baseball falling from the sky, especially one with 45 written on it, could have come from only one place, he reasoned, and he carried it in the elevator up to the DiMaggios' floor. No one had been hurt and the ball was still in good shape. Everything now seemed charmed.

The Yankees were off the next afternoon and rain canceled the game on the afternoon after that—July 4. For Joe it was like he was frozen in place, frozen as a newly crowned king. The newspapers included many drawings of DiMaggio; one artist drew DiMaggio's hitting streak as the eye of a storm around which many other events swirled. A writer suggested that given all the money that the Yankees were making off the streak,

DiMaggio deserved a generous bonus. A top-of-the-page headline read: NATION HAILS DIMAGGIO'S FEAT.

Joe and Dorothy and her parents could recall how just six months earlier, during the visit to Duluth, he had walked unbothered through the town and into a flower shop where he had bought a bouquet of American Beauty roses for the Olsons' home. It seemed impossible that he would be able to run an errand so unmolested now, anywhere.

Fan mail arrived from all over the country, scores of letters each day both to his home and to the Stadium. Many of the envelopes came with a lucky thingamabob inside—a bracelet or a small stone or a few lines of bad, original poetry or something soft to rub. People everywhere wanted in, wanted to feel in some small way a contributor to the streak. With the volume of mail being far too much for him or Dorothy to handle, DiMaggio turned the letters over to the Yankees' front office to be opened.

Though the Yankees were washed out on Independence Day, baseball was played in Boston, Chicago, Cincinnati, Cleveland and Detroit. Each of those games paused in the middle or late innings so that those in the stadium could listen to some words from Roosevelt. He gave a short and pointed speech that denounced isolationism—men like the aviator Charles Lindbergh had been preaching exactly that, or, worse, an alliance with Germany—and the President urged people to overcome their fears as he appealed again for national unity. Americans needed to rally together with a common purpose, the voice said. "We must pledge our work, our will and if necessary our lives."

Listeners had gathered in St. Patrick's Cathedral in New York and around the Liberty Bell in Philadelphia and at theaters and public squares across the land, and when Roosevelt had finished speaking the newly appointed Chief Justice Harlan Fiske Stone led the nation in reciting the pledge of allegiance. The fans in the baseball stadiums rose at their seats and the ballplayers stood on the top steps of their dugouts, caps held over their hearts. Three days earlier, the U.S. had registered more than 750,000 21-year-olds for the service draft; the Japanese had just drafted a million of their own. On the *Boston Herald* editorial page, a piece titled DIMAGGIO DOES IT weighed Joe's feat against Keeler's.

Next to that appeared an editorial on Russia's defense strategy; just above the DiMaggio story ran an analysis of a British general who had faltered in the field and thus been dismissed.

———

THE BAT CAME back, just in time for the July 5th game. Peanuts, wearing a tailored white suit, appeared with it at the Yankees clubhouse. He and Spatola had tracked it down to some guy a few miles north of Newark in Lyndhurst. Just how they had tracked it down Peanuts didn't say.

The good fellows of Newark were fully attuned to the hitting streak and they too wanted to put a mark upon it. One of the police guys that DiMaggio knew from around the Vittorio Castle, a detective who had once been willing (when it became necessary due to an unfortunate misunderstanding) to testify in court on behalf of Richie the Boot's honorable intentions, had given Joe a Winchester 21 shotgun engraved with DiMaggio's name and the date June 30, 1941, the day after he'd passed Sisler's mark. What Joe would do with a duck-hunting gun wasn't immediately clear, but still he appreciated the gift.

In the July 5th game against the Athletics, before a crowd of some 20,000, in his first at bat on the first pitch he saw, DiMaggio hit a home run into the Yankees bullpen, caught there on the fly by the coach John Schulte. Now the streak was at 46 consecutive games. Afterward, wearing a double-breasted suit with a kerchief in his pocket, DiMaggio autographed the barrel of the bat he had used to hit the home run that broke Keeler's record. The bat would be flown to San Francisco via United Airlines; United had a stewardess, Polly Ann Carpenter, on hand to witness the autograph and then carry the bat across the country to be raffled off at the Seals doubleheader the next day, to benefit the USO. Before the first game at Seals Stadium a telegram arrived from FDR himself commending the USO's "essential and patriotic duty" and adding, "I am deeply impressed by the invincible Joe DiMaggio surrendering his favored and record-breaking bat to the USO cause."

DiMaggio sent a telegram as well and wired money to buy 100 of the 25-cent tickets. "If I win it, raffle it over again," the telegram read, and DiMaggio added: "Tell all my friends I am appreciative of the hundreds

of telegrams and air mail letters sent to me in the past several days." Between games at the same stadium where eight years earlier Joe had begun his professional career, Giuseppe and Rosalie DiMaggio presented the bat to the winner of the drawing, a young San Franciscan named Jim Osborne. The bat raffle had raised $1,678.

More than 10,000 fans turned out to see the Seals that day, July 6th; at Yankee Stadium there was six times that—60,948 and for the second time in six days the Yankees' largest home crowd of the year. Hours before the doubleheader against the A's began, before the Stadium gates had opened, fans had formed lines outside. The rain of recent days had cooled the air and there were clouds mixed into the blue sky. Each ticket had on its face an image of Lou Gehrig, and it was Gehrig who would be honored this day.

Nearly five weeks had passed since his death and in centerfield, next to the flagpole and the monument to Miller Huggins, a granite block now stood, wreathed and bearing a newly cast bronze plaque. Before the game, the Yankees and Athletics players assembled in the outfield. Gehrig's widow, Eleanor, stood in a dark dress next to the monument. Dickey and McCarthy together lifted a draped American flag to unveil the plaque which read, below Gehrig's name: "A man, a gentleman and a great ballplayer whose amazing record of 2,130 consecutive games should stand for all time. This memorial is a tribute from the Yankee players to their beloved captain and former teammate."

In the brief eulogies that followed, Mayor Fiorello La Guardia said that Gehrig "will be remembered as long as baseball remains and as long as good government exists." Connie Mack advised "the army of youths of America to follow in his footsteps." Dickey got out that Gehrig was "the greatest first baseman and pal in the history of the game" before he broke down and couldn't go on. Lou's parents were there, sitting together behind the Yankees dugout.

A quiet settled over the crowd during these proceedings, a near silence through which the public address system crackled and the speakers' voices rang and echoed. There was in DiMaggio and the other Yankees a return of the feelings they'd experienced in Detroit during those dark, dreary days in the beginning of June when the news came that Gehrig was

gone. Back then, the hitting streak had been in its first days and DiMaggio was still dogged by his early season slump and the Indians were regarded as the favorites in the American League.

Now, against the A's, the Yankees would win both ends of the double-header and they would do so behind DiMaggio. He had four hits in the first game. In the second he had a long triple and a single; four RBIs all told. In centerfield he had never been more alive. He caught 10 balls in the doubleheader and one observer described "no less than eight" as "breath-taking." He went deep into centerfield to steal, with a leap, a triple from Bob Johnson in the opener. Then in the ninth inning of the rain-spattered nightcap, Johnson hit another one over DiMaggio's head and Joe, loping through the rain and slosh, covering ground out near the granite block that bore Gehrig's name, calmly, over his shoulder and still on the run, made the catch. It was Lou Gehrig's Day at Yankee Stadium but these Yankees were beyond a doubt Joe DiMaggio's team. Since leaving Detroit on the heels of Lou's death he had batted .409. He had driven in 35 runs in 27 games. He had hit 11 home runs and he had struck out only twice. The Yankees in that time had gone 23–4 and had risen from fourth place to first, 3½ games ahead of the Indians. "DiMaggio," said McCarthy, "is the greatest ballplayer in the game."

After the final out the fans rushed onto the field, this time with particular zeal. Some grabbed handfuls of dirt and grass, and many went straight for DiMaggio. He had to really run for safety, feinting and dodging his way to the dugout. He would be leaving town again, bound first for the All-Star Game in Detroit with Dickey, Gordon, Keller, Ruffing and Russo, and then the Yankees would travel for two weeks more. The train for Detroit left the next day. This night DiMaggio would spend with Dorothy. They would stand together on the penthouse terrace and look out over all of New York City. The moon was low and big and nearly full.

Chapter 23

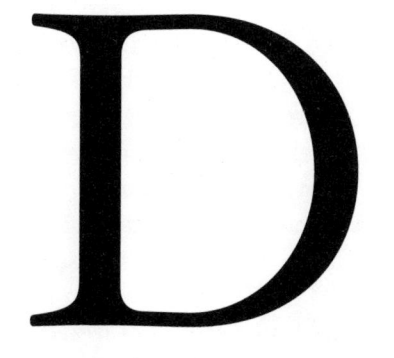IMAGGIO WAS HARDLY the only lure for the nearly 55,000 fans now settling in at Briggs Stadium. There were stars all over the field for this game, the most anticipated of the season. Rapid Robert Feller would pitch for the American League; lanky Ted Williams, at .405, would bat cleanup; old Double X, the Red Sox' burly Jimmie Foxx, would come off the bench as the only player to have been chosen for every All-Star Game since it began in 1933. Little Dominic DiMaggio had made it for the first time, as a backup to big brother Joe. And the Detroit fans would see National League players that they had only read about: the Cardinals' big Johnny Mize, who swung not two but three bats as he swaggered off the on-deck circle, and his teammate, spikes-up Enos Slaughter. The Dodgers' sensational Pete Reiser, batting .360 and at age 22 the baby of the All-Stars, would play centerfield. For a baseball fan anything seemed possible in a game like this. The Mutual Broadcasting System would air every inning from coast to coast. The sun was high and

bright, the air crisp, and even before the playing of the national anthem a marching band struck up in front of the stands. Bunting hung from the stadium facades. Joe Louis sat with an entourage behind the American League dugout. The Tigers' own Rudy York was in the lineup at first base.

The crowd hadn't come only for DiMaggio, but even in this gathering of baseball's best there was an aura around Joe. Many fans had seen the latest newsreel at the movies. After footage of the first test flight of the B-19—the pride of the U.S. military and, as the narrator assured, "the finest bomber in the world"—there appeared short segments about the FBI having rounded up some suspected spies and about Army nurses doing a gas mask drill at Fort Dix. Then came the sports recap and scenes of DiMaggio extending his hitting streak past Sisler in front of that teeming crowd at Griffith Stadium.

In Detroit even the other All-Stars approached DiMaggio as if he were an attraction. During batting practice Williams came around with a camera and snapped pictures of Joe taking his swings. DiMaggio showed a smile and shook his head. Maybe Williams was just goofing, or maybe he was paying honest homage to old Dead Pan Joe. ("I've been down on myself, but I've never heard of Joe getting unsettled," Williams had said.) Or maybe this was a reminder to DiMaggio, a way for Williams to say: I'm here too.

Thought Bobby Doerr, the American League's starting second baseman: *DiMaggio's hitting streak is a challenge to Ted. He sees it as a personal challenge.*

Before DiMaggio had arrived at the Book-Cadillac Hotel, before he had checked in beneath the chandeliers along with the other Yankee players (and with Art Fletcher who had been invited to coach third base), it had occurred to Joe that he had better get a hit in the All-Star game. It was simply a grand exhibition, of course, and the statistics of the game would not count in the regular-season record. His hitting streak, everyone agreed, would remain intact no matter what happened in Detroit. *But what would people say?* DiMaggio thought. *If I don't get a hit in this game, will they say that truly in spirit the streak was stopped? Will they say that I couldn't do it against the National League?*

Even as the exhilaration from breaking Keeler's record lay still warm

inside him, DiMaggio could not help turning over such thoughts in his mind. In the stands at the All-Star game there would be people who had never seen him play, and who would measure him by what he did—or did not do—in this game. Even now there were those fans and reporters who remembered, and would expressly rehash, DiMaggio's appearance in the 1936 All-Star game as a rookie when he had gone 0 for 5 and played poorly in the field and the American League had lost. Never would DiMaggio himself forget that game. Whatever the statistics guys had now decreed regarding the streak, people would be watching in Detroit, and listening everywhere and forming opinions of their own. To DiMaggio, it felt important that he get a base hit in the game.

The fans cheered lustily and sustained a long applause when DiMaggio came to bat in the bottom of the first inning. The Dodgers' right-hander Whitlow Wyatt got ahead 0 and 1 and on the next pitch DiMaggio popped the ball up near third base, where the Cubs' Stan Hack caught it in foul ground.

He flew out deep to Reiser in the fourth and he drew a walk from Bucky Walters in the sixth. Only a handful of players had stayed in the game from the beginning—DiMaggio, Williams, the Senators' Cecil Travis—and in the top of the seventh inning Dominic had been put into rightfield, replacing the Indians' Jeff Heath. Red Barber was calling the game on MBS: *"We have the two American League DiMaggio brothers in the same outfield....There they are shoulder to shoulder for the first time in the big show."* The White Sox' Edgar Smith had come in to pitch for the American League.

DiMaggio was hitless when he came to bat with one out and no one on base in the eighth inning. The National League led 5–2 after a pair of two-run homers by the Pirates shortstop Arky Vaughn. Joe dug in against the fourth National League pitcher, the Cubs' hard-throwing Claude Passeau. *"And here's Joe DiMaggio who hasn't had a hit today,"* said Barber. Passeau wore the Cubs' new road uniform, a bright and metallic blue. The count went to 0 and 2. *"DiMaggio stands, his feet widely spaced...."* And then the pitch.

Barber: *"Swung on, there's a line drive belted deep into left center, Reiser comes over, he can't get it, it's through for an extra base. DiMag has another hit! He's coming into second base and holds on with a double. Of course this*

is unofficial but it's his 49th consecutive game he's hit safely. This has nothing to do with the record books or his consecutive game streak but you know and I know that this is a very important ball game, and we all know that he just sent out a line drive into leftfield for a solid double. They can't stop him!" Behind Barber you could hear the noise of the approving and appreciative crowd.

Williams came up next and struck out looking. Then Dominic stepped in.

Barber: *"He is the only All-Star player on either side who is wearing glasses. . . . He is not nearly as big as Joe."*

Dominic fouled off Passeau's first pitch.

Barber: *"Nothing and one. This is the brother act, the greatest in the major leagues today. There's the big DiMaggio who's the leader of the three brothers at second. There's Dom at the plate trying to get brother Joe in. . . Passeau in position. Big, rugged righthander. There's a drive into right center. It's in for a base hit! Joe is scoring, Slaughter throws into second base and the brother act clicks for a run. A double by Joe and a single by Dom."*

The score was still 5–3 when the eighth inning ended and before the ninth inning began Barber read a service announcement appealing to young men to sign up for "Army aviation cadet training." Early in the game, the Chicago announcer Bob Elson, who called the first 4½ innings, had also read an Army recruitment ad.

In the bottom of the ninth Passeau was still on the mound and the National League still held a two-run lead. The American League, though, had loaded the bases with one out.

Barber: *"What is the situation? The tying run at second, the winning run at first, and no less a person than Joe DiMaggio at the plate."*

After falling behind 0 and 2 DiMaggio stepped out of the batter's box and wiped a film of sweat off of his brow.

Barber: *"Keltner off third, Gordon off second, Travis off first. One out. DiMaggio behind now nothing and two. Passeau delivers. There's a ground ball to short. Miller has it, the throw to second one out, the throw to first. . .not in time. And it's a force play at second, one run is in. Billy Herman's hurried throw was not in time and was also on the home plate side of first and McCormick had to get off. DiMaggio, who was running for dear life, beats the throw."*

With the double play averted, the American League still had life. Herman felt lousy about his poor throw. The National League infield-

ers all came together around Passeau. Williams was striding to the plate.

Barber: *"And how do you like this for a setting? Two outs, the tying run at third, the winning run at first, last half of the ninth inning and the .400 hitter of today at the plate, Ted Williams. Lefthand batter. Passeau ready. Delivers high outside. Danning bluffs a throw to third and Gordon ducks back. Second base is open. . . . I wouldn't have missed this for anything.*

"Now Williams leans over the plate. 5 to 4 National League. . . . Passeau righthanded. Williams swings and fouls it back. One and one. . . . Passeau has been the anchor pitcher. He took the mound with the American League behind. Suppose you know what that means. It means they were swinging for keeps. Harder than ever if anything. Claude ready. Delivers. Williams takes high inside for ball two. Two balls, one strike. . . . Passeau standing back of the hill. Frank McCormick at first base on the corner against the great DiMaggio. . . .

"Joe Gordon the tying run leads down off third. Passeau pitches, Williams swings. There's a high drive going deep, deep. . . it is a home run against the tip-top of the rightfield stands!. . ."

Loud and chaotic sounds burst abruptly onto the broadcast, and then there was near silence, only the distant rumbling of the crowd, for 22 seconds, until Barber came back: *"Well I hope you could hear some of what we said before 55,000 voices rose in a wave of noise that was not to be denied, Mutual microphone or anything else. Ted Williams just missed by a couple of feet hitting the ball completely out of the park, completely over the tip-top of the rightfield stands. . . a tremendous home run that brought in three runs and turned what looked to be a National League win into an American League 7–5 win."*

At home plate DiMaggio shook Williams's hand and then watched him skip over to the dugout, the big red number 9 bouncing on his back. You could have lit up a night game with Williams's grin. In the exultant clubhouse, the American League manager Del Baker wrapped both his arms around the home run hero. "I'd kiss that Williams in the public square if they'd ask me!" he said. The president of the American League, Bill Harridge, appeared and vigorously shook Williams's hand. So did Clark Griffith. A bunch of players—York and Keller and Foxx and Dominic—good-naturedly ambushed Williams at his locker. DiMaggio went and sat beside Williams for a moment and put his right arm across

Williams's back. Then the writers came and Williams laughed and re-counted. "It was a fast one, letter-high, that's what it was," he said. Williams seemed almost overwhelmed by all that was happening. He sat in front of his locker with his Red Sox uniform on for quite some time, even after the reporters had begun to move away.

DiMaggio was pleased that he'd hit safely in the game, and also very pleased that the American League had won. Of the team's seven runs he had scored three and driven in one. As the fuss around Williams continued and the players shouted in the showers—"Now the National League knows how Billy Conn felt in the 13th round!" someone called out—DiMaggio wondered, as he had wondered before, how he might feel when his hitting streak ended, whether he would miss the tension and attention that had become part of his every day, or whether he would feel grateful that it was gone. What would happen to that rare, wonderful thing: the sense of to-getherness in the locker-room after each game in which he'd extended the streak? Or would he feel freer and less put-upon?

"I will probably be relieved when someone stops me," he had said be-fore arriving in Detroit, only to add in the next moment, "I want to keep it going for as long as I can." Inside DiMaggio were both of these feelings and he could not say which was the stronger one.

He shaved and combed his hair and spent time carefully putting on his suit. He said a quick goodbye to Dominic. It was late in the afternoon and the temperature outside could not have been above 80 degrees. It felt like a day in September. Fans called out to him in the parking lot and there would be others waiting for him when he got back to the hotel. *I wish Lefty was around*, DiMaggio thought.

He could remember staying close to the Benjamin Franklin Hotel with Gomez, and he could remember facing Johnny Babich in Shibe Park and then the telegram that had called him to the hospital in Philadelphia. The boy had died, DiMaggio later learned. He could remember the hot, hot day in Washington and the young people who had come to him on the field before the games.

In New York, Henrich had taken this All-Star break to get married to a nurse. Les Brown and his Band of Renown had arrived to begin their en-gagement at the Log Cabin in Armonk. Soon DiMaggio and the other All-

Star Yankees would meet the team for their three games in St. Louis, and next the Yanks would go to Chicago and then to Cleveland after that. In those places, DiMaggio understood, there would not be a field full of All-Stars to disperse the incoming light. Instead in each city, only the home team, the Yankees and him.

AND THAT NIGHT the sun went down, and the morning next it rose.

Sensational

JOE DIMAGGIO

Will Seek To Hit Safely In His

49th

Consecutive Game.

Thur. Nite, July 10

AT ST. LOUIS

Browns vs. Yankees

Sportsman's Park–8:30 P.M.

Tickets Now on Sale at Browns Arcade Ticket Office—

Phone, CHestnut 7900

The signs hung as posters at the St. Louis train station and ran as ads in the local papers, and stood stacked as circus handbills on the counters in the lobby of the Chase Hotel. DiMaggio had become a traveling sideshow's principal act. Instead of swallowing fire or walking barefoot on a bed of broken glass the Sensational DiMag would perform a kind of high-wire act: get a base hit or fall. Though the forecast called for a summer storm, advance ticket sales were the best they had been for a Browns game all season.

This was George Sisler's hometown and on the morning of the game he and DiMaggio met for breakfast. Sisler's hairline began high upon his scalp. He wore a loose-fitting plaid sports jacket and a tie with thick stripes, and pens in the breast pocket of his shirt. He was 48 years old,

working in retail and nearly two decades removed from the day he ran his hitting streak to 41 games. DiMaggio, at their breakfast table, looked as if he had stepped from a magazine advertisement; his creaseless, wide-shouldered suit fit him like he was born to wear it. In 1940, the Custom Tailors Association had named DiMaggio the eighth best-dressed man in the United States.

Sisler smiled broadly and congratulated DiMaggio on the streak and then later, before the game that night, he congratulated him again in a ceremony at home plate. Sisler was the greatest player in the history of the St. Louis Browns. "I hope Joe makes it 49 but with nothing more than a single," Sisler said into a microphone to cheers and laughter from the stands. There were 12,682 fans in Sportsman's Park, more than three times what a typical night game would bring. Thunder rumbled out over the Missouri plains and many people had umbrellas at their sides. Normally the Browns were the worst attended team in either league.

DiMaggio singled before the game was 10 minutes old, in the first inning, on the second pitch he saw. The shortstop Alan Strange couldn't get to DiMaggio's ground ball deep in the hole. By the third inning lightning streaked the sky and in the bottom of the sixth the deluge arrived, stopping the game with the Yankees ahead 1–0 and DiMaggio's base hit officially in the books. After half an hour, with rain still falling in sheets, the umpires sent everyone home. Gomez had pitched five innings for the win.

During the game the next afternoon, water still soaked some areas of the grass and earthworms could be found in the miry edges of the outfield. It was on such days, if the Yankees were in high spirits—and as winners of 10 straight now they certainly were—that the players might conspire to play a little trick on young Phil Rizzuto.

Scooter hated insects, worms, anything that crawled, and when he tossed his glove onto the grass behind shortstop at the end of each inning in the field, it lay there vulnerable to mischief. On his way in from leftfield Keller would furtively slip a fresh and slippery worm into one of the fingers of Rizzuto's glove. The next inning the Yankees would all watch as Rizzuto slid the glove onto his hand and then after a brief look of puzzlement passed over his face, he would suddenly tear it off, frantic and fling it into the air and run from the spot where the glove had land-

ed. How the Yankees laughed! Henrich doubled over in the outfield. The umpires snickered too. The joke echoed again each inning as Rizzuto, spooked and suspicious, picked up his glove and looked warily inside it—*any more worms?*—before carefully, fearfully putting it on. Scooter was one of the team now, batting better than .300 and himself on a nifty little hit streak of 14 games.

At many times McCarthy would not tolerate such practical joking, seeing it as unprofessional, disrespectful even, and not in the Yankee way. But now the manager felt happy and relaxed. He was confident the Yankees would win the pennant. DiMaggio had lifted everyone. By the time the Yankees left St. Louis they had won 12 consecutive games, the longest streak of McCarthy's tenure. DiMaggio had run his hitting streak to 50 straight by singling in the first inning, and then added two more singles and a ninth inning home run. His 20 home runs and 73 RBIs both led the major leagues. The next day he made it 51 in a row with a fourth-inning double over the head of Browns centerfielder Walt Judnich, a hit that scored the newly married Henrich and helped knock Elden Auker out of the game. "DiMaggio is liable to go on indefinitely," McCarthy said.

In Chicago, he extended the streak to 52 and then 53 games before a doubleheader crowd of 50,387, the largest at Comiskey Park in eight years. The irascible Jimmy Dykes, just back from a suspension for hurling particularly obscene and abusive language at an umpire, had saved his two best starting pitchers, Ted Lyons and Thornton Lee, so that they could take on DiMaggio and the Yanks. But DiMaggio had three hits in the first game, and a hard single to right centerfield off Lee in the nightcap. The Yankees won both games. The White Sox had fallen out of the pennant race, 13 games back of New York, eight back of the second-place Indians, four behind Boston. But the fans at Comiskey did not seem to much care about their team's fortunes; they were there for the tingling they got when the game announcer took up his megaphone along the third base line and announced, "Now batting for the Yankees, Joe DiMaggio."

IN CHICAGO, AS in every big city in the country, the bestseller list included *Blood, Sweat and Tears,* a collection of speeches by Winston

Churchill. The book's title came from the short address he'd given to the House of Commons a year earlier, upon taking over as Britain's prime minister. "I have nothing to offer but blood, toil, tears and sweat," Churchill had said. "You ask what is our policy? I will say: It is to wage war...with all our might and with all the strength that God can give us...against a monstrous tyranny never surpassed in the dark and lamentable catalogue of human crime." Now, as Churchill's book weighed upon so many nightstands, the U.S. was sending cargo boats full of the rations that Britain so badly needed: milk, meat, eggs, cheese. On the docks in England hungry workers nipped immediately into the store, sucking eggs right out of their shells.

In Washington, D.C., Congress was moving to extend the first term of service for draftees to longer than a year. A few days before, the U.S. Navy had taken over Iceland at that country's bidding and as a means, Roosevelt said, of protecting America's defensive frontier. Was there any stopping the Nazis as they heightened their attack on Russia, moving on three fronts to Moscow, Kiev and Leningrad? You could forgive the people if sometimes the news, the big, bold-type war headlines, and the sports stories with the ongoing drama of DiMaggio got jumbled together. Before the Yankees' second game in St. Louis—game 50 for DiMaggio—two teams of soldiers stationed nearby had played an exhibition game on the field at Sportsman's Park. In San Francisco the *Call-Bulletin* illustrated the shifting fronts of battle in a daily War-O-Graph; the *Chronicle* still ran its DiMag-O-Log.

The hundreds of Italians now interned in Fort Missoula and other camps—those who had sabotaged a boat in a U.S. harbor, or who were suspected of spying or who had come over to work and stayed on illegally—were told they would not be allowed to leave and go home. As one British government official declared, the war did not now merely engage soldiers and sailors, but civilians too. *The Washington Post* ran stories that compared DiMaggio to other great Italian innovators: Dante, Donatello, Galileo. So if DiMaggio was Italian—and surely the green-white-and-red flags in bleachers on the road as well as at home were waved for him—he was a majestic Italian, freed by his achievement and his bearing from the prejudice and disdain of even the smallest-minded isolationists

and bigots in the land. In the hearts of the people, he was America's Joe. The bench jockeys on opposing teams held their harsh tongues now when DiMaggio came to bat. He belonged to everyone.

In the flyspeck town of Glendive, Montana, in the white dawn of another day, a man walked into a small breakfast shack, a slapped-up place with maybe eight spots to sit. He wore a wide, dark cowboy hat and weathered boots and old blue jeans. He was tall with a broad back and a bow in his gait and a face like leather. He might spend all day and even the night out on the range. A step through the doorway of the breakfast shack the cowboy looked at the man behind the counter and nodded his head. Already by his presence the cowboy's order was placed—griddle cakes, three eggs easy, coffee black. He shared a look with the counterman. "He get one?" the cowboy said. And the counterman nodded and put down the cup of coffee. "Yes. He did. He got one." They didn't even need to say his name.

All across the Western expanse that summer—across the dustblown farm towns through Idaho, Oregon, New Mexico, Wyoming—DiMaggio made the papers, a short front-page report or a longer AP or UPI article with his name splashed across the top. Even in these places, tiny and remote, a base hit by DiMaggio could seem like local news.

The baseball reporters were not referring to him as Giuseppe much anymore, preferring to reach into a stable of grander names: Jolting Joe or the Jolter, or the Yankee Clipper once in a while. They called him DiMaggio the Magnificent, or the Great DiMag or Joseph the Great or, simply, the Great Man. No longer did fans or scribes argue the merits of Mize or Foxx or Greenberg or Medwick or any other current ballplayer against DiMaggio. There was no competition. Instead, the writers argued in print whether or not DiMaggio now belonged in baseball's alltime outfield, whether his preposterously long hitting streak on top of all else he had done was enough to knock Tris Speaker out of centerfield and let DiMaggio stand between Ruth and Cobb.

After he'd made it 53 straight games the *Chicago Tribune* ran an editorial titled MR. DIMAGGIO AS SEEN FROM OLYMPUS. Perhaps Joe wasn't quite in a league with the Greek immortals, the article allowed, but by now he must have gotten their attention up there; if Zeus hadn't actually been among that outsized doubleheader crowd at Comiskey Park, then

surely, the *Tribune*'s writer concluded, "he had tuned in from time to time to Bob Elson's" play-by-play report on WGN.

Marie's scrapbook swelled in San Francisco, and Maury Allen's fattened in Brooklyn. A cartoon in the *World-Telegram* depicted an imagined office of baseball records, a man bent over a desk scribbling madly: the Yankees had won 14 straight, 18 of 19, 28 of 32. Papers and thick books were stacked high on the floor and the shelves around the scribbling man, and from the side of the office a secretary, Miss Phidgit she was named, called out: "We're going to need a new filing cabinet for DiMaggio."

Keeler had now receded deeply into the background. A few stat-mongers had tried to raise the specter of the longest-ever professional hitting streak of 69 games set in 1919 by a guy named Joe Wilhoit playing for the Western League's Wichita Witches; but that was a Class A circuit, a low-level minor league populated with ballplayers long forgotten or never known, so that record couldn't truly rate. Really, the only long streak that did have some purchase, that still rang in some people's minds, had occurred in California in the Pacific Coast League, a notch below the majors. It wasn't the Show, not at all, but scores of good big leaguers and tough pitchers had played in the PCL. That league's record hitting streak was 61 games long, run off eight years earlier by a highly touted rookie outfielder for the San Francisco Seals, an 18-year-old kid, Joe De Maggio.

Chapter 24
They Didn't Know Then

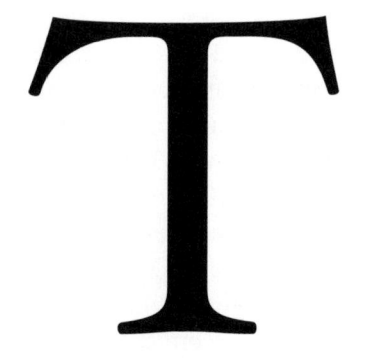HE WORLD AROUND him was different then and he a different man—brand new to professional ball. It was a blur to him as it happened, and a blur in his memory now, and what he remembered most about that hitting streak of 1933 was the tiredness, deep and bony, that dug into him from all the games and the doubleheaders day after day after day: 61 games in eight weeks. *I am not used to playing baseball every day,* DiMaggio thought as that Seals season wore on. He didn't much go for the long bus rides, nor for being on the road. The arc of DiMaggio's baseball career was then much closer to his club team and to imposing his will upon the North Beach playground than it was to the major leagues. In winter and spring he'd head to Funston Park, just a block from Galileo High—where, at his age of 18, he might still have been enrolled—and spend a couple of hours chasing down balls for the older fellows, Joe and Louis Toboni or some of the regulars playing for the Mission Reds. They'd pay DiMaggio two bits for his trouble. He'd cop a couple of cigarettes off them too.

With the Seals that rookie year he earned $225 a month. If DiMaggio—or his doubting Papa—had any question as to what kind of ballplayer he was, the proof was right there on payday. The Seals got their money's worth and more, especially as the streak continued and DiMaggio neared and then passed the old Pacific Coast League record of 49 straight games held by the long-retired Oakland Oaks first baseman Jack Ness. The crowds grew at Seals Stadium and even then, in the bleakest heart of the Great Depression, as teams and leagues in other cities folded and disappeared, people plunked down a dime for a Seals scorebook. *He's Vince's kid brother, huh?* they would say, paging through. *Not just his brother, Vince's replacement too.* (Vince now played down south for the Hollywood Stars.) At night games free bowls of soup were passed out in the stands and ladies got in free.

By the time his hitting streak reached the high 30s, and the Ness record came clearly into view, Joe's name began to appear in small headlines in the *Chronicle*'s SPORTING GREEN, the sports page that Giuseppe was just barely learning to read, or to make some sense of at least. When Joe hit triples in each end of a doubleheader to run the streak to 46 in a row, the news of it ran clear across the top of the page. Suddenly, three months into his PCL career, Joe was someone whom people thought they might remember for many years. The newspapers and most everybody else misspelled his name: De Maggio or DeMaggio. Joe never bothered to correct anyone.

The club declared July 14, 1933, Joe De Maggio night at Seals Stadium and in the game he extended the streak to 50 straight. Flashbulbs went off when he came to bat. San Francisco mayor Angelo Rossi presented Joe with a gold, engraved watch and gave flowers to Marie and Rosalie. The Seals players chipped in to give Joe a small check in gratitude and the boys from Joe's old neighborhood team, the Jolly Knights of North Beach, came out and presented him with a leather traveling bag. At some games, when one of his old Knights teammates called out to Joe from the seats behind the Seals dugout, he did not even turn to look. Often a sense of distance surrounded him—a quiet, incurious pride. It was as if he were somehow set apart. Sometimes around the locker room and in the dugout things were said that DiMaggio did not quite understand.

He was young and skinny and callow, and in the hotel lobbies of

Portland and Seattle and Los Angeles he wore yellowed T-shirts and torn leather shoes. Only later, when Joe began to believe that the money might stick, and began to hear whispers that a team in the major leagues, the Yankees even, might want to sign him did he agree to buy some real clothes. Then he visited with Joe Toboni, down at Toboni's milliner's shop on Market Street, and Toboni stood DiMaggio in front of a mirror and said he had something to teach him that he needed to learn. *You pull the wide end down through here, then you tighten the knot like this. There you go Joe, that's how you tie a tie.*

During the streak DiMaggio faced pitchers who were bound for or had been in the big leagues—young Johnny Babich and Buck Newsom, veterans Tom Sheehan, Frank Shellenback and others. It didn't matter who the pitchers were, Joe didn't think about that. Not ever. He took his bat and went up and swung.

DiMaggio obeyed superstition that season because he thought that was what ballplayers were supposed to do. *Don't mess with anything when you're going good, kid,* the veterans said. So he kept his right thumb wrapped in tape for the whole length of the hitting streak, well after the bone bruise that had ached at the start of the run in May had healed and faded away. *That's it, don't change a thing,* the veterans said. He was summoned to City Hall and honored there for his streak by a local association of semipro ballplayers. At Cardinal Field in Sacramento, with the streak having climbed into the 50s, an Italian social club came out to honor him too.

It was there, in Sacramento for games 54 through 60 of the streak, that the blur became dizzying. He felt his exhaustion might never leave him. The nights were too hot to get a good unbroken sleep. In games 59 and 60, a doubleheader, DiMaggio reached on infield hits that might have been ruled errors but instead extended the streak. "I've seen batters given hits on much easier chances than those of De Maggio's," the Sacramento Solons pitcher Ed Bryan would say after the game in Joe's defense. But the Solons fans hadn't seen it like that. They became irate. A few zealots stormed angrily toward the official scorer in the press box and police were needed to turn them away. To Joe all of this was strange. Confusing. That people should worry so much about a hitting streak! During games he did not react with excitement or disappointment and for the first time some-

one called him Dead Pan Joe. On the day in San Francisco that Oakland pitcher Ed Walsh Jr., the son of the fine White Sox righthander, stopped the streak at 61 games, DiMaggio was the last man up and his sacrifice fly won the game. "It will take a good man to beat what he has done," Seals manager Ike Cavaney said of the hitting streak.

From those eight weeks only soft and imprecise memories remained with DiMaggio. It seemed to him very long ago, and part of his younger, other self. In 1941, recalling that old Pacific Coast League streak gave the baseball writers another number to hold up to the light—DiMaggio chases De Maggio—and perhaps it gave evidence to any surviving cynics that this streak of '41 was no fluke; DiMaggio was of a special breed. For most people who followed the game, however, and certainly for DiMaggio, that minor league milestone of 61 games seemed unimportant and irrelevant. It was not a number that he spent time thinking about.

In Chicago now the calendar turned to July 15 and DiMaggio's big league hitting streak was a full two months old. Sometimes he felt keenly aware that at any moment it could come to an end. Other times it seemed to him that being on the streak was like traveling on a road that he himself was forging and that the road could go on forever.

AT THE HOTEL Del Prado in Chicago, Lefty had to be careful when he opened the door of their room. He might find the hallway filled with children seeking autographs. Gomez would feign heart-stopping shock at the sight of them and then he would banter and suggest that maybe it was in fact *his* autograph that the kids were after, what with his won-lost record now up to 7–3. Anyway, wrong room. "DiMaggio's not here," Lefty would say although of course DiMaggio *was* there, lying on the top of the bed with his long legs stretched out and crossed, reading his *Superman*; or else standing silently beside the window, smoking. When DiMaggio went out in Chicago—maybe, weary of room service, he would try dinner at the Blackhawk or one of the other spots where there was enough buzz and music and distraction that he could, for a short time, be out in the hot night and shielded a little bit too—Lefty would do his best to make sure the hallway was free of lurkers. Then he would help Joe slip

into the elevator, down to the hotel's bottom floor and out the back way.

Sometimes Joe would phone Dorothy and tell her about these crowds and the constant attention that was upon him, and that at times he felt uncomfortable with it all and wished that he could be with her. Dorothy knew this was true; she remembered the difficulty Joe had on the occasions that they went out with Dorothy's Hollywood friends—especially the ones that DiMaggio didn't really know. It was hard for him to sustain himself, to follow the bouncy conversation, to come off as glib. You might have expected Joe to be the worldly one, with his name and his fame, but, really, when there were new and clever people around and all full of talk, it was Dorothy who was at ease, and guiding him. Dorothy wondered whether, as time went on and Joe became more comfortable around different people and with the spotlight that burned ever more brightly, he would still need to rely on her to help him through.

Dorothy thought always of the baby. In her condition how could she not? The thoughts made her feel hopeful and optimistic about her relationship with Joe. They would make a family together! What Dorothy did not know then, as Joe was missing her in Chicago, was that when Joe Jr. was born—on Oct. 23, 1941, 17 days after the Yankees beat the Dodgers to win the World Series—Joe would spend the better part of the night not with Dorothy at Doctors Hospital but at Toots Shor's celebrating and smoking cigars. She did not imagine that during that following off-season in New York, DiMaggio would, more than ever, go out at night without her, leaving her alone, with diapers to change and formula to mix. She had always expected that the real work of child-raising would fall to her (and that Joe would be best for doting on the boy and dandling him on his knee), but when the time came Dorothy did not embrace this responsibility as happily as she thought she might. It was hard and selfless work. Already she had put her own needs and wants into the background for Joe. Now she was doing it for Joe Jr., too. It seemed to her, during the first year of Joe Jr.'s life, that DiMaggio's silences grew longer, his ill temper more acute; she felt sure that there were other women, and she did not like it that Joe too often criticized her in front of their friends.

Nor could Dorothy know then—as she bundled up the daily batch of fan mail to send up to Yankee Stadium—how angry and resentful she

would come to feel. She would leave Joe for a stretch during the 1942 season to go home to Duluth and sit with her mother and father and say the thing that weighed so awfully on her mind. "My marriage is just not going well," she told them. "Sometimes I just want to put it all behind me." Her parents urged her to hang on, to see if, with patience and understanding, she could make things work. It would not be until the fall of 1943 that Dorothy would officially file for divorce, charging Joe with "cruel indifference." DiMaggio was temporarily out of baseball then, a staff sergeant in the Army's special services, and a divorce was not what he wanted. He appealed to Dorothy for another chance, telling her that he would try to make things right between them. For years after the divorce finally went through, in the spring of '44, he would say to people that he and Dorothy might soon reconcile, though they never did.

On those hot July days in New York with DiMaggio's hitting streak now into the 50s, Dorothy did not know that the baby kicking inside her womb would not in the end serve to be a force that held her and Joe together but rather another wedge that drove them apart. She rubbed her big, smooth belly and looked out off of their grand terrace onto the treetops thick with leaves. She followed the streak, as everyone did, through the radio reports. The excitement of what Joe was doing was all around her, in the phone calls, in the mail and on the doorman's lips—"How about that streak, Mrs. Joe!" When Dorothy heard Joe's voice over the telephone line she envisioned him returning home and collecting her in his arms, and she felt that she needed him and that he needed her.

DIMAGGIO STRETCHED THE streak to 54 against the White Sox' Johnny Rigney who, thanks to that broken eardrum, had avoided military induction and who was three months away from marrying a Comiskey. Life was good for Johnny. No wonder he had his fastball. In the second inning, Rigney's 3–2 pitch handcuffed DiMaggio and he lifted a soft flair to short centerfield that the second baseman Billy Knickerbocker flubbed. Error. Some of the Yankee players came out of the dugout and complained that it should have been ruled a hit. On the swing DiMaggio split his bat, the one that had been stolen and then regained with

Peanuts's help, the one that he had hit with in games 1 through 41 in the streak and then used again from 46 through 53. Rigney was booed for walking DiMaggio in the fourth, and booed again when he went to 2–0 against him in the sixth. Then on the third pitch of the at bat, DiMaggio, swinging with a new Louisville Slugger, chopped the ball into the ground in front of the plate. It bounced, then dribbled down the third base line. By the time third baseman Bob Kennedy got to it, DiMaggio was all but across the first base bag. Infield hit for 54. The following game, the last of the four against Chicago, DiMaggio made it 55 in a row when he singled (and later doubled) off of the chubby lefthander Edgar Smith.

DiMaggio had been on the road for nine days now, giving Peanuts time for other pursuits in Newark. He helped to organize and then to lead a group of about 1,000 local Italians on a trip to Rockaway Beach in Queens. "For a day in the sand," he said. Peanuts wore a suit and tie to the beach. He sometimes went by Vincent's barbershop, where one day a guy came in for a shave and brought with him a square clump of turf and sod that he swore he had cut out of the Yankee Stadium outfield after a game the week before. "Got it from right where Joe was standing," the man said. The turf had spike marks in it—Joe's spike marks supposedly—and the man carried it in a cardboard box. His idea was for DiMaggio to sign the box.

At Vincent's and at barbershops like it all the way down through Maryland and right up into New England, the first iterations of Les Brown's *Joltin' Joe DiMaggio*, live from the Log Cabin, could be heard on the swing stations. Before long, with the melody polished and the lyrics updated to reflect the events of DiMaggio's streak, the song would ring out across the country, played many times a day wherever in the United States radios were, and a can't-miss pick on the diner jukeboxes. When Brown and his band went into the Okeh Records studio to lay down tracks for a recording, DiMaggio himself came by the session wearing a light summer suit and sat on a stool in the thick of the big band, cocking an ear to Brown blowing on the saxophone and listening to the song live for the first time: "From coast to coast that's all you'll hear of Joe the one man show/He glorified the horsehide sphere, Joltin' Joe DiMaggio."

He had them all aglow that summer, Joe did, from coast to coast and

on the streets of Chicago where now, on a Tuesday night in the middle of July, DiMaggio was walking toward the La Salle Street train station with a few others: Gomez, a couple of the writers. The street—Van Buren—was nearly empty and unevenly lit but still a few strangers saw him along the way. "Aren't you Joe DiMaggio?" they asked, knowing that he was.

"Yes," said Joe and shook hands without breaking his steady pace. One man came alongside and said that he worked on the trains as a brakeman, and that he too was on his way to the La Salle Street Station. He was late for his shift, he said, but he would risk his boss's ire for the chance to walk and talk with DiMaggio. The man had red hair and said he came from "San Francisco, the Mission District" and asked after Joe's ballplaying brothers. The group turned off of Van Buren and onto La Salle, and the end of the street where the station stood looked bright and busy with people carrying bags. "That's some streak you have, Joe," the man said before breaking off.

The Yankees held a five-game lead on the Indians and had 300 miles to ride to Cleveland for three games that could tighten the pennant race or open it wide. Each of the games would be an event. People were especially excited for the last of the three. Bob Feller was scheduled to pitch and he would once again try to get the better of DiMaggio, who by that point, the folks in Cleveland figured, would be aiming to push his hitting streak to 58 consecutive games.

Chapter 25
Cleveland

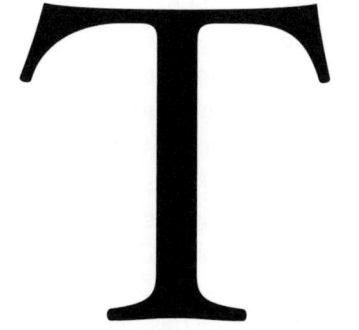HE PEOPLE ARRIVED hours early to the game, herding together outside the Stadium entrance on Third Street and spilling in a great throng onto Lakeside Drive. The weather had broken clear, and a mild evening breeze blew off of Lake Erie and banked through and around the vast vessel of Municipal Stadium. Normally the Indians played only some weekend and holiday games here, but this too was a special occasion. Night game. Yankees. DiMaggio. All of the stadium's 40,000 reserved seats had since been sold and now the push at the ticket stalls was for the rest—the 35,000 general admission tickets that the Indians had put on sale that afternoon.

It's only six blocks but it would be crazy for us to walk, DiMaggio thought as they left the hotel. *Who knows if we would even make it through that crowd with our suits still on.* The Yankees were staying up the hill at the Hotel Cleveland, where from an open window anyone could hear and sense the size and energy of the gathering below. Outside the lobby entrance Joe and Lefty ducked into a cab.

The day before, the Yankees and Indians had played an afternoon game at Cleveland's League Park, and on the first pitch DiMaggio saw from the gangly lefthander Al Milnar he had smashed a sharp single though the middle, extending the streak. Later he reached base on a pop-fly single to short center—the Indians centerfielder Roy Weatherly played DiMaggio so deep it seemed that Weatherly could touch the home run wall behind him. And later still DiMaggio drove a double 400 feet into left center-field. Three hits for Joe, and the Yankees won 10–3. The newspaper in the lobby of the Hotel Cleveland showed a photograph of DiMaggio, deft in a fadeaway slide as he scored the Yankees' second run. He'd hustled home from second base on an infield hit. More magic, the paper said, had been performed by "Joe (Superman) DiMaggio."

"I've got a strange feeling in my bones that you're going to get stopped tonight." The taxi rolled slowly through the choked streets and neared the stadium. The driver was talking to Joe. "I hope you keep the streak going for a hundred games, I do," he said. "But I feel like you're not going to get a hit tonight." Anger shot across Gomez's face and he snapped at the driver to be quiet, just keep driving.

"Creep tried to jinx you!" Gomez, stewing, said to DiMaggio when they stepped out at the players' gate. DiMaggio shrugged, unmoved. All told it had been a 20-cent ride.

By the time the Yankees took batting practice, the seats throughout the huge stadium—at 78,811 it had by far the largest capacity of any major league park—were thick and murmurous with fans. People crowded into the double-decker grandstand and into the outfield bleachers. Down low around the infield there was scarcely room to move in the aisles. Before the start of the series, fans in Cleveland had followed closely the progress and the details of the streak, counting down to DiMaggio's arrival. One newspaper sketch depicted DiMaggio's face on the head of a locomotive charging into town. The official attendance for this game would be 67,463, the largest crowd to attend a baseball game in 1941, and the largest to attend a night game in any stadium, anywhere, ever.

On the field an orchestra played swing tunes, at one point tossing off *Happy Birthday* in honor of Indians shortstop Lou Boudreau who was turning 24. Then the Cleveland manager Roger Peckinpaugh was brought

out and as part of a marketing gimmick was given a brand new refrigerator by the Westinghouse Electric Supply Company. A few within the mammoth crowd were hoping to see DiMaggio's hitting streak stopped by their Indians. Many wanted to see his streak continue. And some people felt both of those things at once, conflicting.

Feller was like that. He couldn't quite bring himself to root for DiMaggio to get a hit against his team, but at the same time as he sat in the dugout in the moments before the game looking out at the great, soughing crowd and the gleaming outfield scoreboard, Feller found himself thinking, *Boy, it would be nice if DiMaggio keeps it going another day. I'd sure like to get a crack at stopping that streak tomorrow. I'd like to be the one on the mound.*

What pitcher wouldn't? The challenge and the excitement around each at bat was motivation enough, and there was also the prospect of immediate fame. Feller's was a widely known name, but for another guy, shutting down DiMaggio would be a notice-maker: the pitcher who stopped Superman.

The Indians' Al Smith, tonight's starter, was skinny and lefthanded, and he threw a lot of soft stuff. He rarely appeared excited about anything. His teammates all called him "Silent Al."

Ground's still wet, DiMaggio thought as he took his batting stance in the top of the first inning. *Might be a slog to first base.* Rain had fallen earlier in the day and he could feel the mud sticking to his spikes. The Yankees already led 1–0, and with one out Henrich stood on second base. Smith started DiMaggio with a fastball, missing high and away.

At third base Ken Keltner shifted his weight, rubbed the palm of his glove, reassumed his crouch. A week earlier he had been an All-Star teammate of DiMaggio's and in the thick of the American League's ninth-inning, game-winning rally in Detroit. Keltner was up and down as a hitter—he drove in 113 runs as a rookie in 1938; he batted just .254 in 1940—but he made the All-Star team because of his glove. He approached the art of fielding assiduously, positioning himself carefully and differently for each batter. Often Keltner stood well in front of the bag, closer to home plate than any other third baseman in the league. He had the reflexes and hands to get away with that. But against DiMaggio, Keltner took the opposite tack. He played very deep and over against the foul line. *I would rather have him sneak a single through the hole than put a double*

past me, Keltner reasoned. He was crisp and heady on the corner, just as Boudreau and Ray Mack were crisp and heady around the second-base bag. *Keltner must be standing on the leftfield grass out there,* DiMaggio thought, glancing down toward him.

On 1 and 0 Smith threw a curveball that broke to the inside corner of the plate. DiMaggio lashed at it, pulling the ball hard and on the ground down that third-base line. It zipped fair past the bag, then into foul ground where Keltner backhanded the ball, straightened his body and threw a pellet to first baseman Oscar Grimes. DiMaggio, on a close play, was out.

Instantly cheers erupted from the stands—*Did you see that play? Best third baseman in the league I tell you! Woulda been a double. What an arm!* A few moments later, when the half-inning ended, applause thundered down again on Keltner as he trotted off the field.

In the top of the fourth inning the score was still 1–0. Smith had run the count to 3 and 2 on DiMaggio, heightening the noisy crowd. Smith relied on several pitches: curveball, changeup, middling fastball and a screwball that could fool you. It was the variety that sustained him. At 33 Smith was on his third team in five years. He had mucked around in the National League—with the Giants and the Phillies—and been cast off before coming to Cleveland and going 15–7 in 1940. He didn't strike out many batters. What he really had going for him was the element of surprise: Smith would use any of his pitches at any time. When he now threw a full-count changeup, DiMaggio fouled it into the stands. Still 3 and 2. *Hang back on this guy,* DiMaggio said to himself. *You can always adjust to that fastball.* The curveball that followed bent too far inside; DiMaggio restrained himself and did not swing. Ball four. Boos rained out of the crowd. Walking DiMaggio, even unintentionally, was rotten play. Smith did not react to the booing, just took the ball and got ready to face Joe Gordon. DiMaggio was now hitless in two times at the plate. *I've seen everything that he's got,* DiMaggio thought. *I'll get one next time up.*

Swiftly, the game moved along. The grandstand shook when the Indians' Gee Walker tied the game at 1–1 with an inside-the-park home run in the bottom of the fourth inning. A visible mist had floated in off the lake and had mixed with the cigarette smoke that wafted from the stands, and the arc lights that encircled the stadium appeared to blur together. Smith

was handling the Yankees fairly easily, and Gomez too had his stuff. Lately, Lefty was feeling as good on the mound as he'd felt in years. He hadn't lost a game since May 12. Watching from the Indians bench Feller felt antsy. He wished it were tomorrow already and that he could get out there and pitch.

Top of the seventh. One out and no one on base. Score still tied at 1–1. *I'm going up swinging this time*, DiMaggio thought. The Cleveland crowd had swung DiMaggio's way for this at bat, rooting for him to get a single and then to stay stranded at first. It was time to get what they had paid for, to witness the Great Man perform. *Awright DiMaggio, let's see what you got.*

From the Yankees dugout Johnny Sturm saw how far back Keltner was standing and thought that DiMaggio might do well to drop down a bunt, although he knew that DiMaggio never would. Smith's first-pitch curveball arrived waist-high and again bent inside. DiMaggio swung and, as if it had been bottled and then uncorked, the play of the first inning unfolded again. The ball whipped down the third-base line, Keltner backhanded it—*No one goes to his right better than this guy*, Feller thought—stood and threw across his body and across the diamond to get DiMaggio, by a stride, at first. Again. *That's twice*, DiMaggio thought jogging back to the bench. *Keltner has my number.* The next batter, Gordon, homered to give the Yankees a 2–1 lead.

And now it was the eighth inning and Smith was tiring badly. The Yankees, on a long rally, had lengthened their lead to 4–1. When Smith walked Henrich to load the bases with one out and bring up DiMaggio, Peckinpaugh came out of the dugout. Aside from the hitting streak, there was a pennant race to consider. The Indians needed to rally back and win this game, then cut the Yankees lead to four behind Feller the next day. Lose, and the Yankees would have a seven-game lead. Peckinpaugh waved for the tall righthander Jim Bagby Jr. to come in from the bullpen. There was half a yellow moon in the sky and it was high up.

DiMaggio knelt on his right knee in front of the Yankees' dugout and rested his left elbow on his left thigh and set his chin upon the back of his left hand and watched Bagby Jr. warm up. Bagby's father had also pitched in the majors and in 1920 he had won 31 games for the pennant-winning Indians. Junior, though, had done nothing close to that; he had less than a .500 record over four so-so seasons. He threw a decent fastball though, especially next to Al Smith's, and he liked to keep it down.

THAT NIGHT, SOUTH of Leningrad, the Nazis and the Red Army were battling in Smolensk. In San Remo, Italy, Mussolini's government had detained 75 American citizens against their will. And in Washington, D.C., the draft lottery had gotten underway. At exactly 7 p.m. a blindfolded Staff Sergeant, Robert W. Shackleton out of Fort Dix in New Jersey, had dipped his hand into a bowl and taken out a small coral-colored capsule with a number inside it. During the two-hour drawing, all of the 750,000 21-year-olds who had registered in early July would have their numbers drawn—some 14,000 from Cleveland, 38,000 from the City of New York. Those whose numbers were pulled from the bowl early on (there were 800 numbers in all; Shackleton drew 196 first) would be inducted no later than September, many as soon as the middle of August. They would be in uniform a few months later, on Dec. 7, when Japanese pilots bombed Pearl Harbor.

In the on-deck circle, DiMaggio rose and swung his two bats a few times and then tossed one away. Johnny Sturm led off from third base. Red Rolfe stood on second. Tommy Henrich took a step off first. In such moments, against the din of the crowd, DiMaggio's wide unflinching stance appeared especially calm, ceremonial even. This would almost certainly be his final turn at bat. Bagby Jr. reared back and threw a fastball an inch or two outside for a ball. The catcher, Rollie Hemsley, complained through his mask that the pitch should have been called a strike. Bagby's next pitch was another fastball, inside this time, that DiMaggio fouled off. Then came a curveball that broke wide. Two and one.

Now it was the fastball again, this one at the knees and DiMaggio swung and caught the top half of the ball, sending it on the ground right to Lou Boudreau, the birthday boy, at shortstop. A certain double play. Just before reaching Boudreau the ball struck something in the grass and leapt abruptly upward; Boudreau raised his glove to catch it at shoulder height, using his bare hand to help. He shuffled the ball to Mack who threw it to Grimes and the double play was complete and the eighth inning was over.

They watched DiMaggio then from the dugout: McCarthy, Rizzuto, Gomez, Dickey, Keller and the rest. As the Cleveland crowd roiled as loudly as it had all night and the Indians came bouncing off of the field—*all right*

fellas we're still in this game!—the Yankees looked to see what DiMaggio would do. The streak was surely finished. Yet he did only what he would have done at any other time. After crossing the first base bag, DiMaggio slowed from his sprint, then turned to his left and continued running out toward shallow centerfield where he bent and, still moving, plucked his glove off the grass. He did not kick the earth or shake his head or pound his fist into the saddle of his glove. He did not behave as if he was aware of the volume and frenzy of the crowd. He did not look directly at anyone or anything. Not once on his way out to centerfield did DiMaggio turn back.

For the rest of the game, in the dugout, DiMaggio remained by himself, the invisible cone around him. Before the end, he nearly had another chance. In the bottom of the ninth inning Gee Walker and Oscar Grimes singled off Gomez and then, with Johnny Murphy in to pitch for the Yankees, pinch hitter Larry Rosenthal tripled. The score was 4–3 with nobody out and if one of the next three Cleveland hitters could knock in Rosenthal the game would be tied; the Yanks, and DiMaggio, might come to bat again. But a ground ball to Sturm at first base kept Rosenthal on third for the first out. The next batter, Soup Campbell, chopped one back to Murphy who caught Rosenthal off the base and got him into a rundown. Out number two. Roy Weatherly's groundout, also straight to Sturm, ended the game.

DiMaggio ran in briskly to the dugout and clacked up the runway to the clubhouse. Although the Yankees had won a tight and important game and had all but put a lock on the pennant, the room remained tentative and hushed. DiMaggio took off his cap and tossed his glove into his locker. The other players all made like they were attending to something important at their own stalls. Not even Gomez, high on his sixth straight win, had anything to say. Through the walls you could hear and feel the rumble of the fans, intoxicated by the night. DiMaggio sat on his stool.

"Well," he said finally, "that's over."

It happened again, then, the towels thrown his way and the gloves tossed jauntily in the air and the guys gathering close and happy around him. *Tough luck, Daig, thought you had one past Keltner. But boy, that was a hell of streak!*

"Suppose it had to end sometime," DiMaggio said. McCarthy threw an arm around him. "You'll start another one tomorrow," he said. For

the photographers Joe posed with his thumbs and forefingers held up in circles—zeros symbolic of his hitless night.

"I'm glad it's over," DiMaggio said to the press. "I've been under a strain." Though a few moments later he amended. "I can't say I'm glad that it's over...certainly I was eager to continue." DiMaggio went back and forth in this way. What he felt was not simple and clean. In one moment he was buoyant, in the next something gnawed inside his chest. It was true that a weight had come off of him, and it was also true, as he would later say, that by losing the streak he felt like he had lost his best friend. To his teammates DiMaggio appeared calm and unbothered.

The news spread over the radio, and the next day in New York and Cleveland and across the country, the end-of-the-streak headlines would run above all else. Page one, top of the page. A cartoon showed Smith and Bagby Jr. as submarines in the high seas, firing away at, and sinking, the Yankee Clipper. Everywhere there appeared small square photos—mug shots—of Smith and Bagby Jr. and often of Keltner too. Like three assassins. Smith looked particularly grim and unsmiling. The three players were linked now and would be linked to this night forever. For each of them, having a role in stopping the streak would be the defining event of their baseball careers, first-paragraph material in their obituaries.

In the Indians clubhouse, Keltner showered and dressed quickly. He brushed aside teammates such as Oscar Grimes who came up to salute him for the plays he'd made on DiMaggio. "We lost the game didn't we?" Keltner said. "There's nothing to congratulate me about." Smith was just as brusque. Fans mustered noisily outside Municipal Stadium and when Keltner and his wife emerged shouts greeted them—some happy, some mad. The crowd started to move in close and a couple of policemen came over and escorted the Keltners to their car. DiMaggio had a lot of friends in Cleveland, the police figured, and you couldn't be sure of what they might do.

People were reluctant to leave. An hour after the game many fans still hung about talking and rehashing while others were just beginning to trundle slowly over the wooden footbridge near City Hall. Cars inched through the forest of walkers and onto the Main Street ramp.

Gradually the Yankees clubhouse began to clear out. Joe, though, was slow to move. He sat on his stool with his uniform on and smoked a

couple of cigarettes. The room had grown quiet again and the Indians' clubhouse boy, an Italian kid named Frank, kept his eyes on DiMaggio. "Scooter, stick around for me, will you," DiMaggio said. So Rizzuto waited as DiMaggio showered and shaved. Rizzuto was the last Yankee left aside from Joe. He would have waited all night if DiMaggio had asked him to.

Finally DiMaggio had slicked back his hair and buttoned his white shirt and clipped his suspenders and snapped straight the sleeves of his suit. They nodded goodbye to Frank, and then, more than two hours after the final play of the game, DiMaggio and Rizzuto stepped out into the night. The crowd had by now given up and gone home. There was no one hanging around to pester Joe. In silence DiMaggio and Rizzuto began to walk, through the moist night air, beneath the lampposts and up the hill toward the Hotel Cleveland. About halfway up there was a little bar and grill. DiMaggio stopped and reached into his pocket. "Shit. Scooter, I left my wallet in the locker room safe," he said. "How much money have you got on you?" Rizzuto pulled out his wallet and opened it. You could hear voices from higher up on the hill, but around them it was quiet. The bar and grill was on the left hand side of the street. "Eighteen dollars."

"Give it here," DiMaggio said. He took the money from Rizzuto and turned to go inside, and Rizzuto followed behind him. "No," said DiMaggio, "you go on. I'm just going to go in here and relax." So Rizzuto continued up the hill and DiMaggio went inside the restaurant, alone, and began the rest of his life.

Often in the weeks and months and years that followed, DiMaggio would think back on the time of the streak—just as so many others in so many places would recall that hot strange summer before the war and would tell their children and their children's children about what DiMaggio had done; and just as the record keepers would log the hitting streak above all others year after year after year and all through the decades of DiMaggio's life—and he would know that in that time he had burst through the bounds of the game, and that he had made something that would live with him always, exalting. Something crowning and indelible. 56.

Epilogue
And The Streak Goes On Forever

OE DIMAGGIO WON 10 pennants and nine World Series in his 13-year career. He was named Most Valuable Player three times and twice finished as the runner-up. He hit 361 home runs and struck out only 369 times. That ratio of 1.02 strikeouts to every home run is beyond extraordinary; of the 129 players who have hit at least 300 career home runs, most have a ratio in the neighborhood of 3 to 1. DiMaggio's 1,537 career RBIs was, at the time of his induction into the Hall of Fame in 1955, 14th on the alltime list, and his total was achieved at the astonishing rate of .89 RBIs per game. He batted .325 over his career and played in 11 All-Star Games. Yet the first line on the Joe DiMaggio plaque that hangs in Cooperstown just to the left of Giants first baseman Bill Terry (the last player before Ted Williams to hit .400 in a season), just to the right of the White Sox supreme knuckleballer Ted Lyons and just above Cubs catcher Gabby Hartnett, reads: HIT SAFELY IN 56 CONSECUTIVE GAMES FOR MAJOR LEAGUE RECORD 1941.

What would DiMaggio's baseball legacy be if, on one of those seem-

ingly insignificant 1-for-whatever days in late May or early June, his hit had not fallen safely? Or if that ground ball to Luke Appling in game 30 had not taken an improbable hop; or if Bob Muncrief had decided to walk DiMaggio after all in game 36; or if Tommy Henrich had been unsuccessful in his bunt attempt and had indeed hit into a double play in game number 38; or if in that same game, DiMaggio's line drive off of Elden Auker had whistled foul?

What if somewhere along the line—perhaps before the newspaper cartoons were drawn and clipped and before the poems were written, before George Sisler's and Wee Willie Keeler's marks were passed and before the song *Joltin' Joe DiMaggio* had made its way into so many jukeboxes— DiMaggio had simply gone hitless for a day? He would be in the Hall of Fame now, certainly, and be remembered as an alltime elite player. But would he have ascended so singularly in his stardom? Would he have quite so dramatically extended his name beyond the circles of the game?

If DiMaggio had hit in only, say, 30 or 35 consecutive games in 1941 would he have even been named that season's Most Valuable Player ahead of Ted Williams and his .406 batting average? Unlikely. No one had hit .400 in 11 years and no one had ever done it with anything like Williams's power. At .406, Williams batted a full 49 points higher than DiMaggio in '41 and hit seven more home runs than DiMaggio did. "It was the 56-game hitting streak which. . .doubtless clinched the verdict," wrote John Drebinger of *The New York Times* after DiMaggio's narrow win in the baseball writers' MVP voting.

Without the far-flung, daily attention that the hitting streak brought him, and without DiMaggio's ability to succeed beneath that glare, to meet and then surpass the expectations of millions day after day after day, would he have risen to the level of living legend? Or might he merely have been another great ballplayer, rather than a figure who for decades after his career ended would be entreated by people, famous and unknown, to, "Tell us about 1941. Tell us about the streak."?

More relevantly to today's perception of DiMaggio as icon: If he had not, in that summer of '41 lured huge audiences and willed an anxious nation to turn its eyes—O.K., its lonely eyes—to him, would the idea of Joltin' Joe as a quintessential, bygone hero nonetheless have presented

itself to Paul Simon and Art Garfunkel 27 years later? (Of the imperishable lyric *Where have you gone Joe DiMaggio? A nation turns its lonely eyes to you. . . .* in the song *Mrs. Robinson,* Simon has said, "The Joe DiMaggio line was written right away in the beginning. And I don't know why or where it came from.")

Paul Simon was hardly a baseball historian, any more than was Ernest Hemingway when, standing at his writer's desk in the early 1950s, he gave DiMaggio literary life in *The Old Man and the Sea* as a symbol of courage (Santiago reveres DiMaggio for his ability to play through the painful bone spurs he endured near the end of his career) and a player who, as the old man says, "makes the difference." The point is not that either of these writers had DiMaggio's hitting streak top of mind, or even that they considered it at all, but simply that there is no doubting the impact that the 56-game run had on the wider perception of who DiMaggio was—that the *idea* of "Joe DiMaggio" was unquestionably colored, however subconsciously, by the streak and its lasting effect.

"That was the crossover event," says Maury Allen who was nine in 1941, and who wrote *Where Have You Gone, Joe DiMaggio?,* a 1975 biography. "The hitting streak was the time when people who didn't know baseball got to know Joe DiMaggio and when people who did know baseball saw that DiMaggio, in some respects, was in a league by himself. Those feelings never ever went away."

Tom Villante, who was 13 years old and living in Queens in 1941 and who would serve as the Yankees bat boy in the '43 World Series and then for two seasons afterward, says, in a sentiment echoed again and again by people who recall the streak from their childhood, "The thing about it is that it was there every day. It just went on and on and he kept doing it and people kept talking about it. He was just in your consciousness and you couldn't help it. And then you started hearing the song about the streak and that made it stick even more."

Consider this. Without the profound elevation in stature that the streak provided, would Joe DiMaggio have been regarded as worthy and appropriate, a real American hero, when, in 1952, he asked, through publicists, to have dinner with the rising movie star and sex symbol Marilyn Monroe?

IN 1969, TO commemorate the sport's centennial season, Major League Baseball commissioned a survey of baseball writers and broadcasters to determine by vote the greatest living players at each position, as well as, it followed, the greatest living ballplayer, period. The results were announced on July 21, one day before the All-Star Game, at a banquet at the Sheraton Park Hotel in Washington, D.C. More than 2,200 people attended including 34 of the 37 living baseball Hall of Famers, the widows of Lou Gehrig and Babe Ruth and all 56 of the players on that year's All-Star teams. "I have been in baseball for half a century," said former Pirate Pie Traynor as he accepted the award for greatest living third baseman, "and this is the greatest event I have ever attended."

Supreme Court Justice Byron White was in the ballroom that night, as were the Secretaries of State, Defense and the Interior. President Richard Nixon sent regrets. He was handling matters relating to Neil Armstrong's having set foot on the moon a few hours earlier, an occurrence that seemed fitting to baseball commissioner Bowie Kuhn as he presided over the banquet. "Baseball," Kuhn explained without irony, "has had a cosmic effect on people because it has promoted human relations and has understood human dignity." Col. Frank Borman, who seven months earlier had commanded the first manned trip into lunar orbit aboard *Apollo 8* and who was now sitting on a dais among ballplayers such as Stan Musial and Satchel Paige, joined in the applause.

One by one the players were cited and honored. "Greatest living catcher: Bill Dickey. . . . Greatest living second baseman: Joe Cronin. . . .Greatest living leftfielder: Ted Williams." Then Willie Mays, 18 years into his career as a centerfielder, was announced as the greatest living *rightfielder* and he bounded to the podium. "Well, what do you know, I played rightfield two or three times in my life," he said good-naturedly. Then he added, "But it would be wrong if centerfield were reserved for anyone but Joe DiMaggio."

It was about then, recall people who were on hand that night, that the murmuring began, the attendees realizing that DiMaggio would also bring home the evening's biggest prize. Soon it was announced: Joe DiMaggio, Greatest Living Centerfielder. Joe DiMaggio, Greatest Living Ballplayer.

The label would immediately, and for the next 30 years, greatly enhance DiMaggio's already formidable aura. He wore the crown regally, bowing slightly and giving a demure smile when the three words preceded his introduction at public events. There was little, if any, public objection that evening or in the days that followed to the choice of DiMaggio—even though this was an ideal subject for sports argument and there certainly seemed room for debate. One candidate with an argument might have been Mays himself, who at that point in 1969 had hit 596 of the 660 home runs he would end up with, and who played centerfield for the Giants with a panache and brilliance that was unmistakably his own.[1]

There was Cardinals outfielder Stan Musial, a three-time MVP and seven-time batting champion who had ended his career in 1963 with 1,951 RBIs (then the fourth highest total of all time) and a National League record 3,630 hits, nearly 1,500 more than DiMaggio had.

There was Mickey Mantle, who had succeeded DiMaggio magnificently as the Yankees centerfielder and who was one year retired from a career in which he clubbed 536 home runs, won three MVP awards of his own and established himself unquestionably as the Greatest Switch Hitter of All Time, if that had been among the honors bestowed.

And of course there was Ted Williams, who had bettered DiMaggio's numbers in virtually every offensive category, outhitting him by 19 points, outhomering him by 160 and reaching base more than 48% of the time to DiMaggio's nearly 40%. Williams had missed almost five full seasons in military service; DiMaggio three. While Williams was inarguably a much, much lesser fielder, he had accumulated his offensive numbers in lineups that were invariably far weaker than those DiMaggio enjoyed.

Yet none of those players ever offered serious complaint about DiMaggio's having the title and the media did little to stir up controversy. DiMaggio was the Greatest Living Ballplayer until the day he died.

Who deserves the title of greatest living ballplayer today? Mays? Musial? Hank Aaron, with his 755 home runs and 2,297 RBIs, his good

---

[1] Sometime in the 1990s DiMaggio was asked by his friend, the writer and boxing aficionado Bert Sugar, whether he thought he would have made the famous over-the-shoulder catch that Mays pulled off against the Indians' Vic Wertz in the 1954 World Series. DiMaggio paused, then replied coyly: "Well, I wouldn't have lost my hat."

speed and good glove? Would anyone make a case for BALCO customer and seven-time MVP Barry Bonds, who, whatever enhancements he may have relied on, still had to actually hit all those home runs, draw all those walks, get all of those 2,935 base hits and play a peerless leftfield? Might some people say that admitted steroid user Alex Rodriguez, sixth on the career home run list at age 35, has a claim? Or Cardinals first baseman Albert Pujols, the only player aside from Al Simmons in the 1920s and '30s to drive in more than 100 runs in each of his first 10 seasons? What about Ken Griffey Jr. who emerged through the steroid era untainted (at the time of his retirement), clubbing 630 home runs and, for the first 12 years of his career anyway, playing a Maysian centerfield? Would the outstanding Phillies' third baseman of the 1970s and '80s, Mike Schmidt, get votes?

From 1969 to '99, the last three decades of DiMaggio's life, there was no doubt who wore the crown. And while he would have been in the running had he never reeled off his hitting streak—a feat, it's worth noting, that DiMaggio himself called his most remarkable career achievement moments after receiving the Greatest Living Ballplayer award—there is little likelihood that he would have beaten the other candidates. "Everybody thought that Williams would win it," recalls Allen, who was then working at the *New York Post* and who attended the event. "He just seemed to have the numbers and he was the Washington manager then. Myself, I voted for Musial, for what he did over 20 seasons—just for being that excellent for that long. So DiMaggio winning it was a surprise.

"In some ways it was DiMaggio's hitting streak versus Williams hitting .406 in 1941 and the voters weighing which one was the greater accomplishment," Allen continues. "Both players did other important things in their careers, of course, but there is no way that DiMaggio would have been named Greatest Living Ballplayer without that hitting streak. No chance at all."

UPON RETURNING TO New York after the end of the streak, DiMaggio was so ardently and unceasingly besieged by autograph-seekers at his apartment that he agreed to set aside some time and hold a special sign-

ing session just for the people who lived in the building. A week later he made an afternoon appearance on Sullivan Street in Greenwich Village where he would give out 1,000 baseballs and 600 miniature bats. He had made similar appearances in years past, and always to exuberant response, but never had it been anything like it was in 1941. The phenomenon of DiMaggio's record-shattering streak burned brightly and he was then 12 games into what would be a 16-game streak that he began the day after being stopped in Cleveland. A line began to form on Sullivan Street 10 hours before DiMaggio showed up. Some kids wore T-shirts with Joe's name and "56" written on them and when the supply of balls and bats ran out many hundreds of people were left empty-handed.

That season and the next, spurred by a suggestion from an editor at the *St. Louis Post-Dispatch*, some sportswriters advocated that DiMaggio change his uniform number from 5 to 56, a fitting reminder of his accomplishment, they said, and perhaps also a fated figure: during the streak, it was pointed out, he had scored exactly 56 runs. DiMaggio dismissed the suggestion without comment but it became an occasional lark in the clubhouse for a teammate to snatch Joe Gordon's uniform—number 6—and hang it beside DiMaggio's number 5. Photographers would try to catch DiMaggio and Gordon standing next to each other during batting practice, DiMaggio on the left, and shoot a picture from behind.

Les Brown's hit song *Joltin' Joe DiMaggio* played regularly on the radio not only in 1941 but for years afterward. When DiMaggio was stationed in Hawaii during World War II he would cringe if the song came on, especially when the other soldiers sang along to the twee background chorus: *We dream of Joey with the light brown bat.* In 1970, upon DiMaggio's turning 56 years old, his friend Reno Barsocchini threw a party for him at Reno's bar on Post Street in San Francisco. This was a milestone, like anyone else's 50th or 60th. Gomez came to the party, as did some of the old guys from North Beach. There were drinks on the house and a blonde hooker for the birthday boy. Joe DiMaggio only turns 56 once.

Away from DiMaggio himself, the number became and still remains a hallmark, a point of absolute reference even beyond the game. Not a week goes by without public mention of DiMaggio's streak, and often several mentions. Predictably, many analysts held up the streak for com-

parison when, at the 2010 Australian Open, Roger Federer reached the semifinals of a Grand Slam event for a record 23rd consecutive time. In a retrospective piece, the *Los Angeles Times* likened the track star Edwin Moses's 122-race win streak from 1977 to '87 to DiMaggio's hitting streak, just as the *Cape Cod Times* invoked the streak in historical comparison to golfer Walter Hagen's winning four straight PGA Championships from '24 through '27. Bassmaster Mike McLelland's recent run of finishing in the money at 14 straight Elite Series fishing events was compared to DiMaggio's streak, as was a club-record 11-game hitting streak run off in the summer of 2009 by infielder Shawn O'Malley of the Class A Charlotte Stone Crabs.

In September of 2010, when Oakland A's second baseman Mark Ellis put together his own 11-game streak, he announced: "I don't think I'm going to break Joe DiMaggio's record."

Modern observers are quick to refer to the streak in any number of contexts. After the Cleveland Indians traded away a reigning Cy Young Award winner for a second consecutive season (CC Sabathia to the Brewers in 2008, Cliff Lee to the Phillies in '09), the *Plain Dealer* suggested that this was the Indians "organizational equivalent" of DiMaggio's streak. When the U.S. luger Erin Hamlin won gold at the world championships to snap a run of 99 straight wins by Germany's women lugers, *USA Today* compared Hamlin to DiMaggio's streak-stoppers Al Smith and Jim Bagby Jr. Last year a *New York Times* writer suggested that the graceful demeanor of the star filly Rachel Alexandra as she raced against and defeated so many colts, was reminiscent of DiMaggio's elegant bearing during his hitting streak. The streak has been leveraged in analogy during debate on the floor of the U.S. Congress and also in courtrooms, including—and this, you can be sure, required some convoluted logic—during the closing arguments of music producer Phil Spector's 2009 murder trial.

And on it goes. A writer for *The Huffington Post* suggested that when the 2010 movie *Avatar* exceeded the record for box-office sales set by *Titanic* 13 years earlier it was akin to a batter shattering DiMaggio's mark. Not long ago an article appearing on popeater.com declared that 'N Sync's U.S. record of 2.4 million copies sold in one week (of their 2000 album *No Strings Attached*), "may be as unbreakable" as Joe DiMaggio's streak of 56 games.

"That number, it is just. . .I guess it's just so big that it's hard to fathom," said the veteran outfielder Adam Dunn, standing in front of his locker before a game. Dunn is a powerful hitter, although with his long swing and his affection for drawing walks, he is not the streaking kind. "In some ways even the name of the man doesn't mean as much as that number does," Dunn went on. "If some other guy had done it we would still know it and we would still look at the number like it was from another world. Everyone understands that Joe DiMaggio was a very good hitter—a very good player—but when you put that number next to him, it makes him, well it makes him different. It makes him better."

Then Dunn said something echoing a notion that had been expressed by other ballplayers on other afternoons, by the Yankees captain Derek Jeter, and by the Hall of Famer Tony Gwynn. "That streak," Dunn said, "pretty much makes it so that DiMaggio won't ever be forgotten."

The View From Here
What Are The Odds?

A distinguished collection of professional thinkers has long debated the likelihood and implications of a baseball player's hitting in 56 consecutive games—Joe DiMaggio in particular, and any big leaguer in general. Scholarly articles have appeared, naturally, in the *Baseball Research Journal*, the flagship publication for the Society for American Baseball Research (SABR) and in the *Journal of Quantitative Analysis in Sports*. Other papers relating to DiMaggio's streak were published in *Sociological Forum*, in the *Journal of the American Statistical Association* and in *Chance*, a magazine that explores the applications of statistics in society. General audiences have found probabilistic analysis of the streak in *The Wall Street Journal*, *The New York Review of Books* and other publications.

The streak has been studied by mathematicians, economists, professors of finance, Ivy League sociologists and by a man who would later become the deputy director of the National Economic Council under George W. Bush. The Nobel Prize–winning physicist Edward M. Purcell took a long and detailed look at the streak, as did an evolutionary biologist so accomplished that the Society for the Study of

Evolution has an award named after him—the Stephen Jay Gould Prize.

In other words, some wicked smart people have gotten into this stuff.

The streak examiners have devised algorithms, run computer simulations, and enlisted teams of undergraduate students to perform dice-rolling experiments. Some folks used a player's game-by-game results as a basis for inquiry, others relied on a player's cumulative statistics over the course of a season (DiMaggio in 1941 etc.), or over several seasons or a career. For some, DiMaggio's batting average served as a point of reference; others factored in the walks that he drew. One man attempted to predict the probability of a hitter who is on a 30-game streak maintaining the streak for 26 more games by drawing upon the past performances of all players during long streaks. A paper on the general streakiness (or lack thereof) among ballplayers sought to weigh game conditions such as runners on base and the handedness of pitchers.

The results? Well, a 1994 study deduced that a streak like DiMaggio's will occur once every 746 years. A rebuttal to that one put it at once every 18,519 years. Other estimates have ranged from a probability of about .001 (or 1 in 1,000) that DiMaggio would have hit in 56 straight in 1941 to .000054 (a little more than 5 in 100,000). Another assessment said that while the chances of DiMaggio himself having hit in 56 straight were only 1 in 3,394, the likelihood that some major leaguer at some time, somewhere, would have done it along the way is a robust 1 in 16. A few years ago a student and a professor working together at Cornell suggested that there was a 42% chance of such a

streak having occurred at some point in baseball history, an overly generous estimate that upon further review the professor himself has felt inclined to question.

The data and statistics can be parsed and deployed in any number of ways to compute the likelihood of a hitting streak. All things considered there is only slightly more consensus on the probability of Joe DiMaggio—or of any major leaguer—having achieved a 56-game hitting streak than there is on the probability of life existing on other planets. Which factors are truly relevant and which are not? Given all the physical and psychological factors that come in to play on a baseball field, who really knows? To conundrums such as the Fermi Paradox and the Drake Equation, let us add The DiMaggio Enigma.

THE SAME BREED of scholars who've pored over DiMaggio's streak have also explored related concepts such as whether an athlete can get "hot" and whether or not there is such thing as a ballplayer who is predictably good in "clutch" situations. The analysts are looking at areas in which they can measure "the influence of chance or random events on the outcomes observed," as the Harvard sociologist Stanley Lieberson wrote in his 1997 paper *Modeling Social Processes: Some Lessons from Sports*. As a whole, sports provides an attractive arena for such study because the results tend to be easily measurable and quantifiable (baskets sunk or not sunk, home runs hit or not hit, etc.) and because the games abide by governing rules that provide a degree of order and some limits upon what can and cannot occur. (A basketball player can't play more

than 48 minutes in a regulation game; a pitcher must stand 60 feet, 6 inches away from home plate and so on.) Compared to a lot of what makes up everyday life, ball games are a controlled experiment.

Study of the "hot hand" in sports grew out of work done in the 1970s by the psychologists Daniel Kahneman (also a Nobel laureate) and Amos Tversky that examined the way that humans perceive and judge probability. Then in 1985 Tversky collaborated with another psychologist, Thomas Gilovich, on a paper that charted shooting patterns in actual NBA games. The study showed that a player having what we might call a "hot hand" had no bearing upon his chances of making a basket. That is, a shooter who has sunk, say, six of seven shots in a game is no more or less likely to sink his eighth attempt than if he had been successful on only one of seven attempts to that point. Just as flipping a coin and getting heads six of seven times does not make the coin any more or less likely to land on heads on the eighth flip than if it has landed on heads just once in seven previous flips. The odds, assuming the coin is perfectly balanced, are 50-50 either way. Similarly, a player's likelihood of sinking that eighth basket (either from the field or from the free throw line; both situations were tested) corresponds to his or her overall shooting percentage.

Subsequent studies tended to echo Tversky and Gilovich's conclusions and similar work was done in baseball. A 1993 paper by Indiana University professor S. Christian Albright charted batters' results over four major league seasons and "failed to find convincing evidence in support of wide-scale streakiness." Sure, a .300 hitter will sometimes have a stretch of 11 hits in 20 at bats, and other

times have a stretch of just one hit in 20 at bats, but that is what is to be expected by pure chance or random variation—again, in the same way that flipping a coin 1,000 times will give you some sequences of 15 heads in 20 flips and other sequences of five heads in 20 flips. (I know; I tried this.) Over a long enough trial, though, the proven .300 hitter will hit around .300 and the coin will land on heads roughly 50% of the time. (I got 509 tails and 491 heads over the course of my 1,000 flips.) Each at bat—like each coin flip and each foul shot—is by this reckoning an independent event unrelated to the at bats that come before or after.

So, did Joe DiMaggio, a career .343 hitter entering the 1941 season, get "hot" when he batted .440 over the final 35 games of his hitting streak? Do any players truly have hot and cold stretches, or are they simply the beneficiaries and victims of randomness? Objective analyses say that hot streaks and slumps are a myth derived from faulty perception. "Ninety-nine percent of what observers see as a player being hot or cold is an illusion," says Red Sox adviser Bill James, baseball's emperor of statistical analysis. "There may be rare cases when a player makes an adjustment or is bothered by an injury, or some other factor enters in that actually changes performance beyond what is expected. But otherwise a hot streak simply is not real."

Of course if you make such a suggestion to a ballplayer he'll look at you as if you have cream cheese on your face. "Whoever says something like that needs to get out from behind his calculator and play some ball," says former NL batting champion Keith Hernandez. "When you are hot you feel hot. When you're in a slump you feel lousy."

"There is no question that sometimes you're going well and other times not so well," says Wade Boggs, a career .328 hitter and a five-time batting champ. "That's just how it is. You try to be consistent but sometimes your mechanics will get messed up or something will get in your way. When you're hot you want to ride it as long as you can."

Batters swear that they go through stretches when the baseball looks to be the size of a grapefruit coming in to the plate, and endure other times when the ball resembles an aspirin. And they aren't the only ones who believe this. Managers regularly strategize around the belief that an opposing batter is "hot," and try to avoid pitching to him. As one of innumerable examples, the Los Angeles Angels felt this way about the Yankees' Alex Rodriguez during the 2009 ALCS. A-Rod had a playoff batting average of .429 and had hit four home runs in 21 playoff at bats before the Angels walked him seven times in his final 18 trips to the plate.

So why would some scientists tend to trust statistical analysis over reports from the front lines? Why rely on untethered data and probability theory rather than on testimony from the players experiencing the events? This lack of trust in the participants brings to mind the old story of Ludwig Wittgenstein, who one day approached an acquaintance with a question.

"Tell me," Wittgenstein began, "why do people say that it was natural for man to assume that the sun went around the earth rather than that the earth was rotating?"

His friend answered: "Well, obviously because it *looks* as if the sun is going around the earth."

And Wittgenstein replied: "But, what would it have looked like if it had looked as though the earth were rotating?"

Thus, it may *look* as though a hitter who knocks out a string of home runs and multihit games is in a hot streak, or that a hitter who strikes out repeatedly while taking a succession of oh-for-fours is in a slump, but how would it look if these stretches were simply the result of random, independent events and chance?

———

THE MOST COMMON approach to computing the probability of a hitting streak involves the application of two statistics: 1) the frequency with which a player gets a hit per time he comes to the plate and 2) the average number of times he comes to the plate each game. The studies that have relied on a player's batting average to determine that first statistic, hit-frequency, are clearly in error. Batting average does not take into account unofficial at bats such as walks and sacrifice hits, even though each of those at bats is in fact an opportunity to get a hit. In many real-life game situations a walk is as good as a hit, as Little League coaches like to say. In determining a player's batting average a walk is as good as a nothing. But in figuring the likelihood of getting a hit in a given game, a walk is as good as an out. It is a missed opportunity.

Joe DiMaggio's career batting average was .325. He had 2,214 career hits in 6,821 official at bats. But when you divide those hits by his career *plate appearances* (7,671), you get .288. (That is, he got a hit 28.8% of the time came to the plate.) I'll call this his career streak average. More relevant to determining DiMaggio's likelihood of putting together a long streak in 1941 is to look at his statistics from '36 through the end of the '40 season. In that five-year

stretch his batting average was .343, his streak average .311.

The accounting for walks (and other unofficial plate appearances) is simple but crucial. Some fans wonder why DiMaggio's peer Ted Williams, whose career .344 batting average is the seventh highest alltime—and much higher than DiMaggio's—never put together a streak of even 25 games. Williams was actually a much weaker candidate for a hitting streak than DiMaggio was because Williams walked so frequently. With 2,654 hits in 9,791 career plate appearances, Williams's streak average is just .271. Even in 1941 when Williams batted .406 to DiMaggio's .357, Williams's streak average was just .305 to DiMaggio's .311. Scores of players are or were better hitting streak candidates than the immortal Williams, including lesser lights such as current Phillies infielder Placido Polanco with a career batting average of just .303, but a streak average of .277.

Let's do this very briefly. Once you have established a player's streak average and his average plate appearances per game (for DiMaggio that number was 4.54 from 1936 up to the start of the 1941 season) you can figure out the likelihood that he will get one or more hits in a game by using a basic formula of probability theory. In DiMaggio's case that likelihood was a hair below 82%—extremely high although hardly unprecedented. To figure the likelihood that he will get a hit in two specific consecutive games, you simply multiply .82 by itself and get about .67 or 67%. Multiply this by .82 again and you get 55% as the probability of a hit in three specific consecutive games and so on. Working it out this way the chances for a 10-game streak are 13.74%, for a 20-gamer 1.89%, for a 30-gamer

.26%, for a 40-gamer .0357% and for 56 straight .0015%.

But that's clearly not our answer. The above formula is for a *specific* 56-game stretch. What we want to know is the likelihood of a given streak at any time over the course of a season, that is, in *any* of the available 56-game stretches, not a particular one. A batter could hit in games 1 through 56, or games 2 through 57, or games 3 through 58 and so on. There are 99 possible ways to hit in 56 straight over a 154-game season. Many of those sequences are overlapping. Now, figuring the probability becomes more complicated. In a 2002 paper published in the *Baseball Research Journal*, Michael Freiman employed a recursive algebraic formula to resolve this issue and ultimately came up with .01%, or one in 10,000, as DiMaggio's chances for hitting in 56 straight at some point in the 1941 season.[1]

Some other studies have used a method like Freiman's, but lately what a lot of people do is simply plug the .82 probability into a computer program and have it run millions of simulated 154-game sequences. Using this approach my neighborhood math genius—the masterly Ben McGill, who by day does quantitative analysis for JPMorgan Chase—determined the likelihood of a 10-game streak as being a robust 99.36% for a batter as efficient as DiMaggio was in 1941. For 20 games it was 37.34%, for 30 games it was 5.28%, and for 40 games just .65%. To hit in 56 in a row? McGill came back with .0231%, or a little more than once every 5,000 seasons. That number will vary depending on the assumptions that you make at the outset of doing the

---

[1] DiMaggio, hobbled by an ankle injury in late August and September, played in just 139 games that year.

calculations.[2] As mentioned, highly skilled mathematicians have used slightly different numbers and gotten a variety of results. Again a fair analogy is to coin flipping. In effect, whether by algebraic formula or computer simulation, you are figuring out a player's hitting-streak probability the same way that you would determine the potential for a certain run of heads in a 154-flip trial. Only in this case the coin is weighted to land on heads about 82% of the time.

I won't go any further in discussing probability theory and I won't attempt to lay out any notation for a number of reasons, the main one being that I am likely to get it wrong. I am, simply put, out of my league. My limited understanding of probability theory—and by limited I mean limited—has been hard-won over the course of researching this book. You can learn the basics of this material without much math training but it is not easy and it requires a commitment to some dense reading. While I was groping my way through some probability formulas I sometimes thought of Jim Harrison, the marvelous writer and eater who in the name of journalistic enterprise once ate his way through a Rabelaisian feast that began with the consumption of an entire gross of oysters. Of the experience, Harrison said: "It is not recommended." Neither is a crash course in probability theory.

I did undertake a series of simple probability tests during my learning. In the process I flipped a lot of coins and rolled a lot of dice. I produced a deck of cards and enlisted family

---

[2] Based on our assumption of DiMaggio getting 4.54 at bats per game, McGill used an 81.61% per-game hit probability to derive these figures. Also, seeking to more closely replicate reality, he ran the same numbers a second time but instead of 4.54 at bats, which is an impossible number for a batter to have in a game, he applied a formula in which he assumed four at bats in half of the games and five at bats in the other half. In this latter model the probabilities for a hitting streak of the various lengths were all very slightly smaller than those listed above.

members to help me test some popular theories of chance. The intention behind these exercises was not to break new ground, of course, but rather just to spend some time thinking about the kinds of things that people think about when they think about this stuff. As luck would have it, though, one experiment yielded a nice illustration of an important point about probability perception that connects to DiMaggio's streak.

One evening, my six-year-old daughter and I sat down and took out the Scrabble tiles. We separated out one of each letter of the alphabet, then put those 26 tiles in a soft, black-and-white top hat of the kind that the Cat in the Hat might wear. I asked my daughter to pull out letters one at a time, three pulls in each trial. We did not replace each letter immediately upon looking at it, but after taking the three out we put them all back into the hat, shook it wildly around and began again. My daughter's first three draws, in precise order, went like this:

$$E \; Q \; K$$
$$Y \; Q \; B$$
$$B \; A \; G$$

"Mommy, I got a word!" she shouted out to my wife. "I got a word on my third turn!" Indeed she had. The chances of drawing, in order, a specific three-letter combination in this scenario is one in 15,600 (that is, $\frac{1}{26} \times \frac{1}{25} \times \frac{1}{24}$). If we assume that at that point in her development as a reader there were 100 three-letter English words that my daughter would have recognized (excluding those that repeat letters such as *mom* or *boo*), then the chances of her pulling one of those words on

any turn is 1 in 156; doing it in just her third turn was surely beating the odds. It was not, however, more improbable than the fact that she pulled Q in the second position in each of the first two turns (the odds of that are 1 in 625) or that she pulled consecutive B's in the second and third turns (1 in 624). It's just that those events didn't mean anything to her. Seeing a word you know is exciting. Hauling out a couple of random Q's, however unlikely that may be, is not.

How does this relate to DiMaggio's hitting streak? Well, we perceive his hitting in 56 straight games as being the most unlikely thing that a batter could do over that span. But in fact whatever the final odds are of that streak, other 56-game combinations are even less probable. Remember that DiMaggio was considerably more likely to get a hit in any given game than not to. Hitting in, say, 49 out of 56 games is of course more probable than hitting in 56 straight if we allow those hitless games to fall anywhere in the series. But if we demand a specific sequence, such as: hit in 19 straight, go hitless for two, hit in 10 straight, go hitless for four, hit in six straight, go hitless for one, and finally hit in 14 more, then the probability becomes even more remote than hitting in 56 straight. That we are amazed by one sequence and not by the other is essentially a matter of perception, not a matter of probability.

My daughter and I did an additional 30 trials that night without getting another word that she knew, and still she regarded her efforts, quite correctly, as a success.

———◆———

IN 2008 A Cornell graduate student named Sam Arbesman and his adviser, Steven Strogatz, an applied mathe-

matics professor, wrote an op-ed piece for *The New York Times* that was titled, *A Journey to Baseball's Alternate Universe*. The two men were out to test just how improbable DiMaggio's streak was and, "using a comprehensive collection of baseball statistics from 1871 to 2005," they wrote, "we simulated the entire history of baseball 10,000 times in a computer." The key statistic was each player's probability of getting a hit in a game—such as the 82% for DiMaggio in 1941 that was noted earlier. The computer model was not much different in approach from the many models that preceded it (it too generated information by virtually flipping a series of weighted coins) but it was far more exhaustive. The published results were jarring. "Forty two percent of the simulated baseball histories have a streak of DiMaggio's length or longer," Arbesman and Strogatz wrote. "In other words, streaks of 56 games or longer are not at all an unusual occurrence."

What?

The piece was immediately set upon, its validity questioned by a range of mathematicians, stat geeks and other concerned baseball fans. A major recurring objection was the study's failure (again, like most of those before it) to account for game-by-game variation. It relied on a distribution of probability that did not necessarily correspond to real events. Surely a hitter might have a better chance of getting a hit on one day, facing pitcher X under Y circumstances, than he does of getting a hit on another day, facing pitcher W under Z circumstances. How then, the naysayers complained, can you accept a study that assigns an unvarying percentage chance of a batter getting hit?

Another objection to Arbesman and Strogatz's findings,

by an inquisitive blogger named Stuart Rojstaczer, pointed out that their model didn't consider what really happened; it paid no mind to the roughly 130 years of data that's readily available about major league hitting streaks. The computer simulation revealed its shortcomings by greatly overprojecting the frequency of 20- and 30-game hitting streaks as compared to the number of those streaks that have actually occurred. "An uncalibrated model," Rojstaczer asserted, "is gibberish." He charted a simple graph on an X/Y axis, using the real-life frequency of major league hitting streaks (30–34 game streaks occur about every four years; 35–39 gamers about every 12 years etc.) and by extending the graph into the 50s suggested that DiMaggio's streak would come along once every 1,300 years.

Arbesman and Strogatz were inclined to agree with and appreciate the criticism (Rojstaczer's work in particular was "brilliant in its simplicity," the egoless Strogatz told me), so they set out to construct some new, better models. This time they ran simulations that added random variation to the probability of getting a hit in any given game. Rather than the probability being a constant, say, 81% (the number that they derived for DiMaggio), it was 71% in one game, 91% in another and so on. (Remember that Arbesman and Strogatz didn't just do this for DiMaggio but for all batters, most of whom had a lower hit-probability than DiMaggio, some of whom had a higher one.) These new models produced a somewhat altered probability of a "DiMaggio-like streak"—one set of trials calculated an 18% chance of it having happened since 1905—but the suggested likelihood of long streaks still turned out to be far greater than actual results bear out.

So, how does Strogatz like his streak-calculation models now? "You know, I'm pretty sure that they're wrong," he told me over the phone. "Demonstrably wrong. There are things in these simulations, including an artificial steadiness even in our more nuanced models, that are just systematically faulty."

The central problem with the Arbesman-Strogatz approach is the same one that undermines so many others. Baseball players are not coins, or dice or Scrabble tiles in the bottom of a hat. The number of factors that might influence the likelihood of a hit in a particular game or at bat are simply too many to properly account for. You'd have to address not only each opposing pitcher's skill but how well rested he is, and, more daunting, his intentions and psychological makeup. You'd have to weigh the positioning of fielders, the softness of the ground, and the temperature and humidity of the air. What about rain or darkness that might shorten a game? And was the batter up at night with a stomach bug? Is his hamstring sore? His finger? His wrist? Is he worried that his girlfriend is ticked off because he never came home on Saturday night? Did a "fan" yell something horribly offensive at him as he stood in the on-deck circle? Is he thinking about the streak or not? Which way is the wind blowing? What is the batter's general temperament, and even if we could know that then what temperament is best suited to a hitting streak? And so on and so on and so on. Even supposing we could answer these questions, how would we know what impact each circumstance might or might not have on the game? How could that influence possibly be measured?

To say that the probability studies of hitting streaks are

naive to psychological factors is a massive understatement. As Robert Remez, a wonderful thinker and professor of psychology at Barnard, said to me, "These experiments are kind of like the stoned guy who is looking for his car keys under the lamppost rather than where he dropped them because that's where the light is."

Virtually all attempts to unravel The DiMaggio Enigma use some sort of what's known as a Bernoulli trial; that is, the coin-flipping model. People deploy Bernoulli trials in studying hitting streaks because it's a method that "works" to provide an answer that has some logic to it. That's where the lamppost light is. The problem is this: Instead of flipping the same weighted coin, say, 10,000 times, what you really need to do is flip 10,000 different coins, each of them minutely nuanced, one time each.

Might some other method be better suited to calculating hitting streak probability? Given that the pitcher-batter confrontation is to a large extent a strategic battle—and especially so when a pitcher bears down hoping to stop a streak—it may be that we could learn something about hitting streaks by applying game theory, a method that is often used to predict economic or military behavior. Game theory addresses situations that are more (or entirely) dependent upon strategy rather than upon chance. The approach would lead to questions such as, "If a batter comes up knowing, as the pitcher knows, that he needs to get a hit to extend a streak, is it to his advantage to swing at the first pitch or not?" There are many other relevant questions that might be asked and valuable answers potentially derived. Yet it is difficult to see how any probabilistic conclusions could be drawn from any of them. In the end, game theory

is not likely to yield anything more than some peripheral insight into optimal hitting streak behavior.

It's also conceivable that hitting streaks could be a conundrum suited to Bayesian analysis, or conditional probability, in which new events and information impact and recalibrate probabilistic estimates.[3] That is, at bats would not necessarily be treated as independent events, but as being influenced by things that have happened before it. While some of the math pros I spoke with thought that Bayesian analysis might *theoretically* have some use in looking at streaks, the obstacle, as ever, lies in knowing what conditions to factor in and how to weigh them. It's easy to see that in practice this method won't work either.

So, back to the Bernoulli trials. Naturally, the people who have studied the probability of hitting streaks using these trials have considered the uncertainty caused by the almost infinite factors that attend each at bat; in their papers the experimenters typically introduce that point in a hedging paragraph or two. But many are willing to accept this uncertainty and, in effect, dismiss it. To them, those many factors are not truly relevant to the probabilistic measurement. It is like suggesting that rolling a die on a wooden table versus a plastic one, or on a sunny day versus a cloudy one might impact the chances that the die will turn up "3". Really, the chances are 1 in 6 regardless of the surface or the weather.

"You can try to factor in all those things a batter is go-

---

[3] There are some nicely laid out examples of Bayesian analysis, named for its progenitor, the 18th century mathematician and Presbyterian minister Thomas Bayes, as well as many other intriguing thoughts on randomness and chance in Leonard Mlodinow's 2008 book, *The Drunkard's Walk: How Randomness Rules Our Lives*. Mlodinow examines some sports occurrences in the book and very briefly touches on DiMaggio's streak.

ing through until you are blue in the face," said Jim Lack-ritz an emeritus professor of information and decision systems at San Diego State, whose 1996 paper *Two of Baseball's Great Marks: Can They Ever Be Broken?* demonstrated that the odds of someone hitting .400 again are much better than the odds of someone hitting in 56 straight games. "But ultimately it won't have much impact on the probability of a hitting streak."

That's where I disagree. It's certainly true that the best statistical models can work to establish a fair distribution of probability. And it's also true that many of the myriad in-game factors may mitigate themselves over a period of time, a full season say, meaning that hazarding a rough probability estimate can make sense. That's why sophisticated stat processors like Bill James can sometimes do a reasonably good job of predicting player performance and why decades-old, dice-and-card board games such as Strat-O-Matic and APBA can sometimes come fairly close to replicating a player's statistics over a given year.

But trying to estimate hitting streaks doesn't follow. First of all, even an extraordinary streak of 40 or 50 games is a very small sample size and thus very likely to have departed from any underlying probability. More relevant: The conditions of a streak are far less knowable or predictable than the conditions in "regular games." There is no such thing as an "ordinary" at bat when a hitting streak is on the line. These are highly charged and highly unusual events. The batter himself, the pitcher, the runners on base, the fielders, the managers and the fans are all to some larger or smaller degree impacted by the fact that a streak is in progress. There is simply no way to gauge this impact or its consequences.

Consider another result of Arbesman and Strogatz's simulation. It revealed the players who most often had the longest hitting streak during those 10,000 baseball histories. The list—headed by 19th century ballplayers such as Hugh Duffy and Wee Willie Keeler—is much like one that Michael Freiman produced in his paper six years earlier and also similar to one published by LSU finance professor Don M. Chance in the October 2009 issue of *Chance*. (Now what are the Chances of that combination?) Chance ranked the top 100 hitters of all time in terms of who was most likely to have had a long hitting streak. In short, he figured the list by determining his own version of streak average[4] and also factoring in the length of a player's career. Obviously, the longer the career went on, the greater was the opportunity for a streak to occur.

Chance's list in some regards feels spot on. Ty Cobb, Keeler and George Sisler were each ranked among the top five most likely to have a long hitting streak and each does in fact have one of the five longest hitting streaks of all-time. But of the other top 20 most-likely on Chance's list, 15 have never had a streak of even 30 games, and none but the three mentioned have hit in more than 31 straight. DiMaggio was 28th on his list; Pete Rose was 53rd. These inconsistencies hardly render the list wrong or without relevance—no one would expect real life results to ex-

---

[4] Chance didn't exactly use total plate appearances to derive this average. He argued that appearances that result in intentional walks or sacrifice bunts should be left out and not held against the hitter in computing his streak average (again, my term) because these aren't true opportunities to get a hit. That, in my mind, is a mistake on his part. A sacrifice bunt might sneak through two fielders or die on a swatch of wet grass and go as an infield single; a batter could reach out over the plate during an intentional walk and smack the ball for a hit—as Kelly Leak did for the Bad News Bears in 1976 and as Miguel Cabrera did for the Florida Marlins in 2006. Any time that a batter steps into the box he has an opportunity to get a hit.

actly mimic probabilistic estimates—but it does seem far enough off from actual events to at least give pause. Maybe guys who go on hitting streaks have something about them that guys who don't don't.

Other recent work more pointedly addresses the disparity between probability guesses and actual player performance. Jim Albert, a math professor at Bowling Green, concluded in a 2008 study that while his probability model "explains most of the streaky hitting in baseball," it also made clear that "there are some players that appear to exhibit more streakiness than one would predict." Then there's the 2008 paper by Trent McCotter, then a student at North Carolina, titled *Hitting Streaks Don't Obey Your Rules*. McCotter took every batter's game log from 1957 through 2006 and randomly shuffled these game logs 10,000 times to see what hitting streaks would materialize. His results revealed that there were *more* actual hitting streaks than were predicted by chance. (More or less is not really the issue here. The main point, for our purposes, is that reality did not match up with probability theory.) McCotter's study, as he summarized, "seems to provide some strong evidence that players' games are not independent, identically distributed trials, as statisticians have assumed all these years and may even provide evidence that things like hot hands are a part of baseball streaks." So, might some hitters be more streak prone than others who produce hits at a similar rate?

"From a statistical standpoint you'd like to say that it's simply a reasonable fluke that of all the .325 hitters DiMaggio was the one to put together the longest streak, but there is a very serious stumbling block to that thinking," says Bill James. "And that is the 61-game hitting streak that DiMag-

gio had in the Pacific Coast League. How do you account for for the fact that there was one player having two streaks of that length? You can't. It makes you think that other things must be in play."

———

WAS THERE SOMETHING about Joe DiMaggio that suited him to hitting streaks? If so, was it tied to his unwavering style of play, an approach and commitment to every game that made him, according to peers, the most consistent player they were ever around? Was there something relevant to DiMaggio's unflagging hustle, a trait shared by Pete Rose, history's other great hit-streaker? And what to make of DiMaggio's extraordinary combination of power and a propensity to make contact—an ability that appears to have some usefulness in maintaining hitting streaks. Home runs cannot be fielded after all, while strikeouts have no chance of worming their way to a fluke hit.[5] Maybe DiMaggio's acute self-consciousness helped him. Behavioral research has suggested that people who are generally self-conscious, as DiMaggio clearly seemed to be, are more easily able to thrive in situations that cause a high level of self-consciousness (such as a hitting streak) because those people are more accustomed to being in that frame of mind. Undoubtedly DiMaggio had a keen understanding of the need to seize important moments on the baseball field and also had the ability to seize them.

One factor that leads many players, as well as most math

---

[5] Not only is DiMaggio's career rate of 1.02 strikeouts per home run by far the lowest of any player with 350 or more home runs, during his streak in 1941 he struck out only five times while hitting 15 homers. Nobody hits like that.

professors, to say that the streak will not be broken is the extent to which it lords above all others. This is baseball's ultimate statistical outlier. No one has gotten to within even 80% of the record. Having the single-season streak record at 56 and the next highest streak at 44 is analogous to Roger Maris's single-season home run record of 61 being followed by a runner-up at 48. In fact there have been 28 player seasons of between 48 and 61 homers.[6] Hank Aaron's career home run record of 755 would be followed not by Babe Ruth's 714 and Willie Mays's 660, but by some player's 593. Hack Wilson's single-season standard of 191 RBIs would be seconded by 149, while in fact the RBI totals of 45 player seasons have fallen between those numbers. All other major records—Orel Hershiser's stretch of scoreless innings (49), Pete Rose's career hits (4,256) etc.—have a next-best that, relative to DiMaggio's lead, is breathing down their necks.

"DiMaggio's is a number that just doesn't seem like it can be explained," says Hall of Famer and career .338 hitter Tony Gwynn. Ed Purcell, the late, great physicist whose work engendered much of the hitting streak analysis and debate, agreed. In Purcell's evaluation, DiMaggio's streak was the only event in baseball history that defied probabilistic explanation.

In the end, The DiMaggio Enigma persists. The scads of probability studies are intriguing and useful in providing a framework for thought. They confirm the intuitive understanding that the likelihood of anyone at any time having

---

[6] I am excluding from all home run discussion the dubious achievements of the Steroid Era, 1996 through 2004. In that time there were an additional 23 player seasons that eclipsed 48 home runs, including six that surpassed 61, polluting the record book.

reeled off a streak of 56 games is much higher than the likelihood of Joe DiMaggio in particular having done so. And they confirm in a general sense that some players—by statistics alone—are more likely than others to go on a hitting streak. But ultimately we get few solid answers.

If there is life on Earth but none yet observed on any of the other planets in our solar system, can we make a guess as to the probability that alien life is thriving somewhere out there in the cosmos? Who could possibly say? We only know that there is life on Earth. And when it comes to baseball and to hitting streaks, there is at least one thing that we can say for sure: Through the end of the 2010 season 17,290 players were known to have appeared in the major leagues. Only one of them had ever hit in 56 straight games.

At Yankee Stadium, DiMaggio leaving the field after Game 48

DiMaggio with Les Brown as he plays "Joltin' Joe DiMaggio"

DiMaggio scoring in Game 56

Acknowledgments

ANY PEOPLE ALLOWED themselves to be peppered with my questions and inquiries over the course of writing this book and I'm grateful to all of them for what they shared: their memories, their insights and, most precious of all, their time. My gratitude begins with the ballplayers from 1941, those who helped bring me onto the field and into the game. A great tip of the cap to the late Dominic DiMaggio, who was patient and gracious at a time in his life when he had every excuse not to be. And to Dom's daughter Emily for her own thoughts. And to Dom's son Dominic Paul. I owe thanks to Bobby Doerr, Benny McCoy, the late Herman Franks and the late Rapid Robert, Bob Feller; to Al Brancato and Marty Marion and Yogi Berra (by way of the exceedingly helpful Art Berke). I enjoyed and was inspired by few conversations more than the several that I had talking baseball with Rugger Ardizoia and Charlie Silvera. I'm also indebted to some important offspring, particularly Charles Keller and Robert Cleveland Muncrief III.

My reporting in San Francisco and North Beach was enriched by numerous longtime residents of the city including Dante Santora and Dick Boyd; Art Peterson of the Telegraph Hill Society; the seemingly indefatigable Alessandro Baccari Jr.; Father Paul Maniscalco and Father Armand Oliveri at the church of Saints Peter and Paul; Gil Hodges III and Trevor Noonan at Liverpool Lil's; David Wright and David Wees at Café Divine; Ida Debrunner and Suzanne Debrunner (and their wonderful photo album) on Taylor Street; Joe Toboni Jr.; Joseph Alioto Jr.; Betty at Galileo High. Telephone conversations with Patti Barsocchini were also very helpful, as were those far-reaching ones with Sam Spear.

Visiting San Francisco would have been far less enlightening, as well as less enjoyable, without the company and guidance of the late Ron Fimrite. I wish I could thank Ron for that again, in person, and also for bringing me to his beloved Washington Square Bar & Grill and introducing me to Michael McCourt, a splendid bartender and also a source for this book.

Several writers helped fill in the landscape, not only with their work, but, more pointedly, in our conversations. Among them: Robert Creamer, Ray Robinson, Dave Anderson, Roger Kahn and the late Maury Allen. They were also among those who escorted me back to 1941, as did Mario Cuomo and Gay Talese.

To Tom Villante: Thank you for your clarity and your precision, again and again.

In New Jersey, special gratitude goes to Bina Spatola and to Larry Chiaravallo, and a nod to Dr. Richard Boiardo. In East Harlem, thanks to Albert Luongo and to Jimmy and Joey.

Among the many others who provided salient wisdom or detail, or both: Bert Sugar, Ed Moose, Orin Dahl, Al Kaufman, Kristi Jacobson, Rich Lindbergh, Andrew Crichton, Nick Peters, Norman Goldberger, George Bailin, Richard Goldstein, Stan Moroknek, Sam Goldman, Paolo Corvino, Sheila King in Chicago and Tucker Anderson.

Many active, or just retired, major leaguers lent me an ear and gave me their voices on any number of relevant subjects, including (but not limited to): Clint Barmes, Luis Castillo, Ryan Church, Adam Dunn, Ken Griffey Jr., Todd Helton, Derek Jeter, Nick Johnson, Dan Murphy,

Jimmy Rollins, Aaron Rowand, Ichiro Suzuki, Gary Sheffield, Matt Stairs, Nick Swisher, Robin Ventura, David Wright and Ryan Zimmerman.

Other players, from the 1970s and '80s, were helpful too, especially: Don Baylor, Wade Boggs, George Brett, Ken Griffey Sr., Tony Gwynn, Keith Hernandez, Carney Lansford, Larry McWilliams, Ron Reed and Pat Zachry.

Pete Rose gets a big thank you just for being himself.

For helping me parse through matters of mind and probability, many thanks to: Robert Remez, Steven Strogatz, Alan Goldberg, Bill James, Jim Lackritz, Benjamin McGill, Gordon Bower and Stanley Lieberson.

For other important illuminations, thanks to Steve Hirdt, Walt Hriniak, Marty Brennaman, Rick Cerrone, Marty Appel, David Robbeson, Don Chance, Richard Hartman and two careful arbiters, Michael Duca and Ivy McLemore.

This book would not have gotten done had I not received help in facilitating access, interviews and materials. For such help I am grateful to Phyllis Merhige, Eric Mann, Jay Horwitz, Corey Kilgannon, Joe Posnanski, Bob Richardson, Betsy Gotbaum, Ethan Wilson, Greg Casterioto, Padraic Boyle, Shirley in Cleveland, Andrew Krueger, David W. Smith, Patricia O'Toole, David Ouse, Jack O'Connell and Jim Nagourney.

At the Yankees, thanks to Randy Levine, as well as to Tony Morante.

At the Baseball Hall of Fame in Cooperstown, special thanks to the indispensable Bill Francis. Also to Benjamin Harry, Freddie Berowski and Brad Horn. Thank you as well to my guides at the Louisville Slugger Museum and Factory, especially to bat-turner Garrik Napier and to then curator Dan Cohen.

A quiet thanks as well to those of you who gave me your time and thoughts or otherwise assisted on the book but asked not to be mentioned by name.

A list of materials that I used follows in a bibliography, but I would like to cite two descriptions in particular: Tommy Henrich's account of the moment Joe DiMaggio realized his bat had been stolen, and Phil Rizzuto's account of the night the hitting streak ended, both from HBO's *Where Have You Gone, Joe DiMaggio?* Also, a special citation to Joyce Hadley's book, *Dorothy Arnold: Joe DiMaggio's First Wife*.

Now, a little closer to home:

This book wouldn't be here without the encouragement and guidance of Andrew Blauner, my agent, adviser and all-around savior. I'm grateful for Andrew's intelligence and clear thinking, and perhaps most of all his abiding sense of decency.

The book was greatly improved by the sharp, thoughtful and careful attention of David Bauer. Sense and sensibility in one. I feel lucky to have had David as an editor.

I'm grateful to Kevin Kerr, a consummately professional and, in my experience, peerless copy editor. And to Sarah Kwak for her hard, thorough and creative work in making sure that we got things right. Many thanks as well to designer Stephen Skalocky and to photo editor Cristina Scalet.

I was helped by Christy Hammond, who kindly excavated materials in Detroit, and by Matthew Parker, who did fine research in New York.

Thank you in a big way to Terry McDonell for believing in the book from the start and then for supporting it. And a big thank you to Richard Fraiman for the same.

Thanks to everyone at *Sports Illustrated* and Time Home Entertainment Inc. who kept things afloat: to the terrific, multitalented Stefanie Kaufman and the wonderfully diligent Allison Parker; to Joy Butts, Tom Mifsud, Helen Wilson, Scott Novak, Emily Christopher, Malena Jones and Lee Sosin.

To Amy, for your fine eye and your counsel at every step of this process (and for your excellent work in Newark) and for your support and companionship and generosity, and for far more than I can here put into words, I embrace you and thank you and thank you again.

In Kathrin Perutz, my eternal guide to defying gravitas, and in Michael Studdert-Kennedy, who sees to the heart of things, I had the two best teachers alive. They were, and are, my inspiration. Thank you for all of it. Thank you for having me.

Kostya Kennedy
New York
2011

Selected Bibliography

BOOKS

Alexander, Charles C. *Rogers Hornsby: A Biography*. New York: Henry Holt and Co., 1995

Allen, Maury. *Where Have You Gone, Joe DiMaggio?* New York: Dutton, 1975

Auker, Elden and Keegan, Tom. *Sleeper Cars and Flannel Uniforms*. Chicago: Triumph Books, 2001

Barber, Red and Creamer, Robert. *Rhubarb in the Catbird Seat*. Garden City, New York: Doubleday, 1968.

Barolini, Helen et al. *Images: A Pictorial History of Italian Americans*. Staten Island, New York: Center for Migration Studies (Fondazione Giovanni Agnelli), 1981

Blount, Roy, Jr. (co-author) *Williams and DiMaggio, The Stuff of Dreams*. Winnetka, Illinois: Rare Air Media, 1999

Cataneo, David. *I Remember Joe DiMaggio*. Nashville, Tennessee: Cumberland House, 2001

Considine, Bob. *Toots*. New York: Meredith Press, 1969

Cramer, Richard Ben. *Joe DiMaggio: The Hero's Life*. New York. Simon & Schuster, 2000

Csikszentmihalyi, Mihaly. *Flow: The Psychology of Optimal Experience*. New York: Harper & Row, 1990

Davis, Kenneth S. *FDR, Into the Storm, 1937–1940: A History*. New York: Random House, 1993

_____. _FDR, The War President, 1940–43: A History_. New York: Random House, 2000

DiMaggio, Dom with Gilbert, Bill. _Real Grass, Real Heroes_. New York: Kensington Pub. Corp., 1990

DiMaggio, Joe. _Baseball for Everyone_. New York: Whittlesey House, 1948

_____. _Lucky to Be a Yankee_. New York: Grosset & Dunlap, 1957

_____, as told to Ross, John M. _The Joe DiMaggio Story, A True Book-Length Feature_

Dowson, Ernest. _The Poems of Ernest Dowson, 1896_. New York: John Lane Company, 1915

Eig, Jonathan. _Luckiest Man: The Life and Death of Lou Gehrig_. New York: Simon & Schuster, 2005

Eliot, T.S. _Collected Poems 1909–1962_. New York: Harcourt, Brace & World, 1963

Feller, William. _An Introduction to Probability Theory and Its Applications_. New York: Wiley, 1968

Hadley, Joyce M. _Dorothy Arnold, Joe DiMaggio's First Wife_. Oak Park, Illinois: Chauncey Park Press, 1993

Hill, Art. _Don't Let Baseball Die_. Au Train, Mich.: Avery Color Studios, 1979

Hemingway, Ernest, _For Whom the Bell Tolls_. New York: Scribner, 1940

_____. _The Old Man and the Sea_. New York: Scribner, 1952

Henrich, Tommy and Gilbert, Bill. _Five O'Clock Lightning_. New York: Carol Publishing Corp. 1992

Honig, Donald. _Baseball When the Grass Was Real_. New York: Coward, McCann & Geoghegan, 1975

_____. _Baseball Between the Lines_. Lincoln, Nebraska and London: University of Nebraska Press, 1976

Huhn, Rick. _The Sizzler: George Sisler, Baseball's Forgotten Great_. Columbia, Missouri: University of Missouri Press, 2004

Immerso, Michael. _Newark's Little Italy: The Vanished First Ward_. New Brunswick, N.J., and Newark: Rutgers University Press and Newark Public Library, 1997

James, Bill and Neyer, Rob. _The Neyer/James Guide to Pitchers_. New York: Simon & Schuster, 2004

James, Bill. _The New Bill James Historical Baseball Abstract_. New York: Free Press, 2001

Johnson, Dick and Stout, Glenn. *DiMaggio: An Illustrated Life*. New York: Walker and Co., 1995

Johnson, Steven. *The Invention of Air*. New York: Riverhead Hardcover, 2008

Kyvig, David E. *Daily Life in the United States, 1920–1940*. Chicago: Ivan R. Dee, 2004

Lindberg, Richard C. *Total White Sox*. Chicago: Triumph Books, 2006

Lagumina, Salvatore J. *Wop! A Documentary History of Anti-Italian Discrimination in the United States*. San Francisco: Straight Arrow Books, 1973

Lee, Sandra S. *Italian Americans of Newark, Belleville and Nutley*. Charleston, South Carolina: Arcadia Publishing, 2008

Lukacs, John. *Blood, Toil, Tears and Sweat: the Dire Warning*. New York: Basic Books, 2008

Madden, Bill. *Pride of October: What It Was to Be Young and a Yankee*. New York: Warner Books, 2003

Malta, Vince. *A Complete Reference Guide: Louisville Slugger Professional Player Bats*. Concord, Calif.: Black Diamond Publications, 2007

McElvaine, Robert S. *Mario Cuomo: A Biography*. New York: Scribner's, 1988

_____. *The Great Depression, America, 1929–1941*. New York: Times Books, 1984

McKim, Vaughn R. and Turner, Stephen P. (editors). *Causality in Crisis? Statistical Methods and the Search for Causal Knowledge in the Social Sciences*. Notre Dame, Indiana: University of Notre Dame Press, 1997

Mlodinow, Leonard. *The Drunkard's Walk: How Randomness Rules Our Lives*. New York: Pantheon Books, 2008

Mondello, Salvatore. *A Sicilian in East Harlem*. Youngstown, New York: Cambria Press, 2005

Monroe, Marilyn with Hecht, Ben. *My Story*. Lanham, Maryland: Taylor Trade Publishing, 2007

Moore, Jack B. *Joe DiMaggio, a Bio-Bibliography*. New York: Greenwood Press, 1986

Moreno, Barry. *Italian Americans*. Hauppauge, New York: Barron's Educational Series, 2003

O'Neal, Bill. *The Pacific Coast League, 1903–1988.* Austin, Texas: Eakin Press, 1990

Ritter, Lawrence S. *The Glory of Their Times.* New York: Macmillan, 1966

Robinson, Ray. *Iron Horse: Lou Gehrig in His Time.* New York: W.W. Norton, 1990

Rose, Pete and Golenbock, Peter. *Pete Rose on Hitting.* New York: Perigee Books, 1985

Rose, Pete and Kahn, Roger. *Pete Rose: My Story.* New York: Macmillan Publishing Co., 1989

Rozanov, Y.A. *Probability Theory: A Concise Course.* New York: Dover Publications, 1977

Schneider, Russell. *Tales from the Tribe Dugout.* Champaign, Ill.: Sports Publishing LLC, 2002

Schoor, Gene. *Joe Di Maggio, The Yankee Clipper.* New York: J. Messner, 1956

Shapiro, Milton J. *The Phil Rizzuto Story.* New York: Messner, 1959

Sickels, John. *Bob Feller: Ace of the Greatest Generation.* Washington, D.C.: Brassey's Inc. 2004

Silverman, Al. *Joe Di Maggio, The Golden Year.* Englewood Cliffs, N.J.: Prentice-Hall, Inc., 1969

Spalding-Reach: *Official Baseball Guide.* New York: American Sports Publishing Co., 1941

Talese, Gay. *Unto the Sons.* New York: Knopf, 1992

Turner, Jonathan H. *On the Origins of Human Emotions.* Stanford, Calif.: Stanford University Press, 2000

Westcott, Rich. *Philadelphia's Old Ballparks.* Philadelphia: Temple University Press, 1996

Whittingham, Richard (compiler and editor). *The Di Maggio Albums.* New York: G.P. Putnam's, 1989

AUDIO and VIDEO

1941 Major League All-Star Game. MBS radio. Red Barber and Bob Elson

1991 Major League All-Star Game. CBS television. Joe DiMaggio–Ted Williams interview

Bands That Played the Blackhawk. Compiled by: Karl Pearson

Baseball. PBS Home Video. Directed by: Ken Burns

Buck Privates. Universal Pictures. Directed by: Arthur Lubin. Starring: Bud Abbott and Lou Costello

Joe DiMaggio: A Hero's Life. PBS American Experience. Producer: Mark Zwonitzer. Narrator: Richard Ben Cramer

The Phantom Creeps. Volumes 1 and 2. Alpha Video.

This Week in Baseball, 1978, Major League Baseball Productions.

Toots. His Town, His Saloon. Catalyst Films. By Kristi Jacobson

Tribute to Lou Gehrig. NBC radio

We Choose Human Freedom. Franklin D. Roosevelt radio address, May 27, 1941

Where Have You Gone, Joe DiMaggio? HBO Home Video. Executive Producer: Ross Greenburg

ARTICLES and PAPERS

Albert, Jim. "Streaky Hitting in Baseball," *Journal of Quantitative Analysis in Sports*; Volume 4, Issue 1, 2008

Albright, S. Christian. "A Statistical Analysis of Hitting Streaks in Baseball," *Journal of the American Statistical Association*; December, 1993

Arbesman, Samuel and Strogatz, Steven H. "A Monte Carlo Approach to Joe DiMaggio and Streaks in Baseball."

_____. "A Journey to Baseball's Alternate Universe," *The New York Times*; March 30, 2008

Baumeister, Roy F. and Showers, Carolin J. "A Review of Paradoxical Performance Effects: Choking Under Pressure in Sports and Mental Tests." *European Journal of Social Psychology*, Vol. 16, Issue 4, 1986

Blahous, Charles. "The DiMaggio Streak: How Big a Deal Was It?" *Baseball Research Journal*; No. 23, 1994

Breaux, O.P. "An Algorithm for Objective Measurement of Hitting Streaks," Personal correspondence to the National Baseball Hall of Fame and Museum; April 3, 1996

Brown, Bob and Goodrich, Peter. "Calculating the Odds: DiMaggio's 56-Game Hitting Streak," *Baseball Research Journal*; Number 32, 2003

Chance, Don M. "What Are The Odds?" *Chance*; Vol. 22, Issue 2. June 2009

Fedo, Michael. "Joe DiMaggio Turns His Lonely Eyes Toward the Girl at 2833 West Third Street." *Whistling Shade*: Spring 2003

Freiman, Michael. "56-Game Hitting Streaks Revisited," *Baseball Research Journal*; No. 31, 2003

Gilovich, Thomas; Vallone, Robert; and Tversky, Amos. "The Hot Hand in Basketball: On the Misperception of Random Sequences," *Cognitive Psychology*; Vol. 17, 1985

Gould, Stephen Jay. "The Streak of Streaks," *The New York Review of Books*; Aug. 18, 1988

Hopkins, James D. "The Jazz World in Armonk, 1935–1942." The North Castle Historical Society, Vol. 3, 1985

Kavanagh, Jack. "Streaks and Feats." *Total Baseball* 2nd edition

Lackritz, James R. "Two of Baseball's Great Marks: Can They Ever Be Broken?" *Chance*; Vol. 9, No. 4, 1996

Lieberson, Stanley. "Modeling Social Processes: Some Lessons from Sports," *Sociological Forum*; Vol. 12, No. 1, 1997

McCotter, Trent. "Hitting Streaks Don't Obey Your Rules," *The Baseball Research Journal*; 2008

Nitz, Jim and Jeff. "The Man Who Stopped DiMaggio: Milwaukee's Own Ken Keltner," *Milwaukee History*; Vol. 27, No. 3, 2004

Robbeson, David. "Was Joe DiMaggio's Hitting Streak the Greatest Feat in All of Sports or Merely a Product of Its Time?" *The Walrus*, Oct. 2007

Rojstaczer, Stuart. "Joe DiMaggio's Hitting Streak Revisited," Forty Questions Blog; 2008

Tversky, Amos and Gilovich, Thomas. "The Cold Facts About the 'Hot Hand' in Basketball," *Chance*; Vol. 2, No. 1, 1989

Yoseloff, Anthony A. "From Ethnic Hero to National Icon: The Americanization of Joe DiMaggio." *International Journal of the History of Sport*; Vol. 16, Issue 3, 1999

NEWSPAPERS

The Atlanta Constitution; Boston Herald; The Brooklyn Eagle; The Cape Cod Times; Chicago Tribune; The Cincinnati Enquirer; (New York) *Daily News;*

The Detroit News; The Duluth Herald; Duluth News Tribune; (Philadelphia) *Evening Public Ledger; The Hartford Courant; Los Angeles Times; The Miami Herald; The Minneapolis Journal; New York Journal-American; New York Post; The New York Times; New York Tribune; The New York World-Telegram; Newark News; Newsday; Palm Beach* (Fla.) *Post; Philadelphia Evening Bulletin; The Philadelphia Inquirer; The Philadelphia Record; The* (Cleveland) *Plain Dealer; St. Louis Post-Dispatch; San Francisco Call-Bulletin; San Francisco Chronicle; The* (New York) *Sun; The Washington Post.*

MAGAZINES AND PUBLICATIONS

Collier's; Life Magazine; The Huffington Post; The National Pastime; The New Yorker; Popeater; The Saturday Evening Post; The Semaphores, Telegraph Hill Dwellers, Issue 187; The Sporting News; Sports Illustrated; Time Magazine.

Photo Credits

Page 9: Tom Sande/AP; Page 92: Bettmann/Corbis; Page 93: AP (top), MLB Photos/Getty Images; Page 268: Corbis (top), San Antonio Light/Texas Institute of Culture/National Baseball Hall of Fame Library; Page 269: Bettmann/Corbis; Page 270: Bettmann/Corbis (2); Page 271: Corbis; Page 344: Daily News Archive/Getty Images; Page 345: Bettmann/Corbis (2); Page 368: National Baseball Hall of Fame Library.

Index

362

hindbrain, 87, 89–90
Hirdt, Steve, 196–97
Hitler, Adolf, 25, 42, 63, 82, 126
hitting streak (DiMaggio), 12–13
  All-Star Game and, 282–83
  analysis of, 86–91, 131–39,
    321–43
  bad-hop ground ball ruling
    and, 121–22, 131–39
  bunting and, 146
  DiMaggio's feelings about, 91,
    98, 118, 184–85, 286,
    295–96, 303, 307–8
  Dom's defense of, 194n
  end of, 307
  inexplicability of, 342–43
  legacy of, 311–19
  newsreels, 201–2
  Pacific Coast League, 292,
    295–96, 341
  pitchers and, 189–90
  poetry about, 146, 151
  press and, 83, 121, 124
  probability of, 322–23
  recognition of, 100
  significance of, 12–13, 131,
    187–88, 201–2, 312–16
  Sisler's record and, 219–20
  statistically safe, 266
  teammates and, 184
  tension and, 176–77, 185,
    206–7, 210
  what-if of, 312
hitting streaks
  analysis of, 86–91, 187–97,
    321–43
  Bayesian analysis of, 337
  Bernoulli trials, 336–38
  choking under pressure,
    90–91
  conditional probability and,
    337
  difficulty of, 12–13, 187–88,
    190–94, 192, 248–49
  game theory and, 337
  luck and, 138
  noticing, 83, 85–86
  pitchers and, 189–90
  probabilities of, 322–25,
  as random occurrences,
    327–33
  records, 12
  relief pitchers and, 189
  self-consciousness and, 342

  streak averages, 328
  subconscious mind and,
    89–91
  superstitions and, 193, 295
  talent and, 190–91
  team behavior and, 194–97
  tension of, 192–94
  thinking about, 85–91
  Yankee players, 116, 118
Hitting Streaks Don't Obey Your
  Rules (McCotter), 340
Hoag, Myril, 103, 145
hockey records, 12
Hodges, Gil, 196
Hollywood Stars, 294
Holmes, Tommy, 187, 191, 256,
  257, 259, 260, 263
Homer, Ben, 239
home runs, strikeouts per,
  342n
Hoover, J. Edgar, 104
Hornsby, Rogers, 146, 149, 167
  batting average, 147
Hospital and Home for Crippled
  Children, Newark, 49–50,
  105, 127
hotel lobbies, 212
"hot hand" studies, 324
"hot" streaks, 323–27
House of Fear, The, 157
Hubbell, Carl ("Old Long
  Pants"), 66, 80
Hudler, Rex, 11
Hudson, Sid, 69, 214, 221
Huffington Post, 318
Huggins, Miller, 24, 134, 279

"in the zone," 88
In the Navy, 105
Ickes, Harold, 25
I Am An American Day, 24–26, 29
isolationists, 65
Italian-Americans, 41–50
  ball players, 41–42
  deportation of, 42
  internment of, 290
  Mussolini and, 43
  non-citizen, 42, 42n
  prejudice against, 41–44
  Roosevelt's note on, 149
  sabotage trial, 114
Italy
  Mussolini and, 43
  World War II and, 44–45, 60, 61

Jackson Heights, 198–202, 224
Jackson Heights Hornets, 36, 37,
  106–7, 111, 198–99, 202
James, Bill, 325, 338, 341
Jefferson Hospital, 210
Jennings, Hughie, 230
Jeter, Derek, 188, 319
Jews, 66, 82, 169–70
Joe DiMaggio Night, Seals
  Stadium, 294
Joe DiMaggio's Grotto, 46, 144,
  149, 159, 160, 216–17, 275
Johnson, Bob, 206, 209, 280
Johnson, Hiram, 220–21
Johnson, Walter, 36, 68–69,
  108, 215
Jolly Knights of North Beach,
  294
Jolter Joe DiMaggio, 239, 299, 317
Journal American, 61, 132, 231
Journal of Quantitative Analysis
  in Sports, 321
Journal of the American Statistical
  Association, 321
Journey to Baseball's Alternate
  Universe, A (Strogatz), 333
Judnich, Walt, 289

Kahneman, Daniel, 324
Keeler, Emma, 229
Keeler, Wee Willie, 138, 146, 191,
  243, 258, 263, 267, 339, 340
  baseball career, 228–31
  hitting streak, 226, 228
  playing style, 230
  as a "scientific hitter," 230
  two-season streak, 263n
"Keep the Home Fires Burning,"
  28, 29
Keller, Charlie ("King Kong"), 27,
  31, 32, 33, 35, 41, 70, 98,
  99, 107–8, 117, 122, 124,
  146, 148, 174, 183, 209,
  219, 223, 280, 284, 285
Keltner, Ken, 74, 101, 303–4,
  305, 308
Kemeny, John G., 266
Kennedy, Bob, 299
Knickerbocker, Billy, 298
knuckleballs, 219
Kramer, Jack, 178
Kubel, Joe, 117
Kuhn, Bowie, 261, 314

Laabs, Chet, 30

About The Author

KOSTYA KENNEDY, a senior editor at SPORTS ILLUSTRATED, writes on a wide range of subjects. Before joining SI, he was a staff writer at *Newsday* and contributed to *The New York Times* and *The New Yorker*. He earned an M.S. from Columbia University's Graduate School of Journalism, from which he received a Pulitzer Fellowship. He lives with his wife and children in Westchester County, N.Y.

www.kostyakennedy.com

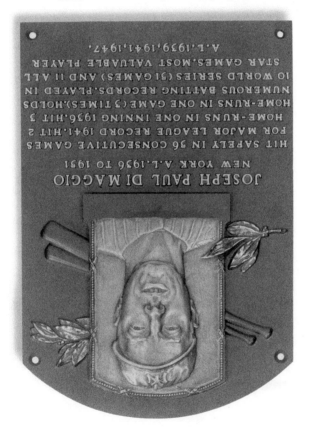

Hall of Fame, Cooperstown, N.Y.